11e

Consumer Behavior

11e

Consumer Behavior

Leon G. Schiffman

J. Donald Kennedy Chair in Marketing
and E-Commerce
Peter J. Tobin College of Business
St. John's University, New York City

Joseph Wisenblit

Professor of Marketing
Stillman School of Business
Seton Hall University, New Jersey

S. Ramesh Kumar

Professor, Marketing
Indian Institute of Management Bangalore

PEARSON

Delhi • Chennai

Credits and acknowledgments borrowed from other sources and reproduced, with permission, in this textbook appear on the appropriate page within text.

Many of the designations by manufacturers and sellers to distinguish their products are claimed as trademarks. Where those designations appear in this book, and the publisher was aware of a trademark claim, the designations have been printed in initial caps or all caps.

Authorized adaptation from the United States edition entitled *Consumer Behavior, 11th Edition*, ISBN: 9780132544368 by Schiffman, Leon G.; Wisenblit, Joseph, published by Pearson Education, Inc., Copyright © 2015, 2010, 2007 Pearson Education, Inc.

Indian Subcontinent Adaptation

ISBN 978-93-325-3764-4

First Impression

Published by Dorling Kindersley (India) Pvt. Ltd, licensees of Pearson Education in South Asia.

Head Office: 7th Floor, Knowledge Boulevard, A-8(A), Sector 62, Noida 201 309, UP, India.
Registered Office: 11 Community Centre, Panchsheel Park, New Delhi 110 017, India.

Printed in India at Pushp Print Services.

In Memory of Leslie Lazar Kanuk
Our Coauthor, Colleague, and Friend

Brief Contents

Contents

Preface

New to the Eleventh Edition

Our guiding principle in writing this edition has been the leaping progress towards the inevitable synthesis of media, entertainment content, and marketing. Not long ago, marketers bought advertising space within information and entertainment content produced by print and broadcast media. Today, media and their contents are often "produced" by consumers. In the past, marketers used media's "audience profiles" in deciding where to place "one size fits all" ads. Today, dynamic-ad-servers customize ads based on consumers' Internet browsing behavior, and marketers use behavioral targeting and employ firms that listen to and analyze what consumers are talking about in social media sites. Marketers that once purchased advertising space in only a few magazines or TV sitcoms, today buy ads through multiple ad exchanges and use predictive analytics that assess the effectiveness of their ads.

- New topics: In this edition, we discuss behavioral targeting, customizing products and promotional messages, predictive analytics, reaching "eyeballs" instead of demographic groups, tracking online navigation and analyzing websites' visits, gauging word-of-mouth and opinion leadership online, consumer-generated advertising, and new media platforms, such as mobile and apps advertising.
- New Technologies and Online Practices: In this edition we also address Americans' usage of new technologies and the online practices of all age subcultures. At a time where the loss of privacy is the subject of an intensive public debate, we have charts showing how leading social networks collect data about consumers and a corresponding judgmental analysis in the chapter on ethics.
- We strengthened the book's principal facet, conceived in its first edition in 1978, which is focusing on the strategic applications of understanding consumer behavior. Our cases feature authentic campaigns that advertisers submitted for recognition by effie Worldwide—a global entity that pays tributes to exceptional marketers. Each chapter opens with a "hands-on" example (some with comments by marketing executives) and exhibits based on recent, empirical data are showcased in all chapters together with guidelines for marketing applications.
- We added sections about sensory audio input, "actual" and "ideal" product-related attitudes, extra measures of cultural values, and empirical data about occupational prestige rankings and social class.
- The presentation about consumers overseas has been updated to include more comprehensive coverage of cross-cultural analysis, charts depicting consumers' spending of disposable income in several countries, brand shares of American products overseas, and profiles of leading global brands.
- Finally, in its first edition, this book was the first one ever to use print ads as illustrations of consumer behavior (a practice that was quickly adopted by all marketing textbooks).

Indian Cases and Examples

There have been significant changes in the Indian context since the previous edition of this book was published. Emergence of cultural aspects that has a mix of western and traditional values, development of digital technologies, the interface between marketing mix elements and technology, cell phone as a medium of communication, and the deepening of western lifestyle in the Indian context are some of the major drivers of change included within the purview of this book. This edition has the objective of providing examples of traditional concepts as well as the impact of contemporary developments like digital tools and social media on the traditional concepts of consumer behavior. A qualitative research case that is grounded in the Indian context has also been added to enable the students to understand how such research techniques that originated in the West can be practiced in the Indian context. This book carries consumer behavior–branding interface examples that are more diverse and in-depth than the earlier edition. Several of these examples have been provided across chapters so that students can connect with the Indian context throughout the text and appreciate the linkages across chapters. Specific emphasis has been given to the examples picked for individual processes (perception, learning, attitude, and personality) as these concepts provide the very foundation for understanding consumer behavior. New perspectives that are important from the Indian context have been introduced in the chapters on Consumer Decision-Making and Communication.

Chapter-by-Chapter Updates: In Detail

Part I: Consumers, Marketers, and Technology

Chapter 1 explains consumer behavior as an interdisciplinary framework. It describes the evolution of marketing, prominent marketing strategies, and marketers' social responsibilities. The chapter details the revolutionary impact of technology on strategic marketing, and the interrelationships among customer value, satisfaction, and retention. It concludes with a model of consumer decision-making. Chapter 2 describes market segmentation, including the demographic, sociocultural, and psychographic bases for segmenting markets. It explores the criteria for selecting target markets, behavioral targeting, and positioning and differentiating products and services.

Chapter 1: Technology-Driven Consumer Behavior

- ***Hands-On:*** Scion
- Technology enriches the marketing exchange
- Behavioral information and targeting
- Interactive communication channels
- Customizing products and ads
- Better pricing and distribution
- Technology and customer satisfaction and retention
- ***Showcased:*** Ownership of mobile devices, prominent online activities, comparing e-readers, an airline's profitability tiers, and an updated model of consumer decision-making.
- ***Ads:*** Scion, PeTA (People for the Ethical Treatment of Animals).

Chapter 2: Segmentation, Targeting, and Positioning

- ***Hands-On:*** Qantas
- Behavioral targeting
- Tracking online navigation
- Geographic location and mobile targeting
- The information "arms race"
- Positioning and repositioning
- ***Showcased:*** Nielsen's segmentation frameworks, samples of psychographic statements, and Target's behavioral targeting
- ***Ads:*** Amul Kool, Count on Shell, Bertolli pasta, V8 100% Original Vegetable Juice, Mack's Earplugs, Campbell's Minestrone, Healthy Choice lunch, TOMTOM GPS, and Fage Total yogurt
- ***Case:*** Porsche

Part II: The Consumer as an Individual

Part II examines the impact of psychological factors on consumer behavior. Chapter 3 discusses the influence of needs, motivation, and personality characteristics. Chapter 4 explores consumer perception, which consists of selecting, organizing, and interpreting marketing stimuli. Chapter 5 describes the learning process and how past shopping experiences affect subsequent buying. Chapter 6 looks at the formation, study, and strategic applications of consumer attitudes.

Chapter 3: Consumer Motivation and Personality

- ***Hands-On:*** Government of Alberta; Vodafone Zoo-Zoo
- ***Showcased:*** Promotional applications of key psychogenic needs, personality characteristics of opinion leaders and innovators, individuals with a high need for uniqueness, materialistic consumers, compulsive shoppers, and vain persons
- ***Ads:*** Levi's, Titan, Godiva, Outward Bound Wilderness, Rock Resorts, Yoplait Light, and Reach Listerine.

Chapter 4: Consumer Perception

- ***Hands-On:*** Lifebuoy
- ***Showcased:*** Sensory audio input and product perception, a price quality relationship "riddle," and brand image updates that create emotional bonds with consumers
- ***Ads:*** Mitchell Eye Centre, Pepsi, Xerox, Crest Whitestrips, Children's Defense Fund, Arrow, Nano Twist, Canadian Dental Association, Gillette Proglide, TVS Scooty, Spy Museum, MADD (Mothers Against Drunk Driving), and Sweet' n Low.

Chapter 5: Consumer Learning

- ***Hands-On:*** Dove Products
- ***Ads:*** Gillette Venus, V8 soups from Campbell's, Mr. Clean Febreze exotic scents, Clorox Bleach Gel, Ragu pasta sauce, Crest Pro-Health, and American Airlines.

Chapter 6: Consumer Attitude Formation and Change

- ***Hands-On:*** Himalaya Hand Wash
- Primary data-based application of the attitude-toward-object-model
- "Ideal," "concept," and "actual" attitudes in developing a new orange juice
- Alumni donations illustration of self-attribution theory
- ***Ads:*** Aleve, Phillips' Caplets, Dole Fruit Bowls, Lysol Wipes, Healthy Choice lunch, V8 Fusion vegetable juice, Method Laundry Detergent, the American Academy for Orthopedic Surgeons, and Pond's Face Wash.
- ***Case:*** Febreze
- ***Case:*** Superfast Handwash

Part III: Communication and Consumer Behavior

Part III addresses communication and persuasion. Chapter 7 covers the elements of communications and overcoming barriers to effective communications. We outline the differences between the broadcasting communications model (which is rooted in mass and traditional media), and the narrowcasting model (which originates in new media, such as online advertising and social media). The chapter then focuses on the message: its structure, persuasive appeal, and effectiveness. Chapter 8 explores communication channels and the transition from print and broadcast media to social media and mobile advertising. We expore the targeting methods used in old and new communication channels, the role of key entities (such as Google and Facebook), and the electronic evolution of traditional media. Chapter 9 examines the credibility of media and personal sources of information, consumers' reference groups, the role of opinion leaders, and the dynamics of word-of-mouth offline and online.

Chapter 7: Persuading Consumers

- ***Hands-On:*** Persuasive Appeals—Fevicol, Sojourner Family Peace Center, ALT magazine, and Clorox Bleach
- Narrowcasting versus broadcasting
- Traditional versus new media
- Addressable advertising
- Measures of message effectiveness
- Timely advertising appeals
- ***Ads:*** Fevicol, MTv with Nano, British Airways, Mistique Ultra Soft Tissue, "I can't believe it's not butter," Aleve, Bucharest's City Police, and Ving hotels.

Chapter 8: From Print and Broadcast Advertising to Social and Mobile Media

- ***Hands-On:*** Impression-Based Targeting
- Targeting segments versus eyeballs

- Real-time bidding and data aggregators
- Retargeting
- Google's consumer tracking and targeting
- Web-search, display, and mobile ads
- Google's "organic results" and "sponsored space"
- Consumers' permissions for apps' information gathering
- Effective social media campaigns
- Owned, paid, and earned social media channels
- Consumers and mobile media
- Measuring the effectiveness of advertising in new media
- Analyzing website visits
- Gauging influence within social networks
- Google Analytics
- Nielsen's Cross-Platform measures
- Traditional media's electronic evolution
- Webisodes, advergames, and branded entertainment
- ***Showcased:*** Google's revenues, number of permissions requested from users by the most popular apps, types of permissions requested, M&M's Mr. Red, declining advertising ad pages, and effective tweeting, Social Media Penetration in India, and Web Users Making Mobile Purchases.

Chapter 9: Reference Groups and Word-of-Mouth

- ***Hands-On:*** Campbell's
- Word-of-mouth in social networks and brand communities
- Klout scores
- Weblogging and twetting
- Buzz agents and viral marketing
- Managing negative rumors online
- Diffusion of Innovations
- ***Showcased:*** Group membership and comparative versus normative influence, characteristics of conformists, product conspicuousness and reference group influence, motivations of opinion leaders and receivers, characteristics and shopping patterns of fashion opinion leaders, sample items used in the self-designation of opinion leadership, and characteristics of risk-averse consumers
- ***Ads:*** MADD, the U.S. Navy, ALT magazine, and PeTA.
- ***Case:*** Keystone Light

Part IV: Consumers in Their Social and Cultural Settings

Part IV examines consumers in their social and cultural settings. Chapter 10 examines the family as a consumption unit and its standing within the social class structure. Chapter 11 describes culture and how it is expressed through values, rituals, and customs. It explains how to measure cultural values, and illustrates Americans' core values with ads and consumers' purchases and priorities. Chapter 12 explores cross-cultural analysis, how to assess marketing opportunities abroad, and whether or not customize products and promotions in global markets.

Chapter 10: The Family and Its Social Standing

- ***Hands-On:*** Toyota's Auris, Yaris, Verso, and Avensis
- Parental styles' and children's development

- Empirical measures of family decision-making
- The role of occupational prestige in determining social class
- Current data about the correlation between education and income
- Enriched descriptions of America's social classes
- ***Showcased:*** Mothers' socialization styles, parental styles and consumer socialization, children's development as consumers, children as three markets, measure of family decision making, occupational prestige rankings, ethics and occupational prestige, seven educational levels and corresponding incomes, descriptions of social classes: "inherited wealth and privilege," "the nouveau rich," "achieving professionals," "faithful followers," "security minded," "the insecure," and "rock bottom."
- ***Ads:*** Listerine Smart Rinse, Mott's apple juice, Lever 2000 soap, Ligne Roset furniture, Rock Resorts, Bad Bath & Beyond, and Brain Candy Toys.

Chapter 11: Culture's Influence on Consumer Behavior

- ***Hands-On:*** Dodge; Dell
- The Rokeach typology and illustrative promotional themes
- Gordon's Survey of Personal and Interpersonal Values
- ***Ads:*** distraction.gov, ISKCON, and ITC.

Chapter 12: Cross-Cultural Consumer Behavior: An International Perspective

- ***Hands-On:*** Patek Philippe; Frito Lay
- Measures of cross-cultural dimensions
- Linguistic and legal barriers in global marketing
- ***Showcased:*** Profiles of leading global brands, five charts depicting prominent nations' consumers' disposable income expenditures, and Japan's VALS.
- ***Ads:*** Philips
- ***Case:*** LG Mobile

Part V: Consumer Decision-Making, Marketing Ethics, and Consumer Research

Chapter 13 integrates the psychological, social, and communication elements into a consumer decision-making model, and discuss the adoption of new products. Chapter 14 addresses marketers' social responsibilities and morals with a focus on ethical issues originating from new media, and, particularly, abuses of consumers' privacy. Chapter 15 details the steps of marketing studies and tools of consumer research.

Chapter 13: Consumer Decision-Making and Diffusion of Innovations

- ***Hands-On:*** GIA; Advil
- ***Ads:*** Cafe Coffee Day, Surf Excel

Chapter 14: Marketing Ethics and Social Responsibility

- ***Hands-On:*** PeTA
- Stages of consumer socialization and exploitive targeting of children
- Manipulative nutritional labeling
- Encouraging overeating and other undesirable consumption
- Abusing consumers' privacy
- Covert marketing

- Consumer ethics
- ***Showcased:*** The impact of irresponsible marketing, regulating targeting children online, alternative (award-winning) designs of nutritional labeling, deceptive or false promotional claims, provocative marketing, promoting social causes, and measuring ethical awareness
- ***Ads:*** Ad Council, NYC Office of Emergency Management.

Chapter 15: Consumer Research

- ***Hands-On:*** Disney's Sophia the First
- ***Showcased:*** The consumer research process, questions for depth interviews, screener questionnaire, focus group discussion guide, projective techniques, survey methods, wording questions, attitudes' measures, sampling methods, and quantitative versus qualitative research.
- ***Ads:*** Gillette
- ***Case:*** Pima Air, Space Museum, and Himalaya Face Wash

Instructor Supplements

Instructor's Manual: This instructor's manual includes lecture outlines, answers to all end-of-chapter questions, additional activities and assignments for your students.

Test Bank (Test Item File): The Test Item File contains more than 1,600 questions, including multiple-choice, true/false, and essay. Each question is followed by the correct answer, the learning objective it ties to, AACSB category, course learning outcome and difficulty rating. It has been thoroughly reviewed by an assessment expert.

Instructor PowerPoints: This presentation includes basic outlines and key points from each chapter. It includes figures from the text but no forms of rich media, which makes the file size manageable. This set was also designed for the professor who prefers to customize PowerPoints.

Additional Reading Material: A chapter on Subcultures and Consumer Behavior describing how subcultures are derived from ethnicity, religion, geographic location, age, and gender.

These resources are available online on the companion website of the book at **www.pearsoned.co.in/leongschiffman**

To Our Families, Colleagues, and Friends

From Leon G. Schiffman and Joseph Wisenblit: During the intense endeavor of making an already successful textbook even better, we were supported and encouraged by our families and friends. Leon Schiffman wishes to thank his wife, Elaine, for her support and devotion; his children and grandchildren: Janet, David, Nikke and Blake Schiffman; Dana, Brad, Alan, and Noah, Reid, and Allison Sherman; and Melissa and Rob and Jordyn and Emily Slominsky.

Joe Wisenblit thanks Alan Pollack for his counsel and support; Eyal Megged for his expertise on new media strategies; Randi Priluck (Pace University) for her insights and research collaboration; Shira Libhaber for her advice in selecting the ads; and his sister, Ilana and her family: Nir, Daniel, Maya, Eli and Saul Wegrzyn.

We are deeply grateful to Marcy Schneidewind for her tenacity and patience in securing the reprint permissions for the ads and exhibits. Special recognition goes to Stanley Garfunkel for many years of friendship and insights about consumer behavior and Shannon Conlisk for her assistance. Thanks to Jenn Pascoe for the book cover artwork.

At Pearson, we thank Stephanie Wall, our steadfast editor; Jackie Martin, our dedicated project manager, and Shyam Ramasubramony.

We thank our colleagues and friends at the Tobin College of Business at St. John's University, in particular: Dean Victoria Shoaf; A. Noel Doherty and the entire St. John's department of marketing for providing a warm and friendly environment in which to conduct research and write, as well as teach. At Seton Hall University's Stillman School of Business, we thank Dean Joyce Strawser and Department Chair Steve Pirog.

Special thanks to our friends and colleagues: Benny Barak, Barry Berman, Joel Evans, William James, Charles McMellon, Susan Caccavale, and Elaine Sherman of the Zarb School of Business at Hofstra University; Martin Topol and Mary Long of the Lubin School at Pace University; Fredrica Rudell of the Hagan School of Business at Iona College; Steve Gould and other colleagues at Baruch College–CUNY; Mark Kay of Montclair State University; and Deborah J. Cohn at New York Institute of Technology.

We also acknowledge Ken Weinstein, Honeywell International; Hank Edelman and Kelley Smith, Patek Philippe; Ross Copper, Gold n Fish Marketing Group; Lancy Herman, Mediamark Research; Moya Amateau, Ipsos Mendelsohn Research; Bill Carroll, Euromonitor International; Diana Schrage, Kohler Company; Mary Lee Keane and Erica Stoppenbach, Effie Worldwide; Helen Priestley, McCain Foods; and Nir Wegrzyn, BrandOpus, U.K.

We are especially grateful to our own consumers, the graduate and undergraduate students of consumer behavior and their professors, who have used the earlier editions of this textbook and provided us with invaluable feedback.

From S. Ramesh Kumar: I express my gratitude to Prof B. Ilango, former Vice Chancellor, Bharathiar University for the constant encouragement and support provided to me at crucial points in my career. I would like to acknowledge my well-wisher Mr S. Swaminathan, Chief Executive, Customer Equity Solutions for his inspiring dialogs with me that deepened my interest in the subject.

I would like to thank my parents and my wife Amrith Ramesh for the support provided to me.

I would like to thank Mr Neeraj Bhalla, Associate Acquisitions Editor at Pearson, for the support he had extended for the work. C. Purushothaman, Production Editor, impressed me with his dedication and efficiency, and I thank him.

I would also like to thank Ms Sanhita Sinha, Editorial Assistant at Pearson, who has gone into great details to execute the proposed adaptation. Her passion towards her job, her intent to get things right, and her efforts to provide the best support after she had understood the nuances of the text will make her an asset to any publishing organization.

Profile of the Indian Adapter

Dr. S. Ramesh Kumar has been with the Indian Institute of Management Bangalore (IIM-B) for the last nineteen years and he has a mix of industry, academic, and research experience of thirty-three years. His areas of interests include branding–consumer behavior interface, cultural values, relationship marketing, and combining online and offline marketing strategies. He was awarded the ICFAI Best Teacher Award by Association for Indian Management Schools (AIMS).

Dr. Kumar specializes in applying marketing and behavioral concepts to the Indian marketing context. His co-authored papers and cases have appeared in *Journal of Integrated Marketing Communication*, *Journal of Brand Management*, *Ivey Business Journal*, *Marketing Review*, *Journal of Customer Behavior*, several case titles in Richard Ivey School of Business's case collection, and IIM B–Harvard Business School series of cases. His book publications include *Consumer Behavior (10th edition) Marketing and Branding-The Indian Scenario, Marketing Nuggets – Conceptual Dimensions in Marketing*, which won the first prize awarded by The Federation of Educational Publishers in India and two edited books on cases in collaboration with Pearson and Richard Ivey School of Business. He has presented papers in several international conferences of repute and has been a visiting scholar in universities abroad.

Credits Page

Professor S. Ramesh Kumar and Pearson wish to thank the following executives for their help and cooperation in procuring the Indian ads, visuals, and permissions:

Mr. Sachin Bangera for P*e*TA India

Mr. R.S. Sodhi and Mr. Priyang Bhatt for Amul

Ms. Rahmat Azmi for ColorPlus

Mr. Karthik Srinivasan and Mr. Vikram Passi for Vodafone

Mr. Sheshank Reddy for Levi's

Mr. Parisi Filippo for United Colors of Benetton

Mr. Sooraj Bhat for Madura Fashion and Lifestyle

Mr. Somprabh Singh for Titan

Mr. Madhurjya Banerjee for Lifebuoy

Ms. Deepika Warrier and Mr. Prakhar Kasar for Pepsi

Ms. Devyani Rohatgi for TVS Motors

Mr. Soumitra Pal for Tata Motors

Mr. Rishi Vasudev for Arvind Limited

Ms. Harman Dhillon for Dove

Mr. Sairam Krishnamurthy for Pond's and Fair & Lovely

Mr. Pratik Mukherjee for Gillette

Ms. Antaash Sheikh for The Himlaya Drug Company

Mr. Shawn Chandy for Park Avenue

Mr. Naveen Raman for Edurite, Pearson

Mr. Chella Pandyan for Mondelez International

Mr. Vineeth Vishwambharan and Mr. Suresh Chand for ITC

Mr. Kapil Kulkarni for Pidilite

Ms. Shweta Chawla for Viacom 18

Mr. Simon Kemp for WeAreSocial

Chanchalapathi Das for Iskcon, Bengaluru

Ms. Nirjhara Rastogi for Philips

Ms. Madhuvanthi Anand for United Spirits

Mr. K. Ramakrishnan and Ms. Devahuti for Café Coffee Day

Ms. Pooja Advani for CavinKare

Mr. Aswath Venkataraman for Surf Excel

Ms. Anna Pospiech for the Himalaya Case Study from Richard Ivey School of Business

Mr. Vinay Kamath for *The Hindu Business Line*

1

Technology-Driven Consumer Behavior

Learning Objectives

1 To understand the evolution of the marketing concept, the most prominent tools used to implement marketing strategies, the relationship between value and customer retention, and the objectives of socially responsible marketing.

2 To understand how the Internet and related technologies improve marketing transactions by adding value that benefits both marketers and customers.

3 To understand the interrelationships among customer value, satisfaction, and retention, and technology's revolutionary role in designing effective retention measures and strategies.

4 To understand consumer behavior as an interdisciplinary area, consumer decision-making, and the structure of this book.

MARKETING is the activity, set of institutions, and processes for creating, communicating, delivering, and exchanging offerings that have value for customers, clients, partners, and society.[1] **Consumer behavior** is the study of consumers' actions during searching for, purchasing, using, evaluating, and disposing of products and services that they expect will satisfy their needs. The core of marketing is identifying unfilled needs and delivering products and services that satisfy these needs. Consumer behavior explains how individuals make decisions to spend their available resources (i.e., time, money, effort) on goods that marketers offer for sale. The study of consumer behavior describes what products and brands consumers buy, why they buy them, when they buy them, where they buy them, how often they buy them, how often they use them, how they evaluate them after the purchase, and whether or not they buy them repeatedly.

People buy cars because they need personal transportation. However, the types of cars people buy are determined not by needs alone, but also by how cars express their owners' characteristics. Therefore, car marketers differentiate their products by how specific car brands and models appeal to buyers' psychology.

Egotism and power are pervasive psychological needs, and marketers often appeal to them in advertisements. The Scion ad in Figure 1.1 invites potential buyers to "Take On the Machine." Toyota positioned Scion as a car for drivers who like to face challenges, and feel powerful and in control of their environment. Positioning is conveying the product's benefits and image to potential (or existing) customers, so that the product stands out distinctly in their minds and is not viewed as a "me too" item. Positioning is an essential component of marketing and explained fully in Chapters 2 and 4.

FIGURE 1.1 Scion: "Take On The Machine"

First, this chapter describes the evolution of the marketing concept, marketing strategies for satisfying consumers' needs, and socially responsible marketing. Secondly, it describes how the Internet and new technologies can improve marketing transactions and benefit marketers and consumers alike. Afterwards, we explain the interrelationships among customer value, satisfaction, and retention, and using technology to design more effective retention strategies. Lastly, we describe consumer behavior as an interdisciplinary subject, how consumers make purchase decisions, and the structure of this book.

Learning Objective

1 To understand the evolution of the marketing concept, the most prominent tools used to implement marketing strategies, the relationship between value and customer retention, and the objectives of socially responsible marketing.

The Marketing Concept

Marketing and consumer behavior stem from the **marketing concept**, which maintains that the essence of marketing consists of satisfying consumers' needs, creating value, and retaining customers. It maintains that companies must produce only those goods that they have already determined that consumers would buy.

The **production concept**, a business approach conceived by Henry Ford, maintains that consumers are mostly interested in product availability at low prices; its implicit marketing objectives are cheap, efficient production and intensive distribution. This approach makes sense when consumers are more interested in obtaining the product than they are in specific features, and will buy what's available rather than wait for what they really want. Before the 20th century, only wealthy consumers could afford automobiles, because cars were assembled individually and it took considerable time and expense to produce each vehicle. Early in the 20th century, Henry Ford became consumed with the idea of producing cars that average Americans could afford. In 1908, Ford began selling the sturdy and reliable Model T for $850—an inexpensive price for that day. Soon he found out that he could not meet the overwhelming consumer demand for his cars, so in 1913 he introduced the assembly line. The new production method enabled Ford to produce good-quality cars more quickly and much less expensively. In 1916, Ford sold Model Ts for $360 and sold more than 100 times as many cars as he did in 1908.[2] In only eight years, Americans got the product that led to our nation's extensive system of highways and the emergence of suburbs and large shopping malls.

Henry Ford's near-monopoly of the car industry did not last. In 1923, as the automobile market was rapidly growing thanks to Ford's mass production, Alfred P. Sloan became president and chairman of General Motors. He inherited a company that was built through takeovers of small car companies that had been producing ill-assorted models unguided by clear business objectives. Sloan reorganized the company and in 1924 articulated the company's product strategy as "a car for every purse and purpose." While Ford continued to produce the Model T until 1927 and stubbornly held onto the production concept, GM offered a variety of affordable mass-produced models, from the aristocratic Cadillac to the proletarian Chevrolet. In addition, Sloan stated: "The best way to serve the customer is the way the customer wants to be served."* About 30 years before the birth of the marketing concept, Alfred Sloan understood the core elements of marketing: all consumers are *not* alike and firms must identify and cater to different customer groups (or segments) and provide solid customer service. Although Ford was the industry's pioneer and considered unsurpassed, within several years GM took over a large portion of Ford's market share and became America's largest car company.[3]

---

* Alfred P. Sloan

As more and more companies studied customers' needs and offered products that satisfied them well, companies began offering more and more versions, models, and features, often indiscriminately. They were guided by the **product concept**, which assumes that consumers will buy the product that offers them the highest quality, the best performance, and the most features. A product orientation leads the company to strive constantly to improve the quality of its product and to add new features if they are technically feasible, without finding out first whether consumers really want these features. A product orientation often leads to **marketing myopia**, that is, a focus on the product rather than on the needs it presumes to satisfy.

Marketing myopia occurs when companies ignore crucial changes in the marketplace and look "in the mirror rather than through the window." For example, in the 1980s, Apple bundled its software and hardware together and ignored customers who wanted to buy them separately. Apple sold its software, which was better than other operating systems, only when installed on its own, expensive computers. In contrast, Microsoft licensed DOS (disk operating system)—the less efficient and harder-to-operate software—to any manufacturer that wanted to install it on its computers. Most consumers bought the less expensive, DOS-operated computers, and for many years Apple was an insignificant player in the industry. Apple focused on its product and lost sight of the fact that consumers wanted to buy hardware and software separately.

Evolving from the production concept and the product concept, the **selling concept** maintains that marketers' primary focus is selling the products that they have decided to produce. The assumption of the selling concept is that consumers are unlikely to buy the product unless they are aggressively persuaded to do so—mostly through the "hard sell" approach. This approach does not consider customer satisfaction, because consumers who are aggressively induced to buy products they do not want or need, or products of low quality, will not buy them again. Unhappy buyers often communicate their dissatisfactions with the product through negative word-of-mouth that dissuades potential consumers from making similar purchases.

Implementing the marketing concept requires sellers to use consumer research, market segmentation, a combination of the product, price, place, and promotion strategies, provide value and result in long-term customer satisfaction and retention.

Consumer Research

Consumers are complex individuals, subject to a variety of psychological and social needs, and the needs and priorities of different consumer segments differ dramatically. To design products and marketing strategies that fulfill consumer needs, marketers must study consumers' consumption behavior in depth. The term **consumer research** refers to the process and tools used to study consumer behavior (see Chapter 16). Consumer research is a form of **market research**, a process that links the consumer, customer, and public to the marketer through information in order to identify marketing opportunities and problems, evaluate marketing actions, and judge the performance of marketing strategies. The market research process outlines the information required, designs the method for collecting information, manages the data collection process, analyzes the results, and communicates the findings to marketers.

Market Segmentation, Targeting, and Positioning

The focus of the marketing concept is satisfying consumer needs. At the same time, recognizing the high degree of diversity among us, consumer researchers seek to identify the many similarities that exist among the peoples of the world. For example, we all have the same kinds of biological needs, no matter where we are born: the needs for food and nourishment, for water, for air, and for shelter from the environment's elements. We also develop or acquire needs after we are born, which are shaped by the environment and culture in which we live, our education, and our experiences. The interesting thing about acquired needs is that many people share the same ones. This commonality of need or interest constitutes a market segment, which enables the marketer to target consumers with specifically designed products and/or promotional appeals that satisfy the needs of that segment. The marketer must also adapt the image of its product (i.e., "position" it), so that each market segment perceives the product as better fulfilling its specific needs than competitive products. The three elements of this strategic framework are market segmentation, targeting, and positioning.

Market segmentation, targeting, and positioning are the foundation of turning consumers into customers. **Market segmentation** is the process of dividing a market into subsets of consumers with common needs or characteristics. It consists of defining or identifying groups with shared needs that are different from those shared by other groups. **Targeting** means selecting the segments that the company views as prospective customers and pursuing them. **Positioning** is the process by which a company creates a distinct image and identity for its products, services, and brands in consumers' minds. The image must differentiate the company's offering from competing ones and communicate to the target audience that the particular product or service fulfills their needs better than competing offerings do. Successful positioning focuses on communicating the *benefits* that the product provides. Because there are many similar products in almost any marketplace, an effective positioning strategy must communicate the product's *distinct* benefit(s). In fact, most new products (including new forms of existing products, such as new flavors and sizes) fail to capture significant market shares and are discontinued because consumers perceive them as "me-too" products lacking a unique image or benefit.

How can consumer behavior enable marketers to understand the consumers at the lower end of the socio-economic spectrum? In the Indian context, Horlicks Asha, a milk food that costs half the price of the existing offerings, was tested in Andhra Pradesh. Coca Cola sold powdered beverage Vitingo at ₹2.50 in Orissa. Pepsi Co. was working on a beverage and snack priced between ₹1 and 5 for people who suffer from inadequate nutrition.

Lower-income value explorers may be slum dwellers (about seven crores of the population) who have a household income of ₹72,000 per year (approx.). They constitute a significant segment of consumers for low-priced or packaged fast moving consumer goods (FMCG) products.*

Hence, marketers need to think how consumer behavior principles can be applied to these contexts and how these principles are different in terms of their application from other contexts.

The Marketing Mix

The **marketing mix (four Ps)** consists of four elements:

1. *Product or service:* The features, designs, brands, and packaging offered, along with post-purchase benefits such as warranties and return policies.
2. *Price:* The list price, including discounts, allowances, and payment methods.
3. *Place:* The distribution of the product or service through stores and other outlets.
4. *Promotion:* The advertising, sales promotion, public relations, and sales efforts designed to build awareness of and demand for the product or service.

Box 1.1 Consumer Behavior as the "Back Office" of a Brand's Success

Ek Tha Tiger, a movie shot in foreign locales with a star-studded cast, earned ₹300 crores at the box office. On the other hand, *Kahaani*, a low-budget film shot in the by-lanes of Kolkata, earned ₹104 crores in 50 days. Although belonging to different genres, these movies were successful because the movie makers had recognized the presence of the right segments[4] and that had triggered certain attitudinal elements among them. Renault Duster and Audi 3 may have had the right marketing mix, elements, and segmentation,[5] but perceptual aspects that interpret pricing and value were also at work. P&G lost at least US$ 50 million when its innovative fruits and vegetables cleaner (spray and solution variants) failed because the habits of the consumers could not be changed. Also, dealers were reluctant to stock the product (attitude creation) as consumers would think that they were selling bad fruits and vegetables that required a cleaner.[6]

Socially Responsible Marketing

The marketing concept—fulfilling the needs of target audiences—is somewhat shortsighted. Some products that satisfy customer needs are harmful to individuals and society and others cause environmental deterioration. Studying consumer behavior results in an understanding of why and how consumers make purchase decisions, so critics are concerned that an in-depth understanding of consumer behavior can enable unethical marketers to exploit human vulnerabilities in the marketplace and engage in other unethical marketing practices to achieve business objectives.

Because all companies prosper when society prospers, marketers would be better off if they integrated social responsibility into their marketing strategies. All marketing must balance the needs of society with the needs of the individual and the organization. The **societal marketing concept** requires marketers to fulfill the needs of the target audience in ways that improve, preserve, and enhance society's well-being while simultaneously meeting their business objectives. Regrettably, some marketers ignore laws and market potentially harmful products.

* The following observations have been sourced from Ratna Bhushan's article "Nestle exploring low-cost infant milk market" published in The Economic Times on 12th August, 2010 and Nupur Anand's article "Slums turn haven for consumer firms" published in DNA on 14th May, 2013.

The societal marketing concept maintains that companies would be better off in a stronger, healthier society and that marketers that incorporate ethical behavior and social responsibility attract and maintain loyal consumer support over the long term. Accordingly, fast-food restaurants should develop foods that contain less fat and starch and more nutrients; marketers should not advertise foods to young people in ways that encourage overeating, or use professional athletes in liquor or tobacco advertisements because celebrities so often serve as role models for the young. An advertising campaign featuring unreasonably slim females with pale faces and withdrawn expressions must be reconsidered because of its potential to increase eating disorders among young women. Of course, eliminating such practices altogether is unreasonable, but curtailing them is not.

Many companies have incorporated social goals into their mission statements and believe that marketing ethics and social responsibility are important components of organizational effectiveness. They recognize that socially responsible activities improve their image among consumers, stockholders, the financial community, and other relevant publics, and that ethical and socially responsible practices are simply good business, resulting not only in a favorable image but ultimately in increased sales. The converse is also true: Perceptions of a company's lack of social responsibility or unethical marketing strategies negatively affect consumer purchase decisions. For instance, McDonald's became the target of television commercials blaming it for heart disease. In the commercial, produced by the nonprofit Physicians Committee for Responsible Medicine, a woman weeps over a dead man lying in a morgue. In his hand is a hamburger. At the end, the golden arches appear over his feet, followed by the words, "I was lovin' it," a twist on McDonald's longtime ad slogan, "I'm lovin' it." A voiceover says, "High cholesterol, high blood pressure, heart attacks. Tonight, make it vegetarian."[7]

A division of Warner Music Group that operates online fan clubs for pop-music stars was forced to pay $1 million to settle charges that it illegally collected personal information from the sites' child users. The Federal Trade Commission charged the company with violating the Children's Online Privacy Protection Act—a law that forbids websites from collecting personal information from users under 13 years of age without parental consent. According to the charges, more than 100,000 users' information was gathered illegally through websites for fans of four pop stars. The four websites "attracted a significant number of children under age 13," according to the lawsuit, and "failed" to meet the requirements established by the children's privacy law.[8] When Google first revealed in 2010 that cars it was using to map streets were also sweeping up sensitive personal information from wireless home networks, it called the data collection a mistake. Subsequently, federal regulators charged that Google had "deliberately impeded and delayed" an investigation into the data collection and ordered a $25,000 fine on the search giant.[9]

There are also many not-for-profit advocacy groups whose mission is to advance causes that are ethically and morally right. Among many others, such causes include animal rights, fighting childhood obesity and overeating, supporting sober and nondistracted driving, fighting drug abuse and deadly diseases, and encouraging environmentally sound practices (see Chapter 15). Figure 1.2 shows an ad by a not-for-profit entity,

Source: PeTA India

FIGURE 1.2 PeTA Advocates Socially Responsible Behavior

People for the Ethical Treatment of Animals (PeTA). It features celebrities and urges us to share the world with animals and not mistreat them. By doing so, we will protect and improve the natural environment.

Learning Objective

2 To understand how the Internet and related technologies improve marketing transactions by adding value that benefits both marketers and customers.

Technology Enriches the Exchange Between Consumers and Marketers

Say you are in a strange city and need a hotel for the night. You pull out your smartphone, search for hotels on Google, and find a nearby one listed at the top of the rankings, with a little phone icon that says, "Call." You tap it, reach the hotel, and ask for a room. And just like that, Google made money. That icon was a so-called "click-to-call ad," and the hotel paid Google for it when you called. Technology has revolutionized the marketing mix, as well as segmentation, targeting, positioning, and customer retention. When consumers use their computers, mobile phones, electronic readers, tablets, and other electronic gadgets, they provide marketers with the kind of information that enables companies to target them immeasurably more effectively than during the pre-Internet days. Thus, online technologies create a "value exchange." Marketers provide value to consumers in the form of information that turns shoppers into sophisticated customers, including opportunities to customize products easily, entertainment content, and much more. While online, consumers provide value to marketers by "revealing themselves," which enables companies to market their products more efficiently and precisely. In other words, consumers "pay" for the Internet's seemingly free content by providing virtually unlimited information about themselves to marketers, who gather, analyze, and use it to target buyers.

Advertisers are offering more and more original content online because viewers are now so accustomed to watching programs on devices like mobile phones and tablets that the lines between traditional television and Internet video have become blurred. Advertisers are also shifting dollars from traditional display advertising to sites like Facebook that can deliver huge audiences. Many advertisers say they worry that with so much new content being thrown at the market on so many different platforms, audiences for individual shows will become even more fragmented and microscopic than they already are.[10]

Surfing online allows consumers to locate the best prices for products or services, bid on various marketing offerings, bypass distribution outlets and middlemen, and shop for goods around the globe and around the clock. They can also compare the features of various product models and engage in social networking with consumers who share the same interests, providing and receiving information about their purchases. Online communications created sophisticated and discerning consumers, who are hard to attract, satisfy, and retain. More than ever before, marketers must customize their products, add value to the physical product or the core of a service, provide the right benefits to the right consumer segments, and position their products effectively. Technology also enables marketers to refine their strategies because they can readily customize their offerings and promotional messages, offer more effective pricing and shorter distribution channels, and build long-term relationships with customers. Marketers that use rapidly advancing technologies to track consumers can identify opportunities for creating new offerings, and improve and extend existing products and services. They can gather comprehensive consumer information by tracking consumers online, requiring prospective buyers to register at their websites, and combining this knowledge with demographic and lifestyle data gathered offline (see Chapter 2).

The following example illustrates a value exchange. At Amazon, buyers can find books instantly, read sample pages and reviews posted by other readers, and begin reading purchased books within minutes after placing their orders (as opposed to going to a physical store, picking up a heavy paper copy, standing in line to pay, and then carrying the book.) Simultaneously, when consumers visit Amazon's website, the company records every aspect of their visits, including the books they looked at, the sample pages and reviews they clicked on, and the time spent on each activity. This enables Amazon to build long-term relationships with customers by developing customized book recommendations that shoppers view upon returning to Amazon's website. Amazon also participates in "information exchange networks" that enable marketers to place ads that "follow" consumers into other websites featuring products that consumers have examined or purchased previously (see Chapter 8).

Consumers Have Embraced Technology

Although many assume that only young consumers visit websites and shop online and "reveal themselves" to marketers, it is not so. The Internet has drastically improved consumers' access to the information they need when they buy products for the first time

Application 1: Importance of Digital Marketing and Branding in India

When it comes to information that is associated with product decisions, 90% of consumers trust sources of information from known contacts. 70% trust consumers' online posts;14% trust company's advertising. 80% of consumers search online for product decisions in a week. Brand-related conversations are on the increase in the online media.[11] User-generated content is rapidly getting created. Consumer engagement and integrity are the two factors that consumers consider to trust a brand.

5.3 trillion ads are shown online each year, 400 million tweets are sent daily, 144,000 hours of YouTube video are uploaded daily, and 4.75 billion pieces of content are shared on Facebook every day.[12]

These pieces of research provide an indication of how digital marketing and word of mouth will change the buying context and may also experience an exponential growth in the emerging markets.

Application 2: Consumer Behavior in a Dynamic and Digital World

Google is an example of how well a product can adapt itself to consumer behavior over time and in a changing environment. People look up anything and everything on Google, one of which is entertainment that has a profound impact on consumers. Google + is all about groups (reference groups in a virtual domain) and You Tube, also from Google, has created a revolution in viral marketing. Google's Android runs millions of apps, Google Chrome offers easy download of softwares, and Google Apps online store can create several applications that are associated with entertainment. Google has evolved itself from a search engine to one that provides diverse services through several platforms and offerings. Consumer behavior had played a significant role in its process of adaption.

SAP is another such instance. The company, mostly associated with business to business (B2B) marketing, has moved into the consumer space with its applications like SUP that can run on Android, iOS, Blackberry, and Recall Plus that consumers can download and use.[13] Intel, with its Atom and Medfield offerings used in consumer computing and mobile applications, is another example of B2B companies that are moving into the consumer space. Consumer behavior in today's context needs to be understood even by B2B marketers. Mobile phones, retailing, and gaming can also be brought together. An interesting example is Mojostreet[14] game from the world of digital marketing. It is a game that is based on the board game Monopoly and has 5.5 million geo-tagged locations in India. Players discover cities, recommend it to others, and the game can be downloaded. It can be used with Facebook accounts and mobile apps. The game has a collaborative association with 150 brands across India at 1300 locations providing loyalty rewards.

Social media and gaming (digital marketing), reference groups, brand associations, association of fun and youth, and retail loyalty (instrumental learning) are some of the concepts that can be associated with Mojostreet's offering.Vstart.mobi is a company that created an innovative pricing model for mobile ads between free downloads of apps that depended on ads and apps that were priced.[15]

---

or replace them. Simultaneously, the Internet enables marketers to gather true behavioral data about consumers because they can observe shopping behavior. Before the Internet, marketers gathered behavioral data by relying primarily on buyers' self reports, which often reflected what consumers wanted the marketers to think about them rather than consumers' *actual* buying patterns. For instance, car manufacturers that enable consumers to design their cars online from the "ground up" can quickly determine which colors, features, and accessories are most popular. They can also find out which combinations of features and car attributes are the most desirable and add models with such configurations.

When consumers compare products online, they look at the features and attributes of various models and brands side-by-side. For example, when comparing digital cameras, the most prominent evaluative attributes include the lens, screen, megapixels, light sensor, weight, and photo editing capabilities. Most websites of companies selling comparable brands offer visitors the opportunity to compare models and brands within a single screen, and offer one-click access to more detailed technical information. By observing consumers' comparisons, marketers can identify their direct competitors and the product attributes that consumers consider the most important. Figure 1.3 depicts a comparison of three electronic readers that resemble the options available to customers online for comparing brands of the same products.

	NOVO	DELONEX	TOME
Size	3.9" × 4.8	3.5" × 4.9	4.0" × 4.1
Weight	7.8 ounces	7.5 ounces	8.6 ounces
Touch Screen	Some models	No	All models
Screen Pixels	600 × 800	758 × 1024	1200 × 1600
Memory	8 GB	16 GB	16 to 64 GB
Battery Life	Up to 8 hours	Up to 11 hours	Up to 12.5 hours
Bookstore	Amazon	Amazon	Amazon and Sony
3G Phone	Available with selected providers	Available with selected providers	Available with all U.S. providers
Overseas Capacity	Yes (roaming charges apply)	No	No
Content Storage	Free ***Cloud***Novo storage for Novo content	Free DeLonex***Sky*** for DeLonex content	Free storage for content and address book, calendar, and bookmarks
Price	$199	$279	$359

FIGURE 1.3 Comparing E-book Readers

Box 1.2 Creating Attitudes Using Digital Marketing

In the times to come mobile applications or *apps* are likely to gain popularity over mobile advertising. The advantage of apps is that a brand can create applications that are in line with the proposition of the brand. For example, Red Bull associates itself with the belief of "high energy" through caffeine and other ingredients. Its association with extreme adventure sports has strengthened over the years. Hence, consumers associate the cognitive belief of providing high energy and the affective (emotional) aspects of the thrill of adventures (even the experience of seeing such visuals) with the brand. Keeping in line with these conceptions, Red Bull launched its gaming app, Kart Fighter.

Similarly, a brand like Café Coffee Day (CCD) known for its associations with friendly groups, associations, and hangouts is likely to strengthen such associations with the mobile application, Four Squares that provides the locations of restaurants and the presence of friends within a locality. Coca-Cola's "happiness" proposition can be strengthened by applications that provide happiness through group contests and togetherness. The fundamental difference between the traditional approach of advertising or marketing communication and the contemporary usage of mobile applications is the involvement levels associated with the usage of the mobile applications by consumers. In the traditional process, the brand's overall associations (or schemas as it is referred to by concepts associated with consumer learning) are created by advertising imagery by repeated exposure and usage of a specific brand. The mobile application approach creates a ritual and repetitive process by which the brand becomes a part of the cycle associated with consumer usage of the app. The conative (or the action- related part of the attitude) associated with "intention to buy the brand" can be converted into "intention to use the app" of the brand. Such an approach adds to the behavioral loyalty associated with the brand.

Interactive and Novel Communication Channels

Traditional advertising is a one-way process in which the marketer pays large sums of money to reach large numbers of potential buyers via mass media, and can assess whether its promotional messages were effective only after the fact, by looking at sales and post-purchase marketing research studies. In contrast, electronic communications enable a two-way interactive exchange in which consumers instantly react to marketers' messages by, say, clicking on links within websites or leaving them quickly. Thus, marketers can gauge the effectiveness of their promotional messages instantly, instead of relying on delayed feedback (see Chapter 7). In addition, many U.S. homes now have TV cable boxes that enable two-way communications between consumers and broadcasters. Many cable companies are experimenting with technologies that allow consumers to select only the commercials they like to see by using their remote controls. Another example of interactivity is the supermarket scanners that keep track of households' purchases and instantly provide personalized coupons at the checkout counter.

Another facet of interactivity is promotional messages that are designed largely by the customers themselves. Audi posted three versions of its ad on YouTubeAudi.com and let consumers select which ending should air; Ford Motor's Lincoln brand started a Twitter campaign that asked people to tweet their most memorable road-trip stories. As another example, a Samsung television ad mocking Apple's iPhone incorporated consumer comments from Twitter into its pitch. The spot shows people talking about different features of the new iPhone as they wait in line for an Apple store to open. One of the customers says, "I heard that you have to have an adapter to use the dock on the new one."* Another young man chimes in, "Yeah, yeah, but they make the coolest adapters."* According to Samsung, this ad was based on hundreds of tweets complaining about or poking fun at specific features of the iPhone 5, such as the need for an adapter if a person wants to use the phone with older speakers, chargers, or other accessories.[16]

Technological innovations sometimes force marketers to alter long-established marketing strategies. Consumers can now skip ads using advanced time-shifting and recording devices. Marketers responded by embedding promotional messages directly into TV shows.

Cross-screen marketing consists of tracking and targeting users across their computers, mobile phones, and tablets. New software enables marketers to try to figure out when a mobile user is the same person as a desktop user. The new technology enables advertisers to "push" ads to mobile phones based on the interests people expressed while surfing the Internet.

Advertising across media platforms is essential. A Nielsen study showed that about 84% of smartphone owners and 86% of tablet owners said they used their mobile device while watching TV at least once during a 30-day period. Nearly half of those tablet owners visited a social networking while watching TV. Therefore, during a broadcast of the MTV Video Music Awards, a well-known rapper appeared in a commercial for Pepsi. At exactly the same time, anyone looking at MTV's website or an MTV mobile application saw interactive ads for the soda maker. Such simultaneous commercial blanketing is aimed at capturing the attention of consumers who watch television while surfing the Web or tweeting.[17]

Digital Marketing tools like YouTube, Twitter, mobile phones, mobile phone applications, and blogs do not offer a concrete strategy to brand managers, if used in isolation. They need to be used in tandem with several consumer behavior concepts to ensure the enrichment of a brand's equity. The following are specific questions that need to be taken into consideration when digital marketing is employed by a brand manager:

- How would a specific strategy of digital marketing fit in with a brand's equity?
- What are the objectives to be achieved by using the digital aspect of marketing?
- How would the chosen digital marketing strategy be in tune with the overall marketing communication associated with the brand?
- How would the digital marketing strategy, along with other forms of a brand's marketing communication, enhance the equity of the brand and the usage of Integrated Marketing Communication or IMC?

For example, Bournville chocolate from Cadbury used digital marketing campaign "Not too sweet" (social media) to target a segment in the age group of 19–30 years (objective).[18] It may be noted that the "bitter chocolate eating culture" is not a part of traditional Indian eating culture and the new segment (youngsters in this age group) is into social media. Hence, social media may be a good choice to enhance the brand's equity. The chosen digital strategy is in line with the earlier television campaigns of the brand that positioned Bournville as "something to be earned" because youngsters reward themselves with several things, as observed by their spending culture.

There are other instances where television campaigns mention about the superiority of the brand's ingredients (attributes of the brand). Finally, the brand's equity was boosted both because of its association with attributes as well as its association with social media. This association is powerful from the viewpoint of "Word of Mouth (WOM)" and for diffusing a positive attitude about the brand among its target segment (feelings, associations, and judgments in Kevin Lane Keller's brand equity model). Bournville's objective of creating an attitude about the brand – among the target segment – was achieved through a proposition

* Suzanne Vranica "Ads Let Viewers Be Mad Men," online.wsj.com, February 2, 2013; Suzanne Vranica, "Tweets Spawn Ad Campaigns," online.wsj.com,

("earned reward"), the attributes of the brand (superiority of the ingredients used), and the brand's association with the target segment through a synergy of traditional and digital media.

Digital marketing, in conjunction with consumer behavior, can be used to enhance brand equity in the following ways:

1. Creating strong brand associations (power of classical conditioning).
2. Creating favorable attitudes.
3. Creating an overall perception of the brand (Gestalt effect).
4. Using group behavior to identify like-minded groups (reference group aspects leading to WOM).
5. Using the power of self-concepts (personality).
7. Capturing new segments (Bournville).

Reference groups are those groups that influence the attitudes, values, and behavior of a consumer. Reference groups are perhaps the most important source of aspiration and social interaction for an individual consumer. With social media exploding in the form of Facebook, Twitter, and YouTube, the visual impact of reference groups along with their opinions form an important aspect of WOM and the impact of visuals (IOV). While there have been attempts to quantify WOM, it is not clear from the academic literature how IOV can be quantified.

Watches, apparels, mobiles, and two-wheelers develop brands that may be an extension of a consumer's personality. Most of these brands contribute to one's self-concept and these aspects have an impact on how an individual associates himself or herself with a respective reference group. A brand like Park Avenue or Allen Solly has a virtual mirror that can provide several choices from the brand and digital marketing (mobile-based) can even enable the consumer to get a quick feedback from his or her friends (the respective reference group) about those choices.

In the days to come, prospective brand managers will be expected to use digital marketing to promote low-involvement (relative to the categories and brands discussed in the previous paragraph) brands or categories.

Racold is a well-known brand name in water heaters. The brand had launched a TV campaign (based on lifestyle research that revealed that Indians feel that taking bath is a ritual that they have to go through) that showed teachers and umpires feeling refreshed and "reborn" after a hot bath every morning.[19]

Racold has an Android application to locate the nearest service centre. They are employing digital marketing initiatives to make use of the potential in India as well as to diffuse its well-known name among consumers.

While reference groups are important for socially-visible categories, there needs to be a conceptual approach to make use of social media for categories that may not have social presence or have a high degree of involvement among consumers. For example, the category of antiseptic lotion may have a low degree of involvement, but it can experience a high degree of situational relevance and that can be captured on Facebook or Flickr or Pinterest. Most professionals would do an extended decision making search on social media when they search for real estate avenues. Racold, for instance, needs to capture appropriate segments and make its product a part of the real estate brand. (The brand also works with builders in the B2B space that may be of interest to its target segments.) Such situational relevance will enable the brand to reach out to several reference groups on the social media. Also, social media will enable the a brand to get visually-linked to a high- involvement category like real estate.

Sunsilk shampoo had used the website www.gangofgirls to build a community of girls (target segment) to exchange tips on hair styling and also interact with the company's hair care specialists.

Box 1.3 The "Digital Intent"

Attitudes include a component called conative aspect that is associated with the intent to buy or the action-based aspect of consumer behavior. With the availability of hardware and software in smart phones, brands like BMW and Mercedez- Benz are using the iPad[20] to enhance the conative component.

Mercedez- Benz has an iPad application called iSales that enables the consumer to visualize and customize a car in a visual domain before they order it. BMW also has an iPad application called the Mobile Car Configurator for a similar purpose. It has launched a mobile show room that attempts to capture consumers in emerging cities like Agra, Jamshedpur, Nashik, and Patna.[21]

Customizing Products and Promotional Messages

Oakley is the world's primary seller of high-end sunglasses. For both men and women, the company offers numerous models designed for a variety of lifestyles and sports, and even Asian-fit glasses. Most of Oakley's sunglasses can be customized. Consumers can select frame colors (often in polished or nonpolished forms), choose from among several lens shapes and colors, select different colors for the ear socks and the Oakley icon, and even have their initials elegantly and discreetly etched on the lenses. In addition, they can choose between nonpolarized and polarized (glare-reducing) lenses. Oakley also offers several models of backpacks where consumers can choose the item's primary and contrast colors, as well as the colors of trim, logo, and zipper tape. At Nike's website, buyers can choose among many models of sneakers in different price ranges, customize the selected shoe using several colors and features (e.g., some models even allow buyers to choose the colors of the Nike swoosh and the laces), and put a personal ID on each shoe. Researchers pointed out that customization requires that customers clearly understand their preferences and express them, and also be involved with the product. This indicates that "high involvement" products (i.e., infrequently purchased and pricey items) represent the best prospects for customization.[22]

Companies can also customize promotional messages. For example, an online drugstore may vary the initial display that returning buyers see when they revisit its website. Buyers whose past purchases indicated that they tend to buy national brands will see a display arranged by brand. Past purchasers who bought mostly products that were on sale or generic brands will see a display categorized by price and discounted products.

Better Prices and Distribution

The Internet allows consumers to compare prices more effectively than ever before. For example, when consumers browse at department stores, they often use their mobile phones to check out the prices of comparable products in other stores. This has forced stores such as Target and Best Buy to match the online prices of rival retailers.[23] Some stores and brands are creating new personal touches that feature gadgets rather than a doting sales staff. One makeup marketer installed in-store touch-screen televisions to demonstrate the perfect smoky eye, something that was once the exclusive domain of makeup artists. Another store enables shoppers to use a touchpad to personalize the lighting and music in dressing rooms (there is also a button in case they need help).[24] As more books are going electronic, Apple unveiled a new version of its iBooks digital bookstore that would reduce the prices of high school textbooks by almost 90%.[25]

Marketers long ago recognized that consumers research expensive products such as electronics online. However, in trying to find the best deals, more shoppers are now going online to research groceries, personal grooming items, and household maintenance products before buying them in physical stores. In turn, marketers have begun to use advanced technologies, such as smartphone apps, to target shoppers in stores.[26]

In addition to better pricing, distribution strategies are also improving. Combating failed package delivery—a prominent problem of online retailers—Amazon has installed large metal cabinets, named Amazon Lockers, in grocery, convenience stores, and drugstores, that function like virtual doormen, accepting packages for customers for later pickup.[27]

Realizing that, sooner than later, electronic systems will replace cash and credit cards, several retailers have been developing mobile-payments systems to compete with similar products from Google and cell phone companies.[28] A "shopping bible" for women—the magazine *Lucky*—has introduced a service that saves women the cost and time of driving; a shopping site called myLuckymag.com directs readers to buy clothing and accessories directly from more than a dozen retailers.[29] Many online merchants now offer an "automatic recurring shipment" feature, which appeals to shoppers who like to order habitually needed products, like paper goods and personal care products, online.

The Web also enables marketers to improve customer service inexpensively. A waiter at a restaurant in New York City had trouble remembering all the ingredients of the intricate menu's item. He snapped pictures of the dishes, developed a system to categorize information, designed a set of icons specifying everything from potential allergens to temperature choices, and constructed a website available to the restaurant's servers. Soon, other restaurants subscribed to this service in order to train staff, do online scheduling, and provide internal discussion forums.[30]

Grocers like Safeway and Kroger are offering individualized prices based on shoppers' behaviors that could encourage them to spend more. Their pricing encourages a buyer to purchase a bigger box of Tide and bologna if the retailer's data suggests that the shopper has a large family, and expensive bologna if the data indicate that the shopper is not greatly price-conscious. As another example, a 24-pack of Brand X bottled water costs $2.71 for Ms. A but $3.69 for Ms. B. Ms. A's loyalty data indicates that she likes Brand X products, but not its bottled water. The store encourages Ms. A to put another Brand X product into her grocery cart, with the hope that she will keep buying it, whereas Ms. B is unlikely even to try Brand X bottled water. Some stores have a mobile app that allows shoppers to scan products. When they do, the store identifies them through their frequent shopper number or phone number, and knows where in the store they are. Special e-coupons are created on the spot. Thus, if someone is in the baby aisle and they just scanned diapers, the store presents them at that point with a coupon for a baby formula or baby food, based on the presumed age of their baby and what food the baby might be ready for.[31]

Learning Objective

3 To understand the interrelationships among customer value, satisfaction, and retention, and technology's revolutionary role in designing effective retention measures and strategies.

Customer Value, Satisfaction, and Retention

Customer value is the ratio between customers' perceived benefits (economic, functional, and psychological) and the resources (monetary, time, effort, psychological) they use to obtain those benefits. For example, diners at an exclusive French restaurant in New York City, where a meal with beverages may cost up to $300 per person, expect unique and delicious food, impeccable service, and beautiful decor. When diners receive what they had expected, they leave the restaurant feeling that the experience was worth the money and other resources expended (such as a month-long wait for a reservation). Other diners may go with expectations so high that they leave the restaurant disappointed. In contrast, billions of customers visit thousands of McDonald's restaurants across the globe and purchase standard, inexpensive meals from servers systematically trained by the McDonald's Corporation to deliver the company's four core standards: *quality, service, cleanliness*, and *value*. Customers flock to McDonald's outlets repeatedly because the restaurants are uniform, customers know what to expect, and customers feel that they are getting value for the resources they expend.

Customer satisfaction refers to customers' perceptions of the performance of the product or service in relation to their expectations. As noted earlier, customers have drastically different expectations of an expensive French restaurant and a McDonald's, although both are part of the restaurant industry. A customer whose experience falls below expectations (e.g., a limited wine list at an expensive restaurant or cold fries served at a McDonald's) will be dissatisfied. Diners whose experiences match expectations will be satisfied. Customers whose expectations are exceeded (e.g., by small samples of delicious food "from the Chef" served between courses at the expensive restaurant, or a well-designed play area for children at a McDonald's outlet) will be very satisfied or even delighted.

Customer Retention

Customer retention involves turning individual consumer transactions into long-term customer relationships by making it in the best interests of customers to stay with the company rather than switch to another firm. It is more expensive to win new customers than to retain existing ones, for several reasons:

1. Loyal customers buy more products and constitute a ready-made market for new models of existing products as well as new ones, and also represent an opportunity for cross-selling. Long-term customers are more likely to purchase ancillary products and high-margin supplemental products.
2. Long-term customers who are thoroughly familiar with the company's products are an important asset when new products and services are developed and tested.
3. Loyal customers are less price-sensitive and pay less attention to competitors' advertising. Thus, they make it harder for competitors to enter markets.
4. Servicing existing customers, who are familiar with the firm's offerings and processes, is cheaper. It is expensive to "train" new customers and get them acquainted with a seller's processes and policies. The cost of acquisition occurs only at the beginning of a relationship, so the longer the relationship, the lower the amortized cost.
5. Loyal customers spread positive word-of-mouth and refer other customers.
6. Marketing efforts aimed at attracting new customers are expensive; indeed, in saturated markets, it may be impossible to find new customers.[32] Low customer turnover is correlated with higher profits.
7. Increased customer retention and loyalty make the employees' jobs easier and more satisfying. In turn, happy employees feed back into higher customer satisfaction by providing good service and customer support systems.

Technology and Customer Relationships

Technologies often enhance customer relationships and retention by engaging consumers with brands. Procter and Gamble is the world's larger manufacturer of beauty and grooming (e.g., fragrances, mouthwash, toothpaste, feminine care) and household care products (e.g., household cleaning, laundry detergents, over-the-counter drugs, and disposable diapers). For every brand, the company's website includes suggestions on how to use the product more effectively. For example, for shampoo, the company provides a "scalp care handbook." For its Gillette shaving blades, the website offers comprehensive advice about facial care and proper shaving. For its detergents, P&G advises consumers how to wash white and colors, which temperature is best for which types of fabrics, and how to handle stains on different materials. Amazon.com sends personalized e-mails to previous buyers announcing newly published books that reflect their interests and are based on past purchases. Nature Valley—the granola bar brand—uses technology inspired by Google Street View. A website called Nature Valley Trail View uses cameras showing hikers, in nearly real time, in the Grand Canyon and other national parks. There is no sales pitch on the site and only a small Nature Valley logo appears on the screen. The marketer's objective is to feature lifestyles that its customers care about, engage them with the brand, and build brand awareness and loyalty.[33]

The opportunities for technology-enabled added value are virtually limitless. Professors can enhance classroom teaching with online networks and tools that enable students to read current and beyond-the-text material and practice and complete assignments from any location and at any time. Online newspapers customized to personal preferences include links to previous articles about consumers' favorite topics and send them e-mails about breaking stories. The most revolutionary example of technology-enabled value added to physical products are Apple's iTunes and its large software selection for editing and posting content online.

Researchers have identified two interrelated forms of customer engagement with marketers: **Emotional bonds** represent a customer's high level of personal commitment and attachment to the company. **Transactional bonds** are the mechanics and structures that facilitate exchanges between consumers and sellers. Savvy marketers always strive to build emotional bonds with customers. Technology, mostly in the form of social media, is the most innovative and versatile tool for engaging customers with companies emotionally and far beyond the selling act.

Box 1.4 Mere Exposure Effect and Digital Marketing

There is research indication that mere exposure to stimuli (or brands) will make the brands likeable in the perceptual field of consumers.[34] Digital media has opened up a revolutionary dimension with regard to this mere exposure effect. Instagram, a photo sharing site, has 140 million followers who have shared 16 billion photos! From across the world, every day, the site receives 45 million pictures.[35] Brands are using digital marketing to be present amidst consumers to make the fullest use of mere exposure effect. Levi's invited consumers to submit their photos for a contest that would give them an opportunity to be a part of their campaign.[36] Nike's "PHOTOID" allowed consumers (Nike has 2.1 million people on its Instagram profile) to personalize sneakers using pictures sent by consumers to social media channels.[37] Red Bull called on consumers to upload their opinion on what they thought of its new line of Editions flavor.[38]

As brands get innovative to sustain their presence on the social media, they are likely to create more intense associations with the brand at the sub-conscious level of a consumer's mind. Red Label tea, along with two celebrities, used mobile media for a contest that attracted over two and a half million people.[39] Wheel detergent gained three million unique engagements with callers when it had used the cell phone for a promotional initiative.[40] Google, after Android's one billion activation mark, announced that its next operating system will be named KitKat in a co-branding initiative with Nestle. 50 million special edition chocolates of the KitKat brand were made to announce this decision in 19 countries.[41]

Social media include means of interaction among people in which they create, share, and exchange information and ideas in virtual communities and networks. Social media use mobile and Web-based technologies to create highly interactive platforms through which individuals and communities share, co-create, discuss, and modify user-generated content. Here are several examples of using social media to engage customers emotionally: Millions of customers take pictures with their cameras and cellphones and post them on shared websites, such as Facebook and Instagram. Because people are spending less and less time looking at magazine ads and TV commercials, marketers came up with "lifestyle advertising," that is, adopting the look and feel of the images consumers find most compelling—the ones they shoot themselves. Some fashion brands created digital ads based on pictures posted by consumers. The Web home pages of several clothing companies now feature real women, rather than professional models, wearing their fashions, and one designer published print magazine ads composed of Instagram photos.

In addition to engaging customers with marketers, social media have transformed market research. Many companies can easily collect input about customers' preferences—sometimes without actively questioning consumers. Writers of TV series monitor discussion groups devoted to making critical and humorous observations about broadcasted episodes and rewrite future storylines based on viewers' comments. Similarly, marketers began testing expensive commercials by featuring them in social media first. Before a recent Super Bowl, marketers asked consumers to play a part in creating or choosing the big-game commercials for that year. A car company started a Twitter campaign that asked people to tweet their most memorable road-trip stories.[42]

In the pre-Internet days, Frito-Lay would have used focus groups, surveys, and depth interviews (see Chapter 16) to develop a new potato chip flavor. Instead, the company invited visitors to the new Lay's Facebook app to suggest new flavors and click an "I'd Eat That" button to register their preferences. Some of the results showed that beer-battered onion-ring flavor was popular in California and Ohio, while a churros flavor was a hit in New York. Frito-Lay planned to produce only three of the flavors from its contest, but gave a $1 million prize to the creator of one of those flavors. Frito-Lay has run the contest overseas and discovered chip flavors like hot and spicy crab in Thailand and pickled cucumber in Serbia. When Wal-Mart wanted to know whether to sell lollipop-shaped cake makers, it studied Twitter chatter. Walmart found that cake pops—small bites of cake on lollipop sticks—were becoming popular and people were talking a lot about them. Estée Lauder's MAC Cosmetics brand asked social media users to vote on which discontinued shades to bring back. The stuffed-animal brand Squishable solicited Facebook feedback before settling on the final version of a new toy. Samuel Adams asked users to vote on yeast, color, and other qualities to create a new beer.[43]

Application 1: Social Media and Consumer Behavior

Has the emergence of social media changed consumer behavior? If yes, in what direction? Are the concepts relevant in the era of social media and digital branding? These are some of the basic questions that need to be addressed before students go through the consumer behavior concepts. While social media has had a profound impact on how consumers behave towards brands and the market place, the appreciation for the basics of consumer behavior have only become stronger. In this digital era, social media is a tool through which consumers interact and the decades old concept of reference groups has come alive in consumer behavior. This is an example of how classic concepts need to be combined with contemporary changes in the environment when consumer behavior concepts are being considered.

Content co-creation with the involvement of the consumer may work for brands like Nike or BMW[44] but may not work for all brands. Kingfisher beer may bring consumers together on a social (digital) platform through a comic theme[45] or Miller High Life[46] may create a sensational theme on the web with television ads to attract consumers but similar approaches may not work for all brands. A brand like Coca-Cola needs to follow an approach that is different from the one associated with Fastrack when it comes to synergizing online digital platforms with conventional communication practices. Web or the social media, mobiles, and the convergence of technology can attract the fashionable youth who is willing to spend money on brands that enhance his or her self-concepts and/or group behavior. The concepts remain the same as they were in the erstwhile years; it is the context in which they are applied that has changed. This combination of concepts and contexts has created unique challenges in the environment.

Lonely Maa from Cadbury had the story of elders suffering from loneliness, Hair&Care campaign featured an upcoming singer on YouTube, and Shoppers Stop campaigns on the YouTube (each having a theme on gifting, loyalty) are some of the examples of how Indian brands have used the online media.[47]

Application 2: Personality and Digital Media

Self-Concept is part of a consumer's personality. There is no academic literature required to illustrate the importance of brands that contribute to the self-concept of consumers. We need to only look at the brands in malls and the advertising that supports these brands – soaps, lotions, creams, deodorants, perfumes, cosmetic surgeries, beauty treatments, hair coloring, organic offerings, and diamond studded dentures to name a few categories. Dove soap had earlier changed the concept of "glamorous beauty" (associated with models and celebrities) into "Real Beauty" (that every woman should feel good about her beauty). It launched a digital campaign that had "self- concept" as its theme. The "Real Beauty Sketch" campaign that was popular on the YouTube showed a lady describing her own appearance to someone who sketches her description. It also had someone known to her describe about the lady's appearance and this visualization was also sketched.[48] The campaign suggested that others' self- concept (the sketched-out version of what the person known to the lady had described about her) was much superior to the lady's sketch that she had described (actual self-concept). Dove is available today in 80 countries, the brand is worth between three to four billion dollars, and the "Real Beauty Sketch" ad has attracted about 55 million viewers within two months of its launch.[49] With the presence of complex diversity across consumers, there are several ways in which digital marketing initiatives can be used in conjunction with personality concepts.

Emotional Bonds versus Transaction-Based Relationships

The objective of discerning customers' emotional and transactional motives when buying from a company is to understand the drivers of customer satisfaction, which lead to customer retention and long-term relationships. As consumers buy more and more online, it has become important to understand what makes them satisfied during electronic transactions. Studies have identified the following determinants of customer satisfaction with online websites and merchants:[50]

1. ***Adaptation:*** The merchant's purchase recommendations match one's needs; one is enabled to order products that are tailor-made; personalized advertisements and promotions; feeling like a unique and valued customer.
2. ***Interactivity:*** Ability to view merchandise offerings from different perspectives; search tool that enables one to quickly locate products; having tools that make comparisons easy; useful information.
3. ***Nurturing:*** Receiving reminders about making purchases; providing relevant information for one's purchases; acknowledgment of appreciating one's business; making an effort to increase business with the customer; cultivating a relationship with the customer.
4. ***Commitment:*** Delivering goods on time; responding to problems encountered; customer-friendly return policies; taking good care of customers.
5. ***Network:*** Customers sharing experiences about their product purchases on the merchant's website; useful network for sharing experiences; shoppers benefit from the community of prospects and customers sponsored by the merchant.
6. ***Assortment:*** Merchant provides "one-stop shopping" for most online purchases; site satisfies shopping needs; merchant carries wide assortment and selection of products.
7. ***Transaction ease:*** Merchant's website can be navigated intuitively; a first-time buyer is able to make a purchase without much help; site is user-friendly and enables quick transactions.
8. ***Engagement:*** The merchant's site design is attractive; enjoyable shopping at the site; feel that the site is inviting; feel comfortable shopping at the site.
9. ***Loyalty:*** Seldom consider switching to another merchant; usually click on the merchant's site whenever needing to make a purchase; like to navigate the site; one's favorite merchant to do business with.
10. ***Inertia:*** Unless becoming very dissatisfied, changing to a new merchant would not be worth the bother; finding it difficult to stop shopping at the site; feeling that the cost in time, money, and effort to change merchants is high.
11. ***Trust:*** Counting on the merchant to complete purchase transactions successfully; trusting the site's performance; feeling that the merchant is reliable and honest.

Some of these determinants are driven primarily by emotions (e.g., engagement and nurturing), whereas others are factors stemming from the mechanics of the transaction (e.g., assortment and transaction ease). One study developed a four-way categorization of transaction-based and emotional bond-based customers' relationships with marketers.[51] Table 1.1 applies this framework to Amazon's customers.

TABLE 1.1 Transaction-Based and Emotional Bond-Based Customer Relationships

FANS	LOYAL CUSTOMERS
High bonds and high purchase levels. Buyers and sellers cooperate and make adjustments, expecting to share the benefits of future transactions. High level of commitment. If Amazon is out of a product, fans are willing to wait till the product is in stock. Fans recommend the merchant: "I go to Amazon first, always." "They have my business." "Their customer support policies are the best I have encountered." "Their prices are always at least as good as those of other merchants selling the same merchandise." "I use one of my credit cards only for my Amazon purchases."	*Frequent purchasers, but without high bonds.* "Amazon is OK. I shop there frequently, but always check prices elsewhere first." They stay with Amazon because of calculative commitment. They may have an Amazon credit card that gives them purchase points and no annual fees. Thus, switching costs or lack of alternative suppliers lock them in. They stay loyal not because they are emotionally attached, but for purely rational reasons. They are unlikely to recommend a seller on their own. Amazon should induce them to become committed emotionally.
High bonds but modest purchase levels. The expectations of these customers have been exceeded and they are satisfied, but they are not heavy buyers, in general. "I don't buy these products often, but when I do, I go to Amazon first. They are great." Marketers should try to make these customers advocates for the store and send them purchase incentives.	*Low bonds and infrequent purchasers.* They are price-sensitive and prone to deals offered by competitors. They regard the product as a commodity and will buy from the seller offering the lowest price. They switch sellers from transaction to transaction. Amazon must ensure that they are satisfied and contact them to ask if they are. Some may become loyal or delighted customers, and eventually fans.

Emotional bonds with loyal customers may sometimes backfire, especially when social media are involved. Seventh Generation faced plunging reviews from its most loyal customers after introducing a new version of its baby wipes—thicker and moister—and discontinuing the older product. A flood of negative reviews on Amazon lowered the wipes' Amazon star rating from 5 to 2.5 stars in mere weeks. In response, the company then offered both the new and old versions of its Free & Clear baby wipes online. The company also sent out boxes of the old wipes with handwritten notes of apology and refunds to disappointed consumers, and e-mailed customers announcing that the old wipes were becoming available again.[52]

Customer Loyalty and Satisfaction

Customers who are highly satisfied or delighted keep purchasing the same products and brands, provide positive and encouraging word-of-mouth to others, and often become "customers for life." In contrast, those who are less satisfied or feel neutral either switch to a competitor immediately, or wait until another marketer offers them a somewhat lower price and then switch. In addition, highly dissatisfied customers spread negative and often exaggerated word-of-mouth.

A widely quoted study that linked levels of customer satisfaction with customer behavior identified several types of customers:[53]

1. ***The Loyalists*** are completely satisfied customers who keep purchasing. The *apostles* are loyal customers whose experiences with the company exceeded their expectations and who provide very positive word-of-mouth about the company to others. Companies should strive to create apostles and design strategies to do so.
2. ***The Defectors*** feel neutral or merely satisfied with the company and are likely to switch to another company that offers them a lower price. Companies must raise defectors' satisfaction levels and turn them into loyalists.
3. ***The Terrorists*** are customers who have had negative experiences with the company and spread negative word-of-mouth. Companies must take measures to get rid of terrorists.
4. ***The Hostages*** are unhappy customers who stay with the company because of a monopolistic environment or low prices; they are difficult and costly to deal with because of their frequent complaints. Companies should fire hostages, possibly by denying their frequent complaints.
5. ***The Mercenaries*** are very satisfied customers who have no real loyalty to the company and may defect because of a lower price elsewhere or on impulse, defying the satisfaction–loyalty rationale. Companies should study these customers and find ways to strengthen the bond between satisfaction and loyalty.

Customer Loyalty and Profitability

Classifying customers according to profitability involves tracking the revenues obtained from individual customers and then categorizing them into tiers.

Marketers must recognize that all customers are not equal. Sophisticated marketers build *selective* relationships with customers, based on where customers *rank* in terms of profitability, rather than merely "striving to retain customers." A customer retention–savvy company closely monitors its customers' consumption volume and patterns, establishes tiers of customers according to their profitability levels, and develops distinct strategies for each group of customers. For example, some stockbrokers program their phones to recognize the phone numbers of high-volume traders to ensure that those calls receive priority. In providing technical support on the phone, customers who have purchased and registered several of a company's products should receive expedited handling. Many New York City restaurants log data on important guests in their computers. One restaurant knows that a well-known food critique prefers his soup served in a cup and enjoys iced tea with cranberry juice in a large glass over lots of ice, a famous rapper likes white Burgundy, and one weekly diner wants only the ends of a loaf in his breadbasket. Restaurant also archive where diners like to sit, when they celebrate special occasions, and whether they prefer their butter soft or hard, Pepsi over Coca-Cola, or sparkling over still water.[54] In contrast, a bank's less profitable customers who, say, make little use of their credit cards or maintain only the minimum balance needed to receive free checking should *not* have penalties waived for bounced checks or late payments. Some companies also identify customer groups that are unlikely to purchase more even if pursued aggressively; such customers are often discouraged from staying with the company, or even "fired" as customers. For example, pay-TV providers became more selective about the customers they want to keep, because of rising programming costs, and focus more on holding onto the subscribers who generate the most revenue and profit, even if that means letting less valuable customers go. Because the pay-TV market is saturated, providers have to rely on raising prices or selling extra services to increase revenue. Thus, lower-end customers who are not taking such services as digital video recorders and broadband became unattractive to retain.[55]

Figure 1.4 depicts a hypothetical classification of an airline's customers along levels of profitability. The figures in the left column show how much money the airline makes per mile in each of its four service classes. The top row represents the number of miles travelled by a given customer. The twelve cells represent the airline's revenue from a given customer based on the amount of miles the customer travelled and the class in which he or she sat. The *diamond* is a customer who travelled at least 250,000 miles in first class in one year, which amounts to $1 million of revenue. The *emeralds* are customers who travel in first class, but not as frequently as the *diamonds,* or customers who travel very frequently in business class. The diamonds and emeralds are the airline's most profitable segments. Airlines provide such travellers with free transportation to the airport, hospitality agents that welcome and check them in, and hosts that usher them into VIP waiting lounges. The diamonds and emeralds receive personal and attentive service during the flight, priority and assistance during luggage collection, and prearranged transportation to their ultimate destinations.

Savvy marketers must also carefully plan customer "demotions." For example, a diamond or an emerald who is some miles short of keeping his or her status at the end of a given year technically must be "demoted" to a lower level, because flight miles are computed annually. However, from a consumer psychology standpoint, people may feel that they did not receive a fair chance to prove themselves as valuable customers within such a limited time frame. Researchers have suggested that minimizing the risk of driving away valuable customers outweighs the additional costs of extending elevated status for another year or two. Companies should enable customers, across all loyalty levels, to maintain their status actively instead of simply having to accept the company's decision. For example, some airlines offer customers who are about to be demoted the opportunity to purchase the revenues (e.g., flight miles) that are "missing" to maintain their elevated status.[56]

The *sapphires* are also a profitable segment, because they fly frequently and in business class. They should receive upgrades to first class as often as possible, but not the extra pampering awarded to the diamonds and emeralds. The *elite* and *select* segments are heavy fliers, mostly in premium economy. The airline should allow them to experience what it is like to fly in business class whenever possible (the beginning of Chapter 2 describes the four in-flight classes at Qantas).

Miles Travelled Annually and Matching Revenues

Airplane's Class and Matching Revenues Per Mile		At least 250,000 miles	At least 150,000 miles	At least 100,000 miles
	First Class ($ 4 per mile)	$ 1,000,000 DIAMOND	$ 600,000 EMERALD	$ 400,000 EMERALD
	Business Class ($ 2 per mile)	$ 500,000 EMERALD	$ 300,000 SAPPHIRE	$ 200,000 SAPPHIRE
	Premium Economy ($ 0.6 per mile)	$ 150,000 ELITE	$ 90,000 SELECT	$ 60,000 SELECT
	Economy ($ 0.3 per mile)	$ 75,000 SELECT	$ 45,000	$ 30,000

FIGURE 1.4 An Airline's Profitability Tiers

Measures of Customer Retention

Companies must develop measures to assess their customer retention strategies, and researchers have recommended the following retention measurement methods:

1. ***Customer Valuation:*** Value customers and categorize them according to their financial and strategic worth so that the company can decide where to invest for deeper relationships and determine which relationships should be served differently or even terminated.
2. ***Retention Rates:*** The percentage of customers at the beginning of the year who are still customers by the end of the year. According to studies, an increase in retention rate from 80% to 90% is associated with a doubling of the average life of a customer relationship from 5 to 10 years. Companies can use this ratio to make comparisons between products, between market segments, and over time.
3. ***Analyzing Defections:*** Look for the root causes, not mere symptoms. This involves probing for details when talking to former customers, an analysis of customers' complaints, and benchmarking against competitors' defection rates.

Companies should develop and implement corrective plans stemming from the results of such measurements. Retention strategies could involve actions to improve employee practices, greater top-management endorsement regarding the value of customers and employees, adjustments to the company's reward and recognition systems, and the use of "recovery teams" to eliminate the causes of defections. Companies can also erect barriers to customer switching. They can bundle products by combining several products or services into one package and offering them at a single price. They can also cross-sell (e.g., sell related products to current customers), use cross-promotions (e.g., give discounts or other promotional incentives to purchasers of related products), provide incentives for frequent purchases, and impose termination costs (e.g., penalties for paying off mortgages early).

Learning Objective

4 To understand consumer behavior as an interdisciplinary area, consumer decision-making, and the structure of this book.

Consumer Behavior is Interdisciplinary

Consumer behavior stems from four disciplines. **Psychology** is the study of the human mind and the mental factors that affect behavior (i.e., needs, personality traits, perception, learned experiences, and attitudes). **Sociology** is the study of the development, structure, functioning, and problems of human society (the most prominent social groups are family, peers, and social class). **Anthropology** compares human societies' culture and development (e.g., cultural values and subcultures). **Communication** is the process of imparting or exchanging information personally or through media channels and using persuasive strategies.

Consumer Decision-Making

The process of consumer decision-making, featured in Figure 1.5, includes the input, process, and output stages of decision-making.

The *input stage* of consumer decision-making includes two influencing factors: the firm's marketing efforts (i.e., the product, its price and promotion, and where it is sold) and sociocultural influences (i.e., family, friends, neighbors, social class, and cultural and subcultural entities). This stage also includes the methods by which information from firms and sociocultural sources is transmitted to consumers.

The *process stage* focuses on how consumers make decisions. The psychological factors (i.e., motivation, perception, learning, personality, and attitudes) affect how the external inputs from the input stage influence the consumer's recognition of a need, pre-purchase search for information, and evaluation of alternatives. The experience gained through evaluation of alternatives, in turn, becomes a part of the consumer's psychological factors through the process of learning.

The *output stage* consists of two post-decision activities: purchase behavior and post-purchase evaluation.

Indian Cultural Canvas and Its Linkages to Brands

In any market, consumer behavior occurs against the backdrop of culture. Individual psychological factors like perception, learning or attitudes have strong linkages with culture or the subculture that is identified in a social context. Despite the radical changes in lifestyles and preferences of Indian consumers over the last few decades, the following examples reflect the deep rooted influence of culture:

- Fast food brands like MTR (a Bangalore-based brand) and Ashirwad (ITC) have offerings that are directed towards traditional preparations in urban markets.
- Ujala, a liquid offering that adds a blue tinge to white clothes, is a successful brand catering to the cultural habit that consumers have followed for decades.
- Fortune, a brand of edible oil, used a "Mother and son" advertising theme in which the mother cooks and carries home-made food for her son who is working in the navy. Mother and child bonding is a strong cultural link adopted in Indian ads because India is a country where family ties, as a part of the social structure, are stronger than it is in most parts of the world.[57] Himalaya brand of medicines and personal care offerings have their origin in traditional remedies that are still popular in some parts of the country.
- Mills and Boons, legendary romantic novels that originated in the United Kingdom a century back, had an Indian author, Astha Atray, and featured Indian models on the cover of his book.[58] The publishers of this series have a database of 1300 writers worldwide. From the viewpoint of consumer behavior, such initiatives are taken by brands (several FMCGs have adopted such an approach) to get associated with the local culture.
- Kurkure, from PepsiCo, closely resembles traditional snacks that can be found in several parts of the country.
- Parachute Advansed introduced "Hot Oil" variant as consumer insights suggested that consumers prefer to use hot hair oils.[59] Heating oil, either for hair application or body application, is a cultural practice in some parts of the country.

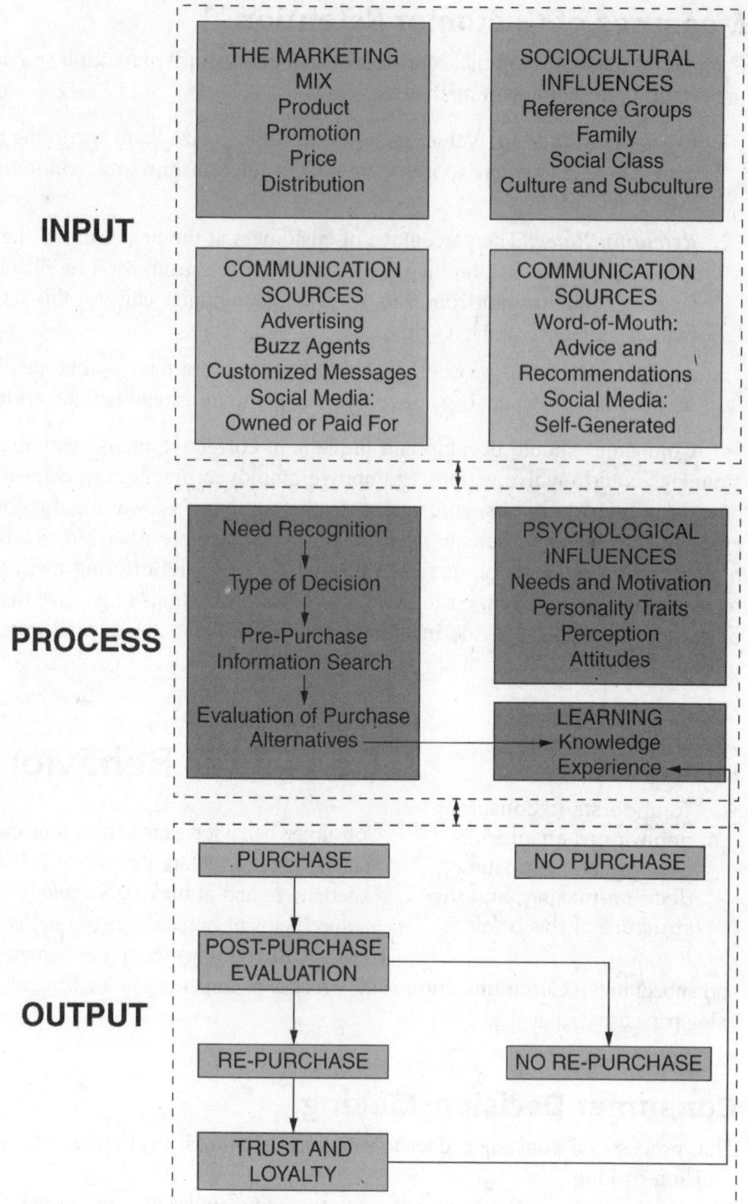

FIGURE 1.5 A Model of Consumer Decision-Making

Unique Marketing Challenges in the Indian Context

For multinational companies with several product categories and price points, the challenge is to market their offerings to several segments of consumers at different socio-economic levels. The poor households earn below ₹1.5 lakhs per annum and form 21% of total households in the country; the emerging middle class households earn between ₹1.5–3 lakhs per annum form around 42% of the households; middle income households that form 23% of the total households earn between ₹3–8.5 lakhs per annum, and the upper middle income households earning over ₹8.5 lakhs per annum form about 14% of the households.[60] This categorization of households is important in terms of its implications on luxury brands, regional brands, and unorganized offerings. Those that are not branded and are sold at a price is significantly lower than branded ones and these offerings may also include "look alike" duplicates of branded offerings. For instance, aspiration-based prestige and luxury brands will have to concentrate on specific geographical markets where the appropriate income groups are present and these may not be restricted only to major cities. The small scale industries need to perhaps concentrate on households that have an income of less than ₹1.5 lakhs per annum. Brand extensions need to be carefully analyzed to ensure that differentiation of offerings are perceived by consumers (for example, how would a brand like Britannia that has offerings at various price points handle its extensions and sub-brands in categories of biscuits, bread, butter, and oats). Interestingly, the heartlands of India,[61] with 400 towns and a population of 100 million Indians, consume 20% of the country's fast moving consumer goods, and there are only four lakh individuals with assets worth a million dollars or more.[62]

Multinational Brands, Indian Values, and Subculture

Nivea, the German brand, had devised an India-centric strategy for its whitening deodorant. Facing stiff competition from several established brands like Axe and Pond's, the brand created a "sleeveless zone" at Mantri Mall in Bangalore. They planned an event, advertised it widely to ensure the target segment of women turned up for the event, get into the "zone", and socialize with a fun-filled agenda. Wearing sleeveless apparel is largely not a part of the Indian women's dressing habit (though such a style has been on the rise but not to the extent of diffusing among the larger cross section of women). The brand recognized that Indian cultural values may not be conducive for a major launch that highlights sleeveless dressing. But it made a very good attempt to connect with the target segment by creating a subculture of "openness" (in this case, being open towards dressing in a manner that is not a part of the mainstream culture). Schwartz model on culture has the dimension that has a continuum of "tradition–openness". Nivea's attempt to create a subculture in this context fits in with the small percentage of consumers open to trying out different styles. The example, with its conceptual fit, illustrates how multinational brands can make an attempt to bring in cultural values that may not be a part of the Indian context.

Quaker Oats has created a sub segment that is interested in health and fitness and would perhaps, like to substitute the traditional Indian breakfast with the more nutritious oats (the brand's proposition). Cultural practices and values are perhaps the strongest with regard to food in any culture.

The Structure of This Book

Part I provides an overview of marketing and consumer behavior and the components of strategic marketing. Chapter 1 explains consumer behavior as an interdisciplinary framework centered on people's consumption-related activities. It describes the evolution of marketing, prominent marketing strategies, and marketers' social responsibilities. The chapter also describes the impact of technology and the interrelationships among customer value, satisfaction, and retention. It concludes with a model of consumer decision-making and an overview of this book. Chapter 2 discusses the process of market segmentation, including the demographic, sociocultural, and psychographic bases for segmenting markets. It also explores the criteria for selecting target markets, behavioral targeting, and differentiating offerings among competitors.

Part II describes the consumer as an individual and explains the psychological factors that affect consumer behavior. Chapter 3 discusses how individuals are motivated and the impact of individual personality characteristics on consumer behavior. Chapter 4 explores consumer perception, which is how individuals select, organize, and interpret the stimuli that they are exposed to. In other word, how the way we view the world around us affects our shopping patterns. Chapter 5 explains how we learn, through applying past experiences and behavior to future purchase decisions. Chapter 6 explores how attitudes, which are cognitions and evaluations of objects, influence buying behavior.

Part III addresses the communication and persuasion process along its components: sender, message, media, receiver, and feedback. Feedback alerts the sender as to whether the intended message was, in fact, received. Chapter 7 introduces the elements of the communication process and explains how to overcome the barriers to effective communications. It then discusses the differences between the traditional broadcasting model of communications, which is rooted in mass traditional media, and the narrowcasting model, which originated in new media such as online advertising and social media. Thereafter, the chapter focuses on the message: Its structure, the persuasive appeal used, and measurements of its effectiveness. Chapter 8 explores the communication channels and the transition from print and broadcast media to social media and mobile advertising. The discussion describes targeting consumers by using different media, and the role of prominent online advertising tools such as Google and Facebook. We then address marketing via social media and mobile advertising, and conclude with discussing the electronic evolution of traditional media. Two sources of communications influence people's purchases: Messages from marketers and information from the consumers' peers, family, word-of-mouth, and their social and cultural groups. Chapter 9 begins with an examination of the credibility of information sources and the groups that consumers use as frames of reference. It continues by describing the characteristics of people, known as opinion leaders, who often influence their peers' buying decisions. We conclude by presenting the dynamics and strategic uses of word-of-mouth, with an emphasis on electronic-word-of-mouth.

Part IV examines consumers in their social and cultural settings. Sociology is the study of the development, structure, and functioning of a society (the most prominent social groups are family, peers, and social class). Anthropology compares human societies' culture and development (e.g., cultural values and subcultures). Chapter 10 examines the family as a consumption unit and its standing within the social class structure. It also explores the characteristics and consumption patterns of various social classes. Chapter 11 describes culture and how it is expressed through values, rituals, and customs. It further describes how to measure cultural values and concludes with a presentation of Americans' core values as illustrated by ads and buying priorities. Chapter 12 describes cultural groups, known as subcultures, that share certain beliefs, values, and customs and exist within a larger society. Membership in a subculture can stem from a person's ethnicity, religion, geographic location, age, and/or gender. Chapter 13 explores cross-cultural analysis, which is a key strategic component for companies pursuing markets in countries other than the United States. It also describes how to assess marketing opportunities abroad and whether or not to customize products and promotions in global markets.

Part V consists of three chapters. Chapter 14 discusses the consumer decision-making process and shows how marketers' strategies and the psychological and sociocultural factors covered in Parts II, III, & IV are linked together. The chapter also describes how consumers react to innovative products and the process by which new products are adopted by individuals and societies. Chapter 15 explores marketers' social responsibility and ethically questionable practices such as exploitive targeting, and covert, manipulative and deceptive marketing. The chapter also examines abuses of consumers' privacy and concludes with a discussion on marketing socially desirable causes and behaviors. Chapter 16 describes the methodology of consumer research, including the distinctions between qualitative and quantitative research design.

Summary

Learning Objective 1: To understand the evolution of the marketing concept, the most prominent tools used to implement marketing strategies, the relationship between value and customer retention, and the objectives of socially responsible marketing.

Marketing is the activity, set of institutions, and processes for creating, communicating, delivering, and exchanging offerings that have value for customers, clients, partners, and society. Consumer behavior consists of consumers' actions taken while searching for, purchasing, using, evaluating, and disposing of products and services that they expect will satisfy their needs. Consumer behavior influences how marketers can communicate and deliver products that offer value to customers and society and explains how individuals make decisions to spend their available resources on products and services. Marketing and consumer behavior stem from the marketing concept, which maintains that the essence of marketing consists of satisfying consumers' needs, creating value, and retaining customers. Companies must produce only those goods they have already determined that consumers will buy. Marketing myopia is a focus on the product rather than on the needs that the product presumes to satisfy. The marketing mix (also known as the Four Ps) consists of product, price, place (distribution), and promotion. Market segmentation, targeting, and positioning are the foundation of turning consumers into customers. Market segmentation is the process of dividing a market into subsets of consumers who share common needs or characteristics. Targeting means selecting the segments that the company views as prospective customers and pursuing them. Positioning is the process by which a company creates a distinct image and identity for its products, services, and brands in consumers' minds. The societal marketing concept requires marketers to fulfill the needs of their target markets in ways that improve, preserve, and enhance society's well-being and simultaneously meet their business objectives.

Learning Objective 2: To understand how the Internet and related technologies improve marketing transactions by adding value that benefits both marketers and customers.

Technology has revolutionized the marketing mix, segmentation, targeting, positioning, and customer retention. When consumers use their computers, mobile phones, electronic readers, tablets, and other electronic devices, they provide marketers with the kind of information that enables companies to target them immeasurably more effectively than during the pre-Internet days. Online technologies create a "value exchange": Marketers provide value to consumers in the form of information, opportunities to customize products easily, entertainment content, and much more. While online, consumers provide value to marketers by "revealing themselves," thereby enabling companies to market their products more efficiently and precisely. Surfing online allows consumers to locate the best prices for products or services, bid on various offerings, bypass distribution outlets and middlemen, and shop for goods around the globe and around the clock. Online communication abilities have created sophisticated and discerning consumers, who are hard to attract, satisfy, and retain. More than ever before, marketers must customize their products, add value to the physical product or the core of a service, provide the right benefits to the right consumer segments, and position their products effectively. Technology also enables marketers to refine their strategies because they can readily customize their offerings and promotional messages, offer more effective pricing and shorter distribution channels, and build long-term relationships with customers. By using rapidly advancing technologies to track consumers, marketers can identify opportunities for creating new offerings, as well as improving and extending existing products and services. They can gather comprehensive consumer information by tracking consumers online, requiring prospective buyers to register at their websites, and combining this knowledge with demographic and lifestyle data gathered offline.

Learning Objective 3: To understand the interrelationships among customer value, satisfaction, and retention, and technology's revolutionary role in designing effective retention measures and strategies.

Customer value is the ratio between customers' perceived benefits and the resources they use to obtain those benefits. Customer satisfaction is customers' perceptions of the performance of the product or service in relation to their expectations. Customer retention involves turning individual consumer transactions into long-term customer relationships by making it in the best interests of customers to stay with the company rather than switch to another firm. It is more expensive to win new customers than to retain existing ones. Technologies allow marketers to retain more customers, and collect highly sophisticated data about shoppers' preferences and post-purchase evaluations. Consumers who are highly satisfied or delighted keep buying the same products and brands, provide positive word-of-mouth to others, and often become "customers for life." Those who are less satisfied or feel neutral either switch to a competitor immediately or wait until another marketer offers them a somewhat lower price and then switch. Dissatisfied customers spread negative and often exaggerated word-of-mouth. Internal marketing is marketing the organization to its personnel.

Learning Objective 4: To understand consumer behavior as an interdisciplinary area, consumer decision-making, and the structure of this book.

Consumer behavior stems from four disciplines: Psychology is the study of the human mind and the mental factors that affect behavior. Sociology is the study of the development, structure, functioning, and problems of human society. Anthropology compares human societies' culture and development. Communication is the process of imparting or exchanging information.

The process of consumer decision-making consists of the input, process, and output stages. The input stage includes two influencing factors: the firm's marketing efforts and sociocultural influences. This stage also includes the methods by which information from firms and sociocultural sources is transmitted to consumers. The process stage focuses on how consumers make decisions. Psychological factors affect how the external inputs influence the consumer's recognition of a need, pre-purchase search for information, and evaluation of alternatives. The output stage consists of two post-decision activities: Purchase behavior and post-purchase evaluation.

This book includes five parts. Part I provides an overview of marketing and consumer behavior and the components of strategic marketing. Part II describes the consumer as an individual and explains the psychological factors that affect consumer behavior. Part III addresses the communication and persuasion process, the revolutionary impact of new media, and the roles of reference groups, opinion leaders, and word-of-mouth. Part IV examines consumers in their social and cultural settings. Part V includes discussions of the consumer decision-making process, consumers' reactions to innovative products, marketers' social responsibility and ethically questionable practices, and the methodology of consumer research.

Review and Discussion Questions

1.1. Describe the interrelationship between consumer behavior and the marketing concept.

1.2. A company is introducing a new E-book reader. Suggest segmentation, targeting and positioning strategies for the new product.

1.3. Define the societal marketing concept and discuss the importance of integrating marketing ethics into a company's philosophy and operations.

1.4. Describe how technology enhances the exchange between marketers and consumers.

1.5. It is often said that consumers receive "free" content online. Is this true? Why or why not?

1.6. Discuss the interrelationships among customer expectations and satisfaction, perceived value, and customer retention. Why is customer retention essential?

1.7. How can marketers use technology to improve customer retention and enhance their bonds with customers?

1.8. Discuss the role of the social and behavioral sciences in developing the consumer decision-making model.

Hands-on Assignments

1.9. Locate two websites that you visit regularly and discuss how they can (and probably do) track your behavior and enable marketers to target you more effectively.

1.10. Locate two examples (one advertisement and one article) depicting practices that are consistent with the societal marketing concept and two examples of business practices that contradict or ignore this concept. Explain your choices.

1.11. Locate two examples of technological innovations designed to enhance customer retention and discuss them.

Key Terms

- anthropology *19*
- communication *19*
- consumer behavior 2
- consumer research *4*
- cross-screen marketing *10*
- customer retention *13*
- customer satisfaction *13*
- customer value *13*
- emotional bonds *14*
- internal marketing *23*
- market research *4*
- market segmentation *4*
- marketing *2*
- marketing concept *3*
- marketing mix (four Ps) *5*
- marketing myopia *4*
- positioning *4*
- product concept *4*
- production concept *3*
- psychology *19*
- selling concept *4*
- social media *14*
- societal marketing concept *5*
- sociology *19*
- targeting *4*
- transactional bonds *14*

2

Segmentation, Targeting, and Positioning

Learning Objectives

1. To understand the interrelationship among market segmentation, targeting, and positioning and how to select the best target markets.
2. To understand the bases used to segment consumers, including demographics, psychographics, product benefits sought, and product usage-related factors.
3. To understand behavioral targeting and its key role in today's marketing.
4. To understand how to position, differentiate, and reposition products.

MARKET SEGMENTATION, targeting, and positioning are the foundation of turning consumers into customers. **Market segmentation** is the process of dividing a market into subsets of consumers with common needs or characteristics. Each subset represents a consumer group with shared needs that are different from those shared by other groups. **Targeting** consists of selecting the segments that the company views as prospective customers and pursuing them. **Positioning** is the process by which a company creates a distinct image and identity for its products, services, and brands in consumers' minds. The image differentiates the company's offering from competition by communicating to the target audience that the product, service, or brand fulfills their needs better than alternatives.

The emerging Indian market embodies several aspects of segmentation and positioning and poses unique challenges to marketers in terms of combining segmentation bases and positioning associations. The dynamic nature of lifestyles of consumers and the proliferation of brands create complexities that affect both positioning and repositioning of brands. There is no single base on which a market like India can be segmented. There are combinations of bases ranging from demographics to psychographics and cultural sensitivity that needs to be analyzed in any kind of positioning strategy. In addition, there are brands that have been a part of the Indian context for decades and such old associations of brands also need to be considered. Successful brands that have managed such changes in the environment from the viewpoint of positioning and repositioning associations include Lifebuoy, Horlicks, Santro, Titan, Park Avenue, Dettol (soaps), 5Star, Hero (motorcycles), and Parachute (hair oil).

Segmentation, targeting, and positioning are interrelated and implemented sequentially. For example, airlines traditionally offered three in-flight service choices: first class, business class, and economy (or coach). Because more and more flyers used their frequent flyer

First *Source: Qantas Marketing*

Business *Source: Qantas Marketing*

Premium Economy *Source: Qantas Marketing*

Economy *Source: Qantas Marketing*

FIGURE 2.1 Qantas Market SegmentsFirst

awards to upgrade their seats from coach to business or first class, airlines have steadily lowered the level of service and amenities in first and business classes, and these alternatives lost their appeal over economy class. Rather than pay the high fares for first or business class on commercial airlines, many first and business-class flyers switched to flying on shared, private and corporate jets. When some airlines realized that the traditional in-flight classes—first, business, and economy—no longer attracted three distinct customer segments, they redesigned their services. In order to illustrate such redesigns, the photos in Figure 2.1 show the four classes that Qantas now offers. The redesigned First class offers small, room-size private spaces; seats that turn into flat beds; designer linen and towels; gourmet food and a large selection of wines and alcoholic beverages; personal attention (one flight attendant for every two or three passengers); and elaborate pre- and post-flight amenities. Business class features generously reclining seats that become nearly flat beds, delicious food and drinks, a personal kit with expensive cosmetics and grooming products, and pre- and post-flight services. Qantas also realized that there is a new segment of flyers: passengers who are willing to pay more for larger seats and more legroom, but not for extras such as fancy meals, free alcohol, and pricey toiletries. To this newly discovered segment, Qantas offers Premium Economy, which features larger and more spaciously placed seats that recline more than those in coach. Qantas also redesigned its Economy class with more comfortable seats and an open buffet of refreshments during the flight.

Qantas targets four distinct segments: coach passengers; premium economy, which costs 50% more than coach; business class, which costs twice as much as premium; and first class, which often costs three or four times as much as business. The four alternatives are clearly differentiated: an almost hotel-like privacy and sleeping accommodations, personal attention, and luxurious amenities in first class; privacy, beds, and extensive amenities in business class; more space, legroom, and generously reclining seats in premium economy; and improved seating and food service in coach.

This chapter describes the criteria and bases for selecting target markets, introduces a new strategy called behavioral targeting, and concludes with a discussion of positioning and repositioning strategies.

Learning Objective

1 To understand the interrelationship among market segmentation, targeting, and positioning and how to select the best target markets.

Market Segmentation and Effective Targeting

All consumers are not alike because they have different needs, wants, and desires, and different backgrounds, education levels, and experiences. Therefore, marketers must offer alternatives that correspond to the needs of different consumer groups or segments. For example, Marriott offers hotel accommodations to travelers, but different travellers have different needs. Thus, JW Marriott offers fine, elegant accommodations with extensive amenities and superior service. The Courtyard by Marriott hotels are conveniently located near cities' business districts and provide quality stays for business travellers. Fairfield Inn & Suites by Marriott offer modestly priced rooms, and Residence Inn by Marriott hotels are designed for long stays of business travellers. Like Marriott, most companies of consumer goods and services provide multiple products for different market segments.

Market segmentation, strategic targeting, and product (or service) positioning are the key elements of marketing consumer goods and services. They enable producers to avoid head-on competition in the marketplace by differentiating their products on the basis of such features as price, styling, packaging, promotional appeal, method of distribution, and level of service. Effectively catering to the distinct needs of consumers by offering them clearly differentiated products is significantly more profitable than mass marketing, in spite of the much higher research, production, advertising, and distribution costs that accompany segmentation and strategic targeting.

Marketers use segmentation research to identify the most appropriate media in which to place advertisements. All media vehicles—from Facebook, Google, and Twitter to TV, radio stations, newspapers, and magazines—use segmentation research to determine the characteristics of their audiences so that they can attract advertisers seeking to reach a given audience. For example, The New York Times and The Wall Street Journal offer separate editions for readers in different areas of the world, as well as online editions that can be customized according to the reader's interests.

Before describing how market segments are identified, we must point out that not every segment is viable or profitable. To be an effective target, a market segment must be identifiable, sizeable, stable and growing, reachable, and congruent with the marketer's objectives and resources.

Identifiable

Marketers divide consumers into separate segments on the basis of common or shared needs by using demographics, lifestyles, and other factors named "bases for segmentation." Some segmentation factors, such as demographics (e.g., age, gender, ethnicity), are easy to identify, and others can be determined through questioning (e.g., education, income, occupation, marital status). Other features, such as the product benefits buyers seek and customers' lifestyles, are difficult to identify and measure.

Sizeable

To be a viable market, a segment must consist of enough consumers to make targeting it profitable. A segment can be identifiable, but not large enough to be profitable. For example, athletic and slim men with wide shoulders and narrow waists often have to buy suits with trousers that are larger than they need (and have them retailored). Other than high-end fashion designers such as Prada and Dolce & Gabbana, most American clothiers make suits only for men who have more generous waists than the relatively small segment of very athletic men.

Stable and Growing

Most marketers prefer to target consumer segments that are relatively stable in terms of lifestyles and consumption patterns (and are also likely to grow larger and more viable in the future) and avoid "fickle" segments that are unpredictable. For example, teenagers are a sizeable and easily identifiable market segment, eager to buy, able to spend, and easily reached. Yet, they are also likely to embrace fads, and by the time marketers produce merchandise for a popular teenage trend, interest in it may have waned.

Reachable

To be targeted, a segment must be accessible, which means that marketers must be able to communicate with its consumers effectively and economically. With the diversification of magazines (and their online versions), the emergence of TV channels that target narrowly defined interests, and the growth of new media (e.g., sending ads to cell phones), marketers have significantly more avenues for reaching unique segments and can also do so with customized products and promotional messages.

Whether in print or online, magazines and leading newspapers have been one of the best media used to reach narrowly defined market segments. Magazines focus on specific areas of knowledge, interest, or hobbies, such as travel, science, literature, art, home decorating, architecture, occupation, and any leisure activity conceivable. Magazines and newspapers provide extensive profiles of their readers to advertisers wishing to reach groups of consumers with specific characteristics. Table 2.1 describes the readers' profiles of prominent print media.[1] In addition, The Wall Street Journal's readers have an average net worth of $1.6 million; 31% have liquid assets of more than $1 million; 50% spend more than $1,000 with their credit cards per month; 89% visit museums and antique shows regularly; 87% attend the theater, concerts, and the opera. Advertisers use audience profiles in deciding where to place their ads. For example, ads for the opera and the theater often appear in The Wall Street Journal, and ads for educational and pricey cruises are regularly featured in the National Geogtraphic Traveller.

TABLE 2.1 Readers' Profiles of Selected Media

PUBLICATION	AUDIENCE & MEDIAN HOUSEHOLD INCOME	GENDER	MEDIAN AGE	EDUCATION	OCCUPATION
Scientific American	2.8 million $90,000	70% men 30% women	47	62% college + 31% postgraduate 7% unreported	52% managerial 19% decision makers, high tech 13% owner, partner 16% unreported
National Geographic Traveller	7.3 million $72,000	55% men 45% women	42	69% college +	31% professional, managerial
National Geographic	6.7 million worldwide 5.2 million US $68,000	56% men 44% women	45.6	66% college	27% professional, managerial
The Wall Street Journal	911,000 $285,000	63% men 37% women	45	100% college +	Majority are impressive earners and investors

Source: Based on www.scientificamerican.com/mediakit/assets/pdf/audience_demoprofile.pdf wsjmediakit.com/downloads/gny_audience_profile.pdf?12060903

Box 2.1 Importance of Micro-segmentation

Micro-segmentation and narrow-casting are important for the cell phone industry in India. Airtel has a base of about 140 million in the country. Apart from messages, four billions calls are made and received everyday; 80% of the services are basic offerings and micro-segments can range from 5000—300,000 consumers.[2] This reflects the need for several bases of segmentation – benefits, psychographics (lifestyle aspects to know the needs that may be symbolic, other than functional benefits), demographics like urban verses rural, and customization based on needs.

Congruent with the Marketer's Objectives and Resources

Not every company is interested in or has the means to reach every market segment, even if that segment meets the four preceding criteria. For example, in contrast to the four in-flight options that Qantas provides, Southwest Airlines offers only one class of service because its business objective is to provide uniform, inexpensive, no-frills air transportation.

Applying the Criteria

To demonstrate the application of the criteria to selecting a target market, let's assume that Perry & Swift, an investment management firm, is considering adding a hedge fund to its financial services. The company has determined that it has the resources to do so and that adding a hedge fund is congruent with its objectives. Because hedge funds are risky and require sizeable financial investments, their target market is wealthy households with high net worth. Using a P$YCLE Segmentation System, which is part of a database entitled Nielsen NyBestSegments, Perry & Swift identifies a segment entitled *Financial Elite* whose members are the most affluent Americans with the highest amount of income-producing assets. Members of this segment invest in a large variety of financial growth tools, such as stocks, bonds, mutual funds, investment-focused life insurance, and real estate, mostly through financial investment firms. Within this broad group, Nielsen's system features two more precisely defined segments: the *Wealth Market* and *Business Class*. Table 2.2 illustrates how Perry & Swift applied the criteria for effective targeting to the two segments.[3]

TABLE 2.2 An Illustration of Effective Targeting

	WEALTH MARKET	BUSINESS CLASS
The segment is identifiable by its demographics	Millions in assets, median household income $137,000, 55+ years old, have graduate and postgraduate education. Kids are grown and have their own families.	Wealthy, median household income $101,000, 45–64 years old, have graduate and postgraduate education. Kids are away from home studying.
Is the segment likely to be profitable?	2.28% of the 2,659,000 U.S. households. Members use many brokers and financial advisers.	1.97% of the U.S. households. Members trade financial instruments frequently.
Is the segment stable?	Members invest regularly in a mix of short- and long-term instruments.	Members are still working and wish to accumulate more wealth before retiring.
How can the segment be reached?	Live in wealthy suburbs or in the wealthiest areas of large cities. Belong to country clubs and read financial magazines.	Live in wealthy suburbs or in the wealthiest areas of large cities. Attend horse races and read financial magazines.
Members' financial aspirations and objectives	Although they hold diversified financial portfolios, are reluctant to invest in risky instruments. Their home(s) are paid for, as is their children's education. Somewhat receptive to making risky investments as part of trust funds they have set up for their grandchildren.	Kids are in expensive schools. Expect to pay for kids' graduate and postgraduate education. Some are looking to buy a second home. Have made successful, risky financial decisions in the past. Feel that they are still young enough to make up for bad investment decisions, if necessary.

Source: Based on selected data from MyBestSegments at claritas.com (May 2012).

As shown in Table 2.2, both segments are likely to be profitable, and Perry & Swift can pursue both or either one. Let's assume that the company decided to focus on the Business Class segment because it has higher growth prospects than the Wealth Market: its members are younger and still accumulating wealth. Therefore, they invest in long-term investments, and their financial aspirations and objectives indicate that they are willing to take greater financial risks, while members of Wealth Market invest in less risky financial instruments. The firm should use Nielsen's ZIP Code geodemographic tool, which is described later in this chapter, to determine which geographic areas of the country include subtantial numbers of the Business Class segment. Then, it should use salespersons and local advertising to recruit customers.

Learning Objective

2 To understand the bases used to segment consumers, including demographics, psychographics, product benefits sought, and product usage-related factors.

Bases for Segmentation

A segmentation strategy begins by dividing the market for a product into groups that are relatively homogeneous and share characteristics that are different from those of other groups. Generally, such characteristics can be classified into two types: behavioral and cognitive.

Behavioral data is evidence-based; it can be determined from direct questioning (or observation), categorized using objective and measurable criteria, such as demographics, and consists of:

1. ***Consumer-intrinsic*** factors, such as a person's age, gender, marital status, income, and education.
2. ***Consumption-based*** factors, such as the quantity of product purchased, frequency of leisure activities, or frequency of buying a given product.

Cognitive factors are abstracts that "reside" in the consumer's mind, can be determined only through psychological and attitudinal questioning, and generally have no single, universal definitions, and consist of:

1. ***Consumer-intrinsic*** factors, such as personality traits, cultural values, and attitudes towards politics and social issues.
2. ***Consumption-specific*** attitudes and preferences, such as the benefits sought in products and attitudes regarding shopping.

The bases for segmentation are discussed next and separately. However, in reality, marketers use multiple bases. For example, although demographics and lifestyles (or psychographics), which are the most widely used bases, are discussed separately, every psychographic classification of consumers includes their demographics. Whereas demographics *determine* consumers' needs for products (e.g., males and females buy different products) and the ability to buy them (e.g., income), psychographics *explain* buyers' purchase decisions and choices. For example, being a student and having limited financial resources are demographic factors, but how students spend their resources is a function of their lifestyles, values, and interests. Some students buy expensive designer brands, whereas others rummage for clothes in thrift and vintage clothing stores. Some students go to sports events, while others go to the latest nightclubs. As shown in Figure 2.2, Color Plus has developed strong associations of user benefits and feelings as a differentiation among higher-end casual apparel brands.

Source: Raymond

FIGURE 2.2 Color Plus

Demographics

Demographic segmentation divides consumers according to age, gender, ethnicity, income and wealth, occupation, marital status, household type and size, and geographical location. These variables are objective, empirical, and can be determined easily through questioning or observation. They enable marketers to classify each consumer into a clearly defined category, such as an age group or income bracket. Similarly, one's social class is defined by computing an index based on three objective and quantifiable variables: income (number of dollars earned), education (number of years studied for the highest degree held), and occupation (prestige scores associated with various occupations). As discussed later, consumers' geographic locations and zip codes can be easily matched with their demographics.

All segmentation plans include demographic data for the following reasons:

1. Demographics are the easiest and most logical way to classify people and can be measured more precisely than the other segmentation bases.
2. Demographics offer the most cost-effective way to locate and reach specific segments, because most of the secondary data compiled about any population consists of demographics Top six metros account for 40% of the domestic expenditure while rural

markets account for almost 50% of the durable categories. ITC Lifestyle, Shoppers Stop, and Spice Hotspot have tier-2 cities as their focus. The 22 key urban towns outside the metros and another 39 cities with 5094 towns account for 70% of the urban consumption.[4] Another example in the credit card market is the case of American Express that targets households with income above ₹800,000 per annum because such households are likely to spend more than other relatively lower- income range households and are also prompt in payment.[5] For the company, the volume of expenditure a card holder makes is important as it charges 2.5% commission from merchants (against the industry norm of one per cent). Credit cards account for just two per cent of consumer spends in India and American Express also offers charge cards (a consumer deposits an amount every month and spends on it). Hence, it may have a demographic segmentation base that is different from other credit card brands to suit its target segment.

India produces 5.2% of the world's production of coffee, but the internal consumption is a small percentage. With cafes in urban India and the association of youth, Nescafe introduced a campaign to attract the youth by using a well-known celebrity popular with the youth segment.[6]

3. Using demographics, marketers can identify new segments created by shifts in populations' age, income, and location.
4. Demographics determine many consumption behaviors, attitudes, and media exposure patterns. For example, many products are gender-specific and music preferences are very closely related to one's age. Therefore, local radio stations specializing in various types of music are an efficient and economical way to target different age groups. Leisure activities and interests, as well as the media people read or watch, are functions of their ages, education, and incomes.

Next, we describe the most prominent demographics used in segmenting markets and targeting consumers.

Age

Product needs often vary with consumers' age, and age is a key factor in marketing many products and services. For instance, younger investors—in their mid-20s to mid-40s—are often advised to invest aggressively and in growth stocks, whereas people who are older and closer to retirement should be much more cautious, keep a significant portion of their assets in bonds (which provide stable and safe income), and avoid risky, long-term investments. Age influences segmentation. Pond's Miracle age-defying cream targets women who are into their middle age and have the aspiration to look younger. Fair & Lovely targets younger women, perhaps teens and young adults who may later graduate to other skin care offerings. Rexona soap targets young married couples. Cadbury Gems, aimed at children, is now attempting to redefine its segment by targeting the older generation with its new tagline, "Raho Umarless".

Cognitive age (psychological mindset of the consumer rather than the biological age) may also be an important segmentation base for brands that target the youth. There may be a secondary segment that buys watches and jeans to feel and look younger. For example, a brand like Fastrack or Nike may appeal to a 45 year old consumer who is under the influence of cognitive age. In such a case, the brand manager faces a challenge to reconcile preferences of the biological and cognitive age.

Many marketers cater to the needs of 18- to 34-year-old consumers, known as Millennials. For example, as MTV's audience got older, the network developed programs specifically aimed at this segment, and Keds—positioned as "The Original Sneaker"—has started a campaign allowing millennials to express their creativity using Keds sneakers as the canvas for drawing pictures.[7]

With coffee being linked to modernity, Amul Kool Café, shown in Figure 2.3, targets young consumers who have a positive attitude towards modernity. Every summer, movie studios compete for young adult viewers, because teenagers and people in their very early 20s go to movies frequently and many see the same movies more than once. Therefore, in recent years, Hollywood's summer staples have been sequels and prequels to the movies that have previously been hits among these age groups (e.g., movie series such as Harry Potter, Twilight, and The Hunger Games).[8]

Although the Internet is often described as a "young" medium, consumers of all ages go online regularly. However, people of different ages use online access differently, as featured in Figure 2.4. Not surprisingly, people go online less frequently as they age, but continue using social networking sites and e-mail. Surprisingly, buying online varies only somewhat across age groups.[9]

Gender

Many products and services are inherently designed for either males or females, but sex roles have blurred, and gender is no longer an accurate way to distinguish among consumers in some product categories. Today, more and more magazine ads and TV commercials depict men and women in roles traditionally occupied by the opposite sex. For example, many ads reflect the expanded child-nurturing roles of young fathers in today's society. In contrast, some companies of "men's products" are targeting women specifically. For instance, Van Gogh Blue, a vodka brand, has been targeting 25- to 44-year-old female consumers with a somewhat provocative campaign entitled "You Unbottled."[10] Other companies have introduced gender-specific

Source: Amul

FIGURE 2.3 Appealing to Young Consumers

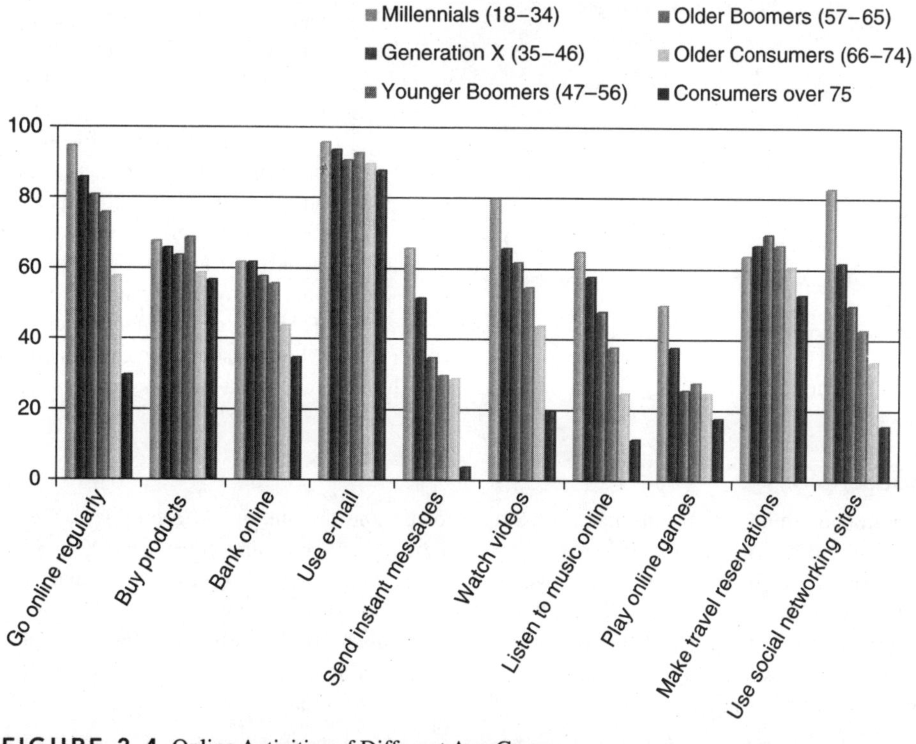

Source: Based on selected portions of a report issued by Pew Internet (accessed May 2012).

FIGURE 2.4 Online Activities of Different Age Groups

versions. Frito-Lay overhauled all of its calorie-conscious snacks, making them more appealing to women, and introduced 100-calorie packages of snacks.[11] Recognizing that many advertisers target women 25 to 35, the cable channel VH1 introduced shows to attract them, such as a reality show entitled Mob Wives, which portrays the lives of women who were born, or married, into reputed organized-crime families.[12]

Source: Shell Oil Company

FIGURE 2.5 Appealing to Women and Changing Gender Roles

Women have traditionally been the main users of such products as hair coloring and cosmetics, and men have been the main users of shaving tools and preparations. However, men's grooming products are becoming a fast-growing sector as more men use exfoliators, toners, aftershave creams, and cooling and tinted moisturizers. In the past, women bought skin products for men, but today men are buying such products themselves. Recognizing that many men feel embarrassed to be seen looking for cosmetics, many department stores have redesigned the areas where men's grooming products are sold. For example, they now display large signs over the men's grooming products section, so that men will not confuse men's skin care products with women's cosmetics. Although women's products are generally placed behind counters and with salespeople standing in front and ready to advise, men's products are displayed on open shelves, because many men do not like to speak with salespersons. The store sections where men can buy grooming products feature TVs tuned to sports or financial channels, and semiprivate areas where men can try shaving creams, moisturizers, and other products.[13]

Gender-based segmentation is being explored by marketers in India. Fair and Handsome fairness cream for men, Park Avenue's beer shampoo for men, brands like Allen Solly, and Van Heusen offering their fashion apparel to the women segment are examples of established brands getting into women segments. Pleasure and Scooty Pep brands of two-wheelers are also examples of how gender segmentation can work when consumerism catches up in an environment.

The ad in Figure 2.5 illustrates targeting women and also shows how stereotypes—such as that women cannot change a car's oil—are no longer true.

Families and Households

Many families pass through similar phases in their formation, growth, and dissolution. At each phase, the family unit needs different products and services. For example, brides are generally happy and spending consumers. Young, single people, for example, need basic furniture for their first apartment, whereas their parents, finally free of child rearing, often refurnish their homes with more elaborate pieces. The **family life cycle** is a classification of the phases that most families go through; each stage represents an important target segment to many marketers (see Chapter 10). A study investigated the impact of major life events on consumption and discovered that occasions such as moving, marriage, a child's birth or adoption, the death of a close family member, significant changes in one's employment, and caring for older relatives are viable segmentation variables when used together with age cohorts.[14]

Traditionally, most marketers have targeted families. They researched the number and kinds of households that buy and own certain products and the media profiles of household decision makers, and then developed appropriate marketing appeals. More recently, marketers began targeting specific marital status groups, such as singles, divorced individuals, single parents, and dual-income married couples without children. For instance, urban, one-person households with incomes greater than $75,000 tend to buy premium alcoholic drinks and beer, books, organic products, and fresh produce, and to shop in green markets and specialized food stores rather than in conventional supermarkets.

Social Class

Income is an important variable for distinguishing between market segments, because it indicates an ability or inability to pay for a product model or brand. Income is often combined with other demographic variables to define target markets more accurately. To illustrate, a combination of high income and age identified the Affluent Elderly segment. Income has also been combined with both age and occupational status to single out the Yuppies, a sought-after subgroup of the baby boomer market (see Chapter 12).

Education, occupation, and income are closely correlated; high-level occupations that produce high incomes usually require advanced education and are more prestigious than occupations requiring less education. Social class is an important base for market segmentation in the form of a weighted index of education, occupation, and income. **Social class** is a hierarchy in which individuals in the same class generally have the same degree of status, whereas members of other classes have either higher or lower status. Studies have shown that consumers in different social classes vary in terms of values, product preferences, and buying habits (see Chapter 10).

Conditions that affect social classes often have a direct effect on marketing. For example, Procter and Gamble (P&G), the world's largest maker of consumer goods and advertiser, has been worried about the financial hardship of America's middle class, which it believes will be long lasting. P&G's definition of "middle class" is households with annual income between $50,000 and $100,000, which amounts to 40% of the country's households. These families are P & G's core customers and, with their net worth declining following the financial crisis and the increased costs of children's education, they have become more price conscious. In response, like many other companies, P & G introduced lower-priced lines of many of its goods, despite the negative impact of this action on the company's earnings.[15] Looking at the other aspect of recessionary times, during the financial crisis very affluent people avoided being seen leaving expensive stores and carrying shopping bags bearing the stores' logos. After the financial markets recovered, the same consumers resumed buying extraordinarily expensive products (e.g., at Neiman Marcus, Chanel coats that cost $9,000 and women's Christian Louboutin shoes that sell for $800) and these goods' prices went up.[16]

Ethnicity

Marketers segment some populations on the basis of cultural heritage and ethnicity because members of the same culture tend to share the same values, beliefs, and customs. In the United States, African Americans, Hispanic Americans, and Asian Americans are important subcultural market segments (see Chapter 12). Culturally distinct segments may be prospects for the same product, but marketers should target them using different promotional appeals. For example, *Cosmopolitan* magazine and other media have started targeting Latin women, a segment that, for a long time, went unnoticed by most media. *Cosmopolitan Latina* targets American-born, bilingual Latinas. *Cosmopolitan* also has editions for women in Argentina, Mexico, and Colombia.[17] Similarly, L'Oreal USA collaborated with Telemundo (an American TV network that broadcasts in Spanish) in building a website for Hispanic consumers.[18]

Box 2.2 Geographical Segmentation and the Indian Context

Geographical segmentation base is very relevant in the Indian context. LG Electronics planned to launch microwaves for specific dishes popular in the east and southern regions. Cavinkare's Meera shampoo targets South India with its variants. Godrej sells a green variant of Godrej No. 1 in Tamil Nadu and Punjab. Barista Coffee sells South Indian dishes in some parts of Karnataka. Future group planned to introduce different variants of rice under its brand Ektaa for different regions.[19] The taste of tea varies depending upon the cultural aspects associated with taste in different regions of the world. Hence, tea brands make changes in the respective blend that reaches a specific geographical area.

Geodemographics

Where a person lives determines some aspects of consumption behavior. For example, climates determine the types of clothing most people own, and fashions and styles in large cities are often very different from those in nonurban areas. Local customers, as opposed to visiting tourists, are also a distinct segment. For instance, one study investigated the "local resident gambler" segment in Las Vegas and found that the gaming habits of this group were distinctly different from those of tourists—a segment on which most marketing studies have focused.[20] Hindustan Unilever* does not generally alter the positioning of its brands. But in

* Hindustan Unilever is the Indian subsidiary of the global Unilever brand. In this book, it has also been referred to as Unilever India to help the global leader relate to it.

the light of environmental issues of sustainability, the company had decided to do so.[21] For instance, the germ killing action of Lifebuoy can prevent diseases and Surf Excel may have a proposition that would help save water.

The most popular use of geography in strategic targeting is **geodemographics**, a hybrid segmentation scheme based on the premise that people who live close to one another are likely to have similar financial means, tastes, preferences, lifestyles, and consumption habits (as an old adage states, "Birds of a feather flock together"). The primary application of geodemographics is **PRIZM**, offered by Nielsen's MyBestSegments service. Marketers can locate each of PRIZMS's 66 segments according to their postal ZIP Codes. The residents of most ZIP Codes include more than one PRIZM segment, and Nielsen's ZIP Code Look-Up details the relative percentage of each segment within each local population in the United States. If you go to the Look-Up and enter your residence's ZIP Code, you will find out the characteristic of the segments residing in your area and their relative sizes (claritas.com). The sixty-six segments are also classified according to levels of population density (urbanization) and affluence, and placed into one of several Lifestage Classes. These groups are similar to the stages of a typical family's evolution (see Chapter 10). In recent years, Nielsen developed two additional segmentation measures: P$YCLE (based on the household's wealth) and ConneXions (based on the household's receptivity to new technologies). Table 2.3 describes Nielsen's segmentation frameworks.

TABLE 2.3 Nielsen's Segmentation Frameworks

NAME	DESCRIPTION
PRIZM	Household segmentation model that groups consumers into 66 PRIZM segments based on socioeconomic ranking, consumer behavior, and media exposure patterns. Each segment is assigned into an SER (socioeconomic rank) based on neighborhood data for income, education, occupation, and home value.
Urbanization Classes	Assigns the 66 segments into 4 types of population density: Urban, Suburban, Second City, and Town & Rural
Social Groups	Each of the 66 segments is classified according to its levels of affluence and urbanization.
Lifestage Classes	Each of the 66 segments is classified into one of the following classes: Younger Years (2 types): 35 years old or younger without kids; middle age without kids at home. Family Life: households with kids living at home. Mature Years (2 types): over 55 years old; ages 45–64 without children living at home.
Lifestage Groups	Each of the 66 segments is classified according to its levels of affluence and Lifestage Classes.
P$YCLE	Every U.S. household is classified into one of 58 consumer segments based on the household's finances and wealth.
Income-Producing Assets (IPA)	Each of the 58 consumer segments is classified into one of seven IPA groups based on retirement accounts, cash, demand deposits, stocks, money market funds, and other assets that can be liquidated easily. Then, each of the 58 segments is classified according to the Lifestage Classes.
ConneXions Groups	Fifty-three segments based on the household's willingness to adopt new technologies early. The segments are: High Tech, Mid Tech, Low Tech, and No Tech. The segments are then classified according to the Lifestage Classes.

Box 2.3 Price as a Dominant Base for Segmentation

Sometimes, price may be a dominant segmentation base though it may not be the only base. Google promoted its Android operating system to several late entrants like Micromax and Spice mobiles. This was an attempt to come out with below US$ 100 mobile phones that would have features comparable with high end phones.[22] This is an important base in a country where 42% of the population is earning less than US$ 1.25 per day.

Green Consumers

Green consumers are attractive prospects for many products and marketers have explored targeting them. One study identified three types of green consumers:

1. ***Environmental activists:*** "green" enthusiasts and people who adopt lifestyles focused on health and sustainability. They seek foods from farms that not only produce organic products, but also cut down on water use, power use, and trash.
2. ***Organic eaters:*** concerned about sustaining their own health and not so much about sustaining the planet.
3. ***Economizers:*** experimenting with buying eco-friendly products in order to save money.[23]

Another study identified four groups of green consumers:[24]

1. ***True Greens:*** persons who have adopted environmentally friendly behaviors. They try to convince friends to use environmentally friendly products, and avoid buying products that have a negative environmental impact. They switch brands for ecological reasons and are willing to make personal sacrifices to protect the environment. Furthermore, they maintain that the government should do more to protect the environment and educate children regarding future environmental protection, and want companies to be transparent when marketing environmentally friendly products.
2. ***Donor Greens:*** These individuals feel guilty about their lack of environmentally sound buying behavior, and sometimes consider environmental impacts when purchasing products. They are willing to sacrifice financially to support the environment, but unwilling to change their shopping behaviors.
3. ***Learning Greens:*** These persons are still learning about environmental issues, but are not actively engaged in ecological causes. They seek easy ways—that do not involve big changes in consumption behavior—to support the environment and sometimes consider environmental impact when purchasing products, but are skeptical about environmentalists' claims.
4. ***Non-Greens:*** People who do not care about wildlife or environmental issues. They neither engage in environmentally friendly behaviors, nor feel guilty about adversely impacting the environment. Although some of them acknowledge environmental problems, they still buy ecologically unsound products, do not look for green seals when shopping, and believe that it is okay for large companies to act in ways that have negative effects on the environment.

Yet another study divided consumers according to a *spectrum of green,* on which the *darkest greens* are consumers who are willing to pay a premium for eco-friendly products in order to help reduce global warming, and the *lightest greens* are mostly concerned about saving money on their energy bills, rather than saving the planet.

Personality Traits

Many psychographic factors overlap with personality characteristics or traits. Through personality tests—which consist of questions or statements presented to respondents—researchers can study consumers' personality characteristics and apply them in segmenting markets (see Chapter 3). For example, consumers who are open-minded and generally perceive less risk than others in trying new things are likely to be **innovators**—that is, more likely to buy a new product when it is first introduced and before many other consumers buy it. Therefore, marketers of new products must identify these individuals (and also find out their demographics, lifestyles, and values) and target them during introductions of the new products. Furthermore, if personality tests also discover that innovators tend to score high on "exhibition"—a trait where a person wants to be the center of a group—the promotion directed at this group should encourage the innovators to initiate positive word of mouth and tell others about new products.

Psychographics, Values and Lifestyles

In marketing, lifestyles are named **psychographics**, which include consumers' *activities*, *interests*, and *opinions*. In consumer research, psychographics consists of creating statements and asking respondents to indicate their level of agreement or disagreement with each statement. The dimensions studied include consumers' buying patterns, opinions about consumption and/or social issues, values, hobbies, leisure activities, and many other dimensions. There are no standardized definitions of psychographic dimensions (such as an "active lifestyle" or consumer types like an "impulse buyer" or a "green consumer"), because almost all psychographic terms are defined in the scope of specific studies. Nevertheless, because they are so versatile, psychographics are widely used, and, together with demographics, are included in almost all segmentation frameworks. Table 2.4 shows a sample of psychographic measures Figure 2.6 shows an ad that targets affluent travellers who like to explore new cuisines.

VALS™ (an acronym for "values and lifestyles") is the most popular segmentation system combining lifestyles and values. Drawing on Maslow's need hierarchy and the concept of a person's "social character" (see Chapter 3), researchers at Strategic Business Insights developed a segmentation scheme of the American population known as VALS. It classifies America's adult population into eight distinctive subgroups (segments) based on consumer responses to both attitudinal and demographic questions. Figure 2.6 is a diagram of the VALS segments, and Table 2.5 describes the eight VALS segments.

Examining the diagram from left to right, there are three *primary* motivations: the *ideals motivated* (these consumer segments are guided by knowledge and principles), the *achievement motivated* (these consumer segments are looking for products and services that demonstrate success to their peers), and the *self-expression motivated* (these consumer segments desire social

TABLE 2.4 Samples of Psychographic Measures

PSYCHOGRAPHIC FACTOR	SAMPLE STATEMENTS
Values and goals*	• Sense of belonging • Fun and enjoyment in life • Warm relationship with others • Self-fulfillment • Being well respected
Attitudes toward Life**	• Financial security is important to me • My greatest achievements are ahead of me • I am more conventional than experimental • I would rather spend a quiet evening at home than go to a party • My social status is an important part of my life
Apparel and Fashion**	• I buy clothes I like regardless of current fashion • My friends often ask me for advice on fashion • Men do not notice women who do not dress well
Gift Giving**	• I generally give gifts because people expect me to • I try to give gifts that carry personal messages to recipients • Gifts always communicate love and friendship
Control of Life**	• I find it hard to speak in front of a group • When I make friends I always try to make the relationships work • I enjoy making my own decisions • Others usually know what's best for me
Buying Online**	• It requires too much time to set up accounts with online stores • The look of a website is an important factor in my buying decisions • I tell others about my experiences in buying online
Leisure Activities***	• Played adult games (e.g., cards or mahjong) • Visited art gallery or museum • Went hunting or shooting • Went to the movies • Attended a sporting event

* Responses use an "extremely important" to "extremely unimportant" scale

** Responses use a "strongly agree" to "strongly disagree" scale

*** Responses use a "frequently" to "never" scale

Source: Unilever

FIGURE 2.6 An Appeal to Sophisticated Consumers Who Travel and Explore New Destinations

TABLE 2.5 Descriptions of the VALS™ Segments

SEGMENT NAME	MOTIVATION AND RESOURCES	SELECTED DEMOGRAPHICS	VALUES AND CONSUMPTION PATTERNS
Innovators	Abundant resources; motivated by ideals, achievement, self-expression, and self-esteem.	10% of the U.S. population. Median age 45. 65% are married and 72% work full time.	Successful, sophisticated, and curious. Receptive to new ideas and technologies, and buy niche products and services. Concerned about how their purchases express their tastes and personalities. Cultivate tastes for the finer things in life.
Thinkers	Motivated by ideals and have solid resources.	11% of the U.S. population. Median age 56. 75% are married and 55% work full time.	Mature, satisfied, and comfortable; value order and responsibility. Well educated and informed about world, wish to broaden their horizons and open to new ideas. Practical consumers, who look for durability, functionality, and value in products.
Believers	Motivated by ideals and have moderate resources.	16.5% of the U.S. population. Median age 52. 63% are married and 47% work full time.	Conservative, conventional with traditional beliefs, whose priorities are family, religion, and community. Follow routines focused on their homes, families, and social or religious organizations. Predictable consumers who buy established brands, favor U.S. products, and are brand loyal.

(Continued)

TABLE 2.5 *(Continued)*

SEGMENT NAME	MOTIVATION AND RESOURCES	SELECTED DEMOGRAPHICS	VALUES AND CONSUMPTION PATTERNS
Achievers	Motivated by desire for achievement and have solid resources.	14% of the U.S. population. Median age 41. 72% are married and 70% work full time.	Goal-oriented and committed to career and family. Their lives are focused on family, religion, and work. Live conventionally, are politically conservative, and seek predictability and stability. As consumers, they favor products that demonstrate success to their peers.
Strivers	Motivated by achievement and have moderate resources.	11.5% of the U.S. population. Median age 28. 34% are married and 52% work full time.	Trendy, fun loving, and seek approval from others. Don't have enough resources to meet their desires and impulsively buy stylish products that emulate the purchases of people with greater material wealth. Lack the skills they need to move ahead.
Experiencers	Motivated by self-expression and have solid resources.	13% of the U.S. population. Median age 24. 25% are married and 52% work full time.	Young, enthusiastic, and impulsive consumers who seek variety and excitement and savor the new, offbeat, and risky. Favor exercise, sports, outdoor recreation, and social activities. Spend a lot on fashion and entertaining and concerned about appearing "cool."
Makers	Motivated by self-expression and have moderate resources.	12% of the U.S. population. Median age 46. 68% are married and 59% work full time.	Express themselves by building houses, raising children, and fixing cars. Practical people, who value self-sufficiency, live traditionally, and have little interest in what lies beyond their family lives. Prefer value to luxury and buy practical products.
Survivors	No strong primary motivation and low resources.	12% of the U.S. population. Median age 70. 45% are married and 13% work full time.	Live narrowly focused lives and often believe that the world is changing too quickly. Comfortable with the familiar and concerned with safety and security. Brand loyal and seek discounts. As a group, they are a modest market for most products and services.

Source: Reprinted with permission of Strategic Business Insights; www.strategicbusinessinsights.com/VALS

or physical activity, variety, and risk). Furthermore, each of these three major self-motivations represents distinct attitudes, lifestyles, and decision-making styles. Examining Figure 2.7 from top to bottom, the diagram reveals a continuum in terms of resources and innovation—that is, *high resources-high innovation* (on the top) to *low resources-low innovation* (on the bottom). This range of resources/innovation (again, from most to least) includes the range of psychological, physical, demographic, and material means and capacities consumers have to draw upon, including education, income, self-confidence, health, eagerness to buy, and energy level, as well as the consumer's propensity to try new products.

Each of the eight VALS segments contains between 10 and 17% of the U.S. adult population, with Believers, at 17%, being the largest VALS group. In terms of consumer characteristics, the eight VALS segments differ in some important ways. For instance, *Believers* tend to buy American-made products and are slow to alter their consumption-related habits, whereas *Innovators* purchase top-of-the-line and new products, especially innovative technologies. Therefore, for example, it is not surprising that smart marketers of the first intelligent in-vehicle technologies (e.g., global positioning devices) targeted innovators, because they are early adopters of new products.

Benefit Segmentation

Benefit segmentation is based on the benefits that consumers seek from products and services. The benefits that consumers look for represent unfilled needs, whereas buyers' perceptions that a given brand delivers a unique and prominent benefit result

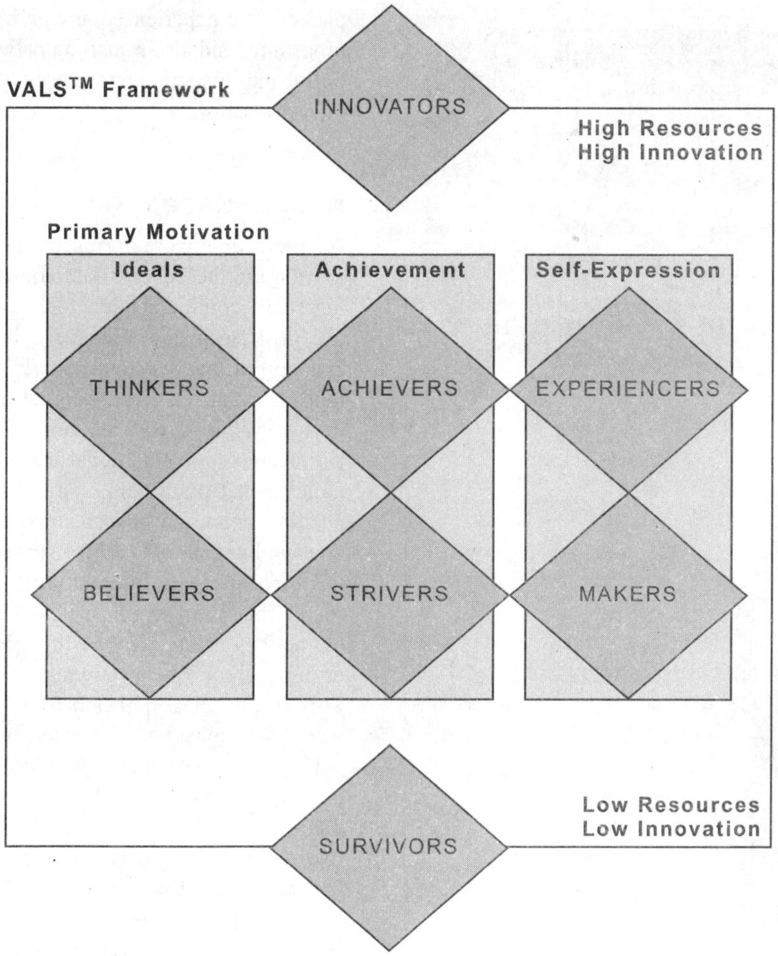

Source: Strategic Business Insights VALS

FIGURE 2.7 Diagram of the VALS™ Segments

in loyalty to that brand. Marketers of personal care products, such as shampoos, soaps, and toothpastes, create different offerings designed to deliver specific benefits. Colgate is probably the world's most sophisticated marketer of personal care products, and its line of toothpastes is an excellent example for understanding the benefits that consumers seek in regard to care for their teeth and oral hygiene. Colgate's website includes a link entitled "Search by Benefit." Toothpastes are classified into four benefits: (1) long-lasting fresh breath; (2) plaque and gingivitis protection; (3) sensitivity relief; and (4) tooth whitening. For example, *Colgate Total* provides 12 hours of germ fighting, which other toothpastes do not. *Colgate Max Fresh* wipes out bad breath. *Colgate Sensitive Pro-Relief* is for people who have sensitive gums. Other Colgate versions whiten teeth, protect enamel, prevent cavities, fight tartar, combine mouthwash with toothpaste, and provide many other benefits. In addition, the *Colgate Pro-Clinical* line includes three versions—daily cleaning, daily whitening, and daily renewal—and is presumably aimed at encouraging consumers to brush their teeth three times a day.[25] The V8 ad in Figure 2.8 reflects the product's primary benefit, which is consuming vegetables.

A study identified three groups of benefits that consumers commonly seek when visiting each of three service providers: a dentist, a hairdresser, and a travel agent. The study also discovered that consumers' loyalty levels to their service providers correlated positively with the benefits these consumers believed they had received.[26] Service providers can use the findings to improve customer retention. For example, dentists can enhance patients' confidence by post-visit contacts inquiring if patients had experienced any problems following a dental procedure, and also e-mailing patients press clippings featuring the dentist's appearances at conferences or media interviews.

Media-Based Segmentation

As more and more forms of media emerge, marketers must study the benefits that consumers seek from adopting these communication tools, so that they can advertise in these media effectively. In one study, consumers singled out *immediacy, accessibility,* and *free cost* as the most relevant features of digital newspapers, while identifying *writing style* and more *depth* and *details* as the key features of traditional newspapers. These findings indicate that publishers of traditional newspapers should position online and paper newspapers as complementing one another and that the two versions represent opportunities for somewhat different types of ads.[27] Another study found that car buyers substituted information searches online for reading print ads in order to reduce the amount of time spent on negotiating prices with car dealers.[28] This means that marketers should approach car buyers who have consulted the Internet differently than those who have not. Another study identified six types of benefits sought by users of mobile electronic devices (see Table 2.6).[29] A Canadian study identified three distinctive segments of online consumers and their characteristics, which are listed in Table 2.7.[30] As illustrated in this table, marketers should study consumers' demographics and their Internet navigation patterns and segment them accordingly.

Source: Strategic Business Insights VALS

FIGURE 2.8 V8's Benefit: Consuming Vegetables

Usage Rate Segmentation

Usage rate segmentation is reflects the differences among heavy, medium, and light users, and nonusers of a specific product, service, or brand. Marketers of many products, such as soup, laundry detergent, beer, and dog food, have found that a relatively small group of heavy users accounts for a disproportionately large percentage of the total product usage. For example, about 25% of all those who drink beer account for about 75% of all beer consumed. Therefore, most beer companies direct their advertising campaigns to heavy users rather than spend money trying to attract medium or light users. This also explains the successful targeting of light beer to heavy drinkers under the positioning that it is "less filling" (and thus can be consumed in greater quantities) than regular beer.

Targeting heavy users is a common marketing strategy and is often more profitable than targeting other user categories. However, catering to this segment requires a lot of expensive advertising because all competitors target the same heavy users. Some marketers prefer to target light and medium users with products that are distinct from those preferred by heavy users. For example, though India has several segments that are price-sensitive, brands also target higher-end segments that are prepared to pay more for better value of the offerings like Haier, the durable brand from China, aims to capture the higher value price point.[31]

Usage rate segmentation also focuses on the factors that directly affect the usage behavior. For instance, a study of supermarket customers found differences between two segments of buyers in terms of usage frequency, defined as the number of times per week buyers visited the supermarket. The researchers also examined usage frequency in relation to buyers' reasons

TABLE 2.6 Benefits That Consumers Seek When Using Mobile Devices

LOCATION INFORMATION	COMMUNICATION	SPORTS AND ENTERTAINMENT	VALUE-ADDED SHOPPING	FINANCIAL SERVICES
Directions to location; location of the place where they are; weather and news reports	Sending and receiving email, pictures, and texts; chatting with strangers	Receiving sports-related information; accessing adult entertainment; gambling and gaming online; downloading music	Comparing prices; receiving coupons and sales alerts; receiving product information	Banking; trading stocks; filing insurance claims; bidding at auctions; buying tickets; making currency conversions

Source: Based on Gillian Sullivan Mort and Judy Drennan, "Marketing M-Services: Establishing a Usage Benefit Typology Related to Mobile User Characteristics," *Database Marketing & Consumer Strategy Management*, 12 no. 4 (2005): 327–341.

TABLE 2.7 Segments of Online Consumers

CHARACTERISTICS	BASIC COMMUNICATIONS	LURKING SHOPPERS	SOCIAL STRIVERS
Percentage of total & gender	39% 75% female	39% 52% female	22% 57% female
Age	41% under 35 41% 35–54 19% over 54	31% under 35 48% 35–54 21% over 54	49% under 35 31% 35–54 20% over 54
Income	39% $49,000 or less 35% $50,000–74,000 26% $75,000 and up	40% $49,000 or less 23% $50,000–74,000 37% $75,000 and up	54% $49,000 or less 27% $50,000–74,000 19% $75,000 and up
Internet use	12.4 hours per week	16.7 hours per week	20.7 hours per week
E-mail	High	Regularly	Regularly
Browsing	Some	High	Some
Shopping	Some	Very high	Some
Blogging	Low	Some	Very high
Chatting	Low	Low	Very high
Video streaming	Low	Some	Very high
Downloading	Low	Some	Very high

Source: Based on Muhammad Alijukhadar and Sylvain Senecal, "Segmenting the online consumer market," *Marketing Intelligence and Planning*, 29 no. 4 (2011): 421–435.

for purchasing at that chain, levels of expenditure at the store, travel times to the store and modes of transportation, and whether buyers came in from home, a job, or were simply passing by.[32]

Rate of usage is strongly related to **product awareness status**, which is the degree of a consumer's awareness of the product and its features, and whether or not he or she intends to buy it reasonably soon. The consumer's degree of awareness of the product, along with whether the consumer is unaware and needs to be informed about the product, represent distinct targeting opportunities. A related factor is **product involvement**, which reflects the degree of personal relevance that the product holds for the consumer (see Chapter 5). A study identified three clusters of consumers based on their varied involvement with a wine's "background or history" (i.e., its "appellation of origin") and found significant differences among the clusters in terms of knowledge of wine brands and wine purchases.[33]

FIGURE 2.9 Usage Occasion: Spring Break

Source: Devin Benner CEO McKeon Products Inc.

Usage Occasion Segmentation

Vicco turmeric cream used the occasion of "marriage" as a segmentation base decades back. Marie biscuits have been associated with tea time or family time by Indian brands. When there are guests at home, many consumers prefer basmati brand of rice like Kohinoor. Dettol initially positioned itself as a soap that can protect against germs when one goes through a dusty environment – not uncommon in India. Café Coffee Day is sought after by youngsters for socializing occasions.

Many marketers promote their offerings for holidays or seasons. The greeting card industry, for example, promotes special cards for a variety of occasions that seem to be increasing annually with such additions as Grandparents' Day, Secretaries' Day, and so on. The florist and candy industries promote their products for Valentine's Day and Mother's Day, the diamond industry promotes diamond rings as an engagement symbol, and makers of expensive wristwatches and fountain pens often promote their products as graduation gifts with heavier advertising during the May–June graduation season. As consumers purchase more products online, the marketers of Campbell's Soup, Kraft, Hershey, Kellogg, and other prominent brands have been promoting their products online before the holidays, because consumers spend more money during the weeks before New Year's Eve.[34] The ad for Mack's Earplugs in Figure 2.9 promotes using the product during spring break.

Box 2.4 Loyalty, a Powerful Segmentation Base

Shoppers Stop has about 1.8 million loyalty cards that account for 73% of the total sales value.[35]

The company used the existing loyalty base (loyalty as a segmentation base) of consumers to locate areas where it had set up new stores. It also estimated the impact of cannibalization of the new stores on places where the shoppers had been visiting before these new shops were opened.

Learning Objective

3 To understand behavioral targeting and its key role in today's marketing.

Behavioral Targeting

Behavioral targeting consists of sending consumers personalized and prompt offers and promotional messages designed to reach the right consumers and deliver to them highly relevant messages at the right time and more accurately than when using conventional segmentation techniques. This method is enabled by tracking online navigation, current geographic location, and purchase behavior.

Tracking Online Navigation

Tracking consumers' navigation online includes:

1. Recording the websites that consumers visit.
2. Measuring consumers' levels of engagement with the sites (i.e., which pages they look at, the length of their visits, and how often they return).
3. Recording the visitors' lifestyles and personalities (derived from the contents of consumers' blogs, tweets, and Facebook profiles).
4. Keeping track of consumer' purchases, almost purchases (i.e., abandoned shopping carts), and returns or exchanges.

Long stays and repeat visits to sites indicate a high level of product involvement and purchase intention. Because websites are versatile, marketers can respond quickly to consumers' purchase interests and intentions. For example, customers who visit an online store in search of digital cameras are asked whether they want the cameras displayed by brand or by price. Then, when they visit again, in an attempt to "convert" visitors into buyers, the cameras are immediately displayed in the order the customers preferred during their initial visits.

Geographic Location and Mobile Targeting

Smartphones and GPS devices have created highly effective targeting opportunities. For example, Broadway theaters in New York City can offer unsold seats for the same day's performance at discounted prices by sending messages to the mobile phones of people travelling by cabs through the city's theater district, because a cab's GPS device shows its location on tracking devices.

Customers' mobile devices brought upon problems for brick-and-mortar retailers. Customers frequently engage in **showrooming**, which occurs when consumers use smartphones to scan the bar codes of products displayed in physical stores and then check the items' prices online in order to purchase them at the lowest prices. In order to combat showrooming, some physical stores started **geofencing**, which consists of sending promotional alerts to the smartphones of customers who opted into this service, when the customers near or enter the store.[36]

Purchase Behavior

Many marketers are now using **predictive analytics**, which are measures that forsee consumers' future purchases on the bases of past buying information and other data, and also evaluate the impact of personalized promotions stemming from the predictions. Some of the questions that can be answered by predictive analytics include:

1. When leaving a given page, what content and pages are visitors likely to look at next?
2. Which websites' features (and combinations of features) are likely to persuade people to register with a website?
3. What are the characteristics of visitors who are likely to return to a website and why?
4. What factors make visitors click on specific ads?

Predictive analytics often focuses on *noticing* significant changes in a consumer's buying behavior, because such changes often alert marketers that consumers are going through significant life events, such as the arrival of a new baby, upcoming marriage, and even divorce; during such times, consumers are inclined to spend more money and shop less carefully. For example, Target developed a model that detects changes in women's buying pattern to identify their pregnencies early on. Figure 2.10 describes how this model was used to market baby-related products to Susan, a hypothetical Target shopper. After Susan started buying several products that she had never bought before, Target's predictive analytics signaled that these purchases strongly indicate that Susan is expecting a baby. Using this data and a lot of additional information, Target then started sending Susan applicable promotional offers and also took steps to conceal its spying on her.[37]

The Information "Arms Race"

Collecting and analyzing the right data are the foundations of effective behavioral targeting. Marketers strive to anticipate occurrences and events in consumers' lives that affect the consumers' shopping. Marketers are also eager to discover information about people's interests and the social networks with which they connect online. Because of its strategic importance, the competition for more and more data about consumers has become extraordinarily fierce.

Mobile phones can be used in an innovative manner by a well-known brand for segmentation purposes.

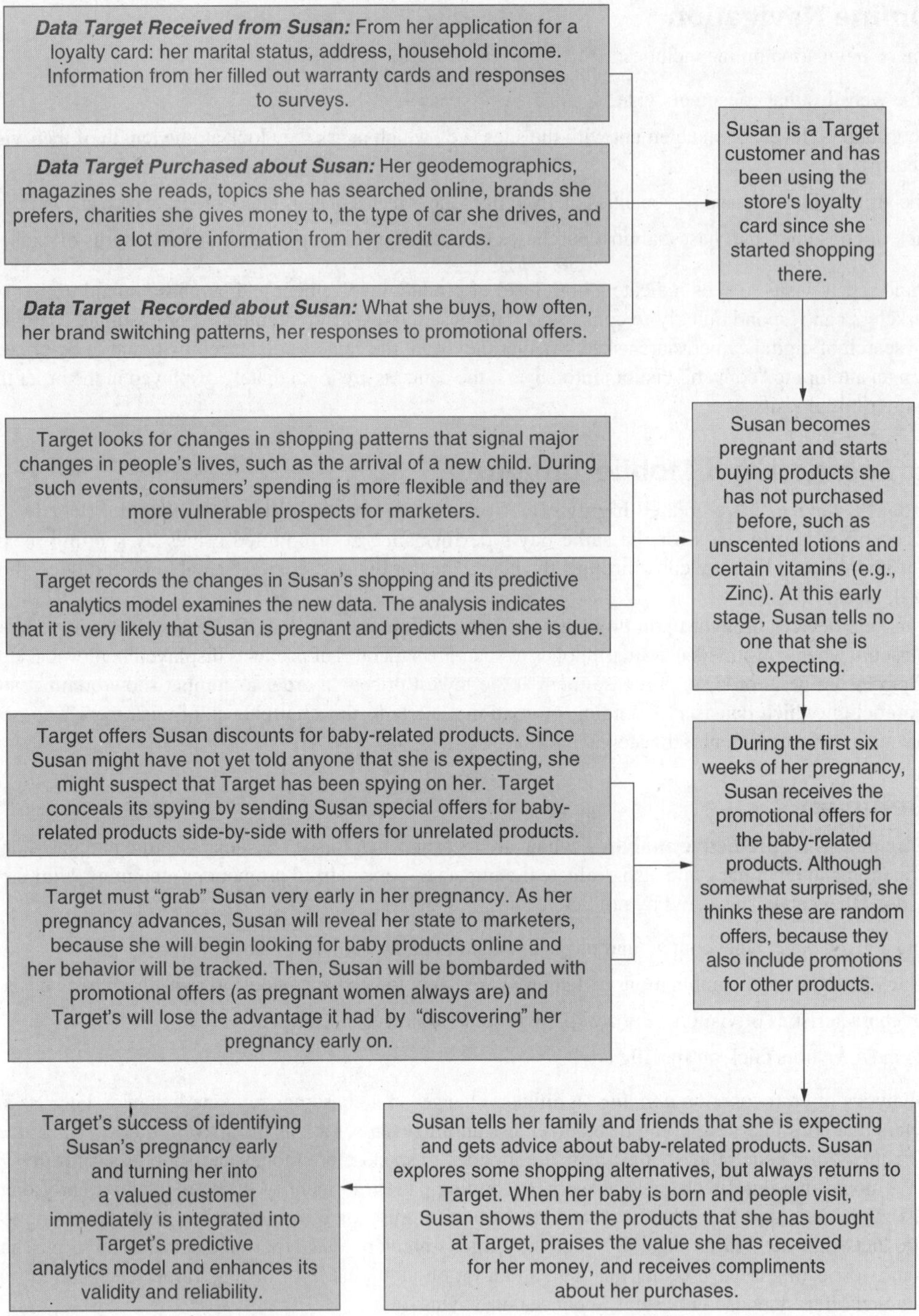

Source: From Charles Duhigg, "How Companies Learn Your Secrets," nytimes.com February 16, 2012

FIGURE 2.10 Behavioral Targeting

Toyo Tag is a logo from Toyota that can be photographed by a consumer using his mobile.[38] Through this approach, the consumer can have a one-on-one interaction with the company on a variety of issues like prices, models, availability, features, and so on. A marketer can observe the pattern and identify segments of consumers based on several bases that are used for dividing markets – readiness into buy (prospective buyers who are at the advanced stage of buying cars), price-oriented buyers (who have their queries only on pricing aspects), loyal consumers (consumer who would like to have a repeat buy of the same brand), and consumers who are adventurous (who have their queries on several lifestyle-based aspects associated with outdoor life and adventure). This example illustrates the fact that the classical approach to segmentation is important while marketers attempt to make their approaches using contemporary technologies. Perhaps, Indian brands like Santro, Figo, and other brands would follow suit to emulate such an approach as mobile technologies are evolving in this country.

Online marketers customize ads to users based on the users' past activities, which are tracked and collected via "cookies," which are bits of computer code placed on browsers to keep track of online activity. Acxiom integrates what it knows about consumers' offline, online, and even mobile selves, and creates in-depth behavior portraits known as "360-degree view" on consumers. Chapter 15 addresses the ethics of gathering a lot of personal information about consumers without their knowledge.

Learning Objective

4 To understand how to position, differentiate, and reposition products.

Positioning and Repositioning

After segmenting the market and selecting targeting prospects, marketers must persuade prospective buyers to buy the products that they offer, rather than competing products. **Positioning** is the process by which a company creates a distinct image and identity for its products, services, or brands in consumers' minds. The image and unique identity are called a "position." The position, which is intangible and exists only in the consumer's mind, represents how marketers want consumers to *perceive* products and brands (see Chapter 4). The result of effective positioning is a unique perception of the product in consumers' minds relative to competing offerings. Most new products fail because consumers perceive them as "me-too" offers that do not provide any advantages or unique benefits over competitive products because they are not positioned effectively.

The positioning process includes the following steps:

1. Defining the market in which the product or brand competes, who the relevant buyers are, and the offering's competition.
2. Identifying the product's key attributes and researching consumers' perception regarding each of the relevant attributes.
3. Researching how conumers perceive the competing offerings on the relevant attributes.
4. Determining the target market's preferred combination of attributes.
5. Developing a distinctive, differentiating, and value-based positioning concept that communicates the applicable attributes as benefits.
6. Creating a positioning statement focused on the benefits and value that the product provides and using it to communicate with the target audiences.

Marketers of different brands in the same category differentiate their labels effectively by stressing the benefits that their brands provide. The benefits must reflect product attributes that research studies have found are relevant and important to consumers. Positioning is especially difficult among commodities, where the physical characteristics of all the brands are identical, such as water. Nevertheless, marketers offer many brands of mineral water that range in price and are positioned differently.

Box 2.5 Category Membership and Point of Parity in Segmenting and Positioning

Category membership and point of parity[39] are important concepts in segmentation, especially when a brand attempts to create a subcategory. Consumers under such a situation need to know the competitive offerings of the brand (category membership) and how diverse is the differentiation of the brand among the competitive offerings (how differentiation emerges from point of parity). Colgate introduced Aroma Therapy body wash. Milkfoods introduced yogurt (sweetened curds that are popular in developed markets as a health food). Under such a situation, consumers need to know that the body wash is competing with soaps; yogurt, though it competes with curds, is a healthier option.

The brand creating the subcategory also needs to ensure that there is no confusion among the consumers about the category itself. For instance, consumers may confuse flavored yogurt to be competing with ice creams! Dove's advertisement illustrates the point. The brand introduced a moisturizing bar and showed how it is superior by comparing its offering with "ordinary soap". Another aspect of point of parity is associated with the differentiation aspect of the brand. Close up toothpaste has the proposition of fresh breath. In Europe, though consumers liked the point of difference, the purchase intention was low as they also expected point of parity associated with the brand on tartar protection and prevention of decay.[40] Vanish liquid is also another example to reflect the usefulness of category membership. The brand came out with a campaign "Which side are your clothes on?"– Comparing Vanish with chlorine bleach. This clearly conveys to the consumers that the brand competes with several other offerings that may involve chlorine (and many of these may be in the unorganized sector).

TABLE 2.8 Positioning, Advertised Benefits, and Prices of Bottled Water Brand

BRAND	DESCRIPTION	POSITIONING, UNIQUE BENEFIT	PACKAGING	PRICE*
Tŷ Nant,	From Wales. Award winning. Served at top hotels and restaurants.	Style. Status. Attention-grabbing bottle.	Cobalt or red glass, elegant bottle.	$2.50
Voss	From Norway. From a virgin aquifer that was shielded by ice and rock for centuries.	Purity.	Cylindrical, frosted glass, modern, engraved font.	$3.50
Fiji	From the rain forest. The company is committed to conservation.	Environmental—"drink with a clear conscience."	Conventional glass bottle, printed label.	$2.50
Jana	From Croatia. Artesian water from deep beneath the surface. Pure and balanced.	The perfect pH**.	Conventional tall bottle, printed label.	$2.25
GOTA	From the Guarani Aquifer in Argentina, which is one of the purest reserves of underground water on earth, consists of sandstones deposited 200 million years ago, and is overlaid with igneous basalt of low permeability, which provides a high degree of containment.	Perfectly selected by nature. Provides minerals that help one's body remain young, healthy, and lively.	Clear glass, unconventional clear glass bottle with elegant, dark print.	$3.80

Notes:
* Price of 1 liter bottle
** pH is a measure of a liquid's acidity level.

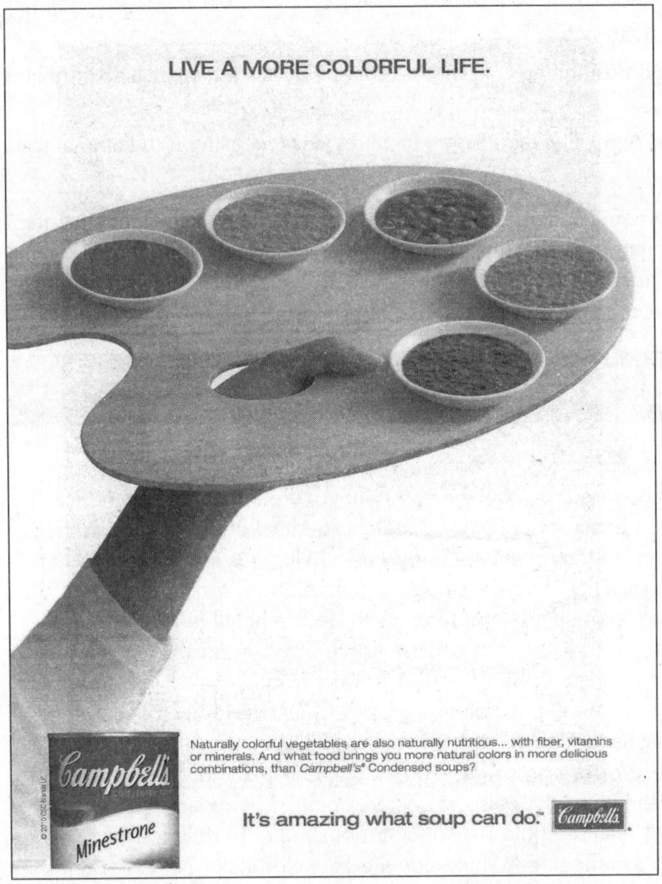

Source: Campbell Soup CompanyFebruary 16, 2012

FIGURE 2.11 An Illustration of Umbrella Positioning

Table 2.8 describes the positioning claims, unique benefits, and prices of several brands of bottled water.

The result of successful positioning strategy is a distinctive brand image on which consumers rely in making product choices. A positive brand image also leads to consumer loyalty, promotes consumer interest in future brand promotions, and "inoculates" consumers against competitors' promotions. When new products arrive and the marketplace becomes more crowded, it is increasingly harder to create and maintain a distinctive brand image among many competing ones.

The positioning strategies used most often are: umbrella positioning, premier position, positioning against competition, key attribute, and finding an "unowned" perceptual position. It must be noted that these strategies are not mutually exclusive and often overlap.

Umbrella Positioning

Umbrella positioning is a statement or slogan that describes the universal benefit of the company's offering. At times, this statement does nor refer to specific products. For example, Campbell's slogan, "Soup is good food," promotes *all* soups without any reference to the Campbell's brands. The slogan has been very effective, because the company dominates the soup market, and most consumers immediately think of Campbell's when they hear the word "soup." Figure 2.11 features a Campbell's ad that promotes soup as a way to "live a more colorful life," without mentioning any specific product attributes.

* McDonald's

A classic example of umbrella positioning includes the scores of slogans that McDonald's has used over the years, such as: "You deserve a break today" (1971); "Nobody makes your day like McDonald's can" (1981); "Food folks and fun," (1990); "Make every time a good time" (2002); and "I'm Lovin' It" (2003)*. Other examples are: Nike's "Just Do It" (launched in 1998), DeBeers's "A Diamond Is Forever" (launched in the 1940s). A cup of Maxwell House coffee is "good to the last drop," and a cup of Folgers is "the best thing about waking up." Among airlines, American "does what it's doing best," and United is "the friendly skies."

Premier Position

This positioning strategy focuses on the brand's exclusivity. For example, the "snobby" positioning of The New York Times is "All the news that's fit to print." Sometimes, the brand centers on the belief that the higher the product's price, the higher its exclusivity. For example, the marketer of Joy (a fragrance brand) positioned it as "the costliest perfume in the world." Although all prestigious fragrances are very expensive, no other perfume marketer has claimed that its product is the *most* expensive. Chapter 4 describes the concept of price-quality relationship.

For years, L'Oreal's hair coloring product presented women with an unstated but obvious question: "Why should I use this product?" and then provided an answer in the form of a positioning statement: "Because I'm Worth It" (coined in 1971). In the age of feminism, this slogan sounds arrogant because it strongly implies that only a woman's physical appearance counts more than her profession and knowledge. Thus, L'Oreal changed its positioning to "Because We're Worth It." In addition to being a more timely tagline, the new slogan can also be readily translated into many languages.[41] Chapter 13 describes the importance of translating brand names and advertising themes to other languages.

Box 2.6 Positioning and Primary and Secondary Associations in Positioning Brands

After a brand accomplishes its positioning slot, should it have a single association in the mind of the consumers or can it have multiple associations?

Brand Positioning is about a distinctive image or proposition or value that differentiates a brand from its competitors – it can be with regard to competitors, benefit or application in a specific situation or product class, attribute or user imagery. The concept of primary and secondary brand associations is important from the view of positioning as these two concepts are closely intertwined. Strongest of the brands have a single association or proposition, Santoor for youthful and ageless skin, Fastrack for urban fashion, Horlicks for health, Café Coffee Day for socializing and fun, Clinic Plus for the young daughter, and Moov as an ache remedy. The secondary associations of a brand need to be linked to the primary association that is created through the basic positioning.

Over a period of time it is challenging for a brand to sustain its original association and also make it contemporary amidst environmental changes. Lifebuoy's associations are different from Lifebuoy Clini-care 10, a higher-priced offering.

Positioning against Competition

Some positioning statements acknowledge competing brands. For example, Avis claims that "We're No. 2. We Try Harder" and indirectly acknowledges the existence of Hertz, the number-one brand in car rentals. The positioning of 7Up as the "Uncola" recognized that Coke dominates the soft drink market. Contrasting one's brand with competitors is very effective in positioning and differentiation, as illustrated by the Healthy Choice in Figure 2.12. The first ad positions Healthy Choice as a more nutritional lunch than Italian sub sandwiches and the other ad makes the same claim in comparison of prepared salads.

Key Attribute

Positioning based on relevant attributes often expresses the brand's superiority. The marketer of Bounty, a paper towels brand, initially positioned it as "the quicker picker upper" (presumably against Viva, its major competitor), later on as "the quilted picker upper," and then as "the clean picker upper." During an economic downturn, Bounty altered its positioning and appealed to consumers' frugality using the following statements: "With one sheet of Bounty, you'll have confidence in your clean," "One sheet keeps cleaning," and "Thick and absorbent Bounty helps you clean up quickly and easily, so you get more out of each day."[42]

Source: (Left & Right) Reprinted with permission of ConAgra Foods, Omaha, Nebraska

FIGURE 2.12 Differentiation: Healthy Choice versus Italian Subs and Prepared Salads

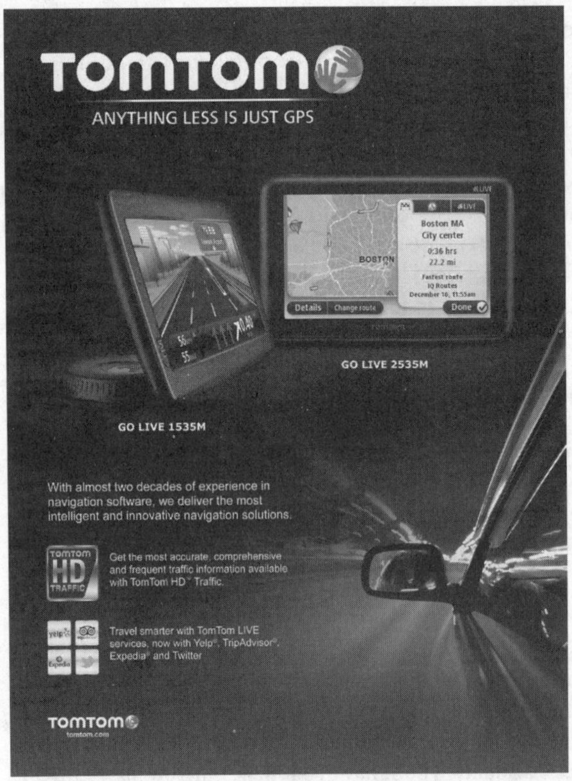

Source: With permission of TomTom, Intl.

FIGURE 2.13 Positioning Focused on a Key Product Attribute: A High-Definition GPS

Believing that consumers use brands to express their identities, some marketers have repositioned their products from focusing on functional attributes to focusing on how the products fit into a consumer's lifestyle. However, one study indicated that this approach is undesirable, because consumers' need for "self-expression" can be satiated not only by a brand's direct competitors but also by brands from unrelated product categories.[43]

The ad in Figure 2.13 features a high-definition GPS device that provides the most current traffic information. Thus, the ad's tag line—"Anything Less Is Just GPS"—proclaims the brand's superiority because of its high-definition display.

Un-Owned Position

Linguistically, perception is not a physical object and cannot be "owned." In marketing, the term "un-owned" position loosely means a perception that is not clearly associated with a brand or product. For example, in New York City, the Daily News newspaper specializes in sensationalized stories for readers without much education. In contrast, The New York Times focuses on artices written by famous and credible journalists for educated readers. *Long Island Newsday* positioned itself as "On top of the News and ahead of the Times," and targeted readers who wanted a newspaper that was not as "trashy" as The Daily News, but also not as highbrow as The New York Times.

Because unfilled or un-owned perceptual positions present opportunities for competitors, sophisticated marketers create many distinct product versions, often under the same brand, in

FIGURE 2.14 Fage Yogurt's Thickness: A Key Attribute and Occupying an "Un-Owned" Position

order to fill as many positions as possible. For example, Good Day biscuit is a ₹1500 Crore[44] brand that had used occasion as a segmentation base 25 years ago, positioning it as a healthier alternative to glucose biscuits[45] or cream biscuits that consumers were having with tea. The brand had started with a butter variant and later, over time, added cashew and other variants (this could be associated with some aspects of brand revitalization that is used to adapt the brand to changes in the environment). Vaseline cream, positioned on "healing", offered several variants – one for mositurising, one for fairness, and one for healing cracked heels.

The un-owned position must be in the consumer's mind and not the marketer's. Stated differently, marketers must not look in the mirror (at themselves), but through the window, at consumers. For example, in 1967, a biochemist working for New York's Rheingold Brewery observed (figuratively, he looked in the mirror) that there was no beer catering to diet-conscious drinkers and introduced Gablinger's Diet Beer. The product failed because heavy beer drinkers—who account for more than 80% of all the beer sold—were not diet conscious. Later on, using the same beer formula, Miller introduced Miller Lite as the "less filling" beer, and the product was a great success. Miller discovered (figuratively, by looking at the outside) that heavy beer drinkers wanted a less filling beer so that they could drink more beer without feeling filled. The exact same physical product failed when it was positioned as a diet beer, but succeeded handsomely when it was positioned as a less-filling beer. Beer drinkers perceived the second positioning as beneficial. The Fage yogurt ad in Figure 2.14, for a "Ridiculously thick yogurt," stresses thickness as the product's primary benefit, and also distiguishes Fage from the "much thinner" American yogurts.

Repositioning

Repositioning is the process by which a company strategically changes the distinct image and identity that its product or brand occupies in consumers' minds. Companies do so when consumers get used to the original positioning and it no longer stands out in their minds. Similarly, when consumers begin to view the old positioning as dull, marketers must freshen up their brands' identities. At times, too many competitors stress the same benefit in their positioning, so marketers must uncover other attributes that consumers perceive as important. For instance, at present Fage Greek yogurt is "ridiculously thick" and Chobani (a competing brand of Greek yogurt) is marketed as "authentic, real, and indulgent." Let's assume that a new brand of Greek yogurt is introduced as "thickly authentic." If the new brand begins to gain market share, Fage and Chobani will have to reexamine their positioning claims. Table 2.9 features instances of how positioning in India has evolved over the ages.

Another reason to reposition a product or service is to appeal to a new segment. For example, GM tried for years to convince younger consumers that Oldsmobile was not an "old folks" car and tried to reposition it as being "not your father's Oldsmobile." However, this effort failed because the "old folks" image of the brand was strongly set in the minds of car buyers, and GM stopped making this formerly highly successful brand.

A major factor that fueled the financial crisis of fall 2008 was consumers' excessive borrowing in the form of home equity loans. Traditionally, Americans looked forward to paying off their mortgages (the ritual of burning the mortgage note was an

TABLE 2.9 Examples of Repositioning in the Indian Context

PAST POSITIONING	SUBSEQUENT REPOSITIONING
Raymond's fabric positioned itself as a guide for well-dressed male in the eighties	The brand positioned itself as one associated "complete man" who also cares for his family (Relationships)
Dettol was an antiseptic lotion	Dettol was positioned as a tool for the housewife to take care of her family
Horlicks, for decades, was milk additive that provides nutrition	Horlicks was positioned to growing kids who would like to become taller, stronger, and sharper
Cadbury (molded/slab) version was positioned as a gift for kids	Cadbury was positioned as a chocolate for adults to celebrate everyday moments
Titan watches were positioned as a gift	Titan watches were positioned with a Celebrity association that suggested aspiration ("Be more")
Liril soap was positioned as a refreshing soap	Liril was positioned with product attributes that is beneficial

American tradition) and associated the term "second mortgage" with desperate borrowing, as a last resort. However, over the years, bank marketers repositioned this negatively perceived loan by luring consumers to get "equity loans" and use the funds for discretionary spending. In reality, an equity loan is a positive expression of the negatively perceived second mortgage. Consumers responded and used equity loans excessively and increasingly unwisely because the banks brilliantly repositioned the dreaded second mortgage. The banks convinced consumers to take advantage of their homes' appreciation and borrow money against the value of those homes. Banks advertised the new credit lines with such statements as "There's got to be at least $25,000 hidden in your house. We can help you find it." Marketers also replaced the term "equity loans" with "equity access," because a "loan" means borrowing, whereas consumers associate "access" with having resources. As the market for these lines of credit grew, the repositioning statements became bluntly aggressive, with slogans such as: "Is your mortgage squeezing your wallet? Squeeze back," "The smartest place to borrow? Your place," "The easiest way to haul money out of your house," and "You've put a lot of work into your home. Isn't it time for your home to return the favor?" The repositioning of the second mortgage was a spectacular success and since the 1980s equity loans ballooned from $1 billion to $1 trillion.[46] Apparently, consumers' needs were fulfilled, but the same strategies that filled these needs destabilized the world's financial structure.

Perceptual Mapping

Perceptual mapping is constructing a map-like diagram representing consumers' perceptions of competing brands along relevant product attributes. Perceptual maps show marketers:

1. How consumers perceive their brands in relation to competition.
2. How to determine the direction for altering undesirable consumer perception of their brands.
3. Gaps, in the form of un-owned perceptual positions, that represent opportunities for developing new brands or products.

The aim of perceptual mapping is to develop repositioning strategies and fine-tune the images (i.e., consumers' perceptions) of products and services. Figure 2.15 features a perceptual map of 10 well-known stores. It represents a hypothetical study in which researchers asked consumers how they perceived 10 stores along two dimensions: (1) "innovative" versus "traditional" and (2) "luxurious" (high-end) versus "thrifty" (low-end). The additional adjectives listed in the four quadrants represent words used to characterize the stores by the study's subjects. For example, consumers viewed Barneys as a very innovative, high-end store, and, additionally, as creative and up-to-date. On the map, Barneys stands by itself and far from Bloomingdale's, its closest competitor. In contrast, consumers perceived Macy's and Old Navy similarly and as rather non-distinct variety stores (note that this is a *hypothetical* example). The management of Macy's should recognize that it has a problem: consumers did not perceive the store accurately, because, in reality, it is neither very thrifty nor traditional. This indicates that the store's promotional messages must focus on "correcting" this image and convincing consumers that Macy's is more high-end than Old Navy. The study's respondents viewed Modell's and H & M as close competitors, and the Gap and Banana Republic as close competitors and middle-of-the-road in terms of pricing and innovativeness. To management, this indicates that the two stores must be positioned more clearly in consumers' minds. Bergdorf Goodman and Saks 5th Avenue were perceived as high-end competitors, and with Saks as a more traditional store.

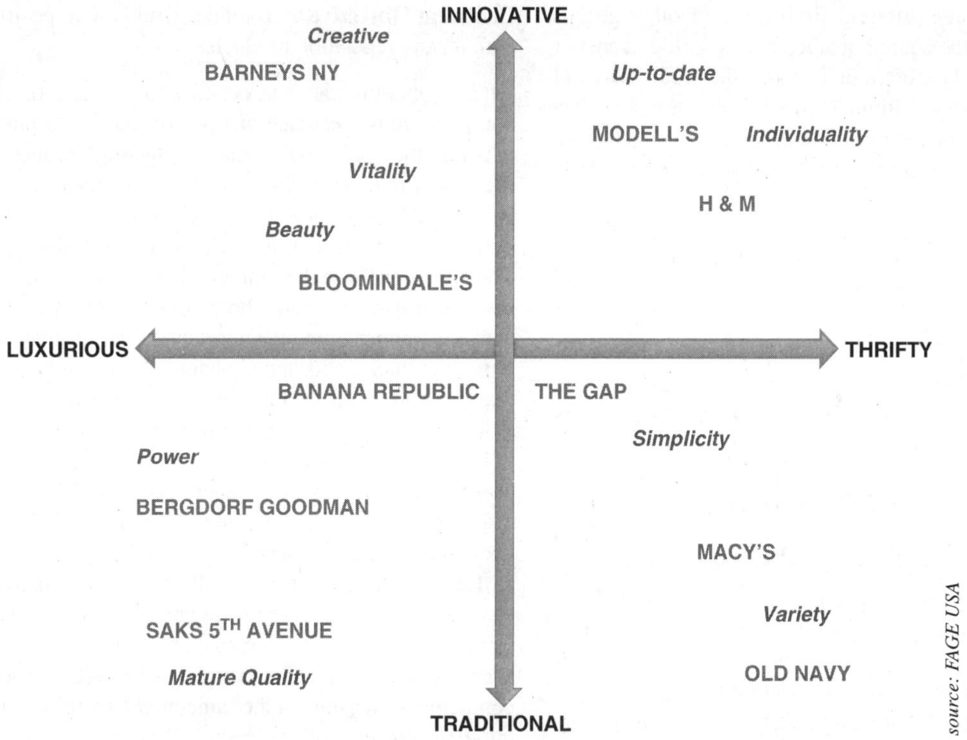

FIGURE 2.15 A Perceptual Map of Well-Known Stores

Box 2.7 Niche Markets and Online Shopping

Internet commerce is likely to grow exponentially (with the current growth rate of 80%) in the Indian context with 200 million internet users and an online market of US$ three billion (excluding travel). Brands are likely to pursue niche markets that have special requirements (though may not be in line with the typical definition of niche that needs to be premium). Hopscotch[47] is an e-retailer for infants that has a list of about 400 brands (international and domestic) targeting mothers with infants. There are about one lakh consumers for the brand that deals with offerings not available in neighborhood stores. These stores get 40% of their orders from non-metro cities.

Summary

Learning Objective 1: To understand the interrelationship among market segmentation, targeting, and positioning and how to select the best target markets.

Market segmentation consists of dividing a potential market into distinct subsets of consumers. Each subset represents a consumer group with common needs and characteristic. Targeting means selecting one or more segments and approaching each one with a specially designed marketing mix. Besides aiding in the development of new products, segmentation studies assist in the redesign and repositioning of existing products, in the creation of promotional appeals, and in the selection of advertising media. To be a viable target market, a segment must be identifiable, sizeable, stable or growing, accessible, and congruent with the marketer's objectives and resources.

Learning Objective 2: To understand the bases used to segment consumers, including demographics, psychographics, product benefits sought, and product usage-related factors.

A segmentation strategy begins by dividing the market for a product into groups that are relatively homogeneous and share characteristics that are different from those of other groups. Broadly speaking, the shared characteristics include consumers' behaviors (e.g., how often do they buy the product) as well as their cognitions (e.g., attitudes towards new products). The bases for segmentation include demographics, personality and psychographics, geodemographics, product benefits, media exposure, usage rate, and usage occasion.

Learning Objective 3: To understand behavioral targeting and its key role in today's marketing.

Behavioral targeting consists of sending consumers personalized and prompt offers and promotional messages based on marketers' tracking of one or more of the following factors: online navigation, current geographic location, and purchase behavior. The objective of behavioral targeting is to reach the right consumers and deliver highly relevant messages to them at the right time more accurately than when using conventional segmentation techniques. Many marketers use predictive analytics, which consists of methods predicting consumers' future purchases on the bases of past buying information and other data, and evaluating the impact of personalized promotions stemming from the predictions. Collecting the right data and analyzing it strategically are essential to effective behavioral targeting. Marketers collect and use information about consumers' interests, personal lives, and the social networks with which they connect online for targeting them with customized products and promotional messages.

Learning Objective 4: To understand how to position, differentiate, and reposition products.

After segmenting the market and selecting targeting prospects, marketers must persuade prospective buyers to buy the products that they offer, rather than competing products. Positioning is the process by which a company creates a distinct image and identity for its products, services, or brands in consumers' minds. The image and unique identity are called a "position." The "position," which is intangible and exists only in the consumer's mind, represents how consumers perceive the product. Positioning is more important to the ultimate success of a product than are its actual characteristics, although products that are poorly made will not succeed on the basis of image alone. The result of effective positioning is a unique perception of the product in the mind of the consumer. Most new products fail because consumers perceive them as "me too" offers that do not provide any advantages or unique benefits over competitive products.

Repositioning is the process by which a company intentionally changes the distinct image and identity that its products, services, and brands occupy in consumers' minds. Several reasons may force marketers to reposition products, such as many competitors focusing on the same product attribute in positioning their offerings.

Perceptual mapping consists of constructing a map-like diagram representing consumers' perceptions of competing brands along relevant product attributes.

Review and Discussion Questions

2.1. What is market segmentation? How is the practice of market segmentation related to the marketing concept?

2.2. How are market segmentation, targeting, and positioning interrelated? Illustrate how these three concepts can be used to develop a marketing strategy for a product of your choice.

2.3. Apply the criteria for effective targeting to marketing a product of your choice to college students.

2.4. Discuss the advantages and disadvantages of using demographics as a basis for segmentation. Can demographics and psychographics be used together to segment markets? Illustrate your answer with a specific example.

2.5. Select at least two segmentation bases that should be used jointly to segment the market for each of the following products and explain your choices: (1) men's denim pants; (2) women's cocktail dresses; (3) hybrid cars; (4) e-readers.

2.6. Some marketers consider benefit segmentation to be the segmentation approach most consistent with the marketing concept. Do you agree or disagree with this view? Why?

2.7. Regent Seven Seas Cruises and Royal Caribbean International are two companies in the vacation and travel industry. After looking at their websites, describe the kind of consumers that each company is seeking to attract. Also, describe how either company can use demographics and psychographics to identify TV shows and magazines in which to place its advertisements.

2.8. How can a marketer for a chain of health clubs use the VALS™ segmentation profiles to develop an advertising campaign? Which segments should be targeted? How should the health club be positioned to each of the segments targeted?

2.9. Using one of the frameworks described in Table 2.3, find at least two suitable segments for one of the following products: (1) SUVs; (2) financial retirement plans; or (3) LED TVs. Using Nielsen's online Zip Code Look-Up, identify the closest location of consumer clusters belonging to these segments to your home. Describe the segments you chose and why, and the locations you looked up.

2.10. Explain how marketers can use each of the following pieces of data in predictive analytics:

a. The websites consumers visit.

b. Consumers' levels of engagement with visited websites (i.e., the pages viewed, length of visits, frequency of return to the site).

c. Visitors' and consumers' interests, lifestyles, and personalities (e.g., from the contents of their blogs, tweets, and Facebook profiles).

d. Visitors' purchases, almost purchases, abandoned carts, and product returns and exchanges.

2.11. How would you segment the market of consumers who would like to order Oakley sunglasses online? Explain your answer.

2.12. Describe the stages of the positioning process and apply them to positiong a product of your choice.

2.13. How is the understanding of consumers' perceptions of a product's attributes used to position a brand within that product category?

2.14. What is the relationship between benefit segmentation and positioning?

2.15. Why do marketers have to reposition their brands? Illustrate with examples.

2.16. What are perceptual maps, and how are they used in positioning brands within the same product category? Illustrate your answer with the chapter's discussion of eye drops and toothpaste.

2.17. Describe the relationship between behavioral targeting and predictive analytics.

Hands-on Assignments

2.18. Select a product and brand that you use frequently and list the benefits you receive from using it. Without disclosing your list, ask a fellow student who uses a different brand in this product category (preferably a friend of the opposite sex) to make a similar list for his or her brand. Compare the two lists and discuss the differences and similarities among the benefits that you and your friend seek from the same product category.

2.19. Does your lifestyle differ significantly from your parents' lifestyle? If so, how are the two lifestyles different? What factors cause these differences?

2.20. Visit two websites that you are familiar with and write down every click that you make and the patterns and the navigation patterns and times of your surfing. Then, describe how a marketer—of a product of your choice—who had tracked your Web visits to the sites could use the observation of your surfing in designing a customized advertising message directed at you.

2.21. The owners of a local health-food restaurant have asked you to prepare a psychographic profile of families living in the community surrounding the restaurant's location. Construct a 10-item psychographic questionnaire that measures a family's dining out preferences..

2.22. Find three print advertisements directed at three different clusters, each one belonging to one of the three frameworks listed in Table 2.3: PRIZM, P$YCLE, and ConneXions. Explain your choices.

Key Terms

- behavioral data *31*
- behavioral targeting *44*
- benefit segmentation *40*
- cognitive factors *31*
- innovators *37*
- demographic segmentation *31*
- family life cycle *34*
- geodemographics *36*
- geofencing *45*
- market segmentation *26*
- perceptual mapping *52*
- positioning *26*
- predictive analytics *45*
- PRIZM *36*
- product awareness status *43*
- product involvement *43*
- psychographics *37*
- repositioning *51*
- showrooming *45*
- social class *35*
- targeting *26*
- umbrella positioning *48*
- usage occasion segmentation *44*
- usage rate segmentation *42*
- VALS *38*

Case One: Porsche

"How Porsche Created New Relevance for a Revered Icon"

Lead Agency: **Cramer-Krasselt**
Contributing Agencies: **Struck Axiom/OmnicomMediaGroup**

Strategic Challenges

Was America's luxury sports car category on the ropes? With the uncertain economic times, it seemed no one needed a sports car and it was no longer publicly acceptable to share a longing for one—let alone the sports car of all sports cars, a Porsche.

This was the problem weighing on the minds of the Porsche team in 2010. In the larger sports car category, which was down 56%, Porsche was experiencing precipitous declines. Since 2007, sales of the 911—Porsche's revered icon, and the heart and soul of the brand—were down 54%. Not only were 911 sales down dramatically, sales of *all* two-door Porsche sports cars (including the 911, Boxster, and Cayman) had fallen an unprecedented 58%. Thus, the loss of relevance and diminished road presence of the 911, Porsche's flagship model, had wide reverberations that strongly affected the very identity of Porsche.

The key challenge: Figuring out how to sell a product that's synonymous with success and status during a time when affluent consumers were examining, reexamining, and justifying each and every purchase.

The challenge was exacerbated by several factors. Porsche had no new product to generate buzz. In fact, the 911 was in the last year of its current model cycle, and the new 911 model, the Type 991, had already been publicly announced and was eagerly anticipated by Porsche enthusiasts. Those who were interested in buying a new 911 were on the sidelines, waiting for the new model, and some dealers were taking orders. To meet its aggressive sales goals, Porsche knew it had to reach beyond its core enthusiasts, and establish brand relevance with a larger audience, many of whom had never owned or considered a Porsche before. Porsche intended to sell its current $80,000-plus vehicle without any major promotional or pricing programs, and with a communications budget that was half that of its closest competitor.

Objectives

1. Change Brand Perceptions: Within the challenging economic environment, the company had to make the Porsche 911 and mid-engine models (Boxster and Cayman) relevant and worth their price.
2. Dealer Lead Generation: With the 911 sales down 54%, people weren't even putting Porsche sports cars on their shopping lists, and dealers were running low on leads. Porsche had to significantly increase purchase consideration and "find a dealer" requests on its website.
3. Sales: With the new 911 model going into production, the company needed to increase existing 911 sales and ultimately sell the remaining models. To do this, it had to broaden its audience and create new brand relevance—reaching both men and women, many of whom had never even considered a Porsche.

Insights

Porsche assumed that for those who could afford it, the economic downturn had made owning a Porsche socially unacceptable. People didn't want to pull up to their driveway in a shiny new sports car, for fear of looking insensitive to all that was going on around them, including neighbors and friends who might be struggling financially.

This assumption was wrong. Potential customers weren't afraid to spend the money, but the economic times were dictating *how* they spent it. *"I respect and like the 911. I even test-drove one about five years ago before I bought my Mercedes. It's definitely a great sports car, but it didn't have the luxury touches I was looking for. It felt too impractical to drive every day.—It's a great third car, but not a daily driver"* (quote from a customer).

Buying a Porsche wasn't socially unacceptable; it was personally unjustifiable. *"If I bought a Porsche, when would I actually drive it?" "Now isn't the time to buy a weekend toy* (quotes from customers). Customers perceived Porsche as an *epic* sports car.

This perceived epic sports car status of the 911 Porsche kept people away from showrooms and resulted in dated brand images. The timeless shape of the 911 had slowly evolved over the years, but with no radical exterior changes to cue reconsideration, many prospects assumed that the car was more for racing than daily driving. They thought the interior of the cars had nothing more than three pedals and a gear shift, resulting in a rough and uncomfortable ride they wouldn't want to drive daily, making it hard to justify spending more than $80,000. Even though they wanted a sports car, what they needed was one car that could comfortably fill multiple roles—and because they didn't see Porsche as this type of car, they compromised. They settled for luxury cars with less magic but more versatility, even calling them their "compromise cars."

Porsche's research studies discovered that few people realized that the 911s are built to be driven every day, year round. They are not precious, but solid and substantial. The company needed to expand the Porsche 911 and mid-engine driving occasions and let people know that Porsches are comfortable, functional, and intended to be driven every day.

The Big Idea

Porsches are amazing sports cars designed to be driven hard every day, making everyday driving more magical.

Questions

1. Before you read this case, did you believe that Porsche cars were meant to be driven everyday or only for special occasions? Explain your answer.
2. Since it was founded, in 1931, the core of the Porsche brand was "outstanding engineering, tradition, and versatility." How does the "everyday magic" campaign fit within the core's three elements?
3. Was the campaign designed to reposition the Porsche 911? Explain your answer.
4. Although not stated overtly, the campaign targeted *two* segments. Which ones? Explain your choices.
5. Find three print ads for the "everyday magic" campaign (available online) and evaluate their persuasive effectiveness. Do you find any of these ads "unrealistic?" Explain.
6. How would Porsche determine whether the campaign's objectives were achieved?

Source: Effie Worldwide, Effie Showcase Winners. Reprinted by permission. Porsche is a 2012 Silver Effie Winner. For information on Effie's programs for students, visit the Collegiate Effies at www.effie.org

3

Consumer Motivation and Personality

Learning Objectives

1. To understand the dynamics of motives, needs, and goals and how they shape consumer behavior.
2. To understand motivation theories and their applications to consumer behavior.
3. To understand how to identify and measure motives.
4. To understand the scope of personality and theories of its development.
5. To understand how innovativeness and other personality traits influence consumer behavior.
6. To understand the personification of products and brands and its strategic applications.
7. To understand self-image and its impact on consumer behavior.

MOTIVATION is the driving force that impels people to act. It represents the reasons one has for acting or behaving in a particular way. **Needs** are circumstances or things that that are wanted or required, and they direct the motivational forces.

Human beings' most basic needs are biological and fulfilling them sustains physical existence and safety. For example, when parents send their kids to school they expect a physically safe environment. The ad in Figure 3.1 targets drivers by showing parents' concerns for their children's safety when the youngsters get off a school bus. The slogan "It shouldn't be this dangerous" urges drivers to stop when they see flashing lights and ensure that kids get home safely.

Personality consists of the inner psychological characteristics that both determine and reflect how we think and act, which together form an individual's distinctive character. Consumers often purchase products and brands because advertisers have given them "personalities" that differentiate them from competing offerings. **Brand personification** occurs when consumers attribute human traits or characteristics to a brand. A "brand personality" provides an emotional identity for a brand, which produces sentiments and feelings toward it among consumers. For example, consumers often view certain brands as "exciting," sophisticated," or "warm."

Brand personification is a form of **anthropomorphism**, which refers to attributing human characteristics to something that is not human. For example, Figure 3.2 features Zoo-Zoo characters, introduced by Vodafone, to reflect anthropomorphism in the Indian context.

Source: Government of Alberta. Used with permission.

FIGURE 3.1 An Appeal Directed at Safety Needs

Source: Vodafone

FIGURE 3.2 Brand Personification

Application 1: The Power of Virtual/digital Brand Personality

Brands like Volvo, MTV, and clothing retailer Hennes & Mauritz have entered the market with virtual goods.[1] With Facebook and other social marketing websites making their presence felt overwhelmingly, the brands are working on various ways to connect with consumers. Creating awareness, excitement, and even strengthening associations by contemporary images are some of the objectives of these brands. Volvo introduced its virtual goods on the iPhone application, My Town, with a game where players having to check auto dealerships to buy Volvo products. Hennes & Mauuritz also used My Town to get consumers interested in its offerings. MTV used virtual goods to boost the viewership of its Video Music Awards. It used Facebook's Mall World to provide virtual replicas of several fashion accessories used by celebrities.

Are brands attempting to build virtual self-concepts revolving around consumers? Such brand strategies raises interesting questions on virtual brand personality – should there be such a concept? If so, what would be the convergence with a brand's offline brand personality with its online personality? Would consumer segments be interested in trying out different virtual selves and how could marketers get an idea about them? For instance, a brand like TVS Pleasure has used celebrities to convey the self-concept of independence and self-reliance. It may find that youngsters who are in the target segment may like to experience a different kind of "self" on the virtual domain and hence, the challenge for the brand is to balance actual and virtual brand personality. A brand like Axe can be associated with several aspects of the Freudian theory. It may want to develop an extension of such a personality on the virtual domain. A combination of virtual self, consumers' desire to experiment (perhaps with regard to their unconscious desires), and the need for the marketer to respect cultural sensitivity in the Indian context can open up new conceptual challenges for the marketers.

Mercedes in India is perceived as a sporty, innovative, aesthetic, and dynamic brand.[2] The brand sponsors golf tournaments, wine tasting sessions, and events with fashion designers to reinforce such associations.

Application 2: Values, Traits, and Brands

Self-concept, together with values, will be useful to marketers in the Indian market. Given the diversity of segments and psychographics associated with such segments, self-concept and values can provide several insights into brands. A conservative lady belonging to a traditional family may buy gold jewelry both as an investment and to impress others about her status when she attends functions like weddings (Indian weddings are typically associated with such jewelry). A middle-class working woman may buy jewelry to identify with her group of colleagues at the office who had also bought branded jewelry and may prefer a brand like Gold Plus. A working woman holding an executive rank may prefer a brand like Tanishq to express her sense of uniqueness. A lady buying a brand like Tiffany, who is further higher in terms of economic status, may like to be seen with the brand in a social gathering as a symbol of her wealth. The three consumers associated with the different brands of jewelry have a self-concept that is associated with the value of accomplishment. (In this context, accomplishment is reflected through the possession of the respective brand). It is also interesting to note that a consumer's value of accomplishment is driven by a specific personality trait. In the case of the first consumer, it is the trait of affiliation and self esteem; in the case of the second consumer, it may or may not be affiliation and self esteem; in the case of the third consumer, it is the trait of individuality (autonomy) and in the fourth case, and it is the trait of exhibitionism along with self-esteem. Values and traits combine to form an important part of one's self-concept. The other variants of the self-concept so formed (like actual self-concept or social self-concept or ideal self-concept) depend on such combinations of values and traits. The same set of traits may be present across different target segments and the same set of traits or related traits may surface with regard to different contexts (contexts portrayed with regard to the four consumers). Brand associations need to take into consideration several aspects of concepts associated with personality.

This chapter begins with a discussion of consumers' needs and motivation and then describes how consumers' personalities influence their buying behavior.

Learning Objective

1 To understand the dynamics of motives, needs, and goals and how they shape consumer behavior.

The Dynamics of Motivation

Motivation drives consumers to buy and is triggered by psychological tension caused by unfulfilled needs. Individuals strive both consciously and subconsciously to reduce this tension through selecting goals and subsequent behavior that they anticipate will fulfill their needs and thus relieve them of the tension they feel. Whether gratification is actually achieved depends on the course of action pursued. Personality characteristics guide the goals that people set and the courses of action they take to attain these goals.

The foundation of marketing is identifying and satisfying needs. Marketers do not create needs, although in many instances they strive to make consumers more keenly aware of unfelt or dormant needs. Savvy companies define their business in terms of the consumer needs they satisfy rather than the products they produce and sell. Because consumers' basic needs do not change, but the products that satisfy them do, a corporate focus on developing products that will satisfy consumers' needs ensures that the company stays in the forefront of the search for new and effective solutions. By doing so, such companies are likely to survive and grow despite strong competition or adverse economic conditions. In contrast, companies that define themselves in terms of the products they make may suffer or even go out of business when their products are replaced by competitive offerings that better satisfy consumers' needs.

For example, Procter and Gamble defines its business as "providing branded products and services of quality and value that improve the lives of the world's consumers"*—a need-focused definition—rather than stating that the company sells products such as detergents, shampoos, diapers, household cleaners, and dozens of other items (i.e., a product-oriented approach). Similarly, the mission of the Ritz Carlton Hotels and Resorts is not to provide rooms for overnight stays, but "the genuine care and comfort of guests," through providing customers an experience that "enlivens the senses, instills well-being, and fulfills even the unexpressed needs and wishes"** of guests. The diagram in Figure 3.3 illustrates the process of motivation.

Needs

There are two types of human needs: **Physiological needs** are innate (biogenic, primary) and fulfilling them sustains biological existence. They include the need for food, water, air, protection of the body from the outside environment (i.e., clothing and shelter), and sex.

Psychological needs are learned from our parents, social environment, and interactions with others. Among many others, they include the needs for self-esteem, prestige, affection, power, and achievement.

Both types of needs affect our buying decisions. For example, all individuals need shelter from the elements and therefore buy homes. However, the kind of homes they buy is the result of psychological, learned needs. A young Indian executive who is buying an iPhone will satisfy his physiological need (perhaps to quickly order some fast food through the Zomato app) as well as satisfy his psychological need of connecting with his group of friends.

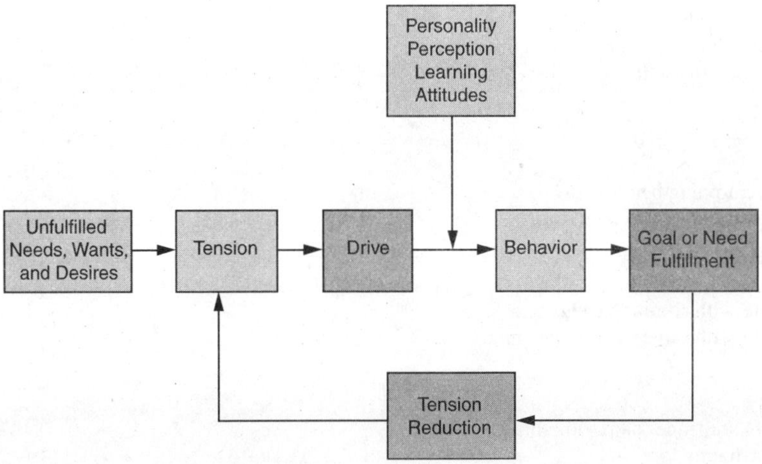

FIGURE 3.3 The Motivation Process

* Proctor & Gamble

** Ritz Carlton

Goals

Goals are the sought-after results of motivated behavior, and all human behavior is goal oriented. There are two types of goals: **Generic goals** are outcomes that consumers seek in order to satisfy physiological and psychological needs. **Product-specific goals** are outcomes that consumers seek by using a given product or service. For example, when a student tells his parents that he wants to become an entrepreneur, he expresses a generic goal. If he says he wants to earn an MBA from Stanford, he expresses a product-specific goal. A consumer wanting an alternative (perhaps a service offered by a laundry or a washing machine) to satisfy his or her needs of convenience associated with cleaning clothes. In a situation where traditional house maids are becoming scarce in Indian metros, this is a generic goal; the consumer wanting to buy a brand of washing machine is a product-specific goal.

As consumption became technology-driven, marketers have become keenly interested in the motivations of bloggers and individuals who post comments online. Such individuals influence other consumers, because people perceive both positive and negative reviews from other consumers as more credible information than advertisements. In fact, many bloggers shape the views of thousands of consumers, and many have documented their influence by following the number of responses that they get to their postings and tweets (see Chapter 9). Marketers would be delighted to have any—even the smallest—degree of influence over online writers whose essays and comments focus on products and consumption, because understanding the motivations of the writers often enables marketers to influence what is being written. One study identified three motivations for blogging: (1) self-expression; (2) documenting one's life (i.e., keeping a diary); and (3) identifying other influential bloggers.[3] Table 3.1 summarizes the motivations of consumers who share information on Facebook.[4]

Need Arousal

Most of an individual's needs are dormant much of the time. The arousal of any need at a specific moment in time may be caused by biological stimuli, emotional or cognitive processes, or stimuli in the outside environment. A drop in blood sugar level or stomach contractions will trigger awareness of a hunger need. A decrease in body temperature will induce shivering, which makes the individual aware of the need for warmth. Most of these physiological cues are involuntary, but they arouse needs that

TABLE 3.1 Motivations of Facebook Users

INFORMATION SHARING
To provide information To share information that might be useful to others To share news
CONVENIENCE AND ENTERTAINMENT
Because it's enjoyable Because it's an easy way to stay in touch with people Because I just like to use it
PASSING TIME
Because I'm bored Because I have nothing better to do Because everyone else is doing it
INTERPERSONAL UTILITY
To meet people with similar backgrounds To meet people with same interests as mine
CONTROL
Because I want someone to do something for me To tell others what to do
PROMOTING WORK
To promote the organization I work for To promote my personal work

cause uncomfortable tensions until they are satisfied. For example, a person who is cold may turn up the heat in his bedroom and make a mental note to buy a warm sweater to wear around the house.

In cognitive arousal, random thoughts can lead to a cognitive awareness of a need to act. For instance, a greeting card company's ad might remind a viewer that her grandchild's birthday is next week, and that it is time to run out and purchase a gift and a birthday card, and be ready for the birthday party. Many promotional messages are cues designed to arouse consumer needs. Without these cues, consumers' needs may remain dormant. Thus, creative marketing messages arouse needs by stimulating a psychological desire or imbalance in consumers' minds. The goal then becomes to act on the desire, and reduce the felt imbalance by buying products.

Selecting Goals

Usually, consumers set purchase-related goals that satisfy more than one need. We buy clothing for protection and for a certain degree of modesty; in addition, our clothing fulfills a wide range of personal and social needs, such as acceptance by others. People with different needs may seek fulfillment by selecting the same goal, and people with the same needs may seek fulfillment via different goals. For example, two people driven by the need for achievement might seek fulfillment in different ways. One may seek advancement and recognition through a professional career, whereas the other may choose to run marathons.

For any given need, there are many different and appropriate goals. The goals that individuals select depend on those individuals' personal experiences and knowledge, physical capacity, prevailing cultural norms and values, and the goal's accessibility in the individuals' physical and social environments. For example, a young woman may wish to get a deep, even tan and may envision spending time in the sun as a way to achieve her goal. However, if her dermatologist advises her to avoid direct exposure to the sun, she may settle for a self-tanning cosmetics instead. The goal object has to be both socially acceptable and physically accessible. If cosmetic companies did not offer effective alternatives to tanning in the sun, our young woman would either have to ignore the advice of her dermatologist or select a substitute goal, such as fair (but undamaged) youthful-looking skin.

The motivation to select goals can be either positive or negative. We may feel a driving force *toward* some object or condition or a driving force *away* from some object or condition. For example, a person may be encouraged to start exercising in order to avoid health problems (i.e., a negative outcome) or in order to look more attractive and dynamic (i.e., a positive outcome). Positive outcomes that we seek are called **approach objects**; negative outcomes that we want to prevent are called **avoidance objects**. For instance, a college is an approach object to a high school graduate who is motivated by the desire for higher education. Another person knows that his parents would criticize him if he does not go to college, so he goes to college to avoid being criticized. Both individuals have the same goal—college education—but are motivated to adopt that goal in opposite ways.

Box 3.1 Goal Selection and Brands in an Emerging Market

With installment system almost a widely-offered provision across several categories of products and services, different categories and brands compete for a share of the wallet of the Indian consumer. Brands need to ensure that the consumers are attracted to both the product category and the respective brand. This is because Indian consumers have a "Product ladder" in their mindset rather than a "Brand ladder". Consumers may not be able to buy all the categories they wish to (approach objects); the cultural habit of saving becomes a barrier for some of these categories. Insurance companies and brands position themselves towards child welfare schemes; milk additives like Horlicks and Bournvita position themselves on health (the consumer may have the choice of a milk additive or fruits or a nutritive food supplement for his/her children, but he may not be able to afford every category). A middle-class working couple will face the dilemma of either buying a two-wheeler for commuting or saving for their children's further education (both are approach objects and the categories may not directly compete with one another). A consumer who is at the bottom rung of the strata and generally uses unbranded offerings may have a cycle for his indulgence (buy a pack of cream biscuit like Oreo in a sachet and then buy a sachet of branded tea in his next purchasing cycle instead of the biscuit). Such a situation presents unique challenges to brands.

Students may refer to the last chapter on "Consumer Research" to have an idea about the concept of laddering that links brand features to benefits and then to the values of consumers. A study in the Indian context is provided in the chapter specified.

Needs and Goals Are Interdependent

Needs and goals are interdependent; neither exists without the other. However, people are often not as aware of their needs as they are of their goals. For example, a teenager may not consciously be aware of his social needs, but may join a number of chat groups online to meet new friends. Similarly, people are aware that they need to buy certain items, but may have different goals when they go shopping. One study contrasted the shopping motivations of pairs of mothers and daughters and discovered that daughters go to malls for recreational or social shopping, whereas their mothers tend to be more purposeful in their shopping.[5] Another study identified several factors that motivate people to go shopping:[6]

1. Seeking out specific goods, such as going to to supermarket to buy foods or a hardware store to purchase needed tools or materials.
2. Recreational shopping occurs when consumers do not have an urgent product need in mind, but go shopping for the personal enjoyment of shopping.
3. Activity-specific shopping, which includes such motivations as sensory stimulation, gift shopping, and bargain hunting.
4. Demand-specific shopping, in which consumers are motivated by such factors as service convenience, store atmosphere, assortment innovations, and assortment uniqueness.

Needs Are Never Fully Satisfied

Human needs are never fully or permanently satisfied. As individuals attain their goals, they develop new ones. If they do not attain their goals, they continue to strive for old goals or they develop substitute goals. For example, a person may partially satisfy a need for power by working as an administrative assistant to a local politician, but this vicarious taste of power may not sufficiently satisfy her need; thus, she may strive to work for a state legislator or even to run for political office herself. In this instance, temporary goal achievement does not adequately satisfy the need for power, and the individual strives ever harder to satisfy that need more fully.

New Needs Emerge as Old Ones Are Satisfied

Some motivational theorists believe that a hierarchy of needs exists and that new, higher-order needs emerge as lower-order needs are fulfilled.[7] For example, a man whose basic physiological needs (e.g., food, housing, etc.) are fairly well satisfied may turn his efforts toward achieving acceptance among his neighbors by joining their political clubs. Once he is confident that he has achieved acceptance, he then may seek recognition by giving lavish parties or building a larger house.

Success and Failure Influence Goals

Individuals who achieve their goals usually set new and higher goals for themselves. They raise their aspirations because success in reaching lower, earlier goals makes them more confident of their ability to reach higher goals. Conversely, those who do not reach their goals sometimes lower their aspirations. For example, a college senior who is not accepted into medical school may try instead to become a dentist.

The effects of success and failure on goal selection have strategic implications for marketers. Goals should be reasonably attainable and advertisements should not promise more than can be delivered; instead, they should only promise what the product is able to live up to. Furthermore, products and services are often evaluated by the size and direction of the gap between consumer expectations and objective performance. Thus, even a good product will not be repurchased if it fails to live up to unrealistic expectations created by ads that overpromise. Similarly, consumers often regard mediocre products with greater satisfaction than is really warranted if the products' performance exceeds their expectations.

When people cannot attain their primary goals, they often set "substitute goals." Although the substitute goal may not be as satisfactory as the primary goal, it may be sufficient to dispel uncomfortable tension. Continued deprivation of a primary goal may result in the substitute goal assuming primary-goal status. For example, a woman who has stopped drinking whole milk because she is dieting may actually begin to prefer skim milk. A man who cannot afford a BMW may convince himself that a new, sporty, and less expensive Japanese car has an image he prefers.

Frustration and Defense Mechanisms

Frustration is the feeling that results from failure to achieve a goal, and **defense mechanisms** are cognitive and behavioral ways to handle frustration. At one time or another, everyone has experienced the frustration that comes from the inability to attain a goal. The barrier that prevents attainment of a goal may be personal (e.g., limited physical or financial resources) or an obstacle in the physical or social environment (e.g., a storm that causes the postponement of a long-awaited vacation). Regardless of the cause, individuals react differently to frustrating situations. Some people manage to cope by finding their way around the obstacle or, if that fails, by selecting a substitute goal. Others are less adaptive and may regard their inability to achieve a goal as a personal failure. Such people are likely to adopt a defense mechanism to protect their egos from feelings of inadequacy.

People cope with frustrations differently. For example, two young women yearn for European vacations that they cannot afford. The coping woman may select a less expensive vacation trip to Disneyland or a national park. The other woman, who cannot readily cope with frustration, may react with anger toward her boss for not paying her enough money to afford the vacation she desires, or she may persuade herself that Europe is unseasonably and uncomfortably warm this year. These latter two possibilities are examples, respectively, of **aggression** and **rationalization**, defense mechanisms that people sometimes adopt to protect their egos from feelings of failure when they do not attain their goals. Other defense mechanisms include **regression**, **withdrawal**, **projection**, **daydreaming**, **identification**, and **repression**. These defense mechanisms are described in Table 3.2. This list of defense mechanisms is far from exhaustive, because individuals tend to develop their own ways of redefining frustrating situations to protect their self-esteem from the anxieties that result from experiencing failure. Marketers often consider this fact in their selection of advertising appeals and construct advertisements that portray a person resolving a particular frustration through use of the advertised product.

In a country where there is a high magnitude of disparity between "haves" and "have-nots", brands in the Indian context need to explore possible ways of using defense mechanisms in the brand's strategy. Consumers at all levels of socio-economic planes have aspirations and desires. The fulfillment of such desires may not be accomplished due to affordability reasons and many of these desires may require an act of indulgence (for example, indulging in luxury brands at a shopping mall to gratify one's self-esteem needs). The environment is dynamic and new needs keep emerging as brands introduce new offerings. A brand like Nike may be interested in sponsoring a sports camp for underprivileged kids to cater to their "Aggression" and in the process be associated with a social cause. The ads of some brands of detergents and kitchen appliances portray feelings of frustration through actors who grapple with their situational problems. They are addressing "Identification" aspect of defense mechanism. CRY (a non- profit organization) and initiatives of Proctor &Gamble on cause-based marketing (consumer would contribute to a social cause by buying a brand) may be associated with "Repression" (an individual not being able to contribute to social progress though he or she would very much like to). Fair &Lovely, Pond's, and TVS Pleasure have ads that may trigger "Daydreaming" that leads the consumer towards these brands. A new brand of edible oil may portray the defense mechanism of "Projection" by reflecting that most edible oils may interfere with tasty food and that she should try the new brand. Similarly, a cooking appliance like rice cooker or an induction cooker brand may use "Rationalization" aspect by projecting that the working woman may not have adequate time due to the limitations of the usual gas stove that needs to be supplemented by the brand. A brand of entertainment service (theatre or a music company that organizes events) can use "Withdrawal" by appealing to consumers to relax from their high-pressure professional goals by choosing the membership of the service.

The advertising appeals need to be formulated taking into account the psychographic motivations of the target segment. As lifestyles become more complex, defense mechanism will be used by marketers in the years to come.

TABLE 3.2 Defense Mechanisms

DEFENSE MECHANISM	DESCRIPTION AND ILLUSTRATIONS
Aggression	In response to frustration, individuals may resort to aggressive behavior in attempting to protect their self-esteem. The tennis pro who slams his tennis racket to the ground when disappointed with his game or the baseball player who physically intimidates an umpire for his call are examples of such conduct. So are consumer boycotts of companies or stores.
Rationalization	People sometimes resolve frustration by inventing plausible reasons for being unable to attain their goals (e.g., not having enough time to practice) or deciding that the goal is not really worth pursuing (e.g., how important is it to achieve a high bowling score?).
Regression	An individual may react to a frustrating situation with childish or immature behavior. A shopper attending a bargain sale, for example, may fight over merchandise and even rip a garment that another shopper will not relinquish rather than allow the other person to have it.

(*Continued*)

TABLE 3.2 (*Continued*)

DEFENSE MECHANISM	DESCRIPTION AND ILLUSTRATIONS
Withdrawal	Frustration may be resolved by simply withdrawing from the situation. For instance, a person who has difficulty achieving officer status in an organization may decide he can use his time more constructively in other activities and simply quit that organization.
Projection	An individual may redefine a frustrating situation by projecting blame for his or her own failures and inabilities on other objects or persons. Thus, the golfer who misses a stroke may blame his golf clubs or his caddy.
Daydreaming	Daydreaming, or fantasizing, enables the individual to attain imaginary gratification of unfulfilled needs. A person who is shy and lonely, for example, may daydream about a romantic love affair.
Identification	People resolve feelings of frustration by subconsciously identifying with other persons or situations that they consider relevant. For example, slice-of-life commercials often portray a stereotypical situation in which an individual experiences a frustration and then overcomes the problem by using the advertised product. If the viewer can identify with the frustrating situation, he or she may very likely adopt the proposed solution and buy the product advertised.
Repression	Another way that individuals avoid the tension arising from frustration is by repressing the unsatisfied need. Thus, individuals may "force" the need out of their conscious awareness. Sometimes repressed needs manifest themselves indirectly. The wife who is unable to bear children may teach school or work in a library; her husband may do volunteer work in a boys' club. The manifestation of repressed needs in a socially acceptable form is called *sublimation*, another type of defense mechanism.

Systems of Needs

Over the years, several psychologists have developed lists of human needs, but there is no single, comprehensive, and commonly accepted list. Although there is little disagreement about physiological needs, there are distinct differences of opinion about defining and categorizing needs with nonphysical origins, that is, psychological (or psychogenic) needs.

Murray's List of Psychogenic Needs

In 1938, the pioneering psychologist Henry Murray prepared an extensive list of psychogenic needs, which represented the first systematic approach to the understanding of nonbiological human needs. Murray believed that although each need is important in and of itself, needs can be interrelated, can support other needs, and can conflict with other needs. For example, the need for dominance may conflict with the need for affiliation when overly controlling behavior drives away friends, family, and spouses. Murray also believed that environmental circumstances strongly influence how psychogenic needs are displayed in behavior. For example, studies have indicated that people with a high need for achievement tend to select more challenging tasks. Also, people with high needs for affiliation are part of large social groups, spend more time in social interaction, and feel lonely when faced with little social contact.

Murray organized his needs into five groups: *ambition, materialistic, power, affection,* and *information* needs. Later on, the psychologist Allen Edwards developed a self-administered *personality inventory* that became one of the most widely used tools in the study of personality traits. Table 3.3 lists the definition and illustrative characteristics of several needs researched by Murray and Edwards that are most relevant to consumer behavior.

Maslow's Hierarchy of Needs

Psychologist Abraham Maslow formulated a theory of human motivation based on the notion that there is a hierarchy of human needs.[8] **Maslow's hierarchy of needs** consists of five levels of human needs, which rank in order of importance from lower-level (biogenic) needs to higher-level (psychogenic) needs. The theory states that individuals seek to satisfy lower-level needs before higher-level needs. The lowest level of unsatisfied needs motivates a person's behavior. When that need is fairly well satisfied, the individual is motivated to fulfill a need in the next level of the hierarchy. When that need is satisfied, the need in the next level

TABLE 3.3 Psychogenic Needs Applicable to Consumer Behavior

NEED	ILLUSTRATIVE CHARACTERISTICS	PROMOTIONAL APPLICATIONS
Achievement: accomplish tasks, succeed, and overcome obstacles.	Do the best and work hard in any undertaking. Be able to do things better than others.	Messages that encourage and illustrate success (e.g., advertising education).
Exhibition: shock or thrill others and be the center of attention.	Tell amusing jokes at parties. Say things that others regard as witty and clever.	Messages showing attention from others when they notice one's possessions (e.g., expensive cars).
Affiliation: spend time, form strong friendships and attachments with others.	Be loyal to and share things with friends. Help friends in trouble. Be confided in by others and told about their troubles.	Messages showing people enjoying themselves in large groups (e.g., vacations, shopping situations).
Power/Dominance: control, influence, and lead others.	Seek leadership in groups. Supervise and direct the actions of others.	Messages showing actual or symbolic dominance (e.g., being a chief executive; owning a powerful car).
Change: seek new experiences and avoid routine.	Doing new and differ like eating in new restaurants, going on trips, and avoiding conventional situations.	Messages stressing novelty, uniqueness, and breaking with routines (e.g., adventure travel and active vacations).
Order: keeping things neat and organized.	Planning and organizing the details in any undertaking. Setting definite times for activities.	Promoting devices that save space and keep things firmly in place (e.g., dividers and organizers for closets, drawers, and garages).

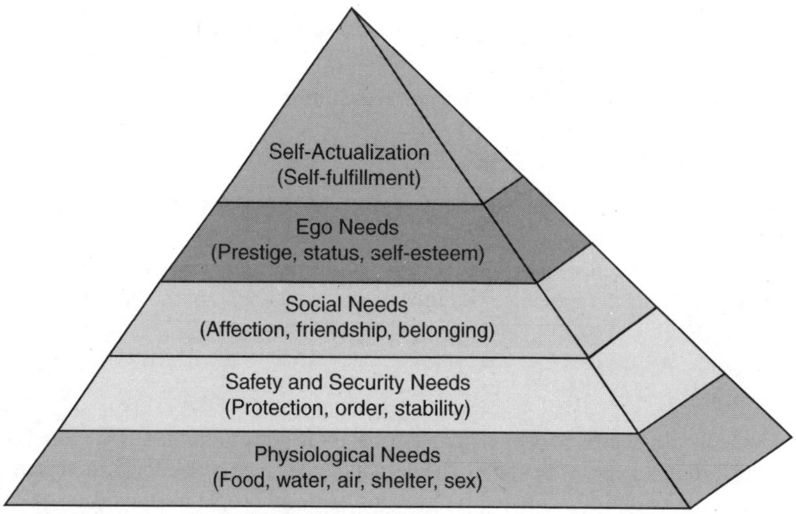

FIGURE 3.4 Maslow's Hierarchy of Needs

is one's primary motivator, and so on. However, if a person experiences renewed deprivation regarding a formerly met lower-level need, that need becomes the dominant factor in the person's motivation, even if only temporarily. For example, if a person who is well off and trying to satisfy his ego needs loses his job, he reverts or "goes back" to trying to satisfy his security needs; if he gets a new job that pays well, thus satisfying security needs, he will once again "move" to a higher level in the hierarchy.

Figure 3.4 presents a diagram of Maslow's hierarchy of needs. For clarity, the levels appear as mutually exclusive. According to the theory, however, there is some overlap among the levels, as no need is ever completely satisfied. Thus, to some extent, all levels of need below the level that is currently dominant continue to motivate behavior. Nevertheless, the prime motivator—the major driving force within the individual—is the lowest level of need that remains largely unsatisfied.

Physiological Needs

Maslow maintained that **physiological needs** are the first and most basic level of human needs. These primary needs, which are required to sustain biological life, include food, water, air, shelter, clothing, and sex—all biogenic needs. According to Maslow, physiological needs are dominant when they are chronically unsatisfied: "For the man who is extremely hungry, no other interest

Source: Levi's

FIGURE 3.5 Use of Maslow's Concept to Connect with Hipsters

exists but food. He dreams food, he remembers food, he thinks about food, he emotes only about food, he perceives only food, and he wants only food."[9]

Safety Needs

After physiological needs have been satisfied, **safety and security needs** become the driving force behind an individual's behavior. These needs are concerned not only with physical safety, but also with order, stability, routine, familiarity, and control over one's life and environment. For example, health and the availability of health care are important safety concerns. Savings accounts, insurance policies, education, and vocational training are all means by which individuals satisfy the need for security.

Social Needs

The third level of Maslow's hierarchy consists of **social needs**, such as love, affection, belonging, and acceptance. Maslow's concept of social needs, affiliations or belongingness has been used by Levi's, as illustrated in Figure 3.5, to connect with hipsters at an individual level.

Egoistic Needs

When social needs are more or less satisfied, the fourth level of Maslow's hierarchy becomes operative. This level includes **egoistic needs**, which can take either an inward or an outward orientation:

1. ***Inwardly directed ego needs*** reflect an individual's need for self-acceptance, self-esteem, success, independence, and personal satisfaction.
2. ***Outwardly directed ego needs*** include the needs for prestige, reputation, status, and recognition from others.

Need for Self-Actualization

According to Maslow, once people sufficiently satisfy their ego needs, they move to the fifth level. The **self-actualization need** refers to an individual's desire to fulfill his or her potential—to become everything that he or she is capable of becoming. For example, an artist may need to express herself on canvas; a research scientist may strive to find a new drug that eradicates cancer. Advertising an organization as one that "lets you do great things," or enables you to "be all you can be," appeals to the need for self-actualization.

Evaluation of Maslow's Theory

Maslow's theory states that higher-order needs become the driving force behind human behavior as lower-level needs are satisfied. The theory says, in effect, that dissatisfaction, not satisfaction, motivates behavior. The need hierarchy has received wide acceptance in many social disciplines because it appears to reflect the assumed or inferred motivations of many people in American society. The five levels of needs are sufficiently generic to encompass most individual needs. The major problem with the theory is that it cannot be tested empirically; there is no way to measure precisely how satisfied one level of need must be before the next higher need becomes operative. The need hierarchy is very closely bound to the American culture (i.e., it appears to be both culture- and time-bound). In non-Western countries, the needs specified by Maslow are ranked differently. Indeed, research indicated that in some countries, safety, love, and belonging are at the apex of the needs pyramid.[10]

Marketing Applications of Maslow's Theory

Despite its limitations, Maslow's hierarchy has been a highly useful framework for marketers. Maslow's needs hierarchy is readily adaptable to market segmentation and the development of advertising and other marketing communications appeals, because there are consumer goods designed to satisfy each of the need levels, and because most needs are shared by large segments of consumers. For example, individuals buy health foods, medicines, and low-fat products to satisfy physiological needs. They buy insurance, preventive medical services, and home security systems to satisfy safety and security needs. Consumers buy personal care and grooming products (e.g., cosmetics, mouthwash, shaving cream), as well as most clothes, in order to satisfy social needs. They purchase high-tech and luxury products, such as elaborate sound systems, high-end wristwatches, sports cars, and expensive furniture, to fulfill ego and esteem needs. Postgraduate college education, hobby-related products, and exotic and physically challenging adventure trips are often sold as ways of achieving self-actualization.

Advertisers and other forms of marketing messages can also use the need hierarchy to position products; that is, to develop a strategy that will make consumers perceive a product or brand as its marketer intends. The need hierarchy is a versatile tool for developing positioning strategies because different appeals for the same product can be based on different needs. For example, a study that tested the appeal of different military recruitment slogans found that the two slogans that resonated well with potential recruits were "Be All You Can Be" and "The Few, the Proud, the Marines." The slogans that most respondents disliked were "I Want You" and "Join the People Who've Joined the Army."[11] Clearly, egoistic and self-actualization needs are the prime motivators behind joining the armed forces.

Box 3.2 Motivation and the Management of Premium and Discounted Items

Several concepts associated with motivation and needs are relevant to marketers in the Indian context, like Maslow's theory of hierarchy of needs, Freudian psychoanalytic theory (discussed later) and product-specific and brand-specific goals. Consumers prefer functional appeals, symbolic appeals or hedonic appeals in brands. Appeals of any kind are also intertwined with the perception of value, which takes into consideration "price-benefits" aspects. Value differs from one segment to another and the concept of motivation has immense applications. With significant retail expenditure of consumers on groceries and food products, discount retailing stores have emerged in the country. Reliance Fresh, for example, has discount offers in several categories through out the year.

The sachet or one-use packaging in several categories motivates consumers who may like to use branded offerings occasionally. These aspects can be associated with survival and security needs for a family that is at the lower end of the socio-economic spectrum. A per capita annual income of around ₹61,564 (per annum) in 2011-12[12] means that most families in India are motivated to save money on daily-use items because they want to spend on children's education, weddings, or on durable categories (like a TV or refrigerator).

There are segments of consumers who may have a high degree of status needs or hedonic needs and indulge in brands that offer the respective gratification. Premium brands are important to consumers with such a motivational pattern. Tanishq in jewelry, Mont Blanc in pens, Omega in watches, iPhones in mobiles, and Volkswagen Beatle in cars are some examples that highlight the importance of symbolic needs. Red Bull in the soft drink category with its energy proposition emphasizes the hedonic or consumption needs of consumers. Premium brands that may be high on symbolic and functional needs or hedonic and symbolic needs have to capture these needs for an appropriate brand image. Brand image is critical in triggering these needs among the respective target segment. The need for affiliation triggers the youth to buy symbolic offerings that signals group affiliation. For instance, Fastrack watches are positioned toward urban youngsters. Motivation-based concepts provide a platform on which both premium and discounted offerings can formulate their communication plans.

A Trio of Needs

Another framework for organizing human needs is known as the trio of needs: the needs for power, affiliation, and achievement (these needs are reflected in Table 3.3 and also in Maslow's needs hierarchy). Individually, each of the three needs can affect consumer motivation.

Power

The **power need** is an individual's desire to control his or her environment. It includes the need to control other persons and various objects. This need appears to be closely related to the ego need, in that many individuals experience increased self-esteem when they exercise power over objects or people.

Affiliation

Affiliation is a well-researched social motive that significantly influences consumer behavior. The **affiliation need** is very similar to Maslow's social need and suggests that behavior is strongly influenced by the desire for friendship, acceptance, and belonging. People with high affiliation needs tend to be socially dependent on others and often buy goods that they feel will meet with the approval of friends. Teenagers who hang out at malls or techies who congregate at computer shows often do so more for the satisfaction of being with others than for the purpose of making a purchase. In Figure 3.6, United Colors of Benetton depicts that the need for equality is triggered by the larger aspect of need for affiliation.

Achievement

Individuals with a strong **achievement need** often regard personal accomplishment as an end in itself. They are self-confident, enjoy taking calculated risks, actively research their environments, and value feedback, often in the form of monetary rewards. People with high achievement prefer situations in which they can take personal responsibility for finding solutions.[13] Because of this, portraying achievement is a useful promotional strategy for many products and services, especially those targeting educated and affluent consumers. (Figure 3.4 represents an appeal based on the need for achievement).

Learning Objective

3 To understand how to identify and measure motives.

The Measurement of Motives

How are motives identified? How are they measured? How do researchers know which motives are responsible for certain kinds of behavior? These are difficult questions to answer because motives are hypothetical constructs; that is, they cannot be seen or touched, handled, smelled, or otherwise tangibly observed. For this reason, no single measurement method can be considered a reliable index of motivation. Instead, researchers usually rely on a combination of research techniques when trying to establish the presence and/or the strength of various motives. By combining several research methods—including responses to questionnaires or survey data (i.e., self-reports of opinions and behaviors) and insights from focus group sessions and depth interviews (i.e., to discover underlying motives)—consumer researchers achieve more valid insights into consumer motivations than they would by using any single technique.

Source: United Colors of Benetton

FIGURE 3.6 A Need for Affiliation

Self-Reporting

Self-reported measures of motives consist of written statements which ask respondents to indicate how relevant each statement is to them. The researchers administering these measures politely ask respondents not to think too much before providing their answers, because, if they do so, they might figure out what the statements measure and not answer honestly. If so, the subjects' responses are likely to reflect not who they *are*, but how they *wish* to be perceived. For example, a respondent who figures out (correctly) that the statement "one does one's best work when the assignment is difficult" measures a person's need for achievement, may "strongly agree" with the statement even if she does not really find it applicable because she wants to be perceived as an achiever. If used correctly, self-reported measures assess people's motives fairly accurately.

Qualitative Research

Frequently, respondents may be unaware of their motives, or may be unwilling to reveal them when asked directly. In such situations, researchers use **qualitative research** to delve into the consumer's unconscious or hidden motivations. Many qualitative methods also termed **projective techniques** because they require respondents to interpret stimuli that do not have clear meanings, based on the assumption that the subjects will "reveal" or "project" their subconscious, hidden motives onto the ambiguous stimuli. The findings of qualitative research methods are highly dependent on the training and experience of the analyst; the findings represent not only the data themselves but also what the analyst thinks they imply. Though some marketers are concerned that qualitative research does not produce hard numbers that objectively "prove" the point under investigation, others are convinced that qualitative studies are sometimes more revealing than quantitative studies (see Chapter 16). The major types of qualitative methods used to study motivation are featured in Table 3.4, together with applicable examples.[14]

Motivational Research

The term **motivational research**, which should logically include all types of research into human motives, has become a "term of art." It refers to qualitative studies conducted by Dr. Ernest Dichter in the 1950s and 1960, which were designed to uncover consumers' subconscious or hidden motivations. Based on the premise that consumers are not always aware of the reasons for their actions, motivational research attempted to discover underlying feelings, attitudes, and emotions concerning product, service, or brand use. This premise reflects Sigmund Freud's psychoanalytic theory of personality, which maintains that unconscious needs or drives—especially biological and sexual drives—are at the heart of human motivation and personality.

When Dr. Dichter, trained as a clinical psychoanalyst in Vienna, arrived in the United States in the late 1930s, he joined a major New York advertising agency rather than establish a clinical practice. Dr. Dichter applied Freud's psychoanalytical techniques to the study of consumer buying habits and used qualitative research to figure out why consumers did what they did. Marketers became fascinated by the glib, entertaining, and sometimes surprising explanations offered for consumer behavior,

TABLE 3.4 Qualitative Measures of Motives

RESEARCH METHOD	DESCRIPTION AND EXAMPLES
Storytelling	Storytelling consists of having customers tell real-life stories regarding their use of the product under study. By using this method to study parents' perceptions of diapers, Kimberly-Clark discovered that parents viewed diapers as clothing related to a particular stage in the child's development. Thus, if their children wore diapers too long, parents became distressed and embarrassed because it was an overt sign of their failure to toilet-train their children. The company introduced its highly successful Huggies Pull-Ups training pants—a product that established a new category in the U.S. diaper industry.
Word Association	In the **word association method**, respondents are presented with words, one at a time, and asked to say the first word that comes to mind. This method is highly useful in determining consumers' associations with existing brand names and those under development. In sentence completion, respondents are asked to complete a sentence upon hearing the opening phrase (e.g., "People who drive convertibles . . .").

(*Continued*)

TABLE 3.4 (Continued)

RESEARCH METHOD	DESCRIPTION AND EXAMPLES
Thematic Apperception Test	Developed by Henry A. Murray, the **Thematic Apperception Test** consists of showing pictures to individual respondents and asking them to tell a story about each picture. For example, Clearasil employed an image of a female looking into a mirror under the caption "Here is a teenager looking into the mirror and seeing pimples." The researchers discovered that teenagers view their lives as fast-paced and socially active and that the discovery of a pimple abruptly disturbs the swiftness of their lives. The resulting advertising depicted a teenage male walking briskly down the street and spotting a pimple on his face in a store window. All motion around him stops. He applies Clearasil, the pimple disappears, and life resumes its pace.
Drawing Pictures	Visual images are often used to study consumers' perceptions of various brands and to develop new advertising strategies. For example, when respondents were asked to draw pictures of the typical Pillsbury cake-mix user, their drawings depicted old-fashioned, chubby females wearing frilly aprons. When asked to draw pictures of the Duncan Hines cake-mix user, their drawings showed slim, "with it" women wearing heels and miniskirts. These findings provided important input to Pillsbury concerning the need to reposition its product.
Photo Sorts	In a study using photo sorts conducted by the advertising agency for Playtex (a manufacturer of bras), respondents received stacks of photos depicting different types of women and asked to select pictures portraying their own self-images. Although many of the respondents were overweight, full-breasted, and old-fashioned in appearance, they selected photos showing physically fit, well-dressed, and independent women. The advertising agency advised Playtex to stop stressing the comfort of its bras in its ads and designed a new campaign showing sexy, thin, and big-bosomed women under the slogan: "The fit that makes the fashion."

Sources: Emily Eakin, "Penetrating the Mind by Metaphor," New York Times, February 23, 2002, B9, Bl 1; Ronald B. Leiber, "Storytelling: A New Way to Get Close to Your Customer," Fortune, February 3, 1997; and Bernice Kramer, "Mind Games," New York, May 8, 1989, 33–40.

especially since many of these explanations were grounded in sex. For example, Dichter told marketers that consumers bought cigarettes and Life Saver candies because of their sexual symbolism, that men regarded convertible cars as surrogate mistresses, and that women baked cakes to fulfill their reproductive yearnings. Before long, almost every major advertising agency in the country had a psychologist on staff to conduct motivational research studies. Table 3.5 includes a sample of product profiles created by Dichter and his colleagues.

TABLE 3.5 Examples of Dichter's Subconcious Interpretations

PRODUCT	SUBCONSCIOUS INTERPRETATION
Baking	Baking expresses femininity and motherhood by evoking nostalgic memories of delicious odors pervading the house when the mother was baking. When baking a cake, a woman is subconsciously and symbolically going through the act of giving birth, represented by the baked product being pulled from the oven. Thus, when a woman bakes a cake for a man, she is offering him a symbol of fertility.
Automobiles	A car allows consumers to convert their subconscious urges to destroy and their fear of death—two key forces in the human psyche—into reality. For example, the expression "step on it" stems from the desire to feel power, and the phrase "I just missed that car by inches" reflects the desire to play with danger. Based on this view, Dichter advised Esso (now Exxon) to tap into consumers' aggressive motives for driving cars in promoting the superiority of its gasoline product. The slogan "Put a tiger in your tank" was developed as a result of his advice. Dichter also maintained that cars have personalities, and that people become attached to their cars and view them as companions rather than objects. This notion stands behind his views that a man views a convertible as a mistress and a sedan as his wife.

(Continued)

TABLE 3.5 (Continued)

PRODUCT	SUBCONSCIOUS INTERPRETATION
Dolls	Dolls play an important part in the socialization of children and are universally accepted as an essential toy for girls. Parents choose dolls that have the kind of characteristics they want their children to have, and the doll is an object for both the parents and the children to enjoy. When Mattel introduced Barbie in 1959, the company hired Dichter as a consultant. His research indicated that although girls liked the doll, their mothers detested the doll's perfect bodily proportions and Teutonic appearance. Dichter advised Mattel to market the doll as a teenage fashion model, reflecting the mother's desire for a daughter's proper and fashionable appearance.
Ice cream	Ice cream is an effortless food that does not have to be chewed and that melts in your mouth, a sign of abundance, an almost orgiastic kind of food that people eat as if they want it to run down their chins. Accordingly, Dichter recommended that ice cream packaging should be round, with illustrations that run around the box panel, suggesting unlimited quantity.

Modern motivational research includes many qualitative methods and procedures and is well established in consumer research.[15] It includes research methods not only from psychology, but also from sociology and anthropology. Qualitative consumer research methods, consisting of focus group sessions and depth interviews, are routinely used by businesses seeking to gain deeper insights into the *whys* of consumer behavior. Motivational research often reveals unsuspected consumer motivations concerning product or brand usage and is often used to develop ideas for promotional campaigns. Qualitative research also enables marketers to explore consumer reactions to product ideas and advertising copy at an early stage, and avoid the costly errors resulting from using ineffective and untested ads. Furthermore, motivational research findings provide consumer researchers with insights that serve as the foundations of structured, quantitative marketing research studies, which employ larger and more representative consumer samples than qualitative studies.

Building on the studies of Dr. Dichter and other motivational researchers, the Qualitative Research Consultants Association (QRCA) was established with the objective of applying an interdisciplinary orientation to consumer motivation research. The membership of QRCA consists of qualitative researchers who regularly conduct focus groups and one-on-one, in-depth interviews for client marketing companies that seek to identify the underlying needs and motives of their customers. Through its publications and conferences, the QRCA has brought about an expansion of the methodologies used in consumer research.

Culture and Need States

In a dynamic environment, the consumer has two mental states—a desired state and the actual state. Decision making models are created when there is a recognized gap between actual and desired states for consumer segments. Most marketing activities rely on the identification of these states for various products and consumer segments. The gap can be in terms of functional/experiential/symbolic aspects of a product.

Though there are several strategies in decision making, there are a number of linkages across stages. Consider a product like iced tea or an electric toothbrush. In the former case, consumers in India are used to having iced tea as a cultural habit and in the latter case the perceived risk and the concept need to be explained. In the former case, brand associations are important even at the need stage. In the case of an electric toothbrush, "primary advertising" is needed to sell the concept to consumers.

While the need stage recognizes various states of the consumer's psyche, marketers have to be careful when it comes to cultural aspects. Eating and cleaning habits, for example, are well entrenched in a society and it is difficult to change them. A fast food brand that attacks traditional food habits in India as non-nutritious (and offers nutrition-based fast food) may not be well-received by consumers. Ariel and Tide (international brands of P&G) introduced bar detergents, given the huge market and the consumer's tendency in India to use bar detergents to clean clothes.

Learning Objective

4 To understand the scope of personality and theories of its development.

The Nature and Theories of Personality

Personality consists of the inner psychological characteristics that both determine and reflect how we think and act. The emphasis in this definition is on *inner* *characteristics*—those specific qualities, attributes, traits, factors, and mannerisms that distinguish one individual from other individuals. As discussed later in this chapter, the deeply ingrained characteristics that we call personality influence the individual's product choices: They affect the way consumers respond to marketers' promotional efforts, and when, where, and how they consume many products or services. Therefore, the identification of specific personality characteristics associated with consumer behavior has been highly effective in the development of market segmentation and promotional strategies.

The Facets of Personality

Psychologists' research into human personality has not been uniform. Some have emphasized the influence of heredity and early childhood experiences on personality development. Others have stressed broader social and environmental influences. Some theorists view personality as a unified whole, whereas others focus on specific traits. Overall, researchers agree on the following: (1) personality reflects individual differences; (2) personality is generally consistent and enduring; and (3) although it is enduring, personality can change.

Personality Reflects Individual Differences

Because the inner characteristics that constitute an individual's personality are a unique combination of factors, no two individuals are exactly alike. Nevertheless, many individuals may possess a single or even a few personality characteristics, but not others. For instance, some people can be described as "high" in consumer ethnocentrism (i.e., unwillingness to accept foreign-made products), whereas others can be described as "low" in ethnocentrism (i.e., not reluctant to buy foreign-made products). Personality enables marketers to categorize consumers into different groups on the basis of one or several traits, because consumers who belong to a given segment are often "high" on a particular personality characteristic, whereas consumers from another segment score "low" on that same characteristic.

Personality is Consistent and Enduring

Generally, an individual's personality tends to be both consistent and *generally* enduring. Indeed, the sibling who comments that her sister "has always cared a great deal about her clothes from the time she was a toddler" is supporting the contention that personality has both consistency and endurance. Both qualities are essential if marketers are to explain or predict consumer behavior in terms of personality. Marketers cannot change consumers' personalities to conform to their products. However, if they know which personality characteristics influence specific consumers' responses, they can appeal to the relevant traits inherent in their target consumers. For instance, if a marketer knows that one of the firm's products attracts consumer innovators, it can create marketing messages that appeal to innovative consumers.

Personality May Change

Although personality is generally enduring, under certain circumstances, personalities change. For instance, major life events, such as marriage, the birth of a child, the death of a parent, or a change of job and/or profession strongly affect personality. One's personality changes not only in response to abrupt events, but also as part of a gradual maturing process: "He's more mature, and now he's willing to listen to points of view that differ from his own," says an aunt after not seeing her nephew for several years.

Theories of Personality

There are three major theories of personality: (1) Freudian theory, (2) neo-Freudian theory, and (3) trait theory. We have chosen them over other theories because each has played a role in the study of the relationship between consumer behavior and personality.

Freudian Theory

The premise of **Freudian theory** is that *unconscious* needs or drives, especially sexual and other biological drives, are at the heart of human motivation and personality. Freud constructed his theory on the basis of patients' recollections of early childhood experiences, analysis of their dreams, and the specific nature of their mental and physical adjustment problems. Freud proposed that the human personality consists of three interacting systems: the id, the superego, and the ego. Figure 3.7 shows the interrelationships among Freud's three interacting systems.

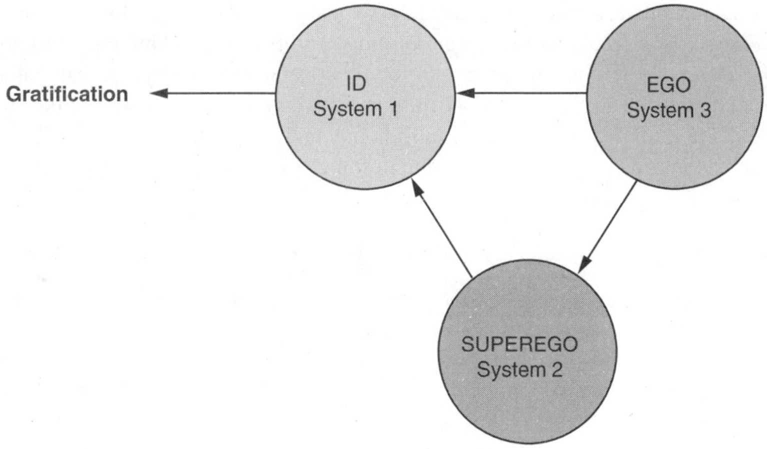

FIGURE 3.7 Freud's Theory

Source: Godiva Chocolates

FIGURE 3.8 An Appeal to Id-Like Primitive Drives: Feeling Like a Diva

The **id** is the "warehouse" of primitive and impulsive drives—basic physiological needs such as thirst, hunger, and sex—for which the individual seeks immediate satisfaction without concern for the specific means of satisfaction. The Godiva ad in Figure 3.8 captures the mystery and excitement aroused by these "primal forces."

In contrast to the impulsive (and selfish) id, the **superego** is the individual's internal expression of society's moral and ethical codes of "proper" or "correct" conduct. The superego's role is to see that individuals satisfy their needs in a socially acceptable fashion. Thus, the superego is a kind of "brake" that restrains or inhibits the impulsive forces of the id. Finally, the **ego** is the individual's conscious control. It functions as an internal monitor that attempts to balance the impulsive demands of the id and the sociocultural constraints of the superego.

Freud emphasized that an individual's personality is formed as he or she passes through a number of distinct stages of infant and childhood development: the *oral*, *anal*, *phallic*, *latent*, and *genital* stages. According to Freudian theory, an adult's personality is determined by how well he or she deals with the crises that are experienced while passing through each of these stages (particularly the first three). For instance, if a child's need for food is not adequately satisfied at the first stage of development, he may become "fixated" at this stage, and, as an adult, his personality will reflect dependence on others. As another example, an individual who is treated impatiently during toilet training may become an adult obsessed with cleanliness and neatness.

"Id" is the seat of sensual, primitive, suppressed pleasure associated with the personality of individuals, as per the Freudian theory. Axe (deodorant), Fastrack (watch), Bourbon (cream biscuits) and Flying Machine (apparel) are some of the brands that had formulated advertising themes[16,17] that are suggestive of the Freudian approach. The US campaign of Old Spice deodorant brand "The Man Your Man could smell like" attracted 47 million likes on the YouTube. The Indian ad, released in 2013, urges men to use the brand to feel "Mantastic" resulting in two million hits in the YouTube in ten days. The model selected for the ad was associated with a sexually controversial ad during the nineties; the build of the campaign along with the tagline was suggestive of fantasy associated with id.

Box 3.3 Brands and Freudian Theory

Parle's Hide&Seek Milano had tried to associate "id" part of Freudian theory (suppressed drives and baser instincts) with the biscuit category. The commercial shows a young man in a historical attire (celebrity) with a princess. The ad evokes pun through its visuals that hints at sexual overtones. The tagline with the visuals suggested that there is a secret behind very Milano biscuit. Fantasies (Freudian in nature and that can be associated with id part of Freud's theory) of movie goers are captured by Bollywood movies through songs, romantic scenes, and fight sequences[18] (to name a few aspects) and these are fantasies that people cannot enact everyday but would like to experience frequently.

Neo-Freudian Personality Theory

Neo-Freudian theory maintains that, in addition to Freud's concepts, social relationships play a crucial role in the development of personality. Several of Freud's colleagues disagreed with his contention that personality is primarily instinctual and sexual in nature. These neo-Freudians believed that social relationships are fundamental to the formation and development of personality. For instance, Alfred Adler viewed human beings as seeking to attain various rational goals, which he called *style of life*. He also placed much emphasis on the individual's efforts to overcome *feelings of inferiority* (i.e., by striving for superiority). Harry Stack Sullivan, another neo-Freudian, stressed that people continuously attempt to establish significant and rewarding relationships with others. He focused on the individual's efforts to reduce tensions such as anxiety.

Karen Horney was also interested in anxiety and studied the impact of child–parent relationships on the individual's desire to reduce feelings of anxiety. Horney proposed that individuals be classified into three personality groups:[19]

1. **Compliant individuals** are those who move *toward* others and wish to be loved, wanted, and appreciated.
2. **Aggressive individuals** are those who move *against* others and desire to excel and win admiration.
3. **Detached individuals** are those who move *away* from others and seek independence, self-reliance, self-sufficiency, and freedom from obligations.

Researchers developed a personality test based on Horney's theory (the CAD test) and used it to study consumer behavior.[20] The initial CAD research uncovered a number of tentative relationships between college students' scores and their product and brand usage patterns. For example, highly compliant students liked name-brand products such as Bayer aspirin, whereas aggressive subjects preferred Old Spice deodorant over other brands (seemingly because of its masculine appeal); and highly detached students were heavy tea drinkers (possibly reflecting their desire not to conform).

Many marketers use aspects of neo-Freudian theories intuitively. For example, marketers who position their products or services as providing an opportunity to belong or to be appreciated by others in a group or social setting are following Horney's characterization of the compliant individual. To illustrate, an ad for a digital camera featuring others complimenting the photographer's pictures appeals to compliant persons. An ad featuring a rider on a black mountain bike riding alone down steep hills appeals to aggressive persons.

Trait Theory

Trait theory represents a departure from the qualitative, nonempirical approaches of the Freudian and neo-Freudian movements. **Trait theory** focuses on empirical measures of personality in terms of specific psychological characteristics, called "traits." Traits are personal characteristics or features that set one person apart from another person. Trait theorists use personality tests (or inventories) that pinpoint individual differences in terms of "high" versus "low" scores on specific traits. Researchers developed tailor-made, single-trait personality tests for consumer behavior studies. These personality tests measure such traits as **innovativeness** (how receptive a person is to new consumer-related experiences or the early consideration and purchase of new products and services), **materialism** (the degree of the consumer's attachment to worldly possessions), and **ethnocentrism** (the consumer's likelihood to accept or reject foreign-made products).

Researchers have discovered that personality traits are linked to consumers' consumption of broad product categories rather than specific brands. For example, a statistical correlation between a given personality trait and whether or not an individual regularly eats peanut butter is more likely to occur than a correlation between that trait and the brand of peanut butter purchased. Furthermore, marketers study the influence of personality on consumption behavior because such knowledge enables them to segment consumers effectively, and develop advertisements that target specific segments. In the next section, we discuss several personality traits that provide particularly useful insights about consumer behavior.

Learning Objective

5 To understand how innovativeness and other personality traits influence consumer behavior.

Personality Traits and Consumer Behavior

We now explore the relationship between personality traits and consumer behavior. We begin with a discussion of the personality traits related to one's receptivity to new products. Afterwards, we examine the personality traits that are closely related to this dimension, which are dogmatism, social character, and the need for uniqueness. We note that these traits apply to the behavior of all consumers, whether or not they are among the first to purchase newly introduced products. Lastly, we describe other consumption-related personality traits, including optimum stimulation level (OSL), sensation seeking, variety or novelty seeking, need for cognition, visualizers versus verbalizers, materialism, fixated consumption, compulsive consumption, and consumer ethnocentrism.

Consumer Innovators and Innovativeness

Innovators are the first to try new products, product line extensions, and services because they are open to new ideas and practices. Their response to newly introduced products is critical to the success or failure of new products. Consumer innovators are enthusiastic about innovative products and can speed up the market acceptance of innovations, because they tell others about their purchases and often show them the new products. Furthermore, as more consumer innovators discuss the new products online, their domains of innovative behavior expand.[21] Table 3.6 presents illustrative opinions of an innovator of high-tech products.

Innovativeness is the degree of a consumer's willingness to adopt new products and services shortly after the products are introduced. One study discovered four motivational factors that inspire consumer innovativeness:

1. ***Functional factors*** reflect interest in the performance of an innovation.
2. ***Hedonic factors*** relate to feeling gratified by using the innovation.
3. ***Social factors*** reflect the desire to be recognized by others because of one's pursuit of innovations.
4. ***Cognitive factors*** express the mental stimulation experienced by using an innovation.[22]

TABLE 3.6 Illustrative Opinions of an Innovator of High-Tech Products

- I'm not brand loyal; I'm always looking for the "best" and "latest" in consumer technology.
- When I go into a technology store, I tend to tell the staff about the products, rather than them telling me.
- My friends often ask me questions before they purchase things dealing with new consumer technologies.
- I enjoy buying and trying very new consumer technology.
- When I see something new in the technology stores that I regularly visit, I "play" with it.
- I often get bored with rather new technological products and give them to my friends.
- I often look at technological websites and blogs, or social network sites, for more information about new technologies.
- I always read the technology section in the newspaper and then go online to check out the new products described.
- Every year, I look up the annual "holiday gift buying guides" because they always feature many technological products.

Whereas most researchers view innovativeness as a single personality trait, one study identified three levels of innovativeness:[23]

1. ***Global innovativeness***—a trait that exists independent of any product-related context and represents the "very nature" of consumers' innovativeness
2. ***Domain-specific innovativeness***—a narrowly defined activity within a specific domain or product category
3. ***Innovative behavior***—actions or responses that indicate early acceptance of change and adoption of innovations (e.g., being among the first to purchase new and different products or services).

As expected, there is a positive relationship between innovativeness and using the Internet and new technologies. One study reported that heavy Internet shoppers saw themselves as being able to control their own future, used the Internet to seek out information, enjoyed change, and were not afraid of uncertainty.[24] Another study found that while online banking was positively associated with Internet-related innovativeness (i.e., domain-specific innovativeness), global consumer innovativeness was negatively related to embracing online banking; these results highlight the importance of researching domain-specific innovativeness.[25] Researchers have also discovered that consumer innovativeness strongly affects consumers' likelihood to purchase brand extensions, and therefore firms introducing such products must target innovative consumers.[26] Several studies showed that consumer innovativeness shaped buying decisions to a greater degree than such factors as price consciousness, value consciousness, and perceived price variation.[27]

Dogmatism

Dogmatism is one's degree of rigidity—the opposite of being open-minded—toward information and opinion contradictory to one's beliefs and views (i.e., closed-mindedness).[28] A person who is highly dogmatic approaches the unfamiliar defensively and with uncertainty and discomfort. In contrast, a person who is less or not dogmatic readily considers unfamiliar or opposing beliefs. Generally, consumers who are not dogmatic prefer innovative products rather than traditional ones.

Highly dogmatic consumers tend to be more receptive to ads that contain appeals from authoritative figures, such as celebrities and experts. In contrast, low-dogmatic consumers are more receptive to messages that stress factual differences, product benefits, and other product-usage information. Researchers found that consumers scoring high on the traits of "openness to experiences" (similar to low dogmatism) and "extraversion" (which is related to personal energy, ambition, venturesomeness, and being outgoing) responded favorably to emotional messages, and were likely to purchase and become loyal to the brand advertised.[29]

Social Character: Inner- versus Other-Directedness

Inner-directed consumers rely on their own inner values or standards in evaluating new products and are likely to be consumer innovators. Conversely, **other-directed** consumers look to others for guidance as to what is appropriate or inappropriate and are unlikely to be consumer innovators. Inner- and other-directed consumers are receptive to different types of promotional messages. Inner-directed people prefer ads that stress product features and personal benefits, whereas other-directed people prefer ads that feature social acceptance and respond favorably to appeals portraying social or group interactions. The ad in Figure 3.9 features an inner-directed person experiencing adventure and wildness by himself. The ad's secondary tagline—"This is Outward Bound. This challenge belongs to you"—focuses on a person's inner-directedness.

Need for Uniqueness

Many consumers acquire and display material possessions because they want to be differentiated from other people. Consumers' **need for uniqueness** is defined as an individual's pursuit of differentness relative to others that is achieved through the acquisition of consumer goods in order to enhance one's personal and social identity. Individuals with a high need for uniqueness adopt new products and brands quicker than others. They prefer creative products that counter conformity and are outside group norms, and avoid the similarity reflected in buying mainstream products.

In each of us, there is another whom we don't know – Carl Jung. In Figure 3.10, Allen Solly brand creatively explores the inner self of consumers with the promise of individuality. Understanding this personality trait is highly pertinent to the fashion industry, because clothing trends and styles are ever changing. Many marketers target people with a high need for uniqueness with marketing stimuli designed to enhance self-perceptions of uniqueness. Illustrative opinions of a consumer with a high need for uniqueness appear in Table 3.7.

Source: Outward Bound

FIGURE 3.9 An Appeal to Inner-Directed Consumers

Source: Madura Fashion and Lifestyle

FIGURE 3.10 A Promise of Individuality

TABLE 3.7 Illustrative Opinions of a Young Executive with a High Need for Uniqueness

- When I travel, I'm always seeking out unusual gifts for myself.
- I'm happy when other people tell me that my taste is "different" and "uncommon."
- I work at maintaining my own unique persona.
- Some of my acquaintances think I'm somewhat of a weirdo in my seeking to be different.
- Standing out and being different is important to me.
- I stop buying brands when everyone starts to buy them.
- Being different is my own personal trademark.

Optimum Stimulation Level

Optimum stimulation level (OSL) is the degree to which people like novel, complex, and unusual experiences (i.e., high OSL) or prefer a simple, uncluttered, and calm existence (i.e., low OSL). Research has found that consumers seeking high levels of optimum stimulation are more willing to take risks, more likely to try new products and be innovative, and seek to maintain high optimum stimulation levels while shopping.[30] A study of college students' tendency to purchase "mass customized" clothes (e.g., a pair of jeans that is specially measured, cut, and sewn so they offer a better fit or appearance) discovered that people with high OSL wanted to: 1. "experiment with personal appearance" (e.g., "I try on some of the newest clothes each season to see how I look in the styles"), and 2. "enhance their individuality" (e.g., "I try to buy clothes that are very unusual").[31]

OSL scores also reflect a person's desired level of lifestyle stimulation. For instance, consumers whose actual lifestyles are equivalent to their OSL scores said that they are "quite satisfied" with their lives, whereas those whose lifestyles are understimulated (i.e., their OSL scores are greater than their lifestyle) felt "bored." This suggests that the relationship between consumers' lifestyles and their OSLs probably influences their choices of products or services and how they manage and spend their time. For instance, a person who feels bored (an understimulated consumer) is likely to be attracted to a vacation that offers a great deal of activity and excitement. In contrast, a person who feels overwhelmed (an overstimulated consumer) is likely to seek a quiet, isolated, relaxing, and rejuvenating vacation.

Box 3.4 Overstimulated Consumer Segments and Marketing Thoughts on Spirituality

In an environment that is increasingly oriented toward hedonism and sensual gratification, spiritual gurus and institutions the world over are increasingly linking thoughts on spirituality to OSLs. While Indian spiritual texts are full of content that emphasizes the need to control sensual gratification thorough senses to achieve inner peace, this message is taking several forms—usually linking the degradation of the quality of life to too much hedonism. The Art of Living's messages of love and peace, ISKCON's messages on control of sensual gratification, and spiritual guru Deepak Chopra's writings trigger thoughts on the pressures of a successful but high-pressure lifestyle to achieve hedonism through materialism. In his Christmas message of 2009, the Archibishop of Canterbury* mentioned that sexual advertising, the culture of independence, and the pressure to become performers from an early age drive children away from of finer aspects of community living.

All these messages can be linked to overstimulated consumer segments who long for inner peace (rest or relief). There seems to a growing awareness on inner-directed tranquility among overstimulated consumers who are the primary target segments for several categories of consumer products. Perhaps these consumers will become less stimulated in the process of achieving the balance between spirituality and hedonism!

Source: *"Children 'Rushed' into Growing Up, Says Archbishop," *BBC World News*, December 26, 2009.

Sensation Seeking

Closely related to the OSL concept is **sensation seeking**: one's need for varied, novel, and complex sensations and experiences, and the willingness to take risks for the sake of such experiences. For example, many teenage males with high sensation-seeking scores engage in "extreme sports" forms of biking, skateboarding, and rollerblading. One study discovered that consumers who scored high on sensation seeking and innovativeness were more likely to incorporate volunteerism into their vacations.[32] The ad for Rock Resorts in Figure 3.11 displays the tagline "BE" as a cue for a sensual experience, and the ad's copy invites guests to "embrace the true spirit" and "sectrets" of a special destination.

Variety and Novelty Seeking

Another trait similar to OSL is variety or novelty seeking. In consumer behavior, **variety and novelty seeking** consists of:[33]

1. ***Exploratory purchase behavior*** includes switching brands to experience new, different, and possibly better alternatives.
2. ***Vicarious exploration*** consists of gathering information about new and different product alternatives and contemplating buying them.
3. ***Use innovativeness*** means using an already adopted product in a new or novel way.

Seeking variety is particularly relevant to technological products (e.g., smartphones), where many models offer an abundance of functions while other provide only basic features. For example, high variety-seeking consumers are likely to purchase the latest smartphones, whereas consumers with low variety-seeking are likely to stick with their existing phones.

Source: RockResorts

FIGURE 3.11 An Appeal to Sensation-Seeking Consumers

Need for Cognition

A **need for cognition (NFC)** measures a person's craving for or enjoyment of thinking. Consumers who are high in NFC respond to ads that contain a lot of product-related information and descriptions, whereas consumers who are relatively low in NFC are attracted to the background or peripheral aspects of an ad, such as an attractive model or well-known celebrity. A study showed that including diagnostic product information in advertising (e.g., information that allows consumers to evaluate product quality and distinguish between brands) increased ad persuasion for high NFC consumers, but not for low NFC consumers.[34] Along the same lines, another study found that individuals low in NFC accepted a marketer's recommended alternatives more readily than high NFC consumers did.[35]

Need for cognition also plays a role in consumers' use of the Internet. Studies showed that high NFC persons were more likely than others to seek product information, current events, and educational resources online.[36] Other studies discovered that people high in NFC concentrated on the objectives of their planned online activities, whereas low-NFC persons were distracted by the vast amount of data on the Web and unable to focus on their intended online activities.[37]

Visualizers versus Verbalizers

Researchers found out that some people prefer the written word as a way of securing information, whereas others are influenced by images. **Verbalizers** prefer promotional messages containing a lot of written, textual, and verbal information. **Visualizers** are more receptive to pictorial images, and include:

1. ***Object visualizers***, who encode and process images as a single perceptual unit.
2. ***Spatial visualizers***, who process images piece by piece.

Individuals scoring high on object visualization tend to score low in spatial visualization, and vice versa. Furthermore, whereas visual artists generally excel in object imagery, scientists and engineers do best with spatial imagery.[38]

Although most ads consist of both verbal and pictorial information, some ads are significantly more visual than others. The Yoplait ad in Figure 3.12 appeals mostly to visualizers; it conveys the yogurt's palatal "richness" with a picture and almost no

FIGURE 3.12 An Appeal to Visualizers

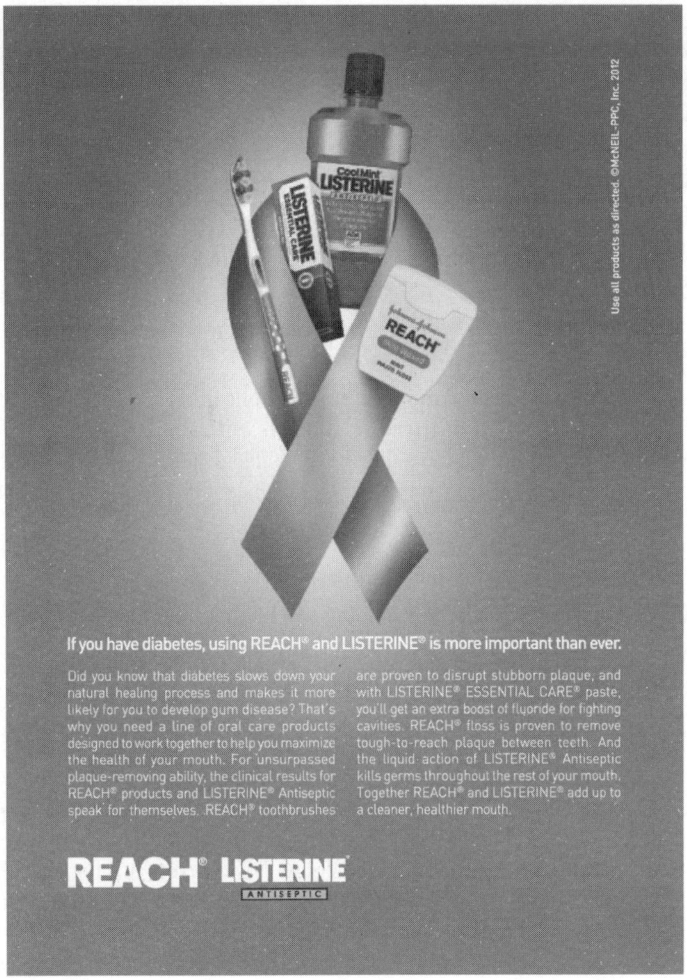

FIGURE 3.13 An Appeal to Both Visualizers and Verbalizers

text. The Listerine ad in Figure 3.13 appeals to both visualizers and verbalizers; it includes a picture that clearly stands out, as well as a lot of verbal information about the product.

Consumer Materialism

Materialism gauges the extent to which an individual is preoccupied with purchasing and showing off physical possessions that are mostly nonessential and often conspicuous luxury goods. A study that compared the extent of consumer materialism among young adults (aged 18 to 35) from China and their American counterparts discovered that the Chinese were more materialistic than the Americans.[39] The study concluded that as the economic conditions in China improved, Chinese society accepted materialism readily. In contrast, as the U.S. economy became uncertain and volatile, young American consumers became more reserved and frugal.

Highly materialistic consumers define themselves by acquiring possessions. They value buying and showing off their belongings, are often self-centered and selfish, live cluttered lives, and often do not experience personal satisfaction or happiness from their possessions alone.[40] In contrast, consumers who are less materialistic do not define themselves by what they possess and are more interested in seeking fulfilling experiences and enjoying them, often with others. They are not particularly impressed by what they and others have, but rather how they enjoy life. One study discovered that "tightwads" spend less than they had intended, because they felt discomfort about paying for their purchases. In contrast, "spendthrifts" felt no discomfort about paying and typically spend more than they intended to.[41] A Canadian study discovered that 25% of people who remembered dreams recalled dreams about buying things. In reality, many of the respondents thought about the products they dreamed about (and sometimes even sought more information about them), told others about their dreams, and even considered purchasing the products dreamt about.[42] Table 3.8 profiles materialistic consumers.

TABLE 3.8 Selected Characteristics of Materialistic Consumers

- Consider purchasing "things" to be very important.
- Enjoy seeking out things that give them pleasure.
- Believe in the saying: "He (she) who dies with the most toys wins."
- Define themselves by what they wear and possess.
- Believe that they feel better off than those who have fewer possessions.
- Enjoy treating themselves to new possessions.
- Feel more important when they go shopping for new things.

Fixated Consumption

In the context of consumer behavior, **fixated consumption** refers to collectors' and hobbyists' tendency to accumulate items that are related to their interests and show them off to friends and others with similar interests. People collect anything: from free items, such as matchbooks from hotels and restaurants they have visited around the world, to glass paperweights that cost thousands of dollars, vintage motorcycles and cars, art, and century-old wines. Fixated consumers share the following characteristics:

1. A passion for and interest in the category of what they collect.
2. Willingness to invest a lot of effort in adding to their collections.
3. Spending a lot of time and discretionary income searching and buying more items for their collections.
4. Aggressively competing in auctions.

Compulsive Consumption

Compulsive consumption is addictive and out-of-control buying that often has damaging consequences for both the compulsive shopper and those around him or her. Examples of compulsive consumption problems are uncontrollable shopping, gambling, drug addiction, alcoholism, and even eating disorders. Furthermore, the ease of online buying has made compulsive shopping more widespread. Research discovered that at least 75% of compulsive buyers are females.[43] Compulsive shoppers purchase items that they do not need and often do not end up using, and many require psychological intervention in order to eliminate or even control severe compulsive shopping. Research suggests that easy availability of credit cards contributes to compulsive consumption behavior, especially among college students.[44] Marketers must ensure that their promotional messages do not encourage irresponsible consumption. Table 3.9 lists several characteristics of compulsive consumers.

A child at a grocery store, seeing a candy jar within his reach, feels like having one and buys it to consume it. A consumer at Food World sees a brand of sweets and has an impulse to buy a box and share it with his or her family. A young teenager at Shoppers Stop sees a dress and has an uncontrollable desire to buy and wear it. The three consumers have a personality trait called impulsivity. Banwari Mittal *et al*[45] provide three pre-requisites for such a purchase – proximity of stimulus, lack of evaluation of attributes (and a disregard for the consequences of the purchase), and a strong emotional surge towards the stimulus. The stimulus is the brand or the product category.

Forum Mall in Bangalore attracts thousands of youngsters during weekends. Ice-cream, jeans, branded apparel, and even watches can trigger impulsivity among some consumers (though such a compulsive purchase is generally limited to low-priced items). Availability of chocolates and magazines near the cash counter of shops (in modern retail) can also be associated with

TABLE 3.9 Illustrative Characteristics of Compulsive Consumers

- Have an irresistible urge to shop as soon as they enter a shopping mall.
- Often buy products they do not need despite having little money left.
- They feel compelled to spend the money they have left at the end a period.
- Feel others would be horrified if they knew about their shopping habits.
- Buy things although they cannot afford them.
- Buy things to make themselves feel better.
- Knowingly write checks that will bounce.

triggers of impulsivity that may be present among a cross-section of consumers. The emotional pull towards the stimulus is an important aspect of impulsivity and every unplanned purchase may not be a compulsive buy. Four million new consumers are estimated to enter the western style liquor market in India every year.

Bacardi, Diageo and United Spirits are customers of Manjushree Technopack, a packaging provider that gets 25 % of its total sale from smaller packs.[46] While miniature bottles may be introduced by brands for a variety of reasons, such a packaging may incidentally appeal to impulsive consumers as well.

Consumer Ethnocentrism

Ethnocentrism is the consumer's willingness to buy or not buy foreign-made products. Highly ethnocentric consumers feel that it is inappropriate or wrong to purchase foreign-made products, because of the resulting economic impact on the domestic economy, whereas nonethnocentric or less ethnocentric consumers tend to evaluate foreign-made products—ostensibly more objectively—for their extrinsic characteristics (e.g., "How good are they?"). A post-9/11 study found that Americans' ethnocentrism increased in the United States as a result of the 9/11 terrorist attacks and natural disasters.[47] Research has also found that ethnocentrism varies by country and product. For example, Mexican consumers are more ethnocentric than their French and American counterparts; and Malaysian consumers, while preferring to purchase slacks, shirts, undergarments, and belts that are locally manufactured, want to buy imported sunglasses and watches.[48] Other evidence shows that some older American consumers, in remembrance of World War II, still refuse to purchase German- and/or Japanese-made products, whereas some German and Japanese consumers feel similarly about American-made products.[49]

Presently, due to globalization and multinational marketing, consumers may not know for sure whether a particular product is domestic or imported. For example, some of the models Toyota sells in the United States are manufactured in Japan, some in the United States, and others are in both countries. Several studies tried to classify products by their "degree of globalization," or "degree of cultural uniqueness." One study showed that, for some consumers, the "country of assembly" and the "country of design" played a role in deciding whether or not to purchase products.[50] A study of business school students in New York City examined eight different products, from green tea to jazz music, to determine if they differ in terms of "degree of globalization," that is, the product's degree of cultural uniqueness.[51]

Marketers successfully target ethnocentric consumers by stressing nationalistic themes in their promotional appeals (e.g., "Made in America" or "Made in France"), because these consumers are more likely to buy products made in their native lands. To illustrate the strategy of ethnocentric appeal, Honda, the Japanese automaker, in an indirect appeal to ethnocentric Americans, advertised that its Accord wagon is "Exported from America" (reinforcing the fact that some of its automobiles are made in the United States). However, a study examining the preferences of UK consumers across eight product categories found that domestic country bias (i.e., a preference for products manufactured in the consumer's country of residence) varied among product categories. This means that domestic manufacturers cannot always expect that local consumers will automatically prefer their offerings over imported ones.[52] Furthermore, one research study found that low-knowledge consumers' product attitudes (i.e., the consumer has little knowledge about the product) have been more strongly influenced by country-of-origin perceptions than high-knowledge consumers' product attitudes.[53] One study showed that highly ethnocentric Chinese consumers did not favor bilingual signs and messages (in Chinese and English) and were thus less likely to buy the advertised products.[54]

Box 3.5 Targeting the Ethnocentric Consumer

In India, Ruf-and-Tuf jeans is a good case of a brand attempting ethnocentrism. Consumers have been used to a number of foreign jeans brands. Arvind Mills, which launched Ruf-and-Tuf, found that the aspirational levels of consumer groups in semi-urban areas were high, but they could afford to buy only cheap clones or duplicates of well-known brands. There was a need for a good quality brand at affordable prices. Ruf-and-Tuf was launched with a celebrity endorsing it and the brand followed this up with a campaign that emphasized its ethnicity. The campaign was effective in ending the perception that only foreign brands have quality in the category of jeans. The brand was given penetration pricing, tailors were trained and roped in to sew the jeans (as against readymade jeans) and the product itself was presented in a unique manner (the fabric plus other accessories were given as a set). Though the discussion about the sustained success of this brand (as a fabric that needs to be tailored) is beyond this chapter's focus, the example reflects how marketing mix elements back a positioning based on positive ethnocentrism. Its tagline was therefore in Hindi and not in English: *Buland Bharat ki Buland Tasveer*—a strong portrayal of a strong India.

Box 3.6 Value Paradox[55] and an Indian Brand –The Indian Context

Fairness creams in India are estimated to have a market of around ₹1500 crores (with men's market estimated to be around ₹500 crores and fairness appears to be a top priority as a criteria for brides).[56] Racial discrimination based on skin color is looked down among most Indians, at least publicly. What is contradictory is that fairness creams in India are a rage and racial sentiments too are widely negated by consumers!

Such a behavior is referred to as value paradox – the contradiction between what an individual considers as desired versus what is desirable (values in real life versus values in an ideal life[57])

Personality and Color

Consumers not only ascribe personality traits to products and services, but some also associate personality characteristics with specific colors. For instance, consumers associate Coca-Cola with red, which connotes excitement. Blue bottles are sometimes used to sell wine because the color blue appeals particularly to female consumers. Yellow connotes novelty and black sophistication. Brands can create a sophisticated, upscale, or premium image (e.g., Miller Beer's Miller Reserve) by using primarily black labeling or packaging. A combination of black and white communicates that a product is carefully engineered, high tech, and sophisticatedly designed. For instance, Nike produced shoes in black, white, and a touch of red for selected models of its sports shoes because this color combination connotes high performance. Many fast-food restaurants use combinations of bright colors, like red, yellow, and blue, for their roadside signs and interior designs because research discovered that consumers associate these colors with fast service and inexpensive food. In contrast, most fine restaurants use sophisticated colors like gray, white, shades of tan, or other soft, pale, and muted tones to underscore their classy environments and good service. Table 3.10 lists various colors, their personality-like meanings, and associated marketing insights.

Box 3.7 India's Macho Bike

Bullet* (from Royal Enfield Motors) is a 50-year-old brand of motorcycle. It has been traditionally associated with a macho image. While several brands are vying with one another on the aspects of contemporary styling and technology, Bullet has become the "Indian Harley-Davidson" among motorcycles. Passionate followers could create the right kind of "buzz" among the youth to make this brand a cult in a niche market. In 2007–08, the brand sold around 38,000 units.

Bullet's example reflects how perception plays a role in shaping the image of a brand in a competitive market in which brand image is vital. The brand has a right gear shift, when motorcycles the world over have moved to the left gear shift. The company has launched a new model with a different brand name, Thunderbird, to target upgraders from small bikes, while another model, the Bullet Machisma 500, targets young bikers. The brand does not advertise as aggressively as others in the market. This helps create its aura of being a prized product and also ensures word of mouth. The brand has done away with discounts, thereby not relating itself to price sensitivity. This strategy, along with the brand's past image, adds to the perception that consumers would buy the brand because they are passionate about the product and what it represents than because of a price deal. The company provides platforms to express this passion: Royal Enfield brand stores attempt to create an experience for prospective buyers. The Indiehumpers Club is a community formed by owners of the bikes and the company has a Web site to encourage online interaction among the owners to enhance affinity (another form by which buzz can spread quickly). The Web site has stories, problems, and solutions about the brand.

In a world that is getting ahead with functionality and benefits, heritage brands with symbolism rather than benefits can be created to hold the consumers' attention—if principles of perception are appropriately applied.

Source: **All About Ads*, NDTV Profit channel (interview with Prahlad Kakkar), October 18, 2009.

Box 3.8 Degrees of Personality Orientation

Thums Up, Fastrack, and Lux are brands that had developed a strong brand personality association, while Sprite, Dettol, and Peter England are brands that had developed a moderate brand personality association. Horlicks, Krack, and Quaker Oats brands have a strong benefit orientation (as observed from the advertisements and brand imagery over a period of time). In the Indian context, marketers have a choice of implicit brand personality associations or explicit brand personality associations. There may be a need to decide why human associations are required for a brand in the context of competitive brands. There may also be categories that may have a strong personality association that may be used by brands to shape their associations or personality, if appropriate to the respective product category.

TABLE 3.10 Personality Traits Associated with Colors

COLOR	PERSONALITY LINK	MARKETING INSIGHTS
Blue	Commands respect, authority	• America's favored color • IBM holds the title to blue • Associated with club soda • Men seek products packaged in blue • Houses painted blue are avoided • Low-calorie, skim milk • Coffee in a blue can perceived as "mild"
Yellow	Caution, novelty, temporary, warmth	• Eyes register it fastest • Coffee in yellow can tastes "weak" • Stops traffic • Sells a house
Green	Secure, natural, relaxed or easygoing, living things	• Good work environment • Associated with vegetables and chewing gum • Canada Dry ginger ale sales increased when it changed its sugar-free package from red to green and white
Red	Human, exciting, hot, passionate, strong	• Makes food "smell" better • Coffee in a red can perceived as "rich" • Women have a preference for bluish red • Men have a preference for yellowish red • Coca-Cola "owns" red
Orange	Powerful, affordable, informal	• Draws attention quickly
Brown	Informal and relaxed, masculine, nature	• Coffee in a dark-brown can was "too strong" • Men seek products packaged in brown
White	Goodness, purity, chastity, cleanliness, delicacy, refinement, formality	• Suggests reduced calories • Pure and wholesome food • Clean, bath products, feminine
Black	Sophistication, power, authority, mystery	• Powerful clothing • High-tech electronics
Silver, Gold, Platinum	Regal, wealthy, stately	• Suggests premium price

Source: From "Color Schemes" by Bernice Kanner in *New York Magazine* 4/3/1989. Reprinted by permission of Bernice Kanner/New York Magazine.

Learning Objective

6 To understand the personification of products and brands and its strategic applications.

Product and Brand Personification

Earlier in this chapter, we introduced the notion of "product personality." **Brand personification** occurs when consumers attribute human traits or characteristics to a brand. A "brand personality" provides an emotional identity for a brand, which produces sentiments and feelings toward the brand among consumers. For instance, consumers perceive Perdue chickens as very fresh, Nike as the athlete in all of us, and BMW as being performance driven. A brand's personality can either be functional ("dependable and rugged") or symbolic ("the athlete in all of us"). A distinct brand personality differentiates the brand from similar offerings, and creates favorable attitudes toward the brand, higher purchase intentions, and brand loyalty.

It may be worthwhile to consider both old and new examples of brand personality in the Indian context. For example, Raymond's "complete man" image suggests a well-dressed, successful male who also values his relationships and the people in his life. Liril was one of the earliest brands to convey a brand personality with associations revolving around "refreshing, indulgent, and vibrant" aspects. Zodiac was probably one of the earliest brands in the readymade apparel category to create a "corporate–executive" type of personality around its brand, with a bearded model reflecting sophistication. LML Vespa created a lifestyle positioning in scooters through a "suave, sophisticated, standing-apart-from-the-crowd" type personality association to break the "value-based, middle-class" personality association of its rival, Bajaj. In women's ethnic wear (sarees), Vimal suggested an "other-directed, gregarious and charming" personality as against the "aloof, proud and classy" personality of the Garden Vareli brand. Lux, the soap brand from Unilever, has a contemporary orientation toward creating a brand personality that has overtones of glamor. Saffola Gold (edible oil), by using the visual of the housewife caring for her husband's health, suggests a "sincere, warm, and caring" personality. Dettol's floor cleaner, with its visual of the housewife taking care of her family, suggests a similar personality that is used in conjunction with the germ-killing action of the brand. Where celebrities are used in ads, the celebrity's personality associations are likely to rub off on the brand. Thums Up, the soft drink brand, has over the years created a macho personality though its advertisements and this is reinforced by the characteristics of the celebrity who promotes the ad.

In India, there is a huge opportunity for brands in the durable categories to develop brand personality associations. Trust, dependability, and friendliness (ranging from product features to after-sales service) are some associations that can be built up in the Indian context among durable categories. Over the years, Santoor soap has used advertising visuals that suggest "charming youthfulness." It is important for a brand to develop a personality and sustain it over time with contemporary changes, in tune with the changing environment. Over the last two decades, Santoor seems to have achieved this aspect effectively. The brand has a significant market share, too, in the category.

Research shows that of all the elements of the marketing mix, promotional messages have the greatest influence in creating a brand personality. One study explored dimensions of brand personality for products marketed by 64 American multinational corporations. It analyzed 270 websites of these corporations, in the United States, UK, France, Germany, and Spain, and discovered five underlying dimensions of brand personality: *excitement*, *sophistication*, *affection*, *popularity*, and *competence*.[58]

Product and brand personifications are forms of **anthropomorphism**, which refers to attributing human characteristics to something that is not human. For example, a study focusing on anthropomorphized products found that the ease with which consumers could anthropomorphize a product was a function of how the product was advertised and the inclusion or absence of references to or depictions of human-like product features. Consumers perceived products presented as having human features more favorably than products without human attributes.[59] One study investigated the relationship between brand personality and two human characteristics:

1. ***Attachment anxiety***—the degree to which people are concerned about whether they are worthy of love.
2. ***Avoidance anxiety***—one's view of others in the context of attachment.

The study discovered that people who were preoccupied with their self-worth and had a negative view of people (i.e., high anxiety and high avoidance) preferred an *exciting* brand personality, whereas those with high anxiety and a favorable view of people (i.e., low avoidance) preferred a *sincere* brand personality. Many researchers have advised marketers to study the personality traits of their consumers before personifying their brands in promotional messages.[60]

Consumers personify brands because marketers have given their offerings human characteristics through repetitive and effective advertising. For example, the M&M "person" (see Figure 8.4) originated from asking consumers: "If an M&M (a chocolate-coated peanut variety) were a person, what kind of person would it be?" For decades, the M&M "person" has been one of America's best-loved and most widely recognized characters. The manufacturer of Mr. Coffee—an automatic-drip coffee maker—unexpectedly found that, in focus groups, consumers referred to Mr. Coffee as if it were a person, with such expressions as "he makes good coffee" and "he's got a lot of different models and prices." The brand's marketer then personified the machine and, in subsequent studies, discovered that consumers perceived Mr. Coffee as "dependable," "friendly," "efficient," "intelligent," and "smart." In several focus groups, participants described several well-known brands of dishwashing liquid as "demanding taskmasters" and "high-energy people." In another study, French young adults (aged 18 to 23) perceived Coca-Cola as friendly, creative, charming, and elegant (among other characteristics), and that such perceptions led to trust, attachment, and commitment to the brand.[61]

Box 3.9 Love Relationships and Brands

Sternberg's classification on relationships – originally developed towards interpersonal relationships – has interesting implications for Indian brands.[62] While marketers in this era are using quantitative concepts like customer lifetime value, a brand manager also needs to be sensitive to the qualitative aspects of consumer behavior. Intimacy, commitment, and passion are some of the components that have been drawn from Sternberg's theory. Intimacy is how well a consumer knows his or her brand. Can this be applied to a luxury brand like Mont Blanc or to a beauty care brand like Lakme? Commitment is about long-term association and it may or may not have intimacy. A mother's commitment to a brand like Horlicks because she believes that the brand can make her children "Taller, sharper and stronger" – the proposition of the brand. Passion is all about emotional and physiological arousal and a brand like Red Bull fits in well on such a platform. Of course, each of these three elements can exist in isolation or with the other two in degrees depending upon how the brand associations are created and nurtured.

Some consumers become "brand zealots" and develop a relationship with brands beyond the functions of these products. An example of this behavior is VW Beetle owners who give their cars names, and who have been seen talking to their vehicles and affectionately stroking them. Another example is the Harley-Davidson motorcycle owners who go so far as to get Harley tattoos. One friend of the authors refers to his garbage disposal as "Garby," and calls his expensive cappuccino machine "Princessa," whom he usually praises for making a lot of froth and seldom rebukes for making too little.

Govers and Schoormans[63] proposed the concept of product personality and stated that products or product variants defined by size, price, or appearance carry human associations (to be differentiated from the identity of a brand associated with a specific name). Let us see how this concept is applicable to the Indian context, where a large number of unbranded products exist in the unorganized sector. An unorganized offering is one that does not have a brand name, is sold within a small geographical area surrounding the place of manufacture and is generally low in price and quality as compared to branded offerings. Product categories that have a large chunk of their market in the unorganized sector include watches, biscuits, mineral water, apparel, footwear, small electrical appliances like heaters, fans, and edible oils. With mobile penetration proliferating across the country and the 3G introduction, it may be interesting to look at the differences between the perception of urban and rural consumers with regard to cell phones and, in a competitive clutter, a brand may benefit by identifying specific gaps in associations (with several cell phone brands competing vigorously, brand associations are important with regard to differentiation). There are only a few brands of electric cookers and the category itself is not very popular throughout the country. It may be useful for a marketer of electric cooker brands to analyze the personality of the category itself. Jewelry and perfumes are becoming uni-gender categories (Nivea and Rexona, among other cosmetic brands, have products for both genders) and, therefore, gaining consumer insights into product personality will be useful for marketers. Coffeemakers have not become diffused even in the southern parts of the country (traditionally constituting the largest part of the coffee drinking population) and product personality is likely to be useful when associations are developed for this category. Even in shampoos (a category with a slew of brands), product personality is likely to be useful. Dove's Hair Fall Therapy System (a variant that has "hair fall prevention" as its proposition) advertises its product and suggests that entrenched beliefs among consumers are used to strengthen the product's proposition. The TV advertisement shows a consumer using a widetoothed comb and still finding that hair fall is considerable (it is a common belief that hair fall can also be caused by the use of a wrong comb). The ad then goes on to illustrate the effectiveness of the product when the consumer uses a comb after using the product. This is a high-end product in the category in terms of its price point. Product personality under such a situation will also be useful in developing associations with regard to the product and its use aspects.

The framework in Figure 3.14, which has been applied to personifying many brands of consumer goods, depicts 5 underlying dimensions of a brand's personality—sincerity, excitement, competence, sophistication, and ruggedness—and 15 more narrowly defined characteristics, such as down-to-earth, daring, reliable, upper class, and outdoors.

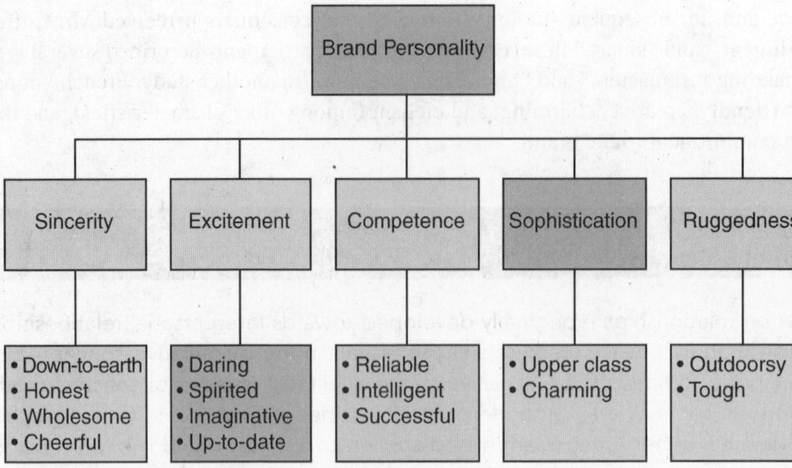

FIGURE 3.14 A Brand Personality Framework

Source: Journal of Marketing Research, 1997. American Marketing Association

Application 1: Brand Personality and Contradictions

A brand that is associated with a specific personality (explicit or implicit) may not want to radically change its personality as it may have an adverse effect on the brand. Cadbury (molded bar version) during the eighties was positioned as a reward for children (child-like personality). Later, it was positioned to adults with adult imagery, projected amidst spontaneous enjoyment bordering on impulsive celebration of daily moments. When Cadbury introduced its Gold variant that had a permissive personality association (the TV ad showed a woman embarrassing men at a place like gymnasium)[64], it may not have gone well with consumers.

Application 2: Brand Personality and Non-conspicuous Products

BSH Home Appliances markets Siemens and Bosch brands of washing machines (a category that is relatively non-conspicuous) and other durables in the Indian market. As they compete in the same price band, brand personality is used to differentiate them in the perception of consumers. Siemens is projected as a future-oriented and innovative brand[65] (its washing machine has the option of either a fast wash or the option of saving energy and water). Bosch is projected more as a sturdy (perhaps stable), value-minded, and peace of mind-oriented offering (security of good and hassle free working).[66]

Product Personality and Gender

A product's personality frequently endows products and brands with gender. For instance, Celestial Seasonings' Tracy Jones was given a feminine persona, whereas Mr. Coffee was given a masculine personality. Products' assigned genders vary by culture: In certain cultures, consumers may perceive coffee and toothpaste to be masculine products, whereas bath soap and shampoo are viewed as feminine. Another study examined the personality characteristics that Hispanic shoppers associate with well-known U.S. retailers. In focus groups conducted in Spanish in several American cities, researchers discovered that Hispanic consumers ascribed personality characteristics to retailers. For example, Walmart was frequently characterized as a detail-oriented, successful businesswoman; Old Navy was described as "a woman who is friendly and gardens"; and Sears as "an elegant man driving an expensive car."[67]

Product Personality and Geography

Consumers associate some brands with geographic locations (e.g., New England clam chowder), and such associations often enhance their memory and the likeability of brands. Interestingly, geographic brand names can be either real or fictitious. For example, Philadelphia Cream Cheese is actually made in Illinois, but many consumers associate it with a city known for its historical role in the founding of the United States. Whether the brand's association with a location is real or fictitious, the perceived location's image enhances the brand's equity. Although Texas Best Barbecue Sauce is made in New Jersey, many Americans associate barbecue with Texas. Similarly, the Old El Paso brand of salsa capitalizes on the Mexican influence in the Southwest. The product is made in Minneapolis, but a brand of salsa named Twin Cities Salsa (i.e., Minneapolis/St. Paul) just does not have the same cachet.

Website Personality

As consumers navigate the Internet, many of them become emotionally attached to certain websites. A recent study identified four personality characteristics of websites: (1) *intelligent* (i.e., searchable, comprehensive, fast, and concise); (2) *fun* (i.e., colorful, attractive, interactive, and dynamic); (3) *organized*; and (4) *sincere* (i.e., straightforward and down-to-earth).[68] These finding suggest that incorporating personality traits into the design of websites can generate more favorable attitudes among visitors and more clicks on the site's pages.

Learning Objective

7 To understand self-image and its impact on consumer behavior.

The Self and Self-Image

Self-image represents the way a person views herself or himself. Perceptions of self are often related to the purchases of products and services, because consumers often select products that are consistent with their self-images and enhance them. In fact, consumers have multiple "selves," because people act differently in different situations. For instance, a person is likely to behave in different ways with parents, at school, at work, at a museum opening, or with friends at a nightclub.

Each individual has an image of himself or herself as a certain kind of person, with certain traits, skills, habits, possessions, relationships, and behaviors. One's self-image originates in a person's background and experience. Many products and brands have symbolic value for individuals because their images are consistent with the ways these people perceive themselves, and consumers buy offerings that are congruent with their self-image and avoid products and brands that are not. A recent study uncovered an interesting correlation between food consumption and self-image. Apparently, as Americans are becoming larger, because of consuming increasingly larger portions and too much food, many people who are overweight see themselves as being of normal or average weight.[69]

Consumer behavior researchers identified four components of self-image:

1. **Actual self-image** is the way consumers see themselves;
2. **Ideal self-image** is how consumers would like to see themselves;
3. **Social self-image** is how consumers feel others see them; and
4. **Ideal social self-image** is how consumers would like others to see them.

Consumers select the type of self-image that guides them in the context of buying situations. For instance, with everyday household products, consumers might be guided by their actual self-images, whereas for some socially enhancing or socially conspicuous products, they might be guided by their social self-images. When it comes to an important and strong personal goal or wish, like losing weight and feeling better about oneself and one's appearance, people are often guided by either their ideal self-images or ideal social self-images.

The concept of self-image has strategic implications for marketers. For example, companies can segment their markets on the basis of relevant self-images and then position their products or services as symbols of such. These strategies reflect the marketing concept: Marketers study the needs of a consumer segment (with respect to both the product category and as the product's or brand's reflection of self-image) and then develop and market an offering that meets both criteria. Jockey—a marketer of undergarments—recognizes the importance of self-image.

The Extended Self

Consumers' possessions can confirm or extend their self-images. For instance, acquiring a sought-after pair of "vintage" Levi jeans might enrich a teenager's self-image, because she might see herself as being more desirable, fashionable, and successful when she wears those pants. Researchers suggested that possessions are extensions of self in the following ways:[70]

1. ***Actually***, by allowing the person to do things that otherwise would be very difficult or impossible to accomplish (e.g., problem solving by using a computer).
2. ***Symbolically***, by making the person feel better (e.g., being considered the "best dressed" at work).
3. ***Conferring status or rank***, for example, being an art collector and owning a rare and well-known masterpiece.
4. ***Feelings of immortality*** by leaving valuable bequests after death.

Titan Raga and Edge are examples to reflect how brands are associated with the finer aspects of Extended Self
For example, in Figure 3.15, Titan Raga stands for beauty, femininity and sensuality. These values make their way into its exquisite timepieces and reflect in its communication. Probably, this is why the brand has evolved from being associated with special occasions to one that celebrates the special moments in a woman's life.*

The Titan Edge, as shown in Figure 3.15, is an ode to perfection and excellence. It epitomizes the ultimate in mastering an art. Simply put, it expresses – there is no other.**

Source: Titan

FIGURE 3.15 Brands and Extended Self

* This observation has been made by Somprabh Singh, Head of Marketing, Titan, India.

** This observation has been made by Manoj K. Chakravarti of IIM-Bangalore, currently Chief Operations Officer, Centre for Corporate Governance and Citizenship, Indian Institute of Management, Bangalore and earlier vice-president and senior advisor, Titan Industries.

Altering the Self

Sometimes consumers wish to change or improve their selves. Clothing, grooming aids or cosmetics, accessories (such as sunglasses, jewelry, tattoos, or even colored contact lenses), and makeovers offer consumers opportunities to enhance their appearance and thereby alter their selves. In using self-altering products, consumers frequently attempt to express their new selves or take on the appearances of particular types of people (e.g., a military person, physician, business executive, or college professor).

Personal vanity is closely related to both self-image and alteration of the self. Vanity is often associated with acting self-important, self-interested, or admiring one's own appearance or achievements. Researchers discovered two types of vanity: (1) *physical vanity,* which is excessive concern with or inflated view of one's physical appearance; and (2) *achievement vanity,* which is excessive concern with or inflated view of one's personal achievements. They found that both vanity types correlated with a high level of materialism, high use of cosmetics, concern with clothing, and importance of belonging to prestigious country clubs.[71] Table 3.11 lists several characteristics of vain people. From a marketing viewpoint, these features indicate that vain consumers: (1) are a lucrative market for personal care and beauty products; (2) welcome promotional messages showing that they attract others' attention; and (3) are receptive to promotional messages featuring personal achievement.

Application 1: I and Others

Sheena Iyengar, in *The Art of Choosing*, says that consumers of iPod felt that their own choice of the brand was more due to utilitarian aspects as compared to other consumers who were more inclined to choose it for social reasons. Such an observation provides several interesting propositions to marketers of luxury brands in the Indian context. While the self-concept of a consumer gets enhanced in the perception of others in terms of status and prestige, the consumer may be fully aware of such a benefit but may continue to believe that such luxury products or brands are bought for utility purposes.

Is it due to the guilt of buying expensive brands? Or is it an ego-defensive mechanism that one is not so irrational to buy an expensive brand? The Indian luxury market across categories has been experiencing a high growth in the recent years and exploration of self-concepts should be useful to marketers.

Application 2: Multiple-selves and Branding

Self-concepts were used innovatively by Philips when it marketed its male grooming kits. "Who U Gonna Be Today"[72] effectively sold the offerings as it depicted a celebrity, John Abraham, in different styles. It perhaps appealed to differing personalities associated with different self-concepts (not to the extent of contradicting one another).

Application 3: Brands, Actual Self, and Ideal Self

Special K cereals (from Kellogg's), with the proposition of weight loss, targeted consumers who would like to slim down. The brand was endorsed by a celebrity who looked fit. The company's Wheat flakes variant showed a housewife who gets over her everyday fatigue by consuming the brand. The ad showed that the housewife would be cheerful to go about the domestic chores if the brand is consumed. Pond's anti-ageing cream suggested that a lady who is noticing wrinkles should use the offering. The ads get linked with the "journey" of the respected target segment from actual self to ideal self and to some extent to the self-concepts associated with social self too. The variations in self-concepts need not necessarily be used with an aspiration-based approach.

With changing lifestyles, a family eating together seems to have become an infrequent practice, at least in urban markets. Cadbury introduced a *Meetha Dinner* contest with the ad caption, "A family that eats together stays together". Such an approach can be related to the ideal self-concept of individual members of a family who may long for such family bonding.

Application 4: Reality to a State of Altered Reality

Self-concepts can be used in several ways by marketers. When a brand of fairness cream carries an aspiration-based appeal that targets middle class girls, the brand may be closer to reality. "Give in to your passion of jewelry" was an ad from the jewelry brand Gitanjali that is also close to reality, appealing to the self-concept of consumers who may want to indulge in the product category of consumption or buying.

Kaya, the beauty care brand, advertised itself on the following lines – "Every beautiful woman you've envied now wants to be you". This may still be closer to reality as it addresses such a self-concept. Yamaha's new bike FZ S advertised itself as "This new year let your bike rule the streets" (Lord of the street). The metaphor of using Lord and perhaps equating it with the feeling the rider may experience as he rides the vehicle on the street is an example of how the concept of the state of altered reality[73] can be used in advertising, taking into consideration the self-concept of the target segment.

Application 5: Brands, Ideal, and Actual-self

Although different types of self-concepts can be used in different ways by marketers, it may be interesting and insightful to know how ideal and actual self-concepts can be differentiated.[74] Ideal self-concepts are applied when a brand would like consumers to recall the attributes and benefits when they choose brands that are in tune with their actual self-concepts (how they perceive themselves actually). A consumer who considers himself sophisticated and classy may choose Hermes brand of accessories. The same consumer may choose a brand that enhances his self-esteem when he chooses a brand of car. He may choose a Hummer brand of car as he perceives that the "adventure/off the road" association enhances his image in the presence of his friends. Fair & Lovely is for a teenager's "ideal self" of looking fair versus the choice of Hamam brand that is tune with her actual self-concept of being amidst the traditional family.[75] Self-schemas seem to be impacting the preferences of consumers.

Application 6: Brand Proposition for a Global Brand

Snickers is positioned in 50 countries as a snack for hunger (basic universal need). In India, the brand had positioned itself with a TV commercial that had a set of cricketers going for practice experiencing hunger and had the tagline "You are not you when you are hungry".[76] This is the usage of malleable-self that includes several self conceptions of a consumer like actual self, bad self and "not me" self.[77]

Application 7: Perception and Its Importance for Brands

Dove's campaign on real beauty[78] shows the importance of actual self (how a consumer perceives herself) and social self (how others perceive her). With the growing importance of personal appearance as a reflection of self-esteem, consumers seem to place importance on social self-concept (how others perceive our appearance rather than how we actually perceive ourselves). Dove's campaign showed an artist painting images of women with their own description of themselves (actual or ideal perception of the self) and comparing it with images of these women based on their description provided by someone else (social actual or ideal self- concept of others perceiving the consumer). The women who had been sketched find that the description of other's self-concept (social self) related to them were much better than the images they had described about themselves. The campaign suggested that others' self –concept (social self) mattered much more than how a consumer perceives herself in terms of appearance (actual or ideal self).

This does not mean that consumers do not have strong actual or ideal self-concepts. It is interesting to note that the Swiss watch brand Raymond Weil (offerings in the range of ₹45,000 to ₹8 lakhs) does not use a brand ambassador as it would like to appeal to a consumers who has an "independent personality and who is capable of making choices with a hunger for precision"[79] (indicating strong actual or ideal self-concept that matters to the Raymond Weil consumer).

TABLE 3.11 Illustrative Characteristics of Vain Persons

- Always want to look their best.
- Always concerned with their appearance.
- Believe that others notice and envy their looks.
- Believe that others find them sexually appealing.
- Obsessed with personal achievements.
- Want their achievements to be highly regarded by others.
- Believe that they are a good example of success.
- Believe that others wish they were as successful as them.

Summary

Learning Objective 1: To understand the dynamics of motives, needs, and goals and how they shape consumer behavior.

Motivation drives consumers to take action by producing a psychological tension caused by unfulfilled needs. Individuals strive to reduce this tension through selecting goals and subsequent behavior that they anticipate will fulfill their needs and thus relieve them of the tension they feel. There are two types of human needs: Physiological needs are innate and fulfilling them sustains life. They include the need for food, water, air, protection of the body from the outside environment (i.e., clothing and shelter), and sex. Psychological needs are learned from our parents, social environment, and interactions with others. Among many others, they include the needs for self-esteem, prestige, affection, power, learning, and achievement. Goals are the sought-after results of motivated behavior; all human behavior is goal oriented and focused on satisfying physiological and psychological needs. Need-driven human activity never ceases because: (1) Needs are never fully satisfied; they continually cause actions designed to attain or maintain satisfaction. (2) As needs are satisfied, new and higher-order needs emerge, cause tension, and induce activity. (3) People who achieve their goals set new and higher goals for themselves.

Learning Objective 2: To understand motivation theories and their applications to consumer behavior.

Human beings share the same biogenic and similar psychological needs. However, different people assign different priorities to psychological needs. Maslow's hierarchy-of-needs theory proposes five levels of human needs: physiological needs, safety needs, social needs, egoistic needs, and self-actualization needs. Other needs widely integrated into consumer advertising include the needs for power, affiliation, and achievement.

Learning Objective 3: To understand how to identify and measure motives.

There are self-reported and qualitative methods for identifying and measuring human motives, and researchers use these techniques in tandem to assess the presence or strength of consumer motives. Motivational research and its current extended form (commonly referred to as qualitative research) seek to delve below the consumer's level of conscious awareness, and identify underlying needs and motives. Quantitative research has proved to be of value to marketers in developing new ideas and advertising copy appeals. Self-reported measures of motives consist of presenting written statements to respondents and asking respondents to indicate how relevant each statement is to them.

Learning Objective 4: To understand the scope of personality and theories of its development.

Personality consists of the psychological characteristics that both determine and reflect how a person responds to his or her environment. Although personality tends to be consistent and enduring, it may change abruptly in response to major life events, as well as gradually over time. Three theories of personality are prominent in the study of consumer behavior: psychoanalytic theory, neo-Freudian theory, and trait theory. Freud's psychoanalytic theory provides the foundation for the study of motivational research, which operates on the premise that human drives are largely unconscious in nature and motivate many consumer actions. Neo-Freudian theory tends to emphasize the fundamental role of social relationships in the formation and development of personality. Trait theory focuses on empirical measures of personality in terms of specific psychological characteristics, called traits, that set one person apart from another.

Learning Objective 5: To understand how innovativeness and other personality traits influence consumer behavior.

Trait theory postulates that individuals possess innate psychological traits (e.g., innovativeness, novelty seeking, need for cognition, materialism) to a greater or lesser degree, and that these traits can be measured by specially designed scales or inventories. Several personality traits are solidly related to innovativeness: dogmatism, social character (i.e., inner- versus other-directedness), and the need for uniqueness. These personality traits, as well as others (such as optimum stimulation level, sensation seeking, variety or novelty seeking, need for cognition, visualizer or verbalizer status, consumer materialism, fixated consumption, compulsive consumption, and consumer ethnocentrism) strongly affect consumption behavior and understanding them enables marketers to develop effective persuasive strategies.

Learning Objective 6: To understand the personification of products and brands and its strategic applications.

Some consumers attribute human-like qualities to products and brands. Marketers who study and understand the meaning of such product and brand personalities can use them to shape consumers' responses to promotional messages and enhance their emotional connections to products and brands. A product's personality frequently endows products and brands with gender. Consumers associate some brands with geographic locations, and such associations often enhance their memory and likeability of brands. Many consumers who are heavy Internet users become emotionally attached to certain websites, and several researchers have studied the ascribing of personality traits to websites.

Learning Objective 7: To understand self-image and its impact on consumer behavior.

Each individual has a perceived self-image (or multiple self-images) that is an expression of his or her traits, habits, possessions, and relationships. Consumers frequently attempt to preserve, enhance, alter, or extend their self-images by purchasing brands that appeal to their self-image(s), and also by shopping at stores that they perceive as consistent with their relevant self-image(s). Consumer behavior researchers identified four components of self-image: (1) actual self-image, (2) ideal self-image, (3) social self-image, and (4) ideal social self-image. Understanding the dimensions of self-image enables marketers to design effective promotional messages targeting various segments.

Review and Discussion Questions

3.1. Discuss the statement "Marketers don't create needs; needs preexist marketers." Can marketing efforts *change* consumers' needs? Why or why not? Can they *arouse* consumer needs? If yes, how?

3.2. Consumers have both innate and acquired needs. Give examples of each kind of need and show how the same purchase can serve to fulfill either or both kinds of needs.

3.3. List the innate and acquired needs that would be useful in developing promotional strategies for the following products and explain how they would be useful: (a) global positioning devices, (b) sunglasses that can be customized online, and (c) smartphones.

3.4. Why are consumers' needs and goals constantly changing? What factors influence the formation of new goals? Apply the concepts of needs and goals to the introduction of a new program by your college or university.

3.5. How can marketers use consumers' failures at achieving goals in developing promotional appeals for specific products and services? Give examples.

3.6. For each of the following products, select one level from Maslow's hierarchy of human needs. Describe how you would use the need you selected in promoting the product to a market segment of your choice. The products are: e-readers, expensive shoes, and vacation homes.

3.7. What are the advantages and disadvantages of using Maslow's needs hierarchy in segmentation and positioning?

3.8. a. How do researchers identify and measure human motives? Give examples.

b. Does motivational research differ from quantitative research? Discuss.

c. What are the strengths and weaknesses of motivational research?

3.9. How would you explain the fact that, although no two individuals have identical personalities, personality is sometimes used in consumer research to identify distinct and sizable market segments?

3.10. Contrast the major characteristics of the following personality theories: (a) Freudian theory, (b) neo-Freudian theory, and (c) trait theory. In your answer, illustrate how each theory is applied to the understanding of consumer behavior.

3.11. Describe personality trait theory. Give five examples of how personality traits can be used in consumer research.

3.12. Research has found that the target market selected by the maker of a digital camera consists primarily of individuals who are other-directed and also have a high need for cognition. How can the camera's marketer use this information in promoting its product?

3.13. Describe the type of promotional message that would be most suitable for each of the following personality market segments, and give an example of each: (a) highly dogmatic consumers, (b) inner-directed consumers, (c) consumers with high optimum stimulation levels, (d) consumers with a high need for recognition, and (e) consumers who are visualizers versus consumers who are verbalizers.

3.14. Is there likely to be a difference in personality traits between individuals who readily purchase foreign-made products and those who prefer American-made products? How can marketers use the consumer ethnocentrism scale to segment consumers?

3.15. A marketer of health foods would like to segment its market on the basis of self-image. Describe how the marketer can use actual self-image and ideal self-image to do so.

Hands-on Assignments

3.16. Find two advertisements that depict two different defense mechanisms (Table 3.2) and discuss their effectiveness.

3.17. Find three advertisements that illustrate the needs for power, affiliation, and achievement and discuss their effectiveness. (Each advertisement should depict one of the three needs.)

3.18. Find two examples of ads that are designed to arouse consumer needs and discuss their effectiveness.

3.19. Interview three friends about their favorite leisure-time activities. Do your leisure-time preferences differ from those of your friends? Which personality traits might explain why your preferences are different from or the same as those of your friends, and how so?

3.20. Find three print advertisements that illustrate concepts from Freudian personality theory and discuss how they do so.

Key Terms

- Achievement need *70*
- Actual self-image *91*
- Affiliation need *70*
- Aggression *65*
- Aggressive individuals *76*
- Anthropomorphism *58*
- Approach objects *63*
- Avoidance objects *63*
- Brand personification *58*
- Compliant individuals *76*
- Compulsive consumption *84*
- Daydreaming *65*
- Defense mechanisms *64*
- Detached individuals *76*
- Dogmatism *78*
- Ego *75*
- Egoistic needs *68*
- Ethnocentrism *77*
- Fixated consumption *84*
- Freudian theory *74*
- Frustration *64*
- Goals *62*
- Generic goals *62*
- Id *75*
- Ideal self-image *91*
- Ideal social self-image *91*
- Identification *65*
- Inner-directed *78*
- Innovativeness *77*
- Innovators *77*
- Maslow's hierarchy of needs *66*
- Materialism *77*
- Motivation *58*
- Motivational research *71*
- Need for cognition (NFC) *81*
- Need for uniqueness *78*
- Needs *58*
- Neo-Freudian theory *76*
- Optimum stimulation level (OSL) *79*
- Other-directed *78*
- Personality *58*
- Physiological needs *61*
- Power need *69*
- Product-specific goals *62*
- Projection *65*
- Projective techniques *71*
- Psychological needs *61*
- Qualitative research *71*
- Rationalization *65*
- Regression *65*
- Repression *65*
- Safety and security needs *68*
- Self-actualization need *68*
- Self-image *91*
- Self-reported measures of motives *71*
- Sensation seeking *80*
- Social needs *68*
- Social self-image *91*
- Superego *75*
- Thematic Apperception Test *72*
- Trait theory *76*
- Variety and novelty seeking *80*
- Verbalizers *82*
- Visualizers *82*
- Withdrawal *65*
- Word association method *71*

4

Consumer Perception

Learning Objectives

1. To understand the elements of perception and their role in consumer behavior.
2. To understand why consumers process only a small amount of the information they receive.
3. To understand how consumers organize consumption-related information.
4. To understand why and how consumers "add" biases to stimuli and the implications of this tendency for marketing.
5. To understand the elements of consumers' imagery.
6. To understand how consumers determine the quality of products and services.
7. To understand consumers' perceived risks and how they handle and reduce those risks.

PERCEPTION is the process by which individuals select, organize, and interpret stimuli into a meaningful and coherent picture of the world. It can be described as "how we see the world around us." Two individuals may be exposed to the same stimuli, but how each person recognizes, selects, organizes, and interprets these stimuli is a highly individual process based on each person's own needs, values, and expectations.

Consumers act and react on the basis of their perceptions, not on the basis of reality. For each individual, "reality" is a totally personal phenomenon, based on that person's needs, wants, values, and personal experiences. Thus, to the marketer, consumers' perceptions are much more important than their knowledge of objective reality. For if one thinks about it, it's not what actually *is* so, but what consumers *think* is so, that affects their actions and their buying habits. And, because individuals make decisions and take actions based on what they perceive to be reality, it is important that marketers understand the notion of perception and its related concepts to determine more readily what factors influence consumers to buy. As shown in Figure 4.1, Lifebuoy has always been at the forefront of saving lives through its promise of germ kill over the decades. In this particular campaign, Lifebuoy spreads the message on how washing hand with soap can help prevent flu and 10 such other infections during monsoons.

Later on, we explain the concept of the **just noticeable difference (JND),** which maintains that any changes in logos and packages must be within certain "limits" in order to ensure that consumers still recognize the items instantly after the changes. Coca-Cola packaged regular Coke in snow-white cans. Many consumers complained that the holiday can was confusingly similar to Diet Coke's silver cans, and the company brought back the familiar, red can immediately. Coca-Cola's white can was above the JND, which resulted in consumer confusion and complaints.

Source: Hindustan Unilever Limited

FIGURE 4.1 Lifebuoy

Box 4.1 Perception and B2B Marketing

Perception is not just confined to consumer products. Intel was perceived by the makers of smart phones and tablets as a chip that was consuming excess power as compared to the ones made by Samsung or Texas Instruments. The company had introduced the chip "Medfield"[1] to get over the competitive situation.

Learning Objective

1 To understand the elements of perception and their role in consumer behavior.

The Elements of Perception

Perception is all about consumers' *subjective* understandings and not *objective* realities. Altering subjective "wisdom" is difficult, or even impossible. For instance, for decades, Science Diet—sold mostly in specialty stores and priced quite high—has been the premier dog and cat food because it was based on the claims that, following scientific laboratory research, the food included vitamins, grains, and other special ingredients. However, in recent years, consumers' preferences changed and pet owners became fond of pet foods that mimicked their own diets, such as natural and organic foods. At this point, Science Diet's claim of engineered nutrition became a liability and its sales sharply declined. The brand's marketer responded with Science Diet Nature's Best, the ingredients of which included lamb, brown rice, soybean meal, and apples. Still, the new offering did poorly because consumers continued to perceive Science Diet as an artificial and unnatural product.[2]

Application 1: Attention Getting is a Prerequisite to Consumers' Perception

Attention occurs when we notice a stimulus and the attention may be voluntary or involuntary. Attention is a prerequisite for perception to take place. The Times of India Bangalore edition dated February 17, 2013 carried an ad that made use of the concept of attention associated with perception.

The first page reports a spate of fire accidents. Most readers were likely to at least spend a few seconds on this front page. Immediately, when the page is turned, there is an ad for Eureka Forbes's FIREGUARD (a gas- based offering that could be used to extinguish fires) with a mild fear appeal.

Moving the consumer from involuntary to voluntary attention on an important issue has been well conceptualized by the brand. It may be recalled that almost three decades back the brand Ceasefire, a similar offering, had made an impact in the market.

Application 2: Technology and Branding at the Point of Sale

United Breweries handles Heineken beer in India where alcohol is a media dark industry. Technology, attention, sensory inputs, and contrast – with regard to sense of sound – were brought together by the brand at the point of sale when it launched the "Voice in the head" campaign.[3]

When a consumer enters the retail outlet, he or she cuts a beam, sensors are set off, and an audio track starts playing. It subsequently stops if the consumer leaves the area. The consumer is attracted by the involuntary attention – music stops (contrast occurs through the stoppage of audio when he leaves the area ear marked for the audio) and keeps him wondering about the source of the audio. The brand had achieved 100% growth during the promotion.

Nevertheless, changing a brand image, or **repositioning**, is necessary. For example, for decades, Chevrolet was positioned as an American icon, with such slogans as "See the USA in Your Chevrolet," Heartbeat of America," and "Baseball, Hot Dogs, Apple Pie and Chevrolet." As GM started to sell the brand globally, it needed a new slogan that would create a united, global perception of the brand. The first new slogan it tried was "Chevy Runs Deep," but this tagline proved to be mundane and unexciting. Subsequently, GM began to advertise Chevrolet under the slogan "Find New Roads," which the company believes to be exciting, flexible, and also easily translated into other languages.[4] Interestingly, the Chevrolet brand name is not included in the new tagline.

Raw sensory input by itself does not produce or explain the coherent picture of the world that most adults possess. Indeed, the study of perception is largely the study of what we subconsciously add to or subtract from raw sensory inputs to produce our own private picture of the world. Human beings are constantly bombarded with stimuli during every minute and every hour of every day. The sensory world is made up of an almost infinite number of discrete sensations that are constantly and subtly changing. According to the principles of sensation, intensive stimulation "bounces off" most individuals, who subconsciously block (i.e., adapt to) a heavy bombardment of stimuli. Otherwise, the billions of different stimuli to which we are constantly exposed might confuse us and keep us perpetually disoriented in a constantly changing environment. However, neither of these consequences tends to occur, because perception is not a function of sensory input alone. Rather, perception is the result of two different kinds of inputs that interact to form the personal pictures—the perceptions—that each individual experiences. One type of input is physical stimuli from the outside environment; the other consists of people's expectations, motives, and what they have learned from previous experiences. The combination of these two very different kinds of input produces for each of us a very private, very personal picture of the world. Because each person is a unique individual, with unique experiences, needs, wants, desires, and expectations, it follows that each individual's perceptions are unique. This explains why no two people see the world in precisely the same way.

Individuals are very selective as to which stimuli they "recognize"; they subconsciously organize the stimuli that they do recognize according to widely held psychological principles, and they interpret such stimuli (give meaning to the stimuli) subjectively in accordance with their personal needs, expectations, and experiences. The following sections examine each of these three aspects of perception: the selection, organization, and interpretation of stimuli.

Application 1: Dissociation of a Brand Name (Brand Revitalizing)

Bajaj, a legendary name in two-wheelers, decided to remove its brand name Bajaj[5] to connect with the "new age" buyers, both in India and abroad (global strategy was the focus of the company). The company had two successful brands, Pulsar and Discover. Reinforcement and revitalizing strategies involve consumer perception. Allen Solly introduced "Color Lab" by which a consumer can choose his "signature colors" and the brand will dye the clothes for him (this association also reinforces the associations of individuality with the brand). Clinic Plus has always been about mother–daughter association and the brand in the recent times shows the mother as the enabler and not as a protector in its ads[6] (the core association has been maintained with a progressive change).

Application 2: Perception is the Anchor for Branding

Sheena Iyengar provides an interesting study that illustrates the role of perception among consumers, even with regard to mundane products.[7] One blind study among consumers in New York reported that a majority of consumers preferred tap water to the expensive mineral water brand, Evian. The next stage of the study was conducted in a restaurant where consumers were offered several brands of mineral water with brand names like L'eau du Robinet and Mount Fuji with the waiter explaining the benefits of these brands. Consumers described the mineral water as being "crispier and smoother", ignorant of the fact that they were all tap water with such names. And L'eau du Robinet in French means tap water!

Sensory Input

Sensation is the immediate and direct response of the sensory organs to stimuli. A **stimulus** is any unit of input to any of the senses. Examples of stimuli (i.e., sensory inputs) include products, packages, brand names, advertisements, and commercials. **Sensory receptors** are the human organs (the eyes, ears, nose, mouth, and skin) that receive sensory inputs. Their sensory functions are to see, hear, smell, taste, and touch. All of these functions are called into play, either singly or in combination, in the purchase, use, and evaluation of consumer products. Human sensory sensitivity refers to the experience of sensation. Sensitivity to stimuli varies with the quality of an individual's sensory receptors (e.g., eyesight or hearing) and the amount (or intensity) of the stimuli to which he or she is exposed. For example, a blind person may have a more highly developed sense of hearing than the average sighted person and may be able to hear sounds that the average person cannot. Figure 4.2 shows an ad for the Mitchell Eye Centre that humorously depicts the consequences of fuzzy vision.

Application 1: Hedonism-the Sensory Trigger

A study published in *Archives of General Psychiatry*[8] has interesting implications for consumer behavior. The study used physiological observations of portions of the brain (such approaches are also used in neuromarketing too). It was concluded that individuals eating chocolates and individuals taking narcotics reflect the same flashes with regard to the portions of their brains (concerned with "self control" and "cravings" regions of the brain).

Essentially, this translates into hedonism (consumption pleasure associated with sensory organs). A consumer who is used to a typical taste of a brand of chocolate (for instance, Cadbury) can get addicted to it. On an extended plane, sensory experiences that are processed by the brain to a greater level (A. R. Rahman's music, for instance) may also be able to create such "cravings". Hedonism and brand loyalty is likely to be researched at a greater depth in the days to come, especially with regard to fast moving consumer goods (FMCG) categories.

Application 2: Culture and Sensory Branding

Indian culture offers several interesting examples of sensory branding. Good Night mosquito coils (smoking away insects), the expectations of consumers on "heat generating " properties of pain balms (like Moov or Iodex), the stinging feel and pungent odor of antiseptic lotions (like Dettol's) and bathroom phenyl (especially the black phenyl) and the strong or *kadak* nature of tea are some interesting examples from the Indian context. Culture and sensory aspects provide valuable insights[9] to marketers.

Application 3: Involuntary Attention and Brand Awareness

Volkswagen, in collaboration with The Times of India, created the world's first "speaking newspaper".[10] Thousands of newspaper readers heard audio messages about the Volkswagen Vento model when they opened the page containing the advertisement of the brand. Capturing attention was taken to new heights by this endeavor.

Application 4: Sensation-Sensory Aspects of Experience and Brand Associations

In an effort to widen the "goodness of coconut" perception, Parachute had extended its proposition (and the brand) to skin lotion category. One of the prerequisites of the skin care category was that the fragrance would not be associated with coconuts (sense of smell). Hence, in order to create a sensual experience[11], the brand had worked on the packaging design and brand communication (sensual experience being enhanced through visuals).

Source: Alberta Eye Centre

FIGURE 4.2 Sensory Input: Mitchell Eye Centre

Sensation itself depends on energy change within the environment where the perception occurs (i.e., on differentiation of input). A perfectly bland or unchanging environment, regardless of the strength of the sensory input, provides little or no sensation at all. Thus, a person who lives on a busy street in midtown Manhattan would probably receive little or no sensation from the inputs of such noisy stimuli as horns honking, tires screeching, and fire engines clanging, because such sounds are so commonplace in

New York City. In situations in which there is a great deal of sensory input, the senses do not detect small changes or differences in input. Thus, one honking horn more or less would never be noticed on a street with heavy traffic.

As sensory input *decreases*, however, our ability to detect changes in input or intensity *increases*, to the point that we attain maximum sensitivity under conditions of minimal stimulation. This accounts for the statement, "It was so quiet I could hear a pin drop." The ability of the human organism to accommodate itself to varying levels of sensitivity as external conditions vary not only provides more sensitivity when it is needed, but also protects us from damaging, disruptive, or irrelevant bombardment when the input level is high.

Most marketing communications appeal to sight and sound. However, smell and touch also represent considerable opportunities for targeting consumers. The importance of smell in communication was strongly supported by two Americans who developed a scientific explanation of how people associate memories with smells (and won the 2004 Nobel Prize in Physiology for this work), as well as other studies demonstrating the impact of fragrance on product and store choices.[12] Scented strips have been part of perfume ads for years, but have also been used by other marketers: for example, scented stickers with coffee aromas were placed on the front page of a daily newspapers, and the scent of chocolate cookies was emitted from ads for milk placed in bus stops. Recognizing that the use of an ambient scent in a retail environment enhances the shopping experience for many consumers and makes the time they spend examining merchandise, waiting in line, and waiting for help seem shorter than it actually is, stores like Abercrombie & Fitch use strong fragrances throughout their facilities. One study discovered that product scent enhanced memory of the product more than ambient scent (i.e., scent in the environment when the product is sold). In addition, when a product was scented, memory of the nonscent-related attributes of the product also increased.[13]

Regarding the sense of touch, several studies indicated that touching a product influences persuasion and that touching could be used as a persuasive tool.[14] Another example of increasing sensory input is to add more merchandise and create more clutter in existing spaces. For example, during periods where consumers feel reluctant to spend money, Dollar General raised the height of its standard shelves and Best Buy tested carrying bigger items, such as bicycles and Segways, to fill in the space created by thinner TVs and smaller speakers.[15]

A sound, like a picture, may be "worth a thousand words." As shown in Table 4.1, many companies have invested large amounts of resources in designing products and packages that emit just the right audio sensory input, after studying how consumers perceive the volumes and pitches of sounds.[16]

The Absolute Threshold

The lowest level at which an individual can experience a sensation is called the **absolute threshold**. The point at which a person can detect a difference between "something" and "nothing" is that person's absolute threshold for that stimulus. To illustrate, the distance at which a driver can note a specific billboard on a highway is that individual's absolute threshold. Two people riding together may first spot the billboard at different times (i.e., at different distances); thus, they appear to have different absolute thresholds. Under conditions of constant stimulation, such as driving through a "corridor" of billboards, the absolute threshold increases (i.e., the senses tend to become increasingly dulled). After an hour of driving through billboards, it is doubtful that any one billboard will make an impression. Hence, we often speak of "getting used to" a hot bath, a cold shower, or the bright sun.

TABLE 4.1 Sensory Audio Input and Product Perception

PRODUCT	SOUND AND ITS CONSUMER MEANING
Snapple	Consumers perceive the sound of the "pop" as an indicator of product safety. When the company came up with the right snap sound, it was able to eliminate the plastic seal around the bottle's cap.
VW Jetta	The car door's "thump" is an indication of quality. The company played and mentioned the door thump in ads for a new model.
Mascara	Consumers perceive the sound and duration of the "click" heard when taking the cover off as indicators of quality.
Eye shadow	A more pronounced "click" heard when opening the compact case symbolizes higher quality.
Tip markers	Consumers like the "screech" because it represents "boldness."
Tampons	Realizing that women dislike opening tampon packages that omit sound, P & G redesigned the product's packaging. The plastic's "crinkle" was carefully balanced and the new adhesive strip makes no sound when opened.
Spray bottle	Method made the nozzle of its spray bottle almost indistinguishable because consumers perceive a quiet nozzle as an indicator of quality.

As our exposure to the stimulus increases, we notice it less. **Sensory adaptation** is "getting used to" certain sensations; that is, becoming accommodated to a certain level of stimulation and becoming less able to notice a particular stimulus.

Sensory adaptation is a problem that concerns many national advertisers, which is why they try to change their advertising campaigns regularly. They are concerned that consumers will get so used to their current print ads and TV commercials that they will no longer "see" them; that is, the ads will no longer provide sufficient sensory input to be noted. In an effort to cut through the advertising clutter and ensure that consumers perceive their ads, some marketers try to increase sensory input—and sometimes, marketers' efforts backfire. For example, the FCC approved rules that require cable operators and TV stations to quiet louder-than-normal TV commercials.[17]

As another example, following consumers' complaints, most department stores have eliminated the roaming spritzers of perfume who, for decades, have been spraying fragrances in stores' aisles assuming that consumers would buy a fragrance after getting a whiff.[18]

Many of the promotional methods aimed at increasing sensory input take the form of ambush marketing or experiential marketing.

Ambush Marketing

Ambush marketing consists of placing ads in places where consumers do not expect to see them and cannot readily avoid them.[19] Examples include brand names stamped on eggs in a supermarket, featured on video screens in taxis, placed in subway tunnels between stations, or featured on doctors' examination tables. Other examples are placing giant, fake pieces of advertised sushi on an airport's baggage carousel; featuring brands on the bottom of the trays where consumers place small personal items during security checks at airports; ads on dry cleaners' shirt boxes; and projecting ads on the sides of large buildings at night in large cities. Additional locations where ads are not expected but have been featured include inside urinals in men's restrooms, on muffin displays, and on the hoods of cars as attendants filled them with gas. Vanilla paired with jasmine aromas were placed in apartments for sale in a Las Vegas condo and scents were added to the handles of men's shaving razors.

Experiential Marketing

Experiential marketing allows customers to engage and interact with brands, products, and services in sensory ways in order to create emotional bonds between consumers and marketing offerings. Examples of this method include consumers' opportunities to closely examine NASCAR's race cars in Times Square, New York City, and Ford asking car owners to hold house parties where guests could see, sit in, and even drive the cars. In an innovative promotion of its Stove Top stuffing brand, during one winter month, Kraft Foods heated several Chicago bus stops featuring ads for the brand. The objective was to convey the product's "warmth" to waiting passengers.

The Differential Threshold

The minimal difference that can be detected between two similar stimuli is called the **differential threshold** or the **just noticeable difference (JND)**. A nineteenth-century German scientist named Ernst Weber discovered that the JND between two stimuli was not an absolute amount, but an amount relative to the intensity of the first stimulus. **Weber's law**, as it has come to be known, states that the stronger the initial stimulus, the greater the additional intensity needed for the second stimulus to be perceived as different. For example, during economic downturn, consumers become very price sensitive and are likely to note even small changes in price. However, during such times, companies feel a squeeze on their profit margins because people are doing more with less. For example, most leading brands of tea, detergents, shampoo, lotions and chocolates in India have been adjusting the weight of different stock keeping units, taking into consideration the price rise. This is to ensure that the reduction in the respective weight of the stock keeping unit is not readily noticeable to consumers.

The JND's Implications for Product Pricing and Improvement

Weber's law has important applications in marketing. Manufacturers and marketers endeavor to determine the relevant JNDs for their products for two reasons. First, they want to prevent changes (e.g., reductions in product size or quality, or increases in product price) from becoming readily discernible to the public (i.e., remain below the JND). Second, they want to ensure that product improvements (e.g., improved or updated packaging, larger size, or lower price) are very apparent to consumers, but without being wastefully extravagant (i.e., they are at or just above the JND).

When it comes to product improvements, marketers very much want to meet or exceed the consumer's differential threshold; that is, they want consumers to readily perceive any improvements made in the original product. Marketers use the JND to determine the amount of improvement they should make in their products. Improvements below the JND will not be perceived and will hurt the credibility of a marketer promoting the product as "new and improved." For example, when Apple came up with some new products for which it claimed sharper displays, many consumers were disappointed because, apparently, the improvements were below the JND and therefore unperceived. However, when Apple introduced Retina Displays, they were hailed as a breakthrough technology because the improvements were far above the JND and easily noticeable.

FIGURE 4.3 Changes in the Pepsi Symbol

Source: PEPSI and the Pepsi Globe are registered trademarks of PepsiCo, Inc. Used with permission

The JND'S Implications for Logos and Packaging

Marketers often want to update their existing package designs without losing the recognition of loyal consumers. They usually make a number of small changes, each carefully designed to fall below the JND so that consumers will perceive only minimal difference between succeeding versions. For example, Figure 4.3 shows Pepsi, as a youth brand, has made itself contemporary and relevant to the times by bringing in appropriate changes in its logo, but the basic elements of the symbol changed only minimally from one update to the next, in order to maintain continuous consumer recognition.

Figure 4.4 illustrates how Xerox, during its more than 100-year history, updated the company's logo many times. However, the logo was always updated carefully, with the JND in mind and without moving too drastically away from the previous logo that consumers readily recognized.

Marketers who do not consider the impact of the JND when introducing new logos may anger their loyal customers. For example:

1. Within a few days after introducing its new logo in several stores, The Gap received negative comments expressing resentment from customers. The firm immediately brought back its well-known and liked logo. Apparently, the new logo was too far beyond the JND of many consumers and too great of a change in The Gap's visual identity.
2. On its fortieth anniversary, the Starbucks name was removed from its logo, leaving only a more stylish illustration of the green mermaid. The company also revealed two future evolutions of its logo to be introduced, successively, on its fiftieth and sixtieth anniversaries. In spite of initial complaints from consumers, the company did not bring the old logo back. Apparently, although the change is clearly above the JND, Starbucks' management believes that, as time passes, consumers will accept it.
3. For decades, Tropicana's brand symbol for its premium juice packaging has been an orange with a straw in it. Then, a new logo was introduced, depicting a large glass of orange juice. Apparently, the change was above the JND. Consumers complained, saying that they could no longer find their beloved premium orange juice in supermarkets and that the new package was similar to inexpensive store brands.

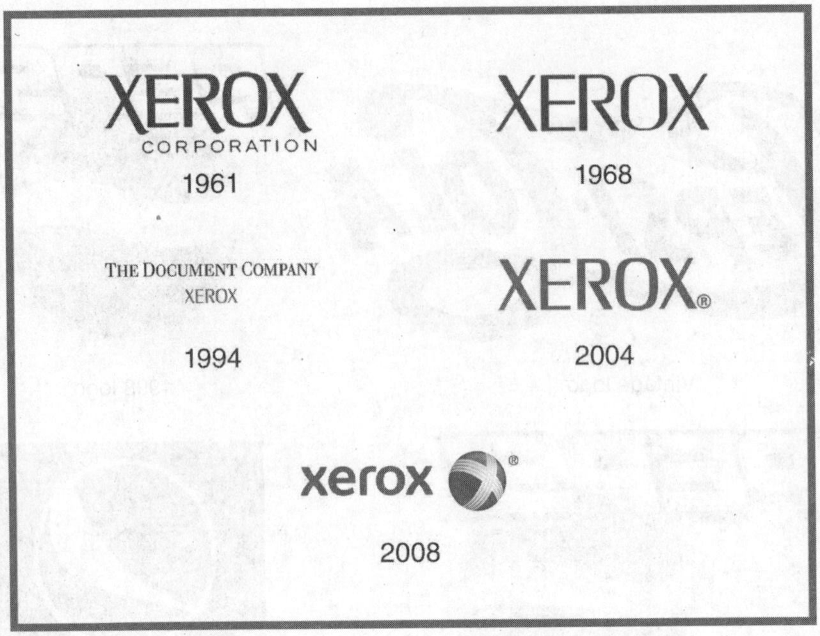

Source: Xerox Corporation

FIGURE 4.4 Changes in the Logo of the Xerox Company

Subliminal Perception

Chapter 3 described how motivation sometimes occurs below one's level of conscious awareness. People can be "stimulated" below their level of conscious awareness as well. That is, they can perceive stimuli without being consciously aware that they are doing so. Stimuli that are too weak or too brief to be consciously seen or heard may nevertheless be strong enough to be perceived by one or more receptor cells. This process is called **subliminal perception**, because the stimulus is beneath the threshold, or "limen," of conscious awareness, though obviously not beneath the absolute threshold of the receptors involved.

The effectiveness of so-called subliminal advertising was reportedly first tested at a drive-in movie theater in New Jersey in 1957, where the words "Eat popcorn" and "Drink Coca-Cola" were flashed on the screen during the movie. Exposure times were so short that viewers were unaware of seeing any message. It was reported that during the six-week test period, popcorn sales increased 58% and Coca-Cola sales increased 18%, but these findings were later reported to be false. Years later, it was discovered that although the simple subliminal stimulus "COKE" served to arouse thirst in subjects, the subliminal command "DRINK COKE" did not have a greater effect, nor did it have any behavioral consequences.

Despite the many studies of subliminal persuasion, there is no evidence that subliminal advertising persuades people to buy goods or services. A review of the research indicates that subliminal perception has no effect on attitudes toward products and consumption behavior, and that most of its effects were "researched" in highly artificial situations.[20] A study from done in a laboratory setting, supports this conclusion. Subjects were asked to keep a running total of numbers flashed on a screen, where they were also exposed to images of either IBM or Apple logos, shown at a speed faster than could be consciously seen. The subjects then performed a creativity exercise. The subjects subliminally exposed to the Apple logo scored higher on the creativity test than those exposed to the IBM logo or to no logo at all.[21] Some interpret these results to mean that a brand can make you perform better. For example, if you wear a swimsuit worn and endorsed by a champion swimmer, you will swim faster. Others argue that the results of the experiment simply mean that a subliminal stimulus may trigger certain associations and motivations, but not necessarily lead to different behavior. However, there is tangential indication that subliminal advertising may reduce antisocial behavior, such as that subliminal antishoplifting messages broadcasted in malls may lower shoplifting rates. However, there is no credible evidence that such advertising can get consumers to engage in shopping—a voluntary and pleasant behavior.

Over the years, there have been sporadic reports of marketers using subliminal messages in efforts to influence consumption behavior. For example, in 1995, Disney was accused of using subliminal messages in the movies Aladdin (where the hero allegedly whispers "good teenagers, take off your clothes" in a subaudible voice) and The Lion King (where the letters "S-E-X" are allegedly formed in a cloud of dust). At times, it has been difficult to separate truth from fiction regarding such alleged manipulations. When some of the subliminal methods were tested methodically using scientific research procedures, the research results did not support the notion that subliminal messages can persuade consumers to act in a given manner. As to sexual embeds, most researchers are of the opinion that "what you see is what you get"; that is, a vivid imagination can see whatever it wants to see in just about any situation. And that pretty much sums up the whole notion of perception: Individuals see what they want to see and what they expect to see.

Learning Objective

2 To understand why consumers process only a small amount of the information they receive.

Perceptual Selection

Subconsciously, consumers are very selective when exposed to stimuli. An individual may look at some things, ignore others, and turn away from still others. In actuality, people receive (i.e., perceive) only a small fraction of the stimuli to which they are exposed. Consider, for example, a woman at a Whole Foods Market. She may be exposed to more than 30,000 products of different colors, sizes, and shapes; to perhaps 300 people (looking, walking, searching, talking); to smells and tastes (from fruit, meat, and sample displays); to sounds within the store (audio announcements, music, cooking demonstrations); and many other stimuli. Yet she manages on a regular basis to visit the store, select the items she needs, pay for them, and leave, all within a relatively brief period of time, without losing her sanity or her personal orientation to the world around her. This is because she exercises *selectivity* in perception.

Which stimuli get selected depends on two major factors, in addition to the nature of the stimulus itself: (1) consumers' previous experience as it affects their expectations (what they are prepared, or "set," to see), and (2) their motives at the time (their needs, desires, interests, and so on). Each of these factors can increase or decrease the probability that a stimulus will be perceived.

The Stimulus

Physical stimuli that affect consumers' perceptions of products and evoke attention include the product itself, its attributes, package design, brand name, advertisements, and commercials (including copy claims, choice and sex of model, positioning of model, size of ad, and typography), and placement of promotional messages within the advertising space. Ads that contrast with their environments are very likely to be noticed. The use of a dramatic image of the product against a white background with little copy in a print advertisement, the absence of sound in a commercial's opening scene, an ad appearing where consumers do not expect it—all offer sufficient contrast from their environments to achieve differentiation and merit the consumer's attention.

Contrast is one of the most attention-compelling attributes of a stimulus. Advertisers often use extreme attention-getting devices to achieve maximum contrast and, thus, penetrate the consumer's perceptual "screen." The Crest ads in Figure 4.5 illustrate a good use of contrast. They evoke contrast because they show two objects—cherries and coffee—colored in white, which is an inaccurate. Crest's benefit comes through clearly: Eating cherries or drinking coffee stains teeth and Crest can remove such stains. Other forms of contrast are unexpected and unrealistic images.

Shocking and unrealistic images provoke attention. The ads in Figure 4.6 are from a campaign created by the Children's Defense Fund, an advocacy group. It depicts the potential tragic, long-term costs of cutting government-financed initiatives for children. One ad depicts a pregnant woman whose head is that of an infant girl and explains that cutting just $4,000 of Medicaid and food stamps from a girl in a low-income home is likely to get her to drop out of school. Then, the teenager might become pregnant, which will cost taxpayers a lot of money because the government pays huge sums for teen pregnancies. A second ad shows a tattooed man in a prison cell, whose head is that of an infant boy. The ad warns that eliminating early education investments now increases the infant's chances of going to prison later by up to 39%, and paying for that imprisonment will cost taxpayers nearly three times more per year than the cost of the child's education. The images of combining infant faces with adult bodies are shocking and make the ads highly noticeable.[22]

Expectations

People usually see what they expect to see, and what they expect to see is usually based on familiarity, previous experience, or a set of expectations. In a marketing context, a person tends to perceive products and product attributes according to his or her

Source: (Left & Right) The Procter & Gample Company

FIGURE 4.5 Contrasts Provoke Attention: Crest Removes Stains from Teeth

own expectations. A student who has been told by his friends that a particular professor is interesting and dynamic will probably perceive the professor in that manner when the class begins; a teenager who attends a horror movie that has been billed as terrifying will probably find it so. Sometimes, stimuli that conflict sharply with expectations receive more attention than those that conform to expectations. One study found that people who believed that they had prepared the dishes they tasted rated the food almost twice as high as others who tasted the same food but did not prepare it.[23] These results have implications for many "I made it myself" products. Marketers should stress the self-preparation aspects in all the promotions for those products, because such statements are likely to enhance their customers' satisfaction.

For years, some marketers have used blatant sexuality in advertisements for products to which sex is not relevant, in the belief that such advertisements would attract a high degree of attention. However, ads with irrelevant sexuality often defeat the marketer's objectives, because readers tend to remember the sexual aspects of the ad (e.g., the innuendo or the model), but not the product or brand advertised. Nevertheless, some advertisers continue to use erotic appeals in promoting a wide variety of products, (see Chapter 7).

Box 4.2 Shock Advertising

Shock advertising[24] (shockvertising) can be used by brands to *get attention* in a cluttered environment. It basically refers to using unusual and unexpected stimuli to gain the attention of consumers. Benetton's "Unhate" Campaign[25] in which US President Obama and Hu Jintao, the then Chinese president, were shown kissing each other is an example. MR Coffee and Tuff[26] shoes of the yesteryear are brands that used sexual innuendos to gain the attention of consumers.

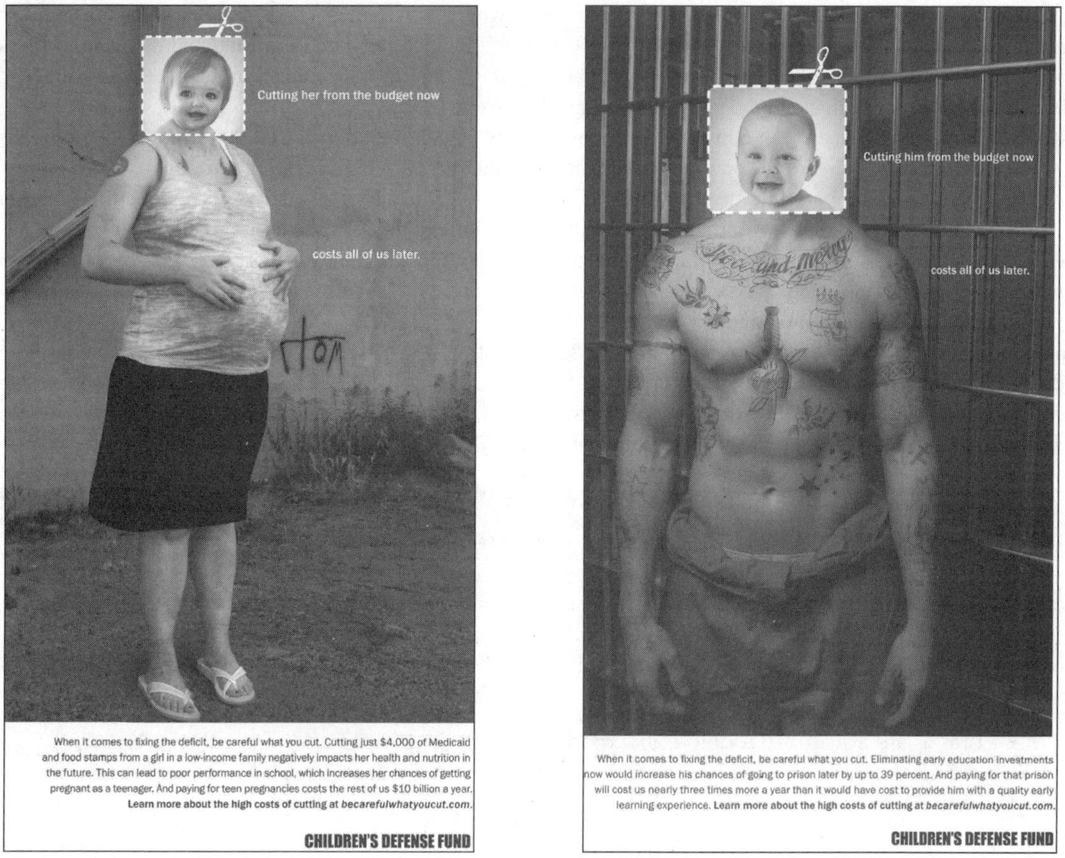

Source: (Left & Right) The Courtesy of the Children's Defense Fund

FIGURE 4.6 Shocking Images Induce Attention: Children's Defense Fund

Motives

People tend to perceive the things they need or want: The stronger the need, the greater the tendency to ignore unrelated stimuli in the environment. A student who is looking for a new cell phone provider is more likely to notice and read carefully ads for deals and special offers regarding such services than his roommate who is satisfied with his present cellular service. In general, there is a heightened awareness of stimuli that are relevant to one's needs and interests and a decreased awareness of stimuli that are irrelevant. An individual's perceptual process simply attunes itself more closely to those elements in the environment that are important to him or her. Someone who is overweight is more likely to notice ads for diet foods; a sexually repressed person may perceive sexual symbolism where none exists.

Marketing managers recognize the efficiency of targeting their products to the perceived needs of consumers. For example, a marketer can determine through marketing research what different segments of consumers view as the ideal attributes of the products they need and wish to purchase. The marketer can then segment the market on the basis of those needs, and vary the product advertising, so that consumers in each segment will perceive the product as meeting their own special needs, wants, or interests.

Selective Perception

As the preceding discussion illustrates, the consumer's selection of stimuli from the environment is based on the interaction of expectations and motives with the stimulus itself. **Selective exposure** occurs when consumers *tune into* messages that they find pleasant or with which they are sympathetic, and they *actively avoid* painful or threatening ones. They also selectively expose themselves to advertisements that reassure them of the wisdom of their purchase decisions.

Consumers exercise a great deal of selectivity in terms of the attention they give to commercial stimuli. **Selective attention** is consumers' *heightened* awareness of stimuli that meet their needs or interests and *minimal* awareness of stimuli irrelevant to their needs. Thus, consumers are likely to note ads for products that would satisfy their needs and disregard those in which they have no interest. People also vary in terms of the kinds of information in which they are interested and the form of message and type of medium they prefer. Some people are more interested in price, some in appearance, and some in social acceptability. Some people like complex, sophisticated messages; others like simple ones.

Perceptual defense takes place when consumers subconsciously *screen out* stimuli that they find psychologically threatening, even though exposure has already taken place. Thus, threatening or otherwise damaging stimuli are less likely to be consciously perceived than are neutral stimuli at the same level of exposure. Furthermore, individuals sometimes unconsciously distort information that is not consistent with their needs, values, and beliefs. One way to combat perceptual defense is to vary and increase the amount of sensory input. For example, because surveys showed that most smokers no longer pay attention to the written warning labels on cigarette packs, some laws now require tobacco firms to feature graphic health warnings on cigarette packs and vary the text of these messages.

Consumers often protect themselves from being bombarded with stimuli by "blocking" some stimuli from conscious awareness. They do so out of self-protection, because of the visually overwhelming nature of the world in which we live. The popularity of such devices as TiVo and DVRs, which enable viewers to skip over TV commercials with great ease, is, in part, an outcome of individuals' quest for avoiding exposure to unwanted stimuli, such as commercials.

Box 4.3 Attention, Contrast, and Consumer Perception of Brand Personality Distinctiveness

Recent research has demonstrated the impact of the subconscious on brand choice in a new direction associated with consumer behavior.[27] There are brands in categories in which consumers are not highly involved (on relative terms) like chocolates, soft drinks, floor cleaners, and snacks. Would you like and choose Bingo brand of snack because

1) These brands are advertised together in a media?
2) The "fun and cheerful" like personality of the brand is distinctive from the floor cleaner brands like Domex, Dettol, and Lifebuoy hand-wash that all have a "killer's" (germ killing action) personality?

The answer seems to be yes. Exposure to multiple brands across categories, when they are advertised together, can have far reaching effects on the choice of a focal brand (in the illustration, it is Bingo). And this happens through consumers' attention (perhaps involuntary, as they just see a spate of ads during a program without any specific intent to watch them) and also the contrast observed by the consumer with regard to the personality associations of the brands they are viewing.

Learning Objective

3 To understand how consumers organize consumption-related information.

Perceptual Organization

People do not experience the numerous stimuli they select from the environment as separate and discrete sensations; rather, they tend to organize them into groups and perceive them as unified wholes. Thus, the perceived characteristics of even the simplest stimulus are viewed as a function of the whole to which the stimulus appears to belong. This method of perceptual organization simplifies life considerably for the individual. The principles underlying perceptual organization are often called **Gestalt psychology** (in German, "Gestalt" means "pattern or configuration"). Three of the basic principles of perceptual organization are figure and ground, grouping, and closure.

Figure and Ground

The term **figure and ground** refers to the interrelationship between the stimulus itself (i.e., figure) and the environment or context within which it appears (i.e., ground). As noted earlier, stimuli that contrast with their environment are more likely to be noticed. A sound must be louder or softer, a color brighter or paler. The simplest visual illustration consists of a figure on a ground (i.e., background). The figure is perceived more clearly because, in contrast to its ground, it appears to be well defined, solid, and in the forefront. The ground is usually perceived as indefinite, hazy, and continuous. The common line that separates the figure and the ground is generally attributed to the figure rather than to the ground, which helps give the figure greater definition. Consider the stimulus of music. People can either "bathe" in music or listen to music. In the first case, music is simply background to other activities; in the second, it is the figure. Figure is more clearly perceived because it appears to be dominant; in contrast, ground appears to be subordinate and, therefore, less important.

Prior experiences affect how figure and ground pattern are perceived. For example, a short time following the destruction of the World Trade Center on September 11, 2001, by hijacked airplanes, one of the authors came across an ad for Lufthansa (Germany's national airline) that featured a flying jet, photographed from the ground up, between two glass high-rise buildings. Rather than focusing on the brand and the jet (i.e., the figure), all the viewer could think about was the two tall glass towers in the background (i.e., the ground), and the possibility of the jet crashing into them. When the author presented the ad to his students, many expressed the same thoughts. Clearly, this figure–ground reversal was the outcome of the painful events that occurred in September 2001.

Advertisers have to put advertisements together carefully to make sure that the stimulus they want noted is seen as figure and not as ground. The musical background must not overwhelm the jingle; the background of an advertisement must not detract from the product. Print advertisers often silhouette their products against a nondistinct background to make sure that the features they want noted are clearly perceived. The Canadian Dental Association ad in Figure 4.7 illustrates how people cannot notice gum disease, but dentists can. The gums are the "ground" that surrounds a "figure." The "figure" is gum disease, which cannot be seen easily, because, unless you are a dentist, the figure and ground are not easily distinguishable when gum disease occurs. In some cases, the blurring of figure and ground is deliberate. A well-known Absolut Vodka campaign ran print ads in which the figure (the shape of the Absolut bottle) was poorly delineated against its ground, challenging readers to search for the bottle; the resulting audience "participation" produced more intense ads and greater consumer attention.

The picture of the woman in Figure 4.8 is another example of figure–ground reversal. How old would you say she is? Look again very carefully. Depending on how you perceive figure and how you perceive ground, she can be either in her early 20s or her late 70s. Marketers must test their advertisements in order to ensure that they do not confuse consumers because there is no clear indication of which is figure and which is ground.

Source: Canadian Dental Association

FIGURE 4.7 Figure and Ground Reversal

Obscuring the Distinction Between Figure and Ground

A marketing technique based on the principle of figure-and-ground consists of inserting advertisements into entertainment content. **Product placement** takes place when the advertised product (i.e., the figure) is deliberately integrated into the TV show or film (i.e., the ground) in one or more of the following ways:[28]

1. The product is used by the cast (e.g., in such shows as Survivor and American Idol).

Source: E.G. Boring, "A New Ambiguous Figure," American Journal of Psychology, Vol. 42 (3), (July 1930): 444

FIGURE 4.8 Depending on One's Perception of Figure and Ground, the Women Is Either Old or Young

2. The product is integrated into the plot (e.g., a Sex and the City episode centered around Absolut vodka was entitled "Absolut Hunk").
3. The product is associated with a character (e.g., the character is also the product's advertising spokesperson).

One study found that a brand integrated and prominently featured in a TV program may produce *negative* feelings toward the brand among viewers who liked the program *a lot*, but those who liked the program *less* were more likely to develop *positive* attitudes toward the brand.[29] Thus, advertisers must be extremely careful in using product placement.

Increasingly and deliberately, consumers avoid watching TV commercials by using time-shifting devices such as DVRs programmed to delay a live broadcast by, say, fifteen minutes, sophisticated remote controls, or the "skip ad" option online. In response, advertisers have been trying to outsmart consumers by creating their own shows (i.e., content). Decades back Liril, the brand that ushered in the lime fragrant soap, had the package of green, the model was dressed in green and the soap's color was also green and the brand's proposition of freshness was covered through thoughtful merging of the figure and ground. These practices show how clever marketers can blur the distinction between figures (i.e., promotional message or symbol) and ground (i.e., the program's content) and expose consumers to advertisements even if the consumers try to avoid them.

Box 4.4 Brands, and Figure and Ground Aspects

Hindustan Unilever launched a sandal variant of Lux with a television ad featuring a well-known celebrity. It was interesting to observe Lux (contemporary and hip association) brand with a sandal variant because Lux had more of a fashion association than the attribute or benefit association linked with sandal–the traditional, nature-based soap for ultimate skin friendliness. The "figure" probably is the Lux's modern and its sustained celebrity associations and Sandal takes the "ground". Making sandal the figure may clash with associations of Lux.

Dettol used a similar figure and ground approach when it introduced the moisturizer variant

Grouping

Grouping refers to people's instinctive tendency to group stimuli together so that they become a unified picture or impression. The perception of stimuli as groups or chunks of information, rather than as discrete bits of information, facilitates memory and recall. Marketers use grouping to imply certain desired meanings in connection with their products. For example, an advertisement for tea may show a young man and woman sipping tea in a beautifully appointed room before a blazing hearth. The overall mood implied by the grouping of stimuli leads the consumer to associate the drinking of tea with romance, fine living, and winter warmth.

We remember and repeat our social security numbers, because we automatically group them into three "chunks," rather than trying to remember nine separate numbers.

Grouping has implications for placing products in supermarkets. For example, as part of a new in-store marketing campaign, Vlasic's pickle jars were moved from the aisles where they had traditionally been placed to locations next to the products with which pickles are eaten, such as hamburgers and buns.[30] The placement of Coca-Cola products in supermarkets is a brilliant example of grouping. The company creates "interaction points" by placing different-size Coca-Cola bottles and its bottled water next to foods with which they are "connected." For example, bottled water is placed near salad bars and family-size bottles of Coke next to takeout counters containing large portions of prepared foods.

Box 4.5 Reinforcing Brand Associations Over a Period of Time

Sustainable core proposition (SCP)[31] advocates that successful brand associations should be nurtured and strengthened over a period of time.

Perceptual principles are important to brands as they are useful in reinforcing brand associations. The challenge for marketers is to maintain the core proposition of a brand over the long term and also to ensure that the images are made contemporary in tune with the changing times. Santoor, with its proposition of youthful and "ageless" skin, has been sustaining a consistent and contemporary image for decades. It also introduced a glycerin variant of the brand featuring a cricket celebrity (during the times of world cup cricket in 2011) and drove home its proposition by showing how the celebrity mistakes the mother of a child to be a prospective "under nineteen" captain!

Nirma's familiar jingle was made contemporary through its associations with the "empowered and modern woman of the house." Sometimes, a well-entrenched brand may not only attempt to sustain its associations; it may also strengthen the associations by introducing a premium variant. Lifebuoy Clini-Care 10 marked over twice the price of the regular variant is an example.[32] The variant has the proposition of offering ten times more germ protection as compared to the original variant. Vespa's (scooter) re-entry into the Indian context at a price of ₹66,000 was heralded by an advertisement as retro-classic in nature. It helped in reinforcing the brand as a symbol of Italian fashion with a hint of nostalgia that captured the retro style (it may be recalled that the brand had a connection with the classic English movie *Roman Holiday*).

Source: (Top & Bottom) The Gillette Company

FIGURE 4.9 Consumers Will "Fill In" The "Missing" Parts of the Gillette Ads

Closure

Closure is people's instinct to organize pieces of sensory input into a complete image or feeling. Individuals need closure, which means that if they perceive a stimulus as incomplete, they are compelled to figure out its complete meaning. If a message they receive is incomplete, they consciously or subconsciously fill in the missing pieces. If the full understanding of a promotional message requires completion and some mental effort, consumers are likely to take the time to figure out its meaning in order to feel closure. For example, the Gillette ads in Figure 4.9, are better remembered than completed ones, because a person facing partial content feels compelled to finalize it so as to achieve closure. Some examples of ads that induce closure include: (1) asking consumers to un-scramble words (e.g., a Clorox ads listing unexpected uses of the product, such as, when unscrambled, read "dog bowl" and a baby's "teething ring"); (2) showing pictures and asking consumers to name the activities or items shown (e.g., Figure 15.3); (3) including words with missing letters and asking consumers to fill in the blanks; and (4) asking consumers to match, say, occupations with people shown wearing different styles of clothes.

The need for closure has interesting implications for marketers. Promotional messages in which viewers are required to "fill in" information beg for completion by consumers, and the very act of completion serves to involve consumers more deeply in the message. In a related vein, advertisers have discovered that they can achieve excellent results by using the soundtrack of a frequently viewed television commercial on radio. Consumers who are familiar with the TV commercial perceive the audio track alone as incomplete; in their need for completion, they mentally play back the ad's visual content from memory.

Learning Objective

4 To understand why and how consumers "add" biases to stimuli and the implications of this tendency for marketing.

Perceptual Interpretation: Stereotyping

The preceding discussion has emphasized that perception is a personal phenomenon. People exercise selectivity as to which stimuli they perceive, and they organize these stimuli on the basis of certain psychological principles. The interpretation of stimuli is also uniquely individual, because it is based on what individuals expect to see in light of their previous experiences, the number of plausible explanations they can envision, and their motives and interests at the time of perception.

Stimuli are often highly ambiguous. Some stimuli are weak because of such factors as poor visibility, brief exposure, high noise level, or constant fluctuation. When stimuli are highly ambiguous, an individual will usually interpret them in such a way that they serve to fulfill personal needs, wishes, interests, and so on. This is the principle that provides the rationale for the projective tests discussed in Chapter 3. Such tests provide ambiguous stimuli (such as incomplete sentences, unclear pictures, or untitled cartoons) to respondents who are asked to interpret them. How a person describes a vague illustration is a reflection not of the stimulus itself, but of the subject's own needs, wants, and desires. Through the interpretation of ambiguous stimuli, respondents reveal a great deal about themselves.

Individuals carry biased pictures in their minds of the meanings of various stimuli, which are termed **stereotypes**. Sometimes, when presented with sensory stimuli, people "add" these biases to what they see or hear and thus form distorted impressions. Several years ago, an ad for Benetton featuring two men—one black and one white—handcuffed together, which was part of the "United Colors of Benetton" campaign promoting racial harmony, produced a public outcry because people perceived it as depicting a white man arresting a black man. Clearly, this perception was the result of stereotypes, as there was nothing in the ad to indicate that the white person was arresting the black person rather than the other way around. Marketers must be aware of possible stereotypes, because these images reflect people's expectations and influence how stimuli are subsequently perceived.

Box 4.6 New Brands, Perceived Value, and Stereotypes

Zynga launched its energy drink at ₹25 for 200 ml when other competitors like Red Bull were selling their offerings at ₹95 for 250 ml. While the brand had enhanced the perceived value among the target segment, the consumer may feel that energy drink is something that is to be seen drinking from a can rather than a new type of packaging that Zynga had introduced.[33] Stereotype is important, especially when self-concept based brands are involved. Interestingly, the brand has positioned itself as an offering that resists sleep (occasion-based segmentation base).

The TVS ad in Figure 4.10 is an example of trying to dispel a stereotype. The ad reflects a young, urban, and modern girl who believes in making her choices and breaking away from the stereotype. The brand has created an imagery that differentiates between the traditional stereotype of a girl who is used to be directed and the modern girl who is confident of making her choices.

There are many reasons behind stereotyping. Generally, people stereotype because it makes the processing of sensory input quicker and easier. For example, many children have been educated to offer their seats on a bus to older persons, because, presumably, older persons are physically weak. On occasion, however, an athletic older person may refuse the offer, or even be insulted by it, because he or she feels that stereotyping all older persons as weak is an insult. Similarly, we often typecast movie stars as, say, "action heroes" and may be reluctant to see a romantic comedy in which they play a leading role. We must note that stereotyping consists of oversimplifying an image either positively or negatively. Therefore, when we pass an H&M store that just opened, we immediately know that it offers fashionable clothing at reasonable prices. In this case, the stereotype is positive and the result of previous shopping and H&M's positive image.

The triggers of stereotyping are physical appearance, descriptive terms, first impressions, and the halo effect.

Source: TVS Motors

FIGURE 4.10 Dispelling a Stereotype

Physical Appearance

People tend to attribute the qualities they associate with certain types of people to others who resemble them, whether or not they consciously recognize the similarity. For this reason, the selection of models for print advertisements and for television commercials can be a key element in their persuasiveness. Culturally, attractive models are likely to be more persuasive and have a more positive influence on consumer attitudes and behavior than average-looking models; attractive men are perceived as more successful businessmen than average-looking men. However, using attractive models without any other considerations does not increase ads' effectiveness. Thus, advertisers must ensure that there is a rational match between the product advertised and the physical attributes of the model used to promote it. For example, highly attractive models are likely to be perceived as having more expertise regarding *enhancement* products (e.g., jewelry, lipstick, perfume), but not *problem-solving* products (e.g., products that correct beauty flaws such as acne or dandruff). The SPYMUSEUM.ORG ads shown in Figure 4.11 poke fun at physical stereotyping with the headline "nothing is what it seems" and a portrayal of people who presumably are spies, although they "do not look like spies." That is, they defy most people's mental images of spies.

Products' physical appearance often influences consumers' judgments. A study indicated that the perceived taste of orange juice and consumers' ability to distinguish between three levels of sweetness were influenced by subtle color variations of the juice and also, somewhat unexpectedly, that such variations influenced perceived taste more than brand and price.[34]

Source: (Top & Bottom) International Spy Museum

FIGURE 4.11 Stereotypes: What Do Spies Look Like?

The shape of packages has great influence on consumers' impressions (as discussed later in this chapter) and affects consumers' expectations. For this reason, ice cream packages are round because this shape was found to communicate abundance. An experimental study investigated how consumers construed the attributes of facial tissue products from print ads, each including one of the following three objects (in varied forms): cats, sunsets, and abstract paintings. The study found that a "fluffy cat" communicated a soft and *expensive* tissue, whereas a "colorful cat" conveyed a soft and *colorful* tissue. Among the sunset images, the "soft sunset" expressed a soft, expensive, and colorful tissue, whereas a "roadside sunset" conveyed a neither soft nor colorful but an inexpensive product.[35]

Descriptive Terms

Stereotypes are often reflected in verbal messages. For example, consumers who eat foods with elaborate names such as "succulent Italian seafood filet" are very likely to rate those foods as tastier and more appealing than those who eat the same foods with such mundane names as "seafood filet." As another example, the common expression "he drives like a real man" connotes fast, aggressive, and even somewhat reckless driving, whereas the expression "he drives like a woman" portrays the driver as effeminate. The ad from Mothers Against Drunk Driving (MADD) in Figure 4.12 dispels the "effeminate" image by stating that slower and less aggressive driving represents more responsible driving for *both* genders.

Although distinct brand names are important to all products or services, associations that consumers make with certain names are particularly crucial in marketing services, because services are abstract and intangible. For example, names such as "Federal Express" and "Humana" (a provider of health services) are excellent names because they are distinctive, memorable, and relevant to the services that they offer. In contrast, "Allegis"—a short-lived brand name aimed at creating a business travel concept by combining United Airlines, Hertz, and Hilton and Westin Hotels under one umbrella—failed because it conveyed nothing to consumers about the type of services it offered.[36]

Advertisers must be careful about using canned stereotypes and "common wisdom" in their persuasive messages. For example, gender-role stereotypes view young boys as having "instrumental" orientation focused on problem solving and young girls as having "communal" orientation focused on relationships and group harmony. A study examined young children's attitudes toward ads that included "instrumental" scripts (e.g., eating a cracker will make you strong) and "communal" scripts (e.g., a cracker is a great snack to have with your friends). The study found that preadolescent children did not necessarily respond more favorably to messages that included stereotypical gender-role attributes.[37]

Source: MADD

FIGURE 4.12 MADD: Dispelling a Negative Stereotype Caused by Descriptive Terms

First Impressions

First impressions tend to be lasting, as illustrated by the saying that "You'll never have a second chance to make a first impression." Because first impressions are often lasting, introducing a new product before it has been perfected may prove fatal to its ultimate success; subsequent information about its advantages, even if true, will often be negated by the memory of its early poor performance. When one retailer put a picture of an aloe vera leaf and the wording "Aloe Vera" on the surface of its mattress, at first impression consumers assumed that aloe vera was a component of the ticking (the mattress cover), and the retailer had great difficulty in dispelling this initial impression.[38]

Halo Effect

The **Halo effect** refers to the overall evaluation of an object that is based on the evaluation of just one or a few dimensions. The linguistic definition of "halo" signifies light, honor, and glory. Thus, in marketing, the term refers to a prestigious image of a product "rubbing off on" other products marketed under the same brand name. For example, consumers who admire Porsche cars will be willing to spend a lot of money on sunglasses and other accessories sold under the same brand name. Historically, the term refers to situations in which the evaluation of a single object or person on a multitude of dimensions is based on the evaluation of just one or a few dimensions (e.g., a man is trustworthy, fine, and noble because he looks you in the eye when he speaks). Consumer behaviorists broadened the notion of the halo effect to include the evaluation of multiple objects (e.g., a product line) on the basis of the evaluation of just one dimension (a brand name or a spokesperson). Using this broader definition, marketers can take advantage of the halo effect when they extend a brand name associated with one line of products to another line. The lucrative field of **licensing** is based on the halo effect. Manufacturers and retailers hope to acquire instant recognition and status for their products by associating them with well-known names.

Tampering with the perceived halo effect of a product or brand can be disastrous. For example, in an attempt to enhance the image of JW Marriott, the Marriott hotel chain's upscale brand, Marriott took over the Righa Royal Hotel, an upscale hotel in New York City, and renamed it the JW Marriott New York. When the new name signs went up, scores of regular, upscale customers, who always stayed at the Righa when visiting New York City, canceled their reservations because they did not want to tell colleagues to contact them at the Marriott. The company restored the Righa Royal Hotel name, with the JW Marriott name included in smaller print.[39]

Traditional and Emerging Stereotypes in Indian Advertising

It may be worthwhile to analyze three aspects related to stereotypes in the Indian context: How have cultural stereotypes been used in ads and to what end? How do traditional and emerging stereotypes in India affect marketing communication? How can brands benefit from stereotypes?

The Use of Stereotypes: A housewife provides warmth, looks after the needs of the family members, is responsible for happiness within the family, is expected to be judicious with her monthly budget, and at times is even expected to sacrifice her comforts and aspirations for the sake of the family/husband. This perhaps is the stereotype of the Indian housewife prevalent in most parts of the country. Such a stereotype has also been widely used by advertisers in India across product categories. Ones that may still be fresh in the memory of older consumers are the Horlicks mother and Surf's Lalitaji. Horlicks showed a caring mother who was concerned about the nutritional value of the food consumed by her children. Complan, a competitive brand in the milk additive market, slightly varied this stereotypical depiction by introducing a (female) dietician advising a group of concerned mothers. Another version of Complan showed a youngish looking mother being taken on a bicycle by her "Complan-nurtured son." On the contrary, for children's educational or health insurance, it is almost always the father who is prominent in ads, depicting that the father is still perceived as the sole or major breadwinner of the family.

The case of Lalitaji used by Surf in the detergent category during the 1980s is an interesting example of how a brand pioneered the concept of communicating the value of a product by using a stereotype in line with the changing consumer mindset even before market liberalization. The traditional hold of pioneering brands was gradually loosening and television channels (though limited in number) were gaining momentum across the length and breadth of the country. In fact, TV viewing began to influence changes in the lifestyles of consumers during the mid- to late 1980s. In 1969, Nirma, an almost unknown brand of detergent, made history by introducing its product at almost half the price of the leading brand, Surf (from Unilever India Ltd, which had several brands in the detergent category). Several years after Nirma was launched, Unilever launched Wheel, a competitive brand of Nirma. In order to hold on to the market share and probably the mindshare of the brand, Surf used a woman in their ads they chose to call *Lalitaji*. Lalitaji was a typical middle-class housewife who bargained hard with vendors (women bargaining with vendors is a cultural practice in India to such an extent that even today a brand in the personal care category uses it in its communication to convey its value proposition). The Surf ad showed Lalitaji telling consumers that half the quantity of Surf would suffice for the same wash as that of the competitive brand. Nirma was not mentioned but it was implied.

Traditional or Emerging Stereotypes? In the 1980s, Vicco, a brand of facial cream that was initially advertised as a turmeric-based cream that was "not a cosmetic," created an advertisement combining culture, occasion and the bridal stereotype. Marriages are big in India and personal grooming of the bride is an important ritual associated with the occasion. Vicco created an ad that showed the friends of the bride applying the cream (instead of the traditional turmeric) on the bride. Vicco used this commercial for a long time. What is more interesting is that Fair & Lovely, a fairness cream (which still dominates the category) used a stereotype more in line with changing trends and incidentally the brand benefited by not getting "tracked" into occasion-based positioning. The brand positioned itself in such a way that consumers perceived a wider, everyday use of the product. Fair & Lovely positioned itself as a fairness cream, which adds to the charm of simply being a girl (the brand later adapted the stereotype in tune with changing times).The stereotype (user stereotype) was a girl in the best of her years wanting to look charming—distinctively different from the occasionbased Vicco. In recent times, Fair & Lovely has created a stereotype that is highly aspirational with a strong desire to succeed in a world dominated by men. Despite traditional gender roles being depicted in a majority of ads to date, there are also ads that have begun to portray the small cross-section of women who are educated and hold professional jobs and who have become the role models for the masses. With lifestyle changes, a strong need for both husband and wife to work in order to lead a reasonably comfortable life and, education being recognized as the route to career growth, aspirations of women have been ignited to the extent that can be used in marketing communication in a realistic manner. Fair &

Lovely created an advertisement in which a girl from the typical middle class succeeds in becoming a cricket commentator—an overwhelmingly male field even now. The stereotype created not only addresses the growing aspirations of women who are still perceived in the "traditional mold" but also uses cricket, which has been a part of the Indian culture for several decades. This is a good example where an emerging stereotype has been created in such a manner that it will appeal to the target segment (girls from middle-class households who nurture dreams of enjoying life together with professional accomplishments).

Product stereotypes have also been used in the context. There have been a few instant coffee brands in the market before Bru. But Bru, launched during the 1970s, used the stereotype of filter coffee (popular in the southern parts of India) to create an association with its offering. After having established itself on the functional attributes of instant coffee, through its comparison with filter coffee, Bru started to use user stereotype in conjunction with the product stereotype that had been created. It introduced urbane and educated-looking youngsters (depicting middle-class families). Most of these campaigns also had an elderly-looking person (stereotype of a middle-class family senior) as a character in the ad. What is interesting to note is that filter coffee has always had a user stereotype associated with the middle-aged/elderly in the minds of consumers and creating a new (emerging) imagery has also involved a traditional one. In the recent times tea brands have been using user stereotypes, which reflect the lifestyles of respective target segments. A brand stereotype (using the attributes of the offering in a category or a user-oriented stereotype) has to be distinctive enough and sustained through marketing communication for a considerable period of time. This ensures that a stereotype is embedded in the psyche of the consumer. To give another example, gifting is a part of the Indian culture and Titan as a watch brand created a stereotype of the brand being gifted in a valued relationship. While consumers would have had several categories of products in their consideration set, Titan the brand name associated itself with the gifting occasion to form a stereotype.

Box 4.7

Force 10 from Liberty associated itself with several trendy products that urban youth use like sunglasses, cola, and jeans. Charms cigarettes (when cigarette advertising was not banned in the country) associated itself with a package design showing jeans. Eveready batteries associated itself with the youth with its "Give Me Red" campaign (red is generally perceived as a color associated with adventure, live activity, and an upbeat mood). Liril soap's initial launch during the 1970s made an excellent convergence of figure and ground with the brand's proposition of "freshness." The pack had a lime image, the soap was green in color and the ad showed a model enjoying herself under a waterfall. Ericsson's initial launch in India refl ected the need to differentiate "figure" from "ground." The brand used excellent humor in its commercial, "One black coffee, please." The commercial showed an attractive woman talking and smiling while using the compact cell phone in a café. A consumer in the restaurant mistakes it to be an invitation from the woman (because he cannot see the phone) and approaches her. The woman fi nishes her conversation and, seeing the man approaching her, mistakes him for a waiter and orders black coffee. While the intention of the brand was to convey the compact benefi t associated with the brand, the humor may have taken the " figure" in the commercial and the brand's proposition may have been associated with the "ground" in the psyche of the consumer. A dipstick study undertaken by the author at that point in time showed that the recall of the commercial's humor was high but the respondents mentioned a competing brand name instead of Ericsson. Incidentally, the brand name mentioned by the respondents was perhaps due to a press campaign by the competing brand at that point in time. The figure needs to be the brand proposition and any creativity (including humor) associated with an advertisement should form the ground.

Allen Solly positioned itself as a semi-formal premium brand in the 1990s, with the slogan "Stop wearing uniforms to work." The brand has leveraged this association to formulate a contemporary association with the slogan: "My world, my way." The brand has also launched casuals for all occasions and the contemporary associations strengthen the old associations with the new products.* Raymond, the apparel company that markets fabric from ₹150 a meter to ₹150,000 a meter,** has managed its associations with luxury and premium aspects over the years in a consistent manner. Hero Honda's Street two-wheeler was positioned as a city bike. But its design was quite similar to an old model called M-80 that was associated with multiple uses and ruggedness. Besides, Street was positioned at the higher price bracket and M-80 was priced much lower. Such aspects may have interfered with the interpretation of the brand and also the positioning associations linked to the brand. Interpretation of value is an important implication with regard to the perceptual process. Coca-Cola introduced glass bottles in 2003 at ₹5 for 200 ml (signaling value to consumers) to widen the market. Volumes improved but this strategy hit the profit

(Continued)

Box 4.7 (Contniued)

margins, forcing the company to withdraw the product.*** Therefore, perceptual interpretation of consumers needs to be balanced with aspects of brand management.

Source: *Sarah Jacob, "With Casuals Allen Solly Now Wears a Brand New Identity," The Economic Times, October 20, 2009.
**Abha Bakaya, "Challenge Is to Keep Coming Out with Products," The Economic Times, October 21, 2009.
***Ratna Bhushan, "Cos Mull Hike in Price of Coke, Pepsi," The Economic Times, October 20, 2009

Effectiveness of Brand Repositioning

Brand positioning and repositioning deal with the mind of the consumer. Brand repositioning is more complex as it has to take into account the perception already created in the mindscape of the consumer. Cadbury successfully repositioned its mold (milk chocolate) variant during the mid-1990s, even managing to change the target segment for the variant—a very difficult task for marketers operating in any kind of market. The body of knowledge concerning brand repositioning is unfortunately not very vast, but the concept is receiving increasing attention with the proliferation of product categories and brands. With brand equity being the driving force behind brands, the ones which are strongly established either in terms of consumer preferences or in terms of recall are under pressure to create a roadmap which will lead to effective repositioning.

Why Is Brand Repositioning Needed?

Brand repositioning is required:

- When new offerings flood the market, and the superiority of the established brand has to be reemphasized.
- When new offerings enter the market, and the established brands may not be in a position to offer either the same features or the variants that are being offered by the new brands (Ambassador and Robin Blue). Hence, there is a need for these established brands to reposition themselves in a timely manner, relying more on the consumer good will they enjoy or by exploring ways to appeal to consumers.
- When a contemporary image is required in some categories due to changing psychographics.
- When brands desire to change their target segment (which may be rare).
- When brands want to advertise improved offerings.
- When motivation to buy the category is low among consumers.

New brands with new products keep entering the competitive marketing context and unless established brands reposition themselves, consumers may not have a contemporary perception of established brands.

Timely Repositioning

Contemporary perception could involve either the image or superior functional utility. Iodex was almost the unassailable leader for several years in the balm market but the brand was forced to reposition itself by Moov, which made rapid strides in the market. Dove is repositioning itself as a superior soap with moisturizers (as against its previous "trial for results" positioning) because of the various new offerings in the market. The Vim challenge was a response to several regional brands emerging in the dish washing detergent market. Esteem's "shall we go for a drive, please" (the son suggesting the drive on Esteem to the father, because he knows that the pleasure of the ride is good enough to ensure his poor exam results do not get his father's attention) repositioning was triggered by the various products that entered the mid-segment passenger car market. If repositioning is not attempted by a brand in a timely manner, the brand may not get a second chance. The powerful positioning of the no-frill Maruti 800 during the mid-1980s could have been preempted by Ambassador not necessarily by the same economy proposition: Ambassador even today is widely acknowledged as a comfortable car for Indian roads and it is also known for its space attribute (some of the recent offerings in the passenger car market are today using this as a strong proposition). The brand could have used this effectively to obtain a favorable perception among a cross-section of consumers. Maruti 800 became almost a legend as much known for derailing Fiat and Ambassador as it is for its fuel economy. Even for FMCGs involving mundane household products, timely repositioning matters in protecting leading brands. The Ujala brand of liquid blue added to whiten clothes made history with its liquid variant. The pioneering (and dominant) brand, Robin Blue, had a powder variant before Ujala was introduced. Powerfully repositioning itself as Robin Blue (even before introducing the liquid variant as a follower) might have reduced the impact of the new entrant because of the favorable brand image Robin Blue had for consumers over the decades. Burnol, the antiseptic cream for burns (it did attempt some sporadic repositioning exercises), which was probably the only brand in the consumers' psyche in that category, no longer seems to occupy the same psychological space. Women continue to cook as before and probably most of them are in a hurry to catch up with the pressures of life. Burnol as a handy brand to overcome the inevitable small burn during cooking could have been a probable brand repositioning strategy. With several categories jostling to get into the mindset of the consumer, a relevant proposition is required for a brand in the "small burn category" to get it into the consideration set of the consumer. The timing of repositioning (in such cases) should be done to ensure that the category does not fade out of the consumer's mind because of a number of other categories emerging to create a generic competition in terms of the share of the consumer's wallet. For example, a brand traditionally used for burns may get forgotten because of several categories of products and offerings like a cream for heels, herbal antisep-tic ones for multiple injuries, corn caps, etc., which attract the consumer's attention and have a share of the consumer's expenditure. Over a period of time, contemporary offerings could erase the consumer's memory of traditional offerings/brands if brand repositioning is not formulated (with or without product attribute improvements). Forhans toothpaste, Zambac, Saibal, the multipurpose antiseptic ointments, Eno, the gas reliever, Waterbury's compound for the "after-cough" recovery, and Crook's Lactocalamine are some of the brands of the yester-year that could have maintained their dominance of the consumer's memory with appropriate repositioning strategies.

Application 1: Brand Repositioning is a Complex and Challenging Exercise

Source: Tata Motors

FIGURE 4.13 Nano Twist

Repositioning involves changing the perceptual aspects of consumers. This can range from a minimum change in packaging or advertisement to major aspects of a brand like marketing mix elements. Such changes also impacts the other offerings in the product-line of the company and it needs to be taken into consideration. Nano was launched with the association of being the "cheapest car"[40]. This may have been also been a result of the wide publicity associated with the prelaunch phase of the brand. The brand later was well-positioned as Nano Twist, as shown in Figure 4.13, a car for youngsters with a number of contemporary features.

Cadbury Gems, the chocolate that has been in the market for several decades, had changed its positioning to kids to repositioning it to tweens and teenagers telling them that "they are not too old to love Gems". This has been done without any change in its product offering.[41] Perhaps the "child-like" qualities seem to have evolved by such repositioning, especially if the changed target segment had grown up with the brand during their formative years.

Application 2: Perception and Foreign Brands[42]

India's British heritage heralded the entry of foreign brands like Vicks, Cadbury, and Horlicks. The post- independence era and the regulated environment ushered in a glamour that was unique to foreign brands like Seiko in watches and 555 in cigarettes (consumers of the erstwhile era shopping in places like Burma Bazar in Chennai substantiates such an origin). This glamour associated with foreign brands and changing lifestyles gave further impetus to foreign sounding names. Park Avenue in readymade wear and Titan in watches (during the era of HMT) of the eighties are still ruling the roost. Western way of lifestyles – even in its *desi* ways – has brought in a host of foreign sounding names. With the onset of the trickle-down effect, such brand names also got diffused into mid-priced segments. Peter England, Hawkins, and Kenstar are examples. Entry of foreign sounding names is equally applicable even to foreign brands that find their entry through collaboration with Indian companies. These brands that have "foreigness" in their names may not be of any threat to well-known foreign brands or even to brands that may not have relatively high awareness (Mont Blanc or Fossil).

Foreign brands that have a local origin will continue to motivate middle-end consumers, provided they add value to their respective offering. Sometimes, foreign brands use the "Country of origin effects" to sound authentic. Stylish warm clothing goes well with the brand Monte Carlo as it may trigger a sense of Italian or European fashion.

Learning Objective

5 To understand the elements of consumers' imagery.

Consumer Imagery

Consumer imagery refers to consumers' perceptions of all the components of products, services, and brands, and to how consumers evaluate the quality of marketers' offerings. Products and brands have images and symbolic values for consumers based on the unique benefits that these products claim they provide. The following section examines consumers' perceived images of products, brands, services, prices, product quality, retail stores, and manufacturers. In Figure 4.14, Arrow's revitalizing and reinforcement strategies are reflected in the trend of fitness and corporate professionalism, along with core proposition of Americanness with which the brand was launched.

Source: Arvind Limited.

FIGURE 4.14 A print ad of Arrow Brand of Formal Wear

Brand Image

The desired outcome of effective **positioning** is a distinct "position" (or image) that a brand occupies in consumers' minds. This mental "position" must be unique and represent the core benefit the brand provides. Most new products fail because they are perceived as "me too" offerings that do not offer consumers any advantages or unique benefits over competitive products. The essence of the marketing concept is to create products that fulfill consumer needs. However, as more and more brands within a given product category fulfill consumers' needs effectively, consumers often rely primarily on the brand's image and claimed benefits in their purchase decisions. Furthermore, in today's highly competitive marketplace, a distinctive brand image is very difficult to create and maintain. For example, the BlackBerry has been a highly successful product and dominated the market, and was probably the first smartphone introduced. However, consumers perceive many newer smartphones as being more fun and exciting than the BlackBerry, which they perceive as mainly suitable for business and not for personal use and multitasking. Clearly, if it is to remain a viable competitor in the smartphone market, BlackBerry must broaden its appeal.[43]

Take, for example, the chore of washing clothes, where the consumer's need is straightforward: To end up with clean clothes. However, the manner in which this need is fulfilled and the clothes are cleaned differs among brands' competitive claims. The *manner* of bringing about the clean clothes (i.e., fulfilling a need) is the brand's claimed benefit. The more unique the benefit and the way it is communicated to consumers, the more likely it is that the perceived image will differentiate the brand from its competitors. A unique perceived image leads to brand loyalty, where consumers buy the brand consistently and neither try nor switch to other brands. Table 4.2 lists the benefit claims and intended perceived images of several detergent brands.[44]

Occasionally, a brand's image must be updated. Consumers often view products that have been around for a long time as boring, especially when newer alternatives are introduced. Sweet'N Low pioneered the artificial sweeteners category, but in recent years had to compete with newer products. The ads in Figure 4.15 show how Sweet'N Low uses pink—the color by which it is widely recognized—to convey a more playful and artistic image. Other examples of brand image updates, focused on creating emotional bonds between the products and consumers, are described in Table 4.3.[45]

TABLE 4.2 Benefit Claims of Detergent Brands

BRAND	BENEFIT	BENEFIT CLAIM
Ecos	Environmentally friendly	Made by Earth Friendly Products and provides power-packed clean without toxins, petrochemicals, bleach, ammonia, phosphates or other harmful ingredients.
Caldrea	Sweet Pea Detergent	Mild but highly effective in removing stains and especially formulated for washing the clothes of babies and children. Tested by dermatologists and includes oils and surfactants derived from plants.
Cheer	Protects against wear and tear	One of the numerous detergent brands made by P&G. Protects against fading, color transfer, and fabric wear. Comes in powder or liquid and with or without bleach.
Ivory Snow	Mild and pure	Also a P&G brand. Provides mild cleansing and purity for a simple clean.
Tide	"Fabric cleaning and care at its best"	The best-selling detergent in the United States and also a P&G brand. The benefit offered is an "umbrella position" (see Chapter 2) within which P&G developed more than 30 versions of Tide, each with a unique benefit. For example, Ultra Tide with Bleach (an alternative to chlorine bleach), Tide Downy (with a touch of softness and freshness), and Tide Free ("No dyes. No perfumes. No worries").

TABLE 4.3 Brand Image Updates Designed to Create Emotional Bonds between Brands and Consumers

BRAND	THEME	ADVERTISING CAMPAIGN
Dell Computer	"More You"	Focused on personalizing technology and getting consumers to think about how they can use the products' features rather than focusing on the products' technical specifications.
StarKist Tuna	"Sorry, Charlie" (reworked)	Reworks the brand's vintage "Sorry, Charlie" slogan. Some refer to ads based on nostalgia as "comfort marketing"—an approach whose objective is to evoke fond memories of mascots and songs.
Quaker Oats	"Go humans, go"	Reflects Americans' optimism and determination to explore new frontiers. It hails the pursuit of dreams and aims at lifting consumers' spirits, and is also articulated in Quaker Oats commercials where the announcer proclaims: "The power of Quaker is in everything we make."
Lay's Potato Chips	"Happiness is simple"	Features actual farmers who grow potatoes used to make the chips. They appear genuine, simple, and plain-spoken. The idea is to get consumers to think of Lay's as a food rather than a snack. The campaign's theme is "Happiness is simple," and the website features a "Happiness Exhibit."
Google	Nostalgia, engaging consumers in technology	Employs classic TV commercials from the 1960s and 70s. It demonstrates how Web ads can be engaging and stir the soul rather than being strictly transactional and informative. For example, a classic 1972 "Hilltop" spot for Coke featured a chorus singing "buy the world a Coke and keep it company." The Google ad asks consumers to send free Cokes around the world to people they have never met through mobile applications and customized vending machines.

(*Continued*)

TABLE 4.3 *(Continued)*

BRAND	THEME	ADVERTISING CAMPAIGN
Mott's Apple Juice	"Words to grow by"	Aimed at mothers of children aged 6 and younger and focused on joining them together. The mothers are invited to share their thoughts on raising a family in a dedicated Web site.
Colonial Williamsburg	"Be part of the story"	The campaign is for an attraction that recreates life in 18th-century Virginia; it is focused on "engagement interaction" and seeks to establish an active role for visitors.

Sources: Mark Hachman, "Dell's 'More You' Ads Mean a Renewed Consumer Push," 7.5.11 online.wsj.com; Stuart Elliott, "Google Remixes Old Campaigns, Adding a Dash of Digital Tools," 3.8.12 nytimes.com; Stuart Elliott, "In New Ads, Stirring Memories of Commercials Past," 1.12.12 nytimes.com; Stuart Elliott, "Sit Under the Apple Tree With Me, Juice Brand Asks," 6.7.10 nytimes.com Stuart Elliott, "Promoting a Potato Chip Using Many Farmers, and Less Salt," May 25, 2010, nytimes.com; Stuart Elliott, "So, Virginia, What's the Story," nytimes.com February 1, 2010.

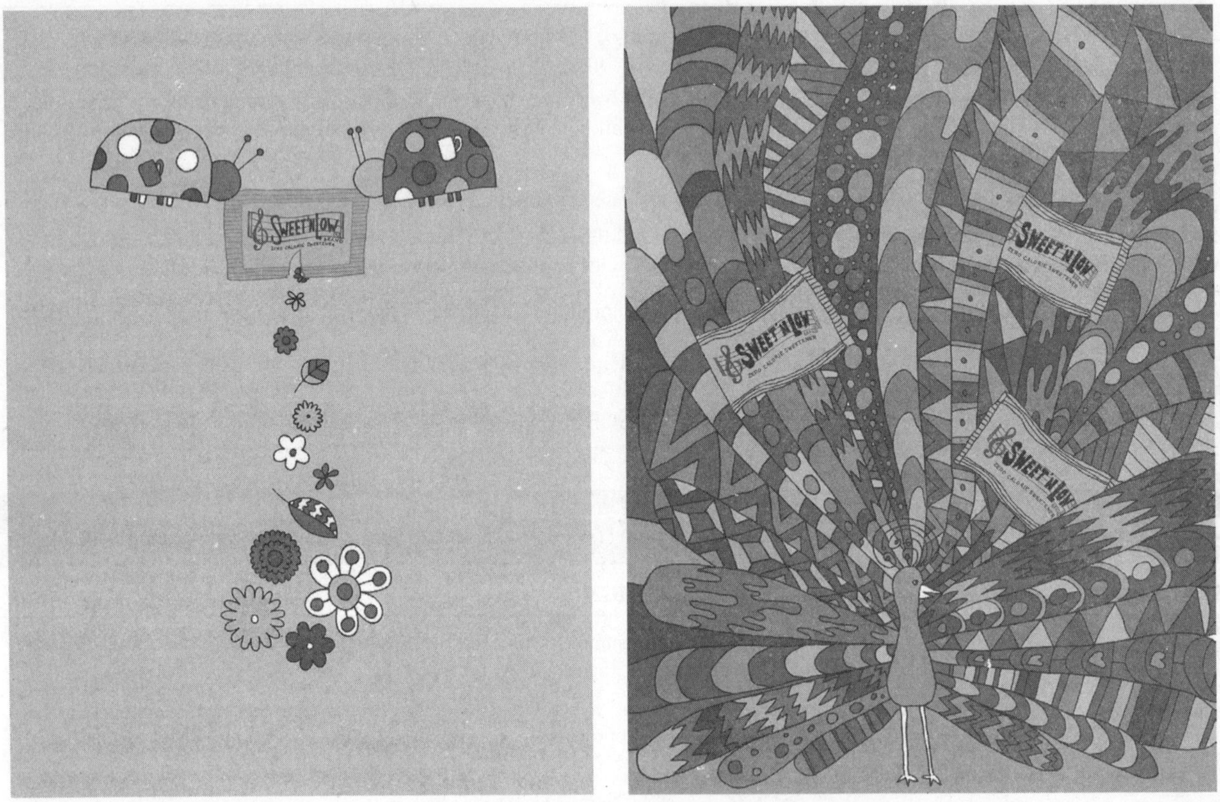

Source: (Left & Right) Cumberland Packing Corporation

FIGURE 4.15 Sweet'N Low's More "Playful" Package Conveys More Fun and a Livelier Image

Box 4.8 Social Media and Brand Perception

Linkages with social media can change the perception of a brand among consumers. Godrej introduced a 3D online environment with online games. Intention to purchase the brand among those who had not heard of the brand went up by 17% and by 35% among those who had heard about it.[46] Fastrack introduced a 50% discount on a Sunday between three to four p.m. to mark its one million likes on its Facebook page and achieved a sale of ₹2.75 crores.[47] In Fastrack's case, such a sales promotion reinforces its "young, trendy, and urban" image.

Package Image

In addition to the product's name, appearance, and features, packaging also conveys the brand's image. For example, the Tide detergent version that predominantly promises stain removal comes in an orange plastic container with a large handle on its side and conveys the "heaviness" of the product, because consumers associate heaviness with the power to remove stains. In contrast, the New Tide Total Care products, which promise scents of fresh morning, rain, and spring days, come in slimmer, slicker packages in brighter shades of orange than the regular Tide, and the handle is angled and congruent with the more sophisticated benefit claim [illegible]his version of Tide. The container of the Ivory Snow detergent is white, round, and without a handle; this implies that th[illegible]gent should be squeezed into the washer, thus supporting the "gentle cleanliness" claim of this brand.

The perception of scent and the associations made with different aromas vary greatly among individuals. For this reason, it is extremely difficult to convey an "image" of a fragrance. To buyers of perfumes, the only tangible evidence of the product's nature and quality is the packaging, the cost of which often accounts for up to 50% of the total cost of the perfume. A study identified several holistic (or Gestalt) designs of packages, each conveying a distinct, prominent brand impression. For each package type, the study also identified the brand personality features that consumers associate with it. Generic images of the package types and the corresponding perceptions appear in Figure 4.16.[48]

Service Image

Compared with manufacturing firms, service marketers face several unique problems in positioning and promoting their offerings. Because services are intangible, image becomes a key factor in differentiating a service from its competition. Thus, the marketing objective is to enable the consumer to link a specific image with a specific brand name. Many service marketers have developed strategies to provide customers with visual images and tangible reminders of their service offerings. These include delivery vehicles painted in distinct colors, restaurant matchbooks, packaged hotel soaps and shampoos, and a variety of other specialty items. Many service companies feature real service employees in their ads (as tangible cues) and use people-focused themes to differentiate themselves.

PACKAGE	MASSIVE	CONTRASTING	NATURAL	DELICATE	NONDESCRIPT
Shape	a 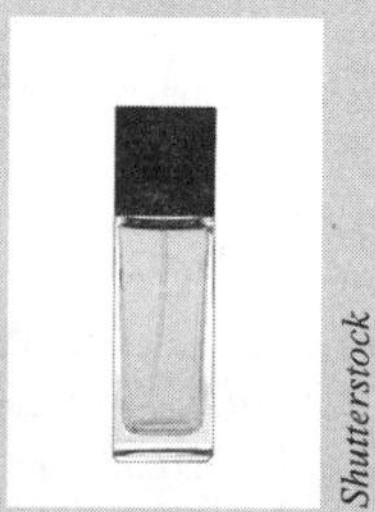	b 	c 	d 	e 
Perceived as	Robust and unelaborative	Nonharmonious and irregular	Harmonious and archetypical	Muted, sleek, delicate, elaborate, and attention-getting	Simple, clean, discreet, undifferentiable from others
Characteristics	Unexciting, unsophisticated but rugged (i.e., strong, robust)	Exciting and rugged but lacking in the necessary ability (i.e., competence)	Sincere and sophisticated	Competent and sophisticated but not rugged	Low sincerity, unexciting and not robust

Source: U.R. Orth and K. Malkewitz, "Holistic Package Designs..." *Journal of Marketing* 72 (May 2008): 64–81.

FIGURE 4.16 Perceptions of Perfume Bottles

The design of the service environment is an important aspect of service positioning strategy, and sharply influences consumer impressions. For example, targeting the dynamic and technologically oriented Generation Y, many stores significantly increased the sensory stimuli provided within the store, including live DJs, dim lighting, scented environments, loud ultra-modern music, flat-screen TVs, and live models. Some Apple stores are open 24 hours and are designed to keep Apple users there even if they are not buying products. Thus, the stores include long tables and chairs with electrical outlets and wireless online access so that Apple users can work on their own projects and also interact with other users. One study indicated that the arousal level within the store environment must match the expectations of the shoppers in order to avoid perceived over- or understimulation.[49]

Perceived Price

Perceived price is the customer's view of the value that he or she receives from the purchase. For example, consumers generally perceive a low price for a meal at a fast-food outlet, as well as a high price for a meal at a gourmet restaurant, as consistent with the value that they receive in both instances and therefore as fair. However, many reasonable consumers may argue that paying about $500 per person for a meal (there are several restaurants in New York City that charge these prices, and the meals do not include wine or alcohol) is unreasonable, because they cannot see how *any* meal can be equivalent to the value of $500.

How a consumer perceives a price—as high, low, or fair—strongly influences both purchase intentions and post-purchase satisfaction. Consider the perception of price fairness, for example. Customers often pay attention to the prices paid by other customers (such as senior citizens, frequent flyers, affinity club members), and sometimes perceive such differential pricing as unfair. No one is happy knowing he or she paid more (sometimes much more) for an airline ticket or a movie ticket than the person in the next seat. Perceptions of price unfairness affect consumers' perceptions of product value and, ultimately, their willingness to patronize a store or a service. Researchers also discovered that perceived price fairness affects customer satisfaction; this indicates that marketers using differential prices must anticipate customers' potential feelings of being exploited.[50]

Products advertised as "on sale" tend to create enhanced customer perceptions of savings and value. Different formats used in sales advertisements have differing impacts, based on consumers' reference prices. A **reference price** is any price that a consumer uses as a basis for comparison in judging another price. Reference prices can be external or internal. An advertiser generally uses a higher *external* reference price ("sold elsewhere at . . .") in an ad offering a lower sales price, to persuade the consumer that the product advertised is a really good buy. *Internal* reference prices are those prices (or price ranges) retrieved by the consumer from memory. Internal reference prices play a major role in consumers' evaluations and perceptions of value of an advertised price deal, as well as in the believability of any advertised reference price. However, consumers' internal reference prices change. For example, as the prices of flat-screen TVs declined sharply due to competition and manufacturers' abilities to produce them more cheaply, consumers' reference prices for this product have declined as well, and they no longer perceive flat-screen TVs as a luxury product that only a few can afford.

The issue of reference prices is complex and the focus of many studies. For example, one study discovered that fair price, rather than expected price, determined consumers' reference price for a new product category, whereas expected price had more impact than fair price on reference prices for existing product categories.[51] Another study showed that reference pricing coupled with limited-time availability (e.g., regularly $599, now $359 and on sale, 3 days only) produced more favorable price and store perceptions than each technique used alone.[52] Still another study illustrated the "right side effect" in relation to consumers' perceptions of discounts. When consumers saw regular and sale prices with the same left digits (e.g., 23 and 22), they perceived larger discounts when the right digits were smaller than 5 than when the right digits were higher than 5. Thus, consumers may perceive a discount from $23 to $22 as providing more value than a discount from $19 to $18.[53] Another study demonstrated that price discounts immediately increased buying intentions and lowered consumers' future reference prices.[54] Generally, a discount of $10 is more appealing on a product whose regular price is $20 than on a product whose regular price is $60. One study discovered that when consumers thought of their reference prices, a $10 discount sometimes seemed less appealing when the price was $20 than when it was $60.[55] These studies illustrate that marketers must be cautious when raising prices and always consider consumers' reference points when they do so.

Naturally, consumers tend to believe that the selling prices of market offerings are considerably higher than their perceived fair prices. When an advertised reference price is within a given consumer's acceptable price range, it is considered plausible and credible. If the advertised reference point is outside the range of acceptable prices (i.e., implausible), it contrasts with existing attitudes and will not be perceived as a valid reference point, thus adversely affecting both consumer evaluations and the advertiser's credibility. When consumers encounter prices that are significantly different from their expectations, they feel inharmonious (i.e., dissonant) and engage in "dissonance reduction" (see Chapter 6). They seek additional information, form cognitions

TABLE 4.4 Consumer Reactions to Unexpected Prices

CONSUMER ENCOUNTERS WITH UNEXPECTED PRICES

↓

CONSUMERS REDUCE DISSONANCE USING ONE OF THE FOLLOWING MODES

SEEKING CONSONANT INFORMATION	**CHANGING ATTITUDE**	**TRIVIALIZING**
↓	↓	↓
Evaluate alternative suppliers Evaluate substitute products Plan to search for additional information Seek consonant information from another retailer or a substitute product (or) remain dissonant	Update Price Expectations ↓ Attribute higher prices to: 1. product quality 2. updated product information 3. product attributes 4. general rising prices	Reduce the importance of: 1. money 2. shop around savings 3. saving money 4. a good deal 5. fair pricing 6. value
↓	↓	↓
Change attitude, trivialize or remain dissonant	Dissonance is reduced	Dissonance is reduced

Source: J. Lindsey-Mulliken "Beyond Reference Price..." *Journal of Product and Brand Management* 12 nos. 2/3 (2003): 141. Emerald Publishing Group

that justify the high price, then consider buying other brands or trivialize some aspects of the buying situation. Table 4.4 explains how consumers handle dissonant situations caused by unexpectedly high prices.[56]

Learning Objective

6 To understand how consumers determine the quality of products and services.

Perceived Quality

Products and services can deliver high quality factually, as determined, say, by experts' judgments of scientific tests. However, if consumers do not perceive offerings as superior products that satisfy their needs and provide value, they will not purchase them, regardless of objective evidence. The perceived quality of products and services is based on a variety of informational cues that consumers associate with the offerings. Some of these cues are intrinsic to the product or service; others are extrinsic. Either singly or together, such cues provide the basis for perceptions of product and service quality. In this section, we first discuss the issues that make evaluating the quality of services more difficult than evaluating the quality of products. We then examine other cues that consumers consider in evaluating quality, including the product's price, its manufacturer, and the store selling it.

Product Quality

Intrinsic cues are physical characteristics of the product itself, such as size, color, flavor, or aroma. In some cases, consumers use physical characteristics (e.g., the flavor of ice cream or cake) to judge product quality. Consumers like to believe that they base their evaluations of product quality on intrinsic cues, because that enables them to justify their product decisions (either positive or negative) as being "rational" or "objective" choices. For example, the package of Hillshire Farm sliced meat was redesigned after studies showed that consumers want to see the meat and care a lot about how it looks. The new package has a transparent window showing the product. It also has a shallower tub, because consumers perceive neatly fanned-out meat in containers as being of higher quality.[57]

More often than not, however, consumers use **extrinsic cues**—that is, characteristics that are not inherent in the product—to judge quality. For example, though many consumers claim they buy a brand because of its superior taste, they are often unable to identify that brand in blind taste tests. The colors of such products as powdered fruit drinks and orange juice are a more important determinant than their labels and actual taste in determining the consumer's ability to identify the flavor correctly. For example, subjects are likely to view purple or grape-colored drinks as "tart" in flavor, and the orange-colored version as "flavorful, sweet, and refreshing." Many studies have shown that the packaging influences consumers' perceptions of products. For example, a study reported that both consumers who rated popcorn's taste as unfavorable and those who rated the same taste as favorable consumed more of the product when the container size was increased.[58] A study that compared how consumers perceive store brands and national brands discovered that consumers used extrinsic cues as indicators of quality.[59] An experimental study of how people judge the quality of two foods—shrimp and cheese—at two price levels and two consumption situations (i.e., elegant and less elegant surroundings) found out that perceived price had a positive impact on perceived quality among highly involved consumers. In addition, elegant surroundings positively affected the subjects' perceived quality of the foods and the pleasure felt when eating them.[60]

In the absence of actual experience with a product, consumers often evaluate quality on the basis of cues that are external to the product itself, such as price, brand image, manufacturer's image, retail store image, or even the perceived country of origin. For example, Häagen-Dazs, an American-made ice cream, has been incredibly successful with its made-up (and meaningless) Scandinavian-sounding name. The success of Smirnoff vodka, made in Connecticut, can be related to its apparent Russian derivation. One study found that the wine region was the most important determinant of consumers' perceived quality of wines and that Napa Valley and Sonoma had the strongest regional images among American vineyards.[61]

Service Quality

It is more difficult for consumers to evaluate the quality of services than the quality of products. This is true because of certain distinctive characteristics of services: They are *intangible*, they are *variable*, they are *perishable*, and they are *simultaneously produced and consumed*. To overcome the fact that consumers are unable to compare competing services side-by-side as they do with competing products, consumers rely on surrogate cues (i.e., extrinsic cues) to evaluate service quality. In evaluating a doctor's services, for example, they note the quality of the office and examining room furnishings, the number (and source) of framed degrees on the wall, the pleasantness of the receptionist, and the professionalism of the nurse; all contribute to the consumer's overall evaluation of the quality of a doctor's services. One study found that online dating services generally fail to meet users' expectations because potential daters want to screen prospective partners by "experiential" attributes (e.g., rapport) whereas online dating providers only enable users to screen by "searchable" attributes (e.g., income). The study also found that using "virtual dates" (thus providing a tangible cue about the service) increased users' satisfaction with the online dating service.[62]

Because the actual quality of services can vary from day to day, from service employee to service employee, and from customer to customer (e.g., in food, in waitperson service, in haircuts, even in classes taught by the same professor), marketers try to standardize their services in order to provide consistency of quality. The downside of service standardization is the loss of customized services, which many consumers value.

Unlike products, which are first produced, secondly sold, and subsequently consumed, most services are first sold and then produced and consumed simultaneously. Whereas a defective product is likely to be detected by factory quality control inspectors before it ever reaches the consumer, an inferior service is consumed as it is being produced; thus, there is little opportunity to correct it. For example, a defective haircut is difficult to correct, just as is the negative impression caused by an abrupt or careless waiter.

During peak demand hours, the interactive quality of services often declines, because both the customer and the service provider are hurried and under stress. Without special effort by the service provider to ensure consistency of services during peak hours, service image is likely to decline. Many marketers try to change demand patterns in order to distribute the service more equally over time. For example, some restaurants offer significantly less expensive "early bird" dinners for consumers who come in before 7:00 p.m.

The most widely accepted framework for researching service quality stems from the premise that a consumer's evaluation of service quality is a function of the magnitude and direction of the gap between the customer's *expectations of service* and the customer's *assessment (perception) of the service* actually delivered.[63] For example, a brand-new graduate student enrolled in an introductory marketing course at a highly reputable university has certain expectations about the intellectual abilities of her classmates, the richness of classroom discussions, and the professor's knowledge and communication skills. At the end of the term, her assessment of the course's quality will be based on the differences between her expectations at the start of the term and her perceptions of the course at the end of the semester. If the course falls below her expectations, she will view it as a service of poor quality. If her expectations are exceeded, she will view the course as a high-quality educational experience.

The expectations of a given service vary widely among different consumers of the same service. These expectations stem from word-of-mouth consumers have heard about the service, consumers' past experiences, the promises made about the service in its ads and by its salespersons, the purchase alternatives available, and other situational factors. If the level of service received significantly exceeds these expectations, the service is perceived as of high quality and generates more customer satisfaction, increased probability of repeat patronage, and favorable word of mouth.[64] Also, marketers should never make promises that they cannot realistically deliver, because such claims raise customers' expectations and significantly increase the likelihood of lower perceived service quality when the service delivered is good, but not outstanding.

The **SERVQUAL scale** measures the "gaps" between customers' *expectations* of the services that they had purchased and their *perceptions* of the services that they had actually *received.* Measuring these discrepancies (or "gaps") includes two factors:

1. **Outcomes**, which focus on whether or not the services purchased were delivered *reliably.* For example, did a flight you took deliver you to your destination?
2. **Processes**, which focus on *how* the core services were delivered. That is employees' responsiveness, assurance, and empathy in handling customers. For example, how polite and understanding were the airlines' people if, say, your flight was delayed and you came close to missing a connection?

The processes enable service companies to exceed, not merely meet, customers' expectations. For instance, Amazon's core service (its "outcome dimension") is selling many types of products and brands. However, Amazon's advantage over competition is exceeding customers' expectations through superior "processes," which consists of its E-book readers and instant and reliable delivery of e-books, advanced database that generates recommendations for customers, shipment tracking system, the ability to preorder books yet to be published months in advance, subscriptions that include unlimited deliveries without shipping fees, and many other options.

Price/Quality Relationship

Look at the six polo shirts in Figure 4.17. Which two are the most expensive? Write their numbers down. Next, look at endnote 48 for this chapter (the chapter endnotes begin at the end of the text) and write down the names of the stores and designers of the shirts you selected, but do not look at the information for the other shirts.[65] Now, look at the two

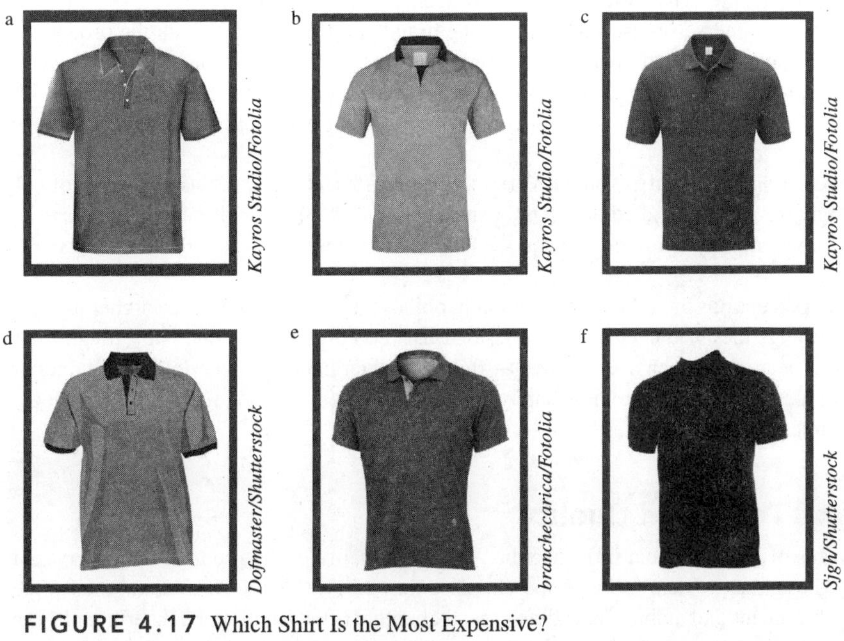

FIGURE 4.17 Which Shirt Is the Most Expensive?

shirts again and decide whether you still believe they are the most expensive. Then, pick two other shirts and repeat this exercise.

Let's assume that you picked shirts 2 and 3 as the most expensive. After looking at the endnote, you discovered that shirt 2 sells at Macy's and was designed by Polonimo, and shirt 3 sells at Camicia—a fashionable store in New York City's Soho area—and was designed by Bertoliani. You now have three pieces of information (i.e., sensory input): The shirts' photos, the stores that carry them, and their designers' names. Thinking of Camicia, you are likely to mentally "group" (associate) it with other fashionable stores in Soho, and the name Bertoliani probably evokes images of fashionably dressed, perfectly groomed, and athletic Italian men drinking espresso in Rome—the ones you saw featured in countless ads. You now decide that shirt 3 is the most expensive and also the most fashionable. However, your fellow classmate—who also picked shirts 2 and 3 initially—believes that the Polonimo shirt sold at Macy's is the most expensive.

You first saw only the photos of the shirts (sensory input), without any additional information. Then, the information about the stores and designers (more sensory input) determined how you "saw" the shirts in your mind. Your mental image of the shirts you had selected—was your subjective interpretation of the three pieces of visual and written sensory input. Unsurprisingly, your classmate's interpretation of the same information was different. After you study this chapter, you will realize why and how what you just experienced happened, and the key role of perception in consumer behavior. The answer to the question "which shirt is the most expensive?" is listed in endnote 66.[66]

Perceived product value has been described as a trade-off between the product's perceived benefits (or quality) and the perceived sacrifice— monetary and nonmonetary—necessary to acquire it. A **price/quality relationship** forms when consumers rely on price as an indicator of product quality; in short, they believe more expensive products are better. Some consumers who decide according to a price/quality relationship are actually relying on a well-known (and, hence, more expensive) brand name as an indicator of quality without actually relying directly on price per se. Because price is so often an indicator of quality, some product advertisements deliberately emphasize a high price to underscore the marketers' claims of quality. Marketers understand that, at times, products with lower prices may be interpreted as lesser quality. At the same time, consumers rely on the price and brand name when evaluating the product's prestige and symbolic value and use more concrete attributes of a product, such as performance and durability, to judge its overall performance. For these reasons, marketers must understand all the attributes that customers use to evaluate a given product and include all applicable information to counter any perceptions of negative quality associated with a lower price. In one study, subjects rated the pain in their wrist, artificially caused by an electric shock, after taking a pain reliever, which was actually a dummy, placebo pill. Half the subjects were told that the medication they took costs $2.50 per dose, and the others learned that it costs 10 cents; in reality, all subjects received identical pills. Eighty-five percent of those who received the more expensive pill reported significant pain reduction, whereas only 61% of those who took the cheaper pill reported such relief. Clearly, consumers tend to believe that more expensive medications are more effective; this finding is consistent with previous research showing that consumers perceive generic drugs to be less effective than brand name medications, even though, chemically, the two medications are identical.[67]

In addition to price, consumers also use such cues as the brand and the store in which the product is bought to evaluate its quality. They view price as an indicator of quality if they have little information to go on, or if they have little confidence in their own ability to make the product or service choice on other grounds. When the consumer is familiar with a brand name, or has experience with a product (or service), or the store where it is purchased, price declines as a determining factor in product evaluation and purchase.

Many products and services are sold as "bundles" (e.g., sets of different pens, tickets to a series of ballet performances), and price discounts lead to more sales of bundled products. A study showed that bundle discounts may have unforeseen results in the form of perceptions of lower quality of all the items in the bundle, which will negatively affect future sales when these items are sold individually.[68]

Some price/quality perceptions are related to personal happiness. In one study, the researcher asked readers of a blog to list the 10 most expensive things they had ever bought, and then list the 10 purchases that had brought them the most happiness. Some products—such as boats and expensive weddings—did not deliver happiness per dollar. Still, there was considerable overlap between the most-expensive list and the most-happy list. Many people included their homes, college educations, vacations, and high-priced electronics in both lists.[69]

Store Image and Perceived Quality

Retail stores have images of their own that influence the perceived quality of the products they carry and consumers' decisions about where to shop. These images stem from the merchandise they carry, the brands sold and their prices, the level of service, the store's physical environment and ambiance, and its typical clientele (this can often be determined from the cars parked in the store's parking lot). One study demonstrated that consumers who have a strong positive image of a store did not find negative word-of-mouth about that store credible.[70]

The width and type of product assortment affect retail store image. Grocery retailers, for example, are often reluctant to reduce the number of products they carry out of concern that perceptions of a smaller assortment will reduce the likelihood that consumers will shop in their stores; they carry primarily widely advertised, best-selling brands. In contrast, Whole Foods Markets—a relatively small supermarket chain—has carved itself a profitable niche by carrying a smaller but highly selective range of products in comparison to conventional supermarkets. Whole Foods stores carry organic (perceived as healthier) products, many of which were bought from mom-and-pop producers; all food products carried are screened for artificial ingredients; and the chain no longer sells products with hydrogenated fats. The chain has been much more profitable than conventional supermarkets in spite of its limited product assortment. Clearly, the unique benefit that a store provides is more important than the number of items it carries in forming a favorable store image in consumers' minds. However, because Whole Food's prices are significantly higher than those of other supermarkets, the chain's nickname has become "Whole Paycheck" and made it rough for the company to attract new consumer segments. The company has been planning to open smaller stores carrying less expensive products, but it must first rid itself of its top-dollar reputation, which, unfortunately, has coined a catchy slogan.[71]

Customers often use brand, store image, and price together as a product quality indicators. When brand and retailer images become associated, the less favorable image becomes enhanced at the expense of the more favorable image. Thus, when a low-priced store carries a brand with a high-priced image, the image of the store will improve, whereas the image of the brand will be adversely affected. For that reason, marketers of prestigious designer goods often attempt to control the outlets where their products are sold. When upscale stores sell leftover expensive items to discount stores, they remove the designer labels from these goods as part of the agreements they have with the manufacturers.

Pricing discounts also affect store image. Stores that offer frequent, small discounts on large numbers of items are more likely to be perceived as "discount stores" and less prestigious than stores offering larger discounts on a smaller number of products. This has important implications for retailers' positioning strategies. In times of heavy competition, when it is tempting to hold frequent large sales covering many items, such strategies may result in an unwanted change in store image. For example, Lord and Taylor in New York City, formerly positioned as an upscale, high-class department store, advertises sales so frequently and so often fills its aisles with racks proclaiming bargain prices, that its upscale image has been tarnished, and its customer mix has changed. Marketers must also consider how price reductions of specific products affect consumers' perceptions. Poorly chosen price promotions cause confusion and may detract from consumers' perceptions of the store.

Manufacturer's Image and Perceived Quality

Consumer imagery extends beyond perceived price and store image. Manufacturers who enjoy a favorable image generally find that their new products are accepted more readily than those of manufacturers who have a less favorable or even a "neutral" image. Consumers also associate certain attributes with manufacturers. For example, Apple is perceived as "different" from other computers and smartphones. A Swatch is perceived as commonplace and inexpensive, whereas watches made by Rolex and Patek Philippe are perceived as expensive status symbols.

Institutional advertising is promotion that is designed to promote a company's overall image without overtly referring to specific products. For example, an ad for Siemens—a global conglomerate—used the slogan "The world of tomorrow needs answers that last" and featured energy-producing windmills placed in the open seas. The ad positioned the company as innovative, forward looking, and socially responsible, a corporate image that is likely to be strategically beneficial. For example, if residents of American communities located directly on the ocean perceive Siemens favorably, they would not mind seeing Siemens windmills from their homes, and would not object to them , whereas persons with neutral or unfavorable attitudes towards companies that "invade" their communities might object to and even prevent the placing of the windmills.

Although some marketers argue that product and service advertising do more to boost the corporate image than institutional advertising does, others see both types of advertising—product and institutional—as integral and complementary components of a total corporate communications program. When the reputation of Walmart was tarnished by allegations of unfair labor practices, sexual discrimination, and the publication of data indicating that the company caused most of America's trade imbalance with China, the company published ads stating that "Walmart Is Working for Everyone." In addition, the company's executives appeared on TV talk shows and met with community groups and government officials to dispel the negative associations.[72] Wal-Mart's troubles continued when a consumer advocacy group initiated an ad campaign that posed the question "Where would Jesus shop?" and argued that people of faith should not shop at the store during the holiday season because of the store's bad wages, benefits, and overseas child labor policies. This negative advertising also illustrates using Jesus' "halo effect"—a term discussed earlier.[73]

In Chapter 2 and within the discussion of repositioning, we discussed how banks' advertising triggered irresponsible consumer spending, which contributed to the financial calamity of 2008. Since then, many banks have been running ads that portray them as "warm" and "cozy" corporations. Examples of advertising slogans designed to convey this image include "where bankin's (*sic*) funner (*sic*)," "a better kind of bank," and "we make money with you, not off you."[74] Also, viral messages online can severely, negatively, and almost instantly affect a company's image. For example, Progressive Corporation—an auto-insurance company—sided with a driver who killed another driver whom they had insured, when the deceased driver's family sued the other driver for negligence. Progressive did so to avoid paying $75,000 to the family of the dead driver. One family member then described, in a blog, how Progressive sided with the killer of a person insured by them. The message "went viral" all over the Internet and generated a lot of angry comments against Progressive, as well as threats by many of its customers to cancel their insurance.[75]

Learning Objective

7 To understand consumers' perceived risks and how they handle and reduce those risks.

Perceived Risk

Consumers must constantly make decisions regarding what products or services to buy and where to buy them. **Perceived risk** is the uncertainty that consumers face when they cannot foresee the consequences of their purchase decisions. This definition highlights two relevant dimensions of perceived risk: uncertainty and consequences.

The degree of risk that consumers perceive and their own tolerance for risk taking are factors that influence their purchase strategies. It should be stressed that consumers are influenced by risks that they perceive, whether or not such risks actually exist. Risk that is not perceived—no matter how real or how dangerous—will not influence consumer behavior. The perception of risk is also a function of how the information is presented. For instance, one study discovered that, in evaluating prescription drugs, consumers greatly overestimated the actual likelihood of adverse events when these were described with words such as "common" or "rare." However, when the commercials induced positive moods, consumers engaged in more nuanced evaluation of product risk information and used it in judging the efficacy and other attributes of the products.[76]

In most situations, consumers' perceived risk is a function of multiple factors. The elements of perceived risk are functional risk, physical risk, financial risk, social risk, psychological risk, and time risk, which are listed and explained in Table 4.5.

Perceived Risk Varies

Consumer perception of risk varies, depending on the person, the product, the situation, and the culture. The amount of risk perceived depends on the specific consumer. Some consumers tend to perceive high degrees of risk in various consumption situations; others tend to perceive little risk. For example, adolescents who engage in high-risk activities, such as fast, complicated, and daring rollerblading or bicycling maneuvers, obviously perceived lower risk than those who do not engage in such high-risk activities. High-risk perceivers are often described as **narrow categorizers** because they limit their choices (e.g., product choices) to a few safe alternatives. They would rather exclude some perfectly good alternatives than chance a poor selection. Low-risk perceivers have been described as **broad categorizers** because they tend to make their choices from a much wider range of alternatives. They would rather risk a poor selection than limit the number of alternatives from which they can choose.

An individual's perception of risk varies with product categories. For example, consumers are likely to perceive a high degree of risk (e.g., functional risk, financial risk, time risk) in the purchase of a LED TV set because it is a very new and, so far, "unproven" product in terms of its superiority over HD TVs.

The degree of risk a consumer perceives is also affected by the shopping situation. At first, many consumers felt uncertain about buying products online. The market dominance that online merchants gained over the years indicates that, because of positive shopping experiences and word-of-mouth, consumers now perceive little risk in online shopping. Obviously, this lower level of perceived risk is due to better technologies that enable buyers to examine the product online in greater detail and even "use" some products virtually. One study of online banking demonstrated that most consumers want to use online payments (mostly to meet deadlines and avoid past-due late penalties), but their willingness or unwillingness to do so is a function of their perceived risk of the security of online payment systems.[77] Studies also found that higher levels of consumer trust reduced perceived risk regarding shopping online.[78] Two studies discovered that the amount of product information posted on websites affects consumer risk perception and satisfaction, as well as the relationships among perceived risk, satisfaction, intention to revisit, purchase intent, and the process of the decision making itself.[79]

TABLE 4.5 The Elements of Perceived Risk

TYPE OF PERCEIVED RISK	DEFINITION	EXAMPLE
Functional risk	Product will not perform as expected.	Can the E-book reader operate a whole day without having to be recharged?
Physical risk	Product can harm self and others; risk to self and others.	Is organic unpasteurized milk safe to drink? (Many states do not permit unpasteurized milk, but many greenmarkets carry it because it is organic.)
Financial risk	Product will not be worth its cost.	Will a new and cheaper model of an LED TV monitor become available six months from now?
Psychological risk	Poor product choice will bruise the consumer's ego.	Will I be embarrassed when my friends see me with a mobile phone that is not a smartphone?
Time risk	Time spent in product search may be wasted if the product does not perform as expected.	Will I be forced to compare all the different carriers' calling plans again if I experience a lot of "dropped calls" with the one I selected?

Consumers handle perceived risk differently, and the prominent ways to reduce purchase-related risk are summarized in Table 4.6.

The concept of perceived risk has major implications for the introduction of new products. Because high-risk perceivers are less likely than low-risk perceivers to purchase new or innovative products, it is important for marketers to provide such consumers with persuasive risk-reduction strategies, such as a well-known brand name (sometimes through licensing), distribution through reputable retail outlets, informative advertising, publicity, impartial test results, free samples, and money-back guarantees. Also, consumers can reduce perceived risk by using online resources that enable them to generate side-by-side comparisons depicting detailed charts of the features, prices, and ratings of all the available models within a given product category.

TABLE 4.6 Consumers Can Reduce Perceived Risk

METHOD	DESCRIPTION
Seek information	Consumers seek information about the product and product category through word-of-mouth communication (from friends and family and from other people whose opinions they value), from salespeople, and from the general media. They spend more time thinking about their choice and search for more information about the product alternatives when they associate a high degree of risk with the purchase.
Remain brand loyal	Consumers avoid risk by remaining loyal to a brand with which they have been satisfied instead of purchasing new or untried brands. High-risk perceivers are more likely to be loyal to their old brands and less likely to purchase newly introduced products.
Rely on brand image	When consumers have had no experience with a product, they tend to "trust" a favored or well-known brand name. They often think well-known brands are better and are worth buying for the implied assurance of quality, dependability, performance, and service.
Rely on store image	If consumers have no other information about a product, they often trust the judgment of the merchandise buyers of a reputable store and depend on them to have made careful decisions in selecting products for sale. Store image also provides assurance of return privileges and adjustment in case of dissatisfaction.
Buy the most expensive model or brand	As indicated in the discussion of price/quality relationship, consumers often feel that the most expensive model is probably the best in terms of quality.

Summary

Learning Objective 1: To understand the elements of perception and their role in consumer behavior.

Perception is the process by which individuals select, organize, and interpret stimuli into a meaningful and coherent picture of the world. Perception has strategy implications for marketers because consumers make decisions based on what they perceive rather than on the basis of objective reality. The lowest level at which an individual can perceive a specific stimulus is that person's absolute threshold. The minimal difference that can be perceived between two stimuli is called the differential threshold or just noticeable difference (JND). Consumers perceive most sensory stimuli above the level of their conscious awareness; however, weak stimuli can be perceived below the level of conscious awareness (i.e., subliminally). Research refutes the notion that subliminal stimuli influence consumers' buying decisions.

Learning Objective 2: To understand why consumers process only a small amount of the information they receive.

Consumers' selections of stimuli from the environment are based on the interaction of their expectations and motives with the stimulus itself. People usually perceive things they need or want, and block the perception of unnecessary, unfavorable, or painful stimuli. The principles of selective perception include the concepts of selective exposure, selective attention, and perceptual defense. Which stimuli get selected depends on two major factors, in addition to the nature of the stimulus itself: (1) consumers' previous experience as it affects their expectations (what they are prepared, or "set," to see), and (2) their motives at the time (their needs, desires, interests, and so on). Each of these factors can increase or decrease the probability that a stimulus will be perceived.

Learning Objective 3: To understand how consumers organize consumption-related information.

Consumers organize their perceptions into unified wholes according to the principles of Gestalt psychology: Figure and ground, grouping, and closure. Each of these concepts has important implications for understanding consumer behavior. The term "figure" refers to the promotional message and "ground" represents the environment or context within which the figure appears. Because consumers are bombarded with stimuli, they often actively seek to avoid promotional messages. Marketers try to obscure the difference between figure and ground so that their ads do not "stand out" from the contents of entertainment, such as movies and TV shows. They often use product placements, which occur when an advertised product (i.e., the figure) is deliberately integrated into a TV show or film (i.e., the ground). The perception of stimuli as groups or chunks of information, rather than as discrete bits of information, facilitates memory and recall. People instinctively try to organize pieces of sensory input into a complete image or feeling (i.e., they seek closure). Thus, if they perceive that a stimulus is incomplete, they feel compelled to figure out its complete meaning.

Learning Objective 4: To understand why and how consumers "add" biases to stimuli and the implications of this tendency for marketing.

The interpretation of stimuli is highly subjective and is based on what the consumer expects to see in light of previous experience, on motives and interests at the time of perception, and on the clarity of the stimulus itself. Individuals carry biased pictures in their minds of the meanings of various stimuli, which are termed stereotypes. Sometimes, when presented with sensory stimuli, people "add" these biases to what they see or hear and form distorted impressions. Stereotypes that distort objective interpretation stem from physical appearances, descriptive terms, first impressions, and the halo effect.

Learning Objective 5: To understand the elements of consumers' imagery.

Consumers perceive images of products and brands. The perceived image of a product or service (how it is positioned) is more important to its ultimate success than are its actual physical characteristics. Products and services that are perceived distinctly and favorably have a much better chance of being purchased than products or services with unclear or unfavorable images. The main elements of consumer imagery are consumers' perceptions of brands, packages, services, and prices.

Learning Objective 6: To understand how consumers determine the quality of products and services.

Consumers' perceived quality of products and services is based on a variety of informational cues that they associate with the offerings. Some of these cues are intrinsic to the product or service; others are extrinsic. Either singly or together, such cues provide the basis for perceptions of product and service quality. In the absence of direct experience or other information, consumers often rely on price as an indicator of quality. How a consumer perceives a price—as high, low, or fair—has a strong influence on purchase intentions and satisfaction. Consumers rely on both internal and external reference prices when assessing the fairness of a price. Products and services can deliver high quality factually, as determined, say, by experts' judgments of scientific tests. However, if consumers do not perceive offerings as superior products that satisfy their needs and provide value, they will not purchase them, regardless of objective evidence.

Learning Objective 7: To understand consumers' perceived risks and how they handle and reduce those risks.

Consumers often perceive risk in making product selections because of uncertainty as to the consequences of their decisions. In most situations, consumers' perceived risk is a function of multiple factors. The elements of perceived risk are functional risk, physical risk, financial risk, psychological risk, and time risk. Consumer strategies for reducing perceived risk include increased information search, brand loyalty, buying a well-known brand, buying from a reputable retailer, buying the most expensive brand, and seeking reassurance in the form of money-back guarantees, warranties, and pre-purchase trials. The concept of perceived risk has important implications for marketers, who can facilitate the acceptance of new products by incorporating risk-reduction strategies into their new-product promotional campaigns.

Review and Discussion Questions

4.1. How does sensory adaptation affect advertising effectiveness? How can marketers overcome sensory adaptation?

4.2. Discuss the differences between the absolute threshold and the differential threshold. Which one is more important to marketers? Explain your answer.

4.3. For each of these products—chocolate bars and cereals—describe how marketers can apply their knowledge of the differential threshold to packaging, pricing, and promotional claims during periods of (a) rising ingredient and materials costs and (b) increasing competition.

4.4. Does subliminal advertising work? Support your view.

4.5. How do advertisers use contrast to make sure that their ads are noticed? Would the lack of contrast between the ad and the medium in which it appears help or hinder the effectiveness of the ad?

4.6. What are the implications of figure-and-ground relationships for print ads and for online ads? How can the figure-and-ground construct help or interfere with the communication of advertising messages?

4.7. Why do marketers sometimes reposition their products or services? Illustrate your answer with examples.

4.8. Why is it more difficult for consumers to evaluate the effective quality of services than the quality of products?

4.9. Discuss the roles of extrinsic and intrinsic cues in the perceived quality of: (a) wines, (b) restaurants, (c) smartphones, and (d) graduate education.

Hands-on Assignments

4.10. Find three print examples of the kind of promotional methods that constitute ambush or experiential marketing. Evaluate each example in terms of the effectiveness of the sensory input provided.

4.11. Define selective perception, and relate one or two elements of this concept to your own attention patterns in viewing print advertisements and online commercials.

4.12. Select a company that produces several versions of the same product under the same brand name (do not use one of the examples discussed in this chapter). Visit the firm's website and prepare a list of the product items and the benefits that each item offers to consumers. Are all these benefits believable, and will they persuade consumers to buy the different versions of the product? Explain your answers.

4.13. Apply the concepts that address consumers' perceptions of service quality to evaluate this course at this point.

Key Terms

- absolute threshold *103*
- ambush marketing *104*
- broad categorizers *132*
- closure *113*
- consumer imagery *122*
- differential threshold (just noticeable difference, JND) *104*
- experiential marketing *104*
- extrinsic cues *128*
- figure and ground *110*
- Gestalt psychology *110*
- grouping *112*

- halo effect *117*
- institutional advertising *131*
- intrinsic cues *127*
- just noticeable difference (JND) *98*
- licensing *118*
- narrow categorizers *132*
- perceived price *126*
- perceived risk *132*
- perception *98*
- perceptual defense *110*
- Positioning *122*
- price/quality relationship *130*
- product placement *111*
- reference price *126*
- repositioning *100*
- selective attention *109*
- selective exposure *109*
- sensation *101*
- sensory adaptation *104*
- sensory receptors *101*
- SERVQUAL scale *129*
- stereotypes *114*
- stimulus *101*
- subliminal perception *106*
- Weber's law *104*

5

Consumer Learning

Learning Objectives

1 To understand the elements of learning in the context of consumer behavior.

2 To understand behavioral learning, classical conditioning, and the roles of stimulus generalization and discrimination in developing and branding new products.

3 To understand instrumental conditioning and the objectives and methods of reinforcement.

4 To understand the role of observational learning in consumer behavior.

5 To understand the elements of information processing, including receiving, storing, and retrieving consumption-related information.

6 To understand cognitive learning as a framework for consumer decision-making.

7 To understand consumer involvement and passive learning, and their impact on purchase decisions and the retention and recall of promotional communications.

8 To understand how to measure the results of consumer learning.

LEARNING IS applying past knowledge and experience to present circumstances and behavior. For example, in Figure 5.1, Dove was launched in the year 1957 in the US and it first ventured in the Indian market in 1993[1] with its soap offering. The brand's heritage was associated with moisturization. The proposition of the brand at a deeper level was associated with the "Real Beauty" and motivating women to be confident about themselves.[2] "Real Beauty", mildness of its ingredients (moisturizers), care and trust were some of the associations of the brand that were extended to other categories like body lotion, face wash, deodorants, and hair oil. Dove consumers have had the opportunity to learn about the brand, associate with its benefits and repeat buy the brand as they feel that the brand has been rewarding. These consumers had, perhaps, used several aspects associated with concepts of learning associated with this chapter. Hence, Dove uses the concept of generalization to extend itself into several categories.

The third element of learning is repetition, which, in advertising, means restating the campaign's key message in many forms and communication channels.

Reinforcement, which is the final element of learning, involves rewarding those who try the new product.

Next, we discuss the elements of learning and apply them to developing marketing strategies aimed at getting consumers to try and continue buying new products. The chapter concludes with a discussion of the methods used to measure the results of learning experiences.

FIGURE 5.1 Dove

Source: Hindustan Unilever Limited

Learning Objective

1 To understand the elements of learning in the context of consumer behavior.

The Elements of Consumer Learning

Learning is the process by which individuals acquire the purchase and consumption knowledge and experience they apply to future, related behavior. **Consumer learning** is a process that evolves and changes as consumers acquire knowledge from experience, observation, and interactions with others and newly acquired knowledge affects future behavior. It ranges from simple and often reflexive responses to marketing stimuli (such as packaging, product colors, and promotional messages), to learning abstract concepts and making decisions about purchasing complex and expensive products.

Not all learning is deliberately sought. Though much learning is *intentional* (i.e., it is acquired as the result of a search for information), a great deal of learning is *incidental*, acquired by accident or without much effort. For example, some ads may induce learning—like the new products under a familiar brand name featured in Figure 5.1—without learning being deliberately sought, whereas other ads are sought out and carefully read by consumers contemplating major purchases. Learning consists of four elements: motives, cues, responses, and reinforcement.

Motives

Uncovering consumer motives is the primary objective of marketers, who seek to teach consumers how they can fill their needs by buying certain products and brands. Unfilled needs lead to **motivation**, which spurs learning. For example, men and women who want to take up bicycle riding for fitness and recreation are motivated to learn all they can about bike riding and practice often. They may seek information concerning the prices, quality, and characteristics of bicycles and learn which bicycles are the best for the kind of riding that they do. They will also read any articles in their local newspapers about bicycle trails and seek online information about "active vacations" that involve biking or hiking. Conversely, individuals who are not interested in bike riding are likely to ignore all information related to that activity. The degree of relevance, or "involvement," determines the consumer's level of motivation to search for information about a product or service and, potentially, engage in learning.

Cues

Cues are stimuli that direct motivated behavior. An advertisement for an exotic trip that includes bike riding may serve as a cue for bike riders, who may suddenly "recognize" that they "need" a vacation. The ad is the cue (or stimulus) that suggests a specific way to satisfy a salient motive. In marketing, price, styling, packaging, advertising, and store displays are cues designed to persuade consumers to fulfill their needs by buying specific products.

Only cues that are consistent with consumer expectations can drive motivation. Thus, marketers must provide cues that match those expectations. For example, consumers expect designer clothes to be expensive and to be sold in upscale retail stores. Thus, high-fashion designers should sell their clothes only through exclusive stores and advertise only in upscale fashion magazines. Each aspect of the marketing mix must reinforce the others if cues are to become stimuli that guide consumer actions in the direction the marketer desires.

Box 5.1 Capillary Technologies

Cues, at the point of purchase, are an important aspect to consider when consumers shop. With new technologies and changing lifestyles, there are several opportunities for retail outlets to introduce these cues. Capillary Technologies recognized the hassle consumers go through when they are required to enroll themselves in loyalty programs of retailers (filling in forms, etc.).[3] With minimum details of the consumer, they developed a software that captures customer details at the cash counter (including the items a customer may have bought) based on real-time analytics. The customer gets an SMS – even while he is completing the transaction – about the promotional offer of an item he may be interested in, based on his history of purchases at the store. Employing this technique, the company had experienced a much higher redemption of their offers as compared to traditional sales promotional offers.[4]

Responses

In the context of learning, **response** is an individual's reaction to a drive or cue. Learning can occur even when responses are not overt. The automobile manufacturer that provides consistent cues to a consumer may not always succeed in stimulating a purchase. However, if the manufacturer succeeds in forming a favorable image of a particular automobile model in the consumer's mind, it is likely that the consumer will consider that make or model when he or she is ready to buy a car.

A response is not tied to a need in a one-to-one fashion. Indeed, as noted in Chapter 3, a need or motive may evoke a whole variety of responses. For example, there are many ways to respond to the need for physical exercise besides riding bicycles. Cues provide some direction, but there are many cues competing for the consumer's attention. Which response the consumer makes depends heavily on previous learning; that, in turn, depends on how previous, related responses have been reinforced.

Reinforcement

Reinforcement is the reward—the pleasure, enjoyment, and benefits—that the consumer receives after buying and using a product or service. For the marketer, the challenge is to continue to provide consumers with an ongoing positive product or service, thus reinforcing future purchases. To illustrate, if a person visits a restaurant for the first time, likes the food, service, and ambience, and also feels he or she received value for the money paid, that customer was reinforced and is likely to dine at the restaurant again. If that person becomes a regular customer, the restaurant's owner should further reinforce the customer's continued patronage by, for example, giving the customer a free drink and recognizing the person by name upon arrival. Of course, the quality of the food and service must be maintained, as they are the key elements reinforcing the customer's continued visits. In contrast, if a patron leaves a restaurant disappointed with the quality of the food or the service or feels "ripped off," reinforcement has not occurred. Because of the absence of reinforcement, it is unlikely that the customer will visit the restaurant again.

Box 5.2 Old Brands and New Communication: Applying Learning Theories

The application of learning theories with appropriate marketing research to find out the appropriateness of visuals/copy can be useful for both new brands and brands with which consumers are familiar. Some of the old brands may trigger a strong brand recognition, but consumers may not have either used them in a while and may hence have forgotten about them (though, at some point in time they were familiar with them), or consumers may have perceived a weak link between the brand (stimulus) and the benefit of the brand (reward). This can happen to a number of well-established brands over a period of time when new brands enter the category. For example, in the category of antacids, currently there are several products in tablet and liquid forms available in the market. Eno is a well-known brand in the category and the brand has been in the market for several decades. In an effort to re-establish itself in consumer memory, Eno came out with an interesting campaign that repositioned the brand vis-à-vis new tablet and liquid variants in the category of antacids. The TV commercial showed Eno in comparison with a tablet and a liquid (both unbranded ones) and explained how the product was more effective than the other two variants. Consumers' sensory store may be receptive to the old and familiar brand and consumers may then think about the ad (if repeated frequently) when they have a need for it. This is how the brand enters the short-term memory of the consumer. When the consumer is exposed to such communication over a period of time, the brand name may enter the long-term memory (the process through which consumers are familiar with several brands like Lifebuoy, Titan, Cadbury or Dettol; consumers through generations have seen their ads in print or in other media). The benefit/satisfaction experienced by consumers on using the product will further strengthen consumers' association with the need, benefits, and pleasure associated with the product.

Sometimes, if the brand is very powerful both in terms of stimulus–reward association as well as brand associations (strength of brand associations), it can be revived even after a prolonged length of time (the brand may not have done much during this period of time). Tiger Balm is one such example.[5] But a brand that is completely out of sync with the changing environment will find it difficult to address both associations and rewards in terms of its offerings. Kodak had introduced Easy Share cameras in partnership with Microsoft (pictures could be transferred easily to PCs) in 2005 and QuickTake camera in partnership with Apple.[6] Despite such efforts, the brand was unable to adapt itself to digital photography. This is even after they had invented the digital camera in 1975![7]

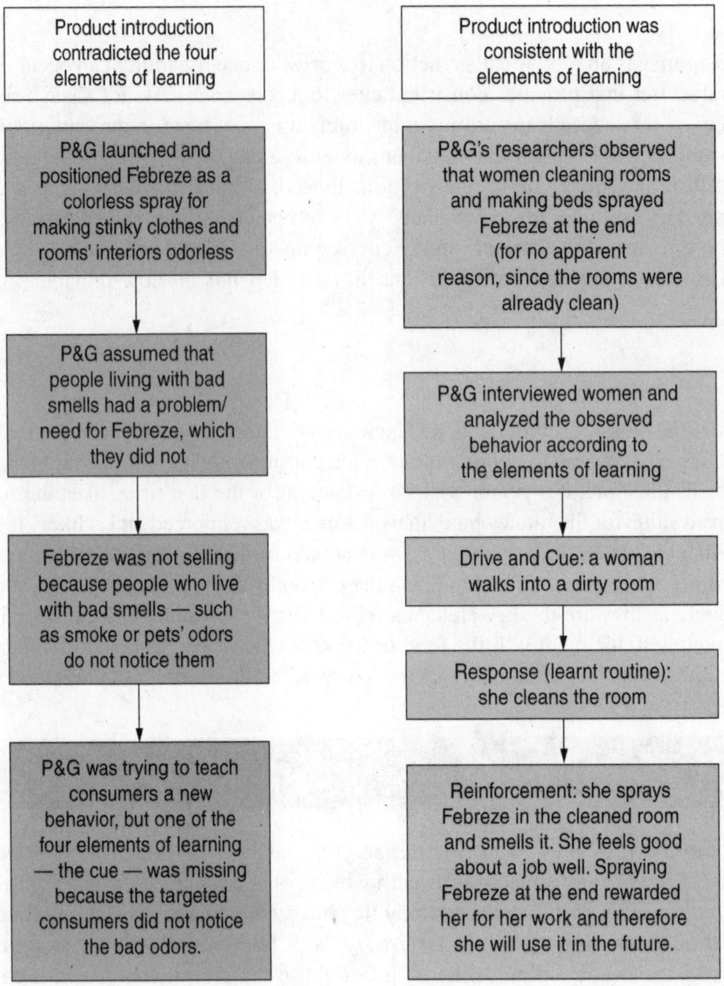

Source: Charles Duhigg, "How Companies Learn Your Secrets," nytimes.com February 16, 2012.

FIGURE 5.2 Procter & Gamble's Febreze

Figure 5.2 applies the four elements of learning to Procter & Gamble's introduction of Febreze, a spray that eliminates bad smells. The chart illustrates the effects of Febreze's initial positioning, which did not follow the principles of learning; the product did poorly. When the product was repositioned in a manner consistent with the principles of learning, it sold much better.[8]

There is no single, universal theory of how people learn. Broadly, there are two models of learning: behavioral and cognitive. Next, we describe these theories and their applications to consumer behavior. Afterwards, we explain how consumers store, retain, and retrieve information, cognitive learning, and how learning is measured.

Learning Objective

2 To understand behavioral learning, classical conditioning, and the roles of stimulus generalization and discrimination in developing and branding new products.

Classical Conditioning

Behavioral learning is sometimes referred to as **stimulus-response learning** because it is based on the premise that observable responses to specific external stimuli signal that learning has taken place. Behavioral learning is not concerned with the *process* of learning, but rather with the *inputs* and *outcomes* of learning; that is, in the stimuli that consumers select from the environment and the observable behaviors that result. Three forms of behavioral learning with great relevance to marketing are classical conditioning, instrumental (or operant) conditioning, and observational (or modeling) learning. Classical conditioning can be used effectively to create subcategories, too. Pond's is a well-known brand. In Figure 5.3, the new subcategory of Men's skin brightness offering (conditioned stimuli) is creatively associated with the unconditioned stimuli of recharge (that elicits associations of recharge of mobile sets that youngsters follow as a ritual).

Source: Hindustan Unilever Limited

FIGURE 5.3 Classical Conditioning

Classical conditioning is viewed as a "knee-jerk" (or automatic) response that builds up through repeated exposure and reinforcement. For instance, if Tyler's friends compliment him on his expensive Prada boots, he is likely to save money to buy a pair of Prada sneakers. If he sees a Prada ad in a magazine, Tyler will immediately recall his friends' compliments and feel good about himself and his prior purchase. Ivan Pavlov, a Russian physiologist, developed the concept of classical conditioning. Pavlov maintained that conditioned learning results when a stimulus that is paired with another stimulus that elicits a known response produces the same response when used alone. Pavlov demonstrated what he meant by "conditioned learning" in his studies with dogs. Genetically, dogs are always hungry and highly motivated to eat. In his experiments, Pavlov sounded a bell and then immediately applied a meat paste to the dogs' tongues, which caused them to salivate. After a number of such pairings, the dogs responded the same way—that is, they salivated—to the bell alone as they did to the meat paste.

Applying Pavlov's theory to human behavior, consider the following situation: For several years during high school, you always watched your favorite TV sitcom—which begins with the show's musical theme—with your best friend and every night at 7:00 p.m. Then you and your best friend went to different colleges. After you settled down in your new dorm, at 7:00 p.m. you turned on the TV to watch your favorite sitcom and the show's musical theme came on. You immediately thought about your friend and felt sad about watching the show alone. Feeling sad when you think about a best friend from whom you are now separated is a natural, human response and is therefore an **unconditioned stimulus** (i.e., a stimulus that occurs naturally in response to given circumstances). Furthermore, before you started watching the sitcom with your friend every night, the show's musical theme was a neutral stimulus that elicited neither behavior nor any feelings. Later on, while watching the sitcom alone, the same music triggered a particular response—feeling sad—so it has become a **conditioned-stimulus** (i.e., a stimulus that became associated with a particular event or feeling as a result of repetition). Feeling sad whenever you hear the music is a **conditioned response** (i.e., a response to conditioned stimulus). The music triggered sadness because of the role of repetition in the process of conditioning. You heard the same musical theme while watching TV with your friend for years, and always at the same time; if you had done so only occasionally, the music would not have triggered sadness. Figure 5.4 depicts Pavlov's model and an analogous example of classical conditioning.

The strategic applications of classical conditioning to consumer behavior are associative learning, repetition, stimulus generalization, and stimulus discrimination.

Classical Conditioning in the Indian Context

The form of association imparted by marketers to brands has important implications for how consumers spontaneously connect with brands. Lux soap can be associated with classical and stylish female beauty (for several decades the brand has been using a contemporary top female actor), and Hamam soap with traditional, ethnic beauty, from their past marketing associations. The same company that markets Lux and Hamam, Unilever India, also has Pears soap that has a gentle, mild, and family association. Pepsi has been associated with fun and happy times, with the brand's use of several cricket and film celebrities in its TVC. The Onida brand of TV was one of the earliest brands in the category to be associated with prestige and status (at a time when TV was considered a status symbol in society). Classical conditioning enables marketers to build and nurture brand associations with specific products.

The following are some examples of how brands have built their associations. It should be noted that as a result of classical conditioning (in the form of associations), brands create a focused perception with regard to consumers: to that extent, classical conditioning is linked to perception (though for conceptual purposes of comprehension, they are treated as distinct academic concepts).

- Margo brand of soap's associations with neem (which is considered good for the skin)over several years (later endorsed by a celebrity)
- Café Coffee Day's associations with relaxation and socializing
- Robin Blue's associations with whiteness of clothes
- Rolex and Omega watches' associations with prestige of the consumer owning them
- Nike's associations with a youthful attitude

- Saffola's association with healthy cooking
- iPhone's associations with technological trends and fashion
- Lux soap's associations with celebrities for several decades

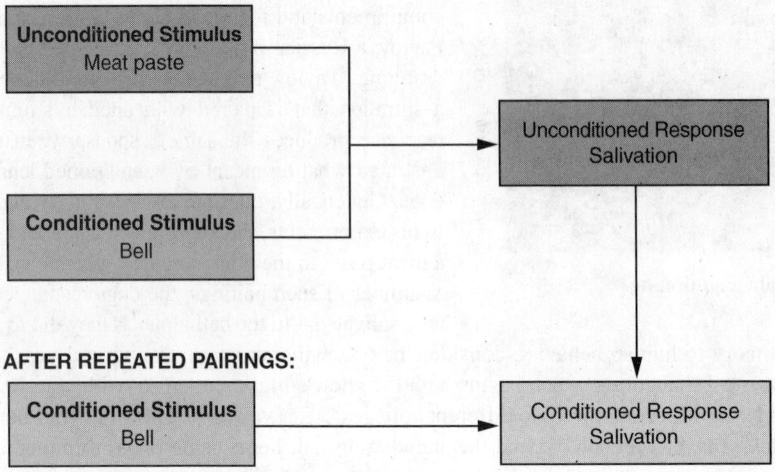

FIGURE 5.4A Classical Conditioning

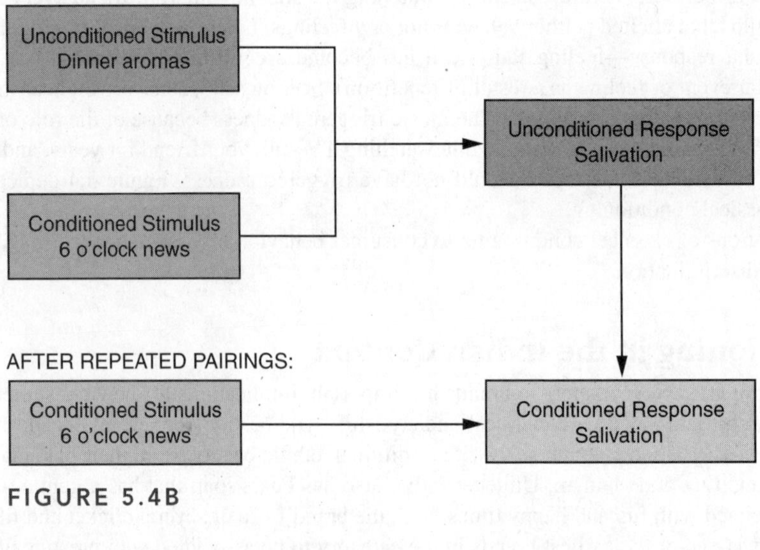

FIGURE 5.4B

Application 1: Brand Associations – The Dilemma of Retaining or Dissociating

While one school of thought believes that brands are forever, there is another school that advocates that old brands should be removed to pave the way for new brands when environment changes over time. A good example is the case of Bajaj. Having built brand names like Chetak, Caliber, Kawasaki, and RTZ, the company has successfully removed these brand names and introduced brands like Discover, Pulsar, Boxer, and Platina. During September 2012 Bajaj Discover became the largest selling motorcycle brand in the world, topping Hero Splendor.[9] The decision to withdraw brands and build new brands and associations is both complex and challenging. Later, 'Bajaj' was dropped from Discover and Pulsar to ensure that the other category associations related to Bajaj do not interfere with these strong brands.[10]

Application 2: What Can a Well-Conditioned Brand Do, Especially When Attitude Creation Is Involved?

Kellogg's, in an attempt to expand its market, had launched an ad comparing its chocolate variant cereal (positioned to children) with *rotis*, a staple food in most parts of the country.

Kellogg's has a global standing as a multinational brand associated with health. With this campaign through *rotis*, the brand has also evoked a cultural association. Here, the unconditioned stimulus is the category of cereals rather than the brand. The conditioned stimulus is the Kellogg's brand name and *rotis*.

It is a good example of attitude creation through classical conditioning associated with the category. Kellogg's, the brand, has been around in India for more than a decade and hence, the conditioning of the brand had been happening for a while.

Application 3: Counter Segmentation and Classical Conditioning

Titan's Zoop brand of watch had used the concept of brand licensing in an interesting manner. Zoop had a tie-up with the movie 'Iron Man 3'. This was to extend its brand, initially positioned for kids, to youngsters in the range of 22–24 years.[11] Counter segmentation is a concept that involves expanding the segment of the brand to include a new segment (especially, when the original segment has been defined narrowly in terms of its appeal). Titan's strategy for Zoop triggers an association with this strategy.

Application 4: Power of Associations

Companies use the power of classical conditioning to extend their brands. Boroplus, a well-known antiseptic cream brand, extended itself into Boroplus Health and Fair Winter cream, Boroplus Intensive Therapy cream for knees and elbows, sun screen protection creams, and summer and winter lotions.[12] Parachute Advansed advertised its Knowledge Center to convey the efficacy of 'deep conditioning' as compared to other conditioners. Extending a brand to a knowledge domain enhances the perception about the functional performance of the brand among consumers. Saffola's Heart Foundation is another example of this kind.

Tang, the well-known brand of juice, was launched in 1959, but its sale improved only after NASA had used it on its space flights (associations with space flights were created among consumers).

Associative Learning

Contemporary behavioral scientists view classical conditioning as learning of associations among events that enable consumers to expect and anticipate events. Rather than being a reflexive action, this is seen as **cognitive associative learning**—not the acquisition of new reflexes, but the acquisition of new knowledge about the world. From this viewpoint, the consumer is an information seeker who uses logical and perceptual relations among events, along with his or her own preconceptions, to form a sophisticated representation of the world.

The Role of Repetition

In advertising, **repetition** is the key to forming associations between brands and fulfillment of needs. For example, having a healthy mouth and good oral hygiene are a human need (i.e., unconditioned stimulus), which many consumers associate with the word "Crest." Why? Because after more than 50 years of *repetitive advertising* and uncountable ads, upon hearing or seeing the name "Crest" consumers think of a premium product for keeping their mouth and teeth healthy and protected from bacteria, diseases, and deterioration. Crest is a *conditioned stimulus* and the consumers' associations are *conditioned responses*. Furthermore, consumers associate Crest with scores of versions of toothpaste, toothbrushes, teeth whitening, flossing, and mouth-rinsing products, all marketed under the Crest brand name. Both the conditioned stimulus and the response are results of hearing or seeing Crest's advertisements again and again—in other words, repetitively.

Repetition increases the strength of the association between two stimuli and slows down forgetting this connection. However, the amount of repetition that aids retention is limited. Although repetition beyond what is necessary for the initial learning aids retention, at some point an individual becomes satiated with numerous exposures, and both attention and retention decline. This effect is called **advertising wear-out**, and marketers reduce it by using different ads expressing the same message or advertising themes, HSBC positions itself as "the world's local bank." An advertising campaign, entitled "Different Values," consisted of about 20 ads centered on the theme that "different values make the world a richer place." The ads illustrated that one's point of view is subjective and reflects one's values and, therefore, the same object can have different meanings depending on one's culture and viewpoint. The featured objects varied, although the central theme remained the same. For example, a container of pills (the object pictured in one of the ads) may represent "prevention" (e.g., vitamins), "cure" (e.g., antibiotics), or "escape" (e.g., illegal substances).

Substantive variations are changes in advertising content across different versions of an advertisement and are appropriate when the marketer wishes to convey more than one product feature. For example, the two ads in Figure 5.5 stress two different attributes of the same product. Varied ads provide marketers with several strategic advantages. Consumers exposed to substantively varied ads process more information about product attributes, and attitudes formed as a result of exposure to such messages are often more resistant to change in the face of competitive attacks.

Although all advertisers use repetition in trying to teach consumers, not everyone agrees on *how much* repetition is enough. Some marketing scholars believe that just three exposures to an advertisement are needed: One to make consumers *aware* of the product, a second to show consumers the *relevance* of the product, and a third to *remind* them of its benefits. This exposure pattern is called the **three-hit theory**. Other researchers suggest that as many as 11 to 12 repetitions are needed to achieve the three objectives. One study indicated that email advertisements that consumers found relevant influenced their learning and attitudes much more than the number of exposures.[13]

QUESTION: Why Did Gillette Use Two Different Ads to Advertise the Same Product?

Source: Courtesy of Gillette.

FIGURE 5.5

Stimulus Generalization

According to classical conditioning theorists, learning depends not only on repetition but also on individuals' ability to "generalize." Pavlov found, for example, that a dog could learn to salivate not only to the sound of a bell, but also to similar sounds such as jangling keys or coins. Responding the same way to slightly different stimuli is called **stimulus generalization**.

Stimulus generalization explains why some imitative me-too products succeed in the marketplace: Consumers confuse them with the original product they have seen advertised. It also explains why manufacturers of private-label brands try to make their packaging closely resemble that of the national brand leaders. They are hoping that consumers will confuse their packages with the leading brand and buy their product rather than the leading brand.

There are four strategic applications of stimulus generalization to branding and managing product lines: product line extensions, product form extensions, family branding, and licensing.[14]

Box 5.3 Generalization in the Indian Context

Eveready introduced LED lanterns running on battery and launched it as a substitute for kerosene-based lanterns in rural India. The product generated ₹75 crores as revenue during the first year, but had to take on duplicates which were of poor quality.[15] This aspect of generalization, linked to the concept of learning, can be found in several categories and brands need to ensure that these duplicates do not erode into their market share.

Source: Campbell Soup Company

FIGURE 5.6 A Product Line Extension: V8 Soups

Product Line Extensions

Product line extensions are additions of related items to an established brand; these are likely to be adopted because they come under a known and trusted brand name.[16] For example, what comes to one's mind upon seeing the V8 symbol? The most likely answer is a small can of vegetable juice sold via vending machines and convenience stores and larger bottles of the brand sold in supermarkets. Most consumers associate drinking vegetable juice and eating vegetables with consuming vitamins, antioxidants, and agents boosting the immune system.

While most consumers associate V8 with vegetables, originally, they did not associate soups with V8. Why did Campbell's (which owns V8), "interfere" with consumers' long-established cognitions by introducing the soups featured in Figure 5.6? Each time consumers bought V8 vegetable juice, they were "rewarded" because the juice tasted good and they were consuming a healthy product. When new products carrying the V8 brand name are advertised, consumers are likely to associate them with the many, prior rewarding experiences of consuming V8 vegetable juice, including the perceived health benefits that are the core of this brand. In learning terms, consumers will apply what they already know about V8 to its new product and probably try the new item. The extension of the V8 line to other products is also a form of family branding, which consists of marketing different products under the same brand name.

Source: Proctor & Gamble

FIGURE 5.7 Mr. Clean's Product Line Extensions

The two Mr. Clean products shown in Figure 5.7 are examples of line extensions under a brand name that has been a best seller since the 1950s and represented by a mascot that consumers view as a strong, tenacious, competent, dependable, and friendly "person" (see Figure 3.2).

Product Form Extensions

Offering the same product in a different form but under the same brand is a **product form extension**. For example, Listerine, a mouthwash in the form of liquid and a leading brand, introduced Listerine PocketPacks—a solid form of its product (see Figure 5.8). Clorox Bleach—one of the most recognized brand names among clothing care products—has been sold only as a liquid since its introduction many decades; building upon the brand's universal recognition as a quality product, the company introduced Bleach Gel.

Family Branding

Another strategy stemming from stimulus generalization is **family branding**, which consists of marketing different products under the same brand name. For example, Campbell's, originally a marketer of soups, continues to add new food products to its product line under the Campbell's brand name, such as chunky, condensed, kids, and lower sodium soups; frozen meals named Campbell's Super Bakes; and tomato juice.

Licensing

Licensing is contractually allowing a well-known brand name to be affixed to the products of another manufacturer. The names of designers, manufacturers, celebrities, corporations, and even cartoon characters are attached, for a fee (i.e., "rented out") to a variety of products, enabling the licensees to achieve instant recognition and implied quality for the licensed products. Some successful licensors include Liz Claiborne, Tommy Hilfiger, Calvin Klein, and Christian Dior, whose names appear on an exceptionally wide variety of products, from sheets to shoes and luggage to perfume.[17]

Corporations also license their names and trademarks to marketers of related products. For example, Godiva chocolates licensed its name for Godiva liqueur. Corporations also license their names and logos for purely promotional purposes: For example, the phrase "Always Coca-Cola" is printed on clothing, toys, coffee mugs, and the like, none of which are made by Coca-Cola.

The number of different products affiliated with a given brand—originating in line and form extensions, family branding, and licensing—will strengthen the brand name, as long as the brand's owner ensures that the additions are of high quality and consistent with the brand's image and positioning. Failure to do so will negatively affect consumer confidence and evaluations of all the brand's products. One study showed that brands that include diverse products are likely to offer more successful brand extensions than brands that include similar products. The study also confirmed that consumers' reactions to the brand's extensions are strongly related to the distinct benefits these items provide.[18]

Source: The Clorox Company

FIGURE 5.8 A Product Form Extension: Clorox Bleach Gel

Stimulus Discrimination and Product Differentiation

Stimulus discrimination, the opposite of stimulus generalization, is the selection of a specific stimulus from among similar stimuli. The core objective of positioning (see Chapter 2) is to "teach" consumers to discriminate (or distinguish) among similar products (i.e., similar stimuli) and form a unique image for a brand in their minds. Therefore, the objective of marketers' persuasive messages is to convey a brand's unique benefits effectively and differentiate it from competition. Unlike the marketers of brands known as "imitators"—which are often obscure or store brands—who hope that consumers will "generalize" by confusing their brands with well-positioned ones, market leaders' objective is to convince and enable consumers to clearly distinguish (or discriminate) between their products and the imitators.

Most product differentiation strategies are designed to distinguish a product or brand from that of competitors on the basis of an attribute that is relevant, meaningful, and valuable to consumers. It is always difficult to unseat a brand leader once stimulus discrimination has occurred. One explanation is that the leader is usually first in the market and has had a longer period to "teach" consumers (through advertising and selling) to view the brand as the best alternative within a given product category. Apple is a prominent example of differentiating a product. Its early ads explicitly stated that Apple's innovative products represent a distinctive and extraordinary way of thinking. These ads' tag line was "Think Different" and they brilliantly conveyed this notion by featuring famous geniuses, such as Albert Einstein and Jim Henson, who thought "outside the box" and came up with ideas that changed the world.

Classical conditioning theory underpins many ways of influencing consumer behavior through repetition, stimulus generalization, and stimulus discrimination. However, although a great deal of consumer behavior is shaped by repeated advertising messages stressing the unique attributes of various brands, consumers also buy the same brands repeatedly because they are continuously rewarded. The role of reinforcements (or rewards) in shaping learning is discussed next.

Learning Objective

3 To understand instrumental conditioning and the objectives and methods of reinforcement.

Instrumental Conditioning

Instrumental conditioning (or operant conditioning) is based on the notion that learning occurs through a trial-and-error process, with habits formed as a result of rewards received for certain responses or behaviors. Like classical conditioning, instrumental conditioning requires a link between a stimulus and a response. However, in instrumental conditioning, the stimulus that results in the most rewarded response is the one that is learned. For example, after visiting stores, consumers know which stores carry the type of clothing they prefer at prices they can afford to pay. Once they find a store that carries clothing that meets their needs, they are likely to patronize it to the exclusion of other stores. Every time they purchase a shirt or a sweater there that they really like, their store loyalty is rewarded (*reinforced*), and they are likely to become repeat customers.

The American psychologist B. F. Skinner constructed the model of instrumental conditioning. According to Skinner, most learning occurs in environments where individuals are "rewarded" for choosing an appropriate behavior. In consumer behavior

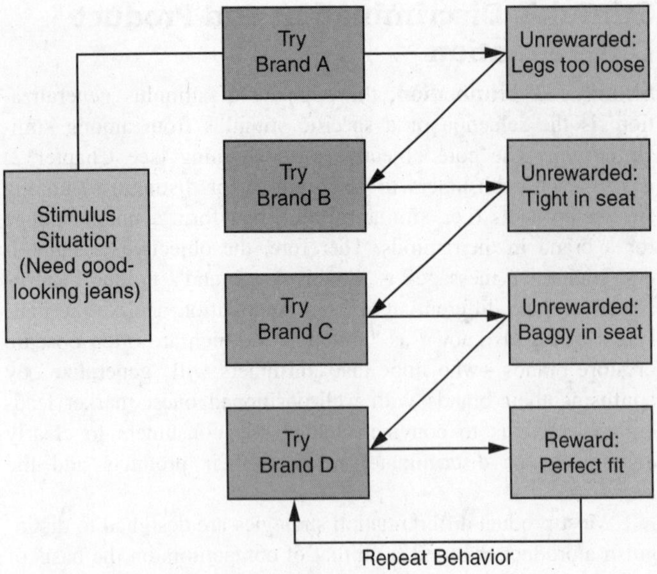

FIGURE 5.9 A Model of Instrumental Conditioning

terms, instrumental conditioning suggests that consumers learn by means of a trial-and-error process in which some purchase behaviors result in more favorable outcomes (i.e., rewards) than others. A favorable experience is the *instrument* of teaching the individual to repeat a specific behavior.

Like Pavlov, Skinner developed his model of learning by working with animals. Small animals, such as rats and pigeons, were placed in his "Skinner box." If they behaved as Skinner desired—such as pressing a particular lever or pecking keys—he rewarded them with food pellets. Skinner and his many adherents have done amazing things with this learning model, including teaching pigeons to play ping-pong and even to dance. In a marketing context, the consumer who tries several brands and styles of jeans before finding a style that fits her figure (i.e., reinforcement) has engaged in instrumental learning. Presumably, the brand that fits best is the one she will continue to buy. This model of instrumental conditioning is presented in Figure 5.9.

Applications 1: Habits and Brands – the Usefulness of Automaticity

Recent research views habit as a behavioral action that is triggered by contextual cues – location, social settings, time, and preceding an event.[19] For example, consumers may have soft drinks at their place of work (location); they may visit Café Coffee Day (location) when meeting up with friends, have Marie biscuits with tea during evenings (time), and may use Parachute after-shower hair gel before going out to a party (event). Habits – according to this research – gets triggered with stable cues and they are triggered automatically (automaticity is the research stream that is associated with this aspect).

Application 2: Habits, Script, and Brands

A research study reports that consumers buying a brand for the eighth time are 97% likely to buy it for the ninth time and those marketers have not studied these habits significantly.[20] Habits are unconscious in nature and even the physiology of consumers seems to accept the routine tasks in its habitual mind, as compared to the thinking-based executive mind.[21] Script is a type of schema that has knowledge of the sequence of actions involved in an event.[22] Habits and script together can have a significant impact on enhancing instrumental learning. Bru coffee, launched during the seventies, was associated with the traditional filter coffee and coffee is a habit in most South Indian households.[23] The brand had made an effort to become a part of the consumer's script.

iPod and iTunes have became a part of the habit of millions of consumers. An iPad app introduced by eBay allows the viewer to order items while they are viewing. For instance, a viewer can develop the habit of ordering a fancy item used by an actor while viewing a TV series. A study by Yahoo/Nielson found that 86% of smart phones and tablet users used the app while viewing the show and 26% of them looked for information related to the show they were watching.[24]

The convergence of technologies and the mobile revolution has opened up several possibilities for script and habits. Google + struggled (135 million users and 500 million account holders) to win over brands against Facebook's 1.1 billion users. A Nielson study reported that on an average, an US user spent 6 hours on Facebook as against 6 minutes and 47 seconds on Google +.[25] Habits, perhaps, are an important reason why Facebook has taken a pioneering lead in the world of social networking.

Application 3: Brand Diffusion and Habits

In instrumental conditioning, other than the response-reinforcement aspect that is instrumental in the formation of loyalty, it may be interesting to note that habit, too, contributes to the reinforcement cycle.

The 'expectation-anticipation-reward-habit' cycle is important for brand loyalty.[26]

Hindustan Unilever had introduced 250 million consumers to the hand washing habit when six million children die every year due to diseases that can be prevented by washing hands.[27] The expectation from the message in the ads of hand wash is the promise of protection from germs, reward (anticipatory) is not falling sick frequently and the habit is washing hands. Lifebuoy, from Hindustan Unilever, perhaps has become a habit among many of the consumers who were introduced to the hand washing practice.

Close up toothpaste has the 12 hour refreshing feeling proposition and the advertisement visuals express the moments with the 'Good morning, Good afternoon, and Good evening' visuals where it is important for the consumer to have refreshing breath . The expectation is protection from bad breadth, the reward is the refreshing breath experienced by the consumers and the brand, Close up, becomes a part of the brushing habit or ritual.

Application 4: Branding and Behavioral Learning Theories

Both classical conditioning and instrumental conditioning can be applied to create brand associations in an environment that is increasingly getting digital. Axe deodorant targets youth in the age group of 18–15 years. The Axe ads received thousands of views on You Tube[28] and there is an opportunity for a brand to be associated with the everyday life of the target segment. Deodorants are chosen more over fragrances in India and the brand made an attempt to create strong associations with its variants. The Axe Dark Temptation was portrayed as being irresistible as chocolate and hence, chocolate associations or words trigger the brand's association. Its 'Call me' campaign resulted in 3.5 million calls to the Axe number. The Axe Angels fan page on Facebook attracted 7,00,000 friends (all these are classical conditioning aspects). Axe Instinct, an online game, was played by three million people and 55% of them were repeat players[29] (instrumental conditioning at work with the repeat players having enjoyed the game-experiential reward).

Reinforcing Behavior

Skinner distinguished between two types of reinforcement that influence the likelihood that a response will be repeated. The first type, **positive reinforcement**, rewards a particular behavior and thus strengthens the likelihood of a specific response during the same or similar situation. For example, a child receives ice cream when passing an ice cream stand and receives pleasure from eating it. Then, whenever he passes by the stand he asks for ice cream. **Negative reinforcement** is the removal of an unpleasant stimulus and it strengthens the likelihood of a given response during the same or similar circumstances. For example, a child has a cold and also hates swallowing pills. Her mother convinces her to take Advil and her cold symptoms go away (i.e., the unpleasant stimulus is removed). Next time she has a cold, most likely the girl will readily agree to swallow a pill, and might even ask specifically for an Advil. Therefore, marketers of headache remedies use negative reinforcement when they illustrate the unpleasant symptoms of an unrelieved headache, as do marketers of mouthwash when they show the loneliness suffered by someone with bad breath. In each of these cases, the consumer is encouraged to avoid the negative consequences and remove the unpleasant stimulus by buying the advertised product.

Either positive or negative reinforcement can be used to elicit a desired response. However, negative reinforcement should not be confused with *punishment*, which is designed to *discourage* behavior. For example, receiving a speeding ticket and having to pay a fine is not negative reinforcement; it is a form of punishment designed to discourage future speeding. But what constitutes "punishment" is tricky. For example, a driver can perceive the fine as "paying" for a bad behavior and continue speeding; this individual apparently believes that each time he speeds he will merely have to pay for his bad behavior. Therefore, in addition to paying fines, speeding drivers receive "points" on their licenses and can lose their driving rights (and the opportunities to speed) if they speed too many times. In a frequently cited study, researchers discovered that when a day care center started "punishing" parents who picked up their kids late by charging them about $3, late pickups actually *increased*, because parents viewed the fine as the price for being tardy.[30] The "punishment" actually legitimized being late and *encouraged* the behavior it was designed to lessen.

Extinction and Forgetting

Extinction occurs when a learned response is no longer reinforced and the link between the stimulus and the expected reward breaks down. When consumers become unsatisfied with a service (e.g., at a restaurant), the link between the stimulus (i.e., the restaurant) and expected satisfaction is no longer reinforced and the consumers won't come back. Behavior that is not reinforced becomes "unlearned."

Note that there is a difference between extinction and forgetting. Diners who have not visited a once-favorite restaurant for a long time simply forget how much they used to enjoy eating there and their behavior is "unlearned" because of lack of use rather than lack of reinforcement. **Forgetting** is often related to the passage of time, and thus is also called "decay. " Marketers overcome forgetting by contacting customers who stopped buying their products and giving them incentives aimed at persuading the customers to start buying their products again.

Customer Satisfaction and Retention

Savvy marketers reinforce customer satisfaction by consistently providing high quality. Marketers must provide the best value for the money and simultaneously avoid raising consumers' expectations beyond what the products can deliver. Companies must not assume that more attractive prices and broader product lines will make customers more satisfied. Instead, companies that create personal connections with customers, and offer diverse product lines and competitive prices, because these are the most effective reinforcements, which bring about repeat patronage. Most frequent shopper programs are based on the notion that the more a consumer uses the service, the greater the rewards. Another form of reinforcement is rewarding customers who refer other customers. One study discovered that although rewards increased referrals, there was no difference in referral likelihood between smaller and larger rewards. In addition, for existing customers with strong ties to the marketer providing the reward, these incentives did not increase referral likelihood.[31] However, several studies discovered that satisfied customers are often fickle and disloyal when a lot of competition exists.[32]

Reinforcement Schedules

Product quality must be consistently high and satisfy customers every time they buy the product—but additional rewards do not have to be offered during every transaction, because *occasional* rewards often effectively reinforce consumers' patronage. For example, airlines occasionally upgrade a passenger at the gate; here, the *possibility* of receiving a reward is the reinforcement and incentive for continued patronage.

Psychologists have identified three reinforcement schedules: Continuous, fixed ratio, and variable ratio. With **continuous reinforcement**, a reward is provided after each transaction, such as a free after-dinner drink or fruit plate always served to regular patrons of a restaurant. A **fixed ratio reinforcement** schedule provides reinforcement every *n*th time the product or service is purchased (say, every third time). For example, a retailer may send a credit voucher to account holders every three months, based on a percentage of the customer's purchases during the prior quarter. A **variable ratio reinforcement** schedule rewards consumers on a random basis. Gambling casinos operate on the basis of variable ratios. People pour money into slot machines (which are programmed to pay off on a variable ratio), hoping for the big win. Variable ratios tend to engender high rates of desired behavior and are somewhat resistant to extinction; apparently, for many consumers, hope springs eternal. Other examples of variable ratio schedules include lotteries, sweepstakes, door prizes, and contests that require certain consumer behaviors for eligibility.

Shaping

Reinforcement performed *before* the desired consumer behavior actually takes place is called **shaping**. Shaping increases the probability that certain desired consumer behavior will occur. For example, retailers recognize that they must first attract customers to their stores before they can expect those customers to do the bulk of their shopping there. Many retailers provide some form of preliminary reinforcement (shaping) to encourage consumers to visit their stores. For example, some retailers offer loss leaders—popular products at severely discounted prices—to the first hundred or so customers to arrive, because those customers are likely to buy more products at the store rather than only the discounted items. By reinforcing the behavior that is needed to enable the desired consumer behavior, marketers increase the probability that the desired behavior will occur. Car dealers recognize that to sell new-model cars, they must first encourage people to visit the showrooms and test-drive the cars. They hope that the test drive will result in a sale. Using shaping principles, many car dealers encourage showroom visits by providing small monetary or other gifts to those who test-drive the cars, and a rebate check upon placement of an order. They use a multistep shaping process to achieve the desired consumer learning.[33]

Massed versus Distributed Learning

As illustrated previously, timing has an important influence on consumer learning. Should a learning schedule be spread out over a period of time, which is termed **distributed learning**, or should it be "bunched up" all at once, which is called **massed learning**? The question is an important one for advertisers planning a media schedule, because massed advertising produces more initial learning, whereas a distributed schedule usually results in learning that persists longer. When advertisers want an immediate impact (e.g., to introduce a new product or to counter a competitor's blitz campaign), they generally use a massed schedule to hasten consumer learning. However, when the goal is long-term repeat buying on a regular basis, a distributed schedule is preferable. A distributed schedule, with ads repeated on a regular basis usually results in long-term learning that is relatively immune to extinction.

Learning Objective

4 To understand the role of observational learning in consumer behavior.

Observational Learning

Observational learning (or modeling) is the process through which individuals learn behavior by observing the behavior of others and the consequences of such behavior. For this type of learning to occur, reinforcement must take place. For example, Joe—a commuter—notices that more and more train riders are using e-readers, so he buys one to try it out, knowing that he has 30 days to return it. Then, a conductor whom Joe knows and sees daily compliments him on the purchase and also asks questions about the device. Joe's purchase was the result of observational learning. Because the conductor's compliments reinforced his purchase (and also because he likes the device and it works well), Joe decides to keep the device.

Advertisers recognize the importance of observational learning in selecting the models they feature in advertisements, whether celebrities or unknowns. If a teenager sees an ad that depicts social success as the outcome of using a certain brand of shampoo, she will want to buy it. If her brother sees a commercial that shows a muscular young athlete eating Wheaties—"the breakfast of champions"—he will want to eat it, too. Indeed, a lot of advertising is based on observational learning. Many ads feature likeable models achieving positive outcomes to common problem situations through use of the advertised product. Children learn much of their social and consumer behavior by observing their older siblings and parents. They imitate the behavior of those they see rewarded, expecting to be rewarded similarly if they adopt the same behavior. The Ragu ad in Figure 5.10 illustrates a child's observational learning from his grandfather.

Box 5.4 Classical Conditioning, Observational Learning, and Brands

Sensodyne versus Colgate Sensitive toothpaste (both brands are premium-priced ones with therapeutic benefits) provides an interesting example with regard to the application of observational or vicarious learning associated (classical conditioning) to brands. Colgate (a well-known brand in toothpaste category) introduced its Sensitive toothpaste in departmental stores in the early 2000. Subsequently, after a few years it started advertising on TV channels. The ad showed a consumer experiencing agony when she ate something cold (due to sensitivity of teeth) and the pain killing action of the brand was highlighted. It was implied that consumers who had a similar problem would see the ad, put themselves in the position of the model in the ad, and experience the brand (observational learning).

Sensodyne toothpaste (although a new brand in India, it is a multinational brand) advertised the brand being endorsed by a doctor (the visual shows a person in a white coat). It was interesting to note that Sensodyne had overtaken Sensitive in terms of market share within two years of its launch.[34]

This raises interesting questions. Colgate, decades back, used to associate itself (and even now for one of its variants) with doctors. Given the mere exposure of 'brand–doctor' association in the category, does such an association work better for a therapeutic offering like Sensodyne? This is despite the powerful Colgate brand name being associated with Sensitive. How should Colgate Sensitive counter the problem? Other marketing mix elements may be important in this scenario, but brand associations play a dominant role in making an impact on consumers in such categories. Pepsodent, a brand of toothpaste from Unilever, too, had launched its higher-priced variants with doctor's endorsement.

Source: Unilever

FIGURE 5.10 Eating Ragu Is Fun: Observational Learning from Grandfather to Grandson

Learning Objective

5 To understand the elements of information processing, including receiving, storing, and retrieving consumption-related information.

Information Processing

A lot of learning occurs through consumer thinking and problem solving. Sometimes we resolve purchase-related dilemmas instantly. In other situations, we search for information and carefully evaluate what we learned. This kind of learning, called **cognitive learning**, consists of mental processing of data rather than instinctive responses to stimuli. Therefore, we examine the structure and components of information processing, which are diagrammed in Figure 5.11, before explaining cognitive learning.

The human mind processes the information it receives. Consumers process product information by attributes, brands, comparisons between brands, or a combination of these factors. The number and complexity of the relevant attributes and available alternatives influence the intensity or degree of information processing. Consumers with higher cognitive abilities acquire more product information and consider more product attributes and alternatives than consumers with lesser ability.

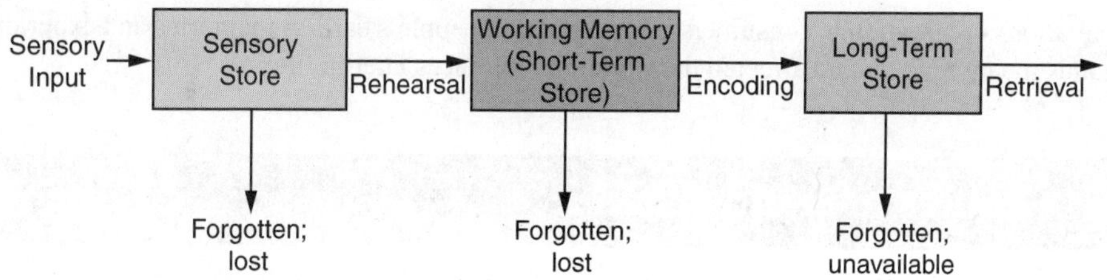

FIGURE 5.11 Information Processing

The more experience a consumer has with a product category, the greater is his or her ability to make use of product information. Greater familiarity with the product category also increases learning during new purchase decisions for items within the same category. The components of information processing are storing, retaining, and retrieving information.

Storing Information

The human memory is the center of information processing. Information processing occurs in stages and in three sequential "storehouses" where information is kept: The sensory, short-term, and long-term stores.

Sensory Store

The **sensory store** is the mental "space" in the human mind where sensory input lasts for just a second or two. If it is not processed immediately, it is lost. All data come to us through our senses, but the senses do not carry whole images, like a camera. Each sense receives a piece of information (such as the smell, color, shape, or feel of a flower) and transmits it to the brain in parallel, where the perceptions of a single instant are synchronized and perceived as a single image for only a brief moment. Because consumers are constantly bombarded with stimuli from the environment, they subconsciously block out a great deal of information that they do not need or cannot use. For marketers, this means that although it is relatively easy to get information into the consumer's sensory store, it is difficult to make a lasting impression. Furthermore, the brain automatically and subconsciously "tags" all perceptions with a value, either positive or negative; this evaluation, added to the initial perception in the first microsecond of cognition, tends to remain unless further information is processed. This explains why first impressions tend to last and why it is hazardous for a marketer to introduce a product prematurely into the marketplace.

Short-Term Store

The **short-term store** is where information is processed and held for just a brief period. Anyone who has ever looked up a number in a telephone book, only to forget it just before dialing, knows how briefly information lasts in short-term storage. If information in the short-term store undergoes the process known as **rehearsal**, which is the silent, mental repetition of information, it is then transferred to the long-term store. The transfer process takes from 2 to 10 seconds. If information is not rehearsed and transferred, it is lost in about 30 seconds or less. The amount of information that can be held in short-term storage is limited to about four or five items.

An interesting experiment illustrated how the short-term store operates. A researcher walked over to a pedestrian and asked for directions. While the pedestrian was responding, two workmen carrying a large door walked between the researcher and the respondent; while hidden by the door being moved, the researcher switched places with another person. Only about half the pedestrians noticed that they were talking to someone else afterward.[35]

Long-Term Store

The **long-term store** is the mental "space" where information is retained for extended periods of time, in contrast to the short-term store, where information lasts only a few seconds. Although it is possible to forget something within a few minutes after the information reaches long-term storage, it is more common for data in long-term storage to last for days, weeks, or even years.

A study of three generations of automobile consumers discovered that people's earliest memories and experiences regarding cars defined what car brands meant to them and affected their brand preferences later in life.[36]

Application 1 : Routes to Brand Schema

Brand associations reside in schema and due to competitive pressures, it has become imperative for brands to develop strong associations in tune with their sustainable core proposition (the ability of a brand to sustain, nurture, and reinforce their core propositions or associations). Lifebuoy (germ killing action), Santoor (youthful skin), and Horlicks (health for youngsters) are some examples of brands that have been able to sustain their core associations. There are different routes that brands have to take to strengthen their associations. It should be noted that all these routes offer certain basic ideas; they are not to be viewed as mutually independent approaches.

Brand Relationships: Fournier suggested several relationships with brands that can be cultivated by marketers.[37] Interdependence, personal commitment, love, intimacy, partner quality, self-concept, and nostalgic connections are some of them. For example, Dove hair oil hinted at 'grandmother's formulation' when it introduced its campaign (nostalgia). The framework may also be useful for a new entrant. A new brand of telecom services can develop association of personal commitment. Telenor, the telecom company, had its field officers posted close to its mobile towers to redress consumer complaints and address their queries. A trusted brand like Life Insurance Corporation can develop 'partner quality' associations.

Brand Love[38]: Good attributes, strong values (cultural, for example), intrinsic benefits (psychological), self-identify, positive emotions, passionate desire, emotional bonding, and length of use are some of the other aspects through which brands can develop their associations. Parachute Advansed brand advertises the daughter advising her mother about the brand (emotional bonding); Red Bull is all about passion; Fair & Lovely is about social confidence (psychological benefit), and Ujala's blue to be used on white clothes denotes a cultural value.

Application 2: Associative Network and Branding

Associative network consists of nodes. Any concept can be stored in a node like a brand name, person's image, name of a place. The nodes are linked to form an associative network that will have a schema (one provides a total set of associations concerning a set of nodes). A brand like Titan, for example, may be interested in linking several nodes that have favorable associations of the brand.

There is a powerful link between the classical conditioning aspects and the associative networks created in the long-term memory. While classical conditioning may be limited by certain aspects (like advertising wear out), associative network seems to offer tremendous scope for brands to explore several associations from the view point of strengthening them, at least in the Indian context. Sachin Tendulkar, at one point of time, was endorsing 13–14 brands.[39] While advertising wear out is associated with one brand presented in a familiar format, the same phenomenon could have created celebrity wear out with so much of familiarity and exposure with regard to the usage of celebrities. Perhaps it is the power of the associative networks that have made marketers use the same charismatic celebrity across brands. This scenario presents a worthwhile research proposition. Dove, with its 'mild, trusted, and problem solving' associations, is present in soaps, shampoos, deodorants and hair oil.[40]

Should marketers place ads as a part of a TV program to achieve effective outcomes?[41] The Indian Premier League has over a million viewers, ensuring that brands that are advertised gain through familiarity and repeated exposure. Brands that are established also benefit through such strategies. Placing an ad as part of a TV program will depend on a two factors – involvement in the program (as discussed later in the chapter) and relevance or linkage of the advertisement to the program. Consumers who are highly involved in a cricket match may fail to notice an ad for a pain balm if the ad explains the benefit of the brand after a six is scored by a batsman. But in a TV serial centered on a child (theme of the serial), an ad for a tire company, elaborating on how a child is saved from an accident because of the attributes of the brand, may sink in with the audience watching that TV serial.

Information Rehearsal and Encoding

The amount of information available for delivery from short-term storage to long-term storage depends on the amount of rehearsal it receives. Failure to rehearse an input, either by repeating it or by relating it to other data, can result in fading and eventual loss of the information. Information can also be lost because of competition for attention. For example, if the short-term store receives a great number of inputs simultaneously from the sensory store, its capacity may be reduced to only two or three pieces of information.

The purpose of rehearsal is to hold information in short-term storage long enough for encoding to take place. **Encoding** is the process by which we select a word or visual image to represent a perceived object. Marketers help consumers encode brands by using brand symbols. Kellogg's uses Tony the Tiger on its Frosted Flakes; the Green Giant Company has its Jolly Green Giant. Dell Computer turns the *e* in its logo on its side for quick name recognition, and Apple uses its stylish and distinctive insignia.

Processing and remembering a picture takes less time than learning verbal information, but both types of information are important in forming an overall mental image. A print ad with both an illustration and body copy is more likely to be encoded and stored than an illustration without verbal information. High-imagery copy produces greater recall than low-imagery copy, and marketers realize that almost every ad should include some form of an illustration. In one study, consumers were given goals and then asked to memorize ads. The study found that an ad-memorization goal enhanced attention to the body text, pictures, and brand design. A brand-learning goal produced attention to the body text, but also inhibited attention to the pictorial design. One may conclude that text-dominant ads activate brand learning and pictorial-dominant ads activate ad appreciation.[42]

Encoding of commercials is related to the context in which they are featured. For example, while watching TV, some parts of a program may require viewers to commit a larger portion of their cognitive resources to processing (e.g., when a dramatic event takes place versus a casual conversation). When viewers commit more cognitive resources to the program than the ads, they encode and store less of the information conveyed by a commercial. This suggests that commercials requiring relatively little cognitive processing may be more effective within or adjacent to a dramatic program setting than commercials requiring more elaborate processing. Viewers who are very involved with a television show respond more positively to commercials adjacent to that show and have more positive purchase intentions. Recent exposure to related information also facilitates encoding. A study found that publicity about advertising campaigns before they were started facilitated better recall of brands featured in subsequent advertising.[43]

When consumers receive too much information and then have difficulty encoding and storing it, **information overload** occurs. For example, in product categories where several strong brands are heavily promoted, consumers do not remember product information featured in ads that promote new brands. Consumers can also become cognitively overloaded when they receive a lot of information in a limited time. Such overload leads to consumer frustration, confusion, and poor purchase decisions.

Information Retention and Retrieval

Information does not merely remain in long-term storage waiting to be retrieved. It is constantly organized and reorganized, as new chunks of information are received and new links among those chunks are created. For example, a memory of a product's name may be activated by relating it to the spokesperson appearing in its advertising.

Product information stored in memory is brand based, and consumers interpret new information consistently with the way in which it has already been organized. One study demonstrated that "brand imprinting"—messages that merely establish the brand's identity—if conducted before presentation of the brand's benefits, facilitated consumer learning and retention of information about the brand.[44] Studies also showed that a brand's "sound symbolism" (a theory suggesting that the sounds of words convey meanings) and the brand's "linguistic characteristics" (e.g., unusual spelling) affected the encoding and retention of the brand name.[45]

A key component of retention is called **chunking**, defined as the process during which consumers recode what they have already encoded; this process often results in recalling additional relevant information. Marketers have studied the kinds and numbers of groupings (or "chunks") of information that consumers can handle. They discovered that that consumers' recall declined when the chunks featured in advertisements did not match the ones stored in the consumers' minds. Also, consumers who are more knowledgeable about a product category can absorb more complex chunks of information than less knowledgeable consumers.

Retrieval is the process by which people recover information from the long-term store; it is frequently triggered by external cues. For example, when we see a product in the store or on TV, we automatically retrieve the applicable information our brains have stored. If the brand is distinctive and heavily advertised, or if we had a memorable experience using it, the retrieval will be quicker than that for less sought-after brands. Some scientists used brain-imaging technologies, normally used in medicine, to examine information retrieval. For example, when men looked at racy sports cars, their reward centers were activated. In an experiment involving soft drinks, two different brain regions were at play. When some loyal drinkers of Coke and others of Pepsi tasted two soft drinks with the brands unidentified, their brains' reward system was activated. The respondents were then asked which of the two they liked better. Afterward, they were told the brand of the drink they liked better in the blind taste test. At that point, their brains' memory region (where information regarding brand loyalty is stored) was activated and overrode the preferences the participants indicated after tasting the soft drink, but before knowing which brand they had tasted. That is, if the brand they said they liked better was *not* their regular brand, they changed their minds regarding which drink they liked better during the blind taste test.[46]

Unexpected elements improve consumers' ad retention only when those elements are relevant to the advertising message. For example, an ad for a brand of stain-resistant, easy-to-clean carpet shows an elegantly dressed couple in a beautiful dining room setting where the man inadvertently knocks the food, the flowers, and the china to the floor. The elegance of the actors and the upscale setting make the accident totally unexpected, whereas the message remains highly relevant: The mess can be cleaned up easily without leaving a stain on the carpet. Because this ad is very dramatic, it is likely to be remembered (or retrieved) when the consumer is exposed to any of the elements of the ad thereafter. However, unexpected cues are not the same as incongruent ones. Although consumers notice ads containing cues that are incongruent with the products advertised, they are unlikely to remember them. For instance, a print ad showing a nude woman sitting on a piece of office furniture would very likely attract readers' attention, but would probably not increase the likelihood that the ad purveyor would be remembered or subsequently retrieved. In one experiment, where subjects were manipulated into making choices among four desserts based on memory or on the actual stimuli (the desserts themselves), researchers discovered that memory-based product choices were guided more by feelings (e.g., an urge for tasty food), whereas stimulus-based choices were guided more by deliberative considerations (e.g., the need to follow a sensible diet).[47]

A greater number of competitive ads in a product category leads to lower recall of all brands' advertising claims, because consumers are confused by many competing ads and they find it hard to retrieve information. Under such conditions, ads can activate the retrieval of cues for competing brands. For example, consumers may believe that the long-running and attention-getting television campaign featuring the Eveready Energizer Bunny is an ad for Duracell batteries.

Learning Objective

6 To understand cognitive learning as a framework for consumer decision-making.

Cognitive Learning

Cognitive learning is the systematic evaluation of information and alternatives needed to solve a recognized but unfilled need or unsolved problem. Unlike behavioral learning, which consists of instinctive responses to stimuli, cognitive learning involves deliberate mental processing of information. Cognitive psychologists focus on the roles of motivation and mental processes in producing a desired response, rather than the immediate response to a given stimulus.

Cognitive learning occurs when a person has a goal and must search for and process data in order to make a decision or solve a problem. For a long time, consumer researchers believed that all consumers passed through a complex series of mental and behavioral stages in arriving at a purchase decision. These stages ranged from awareness of the purchase options (exposure to information), to evaluation and preferences regarding the alternatives available, to possibly trying one or more versions of the product, and then buying or not buying it (behavior expressed as adoption or rejection). For example, a consumer looking to purchase a super-slim, point-and-shoot digital camera (the goal) must choose among many brands and models (problem solving). The consumer will first get to know the features of different models (exposure to information resulting in knowledge), then develop preferences and evaluations regarding the different alternatives, and then decide which model to buy and which ones not to purchase (rejection).

The ad for Crest Pro-Health toothpaste in Figure 5.12 is based on cognitive learning. Let's assume that Betty has had her teeth cleaned every six months—as recommended by dentists—and the tartar and plaque on her teeth has been removed regularly. But, as she grew older, her gums became sensitive and occasionally painful. During her regular cleaning, her dentist tells her that she has occasional gingivitis, which is an inflammation of the gums, and advises her to use toothpaste specifically designed to battle this condition. Previously, Betty regarded toothpaste as a "commodity," considered all brands to be similar, and bought whichever brands were on sale. But, following her dentist's advice, she now faces a new problem and unfilled need: Finding a toothpaste specifically designed to fight gingivitis. She then sees the Crest ad, and, although Crest Pro-Health is more expensive, she starts using it. Subsequently, her gums no longer hurt and her dentist compliments her on her excellent oral hygiene. Betty engaged in cognitive learning: She faced a problem, looked for a solution, read about the benefits of Crest Pro-Health in the ad, and started using the product consistently, which resulted in relief from pain and thus reinforced what she had learned.

Researchers developed several models depicting sequential information processing and cognitive learning, which are featured in Table 5.1. Although the models use different terms to designate the sequences they depict, in essence they all follow the three-stage generic sequence listed in the table's leftmost column.

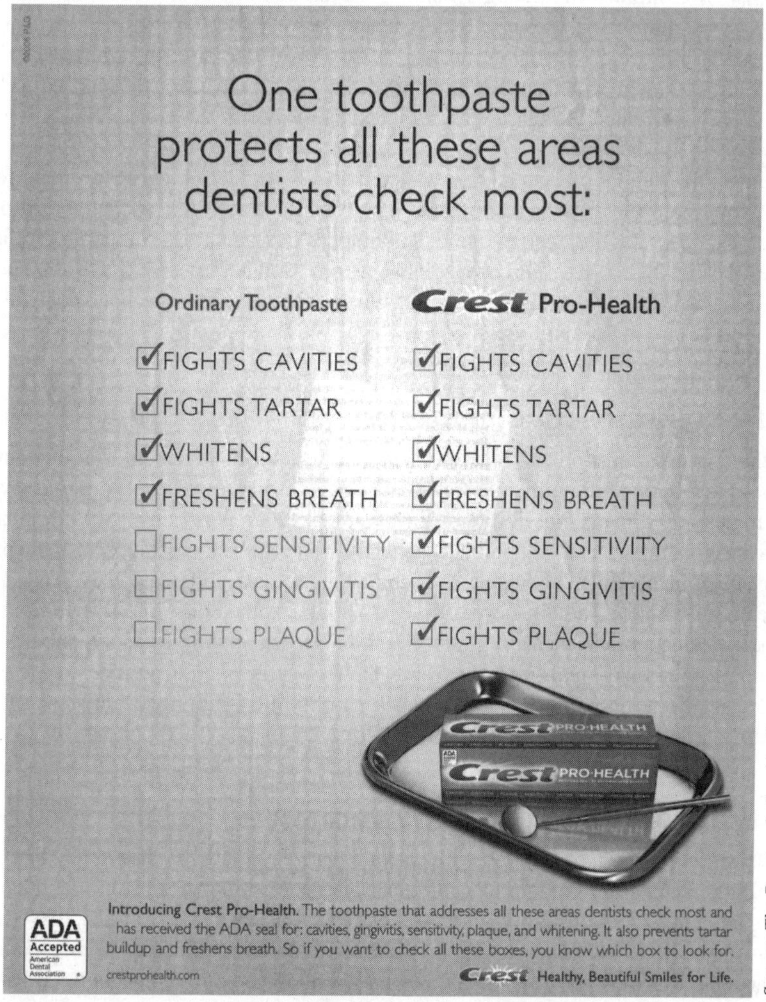

Source: The Proctor & Gamble Company

FIGURE 5.12 Cognitive Learning: Crest Pro-Health

TABLE 5.1 Representations of Cognitive Learning

GENERIC STAGES OF COGNITIVE LEARNING	TRI-COMPONENT ATTITUDE MODEL	AIDA	INNOVATION ADOPTION	INNOVATION DECISION-MAKING
Knowledge	Cognitive	Attention	Awareness	Knowledge
Evaluation	Affective	Interest and Desire	Interest and Evaluation	Persuasion
Behavior	Conative	Action	Trial and Adoption	Decision and Confirmation

Learning Objective

7 To understand consumer involvement and passive learning, and their impact on purchase decisions and the retention and recall of promotional communications.

Consumer Involvement and Hemispheric Lateralization

Initially, marketing scholars believed that complex processing of information applied to all purchases, expensive and cheaper alike. Later on, theorists realized that many purchases, especially routine ones, do not involve extensive information processing and evaluation. Such purchases are of minimal personal relevance, as opposed to highly relevant, search-oriented purchases. This understanding led to the conceptualization and study of consumer involvement.

Consumer involvement is the degree of personal relevance that the product or purchase holds for the consumer. **High-involvement purchases** are very important to the consumer (e.g., in terms of perceived risk) and thus provoke extensive problem solving and information processing. Under this scenario, both automobiles and dandruff shampoo can represent high-involvement purchases: The automobile because of its high perceived financial risk (to most people), and the shampoo because of high perceived social risk (to some people). **Low-involvement purchases** are not very important, hold little relevance, have little perceived risk, and provoke limited information processing.

Measurements of Consumer Involvement

There is great variation in the conceptualization and measurement of consumer involvement. Throughout the marketing research literature, "involvement" has been defined in numerous ways, including product involvement, brand involvement, and advertising involvement. Because there is no universal definition of involvement, there is no single way to measure it. Some measures gauge cognitive factors, such as the importance of a purchase to a buyer and the risk perceived with the purchase; other measures focus on the behavioral aspects of involvement and appraise such factors as the search for and evaluation of product information. The most popular measurement tool is self-administered surveys that assess the consumer's cognitions or behaviors regarding a particular product or product category, and measure involvement on a continuum (not as a dichotomy). For example, a scale measuring involvement with, say, e-books might require respondents to express their attitudes on five-point, bi-polar **semantic differential scales** on ranges between paired adjectives, such as important—unimportant, relevant—irrelevant, exciting—unexciting, priceless—worthless, and interesting—boring.

Strategic Applications of Consumer Involvement

Marketers aspire to create customers who are involved with the purchase and view the brand they buy as unique. Many studies have shown that high involvement with the product category, and also perception of a given brand as superior, leads to brand loyalty.[48] Although there is no generalized profile of a highly involved consumer, many studies have investigated the personal characteristics related to involvement level. For example, researchers found a relationship between ethnicity and involvement; appeals portraying Hispanic identities were effective in advertising low-involvement items, but not high-involvement products.[49]

Research indicates that the context in which the promotional message appears has an impact on involvement. One study discovered that consumers who were highly involved in the sports program they watched recalled commercials significantly better than those who were less involved with the program.[50] Another study found that involvement with video games affected brand memory. Players who were initially unfamiliar with the game, but became highly involved with it while learning how to play, recalled many of the brands embedded in the game. When they became experienced players, they became less involved with the game and recalled fewer of the brands it featured.[51] Many marketers now show avatars—animated, virtual-reality, people-like figures—in websites. Avatars have been effective, and studies have found that this is because they often engage consumers in learning about and becoming involved with products and services. One study discovered that *attractive* avatar sales agents were effective in selling to consumers with moderate product involvement, whereas *expert* avatars were more effective sales agent for products with high involvement levels.[52] In addition to increasing product and brand involvement, marketers must also expand customer involvement with their ads; they can use sensory appeals, unusual stimuli, celebrity endorsers, and scores of innovative techniques online to increase the persuasiveness of their promotions.

Highly involved consumers engage in long-term relationships with products and brands, and increasing involvement levels enhances these bonds. The best strategy for increasing the personal relevance of products to consumers is the same as the core of modern marketing: Providing benefits that are important to customers, differentiating the offering from its competition, improving the product and adding relevant benefits (especially as competition intensifies).

Hemispheric Lateralization

Hemispheric lateralization (split-brain theory) stems from medical research done in the 1960s; its premise is that the human brain is divided into two distinct cerebral hemispheres that operate together, but "specialize" in processing different types of cognitions. The left hemisphere is the center of human language; it is the linear side of the brain and primarily responsible for reading, speaking, and reasoning. The right hemisphere of the brain is the home of spatial perception and nonverbal concepts; it is nonlinear and the source of imagination and pleasure. Put another way, the left side of the brain is rational, active, and realistic; the right side is emotional, metaphoric, impulsive, and intuitive. Some argue that computers emulate many of the sequential functions of the left side of the brain and that we should employ the imaginative, right brain to a greater degree in making business decisions.[53] Figure 5.13 shows an American Airlines ad literally depicting the split-brain theory.

Passive Learning

A pioneer consumer researcher applied hemispheric lateralization to watching TV. He theorized that when consumers watch advertising on TV, they "passively" process right brain, pictorial information.[54] The researcher considered TV a primarily pictorial medium, and TV viewing as a right-brain activity, consisting of passive and holistic processing of images

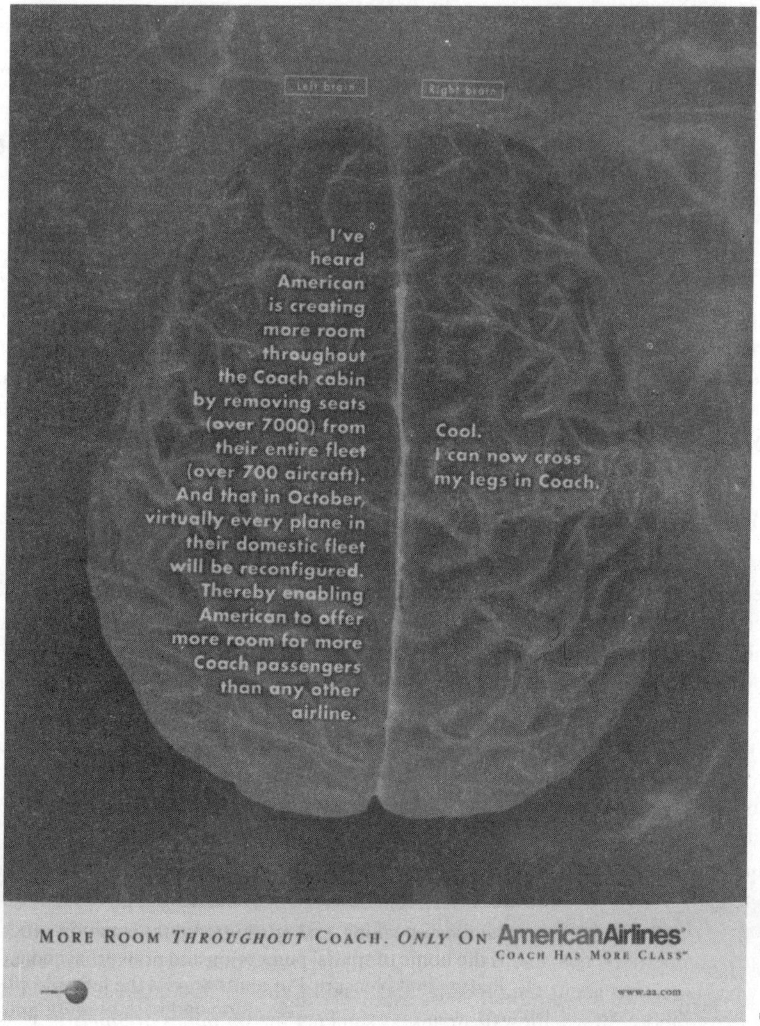

Source: American Airlines

FIGURE 5.13 Hemispheric Lateralization

viewed on the screen. He also maintained that TV is a low-involvement medium. The core of cognitive learning is that consumers deliberate about purchases, seek and evaluate applicable information, form attitudes toward the purchase alternatives available, and then make purchase decisions. According to these models, behavior *follows* the cognitive processing of information. In contrast, advocates of **passive learning** maintain that repeated exposure to TV commercials, which is low-involvement information processing, induces purchases *prior* to consumers' information processing and the formation of attitudes.

As opposed to TV, printed, verbal and static information in newspapers is processed by the brain's left side. Therefore, print media are considered high involvement. Accordingly, the processing of printed advertising takes place in the left brain, and along the cognitive learning sequences featured in Table 5.1. In contrast, advertising that consists mostly of moving images and pictorial information is processed holistically by the right side of the viewer's brain, with minimum involvement.

The right brain's passive processing of information is consistent with classical conditioning. Through repetition, the product is paired with a visual image (e.g., a distinctive package) to produce the purchase of the advertised brand. Accordingly, during passive learning and exposure to low-involvement media, continuous repetition of advertisements is the key factor in producing purchase behavior. This line of thinking also suggests that television commercials are most effective when they are of short (15 or 20 seconds) and repeated frequently. Right-brain information processing underscores the importance of the visual components of advertising. Strong visuals in TV commercials and in-store displays generate familiarity with the brand and induce purchase behavior. Pictorial cues are more effective at generating recall and familiarity with the product, whereas verbal cues (which trigger left-brain processing) generate cognitive activity that encourages consumers to evaluate the advantages and disadvantages of the product.

Learning Objective

8 To understand how to measure the results of consumer learning.

Outcomes and Measures of Consumer Learning

For marketers, the goals of consumer learning are increased market share and brand-loyal consumers. These goals are interdependent: Brand-loyal customers are the core of a stable and growing market share, and brands with larger market shares have disproportionately large numbers of loyal buyers. Marketers' promotions are designed to teach consumers for whom the brands promoted provide the best solutions for satisfying unfilled needs. Thus, marketers must measure to what extent consumers have learned the information contained in promotional messages. The most popular measures of consumer learning are recognition and recall of messages and attitudinal and behavioral evaluations of brand loyalty.

Recognition and Recall Measures

The purpose of recognition and recall tests is to determine whether consumers remember seeing an ad and the extent to which they have read it and can recall its content. Recognition tests are based on **aided recall**, whereas recall tests use **unaided recall**. In a **recognition test**, the consumer is shown an ad and asked whether he or she remembers seeing it and can remember any of its salient points. In a **recall test**, the consumer is asked whether he or she has read a specific magazine or watched a specific television show, and, if so, whether he or she can recall any ads or commercials seen, the product and brand advertised, and any notable points about the offerings promoted.

For example, the **Starch Readership Ad Study** evaluates the effectiveness of magazine advertisements according to three criteria: Noticing the ad, associating the ad with the brand advertised, and involvement with the ad (defined as having read most of the ad text). At the start of a Starch survey, respondents are presented with a magazine issue and asked whether they have read it. Those who respond positively are then shown each ad that had appeared in that issue—with the brand name concealed—and asked questions that measure recall and recognition of the ad. The study output consists of tagged advertisements, with the tags showing the percentage of readers who have "noticed" each ad, were able to "associate" the ad with the brand advertised, and "read most" of the ad's copy. Advertisers can then gauge the effectiveness of each ad by comparing its scores on the Starch measures to similar-sized ads, competitors' ads, and their own prior ads. Starch also appraises consumers' intentions to buy and likelihood to engaging in word-of-mouth about the product after reading the ad. A study using Starch readership scores demonstrated that consumers received more information from advertisements for *shopping products* (e.g., high-priced clothing and accessories) than from ads for *convenience goods* (e.g., low-priced items purchased routinely). Surprisingly, they also received less information from ads for *search products*, that is, very expensive, durable items purchased infrequently and following an extensive information search. These findings show that marketers may not be including enough information when advertising search products.[55]

Brand Loyalty

Brand loyalty is a measure of how often consumers buy a given brand; whether or not they switch brands and, if they do, how often; and the extent of their commitment to buying the brand regularly. To marketers, a high degree of brand loyalty is the most desired outcome of consumer learning and an indication that they have effectively "taught" consumers a given behavior (i.e., buying the marketer's brands consistently). Marketers agree that brand loyalty has two components—behaviors and attitudes—and that both must be measured. Attitudinal measures gauge consumers' overall feelings about the brand, including their future purchase intentions. Behavioral measures focus on observable, factual behaviors, such as the quantity purchased, purchase frequency, and repeated buying.

Behavioral learning scientists who favor the theory of instrumental conditioning believe that brand loyalty results from an initial product trial that was reinforced through satisfaction, which led to repeat and continuous patronage. In contrast, researchers of cognitive learning believe that consumers engage in extensive problem solving, information search, and evaluation of alternatives that eventually lead to a strong brand preference and ongoing purchase behavior. Nevertheless, consumer behavior researchers agree that if a consumer finds many brands in a particular category to be "acceptable," he or she is unlikely to be brand loyal. Therefore, marketers must differentiate their products from competition so that they stand out and consumers become reluctant to view other brands as "acceptable."

The degree of brand loyalty depends on three factors: (1) the consumer's risk aversion or variety seeking; (2) the brand's reputation and availability of substitute brands; and (3) social group influences and peers' recommendations. There are three types of brand loyalty:

1. **Covetous brand loyalty** includes no consistent purchase of a given brand, in spite of strong attachment to it.
2. **Inertia brand loyalty** is purchasing the brand because of habit and convenience, but without any emotional attachment to it.
3. **Premium brand loyalty** means high attachment to the brand and repeat purchase.[56]

Low involvement with a given product category results in habitual buying without emotional attachment to any brand (i.e., inertia loyalty). Consumers perceive minor or no differences among brands and buy a brand repeatedly only because of familiarity and convenience. Premium loyalty represents truly brand-loyal consumers. They are committed to the brand, unlikely to switch to other brands, and likely to go out of their way to buy the same brand (e.g., if a supermarket ran out of their brand, they would drive to another store).

Brand Equity

High brand loyalty greatly increases a brand's monetary value. The term **brand equity** represents the intrinsic value of a brand name. This value stems from the foundations of brand loyalty: The consumer's perception of the brand's superiority, the social esteem that using it provides, and the customer's trust and identification with the brand.

Brands that are heavily promoted for extended periods attain ample name recognition and consumer loyalty, which result is high brand equity. Because of the escalating costs of developing new products and their high failure rates, many companies capitalize on their brands' equity in the forms of family branding and product line extensions rather than launching new brands. Brand equity facilitates the acceptance of new products, allocation of preferred space by distributors, and charging premium prices. Brand equity is most important for low-involvement purchases, such as inexpensive consumer goods that are bought routinely and with little processing of cognitive information. In such circumstances, the most important strategy is continuous advertising designed to prevent extinction and forgetting.

Brand names are the most valuable assets of marketers of consumer goods and services. Among the best-known brands are Apple, Coca-Cola, Campbell's, Disney, Google, Hallmark, and Sony. These names are global, "cultural icons" and enjoy powerful advantages over the competition. According to studies, some the highest equity brands are: Among airlines—Alaska/Horizon, Hawaiian, Delta, and United; among luxury cars—Mercedes-Benz, BMW, Lexus, Acura, Infiniti, Porsche, and Audi; among sports apparel—UnderArmour, Nike and Columbia; and among household cleaners— Lysol All Purpose, Clorox, and Mr. Clean Multi-Purpose.[57]

Summary

Learning Objective 1: To understand the elements of learning in the context of consumer behavior.

Learning is the process by which individuals acquire the purchase and consumption knowledge and experience they apply to future, related behavior. Consumer learning is a process that evolves and changes as consumers acquire knowledge from experience, observation, and interactions with others and newly acquired knowledge affects future behavior. It ranges from simple and often reflexive responses to marketing stimuli (such as packaging, product colors, and promotional messages), to learning abstract concepts and making decisions about purchasing complex and expensive products. The elements of learning are motives (drives), cues, responses, and reinforcement.

Learning Objective 2: To understand behavioral learning, classical conditioning, and the roles of stimulus generalization and discrimination in developing and branding new products.

Behavioral learning (also referred to as stimulus-response learning) maintains that observable responses to external stimuli signal that learning has taken place. Behavioral learning focuses on the inputs and outcomes of learning; that is, on the stimuli that consumers select from the environment and the behaviors that result. There are three forms of behavioral learning: classical conditioning, instrumental (or operant) conditioning, and observational (or modeling) learning.

Classical conditioning (also known as Pavlovian conditioning) is learning where repetion causes the conditioned stimulus to signal the occurrence of the unconditioned stimulus. The strategic applications of classical conditioning to consumer behavior are associative learning, repetition, stimulus generalization, and stimulus discrimination.

Learning Objective 3: To understand instrumental conditioning and the objectives and methods of reinforcement.

Instrumental learning theorists believe that learning occurs through a trial-and-error process in which positive outcomes (i.e., rewards) result in repeat behavior. Both positive and negative reinforcement can be used to encourage the desired behavior. Reinforcement schedules can be total (consistent) or partial (fixed ratio or random). The timing of repetitions influences how long the learned material is retained. Massed repetitions produce more initial learning than distributed repetitions; however, learning usually persists longer with distributed (i.e., spread out) reinforcement schedules.

Learning Objective 4: To understand the role of observational learning in consumer behavior.

Observational learning (or modeling) is the process through which individuals learn behavior by observing the behavior of others and the consequences of such behavior. Advertisers recognize the importance of observational learning in their selection of models, whether celebrities or unknowns. Many ads feature likeable models achieving positive outcomes to common problem situations through the use of the advertised product.

Learning Objective 5: To understand the elements of information processing, including receiving, storing, and retrieving consumption-related information.

The human mind processes the information it receives. Consumers process product information by attributes, brands, comparisons between brands, or a combination of these factors. The number and complexity of the relevant attributes and available alternatives influence the intensity or degree of information processing. Consumers with higher cognitive abilities acquire more product information and consider more product attributes and alternatives than consumers with lesser ability. The elements of memory are the sensory store, the short-term store (or working memory), and the long-term store. The processes of memory include rehearsal, encoding, storage, and retrieval.

Learning Objective 6: To understand cognitive learning as a framework for consumer decision-making.

Cognitive learning is the systematic evaluation of information and alternatives needed to meet a recognized unfilled need or solve a problem. Unlike behavioral learning, which focuses on largely instinctive responses to stimuli, cognitive learning consists of deliberate mental processing of information. Instead of focusing on repetition or the association of a reward with a specific response, cognitive theorists emphasize the role of motivation and mental processes in producing a desired response. Several models of cognitive learning are discussed throughout this book.

Learning Objective 7: To understand consumer involvement and passive learning, and their impact on purchase decisions and the retention and recall of promotional communications.

The consumer involvement model proposes that people engage in limited information processing in situations of low importance or relevance to them, and in extensive information processing in situations of high relevance. Hemispheric lateralization (split-brain) theory gave rise to the notion that television is a low-involvement medium that results in passive learning and that print and interactive media encourage more cognitive information processing.

Learning Objective 8: To understand how to measure the results of consumer learning.

Measures of consumer learning include recall and recognition tests, and attitudinal and behavioral measures of brand loyalty. Brand loyalty consists of both attitudes and actual behaviors toward a brand, and both must be measured. For marketers, the major reasons for understanding how consumers learn are to teach consumers that the marketers' brand is best and to develop brand loyalty. Brand equity represents the intrinsic value of a brand name. This value stems from the foundations of brand loyalty: The consumer's perception of the brand's superiority, the social esteem that using it provides, and the customer's trust and identification with the brand.

Review and Discussion Questions

5.1. How can the principles of: (a) classical conditioning and (b) instrumental conditioning be applied to the development of marketing strategies?

5.2. Describe in learning terms the conditions under which family branding is a good policy and those under which it is not.

5.3. Neutrogena, a company known for its "dermatologist recommended" skin care products, introduced a line of shaving products for men. How can the company use stimulus generalization to market these products? Is instrumental conditioning applicable to this marketing situation? If so, how?

5.4. Which form of learning—classical conditioning, instrumental conditioning, observational learning, or cognitive learning—best explains the following consumption behaviors: (a) buying a six-pack of Gatorade, (b) preferring to purchase jeans at a Diesel Store, (c) buying an e-reader for the first time, (d) buying a new car, and (e) switching from one cell phone service to another? Explain your choices.

5.5. Define the following memory structures: Sensory store, short-term store (working memory), and long-term store. Discuss how each of these concepts can be used in the development of an advertising strategy.

5.6. How does information overload affect the consumer's ability to comprehend an ad and store it in his or her memory?

5.7. Discuss the differences between low- and high-involvement media. How would you apply the knowledge of hemispheric lateralization to the design of TV commercials and print advertisements?

5.8. Why are both attitudinal and behavioral measures important in measuring brand loyalty?

5.9. What is the relationship between brand loyalty and brand equity? What role do both concepts play in the development of marketing strategies?

5.10. How can marketers use measures of recognition and recall to study the extent of consumer learning?

Hands-on Assignments

5.11. Imagine that you are the instructor of this course and that you are trying to increase student participation in class discussions. How would you use reinforcement to achieve your objective?

5.12. Visit a supermarket. Can you identify any packages where you think the marketer's knowledge of stimulus generalization or stimulus discrimination was incorporated into the package design? Note these examples and present them in class.

5.13. Find two ads: one targeting the left side of the brain and another targeting the right side. Explain your choices.

Key Terms

- advertising wear-out *146*
- AIDA *159*
- aided recall *162*
- behavioral learning (stimulus-response learning) *142*
- brand equity *163*
- brand loyalty *163*
- chunking *157*
- classical conditioning *143*
- cognitive associative learning *145*
- cognitive learning *154*
- conditioned response *143*
- conditioned stimulus *143*
- consumer involvement *160*
- consumer learning *140*

- continuous reinforcement *152*
- covetous brand loyalty *163*
- cues *140*
- distributed learning *153*
- encoding *157*
- extinction *152*
- family branding *148*
- fixed ratio reinforcement *152*
- forgetting *152*
- hemispheric lateralization (split-brain theory) *161*
- high-involvement purchases *160*
- inertia brand loyalty *163*
- information overload *157*
- innovation adoption *159*
- innovation decision making *159*
- instrumental conditioning (operant conditioning) *149*
- learning *138*
- licensing *148*
- long-term store *155*
- low-involvement purchases *160*
- massed learning *153*
- motivation *140*
- negative reinforcement *151*
- observational learning (modeling) *153*
- passive learning *162*
- positive reinforcement *151*
- premium brand loyalty *163*
- product form extensions *148*
- product line extensions *147*
- recall test *162*
- recognition test *162*
- rehearsal *155*
- reinforcement *141*
- repetition *145*
- response *141*
- retrieval *157*
- semantic differential scale *160*
- sensory store *155*
- shaping *152*
- short-term store (working memory) *165*
- Starch Readership Ad Study *162*
- stimulus discrimination *149*
- stimulus generalization *147*
- three-hit theory *146*
- tri-component attitude model *159*
- unaided recall *162*
- unconditioned stimulus *143*
- variable ratio reinforcement *152*

6

Consumer Attitude Formation and Change

Learning Objectives

1 To understand what attitudes are, how they are formed, and their role in consumer behavior.

2 To understand the tri-component attitude model and its applications.

3 To understand the structures of multi-attribute models and their use in altering consumers' attitudes.

4 To understand how to alter consumers' attitudes by making particular needs prominent.

5 To understand the role of cognitive elaboration in altering attitudes.

6 To understand how attitudes can precede behavior in the form of cognitive dissonance and the resolution of conflicting attitudes.

7 To understand the ways people assign causality to events and apply this knowledge to consumer behavior.

AN ATTITUDE is a learned predisposition to behave in a consistently favorable or unfavorable way toward a given object. In the context of consumer behavior, an "object" can be a product, brand, service, price, package, advertisement, promotional medium, or the retailer selling the product, among many other aspects of consumption.

Attitudes are learned from direct experience with the product, **word-of-mouth**, exposure to mass media, and other information sources that consumers are exposed to. Attitudes reflect either favorable or unfavorable evaluations of the attitude object and motivate consumers to either buy or not buy particular products or brands. Consumers buy products toward which they have positive and favorable feelings; therefore, marketers must ensure that consumers maintain these attitudes following the purchase so that they keep buying same products repeatedly.

Marketers who introduce new items strive to form favorable consumer attitudes toward the new products in order to get consumers try them, like them, and continue buying them. Doing so is difficult because people are often unreceptive to the unfamiliar, at least initially. One way to establish positive consumer attitudes toward new products is to capitalize on products that consumers already like and buy regularly. For example, Figure 6.1 presents an ad for Himalaya's Pure Hands. When a new product is introduced in a market that is unfamiliar with it, the brand has to build an attitude toward both the category and the brand. Hand sanitizer is a very new category in India and so the ad explains the concept of a sanitizer and the necessity for such a product (through the mention of swine flu, along with other infections) in order to build attitudes toward the brand and the category.

Box 6.1 Apple vs Blackberry –Lessons on Attitude Creation

Apple has been in the lead the coolest of innovations likeiPod, iPhone, and iPad. These offerings offered several "cool" features that several consumers were addicted to – video/picture sharing, seamless connection with apple devices, iTune downloads, linkages with Nike (Nike Plus), variety of apps that were downloaded several million times. Blackberry created a "cool offering" of receiving emails on the go but failed to evolve such features over a period of time. Its Bold 9000, Storm, BB 10 variants like Play Book[1,2] tablet (without an e mail), and its apps failed to offer features that were as exciting as that of Apple. The "cool" benefits are created through a set of features and consumers who initially like the brand Apple affect-aspect of attitude tend to develop a cognitive structure that underlies the affect. "Apple has fun features that I can share with my friends." is a cognitive association that may merge from such cognitive structures. These structures are difficult to change and when a brand continues to update its features and offerings (same/related or different category), the cognitive structure gets strengthened and can lead to loyalty towards the brand. The word of mouth about Apple may be an outcome of such a combination of such cognition and affect. There needs to be a strong association between attitudes and the beliefs created in the cognitive structure of a brand. The cognitive beliefs that are associated with attitude towards a brand is known as evaluative cognitive consistency[3,4] and hence, brands that have a strong cognitive structure are likely to develop a strong attitude among its consumers.

Micromax and Karbonn mobiles offer low-budget and successful smart phones. The idea of "Cool" features at "value-for-money" prices is also an example of the creating strong cognitive structures.

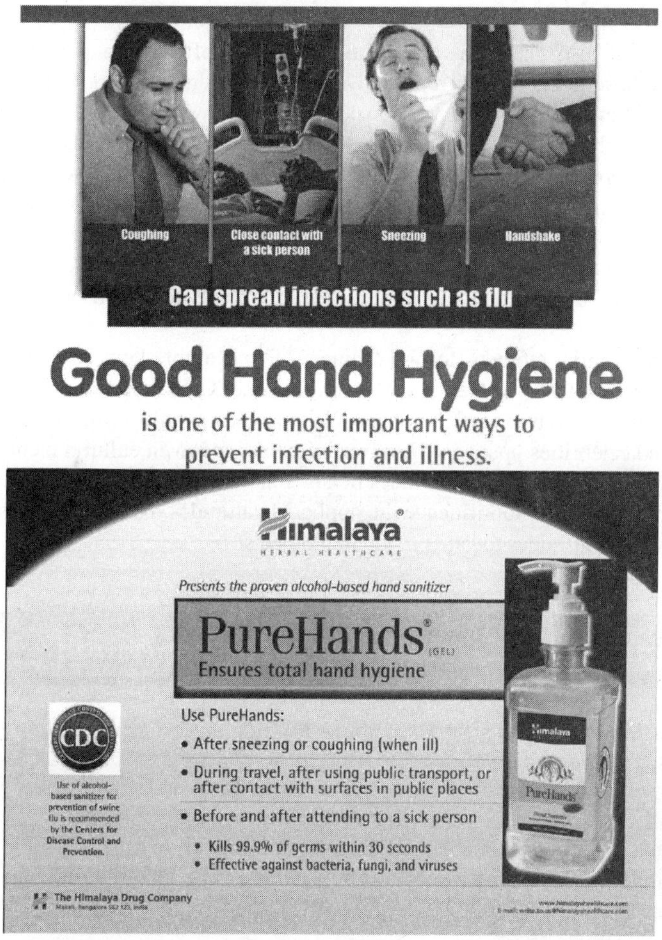

Source: The Himalaya Drug Company.

FIGURE 6.1 Building an Attitude Towards the Brand

Learning Objective

1 To understand what attitudes are, how they are formed, and their role in consumer behavior.

Attitudes and Their Formation

As consumers, all of us have many attitudes toward products, services, advertisements, the Internet, and retail stores, among many others. Whenever we are asked whether we like or dislike a product (e.g., Black and White cookies), a service (e.g., American Airlines), a particular retailer (e.g., J. Crew), a specific direct-online marketer (e.g., Amazon.com), or an advertising theme (e.g., "Snickers Satisfies"), we are being asked to express our attitudes. By studying consumers' attitudes, marketers try to determine whether consumers will accept new products the company is considering, gauge why market segments were not persuaded by promotional themes, or learn how target customers are likely to react to new products, packages and the like. To illustrate, Nike or Reebok frequently study consumers' attitudes towards the functional and aesthetic design of athletic footwear. They regularly gauge reactions to their latest advertising and other marketing messages designed to form and change consumer attitudes. Attitudes are cognitions and not easily observable, but researchers can assess them by asking questions or making inferences from behavior. For example, if a researcher questions a student and discovers that he purchases Lady Gaga recordings from iTunes often and listens to them a lot, the researcher will *infer* that the student likes Lady Gaga and has a positive attitude towards her (and also towards iTunes).

Attitudes are directed at objects, such as products, product categories, brands, services, promotional messages, websites, media, retailers, and many other entities. We must note that although attitudes generally lead to behavior, they are not synonymous with behavior. Sometimes, attitudes reflect either a favorable or an unfavorable evaluation of the attitude object, which might or might not lead to behavior. Attitudes might propel consumers *toward* a particular behavior or repel them *away* from such.

Consumers Learn Attitudes

Consumers form new attitudes and also change existing attitudes. They often form positive attitudes towards new items under the same brand that they have been buying repeatedly and have been satisfied with. Nevertheless, consumers often try new products, product models, and different brands. If such trial purchases meet or exceed their expectations, then they develop favorable attitudes toward those objects. Generally, the more information consumers have about a product or service, the more likely they are to form attitudes about it, either positive or negative. However, if the product is irrelevant to them, the consumers will not cognitively process any of the available and applicable information. Furthermore, consumers often use only a limited amount of the information available to them. Typically, only two or three prominent beliefs about a product play a role in the formation of attitudes, and less important beliefs carry little weight. Therefore, advertisements should be focused on the key points that differentiate products from competitors, and not detail too many of the products' features.

How do consumers form their initial attitudes toward "things"? For example how do young adults form attitudes toward Hanes or Calvin Klein underwear, or J. Crew or Gap casual wear, or Anne Klein or Brooks Brothers business clothing? Would they buy their underwear, casual wear, and business clothing at Walmart, Sears, Saks Fifth Avenue, or Nordstrom? How do family members and friends, admired celebrities, mass-media advertisements, and even cultural memberships, influence the youngsters' attitudes about buying apparel? Why do some attitudes persist for a long time while others change often? Marketers must know the answers to such questions in order to influence the applicable attitudes. Next, we discuss the sources and factors that play a role in determining consumers' attitudes towards marketing objects.

Application 1: Components of Attitude in Branding Action

TVS advertised its XL Super moped using the three attitudinal components that may have an impact on both the attitude towards the brand as well as the attitude of consumers towards the ad. The ad started with the conative component of "no cheque book required and easy instalment buy", a criterion that would appeal to the non-urban buyer too. The ad also had a sense of belongingness indicating "our vehicle and the vehicle for our village" (affective aspects) and was positioned as a reliable vehicle (cognitive). Given the fact that mopeds are themselves a part of the non-urban culture, the ad's message had blended well with the product.

Application 2: Category Involvement and Involvement with Brands

Attitudes and involvement levels are linked. They have an important impact on how consumers get involved in a category versus the brands in the category. This is important as consumers getting associated with brands due to persuasive advertising may behave differently from those who are involved both with the product category as well as the brands in the category[5]. Usually, in an evolved category in terms of penetration like tea, consumers are likely to be acquainted with the category and will be able to differentiate between the ads of brands. Red Label (Nature care variant) advertised its proposition of providing immunity that prevents consumers from falling ill. But in a relatively less-penetrated category like toothpaste[6], brands may have to create category involvement along with a proposition for brands to diffuse into the market faster. Such an approach is required to ensure that brands do not get lost in the advertising clutter.

Sources of Attitude Formation

Personal experience, family and friends, media, the Internet, and (increasingly) social media strongly affect attitudes. A primary source of attitudes toward products is the consumers' direct experiences in trying and evaluating them. Recognizing the importance of direct experience, marketers attempt to get consumers to try new products by offering cents-off coupons, free samples, and other inducements. If consumers try and like the new products, they will form positive attitudes and buy them again. In addition to personal experience, the family strongly impacts people's initial shopping-related attitudes (see Chapter 10). For instance, young children who were rewarded for good behavior with sweet foods and candy often retain a taste for (and positive attitude toward) sweets as adults.

Marketers increasingly use online advertising to shape the attitudes of small and specialized consumer niches, because new technologies enable them to customize advertising messages and also some products. Online, marketers can target consumers on the basis of their demographic, psychographic, or geo-demographic profiles with personalized product offerings (e.g., watches or sets of golf clubs for left-handed people), and messages demonstrating that they understand consumers' special needs and desires. Targeted online marketing can shape attitudes more effectively than other media because the promotional messages address the needs and concerns of precise micro-segments, whereas messages carried by traditional media generally reach diverse and large segments, as well as many consumers who have neither need for nor interest in the product advertised. Research has also shown that attitudes stemming from direct experience (e.g., product usage) are more enduring and resistant to competitors' messages than attitudes originating from promotional messages only (i.e., those developed without trying the product).

Attitude Formation Toward Product Categories/Brands

Though a number of articles deal with attitudes towards brands, marketers are not interested only in brands. They are also interested in product categories, especially when new product categories come into a market. Brands can diffuse in a specific market only when awareness about a new product category is created and a favorable attitude is built up toward these categories. When a new product category is introduced, the market does not usually have too many brands. Washing machines, vacuum cleaners, and water filters are a few examples in the Indian context. Consumers form an attitude toward the category as for Zero B, discussed earlier. A small section may start trying out the product. The new category gets diffused through word of mouth and also through communication strategies of the few brands in the market. It takes time for a category to be "created" in the minds of a larger number of consumers. Once many consumers start using the product, consumer familiarity with regard to the product category is established. Digital watches, for instance, were introduced in the late 1970s when not many consumers were familiar with automatic watches. But now digital watches are well-accepted and consumers are familiar with the product category. A number of brands enter a new category over a period of time. This results in a number of positioning strategies and brand associations/images. Eventually, consumers develop attitudes toward various brands. This, in turn, affects their decision-making with regard to brand preferences. The marketing implication is that the pioneer in a new product category should build its brand effectively to ensure that consumers have a top-of-the-mind recall with respect to the brand. Videocon in washing machines and Aquaguard in water filters seem to have effectively adopted this approach when they entered the market early. Samsung and LG were late entrants in several categories of durable products. But these brands have been able to create very positive attitudes among consumers with their products and marketing communication. These brands now have a substantial share of the market in a number of categories.

Box 6.2 Brands in the Gold Category and Credibility Factor Linked to Celebrities

Gold is a part of the Indian culture and the southern markets of India accounts for 40% of the total sales. There have been branded offerings in the category and retail brands have advertisements that feature male celebrities like Amitabh Bachchan.[7] Likeability and a feeling of trust are core associations linked to gold. While women are consumers who eventually use the offerings, the strategy of using male celebrities is to get the male member's attention with regard to the choice of the retail outlet. It is interesting to see that most of the celebrity brand ambassadors have a strong association with the type of roles that they have donned in movies. The aura of trust and credibility associated with these roles and the respective celebrity is likely to influence the affective element of the attitudes of consumers.

Box 6.3 Category Building and Brand Building

A good example of how a brand had developed a category and also ensured that it had built its brand is the case of Dabur's Real juices.[8] The brand was introduced in 1997 and it created beliefs about the benefits of pure juices (concept-selling using cognitive beliefs). It had created 20 flavors, introduced a film celebrity to show case the benefits of healthy pure juices (an affective support of introducing a celebrity to be associated with the brand to provide support to the cognitive beliefs on the benefits of juices), and launched the Activ sub-brand to reflect the cognitive beliefs concerning "no added sugar, vegetable plus fruit combinations and added fibre." The brand had a market share of 52% as on September 2012 (one and a half decades after introduction of in the brand in the category). The brand had not only created the category, but had also ensured that its brand image (perception) was being cultivated over a period of time.

The Role of Personality Factors

Personality traits significantly influence the formation of attitudes. For example, individuals with a high **need for cognition** (i.e., those who crave information and enjoy thinking) are likely to form positive attitudes in response to promotions that include a lot of detailed, product-related information. In contrast, consumers who are relatively low in this need are more likely to form positive attitudes in response to ads that feature attractive models or celebrities, or other peripheral cues about the products advertised. Attitudes toward new products are particularly influenced by personality characteristics related to one's innovativeness (see Chapter 3).

Attitudes Are Consistent with Behaviors

Similar attitudes consistently lead to the same behaviors. However, despite their consistency, attitudes are not permanent and can change either seldom or frequently. Normally, we expect consumers' behavior to correspond with their attitudes. For example, if a study showed that Mexican consumers prefer Japanese cars over Korean automobiles, we would expect that a Mexican consumer will buy a Japanese car when he replaces his current vehicle. However, circumstances often disrupt the consistency between attitudes and behavior. For example, the Mexican consumer might be unable to afford the car he prefers and buy the Korean car instead. In this case, affordability is a "situational" factor.

Box 6.4 Ahead of Its Time?

Vacumizer was a brand that offered to preserve freshness of food. It was launched in the mid-nineties with a unique concept of a pump being used to create a vacuum to preserve food and, thereby eliminating the rancidity that may set in after the food is cooked and stored. The product offering was ahead of its time as consumers did not want freshness benefit for such a purpose.[9] Creating beliefs and attitudes in tune with the needs of consumers at a given point in time is important.

Attitudes Occur within Situations

Attitudes occur within and are affected by situations. In this context, "situations" are events and circumstances that influence the relationships between attitudes and behaviors at particular times. Situations can cause consumers to behave in ways seemingly inconsistent with their attitudes. For instance, if Margaret purchases a different brand of sun protection lotion each time she runs low, her brand switching may reflect a negative attitude toward towards the brands she has tried. In reality, she may have purchased different brands because she wanted to save money and bought only the ones on-sale. The opposite may also be true. If Edward stays at a Hampton Inn each time he goes out of town for business, we may erroneously infer that he has a particularly favorable attitude toward Hampton Inn. In fact, Edward may find Hampton Inn to be merely "acceptable" and prefer to stay at the Hilton or Marriott. However, because he owns his own business and travels at his own expense, he may feel that Hampton Inn is "good enough."

Consumers may have different attitudes toward a particular object, each corresponding to particular circumstances. For instance, when Scott replaces his old station wagon, he considers buying a new SUV, so that he can drive his children and their friends to after-school and weekend activities comfortably. However, when he realizes how expensive driving the SUV to work—30 miles each day—would be, he reconsiders his intention. Then, he speaks with a co-worker who owns a Ford Escape Hybrid SUV and finds out that his colleague is very satisfied with the car's gas mileage. The gas mileage is better than Scott's old car and he finds the car affordable. He then purchases a Ford Escape so that he can save money on gas and drive his children and their friends to their after-school and weekend activities.

When studying attitudes, researchers can easily misinterpret the relationship between attitudes and behavior, unless they consider the context of the situation. Table 6.1 lists situations that might influence consumer attitudes.

TABLE 6.1 Examples of Situations That Influence Attitudes

PRODUCT/SERVICE	SITUATION	ATTITUDE
Energizer Batteries	Hurricane is coming	"I know that the hurricane is going to knock out my electricity, so I'd better be prepared."
Mini Cooper	Buying a new car	"With gas prices so high, I've got to trade in my SUV and buy a car that gets 30 mpg!"
Cheerios	High cholesterol	"They've been advertising how Cheerios can lower cholesterol for so long that it must be true."
The Wall Street Journal	Extra cash on hand	"I have to decide whether to invest in stocks or just put my money in a money market fund."
Delta Airlines	Friend's bachelor party	"My friend's bachelor party is in Las Vegas, and I want to be there."
Maxwell House Coffee	Need to stay awake	"I had a late date last night, but I've got a lot of work to do this morning at the office."
Stouffer's Easy Express Meals	Want dinner at home	"I'm tired of eating out night after night."

Application 1: Category Beliefs, Brand Beliefs, and the Changing Environment

In recent times, it is interesting to see shifts in category and brand beliefs as marketers use advertising to alter or create these changes. Tea is a drink traditionally associated with refreshment and hedonic taste. Red Label's (Nature care variant) positions the brand as a beverage that adds to health or prevents ailments. Tea, biscuits (from Britannia), cereal (Quaker oats), juices (Tropicana), and milk additives (Horlicks and Bournvita) are several categories that have their messages on the health platform. On the other hand, the two-wheeler brands like Duro 125 positions itself as a functionally- oriented (its press ads) vehicle with 15–18 features when several competitive brands are using the symbolic appeal. In this era of proliferation of brands, a brand would want to take the decision of sustaining or not sustaining the traditional belief systems associated with the respective category, within a category. The dominant brand in the baby-care product category, Johnson & Johnson, had an advertisement that had a doctor endorsing the brand for her baby. The affective component associated with the legendary mother–baby relationship in the J&J ad was backed up with a cognitive argument (the doctor endorsing the brand for her baby).

Application 2: Kellogg's Cereals and Cultural Habit

When Kellogg's entered India in the nineties, its proposition of using cold milk with its cereals (western consumers are used to mixing cold milk) was not accepted by the consumers. The feeling was that using cold milk with cornflakes would not taste good. But over a period of time, Kellogg's realized that Indians preferred to use hot milk, a strong cultural habit in India. After almost two decades, a 2013 ad of the brand showed a mother and son at the dining table with the mother suggesting that they add hot milk (instead of the son's suggestion of adding cold milk) and chocolate sauce to the cereals. This example illustrates the consumer behavior's conceptual axiom that a brand should follow entrenched cultural practices rather than opposing. This seems to have had realistic value in this example of Kellogg's cereals.

Learning Objective

2 To understand the tri-component attitude model and its applications.

The Tri-component Attitude Model

Researchers constructed several models that explain how attitudes affect behavior. First, we examine the tri-component model, and then describe multi-attribute frameworks. The **tri-component attitude model** maintains that attitudes consist of three components: Cognitive, affective, and conative, as shown in Figure 6.2.

Box 6.5 Retailers, Technology, and Attitudes

Tesco provides an interesting example of backing up its low prices with effective strategies that provides conative strength. Using the latest technology, the company introduced "price munch", a promotional initiative.[10] Before the customer checks out of the store, the products selected by him or her are screened for competitive prices by the retailer. If the prices are lower at Tesco, a message is generated as "Congratulations, your shopping at Tesco was cheaper." If the prices are higher at Tesco, there is a voucher issued for the price difference! No wonder, at Tesco, redemption rate of promotional coupons is 14% when the industry average is around one per cent.

The Cognitive Component

The **cognitive component** consists of a person's *cognitions*, that is, the knowledge and perceptions of the features of an attitude object that the person acquired from direct experience with the attitude object and information from various sources. This knowledge and perceptions commonly are expressed as *beliefs*; that is, the consumer believes that the attitude object possesses or does not possess specific attributes. Table 6.2 illustrates the beliefs of a hypothetical consumer about two TV technologies. In Figure 6.3, Park Avenue, a well-established brand with strong cognitive aspects with regard to its features, has entered the women apparel offerings. Cognitive beliefs about a brand is a powerful driver when a brand wants to become a gender-specific brand.

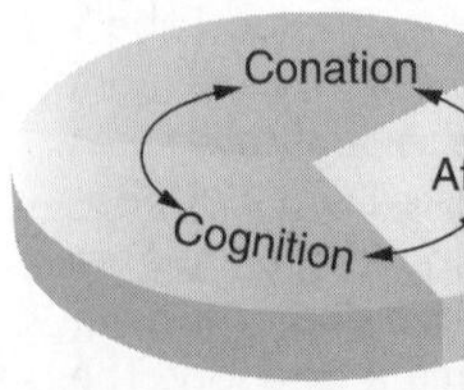

FIGURE 6.2 Tri-Component Attitude Model

The Affective Component

The **affective component** represents the consumer's *emotions* and *feelings* regarding the attitude object, which are considered *evaluations*, because they capture his or her global assessment of the attitude object (i.e., the extent to which the individual rates the attitude object as "favorable" or "unfavorable," "good" or "bad").

Affect-laden experiences also manifest themselves as "emotionally charged states" (e.g., happiness, sadness, shame, disgust, anger, distress, guilt, or surprise). These and other emotional states may enhance or amplify the experience itself, as well as subsequent recollections. For instance, if a person visiting a shopping center feels particularly joyous during

TABLE 6.2 Beliefs about Two TV Technologies

PRODUCT ATTRIBUTE	LED TV	3D TV
Off-angle viewing	Image fades slightly from the right.	Excellent image from all angles.
Screen reflectivity	Small	Medium.
Motion blur	Negligible	Negligible.
Color saturation	Excellent	Good.
Remote control ease of use	His friend had used it easily when they watched TV together.	His friend has had the TV for 3 months, but could not use it without consulting the manual.
Compatibility with cable company's DVR.	His friend said it took him 15 minutes to connect the TV and DVR.	His friend had to call the cable company and have them come to his house to connect the TV and DVR.

Source: Park Avenue

FIGURE 6.3 Park Avenue for Women

TABLE 6.3 Measuring Consumers' Feeling and Emotions about Aramis Aftershave

For the past 30 days you have had a chance to try Aramis Aftershave. We would appreciate it if you would identify how your face felt after using the product during this 30-day trial period. For each of the words below, please mark an "X" in the box corresponding to how your face felt after using Aramis Aftershave.

	VERY				NOT AT ALL
Relaxed	[]	[]	[]	[]	[]
Attractive looking	[]	[]	[]	[]	[]
Tight	[]	[]	[]	[]	[]
Smooth	[]	[]	[]	[]	[]
Supple	[]	[]	[]	[]	[]
Clean	[]	[]	[]	[]	[]
Refreshed	[]	[]	[]	[]	[]
Younger	[]	[]	[]	[]	[]
Revived	[]	[]	[]	[]	[]
Renewed	[]	[]	[]	[]	[]

TABLE 6.4 Semantic Differential Scales Measuring Consumers' Attitudes Toward Aramis Aftershave

Compared to other aftershaves, Aramis aftershave is:

Refreshing	[1]	[2]	[3]	[4]	[5]	[6]	[7]	Not refreshing
Fragrant	[1]	[2]	[3]	[4]	[5]	[6]	[7]	Not fragrant
Pleasant	[1]	[2]	[3]	[4]	[5]	[6]	[7]	Unpleasant
Appealing to others	[1]	[2]	[3]	[4]	[5]	[6]	[7]	Unappealing to others

shopping there, he will spend more time doing so and recall with great pleasure the time spent at the shopping center. In addition, he may encourage his friends to visit the center. Table 6.3 illustrates the measurement of consumers' feelings and emotions toward a product.

Another measure of a person's emotions toward an object, shown in Table 6.4, is a **semantic differential scale**, which is a type of rating scale consisting of a series of bi-polar adjectives (e.g., good/bad, pleasant/unpleasant) anchored on a continuum. Many researchers believe that a person's attitude can be derived directly from this measure because, presuamably, the scales reflect beliefs cognitions, as well as emotions toward the attitude object.

The Conative Component

The **conative component** reflects the likelihood that an individual will undertake a specific action or behave in a particular way with regard to the attitude object. In consumer research, the conative component is treated as an expression of the consumer's *intention to buy.* Buying intention scales are used to assess the likelihood of a consumer purchasing a product or behaving in a certain way. Table 6.5 shows examples of intention to buy measures. Interestingly, consumers who are asked to respond to an intention to buy question appear to be more likely to actually make a brand purchase for positively evaluated brands (e.g., "I will buy it"), as contrasted with consumers who are not asked to respond to an intention question. This suggests that a positive brand commitment in the form of a positive answer to an attitude intention question positively affects the actual brand purchase.

TABLE 6.5 Intention-to-buy Measures

Which of the following statements best describes the chance that you will buy Aramis Aftershave the next time you purchase an aftershave?

_____I definitely will buy it.

_____I probably will buy it.

_____I am uncertain whether I will buy it or not.

_____I probably will not buy it.

_____I definitely will not buy it.

How likely are you to buy Aramis Aftershave during the next three months?

_____Very likely

_____Likely

_____Uncertain

_____Unlikely

_____Very unlikely

Ketchups and soups are categories that have a low penetration in the Indian context. Kissan and Maggi are well-known brands that have been adopting several strategies to enhance the penetration level of these categories. Tasty Treat, an offering from Big Bazaar,[11] (private label) found that consumers were not happy with their kids handling glass bottles of ketchups (for several decades these offerings, advertised for children, have been only available in glass bottles). This conative component that acted as a barrier for purchasing sauces was addressed by the company and it introduced the offering in child-friendly pouches. The brand not only sold a significant number of the offering but also saved on supply chain and production costs. The brand's soup, too, was built on the conative component associated with the habit of drinking soup. The company found that consumers preferred soups in specific quantities and developed appropriate sizes of cups that took into consideration the size of the servings preferred by consumers. Five million servings of soup were sold within two months of the launch of the offering. While several attitudinal strategies focus on cognitive and affective aspects, an emerging marketing context also offers a lot of potential for conative component if insightful consumer behavior is applied.

Application 1: Attitudinal Components and Brands

Cognitive appeals

- Hero Honda created a memorable campaign with its "fill it, shut it, forget it" to highlight its effective mileage.
- Kinetic Honda, the first gearless scooter introduced in India, associated itself with "Himalayan" rally to build the belief that is suitable for Indian roads.
- Gold Plus jewellery with its karatometer (that indicated the purity of gold) enhanced its credibility in a market where credibility is sought after by consumers.
- Activa (scooter) launched a campaign on its mileage and features.
- Affective appeals
- Onida TV developed the tagline "Owners pride, Neighbour's envy" to create a feel good factor about its quality.
- Red bull, the energy drink is associated with consumption pleasure.
- Though Horlicks is built on cognitive appeals, the "mother–child" relationship is a part of the visual that provides the affective appeal.
- Fastrack watches used the "hip and cool" factor to appeal to youth.
- Pleasure, the brand of scooter launched for women by TVS, is based on the likability arising out of "self-reliance, independence, and non-conformist" attitude shown in the brand"s ads.

Application 2: Conative or Intent to Act Aspect of the Attitude

Conative or intent to act is a useful component that can readily be connected with the sales promotional offers at the modern retail outlet in the Indian context. Generally, the sales promotion schemes at, for instance, Reliance Mart are likely to appeal to a large number of consumers from diverse backgrounds. Also, these sales promotional offers are also quite different and more attractive than what is generally found even in large, stores.

Conative component is also useful when a brand promises a futuristic benefit like a savings schemes from Tanishq as saving in gold is a part of the Indian culture. Also, Quaker oats and Kellogg's cereals promise good health (when there is considerable awareness on health issues).

Convenience is another motivating factor that can enhance the conative component. Glam-Up powder cream is a brand that promises to add value to make-up within a minute.[12]

Altering Consumers' Attitudes

Altering consumer attitudes is an important marketing strategy. The goal of leading brands is to strengthen and maintain the existing positive attitudes of customers, so that they will not succumb to competitors' special offers and other inducements designed to win them over. In contrast, in product categories, such as detergents—where Tide is the primary brand—or athletic shoes—where Nike dominates the market—competitors often try to change the strong and positive attitudes consumers have toward the market leaders in an attempt to get consumers to switch brands.

Changing attitudes about products and brands is difficult because consumers frequently resist evidence that challenges strongly held attitudes or beliefs and tend to interpret any ambiguous information in ways that reinforce their preexisting attitudes.[13] There are two primary strategies for changing consumers' attitudes: Changing an offering's overall image, or referring to specific product attributes. Next, we discuss the first strategy. In the following section, which explains multi-attribute models of attitudes, we address the second approach.

Changing Beliefs about Products

The strategy of changing beliefs in order to change attitudes concentrates on changing beliefs or perceptions about the brand itself. This is by far the most common form of advertising appeal. Advertisers constantly are reminding us that their products have "more" or are "better" or "best" in terms of some important product attribute. For example, an ad for Kraft's Miracle Whip claims that using this product makes a tastier turkey sandwich than mayonnaise does. To support this claim, the ad points out that Miracle Whip has "more flavor and half the fat" of mayonnaise.

Information aimed at changing an attitude must be compelling and repeated many times if it is to overcome people's natural resistance to abandoning established attitudes.

Changing Brand Image

The strategy of changing brand image consists of attempting to alter consumers' *overall* assessment of the brand; marketers employ this approach by using inclusive promotional statements designed to set their brands apart from the competition. Examples of such statements include "this is the largest-selling brand" or "the one others try to imitate." An AT&T campaign was designed to enhance the brand's image without any references to products or services offered under the brand name. AT&T's slogan "Rethink 'possible'" was developed to change the attitudes of many who felt overwhelmed by technology in its favor and to increase consumers' confidence in technology, with taglines such as "It's what you do with what we do."[14] As another example, many ads have used the well-recognized phrase "A New Beginning" to bolster a brand's overall image and revive consumer interest.

Changing Beliefs about Competing Brands

Another attitude-change strategy involves changing consumer beliefs about competitors' brands or product categories. For instance, an advertisement for Eclipse chewing gum makes a dramatic assertion of the brand's superiority over other gums by stating: "Most other gums just mask bad breath. We kill the germs that cause it." The ad for Aleve in Figure 6.4 refutes the notion that more pills relieve pain more effectively than fewer pills, and is designed to establish unfavorable attitudes toward Tylenol. Similarly, the ad for Lysol Sanitizing Wipes in Figure 6.1 establishes negative attitudes toward an entire category of competing products. The ad states that Lysol's competitors—paper towels—spread germs, whereas Lysol wipes kill them. The Aleve ad is an example of comparative advertising and the Lysol one depicts a two-sided message (see Chapter 7).

Box 6.6 Emerging Markets and Building Beliefs

Emerging economies present unique challenges to marketers, and attitudes may be useful in such contexts. Pepsi test marketed Gluco+, a beverage with electrolytes and glucose, and Lehar Iron Chusti, a snack fortified with iron.[15] With 55% of Indian women in India being anaemic, these offerings were targeted at rural markets with the price point of ₹two to five (conative aspect being considered). The challenge of marketers in such a context is to develop cognitive beliefs associated with health and a large number of the target segment are daily wage earners.[16] A combination of promotional tools (advertising, messages in local events, sampling, and even customized visuals for rural population) may be required to build such cognitive beliefs.

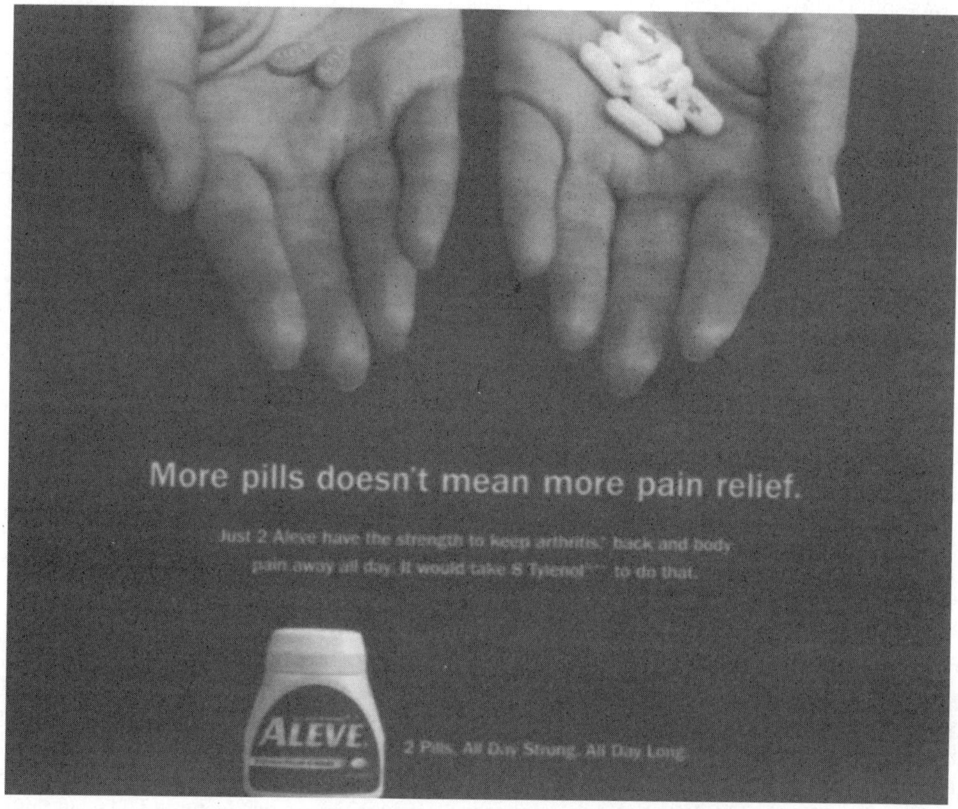

Source: Bayer Healthcare LLC.

FIGURE 6.4 Changing a Belief: "More Pills Doesn't Mean More Pain Relief"

Learning Objective

3 To understand the structures of multi-attribute models and their use in altering consumers' attitudes.

Multi-attribute Attitude Models

Multi-attribute attitude models portray consumers' attitudes as functions of their assessments of the objects' prominent attributes. First, we discuss the attitude-toward-object model and the use of product attribute in changing consumers' attitudes and developing new products. Next, we discuss the attitude-toward-behavior model, the theory of reasoned action, the theory of trying to consume, and the attitude-toward-ad model.

Box 6.7 Contrasting Routes to Nurture Brand Attitude

Sustainable core proposition is an axiomatic route to brands; there may be some exceptions and a brand may deviate from this well-entrenched concept but still nurture an attitude that it had built for many years. Dettol's core proposition of germ killing action or "Be 100% Sure" is sustaining the strong attitudes it had built. Its 1979 campaign had the headline, "Who carries the sword that protects". The brand has 80% share of the market in antiseptic lotions, is the leader in the liquid hand wash market with about 50% share, has 8% share in soaps and has about 10.2% in its kitchen gel (used for utensil cleaning despite strong brands in the category).

Cadbury 5 Star had the proposition of "Deliciously Rich you hate to share it" in the seventies and was a "togetherness bar" in the eighties, a confidence fix during the early nineties, a motivational bar during the late nineties, had a relationship association (boy-girl) during 2001, turned to humor and taste in 2003 that continued in 2005 and the bar was associated with indulgence in 2008. In 2010, "Suresh-Ramesh" campaign was introduced with its humor featuring two brothers. The important change had been that the product was evolving; in this case, the traditional chocolate bar was softer. The digital campaign, "NO hard fillings" too had created significant user-generated content on the internet. In 2014 5Star positioned itself as a cure for "seriousness" and also introduced a sub-brand called Chomp. Dettol was a brand that had followed the sustainable core proposition route to maintain its attitudes and 5 Star is a brand that followed a different route including a different imagery. The context and the category along with the target segment decide the brand's associations in the long term; what is eventually required for a brand is to strengthen consumers" attitude towards it.

*Inputs from Delshad Irani," The Shaken and the Stirred," *The Economic Times*, December 18, 2013, Amit Bapna, " A Clean Break,", *The Economic Times*, December 18, 2013 and Ravi Balakrishnan, " A Star Is Born," The Economic Times, March 5, 2014.

Attitude-toward-object Model

The **attitude-toward-object model** maintains that a consumer's evaluation of a product is a function of:

1. The extent to which the product has (or lacks) each of a given set of attributes.
2. The importance of each of these attributes to the consumer.

In other words, consumers generally have favorable attitudes toward those brands that they believe have better performance on the attributes that they view as important than other brands, and unfavorable attitudes toward those brands that they feel do not meet these criteria.[17]

In a study done to illustrate this model, 96 marketing students rated three brands of smartphones—iPhone, Blackberry, and Android—along the 11 attributes listed in Table 6.6. These ratings represent the students' beliefs regarding the extent to which each brand possesses a specific attribute. Students then indicated the level of importance attached to each attribute. Subsequently, the researchers multiplied the importance "weights" by the ratings for each phone. For example, "long battery life" emerged as the most important attribute in a cell phone (3.77 out of a total of 5 possible points), and the iPhone scored higher on this attribute than the other two phones (2.64), which contributed to its high overall rating. Among the three brands, Blackberry was the only one with a physical keyboard, and therefore scored the highest on this feature (3.34), but this feature has the second-lowest importance rating (1.9), which lowered Blackberry's overall rating.

The totals show that respondents believed that the iPhone is far better than the other two models—but we must note that such perceptions do not necessarily represent the *actual* facts. For example, let's assume that, in reality, the Blackberry's screen resolution is much better than the iPhone's, although consumers *believe* that the iPhone has a better screen. As we already established in our discussion of positioning (Chapter 2), what matters most is how consumers *perceive* the product. Therefore, considering the (hypothetical) results of this study, Blackberry's marketer should promote the brand's screen resolution in its ads in order to "correct" consumers' misperceptions of its product.

Marketers use the attitude-toward-object model in developing promotions designed to change consumers' attitudes in favor of the brands advertised. They do so by adding new product attributes, changing consumers' perceptions of attributes, and also developing new products after researching consumer preferences.

TABLE 6.6 Application of the Attitude-Toward-Object Model

ATTRIBUTE	ATTRIBUTE'S IMPORTANCE	IPHONE		BLACKBERRY		ANDROID	
		PRESENCE OF ATTRIBUTE	PRESENCE × IMPORTANCE	PRESENCE OF ATTRIBUTE	PRESENCE × IMPORTANCE	PRESENCE OF ATTRIBUTE	PRESENCE × IMPORTANCE
Long battery life	3.77	2.64	9.9528	2.34	8.8218	2.31	8.7087
High-resolution screen	3.1	3.62	11.222	2.15	6.665	2.97	9.207
Voice-activated commands	1.8	3.49	6.282	2.25	4.05	2.61	4.698
Carrier provides unlimited data transmission	3.52	3	10.56	2.62	9.2224	2.48	8.7296
Carrier does not require long-term contract	2.43	1.79	4.3497	1.66	4.0338	1.95	4.7385
High-quality camera	3.12	3.51	10.9512	2.07	6.4584	2.84	8.8608
Camera has a flash	2.98	3.44	10.2512	2.62	7.8076	2.83	8.4334
High-resolution video recording	2.52	3.3	8.316	1.93	4.8636	2.67	6.7284
Carrier provides external unlimited data storage	2.72	2.82	7.6704	2.36	6.4192	2.52	6.8544
Physical keyboard	1.9	1.16	2.204	3.34	6.346	2.18	4.142
Smartphone allows multitasking	3.36	3.38	11.3568	2.57	8.6352	2.72	9.1392
TOTALS			93.1161		73.323		80.24

Multimedia-based interactive teaching for children requires creating an attitude among children, as shown in Figure 6.5. The ad uses a celebrity who can relate to the target segment.

Adding an Attribute

Adding a product or brand attribute means either adding an attribute that previously was ignored or adding one that represents an improvement or innovation. For example, to add a previously ignored or unknown attribute or benefit, an ad might point out that yogurt has more potassium than a banana (a fruit associated with a high quantity of potassium). The comparison of yogurt and bananas can enhance attitudes toward yogurt among consumers who wish to take in more potassium.

Another form of adding an attribute is innovation. To illustrate, a bottle of Wish-Bone® Salad Spritzer™ includes a pump that enables consumers to spray a mist of dressing on a salad, thus allowing them to control how much dressing they put on salads more precisely. Figure 6.6 shows an ad for Phillips' Caplets, which are a new form of laxative, because laxatives previously were available only as liquids. The new caplets are also "cramp free," which is a newly added attribute. In addition to portraying an innovative attribute, the ad is also aimed at changing beliefs about a competitor: Within the small print, the ad states that the Phillips' laxative works overnight, whereas its competitor—Miralax—takes up to three days to have an effect. Sometimes, *eliminating* a product feature may change attitudes favorably. For example, after conducting consumer studies, many marketers of personal care products now offer unscented or alcohol-free items.

FIGURE 6.5 Edurite from Pearson

FIGURE 6.6 Adding Product Attributes: Caplets (Not Liquids) and Also Cramp Free

Changing the Perceived Importance of Attributes

In the discussion of benefit segmentation (Chapter 2), we illustrated how different brands provide consumers with different benefits and how they are positioned accordingly. For example, in headache remedies, there is the division between aspirin (e.g., Bayer), acetaminophen (e.g., Tylenol), and naproxen sodium (e.g., Aleve). Marketers of personal care items sell multiple versions of the same product that provide somewhat different, narrowly defined benefits, in order to maintain or gain market share. For instance, Colgate Total provides 12 hours of germ fighting, Colgate Max Fresh wipes out bad breath, and Colgate Sensitive Pro-Relief is for people who have sensitive gums.

Some companies discover product attributes that most consumers pay little or no attention to and feature them in ads. Apparently, Dole discovered that some buyers of prepackaged fruit are unaware that other brands do not immerse the fruit in 100% fruit juice. The objective of the ad in Figure 6.7 is to use consumers' unawareness to differentiate Dole's product.

Developing New Products

Marketers often use the attitude-toward-object model during the development of new products. Consider the following hypothetical example: The Tropicana company is planning to add a new item to its product line. The company's market researchers identified four attributes as the key determinants in consumers' attitudes toward orange juice: Amount of pulp, degree of sweetness, strength of flavor, and color. Then, Tropicana conducted a three-stage study:

1. Using the scales shown in Figure 6.8A, the researchers asked consumers who drank orange juice regularly to describe their "ideal" juice, along the four attributes.
2. Realistically, Tropicana could not produce the "ideal" juice, because it could not offer it at a competitive price. Instead, the respondents rated a "concept" juice representing a product that Tropicana *could* sell. The "concept" juice was similar to the "ideal" one, but not identical.
3. Tropicana *made* an "actual" new orange juice, which consumers tasted and rated.

Source: Reckitt Benckiser

FIGURE 6.7 Changing the Importance of an Attribute: Real Fruit Must Be Packaged in Real Fruit Juice

As Figure 6.8B shows, compared with the "ideal," the "actual" product had too little pulp and was far too sweet, but the flavor of both products was nearly the same. Regarding color, it appears that although Tropicana did not match the ideal or the product concept, the company improved the color in the actual product by making it closer to the ideal. These findings indicate that Tropicana must change the "actual" product so that it matches consumers' preferences, by making it less sweet and adding pulp.

Attitude-toward-behavior Model

The **attitude-toward-behavior model** captures the individual's attitude toward *behaving* or *acting* with respect n object, rather than merely the person's attitude toward the object itself. Using the attitude-toward-behavior model to understand consumers may sometimes be more useful than using the attitude-toward-object model. For instance, a consumer looking for a new car might like Lexus cars (i.e., *positive* attitude towards the *object*), but not be ready or willing to buy an expensive Lexus (i.e., a *negative* attitude towards the *behavior* associated with the object).

A Taiwanese study examined consumers' attitudes toward the *act* (or behavior) of shopping online and revealed that these attitudes reflected nine desired benefits: (1) effectiveness and modern, (2) purchase convenience, (3) information abundance, (4) multiform and safety, (5) service quality, (6) delivery speed, (7) homepage design, (8) selection freedom, and (9) name familiarity.[18]

	1	2	3	4	5	6	
No pulp	☐	☐	☐	☐	☐	☐	Lots of pulp
Not sweet	☐	☐	☐	☐	☐	☐	Very sweet
Weak flavor	☐	☐	☐	☐	☐	☐	Strong flavor
Dim orange	☐	☐	☐	☐	☐	☐	Bright orange

FIGURE 6.8A Semantic Differential Scales

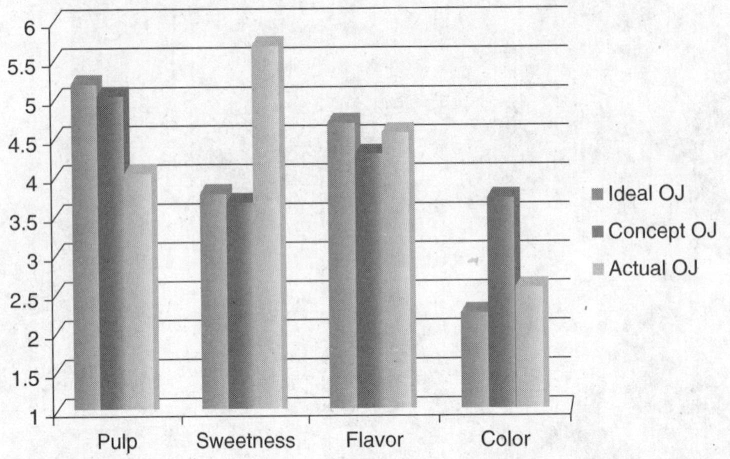

FIGURE 6.8B The "Ideal," "Concept," and "Actual" Compared

Theory of Reasoned Action

Like the tri-component model, the **theory of reasoned action (TRA)** incorporates the cognitive, affective, and conative components. Additionally, it holds that researchers must measure the *subjective norms* that influence a person's intention to act before gauging the level of intention. Subjective norms are the person's feelings as to what relevant others (e.g., family, friends, roommates, co-workers) think of the action the person contemplates. That is, would they support the anticipated action or not. For example, if a student wanted to get a tattoo but first considered whether her parents or boyfriend would approve or disapprove of her contemplated behavior, her consideration of others' opinions is her subjective norm.

Two factors underlie subjective norms: *normative beliefs* that the individual attributes to relevant others, and the individual's *motivation to comply* with the preferences of the relevant others.[19] In order to understand subjective norms correctly, researchers must measure both factors. For instance, the subjective norms of a student contemplating getting a tattoo (i.e., the "purchase") consist of answers to the following questions: (1) Who are her relevant others (e.g., parents and boyfriend)? (2) What are her beliefs about how each relevant other would respond to her tattoo (e.g., "Mom would consider the tattoo an object often associated with gangs, but my boyfriend would love it")? (3) To what extent complying with the preferences of the relevant others plays a role in her decision? In other words, is she sufficiently motivated to defer to the relevant others or not?

Box 6.8 Branding Lessons from My Name Is Khan

My Name is Khan (MNIK), a movie that appealed to audiences across age-groups and socio-economic classes, had linkages with the concepts of consumer behavior that are as important as the charismatic star cast. The movie used a combination of attitudinal concepts anchored in a cultural environment and some topical issues.

Box 6.8 (Continued)

The Mood

There is a long history of Hindu–Muslim interaction and it has become an important part of Indian culture in recent times. Further, people in this part of the world are just about recognizing that differently-abled people need to be treated with special care. Even major cities and public places lack the facilities that are required for them as compared to the Western world. Inter-communal interaction and autism, associated with the main character in the movie, sets the mood for the movie (mood is a non-stimuli-specific emotional state that is lower in intensity than an emotional stimulus and can be a product, service, movie, person or any information input to any of the sensory organs).

Cognitive Beliefs and Affective States

Drawing upon the cognitive and affective aspects of attitudes, *MNIK* delves into several beliefs that are a part of the culture or viewers' psyche:

- A person who has autism cannot think rationally all the time
- A woman settled abroad can take up hair styling as a profession without the social stigma generally attached to such a profession in India
- There is animosity against a particular religion based on some negative acts allegedly committed by a small cross-section of people belonging to the religion
- There is always hope for the husband and wife to unite even against the odds
- Fate plays havoc with a happy family
- There is a need to go to the rescue of people affected by natural disaster
- Indians can gain recognition in the USA (this has been innovatively used by the writer by bringing in autism to achieve this recognition)
- People belonging to a particular religion are not treated well at the port of entry in the USA

All these beliefs have been converted into affective or emotional states in the movie.

In several product categories, branding depends on the extent to which a brand can use emotional or symbolic meanings or associations. A brand like Volvo, known for its safety (cognitive aspects), showed an advertisement that had several people talking about how they were saved from accidents by the brand (emotional). In a similar manner, *MNIK* converts beliefs into emotional states. This is in tune with the mood that was set by the initial frames.

Every belief is converted into emotions and the range of emotions portrayed in the movie are in line with the Plutchik's theory on emotions.* They use both positive and negative emotions to convert beliefs into emotions. Gerald Zaltman, a pioneering qualitative researcher in the area of consumer behavior, observed that marketers rarely use negative emotions and even while they use positive emotions, they do not explore many ways of using such emotions. *MNIK* uses a range of executions to reflect positive and negative emotions. For instance, joy and happiness are captured in the hero's first meeting with the heroine in a beauty parlor (mildly pleasant), his "marry me" (surprise and delight) pestering, and the final wedding (ecstasy) reflect the range of positive emotions. Indian culture involves showing both positive and negative emotions. This is portrayed in the opening of a new parlor by the heroine (happiness) and also the grief expressed in scenes of loss and despair in the movie. The heroine's screams of despair and hatred after losing her son are also examples. The bewilderment of the hero in not understanding the gravity of the situation due his disorder after the violent death of his son (horror), the help rendered by the hero to marooned people (compassion) and, in the process, recalling his son (nostalgia), create high emotional states. There is also a ritualistic element associated with religion in the prayer scenes. The emotional or the affective state associated with any product or service is important because it is the "overall evaluation" of the product in the mind of the consumer (viewer, in this case). While there are many movies that showcase a variety of emotions, the systematic conversion of cognitive beliefs associated with specific cultures into affective states, and the type, frequency, and range of emotions used in the movie makes this product stand out from the viewpoint of attitude creation.

(Continued)

Box 6.8 (Continued)

"Intention to Act": Conative Aspects

Cognitive and affective aspects have an impact on the conative component of attitudes. In this case, it is associated with the word-of-mouth associated with *MNIK*. The digital buzz associated with the movie when this piece was written was around 7 million results produced through just one search engine. At least a part of the buzz may have happened after the movie was launched. The cumulative charisma of the star cast (who have been around for quite some time) adds to emotional states, enhancing the likeability factor associated with the movie.

Note: A version of this text has been published by S Ramesh Kumar in *Hindu Business Line*, March 18, 2010. (www.thehindubusinessline.com/catalyst/2010/03/18/sto-ries/2010031850070200.htm) The text has been used with permission.

Source: *Robert Plutchik, *Emotions and Life: Perspectives from Psychology, Biology, and Evolution* (Washington, DC: American Psychological Association, 2002).

TABLE 6.7 Potential Impediments to Trying to Consume

PERSONAL IMPEDIMENTS
"I wonder whether my nails will be long enough by the time of my wedding."
"I want to try to lose 2 inches off my waist by my birthday."
"I'm going to try to get us tickets for the Jimmy Buffet concert for our anniversary."
"I'm going to attempt to be able to run 5 miles by my birthday."
"I am going to increase how often I exercise from three to five times a week."
"Tonight I'm not going to have dessert at the restaurant."
ENVIRONMENTAL IMPEDIMENTS
"Only the first 500 people at the football game will receive a team cap."
"Sorry, the Jaguar you ordered didn't come in from England on the ship that docked yesterday."
"There are only two cases of Merlot in our stockroom.You better come in sometime today."
"I am sorry. We cannot help you.We are closing the gas station because of an electrical outage."

Theory of Trying-to-Consume

The **theory of trying-to-consume** represents cases where the outcome of a contemplated action (e.g., a purchase), stemming from a positive attitude, is uncertain, but is still being pursued by the consumer. A person trying to consume faces two types of obstacles that may prevent the desired outcome (see examples in Table 6.7):

1. ***Personal impediments,*** such as a consumer who is trying to find "just the right tie" to go with a suit, for less than $50, or a person trying to lose weight, but loves cookies.
2. ***Environmental impediments,*** such as the reality that "just the right tie" costs more than $50, or realizing that one cannot continue eating cookies and lose weight, and that there are no low-calorie cookies that taste good.[20]

Researchers have also studied situations where consumers *fail to try to consume*, and identified two reasons why they do so. First, such consumers do not recognize all the consumption options available. Secondly, they prefer to self-sacrifice or delay gratification.[21]

Attitude-toward-the-ad Model

The **attitude-toward-the-ad model** proposes that the feelings consumers form when they see and hear ads significantly impact their attitudes towards the brands advertised.

Research among Asian Indian U.S. immigrants has explored attitudes toward 12 advertisements and purchase intention of six different products that the ads featured. The study found a positive relationship between attitude toward the advertisement and purchase intention for each of the advertised products; that is, if consumers liked the ad, they were more likely to purchase the product.[22] Other consumer research that examined general attitudes toward advertising in Bulgaria and Romania (recent members of the European Union) found that consumers in those nations were more positive about the institution of advertising (i.e., as a marketing tool) than they were about the actual advertisements used to promote products and services. Furthermore, while the main personal use of advertising in Bulgaria was information acquisition, the entertainment value of advertising was the strongest personal use in Romania.[22]

As shown on Figure 6.9, Oreo positioned itself to teenagers with its overall "attitude towards the brand" dimension (as the world's No. 1 biscuit brand) Also, Figure 6.10 shows how Ashirwad, from ITC, has created an attitude towards the brand in categories associated with commodities.

Source: Mondelez International

FIGURE 6.9 An Ad Visual of Oreo

Source: ITC

FIGURE 6.10 An ad visual of ITC

Application 1: Affect and the Value Offered by a Brand

Sometimes, even brands with strong cognitive beliefs need to be careful while formulating advertising appeal associated with affective aspects (under the assumption that the affective appeal will add to the strong cognitive appeal). Honda's Jazz car launched itself with the affective appeal that questions the seriousness of the individual ("Why so serious"). The brand ended up offering a discount of ₹1.75 lakhs to sell of its stock.[24] The attitudinal aspect may not be the only reason for the brand's performance, but it may be one of the important aspects.

Application 2: Cognitive Beliefs and Brand's Credibility of Arguments

While developing cognitive beliefs, brands must take strong arguments and counter-arguments into consideration.[25] Strong arguments are those that present the facts in a convincing manner and counter-arguments are thoughts of consumers that go against the arguments that are presented. A brand positioned itself as the "brain food" for children. Product claims included several cognitive beliefs like "33% key brain nutrients", the iron in the brand was "bioavailable" and that it contained Omega 3.[26] The findings that were reported in the website of Food Safety and Standards Authority of India (FSSAI) was that most of the claims were not backed up scientifically and the offering cannot be marketed as "brain food".[27]

Learning Objective

4 To understand how to alter consumers' attitudes by making particular needs prominent.

Changing the Motivational Functions of Attitudes

Sometimes marketers must try to change negative consumer attitudes about their products, companies, or marketing practices. Frequently, the negative attitudes are not the result of bad products or promotion, but stem from uncontrollable circumstances. For example, several years ago, the U.S. Food and Drug Administration advised pregnant or nursing women and also young children to eat less canned tuna, due to concerns about the bioconcentration of mercury, a neurotoxin, in the fish. Subsequently, consumption of the three main brands of canned tuna—Bumble Bee, Chicken of the Sea, and StarKist—declined substantially. The three competing brands commissioned an advertising campaign to reverse consumers' negative feelings toward canned tuna. The theme of the campaign was "Tuna the Wonderfish," and through TV and online commercials, print ads, digital screens, posters, and materials placed in gyms and health clubs, it humorously portrayed that eating tuna is fun. Online, "tunathewonderfish.com" featured recipes and wacky characters called "the tuna lovers," and sang the praises of tuna with slogans such as "tuna is good for your heart," "part of a healthy diet," and "great on the go." These messages were designed to restore consumers' confidence in tuna by telling them that eating tuna is not only healthy, but also fun. The product's marketers knew that consumers liked canned tuna but were hesitant to eat it because of information that, although directed at a relatively small segment (i.e., pregnant women), negatively affected the perceptions of many consumers.[28]

The resons (or motivations) behind people's attitudes are known as "functions." Changing attitudes by appealing to consumers' motivations is known as the **functional approach**.[29] Accordingly, attitudes are classified into four functions: The utilitarian function, ego-defensive function, value-expressive function, and knowledge function.

The Utilitarian Function

The **utilitarian function** stems from the belief that consumers' attitudes reflect the utilities that brands provide. When a product has been useful or enabled us to perform certain tasks in the past, our attitude toward it tends to be favorable. One strategy for changing attitudes in favor of a product is by demonstrating to consumers that the product possesses a utilitarian purpose(s) that they may not have considered. The ad in Figure 6.11 illustrates how Lysol Wipes are more utilitarian than paper towels.

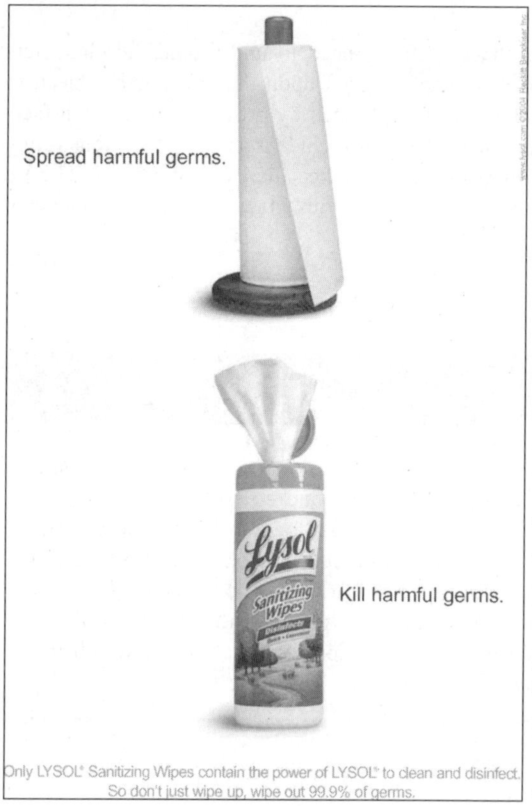

Source: Lysol® is a registered trademark of Reckitt Benckiser Inc.

FIGURE 6.11 An Appeal Based on the Utilitarian Function: Paper Towels Spread Germs but Lysol Wipes Kill Them

Source: Reprinted with permission from ConAgra Foods, Omaha, Nebraska

FIGURE 6.12 Appealing to the Ego-Defensive and Value-Expressive Functions: If You Discover That Your Pants No Longer Fit, Would You Still Believe That Prepared Salads Contain Few Calories?

The Ego-defensive Function

The **ego-defensive function** maintains that people form attitudes in order to protect themselves from sensing doubt and to replace uncertainty with feelings of security and confidence. For example, many consumers believe that salads from restaurants or salad bars—commonly eaten during lunch—are healthy and not fattening. The Healthy Choice ad in Figure 6.12 refutes this belief by humorously stating that such salads are fattening, unlike Healthy Choice, which is positioned as an "honestly labeled healthy lunch." The reference to honesty implies that the other offerings are not labeled correctly.

The Value-expressive Function

The **value-expressive function** maintains that attitudes reflect consumers' values and beliefs, and that marketers can create ads that either support or refute these notions. For example, many nutrition-conscious consumers probably believe that prepared salads are healthy and low in calories. In addition to appealing to the ego-defensive function, the ad in Figure 6.12 also challenges the false belief that prepared salads are healthy and nutritious.

Box 6.9 Value-expressive Function and Youth Brands

Hero Pleasure, a scooter positioned towards women, advertised with the message "Why should boys have all the fun?" Value-expressive function is indicated and this aspect is likely to appeal to young girls who are independent, outdoor-oriented, and are on par with boys in terms of their ambitions, hopes and, dreams.

The Knowledge Function

The **knowledge function** holds that people form attitudes because they have a strong need to understand the characters of the people, events, and objects they encounter. Therefore, many firms use ads centered upon the consumer's "need to know." Accordingly, marketers often try to alter consumers' attitudes in favor of their brands by providing them with facts of which they were unaware. For instance, a message for a new allergy medication might include a bar graph demonstrating the product's superiority by contrasting its allergy symptom relief abilities with those of other allergy medications. The V8 Fusion ad in Figure 6.13 appeals to the knowledge function because it provides consumers with a fact that they may have not known.

Box 6.10 Brands and Attitudinal Functions

The Indian context offers examples of how attitude is associated with specific motivational functions. Charms, a brand of cigarette, advertised as "Charms is the way you are" and sold in denim like packaging during the eighties (currently, cigarette ads are banned in India), 5 Star (Cadbury) as the "togetherness" bar, and Close up with its "close up" smile were the earliest brands to make use of the value-expressive function. Marico's Heart Foundation provided the knowledge function by highlighting health benefits, Vim (liquid variant) advertises on how it effectively cleans a "set of vessels" economically (providing the utility function) and Nomarks soap brand advertises about removing pigmentation, pimples, and other marks indicating the benefit of ego-defensive function (by which the user protects his/her self-image).

Associating Brands with Worthy Objects or Causes

Another way to influence attitudes is to relate them to social or cultural events. The ad for Method detergent in Figure 6.14 associates the product with a worthy cause—ecological concern—by mocking mainstream detergents that come in huge and environmentally harmful jugs.

Research into brand-cause alliances has investigated the relationship between the "cause" and the "sponsor." One study found that although both the brand and the cause benefited from such alliances, less familiar causes benefited more from association with a positive brand than did highly familiar causes.[30] The results of another study indicated that if corporate sponsors do not explicitly reveal their motives for a company-cause or a product-cause association, consumers will form their own beliefs about the connection between the company or brand and the cause.[31] This indicates that sponsors should tell consumers the reasoning behind their sponsorships, rather than allowing consumers to guess, possibly incorrectly, why the sponsorship was formed.

Box 6.11 Overall Attitude and a New Entrant Brand

Traditionally, well-entrenched brands had created the an overall attitude towards brands –Kores, an old brand of photo copier had the tagline "Your guarantee of good impression", Phillips had "If its Phillips you are sure" and Maruti's Esteem had the ad campaign where the son after receiveing bad marks asks his dad if they can go for a drive in the car (Esteem) to cheer up the father's bad mood on seeing his marks.

Renault Duster,an instant success in the Indian market, went in for a campaign that stated "60000 Customers, 29 Awards, No. 1 in Customer Satisfaction, All In Just 10 months". Overall attitude towards a brand, especially a new brand that had demonstrated success through its sale numbers in a short period of time, is an unusual usage of the concepts of attitude.

Source: Campbell Soup Company

FIGURE 6.13 An Appeal Based on the Knowledge Function: Americans Do Not Eat Enough Vegetables, but You Can

Source: © Method Products, Inc: advertising agency: Droga5

FIGURE 6.14 Associating Method Detergent with Ecological Concerns

Learning Objective

5 To understand the role of cognitive elaboration in altering attitudes.

The Elaboration Likelihood Model

The **elaboration likelihood model (ELM)** proposes that attitudes can sometimes be changed by either one of two different routes to persuasion—a central route or a peripheral route—and that the cognitive elaboration related to the processing of information received via each route is different. The central and peripheral routes to persuasion reflect **extensive** and **limited problem solving** (see Chapter 14), and also correspond with **high-** and **low-involvement purchases** (see Chapter 5). The premise of this model is that consumers carefully evaluate the merits and weaknesses of a given product when they consider the purchase to be very relevant. Conversely, consumers engage in very limited information search and evaluation (or little cognitive elaboration) when the purchase holds little relevance or importance for them. Thus, for high-involvement purchases, the **central route to persuasion**—which requires considered thought and cognitive processing—is likely to be the most effective marketing strategy. For low-involvement purchases, the **peripheral route to persuasion**—which requires relatively little thought and information processing—is likely to be effective. In this instance, because the consumer is less motivated to exert cognitive effort, learning occurs through repetition, the passive processing of visual cues, and holistic perception. Highly involved consumers use attribute-based information to evaluate brands, whereas less-involved consumers apply simpler decision rules. In marketing to highly involved consumers, the quality of the argument presented in the persuasive message, rather than the imagery of the promotional message, has the greater impact on the consumption decision.

The route to persuasion has important implications for promotion. For example, comparative ads (see Chapter 7) are more likely to be processed centrally (purposeful processing of message arguments), whereas noncomparative ads are commonly processed peripherally (with little message elaboration and a response derived from other elements in the ad). A study demonstrated that the correlation between a consumer's product involvement and objective product knowledge was higher for *utilitarian* products than for products designed to bring about pleasure (termed *hedonic* products); for hedonic products, the correlation between subjective knowledge and product involvement was higher than for utilitarian products.[32] Assuming that *subjective* knowledge is the result of interpreting the imagery presented in the ad (i.e., the peripheral route) and that *objective* knowledge is the outcome of the factual information the ad provides (i.e., the central route), marketers should consider the product's degree of utilitarianism in selecting either the central or peripheral route in promoting that product.[33]

The central route applies to attitude change when a consumer's motivation or ability to assess the attitude object is high; that is, attitude change occurs because the consumer actively seeks out information relevant to the attitude object itself. When consumers exert the effort to comprehend, learn, or evaluate the available information about the attitude object, learning and attitude change occur via the central route.[34]

In contrast, when a consumer's motivation or assessment skills are low (i.e., low involvement), learning and attitude change occur via the peripheral route and without consumer processing of information that is relevant to the attitude object itself. In such cases, attitude change often is an outcome of secondary inducements such as cents-off coupons, free samples, beautiful background scenery, great packaging, or the encouragement of a celebrity endorsement. Research indicated that, in some low-involvement situations, both central and secondary inducements initially played equal roles in evoking attitudes. However, the central inducement had the greater "staying power"; that is, over time it was more persistent than the secondary one. Additionally, among subjects low in product knowledge, advertisements with terminology and factual data—that is, the central route—produced more favorable attitudes toward brands and ads than secondary cues.[35]

The Ideal Point Model (IPM)

Given the diversity of segments and preferences in the emerging market (with associated demographics and psychographics), the **ideal point model (IPM)**[36] can be used to explore the different dimensions associated with attitudes toward existing brands. This opens up several possibilities for brand managers to segment the market based on attitudinal aspects. Practising marketing managers will find the IPM effective in measuring attitudes. This model captures consumer perception on the "ideal" brand (with ideal features) and compares their perception on existing brands. The components of the IPM are given in Table 6.8.

If the model is applied to a brand of TV, say, "A," the following attributes can be identified.

1. Picture quality
2. Audio quality
3. Usefulness of special features
4. Handling ease
5. Esthetic appeal
6. Compactness

TABLE 6.8 The Ideal Point Model

A_b	Attitude toward the brand
W_i	Importance of attitude *i*
L_i	The 'ideal' performance on attitude *i*
X_i	Beliefs about a brand's actual performance on attitude *i*
n	The number of salient features

Consumers can mark the ideal brand and rate A on the attributes, on a scale of 7 [(1) given to reflect low perception and (7) to reflect high perception about the respective attribute]. The application can, for example, result in the analysis as given in Table 6.9.

The formula for attribute A_b toward the brand can be applied as:

$$A_b = \sum_{i=1}^{n} Wi(Li - Xi)$$

For Brand A, the resulting value is 28.

TABLE 6.9 Analysis of Attributes Following the Ideal Point Model

ATTRIBUTE	IMPORTANCE (WI)	IDEAL (LI)	BRAND A (XI)
Picture quality	7	4	3
Audio quality	4	3	2
Special features	3	2	2 (usefulness)
Handling ease	3	1	1
Esthetic appeal	2	4	1
Compactness	1	3	1

Implications of the Model

A brand can find out how close it is to the "ideal" brand. A value of "0" is ideal because at this point the brand is the 'ideal' brand. The higher the value of a brand, the further away it is from the "ideal" perception of the brand. (the negative sign does not alter the value, as the objective of the model is to measure the distance of a brand from the "ideal" brand. [Wi (Li – Xi) is to be considered.] A brand can improve its attributes and move closer to the "ideal" brand. In the example, except the usefulness of special features, Brand A is further away from the ideal brand on all aspects and requires improvement on these aspects. A brand can shift the importance associated with an attribute. Brand A, for example, can alter the importance on esthetic appeal (on which it is below the ideal brand) through an advertising campaign that stresses the attributes on which it is ranked high. The approach needs to be preceded by research on consumer perception toward this new attribute/benefit. For example, if a shampoo brand wants to shift the importance of attributes by introducing a new benefit—"spreading action to make the roots stronger"—the perception of the consumer needs to be captured before the brand uses this attribute.

In contrast, when a consumer's motivation or assessment skills are low (e.g., low involvement), learning and attitude change tend to occur via the *peripheral route* without the consumer focusing on information relevant to the attitude object itself. In such cases, attitude change often is an outcome of secondary inducements (e.g., rupee-off coupons, free samples, beautiful background scenery, great packaging, or the encouragement of a celebrity endorsement). Research indicates that even in low-involvement conditions (e.g., such as exposure to most advertising), in which both central and secondary inducements are initially equal in their ability to evoke similar attitudes, it is the central inducement that has the greatest "staying power"—that is, over time it is more persistent. Additionally, for subjects low in product knowledge, advertisements with terminology result in the consumer having a better attitude toward the brand and the ad.[37]

An offshoot of the ELM is the *dual mediation model (DMM)*. The DMM adds a link between attitude toward the ad and brand cognitions.[38] It acknowledges the possibility that the central route to persuasion could be influenced by a peripheral cue (i.e., attitude toward the ad). Thus, this model demonstrates the interrelationship between the central and peripheral processes. This model has recently been used in a research study that concluded that an advertisement's effect is important in the formation of an attitude, and therefore the DMM can be employed to explain how advertising impacts consumer behavior.[39]

Learning Objective

6 To understand how attitudes can precede behavior in the form of cognitive dissonance and the resolution of conflicting attitudes.

Cognitive Dissonance and Resolving Conflicting Attitudes

So far, our discussion has maintained the traditional (and rational) view that consumers develop their attitudes *before* taking action (e.g., "Know what you are doing before you do it"). However, there are theories that refute the "attitude precedes behavior" perspective. Specifically, cognitiv dissonance theory and attribution theory provide different explanations as to why and how behavior sometimes *precedes* attitude formation.

Cognitive dissonance occurs when a consumer holds conflicting thoughts about a belief or an attitude object.[40] For instance, after consumers have made a commitment to buy an important and pricy object—for example, made a down payment on a new house or an expensive car—they often begin to feel cognitive dissonance when they think of the unique, positive qualities of the alternatives not selected ("left behind"). When cognitive dissonance occurs after a purchase, it is called **post-purchase dissonance**. Because expensive and important purchases require compromise and choice among similar alternatives (e.g., similar homes in the same community), post-purchase dissonance in such instances commonly occurs, and leaves consumers with an uneasy feeling about their behavior (the purchase decision). Thus, marketers must ensure that these consumers resolve conflicting cognitions by changing their attitudes to conform to their behaviors.[41]

In the case of post-purchase dissonance, attitude change is an *outcome* of an action or behavior already undertaken. The conflicting thoughts and dissonant information that follow a purchase induce most consumers to change their attitudes so that the attitudes become consonant with their purchase behaviors. What makes post-purchase dissonance relevant to marketing strategists is the premise that marketers must help consumers reduce the unpleasant feelings created by the thoughts about alternatives that were "given up." Consumers can reduce their post-purchase dissonance in several ways:

1. Rationalize their decisions.
2. Seek advertisements that support their choices (while avoiding dissonance-creating competitive ads).
3. Try to "sell" friends on the positive features of the purchase made (i.e., "the consumer as a sales agent").
4. Look to satisfied owners for reassurance (e.g., meet homeowners in the community where the newly purchased house is located).

For example, consider a young man who has just purchased an engagement ring for his girlfriend and then sees the following magazine ad: "How can you make two months' salary last forever?" Because the purchase was expensive and the groom-to-be is likely to be experiencing dissonance, the ad might relieve his conflicts because it says that although the engagement ring did cost a great deal, the future bride will cherish it for the rest of her life.

Researchers have discovered different types and levels of dissonance. A study of durable consumer goods identified three segments of dissonant consumers: High-dissonance segment, low-dissonance segment, and "concerned about needing the purchase" segment.[42] As described earlier, consumers can try to reduce cognitive dissonance on their own. In addition, marketers can help consumers do so through ads specifically aimed at reinforcing consumers' decisions. For example, complimenting consumers on their wise decisions, offering them stronger guarantees or warranties, increasing the number and effectiveness of purchase-related contacts (e.g., post-purchase contacts by real estate agents to new home buyers who are waiting to close on the property), or providing more detailed information about the product while it is on order. In reducing dissonance, personal contacts may be more effective than advertisements; several studies indicated that most buyers believe that advertisers stretch the truth about their products in their promotions.[43] A study suggested that overly aggressive salespeople actually induce dissonance because consumers feel that they were "pushed" to make the purchases. Conversely, skilled salespeople can reduce dissonance by providing information and reassurance, and even turn consumers into loyal customers.[44]

Box 6.12 Creating, Nurturing, and Changing Attitudes

There are several approaches to creating and nurturing attitudes. Sometimes, the pioneering brands need to create an attitude. Brylcreem, Palmolive, and Clinic were some of the brands that were associated with the category of hair creams. HMT was associated with watches for a very long time. Titan used both the value-expressive function (lifestyle of gifting) to create an attitude towards its brand and strengthened it using the ego- defensive function ("Be More"). Titan Eye+'s advertisement, "Frames start at ₹395. Compliments come free," uses the ego-defensive function. While digital cameras are generally associated with the knowledge function, Canon's "My Ixus, My Style" emphasizes the value-expressive function. Colgate's Total's "12-hour protection," using a celebrity suggests more of a utilitarian function. Marico's www.heartfoundation.com provides information (knowledge function) on several aspects of heart care. Tata's Croma has a Web site that provides insights on choosing several kinds of durable categories. Santro used a comparative advertising featuring several brands when it entered the Indian market (knowledge function). Kinetic Honda introduced a sophisticated form of scooter (when consumers had developed an attitude toward conventional scooters). It created an attitude by sponsoring the Himalayan rally to reflect the fact that the product was as good as a conventional scooter (knowledge function). The utilitarian function is reflected in product benefits. Horlicks is a milk additive that emphasizes the benefits. It has positioned itself as one that is good for physical and mental growth. In its ads, Sugar Free uses a combination of value-expressive and utilitarian function, situating the product in an emerging culture of health and fitness. Procter & Gamble initiated a social cause-based marketing program by which every unit of purchase with regard to some of its brands contributed to a social cause (association with a cause). IFB, which is advertising its dishwasher, has the caption "Housework on your mind" (utilitarian function), with a visual of a lady in a formal, executive dress suggesting that it would be useful for a working woman.

The type of target segment is important in deciding the specific approach to be employed to create an attitude. With all its "coolness", an iPod or iPhone may require a knowledge-based approach if the target segment consists of youth using Facebook or Orkut and are oriented toward a high-cognitive need as a part of their personality

Resolving Conflicting Attitudes

Attitude-change strategies are designed to resolve actual or potential cognitive conflicts between two attitudes. For example, George is conservative on social issues, a devoted Episcopalian, and also an active Republican. During one presidential elections, the Republican nominee for president was significantly less conservative than George and also a member of another religion. Therefore, George's attitudes conflicted: He wanted to vote for his party, but disliked the party's nominee. George faced a dilemma and had three options: (1) Not vote at all, although he has never missed voting; (2) Vote for the Democratic candidate, which was utterly unacceptable; or (3) Develop more positive attitudes about the Republican candidate and vote for him. After attending the Republican convention as a delegate, speaking to other delegates, listening to the speeches, and even briefly meeting the nominee for president, George decided that the candidate's positions on social issues were, after all, close to his own and also became less concerned regarding the nominee's religion. Thus, George resolved his conflicting attitudes by altering them in favor of the only voting option that was consistent with his past behavior.

In fact, the party's officials recognized that many other Republicans felt the same way that George did before the convention, and they hired marketing consultants whose task was to take measures to change such attitudes. The consultants taught delegates how to address the doubts of their peers during seemingly spontaneous, casual conversations. Also, the speeches and films about the candidate, shown during the convention, included subtle appeals and cues designed to resolve conflicting attitudes. In essence, these measures resembled the strategies that savvy marketers use in similar situations. Of course, George and many others with similar, initial conflicting attitudes were unaware that these strategic communications were taking place during the convention.

Learning Objective

7 To understand the ways people assign causality to events and apply this knowledge to consumer behavior.

Assigning Causality and Attribution Theory

As a group of loosely interrelated social psychological principles, **attribution theory** attempts to explain how people "assign causality" (e.g., blame or credit) to events, on the basis of either their own behavior or the behavior of others.[45] In other words, a person might say, "I contributed to the American Red Cross because it really helps people in need," or "He tried to persuade me to buy an LED, rather than a 3D TV, because he'd make a bigger commission." In attribution theory, the underlying question is *why*: "Why did I do this?" "Why did he try to get me to switch brands?" Making inferences about one's own or another's behavior is an important factor in understanding attitude formation and change.

Many companies sponsor socially beneficial events and causes because they hope that consumers would attribute their efforts to "genuine concern." Research indicates that better "matches" between sponsors and events or causes result in more favorable consumer attributions. Evidence also suggests that consumers are willing to reward high-effort firms (i.e., they will pay more for and/or evaluate the product higher) if they feel that the company has made an extra effort to make better products or provide better consumer services.[46]

Self-perception Attributions

Self-perception attribution reflects the way people see themselves in the causalities they form about prior behaviors and the attitudes they develop thereafter. It is useful to distinguish between *internal* and *external* attributions. Let us assume that Bradley has just used video-editing software for the first time and his video of his South American vacation was well liked by the members of his photography club. After receiving the compliments, if he had thought: "I'm really a natural at editing my digital videos," his statement would reflect an *internal attribution*, because he had given himself credit for the outcome (e.g., his ability, his skill, or his effort). In contrast, if Bradley concluded that his work was due to a user-friendly video-editing program, the assistance of another club member, or just "luck," he would be making an *external attribution*. In the external attribution Bradley might think, "my great video is beginner's luck," whereas in the internal attribution he thought that "the video is good because of me."

Marketers can feature either internal or external attributions in promotions. For instance, ads for video-editing software should persuade users to *internalize* their successful use of the software. If they attribute their photos' quality to their skills rather than the software's capabilities, they would probably buy its new versions. Alternatively, if users *externalize* their success, they would attribute it to "beginner's luck," which is unrelated to the software itself and unlikely to get them to buy updates and advanced editions. Research indicated that appealing to internal attributions persuaded consumers to consider buying the products advertised.[47]

According to the principle of **defensive attribution**, people generally accept (or take) credit for success (internal attribution), but assign failure to others or outside events (external attribution). Thus, promotional messages should encourage

FIGURE 6.15 Internal Attribution for Texting and Driving Accidents

consumers to perceive themselves as the reasons for their success and reassure them that the advertised products will always make them feel this way. Similarly, persuasive messages aimed at getting people to abandon and refrain from socially undesirable behavior should appeal to internal attributions. The OMG ad in Figure 6.15, whose tagline is: "GET THE MESSAGE," bluntly tells drivers who text and drive to attribute the calamities they cause to their own (internal) behavior and not to external causes (e.g., traffic, road conditions).

Foot-in-the-door Technique

The **foot-in-the-door technique** consists of getting people to agree to large requests after convincing them to agree to a small and modest request first. The rationale behind this method is that agreeing to a small request creates a bond between the requester and the requestee. After fulfilling a modest request, the rquestee is likely to fulfill a larger request because of several reasons. First, the requestee does not want to disappoint the requestor, with whom he feels he has bonded. Secondly, the requestee actually becomes interested in the objective of the request. As discussed earlier, cognitive dissonance theory indicates that people tend to develop attitudes to justify prior actions. People's compliance with minor requests and subsequent compliance with more substantial requests is based on the premise that individuals look at their prior behavior (e.g., compliance with minor requests) and conclude that they are the kind of persons who generally agree to requests from others (i.e., an internal attributions). For example, someone who has donated $25 to the Michael J. Fox Foundation for Parkinson's Research is more likely to make a subsequent $100 donation than a person who was asked to donate $100 to begin with. The initial request of $25 was a "foot in the door," and "paved the way" towards a more substantial request.

Some research into the foot-in-the-door technique focused on understanding how specific incentives (e.g., cents-off coupons of varying amounts) influence consumer attitudes and subsequent purchase behavior. It discovered that different-size incentives created different degrees of internal attribution, which, in turn, led to different amounts of attitude change. For instance, individuals who tried brands without any inducements, or bought brands repeatedly, formed increasingly positive attitudes toward the brands (e.g., "I buy this brand because I like it"). In contrast, individuals who received samples were less likely to form positive attitudes about the brands they had tried (e.g., "I tried this brand because it was free").

Contrary to expectations, bigger incentives do not always lead to positive attitude changes. If an incentive is too big, marketers run the risk that consumers will externalize the cause of their behavior to the incentive (i.e., "I did it because I got a large incentive, but I didn't really like the product") and be *less* likely to change their attitudes and purchase the brand again. Instead, what seems most effective are *moderate* incentives, which are significant enough to stimulate initial purchase of the brand, but still small enough to encourage consumers to internalize their positive usage experiences and create positive attitude changes.[48]

In contrast with the foot-in-the-door technique is the **door-in-the-face technique**, in which a large, costly first request that is likely to be refused is followed by a second, more realistic, and less costly request. In certain situations, this technique may be more effective than the foot-in-the-door technique.[49]

Attributions Toward Others

In addition to understanding why people develop causalities about their own behaviors, it is important to understand how they make attributions towards others. As already stated, every time a person asks "why?" about a statement or action of another or other persons (whether family members, peers, salespeople, or marketers), attribution theory applies. To illustrate, in evaluating the words or deeds of, say, a salesperson, a consumer tries to determine whether the salesperson's motives are in his best interests. If he views the salesperson's motives favorably, the consumer is likely to respond accordingly. Otherwise, the consumer is likely to reject the salesperson's words and purchase elsewhere. Suppose, for example, that a consumer orders a new Canon digital point-and-shoot camera from Amazon.com. Because the consumer is going on vacation, she agrees to pay for next-day delivery by FedEx, instead of relying on Amazon's free five-day shipping. If the package with the camera does not arrive when it should, the consumer can attribute the failure to either one or both "others." That is, she can blame Amazon (failing to get the product out on time), FedEx (failing to deliver the package on time), or both (a dual failure). Alternatively, if the weather was very bad, she might attribute the delivery failure to the weather and to neither Amazon nor FedEx.

Attributions Toward Objects

Researchers have also studied consumers' attributions toward objects, which, in the context of marketing, are the products and services purchased. Specifically, when consumers wish to find out why a product met or failed to meet their expectations, they can attribute the product's successful or unsatisfactory performance to the product itself, to themselves, to other people or situations, or to some combination of these factors. To recap an earlier example, when Bradley successfully edited a video of his vacation, he could attribute that success to the software (product attribution), to his own skill (self or internal attribution), to a fellow member in his photo club who helped him (external attribution), or to all three.

Analyzing Self-attributions

After people have made attributions about a product's performance or a person's words or actions, they often attempt to figure out whether the inferences they have made were correct. To illustrate, let's consider two scenarios: (1) an alumnus who is considers donating a large sum to the university where he earned his MBA; and (2) an amateur photographer who is contemplating buying a new and expensive photo printer. Both situations require a substantial outlay of funds, and the fact that they are considered demonstrates that the two persons have made initial attributions of causality: The alumnus believes that the donation will improve the MBA program's reputation and growth, and the photographer believes that the printer will enhance the quality of her work. Both persons are likely to seek reinforcement for their initial attributions, and researchers have identified three factors that they are likely to consider when doing so: Distinctiveness, consistency, and consensus. Table 6.10 explains these factors and describes the photographer and alumnus's hypothetical deliberations.[50]

TABLE 6.10 Reviewing Self Attributions

SCENARIO	DISTINCTIVENESS	CONSISTENCY OVER TIME AND VARIED SITUATIONS	CONSENSUS
An alumnus considering donating money to his MBA program	How distinctive will my contribution be? Do many others make larger donations? Will I become part of a select group if I donate?	Can I afford to donate regularly? Will I be able to contribute money if the university asks for a special donation (e.g., for building a new student center)?	If I ask my friends, would most of them agree that I should make a donation, or will their opinions vary?
An amateur photographer who sees that, when printed on the latest HP printer, her photos look much better	Am I the only one who sees this marked difference, or do other notice the same?	Will I see the same superiority of the HP printer when I take other photos? Or is the advantage I see mostly a function of what this particular photo shows?	If I ask my friends, would most of them agree that my pictures look better when printed on the HP printer, or would some notice the difference and others not?

Summary

Learning Objective 1: To understand what attitudes are, how they are formed, and their role in consumer behavior.

An attitude is a learned predisposition to behave in a consistently favorable or unfavorable way toward a given object. In the context of consumer behavior, object is interpreted broadly to include the product, brand, service, price, package, advertisement, promotional medium, retailer selling the product, and many other aspects. Attitudes are learned from direct experience with the product, word-of-mouth, exposure to mass media, and other information sources. Attitudes reflect either favorable or unfavorable evaluations of the attitude object and they motivate consumers to either buy or not buy particular products or brands. Consumers buy products toward which they have favorable inclinations, so marketers must ensure that consumers maintain positive attitudes following purchases and remain loyal customers.

Attitudes are relatively consistent with the behavior they reflect. However, despite their consistency, attitudes are not necessarily permanent; they do change, and sometimes even frequently. Attitudes occur within and are affected by situations, events or circumstances that influence the relationship between attitudes and behavior. Personality traits significantly influence attitudes.

Learning Objective 2: To understand the tri-component attitude model and its applications.

The tri-component attitude model proposes that attitudes consist of three components: Cognitive, affective, and conative. The cognitive component represents the knowledge and perceptions of the features of an attitude object. The affective component reflects emotions and feelings, which are considered evaluations, because they capture the person's global assessment of the attitude object. The conative component is the likelihood that an individual will undertake a specific action or behave in a particular way with regard to the attitude object (i.e., consumer's intention to buy).

Learning Objective 3: To understand the structures of multi-attribute models and ther use in altering consumers' attitudes.

Multi-attribute attitude models portray consumers' attitudes as functions of their assessments of the objects' prominent features. Multi-attribute models include the attitude-toward-object model, the attitude-toward-behavior model, the theory of reasoned action, the theory of trying-to-consume, and the attitude-toward-ad model. Multi-attribute models can be used when adding product attributes, changing consumers' perceptions of attributes, and developing new products.

Learning Objective 4: To understand how to alter consumers' attitudes by making particular needs prominent.

Altering attitudes according to consumer motivations is termed the functional approach, which classifies attitudes into four functions: The utilitarian, ego-defensive, value-expressive, and knowledge functions. Associating a brand with a well-liked object can also alter attitudes.

Learning Objective 5: To understand the role of cognitive elaboration in altering attitudes.

Attitudes can sometimes be changed by either one of two different routes to persuasion, depending on the degree of cognitive elaboration used when consumers process information. One route requires extensive thought and cognitive processing, and is typically employed in situations where consumers are highly involved and perceive a lot of risk regarding the purchase considered. The second route, which requires relatively little thought and information processing, occurs during less important purchases.

Learning Objective 6: To understand how attitudes can precede behavior in the form of cognitive dissonance and the resolution of conflicting attitudes.

In most cases, attitudes precede and guide behavior. Sometimes, consumers act first and only afterward develop attitudes about actions already undertaken, which creates conflicting thoughts about the attitude object. Because important purchase decisions (i.e., buying a new home) require compromise and choices among similar alternatives, post-purchase conflicts are common. Marketers must ensure that customers resolve cognitive conflicts by changing their customers' attitudes to conform to their behavior.

Learning Objective 7: To understand the ways people assign causality to events and apply this knowledge to consumer behavior.

People assign causality (i.e., blame or credit) to events, their own behaviors, and the behaviors of others. The way people see themselves is reflected in the causalities they form about prior behaviors and the attitudes they develop thereafter. In trying to change consumption-related attitudes, especially with regard to products that require self-participation, marketers must understand how people make attributions, toward others and objects, and also how they analyze their own attributions.

Review and Discussion Questions

6.1. Explain how situational factors influence the degree of consistency between attitudes and behavior.

6.2. Because attitudes are learned predispositions to respond in particular ways, why don't marketers measure only purchase behavior and ignore attitudes?

6.3. Explain a person's attitude toward visiting Disney World in terms of the tri-component attitude model.

6.4. How can the marketer of a "nicotine patch" (a device that assists individuals to quit smoking) use the theory of trying-to-consume? Using this theory, identify two segments of smokers that the marketer should target and explain how to do so.

6.5. Explain how can the product manager of a breakfast cereal change consumer attitudes toward the company's brand by: (a) Changing beliefs about the brand, (b) Changing beliefs about competing brands, (c) Changing the relative evaluation of attributes, and (d) Adding an attribute.

6.6. The department of transportation of a large city is launching an advertising campaign that encourages people to switch from private cars to mass transit. How can the department use the following strategies to change commuters' attitudes: (a) Changing the basic motivational function, (b) Changing beliefs about public transportation, (c) Using self-perception theory, and (d) Using cognitive dissonance.

6.7. Should the marketer of a popular computer graphics program prefer consumers to make internal or external attributions? Explain your answer.

6.8. A college student has just purchased a new Apple iPad. What factors might cause the student to experience post-purchase dissonance? How might the student try to overcome it? How can the retailer who sold the computer help reduce the student's dissonance? How can the computer's manufacturer help?

Hands-on Assignments

6.9. Find two print ads, one illustrating the affective component and the other illustrating the cognitive component. Discuss each ad in the context of the tri-component model.. Why has each marketer taken the approach it did?

6.10. What sources influenced your attitude about this course before it started? Has your initial attitude changed since the course started? If so, how?

6.11. Describe a situation in which you acquired an attitude toward a new product through exposure to an advertisement. Describe a situation in which you formed an attitude toward a product or brand on the basis of personal influence.

6.12. Find advertisements that illustrate each of the four motivational functions of attitudes. Describe how each ad either reinforces an existing attitude or is aimed at changing an attitude.

6.13. Think back to the time when you were selecting a college. Did you experience dissonance after you had made a decision? Why or why not? If you did experience dissonance, how did you resolve it?

Key Terms

- affective component *174*
- attitude *168*
- attitude-toward-behavior model *183*
- attitude-toward-object model *180*
- attitude-toward-the-ad model *186*
- attribution theory *195*
- central route to persuasion *191*
- cognitive component *174*
- cognitive dissonance *193*
- comparative advertising *178*
- conative component *176*
- defensive attribution *195*
- door-in-the-face technique *196*
- ego-defensive function *189*
- elaboration likelihood model (ELM) *191*
- extensive problem solving *191*
- foot-in-the-door technique *196*
- functional approach *188*
- high-involvement purchases 191
- knowledge function *190*
- limited problem solving *191*
- low-involvement purchases *191*
- multi-attribute attitude models *179*
- need for cognition *172*
- peripheral route to persuasion *191*
- post-purchase dissonance *193*
- self-perception attribution *195*
- semantic differential scale *176*
- theory of reasoned action *184*
- theory of trying-to-consume *186*
- tri-component attribute model *174*
- two-sided message *178*
- utilitarian function *188*
- value-expressive function *189*
- word-of-mouth *168*

Case Two: Procter & Gamble

Febreze "Breathe Happy Campaign Launch"

Lead Agency: **GREY**

Strategic Challenges

Febreze was once a breath of fresh air in the category, but the competition caught up.

In 1998, Febreze entered the air care category with a revolutionary product. Rather than simply perfuming the air, its unique formula actually eliminated odors on fabrics and replaced them with a fresh scent. Febreze became known as THE odor-eliminating brand and enjoyed great success. Recognizing a good thing when they saw one, the competition responded by launching similar products that provided the same benefit. "Brand Health" data indicated that P&G had lost its distinct positioning. The company once "owned" odor elimination, but now shared this equity with competitors Glade (category leader by dollar share) and Airwick (third in the category by dollar share).

Air care brands became indistinguishable.

As competitors expanded to offer products similar to Febreze, the category became nebulous. Innovation from any camp was replicated and marketing efforts were immediately countered. Products became increasingly similar with indistinguishable claims. Almost all advertising featured generic imagery, presenting freshness fantasies in idealized worlds. Toxic levels of advertising diluted P&G's marketing efforts and made people unable to tell the brands apart.

Cynical consumers ceased to believe brand claims and Febreze growth declined.

Research revealed that the company's audience (25- to 65-year-old moms who want constant assurance that their homes are clean and fresh) had grown cynical about the category's advertising. Because many cheaper, less advanced brands were making similar claims but did not live up to their promises, people struggled to know whom to believe, and became skeptical about all air care products. Consumers concluded that all brands' claims were overinflated and bought lower-priced products. With Febreze costing up to three times more than its competitors, P&G struggled to sustain sales.

Objectives

1. Restore faith in Febreze's odor-eliminating capabilities in a way consumers will remember.
2. Generate buzz for the Febreze brand and its advertising.
3. Restore the distinctiveness of the Febreze brand.

Insights

People's reactions to bad smells are stronger than their reactions to nice ones.

Focus groups reaffirmed that P&G's audience wanted to create a "welcoming home" by keeping it clean, tidy, and fresh, and that they were concerned about bad smells destroying this atmosphere. The threat of malodors did not only made them uncomfortable, but triggered passionate descriptions of unpleasant smells, reflecting their disgust of uncleanliness. P&G realized that focusing on the problem rather than the solution could help Febreze stand out among the other brands.

What we smell can be more important than what we see.

In-home interviews helped P&G understand Febreze's role in creating a "welcoming home" in greater depth, uncovering the most influential insight: When judging if a home is "welcoming," a messy-looking home can still be clean, but a smelly home can ***never*** be clean. This was best encapsulated by one respondent's comment on the issue: "When you walk into an unappealing room, you can close your eyes, but you can't turn off your nose."

Smelling is believing.

Observations of shoppers in stores revealed that consumers were spraying the product in the aisle after picking it off the shelf. This indicated that firsthand experience of the product is vitally important in influencing the consumer's choice of a brand.

The Big Idea

Involve real people in visceral experiences to prove that Febreze makes even the filthiest places smell nice, no matter what they look like.

Questions

1. Apply the principles of perception to the three insights listed in the case.
2. Are the three objectives aimed at repositioning Febreze? Explain your answer.
3. How would P&G determine whether the campaign's objectives have been achieved?
4. On You Tube, you can find several commercials that "brought to life" the "big idea." Describe three of them and discuss their persuasive effectiveness.
5. Several versions of Febreze are now on the market (febreze.com). Apply the concept of benefit segmentation to three of them.

Source: Effie Worldwide, Effie Showcase Winners. Reprinted by permission. Febreze is a 2012 Bronze Effie Winner. For information on Effie's programs for students, visit the Collegiate Effies at www.effie.org

Case Three: *Lifebuoy/Unilever Asia Private Limited*

"Superfast Handwash"

Lead Agency: **Lowe Lintas and Partners**

Target Markets

The three markets chosen—India, Saudi Arabia, and Pakistan—were the most significant to Unilever because of their sizes and growth opportunities. If it did not "fire" in these markets, Unilever would not be a viable player in the global liquid handwash market.

India: The largest and most valuable among all of Unilever's markets. Lifebuoy was an established brand in India in bar soaps, but the brand's closest competitor owned more than half the market in the liquid handwash category.

Saudi Arabia: The largest market in the Middle East, where Unilever faced a dominant competitor that was growing even larger.

Pakistan: The second largest market in the Indian subcontinent, with two strong Unilever competitors.

Strategic Challenges

In the three countries, antibacterial handwash was widely used, but there were established antibacterial liquids that have been household names for years.

To illustrate the importance of consumers' need for the product and knowledge of its effectiveness, let's consider Argentina. Because of a swine flu outbreak, public messaging exhorted people to wash with soap but did not specify antibacterial soap. Hence, consumers questioned the necessity of an antibacterial soap.

Because Lifebuoy Handwash was high-priced, it was expected to appeal to higher-income groups. This was a difficult issue because, in India, the brand's bar soaps were popular among lower-income groups.

In each of the three markets, competitors offered "all powerful" antibacterial solutions. Consumers perceived these products as "germ killers" that offered long-lasting, all seasons protection.

In Pakistan, India, and Saudi Arabia, Lifebuoy had to create a unique image. It was a new, high-priced entrant to the liquid handwash category, and could not easily take on dominant competitors.

Across the three countries, Unilever wanted to target higher-income mothers who were potential handwash users and convince them to use Lifebuoy Handwash for their families. These mothers had kids aged between 4 and 12 years and were using competitive brands. When it came to protection, the target mothers believed that their families deserved the best and were not willing to compromise. This gave Unilever a foot in the door opportunity. If the company could convince these mothers that Lifebuoy offered the *best* protection, it had a chance to capture meaningful market shares.

Objectives

1. Increase preference for Lifebuoy among higher-income segments (defined by a socioeconomic classification index).

   This would be tracked by a consumer household panel that Unilever commissioned through a retail audit agency.

2. Establish the Lifebuoy proposition as unique and differentiate it from the competition.

   This would be tracked by using quantitative research among consumers after the communication had run for at least a month to measure recall of messaging.

Insights

Through lab research, Unilever could claim that Lifebuoy were better than competitors' products on germ kill: it could kill *even more* germs.

During consumer research studies, when the results of the lab research were shown to them, consumers said this was unbelievable. Proof or no proof, they were unwilling to budge. That's when Unilever realized that beating competitors by going head to head against them would not work.

During the same lab tests that showed that Unilever's product killed *more* germs than the competitors' products, the R&D scientists also discovered that Lifebuoy could kill germs *faster* than the competing products. In fact, Unilever's handwash could protect hands from germs in 10 seconds, whereas all other handwashes took one full minute to do so!

This was exciting, but Unilever did not want to make the same mistake as before of just using facts and figures to position its product. Rather than going in with just the *claim* (what good is a faster handwash anyway?), the company looked extensively for a consumer angle to frame the "faster kill" claim. It was while observing children's habits that the company hit a gold mine!

Universally, children are always in a rush or lazy while doing things they don't particularly enjoy (e.g., eating vegetables, doing their homework, etc.). *When it comes to hand-washing, it is no different.* For kids, it is an unnecessary chore that they do as quickly as possible, as they just want to be finished with it.

So, regardless of how many germs anyone claimed that their product would kill, it would all be rendered useless by the habits of children, who always wash in a hurry.

The campaign titled "Superfast Handwash" used the underlying insight on children's behavior not only to make germ protection in just 10 seconds new and relevant for Lifebuoy, but also to render the competition's perceived high ground on germ protection vulnerable. The double blow of a new parameter of time, combined with the lens of children's habits, managed to dislodge the company's competitors as the last word in germ protection in consumers' minds.

The Big Idea

Lifebuoy Superfast Handwash: 99.9% germ protection in just 10 seconds—because children are always in a hurry, especially when it comes to hand-washing.

Questions

1. Design one TV commercial (a story board) and one print ad that "bring to life" the "big idea."
2. Why didn't Unilever use factual-information (e.g., results of lab tests) about the "faster kill" to differentiate Lifebuoy from competition?
3. How did Unilever use qualitative and quantitative research (see Chapter 16) to develop the positioning claim for Lifebuoy?
4. Does the name "Lifebuoy" convey the product's core benefit effectively? Why or why not?
5. Over time, should Unilever combine the "more germs" and "faster kill" claims into positioning Lifebuoy?
6. It is unlikely that competitors would let Unilever take market shares away from them in the liquid antibacterial handwash category. How can they fight Unilever?

Source: Effie Worldwide, Effie Showcase Winners. Reprinted by permission. Superfast Handwash is a 2012 Bronze Effie Winner. For information on Effie's programs for students, visit the Collegiate Effies at www.effie.org

7

Persuading Consumers

Learning Objectives

1 To understand the elements and persuasive capabilities of communication, as well as the barriers to effective communication.

2 To understand the distinctions between broadcasting and narrowcasting.

3 To understand how to design persuasive messages effectively.

4 To understand the effectiveness and limitations of prominent advertising appeals.

5 To understand how to measure the effectiveness of advertising messages.

COMMUNICATION IS the transmission of a message from a sender to a receiver via a medium of transmission (also named "channel"). In addition to these four components—sender, receiver, medium, and message—the fifth essential component of communication is **communication feedback**, which alerts the sender as to whether the intended message was, in fact, received. Senders *encode* their messages by using words, pictures, symbols, spokespersons, and persuasive appeals, and then the receivers *decode* them. If the messages are to be persuasive, the receivers must decode the messages as the senders intended (see Figure 7.5).

Marketers (the message senders) can choose among numerous persuasive appeals when they design and send advertising messages to consumers (the receivers). The advertising appeal used is the **encoding** of the message. The following ads represent four prominent persuasive appeals. Figure 7.1 shows that when parliamentary elections were held in India, a brand had used a slogan that had striking similarity to an ad campaign of a political party. The brand, Fevicol, had used humor in a contextual manner. Humor is the most widely used advertising appeal. The ad in Figure 7.2 depicts fear and is from a campaign urging victims of domestic violence to seek help before their conditions becomes deadly (the explosives represent abusive fists). Fear is effective in discouraging negative behaviors such as drug abuse and distracted driving. The ad in Figure 7.3 shows a (rather mild) sex appeal. Sex appeals have "stopping power," but must be used carefully, as they may distract consumers from the product advertised if used unwisely. The ad in Figure 7.4 compares washing clothes with added Clorox Bleach to using detergent only. The ad actually "admits" that clothes can be laundered without Clorox. Later on, we explore the advantages and risks of acknowledging alternatives, such as not using the product at all (i.e., a two-sided message), or even mentioning competing brands by name (i.e., comparative advertising) in promotional messages.

Source: Pidilite

FIGURE 7.1 Humorous Appeal

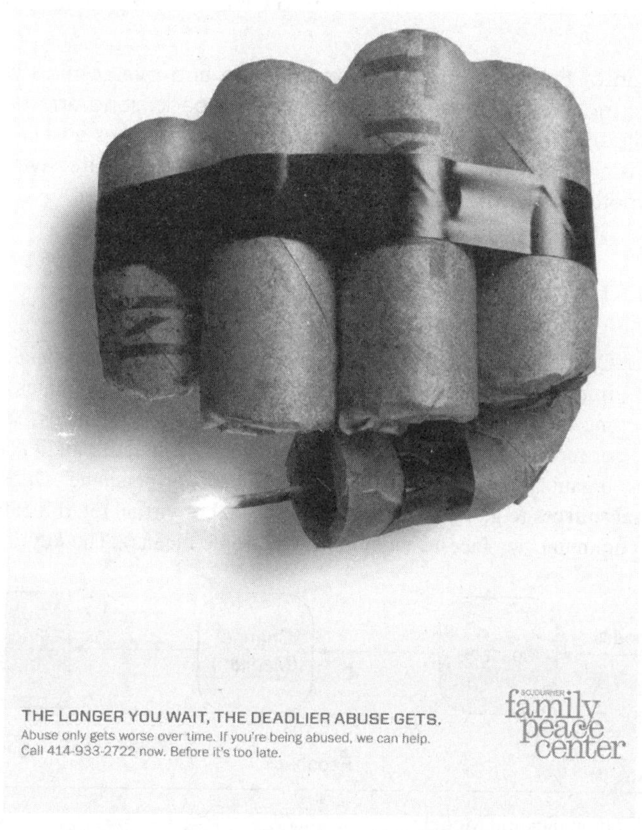

Source: photo copyright Curtis Johnson

FIGURE 7.2 A Fear Appeal: Family Peace Center

Source: photo copyright Curtis Johnson

FIGURE 7.3 A Sexual Appeal: ALT Magazine

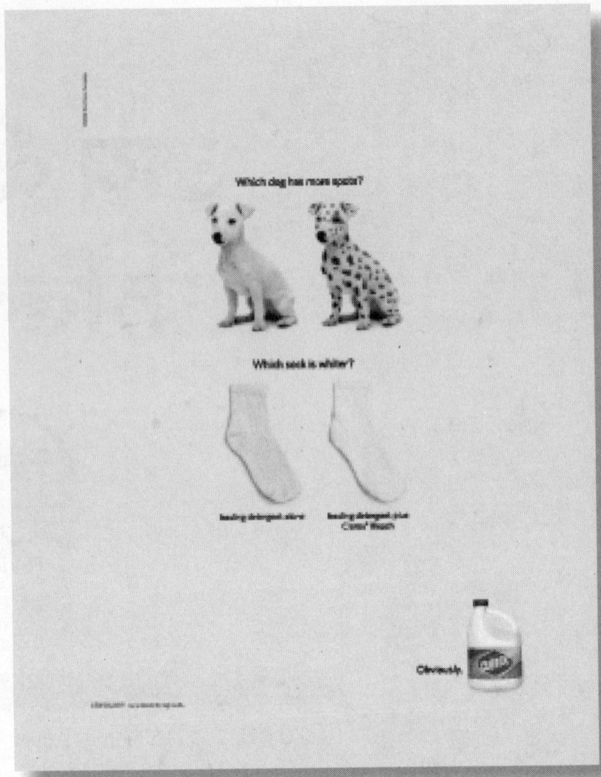

Source: photo copyright Curtis Johnson

FIGURE 7.4 A Two-Sided Message

We begin with a discussion of the elements of communication and overcoming barriers to effective communication. Next, we present two models of media communications: Broadcasting and narrowcasting. Thereafter, we explain the correct structure of persuasive messages and discuss the advantages and limitations of the most popular advertising appeals. After transmitting their ads, marketer must measure the effectiveness of their messages, and they do so by employing the methods discussed in the last section of this chapter.

Learning Objective

1 To understand the elements and persuasive capabilities of communication, as well as the barriers to effective communication.

The Communication Process

Communications can be either impersonal or interpersonal. In marketing, the sources of **impersonal communications** are messages that companies transmit through their marketing departments, advertising or public relations agencies, and spokespersons. The targets, or receivers, of such messages are usually a specific audience or several audiences that the organization is trying to inform, influence, or persuade. The senders of **interpersonal communications** may be either **formal sources** (e.g., a salesperson in a physical or virtual retail location) or **informal sources** (e.g., peers with whom the consumer communicates face-to-face or via electronic means). The key factor underlying the persuasive

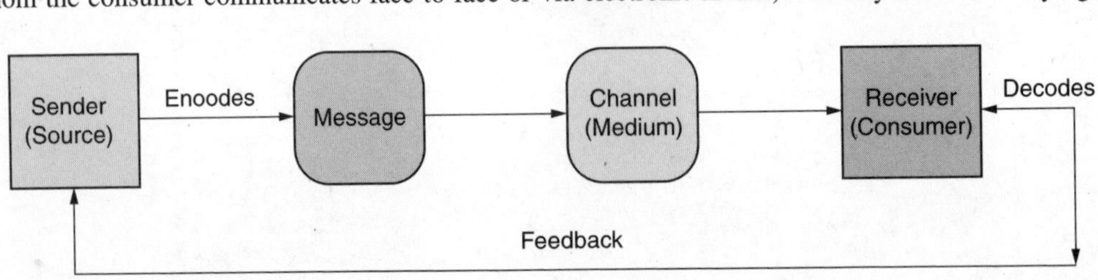

FIGURE 7.5 Communication Model

impact of a personal or interpersonal message received from either a formal or informal source is the source's credibility; that is, the extent to which the receiver trusts and believes the source sending the message. The influence of interpersonal sources can have a great effect on consumers' shopping patterns, and the perceived honesty and objectivity of the sender of the communication can have an enormous impact on how the communication is accepted by the receivers (see Chapter 9).

Compared with impersonal communications in mass media, a key advantage of interpersonal communications is their ability to obtain *immediate* feedback through verbal as well as nonverbal cues. Experienced speakers are very attentive to feedback and constantly modify their messages based on what they see and hear from the audience. Immediate feedback is the factor that makes personal selling so effective, because it enables the salesperson to tailor the sales pitch to the expressed needs and observed reactions of each prospect. Similarly, immediate feedback in the form of inattention serves to alert the college professor to jolt students who text during class. The professor can abruptly and dramatically stop the lecture, firmly ask the "texters" to leave the classroom, and state that the material covered at that point would appear on the next exam. The British Airways ad in Figure 7.6 focuses on the importance of interpersonal communications.

In consumer behavior terms, the sender of the message can be a marketer transmitting an advertisement to consumers or a person telling another consumer about a product. This chapter focuses on the marketer as the source, whereas Chapter 9 discusses consumers as the sources of messages that are transmitted via **word-of-mouth**. **Media** are the channels for transmitting communications. **Traditional media** are the original communications channels that advertisers have used and are generally classified as print (news papers, magazines, billboards) and broadcast (radio, television); these media are impersonal because all receivers get the same message, and the communications are one-way because the receivers cannot interact with the senders. **New media** are online channels, social networks, and mobile electronic devices. These media are drastically more advanced than traditional media because they allow marketers to send personalized messages to individual consumers who can respond to the messages immediately. These responses indicate to marketers whether or not their persuasive efforts have been effective. Chapter 8 explores both forms of media.

Several "barriers" affect the accuracy with which consumers interpret messages. The most prominent ones are selective exposure and psychological noise.

Source: British Airways

FIGURE 7.6 The Importance of Interpersonal Communication

Selective Exposure

Selective exposure refers to consumers' selectivity in paying attention to advertising messages. They read ads carefully for products they are interested in and tend to ignore advertisements that have no interest or relevance to them. Furthermore, technology provides consumers with increasingly sophisticated means to control their exposure to media. Consumers can now control their exposure to mass media and avoid commercials while watching TV by using the pause function when a string of commercials starts and then quickly returning to the broadcast once the ads are over. Viewers can also **time shift** by recording TV shows and viewing them at their leisure while skipping over commercials. Readers of newspapers and magazines online can create personalized editions of these publications and avoid many ads, and satellite radio allows consumers to avoid hearing radio ads altogether. Caller ID, phone answering machines, the government's "do not call" list, and other devices allow consumers to screen out telemarketing and other unsolicited contacts from marketers.

Psychological Noise

Just as telephone static can impair a phone conversation, **psychological noise** in the form of competing advertising messages or distracting thoughts can affect the reception of a promotional message. A viewer faced with the clutter of nine successive commercial messages during a program break may actually receive and retain almost nothing of what he has seen. Similarly, an executive planning a department meeting while driving to work may be too engrossed in her thoughts to "hear" a radio commercial. Marketers use the following strategies to overcome or limit psychological noise:

1. Repeated exposure to an advertising message surmounts psychological noise and facilitates message reception. Thus, repeating an ad several times is a must (see Chapter 5). The principle of redundancy is also seen in advertisements that use both illustrations and text copy to emphasize the same points. To achieve even more advertising redundancy, many marketers now place their messages in such places as video games, movie theaters, elevators, supermarket floors, baggage carousels, subway turnstiles, and even public restrooms (see discussion of **ambush marketing** in Chapter 4).
2. Copywriters often use *contrast* to break through the psychological noise and advertising clutter and attract consumers' attention (see Chapter 4). Contrast includes featuring an unexpected outcome; increasing the amount of *sensory input* (such as color, scent, or sound); and identifying, through testing, message appeals that attract more attention.
3. Digital technologies allow marketers to monitor the consumer's visits to websites, infer the person's interests, and design and send customized promotional messages to that person.

Of course, effective **positioning** and providing value are the most effective ways to ensure that a promotional message stands out and is received and decoded appropriately by the target audience. Advertisements for products that are perceived to be unique and provide better value than competitive products are more likely to be received in their intended ways than other promotional messages within the advertising clutter.

Box 7.1 Experiential Advertising, Brand Imagery, and Involvement Levels in Communication

Schmidt* refers to experiential advertising (or marketing) as the experience cycle associated with sensing, thinking, feeling, acting, and relating with regard to branded products. Experiential advertising deals with multisensory experiences like emotions, fantasy, or hedonism. Physiological consumption means highlighting the consumption of products and this approach has been used by Pepsi and Cadbury in their advertisements. Conspicuous consumption is used by brands like Omega in watches and Hero Honda Hunk in motorcycles and this is associated with self-esteem and the status of consumers. Touch-based experience is applicable to a brand like Liril in soaps that underscores the importance of "refreshing touch" associated with the product. The fantasy experience is associated with the emotional experience of movies and other forms of entertainment. Zoom TV carries several advertisements of films. Well-being experiences are more associated with services. The hoardings of Apollo Hospitals that emphasize the care and attention patients receive are an example.

Experiential marketing is critical to brand imagery. Brand imagery involves powerful associations that brands create, and communication creates and nurtures brand imagery. The Indian context has a diversity of brand imagery across categories: Ujala, the washing liquid blue, when added to white clothes created a strong imagery with the white color, though it was not the pioneer in the category. Titan created the gifting imagery and has managed it well over a period of time. Closeup, the first gel-based toothpaste to be launched in India, created the youth imagery associated with the brand three decades back. Parachute, the coconut oil brand, has created a host of brand associations with the careful use of sub-brands. It has a variant, Therapie, that has a therapeutic association; its Aftershower hair cream and Advansed hair oil have a "modern youth" association; its Jasmine has a traditional association (women in some parts of the country wear jasmine flowers in their hair as a tradition); its Lite has a non-oily association and its Hot Oil has a herbal association. The Himalaya brand has created a contemporary association on a traditional system of medicine (with both its advertising and point-of-purchase communication and its Web site); Johnson & Johnson created a feeling of warmth with its mother–child association. Creating and sustaining brand associations are some of the challenges for marketers.

In several categories, branding often competes with unbranded offerings in the Indian context. Hence, communication has to primarily create the involvement or the personal degree of interest among consumers so that they

(Continued)

Box 7.1 (Continued)

will try branded products. In several categories, especially in FMCGs, rational and emotional aspects need to be blended together to raise the level of involvement among the target segment. Reynold pens pioneered branding in the ball pen category through its features at a time when the market consisted of unbranded offerings. Captain Cook *atta* created involvement with the family association (in a category where less than 2% is branded); Godrej used the tradition of wedding to raise involvement levels in the steel cupboard category (also a category with over 80% in the unorganized or unbranded category). ITC's Mangaldeep incense sticks created involvement in a category that is full of unbranded products. Peter England's affordable proposition raised the involvement levels of consumers at the lower end of the readymade shirt market. Both rational benefits and emotional appeals are useful in categories dominated by unbranded offerings.

Source: *B. Schmidt, *Experiential Marketing: How to Get Customers to Sense, Feel, Think, Act, and Relate to Your Company and Brands* (New York: The Free Press, 1999).

Learning Objective

2 To understand the distinctions between broadcasting and narrowcasting.

Broadcasting versus Narrowcasting

The term **traditional media** is synonymous with broadcast media (or mass media) and consists of channels where all receivers receive the same one-way messages from marketers (i.e., they cannot send direct responses to the messages' sources). In sharp contrast, **new media** are channels of **narrowcasting**, defined as means that permit marketers to send messages that are:

1. ***Addressable*** and directed to specific persons or small audiences rather than groups of consumers.
2. ***Customized*** and based on data gathered from tracing consumers' surfing and clicks online, in combination with other information, to either small groups or individual consumers. The additional data includes the receiver's location (which can be determined from an IP address or a GPS integrated into a mobile device) and information from "cookies" installed on the hard drive of a digital device.
3. ***Interactive*** because, in most narrowcasts, an action by the consumer—in the form of a click on a link or banner—triggers the transmission of a message.
4. More ***response-measurable*** than traditional broadcasted ads because communication feedback is more accurate and received sooner.

Traditional media and communications models that have been used for decades are presently undergoing fundamental changes. Advertisers are unhappy with the current broadcast media because they are reaching increasingly smaller and more fragmented audiences and getting fewer "eyeballs" for the money spend for TV ads. Consumers can avoid commercials with increasing ease, and a large number of broadcasted advertising messages reach many people who are not interested in (and unlikely to purchase) the products advertised. Advertisers complain that the Nielsen ratings do not accurately reflect the ethnic composition of the U.S. population and do not adequately monitor "time shifted" TV viewing. Cable operators realize that they have the means to monitor media viewing more accurately, but are also deeply aware of the privacy concerns of their subscribers. The TV networks, which have lost vast audiences to cable channels, realize that continuing to provide free programming underwritten by advertising revenues generated from reaching massive audiences of prime-time shows—a model in place since the early 1950s—may no longer be feasible. The networks, cable companies, and advertisers agree that the new communications model calls for targeting smaller groups of consumers who are already interested in the products advertised, and to whom they must provide more interactive and enticing ways of viewing promotional messages. In short, driven by technology, communications is going through the greatest changes since the development of spoken and written language, and traditional media are being integrated into or replaced by new media.

Addressable Advertising

Probably, most of the readers have purchased products at Amazon.com, rented a movie at Netflix.com, or traded an item on eBay.com. These premier online merchants analyze the purchase behaviors of their users (including consumers' ratings of the products rented or bought) and utilize this data to make customized, or addressable, recommendations to individual users about future offerings. Thus, **addressable advertising** consists of customized messages sent to particular consumers. These messages are based mostly on the consumers' prior shopping behavior, which marketers have observed and analyzed. In Figure 7.7, MTV is a brand (unconditioned) that is well-linked with the youth over the years.

Tata Nano (conditioned stimuli) associates itself with such a conditioning to get connected with youth and to evoke spontaneous youth associations.

Data aggregators (see Chapter 8) use data from users' browsers, Google, Yahoo!, and Facebook to build models that marketers use to design the different ads customers see, which are also a function of the viewers' demographics and past advertising exposure.[1] A study demonstrated that consumers favor interactive websites where they feel that they receive personalized messages and can easily contact the seller after the purchase, via, for example, chats with the sellers' representatives.[2]

For example, advertising on cell phones is gaining popularity because mobile phones are an ideal forum for personalized advertising. A TV network has teamed up with an online social network to recruit participants for an experiment in addressable and location-based advertising.[3] A publishing company started delivering educational content via cell phones.[4] Several providers of wireless services teamed up with companies by rewarding subscribers who agreed to receive ads on their cell phones with reduced rates and other incentives.[5] As the number of cell phones and other wireless communications devices continues to grow, mobile advertising is likely to become a component of most advertisers' media plans.

Twitter—the most popular short-messaging service—enabled advertisers to send messages to users based on indications of what the users like. For instance, a company that sells soft drinks can elect to show paid ads to Twitter users who are fans of professional football. Twitter can identify a football fan, say, by analyzing whether the Twitter user "follows" football players or commentators, or recirculates Twitter messages from those sources.[6] TV advertisers are now able to vary their spots based on

Source: Viacom 18

FIGURE 7.7 MTv with Nano

audience demographics, changes in weather, sales goals, or the campaigns of competitors. For example, Wendy's designed ads that were customized according to the weather. TV viewers in certain locations saw either a chili spot or a Frosty ad. When it was more than 60 degrees, Wendy's showed the Frosty ads; when it was colder, the chili ad ran.[7] Almost all online newspapers now allow readers to pick and choose only the stories that interest them.

Cable TV operators have a tremendous amount of data about their viewers and are moving away from advertising based mostly on subscribers' geographic locations and the one-message-fits-all approach. For instance, ads for dog food will only go to households that have dogs. One company is experimenting with using data from remote controls to follow what a person is watching, and then matching that information and programs' contents to infer that person's gender and age. It can also use census and syndicated data for further refinement. Then the cable TV company sends targeted ads to individual households.[8]

Box 7.2 Augmented Reality as a Mode of Brand Communication

Augmented reality can add a new dimension to the search process. It also provides a tech-savvy orientation to those consumers who may desire it. It can be a mobile application or *apps* that enables the consumer to get more information through his device instantaneously.[9] Titan had launched such an application for Android phones and iPad for its high-technology, self-energizing offering like watches. A consumer was able to get more information on the film Don 2 when he moved his mobile camera on the poster or ad of the film. These apps also find tremendous potential when consumers shop at modern retail outlets. Quaker Oats, for example, can provide various kinds of information on health and the offering on its app that cannot be accommodated in the conventional package.

Learning Objective

3 To understand how to design persuasive messages effectively.

Designing Persuasive Messages

A **message** is the thought, idea, attitude, image, or other information that the sender wishes to convey to the intended audience, and it can be *verbal* (spoken or written), *nonverbal* (a photograph, an illustration, or a symbol), or a combination of the two. The sponsor, who may be an individual or an organization, must first establish the objectives of the message, select an appropriate medium for sending it, and design (encode) the message in a manner that is appropriate to each medium and to each audience. The objectives of a persuasive message include creating awareness of a service, promoting sales of a product, encouraging (or discouraging) certain practices, attracting retail patronage, reducing post-purchase dissonance, creating goodwill or a favorable image, or any combination of these and other communications objectives.

The source of the message (the sender) must *encode* the message in such a way that its meaning is interpreted by the targeted audience in precisely the intended way. Marketers encode messages by using words, pictures, symbols, spokespersons, and special channels. The message receivers *decode* the messages they receive on the basis of their personal experiences, characteristics, and motives. To encode a message in a form that the audience will understand and thus receive its intended meaning (i.e., decode it successfully), the sender must know exactly what he or she is trying to say and why (i.e., message objectives) and understand the target audience's personal characteristics. According to **cognitive learning** models, (see Chapter 5) exposure to a message leads to interest and desire for the product and, ultimately, to buying behavior. In addition, personality traits affect a person's reactions to various promotional appeals (see Chapter 3).

The decisions that marketers must make in designing a message include selecting images, creating advertising copy, using positive or negative message framing, choosing between one-sided or two-sided messages, and deciding on the order of presentation.

Images and Text

Messages that depict images are often more effective than those with text only, as reflected in the famous saying "One picture is worth a thousand words." The ad for Mistique tissues in Figure 7.8 conveys the product's purpose and effectiveness mostly visually rather than verbally.

Source: SR Foils and Tissue Limited

FIGURE 7.8 Nonverbal Communication

Many studies have investigated the interaction between visual and verbal cues and their ability to attract and capture consumers' attention in likable ways. One study showed that ads' *visual complexity* plays a central role in this regard. Advertisements are visually complex when they contain dense perceptual features and/or when they have elaborate creative designs. The study found that *feature complexity* hurts attention to the brand and attitude toward the ad, whereas *design complexity* enhances paying attention to the ad, raises its comprehensibility, and improves attitude toward the ad. The study demonstrated that marketers must assess the visual complexity of advertisements and use their findings to enhance their ads' "stopping power."[10]

Sometimes, marketers are influenced by the same economic, social, and cultural conditions and thus use similar phrases reflecting these conditions in their advertising copy. For example, given our increasingly busy lives, the growing complexity of technology, and the uncertain economic picture, many marketers have been using the words "simply," "simple," "easy," "honest," and "clear" in their ads. A new brand of orange juice was named "Simply Orange." McDonald's offered "the simple joy of a wholesome breakfast." Ads for one bank declared: "Saving is simple when no one charges you for it"; and ads for Ivory soap urged: "Keep it pure, clean and simple."[11]

Message Framing

Should a marketer stress the benefits to be gained by using a specific product, that is, **positive message framing**; or the benefits to be lost by not using the product, that is, **negative message framing**? Research suggests that the appropriate message framing decision depends on the consumer's attitudes and characteristics as well as the product itself. For example, one study found that persons with a low need for cognition were more likely to be persuaded by negatively framed messages.[12] Another study found that individuals with an *independent self-image* (i.e., who view themselves as defined by unique characteristics) were more persuaded by messages stressing an approach goal (positive framing); those with an *interdependent self-view* (i.e., who view themselves as defined by others) found messages that stress avoidance goals more convincing (negative framing).[13] A study of advertised products that enabled the early detection of disease indicated that positively framed anecdotal messages were less persuasive than negatively framed anecdotal messages.[14] Another study discovered that negative message framing was more effective than positive framing when respondents had less opportunity to process the information in the ad, but less effective when respondents had more opportunity to process the ad content.[15]

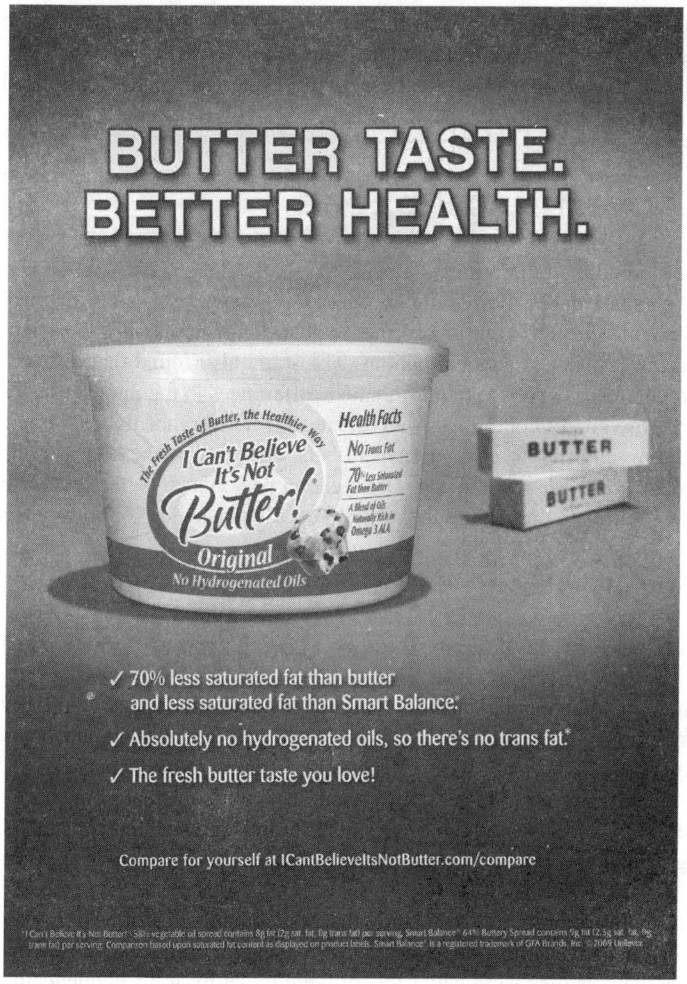

FIGURE 7.9 A Two-Sided Message: I Can't Believe It's Not Butter—a Butter Substitute—versus "Real" Butter

One-Sided versus Two-Sided Messages

Should a marketer pretend that its products are the only ones of their kind, that is, use a **one-sided message**; or should the company acknowledge competing products, that is, use a **two-sided message**? Some marketers stress only positive factors about their products and pretend that competition does not exist. However, when competition does exist and when it is likely to be vocal or obvious, such advertisers tend to lose credibility with the consumer. Figure 7.4 features a two-sided message. Another example is an ad for Ultra Dawn—a dishwashing liquid—proclaiming that the product is twice as strong as "the other guy." It acknowledges competition, but not by name. "I Can't Believe It's Not Butter!" is a butter substitute. Advertisements featuring the product often end with the question, "I Can't Believe It's Not Butter, can you?" The ad in Figure 7.9 is a two-sided message because it acknowledges the product's competitors (that is, butter and butter-substitue brands) without mentioning any.

The credibility of an advertised claim can often be enhanced by disclaiming the superiority of some product features or by not claiming that the product is a universal solution. For example, an ad for a men's hair regrowth product may state that, after clinical testing, whereas almost half the men using the product experienced modest to dense hair regrowth, about a third experienced minimal hair regrowth, and about one-sixth had no regrowth whatsoever. The admission that the product did not always work enhances the credibility of the ad.

The decision of whether to use a one- or two-sided message also depends on the nature of the audience and competition. If the audience is friendly (e.g., if it uses the advertiser's products), if it initially favors the communicator's position, or if it is not likely to hear an opposing argument, then a one-sided (supportive) message that stresses only favorable information is most effective. However, if the audience is critical or unfriendly (e.g., if it uses competitive products), if it is well educated, or if it is likely to hear opposing claims, then a two-sided message is likely to be more effective. Two-sided messages can also be very effective when consumers are likely to see competitors' negative counterclaims or when their predispositions toward the brand are negative.

Order Effects

Is it best to present your commercial first or last? Communications researchers have found that the *order* in which a message is presented affects audience receptivity. For example, on TV, the commercials shown first are recalled the best, whereas those in the middle are recalled the least. When just two competing messages are presented, one after the other, the evidence as to which position is more effective is somewhat conflicting. Some researchers have found that the material presented first produces a greater effect, that is, a **primacy effect**. Others have found that the material presented last is more effective, that is, a **recency effect**. Magazine publishers recognize the impact of order effects by charging more for ads on the front, back, and inside covers of magazines than for the inside magazine pages, because of their greater visibility and recall.

Order is also important in listing product benefits within an ad. If audience interest is low, the most important point should be made first to attract attention. However, if interest is high, it is not necessary to pique curiosity, so product benefits can be arranged in ascending order, with the most important point mentioned last. When both favorable information and unfavorable information are to be presented (as in an annual stockholders' report), placing the favorable material first often produces greater tolerance for the unfavorable news. A study found that revealing the brand name at the onset of a message enhances brand recall and message persuasiveness.[16]

Learning Objective

4 To understand the effectiveness and limitations of prominent advertising appeals.

Persuasive Advertising Appeals

Many researchers have studied the promotional appeals that marketers can use and the factors that influence ad persuasiveness. For example, one study showed that informational appeals were particularly effective in high-involvement situations, whereas positive emotional appeals did better in low-involvement situations. The study also found that different promotional appeals should be used in extensions of existing brands as opposed to new brands. Differences in the impact of various promotional appeals, in both low- and high-**consumer involvement** conditions, were greater for new brands than for brand extensions (see Chapter 5).[17] Another study discovered that, in addition to characteristics of the endorser or the appeal used, people's **need for cognition (NFC)** (see Chapter 3), played a role in responses to ads. The higher a person's NFC, the less he or she is likely to consider peripheral cues, such as endorser likeability, in processing the ad and become persuaded (or not) by ads on the basis of their actual promotional appeals.[18]

The most widely used advertising appeals are comparative, fear, humor, sex, and timeliness.

Comparative Advertising

Comparative advertising is a widely used marketing strategy in which a marketer claims product superiority for its brand over one or more explicitly named or implicitly identified competitors, either on an overall basis or on selected product attributes. Some critics of the technique maintain that comparative ads often assist recall of the competitor's brand at the expense of the advertised brand. However, the wide use of comparative advertising indicates that marketers are confident that comparative ads exert positive effects on brand attitudes, purchase intentions, and actual purchases. Among more sophisticated consumers, comparative ads elicit higher levels of cognitive processing and better recall, and are likely to be perceived as more relevant than noncomparative ads.

Research studies have investigated many aspects of comparative promotions. A study that tested the degree of negativity in comparative messages (by using positive, negative, and mildly negative comparative messages) for several products reported that negative elements in an ad contributed to its effectiveness as long as they were believable or were offset by some elements that made the ad appear neutral.[19] Another study uncovered gender differences in response to comparative ads; comparative ads generated greater levels of brand-evaluation involvement among men but not among women. Among women, attention-getting comparative appeals produced inferences regarding the ads' manipulative intentions and reduced purchase likelihood.[20] Yet another study found that "promotion-focused" consumers (i.e., those focused on the aspirational aspects and the likely positive consequences of a purchase) reacted to comparative messages differently than "prevention-focused" consumers (i.e., those focused on the presence or absence of negative outcomes such as safety). In comparative ads, negative framing led prevention-focused consumers to evaluate the advertised brand positively and the other brand negatively. Among promotion-focused consumers, positive framing led to positive evaluation of the advertised brand but did not affect evaluations of the comparison brand.[21]

There has been considerable concern regarding the potential for comparative advertising to mislead consumers, including several legal actions against companies by the Federal Trade Commission. Consumer advocates have pursued the development of specific measures designed to gauge a comparative ad's ability to mislead consumers. In addition, comparative ads may result in legal disputes. Although the law requires companies to produce "reasonable factual evidence" in support of comparative claims, deciding what constitutes such evidence is difficult.

For example, Pantene has attacked Dove's claim that its conditioner "repairs" hair better than a Pantene conditioner. After both companies presented their supportive studies (one study addressed the differences between "dry combing" and "wet combing"), Dove was forced to limit its claims to its product's adding smoothness and strength to damaged hair. AT&T sued over a Verizon wireless ad featuring a map showing that Verizon has more 3G-type coverage than AT&T. AT&T did not dispute the claim itself but challenged the map. The company claimed that the white spaces shown in the map implied that AT&T has no coverage *at all* in these areas rather than the fact that AT&T has no 3G service in these locations. Campbell Soup initiated a campaign claiming that its Select Harvest soups were "Made with TLC" while Progresso's soups were "Made with MSG." After Progresso responded with its own campaign, both companies filed complaints with the National Advertising Division, which

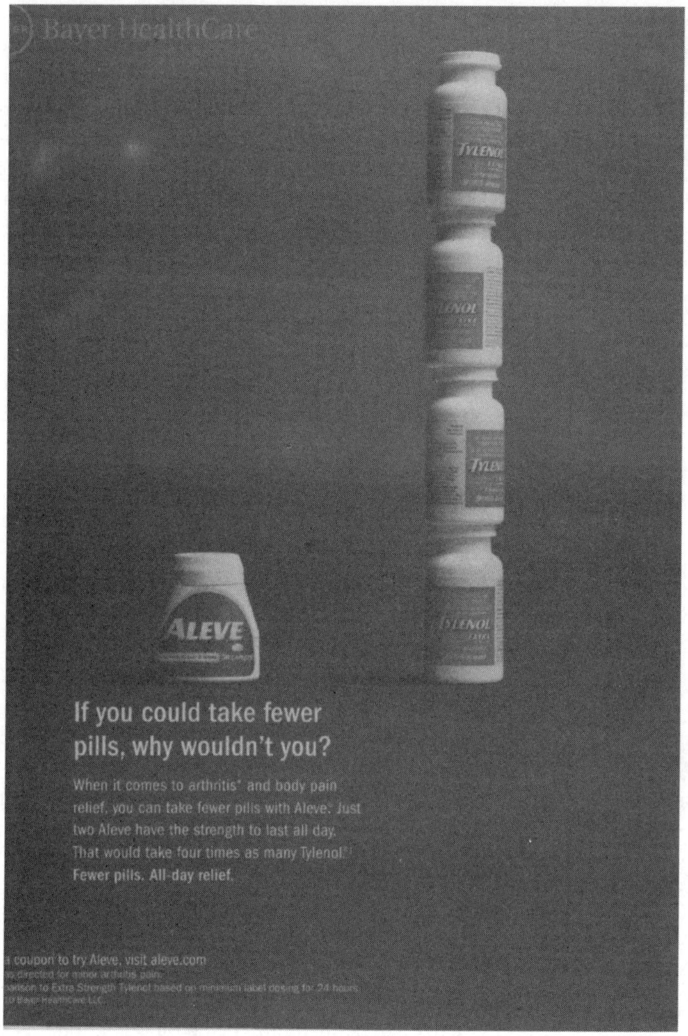

Source: Bayer HealthCare LLC

FIGURE 7.10 Comparative Advertising: Aleve versus Tylenol

recommended that both sides withdraw the comparative ads.[22] The ad in Figure 7.10 compares the relative strength of Aleve's pill with Tylenol's product.

Fear Appeals

Fear is an effective appeal and is often used in marketing communications. Some researchers have found a negative relationship between the intensity of fear appeals and their ability to persuade, so strong fear appeals tend to be less effective than mild fear appeals. A number of explanations have been offered for this phenomenon. Strong fear appeals concerning a highly relevant topic (such as cigarette smoking) cause the individual to experience cognitive dissonance, which is resolved either by rejecting the practice or by rejecting the unwelcome information. Because giving up a comfortable habit is difficult, consumers more readily reject the threat. This they do by a variety of techniques, including denial of its validity ("There still is no real proof that smoking causes cancer"), the belief that they are immuned to personal disaster ("It can't happen to me"), and a diffusing process that robs the claim of its true significance ("I play it safe by smoking only filter cigarettes"). Therefore, marketers should use reasonable but not extreme fear appeals and recognize that fear appeals are not always appropriate. For example, information labels affixed to full-fat, reduced-fat, and nonfat products are likely to be more effective than warning labels. Congruent with the "it can't happen to me" mentality, fear appeals are often used in targeting young people, who often feel overly confident.

Strong fear appeals are often employed to discourage distracted driving caused by using mobile phones and texting, as well as drunk driving. In one study, more females than males said that fear appeals will change distracted driving and suggested using interviews with people who had been affected by distracted driving accidents in advertisements against this behavior. Also, more males than females said that using legal action would discourage distracted driving.[23] The ad featured in Figure 7.11 employs a very graphic image in its fear appeal. One study discovered that a strong graphic threat message had a greater effect for an unfamiliar issue than for a familiar issue. For an issue with which the subjects were very familiar, adding information to a weak-threat fear appeal increased the perceived severity of the undesired behavior. The perceived severity of threat and perceived probability of occurrence significantly influenced people's intentions to adopt the recommended behavior.[24]

Fear appeals are commonly used in antidrug campaigns. Such ads are more likely to be effective if they portray both the negative social consequences of drug use and the physical damage that drugs inflict on one's body. Fear appeals are unlikely to be effective among persons who score high on the personality variable termed **sensation seeking** (see Chapter 3). A high sensation seeker is more likely to use drugs and react negatively to fear-focused antidrug messages, feeling that he or she is immortal. Male and females appear to react differently to fear appeals. A five-month study of high school students discovered that short-term cosmetic fear appeals (such as yellow teeth or bad breath) used in ads to stop or reduce smoking were more persuasive for males, whereas long-term health fear appeals (such as getting cancer later in life) were more persuasive for females.[25]

Many ads arouse fear with images that provoke revulsion: Examples include mutilated bodies from drunk driving accidents, close-ups of lungs destroyed by smoking, and teeth and brains ruined by drug use. Several studies showed that adding

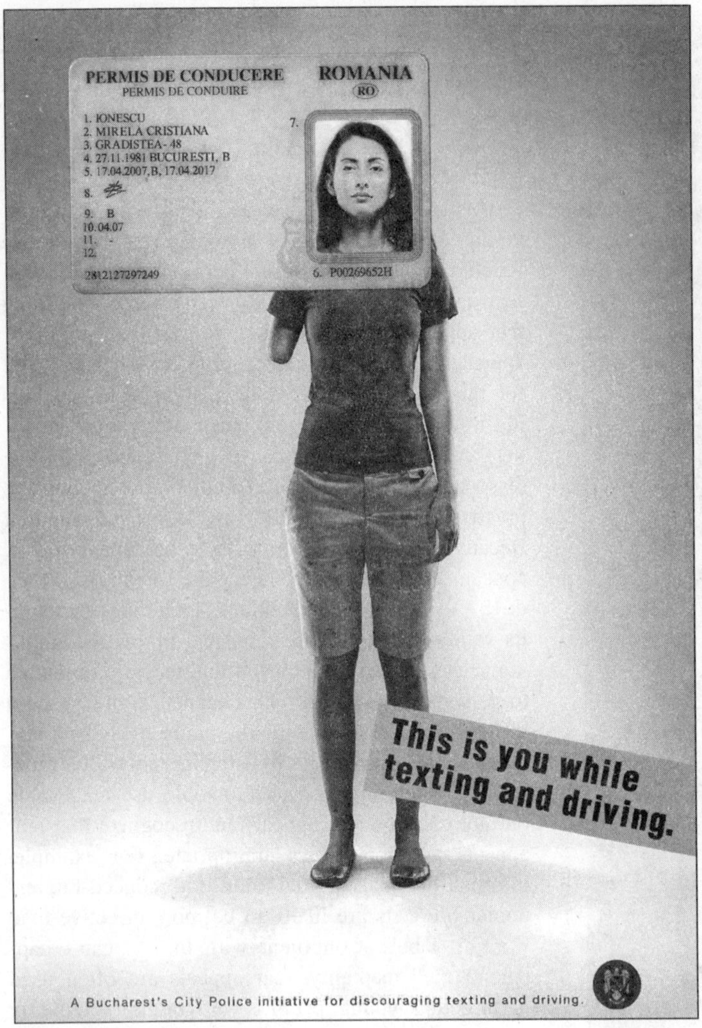

FIGURE 7.11 A Fear Appeal: Discouraging Distracted Driving

Source: Bogdan Nestor - Art Director, Zazvan Soare - Copywriter, Razvan Capanescu - Creative Director

disgust to a fear appeal enhanced message persuasion and compliance beyond that of appeals that elicited only fear.[26] However, portraying disgust might backfire. For example, in a campaign to discourage heavy consumption of soft drinks, New York City's health department featured an ad that depicted a "man drinking fat" and claimed that drinking a can of soda a day makes a person 10 pounds fatter a year. The ad was withdrawn because many complained that it was too revolting, and others claimed that the link between sugar and fat has not been fully scientifically proven.

Based on scores of studies about using fear in advertising, marketers should follow several guidelines:

1. Understand the target audience's reaction to a fear appeal, as well as its previous experiences. For example, those who are already following the behavior recommended but are not yet fully "converted" are likely to react differently than those who are fully "converted." Similarly, different age groups probably react differently to fear appeals, as do persons in different subcultures. Also, people who tried to change their behavior and failed will react differently than those trying to do so for the first time.
2. Beware the boomerang effect. When some persons are exposed to a fear appeal that encourages them to eliminate a strong habit, such as smoking, they may feel angry and resentful and immediately reach for a cigarette in defiance.
3. Realize that changing behavior is a long and complex process. Therefore, persons in different stages of this task react differently to fear appeals.
4. Study the extent to which the fear appeal encourages people to take action but without arousing too much anxiety, because high levels of anxiety may cause people to reject the message or avoid it altogether.
5. Determine whether to use a rational or emotional fear appeal.
6. Plan, over the long term, to repeat advertising using fear appeals. Recognize, though, that repeating these messages too often may reduce their credibility.
7. Accept that some addicts may not respond to fear appeals. For example, many heavy smokers or drinkers do not respond to explicit, clearly visible, and graphic warning labels.
8. Consider alternatives to fear appeals. For example, reward-focused appeals or even portraying humor and happiness when trying to discourage certain conduct may sometimes work better than using fear.

Humorous Appeals

Many marketers use humorous appeals in the belief that humor will increase the acceptance and persuasiveness of their advertising communications. Humor is the most widely used of all advertising appeals; by some estimates, it is used in 80% of all ads.

Therefore, humor is the most studied advertising appeal. The findings of scores of studies on using humor in advertising indicated that:

1. Humor attracts attention and enhances liking of the product advertised.
2. Humor does not harm the comprehension of ads, and, in some cases, it actually aids comprehension.
3. Humor does not always increase an ad's persuasive impact or a source's credibility. For example, one study showed that humor might actually *distract* from cognitive processing of the central benefits of the brand.[27]
4. Humor that is relevant to the product is more effective than humor unrelated to the product.
5. Humor is more effective in ads for existing products than in ads for new products, and more effective in targeting consumers who already have a positive attitude toward the product.
6. Using humor is more appropriate for advertising low-involvement than high-involvement products.
7. The effects of humorous ads vary by the audience demographics.
8. The impact of humor is related to the receiver's personality. For example, higher sensation seekers were found to be more receptive to humorous appeals than lower sensation seekers.[28]

A study developed a measure of a personality trait, named **need for humor** that is focused on a person's tendency to enjoy, engage, or seek out amusement and suggested that these cognitive factors can better explain how consumers respond to humorous advertisements.[29] Another study discovered that ad recall was damaged when the humor was expected, and this adverse effect was more pronounced in individuals with low need for humor.[30] Humorous ads were found to be more memorable when humor was strong and related to the message.[31] Placing product in humorous movie scenes evoked positive emotions.[32]

Humor enables marketers to come up with highly creative ads that can sometimes backfire. For example, Ragu pasta came up with a campaign—designed to form emotional attachment to the product—focused not on the utility of the food, but on its ability to soothe embarrassing childhood memories. One ad showed a young boy entering his parents' bedroom as the accompanying jingle said: "Parents in bed, but it's just 8 o'clock. That's why they taught you that you should always knock." The ad then cut to the boy eating a bowl of pasta with sauce and the song concluded, "You need Ragu, 'cause growin' up is tough. Give him Ragu, he's been through enough." While most consumers found the ad to be creative and funny, some criticized it because of the insinuation of sex.[33] The Ving resorts ad in Figure 7.12 uses humor by showing how parents sometimes wish to "cut off" their noisy children from supposedly restful vacations.

Wordplay

Punning (or wordplay) means a humorous "double meaning." For example, an ad campaign for Moore Paint carried the theme "For those who know more"—with the play on the words "more" and "Moore." The ads appeared mostly in social media, particularly Facebook, rather than traditional media.[34] Data from **Starch Ad Readership Studies** (see Chapter 5) showed that consumers are more likely to read ads that employ puns than those that do not.[35]

Punning can also be used in imagery. For instance, Chuck Norris, a martial arts fighter and actor, lent his name to advertising Era detergent, a value brand priced lower than the premium Tide. The product is advertised as "Chuck Norris approved" with the tagline "a lot of fight for a little dough."[36]

Humor in Advertising: The Indian Way

Humor is often used in ads in the Indian context. Itchguard, a brand that is positioned to treat itches, used a humorous situation of a bridegroom experiencing embarrassing moments when he visits the prospective bride. Polo, the mint, used a student–professor relationship humorously in its advertisements. Humor was also used to introduce a new concept in the former example and in the latter it was used as a kind of fun (given the nature of the category). Ericsson's (mobile phone) "One black coffee, please" advertisement may perhaps bring a nostalgic smile to consumers. It is also equally important that creative humor should ensure that it does not distract consumers from the brand's proposition. There are broadly four ways in which humor has been applied to the Indian context. One approach has been to introduce it in family relationships, another through relationships at an individual level, the third approach to associate fun/humor with group associations, and the fourth through the use of celebrities (for instance, the recent Lehar Kurkure ads featuring Juhi Chawla). These applications range from consumer durable product categories to impulsive products like chewing gum. The recent advertisement for Center Fresh shows the episode between father–son in the context

Source: Rami Hanafi, Viewmasters

FIGURE 7.12 A Humorous Appeal: Parents Daydream about Their Children "Disappearing" while Vacationing at Ving Resorts

of the father reviewing the marks scored by the son, and the brand's proposition of good taste is conveyed humorously through the proposition "The mouth is busy." Hamam's TV commercial shows the "skin glow" proposition being conveyed by the young girl's question, "In which direction does the sun rise?" Pureit, the water purifier brand, introduces the conversation between the mother and son and the brand's proposition of prevention from diseases conveyed during this conversation in a lighthearted manner, with the son's expression adding to the appeal. The Vicks ad for ₹5 too makes use of the mother–son relationship. Aashirvaad sweets has an ad with a "mother-in-law vs. daughter-in-law" situation, reflecting the proposition of good taste.

At the level of individual relationships, humor and fun can be used in different situations to convey the brand's proposition. The Three Roses' proposition of "A good time to talk" between a young couple, or the Quaker Oats' TV commercial announcing the variants of the brand, with the husband proclaiming that for the first time he would frame the rules at home (with the brand's offering for breakfast), are examples of such an approach.

Group associations with humor are widely used when the target segment is the youth. For instance, the Axe Temptation TV ads shows a chocolate man donating bits of himself to people. Sachin Tendulkar in the Aviva insurance ad plays cricket with children and breaks the window pane before the proposition of the brand is conveyed as an interesting example in the services category. Motorola Yuva's advertisement of the classroom situation, in which the professor is fooled into posing for a photograph that is clicked on the phone and distributed everywhere is in tune with the "youth-mobile" trends. Compaq's advertisement for its remote control makes use of the embarrassment that an executive creates for his colleague, using the remote to convey the proposition of remote control in its computers. Closeup's proposition of "close-up" smile was humorously conveyed to a youngster who is suppressing his laughter and another who is able to freely laugh out among a group of friends. Celebrities may be used with any of the approaches depending on the type of product/brand. Samsung uses a celebrity to convey its karaoke feature through a lighthearted execution. There may also be other variants in which humor is used to convey a brand's proposition than the four approaches. A Fevicol (an adhesive) advertisement shows an unbreakable egg laid by a hen that feeds from a container on which "Fevicol" is inscribed and another one shows a bus overflowing with people who are hanging on to it by the windows, doors, etc., depicting a "Fevicol" bind.

A brand's proposition, the extent of relevance to the target segment, and the scope offered by a category for humor (chocolates vs. washing machines, for example) are some important criteria that should be taken into consideration before humor or fun is used in the brand's advertising.

Sexual Appeals

There is a lot of sensual advertising in the print media, the airwaves, and online. Advertisers have been provoking attention with nudity and sex, and promotional messages often include a lot of explicit and daring sexual imagery, extending far beyond the traditional product categories of fashion and fragrance into such categories as shampoo, beer, cars, and travel services, among many others.

Online, marketers have used sexual appeals that are highly innovative and much more daring than those in magazines and network TV. For example, Air New Zealand's safety video on YouTube featured a flight crew that was nude except for body paint applied to mimic uniforms, including neckties on men and scarves on women. Zappos, an online retailer, used a combination of nudity and technology in its campaign. The ads featured naked models in New York City and one ad featured a naked woman riding a Vespa. Other ads showed naked models doing everyday things like jogging, hailing a cab, and playing Frisbee in public. On the Zappos website, viewers were asked to "dress" the naked models with Zappos clothes. Zappos print ads included quick-response codes that, when scanned into smartphones, took users to a website with fictional videos allowing viewers to dress the models.[37]

There is little doubt that sexual themes have attention-getting value, but studies show that they rarely encourage actual buying. Often, sexual advertising appeals detract consumers from the message content and tend to interfere with message comprehension, particularly when there is substantial information to be processed. Because the visual sexual elements in an ad are more likely to be processed than the ad's verbal content, the cognitive processing of the product information may be incomplete. In addition, nudity may negatively affect the product message.

Receptivity to sexual appeals varies among consumers. For example, one study identified two psychological constructs that have an impact on consumers' responses to ads that depict nudity. The first is "sexual self-schema," which is one's cognitive view of the self with regard to sexuality. Sexual schemas originate in persons' past experiences and influence their reactions to sex-related promotional themes. The second is **sensation seeking**, which is the pursuit of novel and exciting sensations and experiences (see Chapter 3). The study discovered that sensation-seeking persons responded favorably to nudity in advertising and that one's sexual schema played only a modest role.[38] Another study indicated that more extroverted people were receptive to sexual appeals and that such appeals should not be used in targeting consumers who are quiet, shy, and reserved.[39] Clearly, marketers must exercise caution in using nudity because not all consumers will react favorably, and some may even feel alienated or offended.

The type of interest that sexual advertising evokes often stops exactly where it starts—with sex. If a sexually suggestive or explicit illustration is not relevant to the product advertised, it has little effect on consumers' buying intentions. This highlights the potential risk of sexually oriented advertising: The advertiser may be giving up persuasiveness to achieve "stopping power." When using sex to promote a product, the advertiser must be sure that the product, the ad, the target audience, and the use of sexual themes and elements all work together. Nevertheless, when sex is relevant to the product, it can be an extremely potent theme. For example, the advertisers of fragrances for either men or women often use highly romantic or suggestive visuals in their ads, implying that use of the fragrance will result in a meaningful or sultry romance.

Timeliness Appeal

During and following the financial crisis of September 2008, many marketers came up with advertising appeals designed specifically for tough economic times. For example, an ad for a health club urged consumers to make "a renewed commitment to lead a healthy life during these challenging times." An ad for a chain restaurant promoting an inexpensive meal used humor by stating: "It's one thing to bail out Wall Street. But who's gonna bail you out?"[40] Other marketers came up with appeals promoting products as affordable and sensible rather than indulgent and fabulous.[41] An ad campaign for a shopping district consisted of ads that did not suggest products to buy but instead listed fun and upbeat things to do, such as catching snowflakes on one's tongue.[42] Finally, some Halloween ads reflected the tough economic times with such appeals as "Incredible savings that are almost scary."[43] Table 7.1 describes advertising themes used during America's down economy.[44]

Box 7.3 Celebrity Appeals in an Emerging Market

Celebrities form an important aspect of reference groups. India is one of the markets in the world where celebrities from diverse fields feature across categories. The psychographic profile of the respective targets segment, associations generated by the specific celebrity, and the associations formed with the brand are important aspects associated with celebrity selection.

Emami has used sixty celebrities since 1974 for several of its brands that include Zandu Balm and Navratna, Fair & Handsome, Emami Vanishing Cream, and Healthy &Tasty edible oil.[45] Besides, the company has also used multiple celebrities for the same brand – Navratna had five, Zandu Balm had six, and Boroplus had four![46]

TABLE 7.1 Advertising Appeals During Economic Downturn

OBJECTIVE	CAMPAIGN THEME
Restore confidence in banks	Humor: "We love Chase and not just because they have a million dollars."
Make people feel good during down economic times	Happiness: Bank of America: "Bank of opportunity"; Coca Cola: "Open happiness"; Western Union: "Yes"; Ads for a Broadway show promise "a happy moment" during "challenging times" and predict better times ahead.
Attract consumers who became more sensible	Advertising products as affordable and sensible rather than indulgent and fabulous. Not appealing to conspicuousness or status. Avoiding aspirational advertising.
Attract buyers who felt uncomfortable about buying real estate	Initially, an ad for an NYC condo proclaimed it to be "not just an address, it's an attitude," and showed beautiful young people dining out or shooting pool. During the economic downturn, new marketing materials promised "clean styling and attractive pricing," and featured a child reaching for a juice box at a local market and an older gentleman leaving the building with his dog.
"Comfort marketing": Appeal to nostalgia	Bringing back vintage characters, themes, and jingles to evoke past fond memories that make shoppers feel better about buying products. Reassuring consumers who demand value for their money that they are buying products that have stood the test of time.
Encourage consumers who are short on cash to paint and renovate their homes themselves	Selling paint: The marketers chose not to show people painting walls or interiors, because such ads remind people that painting is a mundane chore. Instead, they attempted to position paint as the mind-space of the consumers and appeal to their imaginations and emotions. For example, one ad stated that: "To others, a wall is a canvas, an invitation, a blank slate"; the voiceover continued, to a lush soundtrack: "The right color can turn any wall into so much more."

Sources: Stuart Elliott, "Ads That Soothe When Banks Are Failing," nytimes.com, October 7, 2008; Stuart Elliott, "Down Economic Times Elicit Upbeat Consumers," nytimes.com, March 10, 2009; Vivian Toy, "Goodbye, Glitzy Condo Pitches," nytimes.com, August 20, 2010; Patricia Cohen, "Marketing Broadway: Selling Hope for a Song," nytimes.com, December 10, 2008; Andrew Newman, "Using Appeals to Emotions to Sell Paint," nytimes.com, June 7, 2010; Stuart Elliott, "In New Ads, Stirring Memories of Commercials Past," nytimes.com, January 12, 2012.

Learning Objective

5 To understand how to measure the effectiveness of advertising messages.

Measures of Message Effectiveness

Because marketing communications are usually designed to persuade a target audience to act in a desired way (e.g., to purchase a specific brand or product, to vote for a specific candidate), their ultimate test is the receiver's response. Therefore, the sender must obtain feedback as promptly and as accurately as possible. Only through feedback can the sender determine whether and how well the message has been received. **Communication feedback** is an essential component of both interpersonal and impersonal communications because it enables the sender to reinforce or change the message to ensure that it is understood in the intended way.

Compared with impersonal communications in mass media, a key advantage of interpersonal communications is the ability to obtain *immediate* feedback through verbal as well as nonverbal cues. Immediate feedback is the factor that makes personal selling so effective, because it enables the salesperson to tailor the sales pitch to the expressed needs and observed reactions of each prospect. Experienced speakers are very attentive to feedback and constantly modify their presentations based on what they see and hear from the audience. Similarly, immediate feedback in the form of inattention alerts a teacher to jolt a dozing class awake with a deliberately provocative statement such as: "This material will probably be on the next exam."

It has always been very important for sponsors of impersonal communications to obtain feedback as promptly as possible, so that they can revise a message if its meaning is not being received as intended or if the message did not reach (at least in large part) the intended audience. Unlike interpersonal communications feedback, mass communications feedback is rarely direct; instead, it is usually inferred. Senders infer how persuasive their messages are from the resulting action (or inaction) of the targeted audience. Receivers buy (or do not buy) the advertised product; they renew (or do not renew) their magazine subscriptions; they vote (or do not vote) for the political candidate. Another type of feedback that companies seek from mass audiences is the degree of **customer satisfaction** (or dissatisfaction) with a product purchase. They try to discover—and correct as swiftly as possible—any problems with the product in order to retain their brand's image of reliability (e.g., through hotlines and online contacts).

Marketers measure their communications' **persuasion effects**, that is, whether the message was received, understood, and interpreted correctly; and their **sales effects**, that is, whether the messages of a given campaign have generated the sales level defined in the campaign's objectives. In addition, advertisers gauge the **media exposure effects** of their messages by buying data from firms that monitor media audiences (e.g., Nielsen) and conduct audience research to find out which media are read and which television programs are viewed more extensively than others. (see Chapter 8).

The sales effects of mass communications are difficult to assess (although retailers usually can assess the effectiveness of their morning newspaper ads by midday on the basis of sales activity for the advertised product). A widely used method of measuring the sales effects of food and other packaged goods advertising is based on the Universal Product Code (UPC), which is tied to computerized cash registers. Supermarket scanner data can be combined with data from other sources (e.g., media and promotional information) to measure the correlation between advertisements, special promotions, and sales.

Physiological measures track bodily responses to stimuli. For example, *eye tracking* is a method where a camera tracks the movement of the eye across store shelves and gauges the labels or brands to which respondents paid more attention. Another method, *brain wave analysis*, tracks the degree of attention paid to the components of viewed advertisements through monitoring electrical impulses produced by the viewer's brain. *Facial electromyography* (facial EMG) is a technique that tracks the electrical activity and subtle movements of facial muscles so as to gauge the emotions generated by different types of TV commercials.

Attitudinal measures gauge consumers' cognitive responses to messages, including their levels of engagement and involvement with the messages tested. For example, TV programs or commercials are shown in a theater setting and viewers use dials (located in their armrests) to indicate their levels of interest or disinterest in the clips viewed. In self-administered studies, marketers use **semantic differential scales** and **Likert scales** (see Chapter 16) to test ads and find out whether consumers liked the messages and understood them correctly.

Marketers must measure which advertisements are remembered by their target audience(s). In addition to the **recall** and **recognition tests** discussed in Chapter 5 (i.e., the **Starch Ad Readership Study**), researchers use **day-after recall tests** in which viewers of TV shows or listeners to radio broadcasts are interviewed a day after watching or listening to a given program. Participants are asked to describe the commercials they recall. The recall of a commercial and its central theme is evidence of its attention-getting and persuasive power.

Box 7.4 Women and Brands: The Indian Scenario

FIGURE 7.13 Role of Women in the Indian Context and Brand Appeals

In recent times, the position of women has undergone a radical change in the Indian social context. The various roles women play need to be noted to ensure that appropriate communication strategies are being formulated.

Hence, brands need to be careful about the way women are portrayed in advertisements and would want to use such associations with women in culturally permissive ways. While traditional values are still strong, there may be a few progressive sub cultures in terms of permissiveness. The majority of women in India have not experienced empowerment and marketing to women has not changed radically. Marketers must be careful to maintain a delicate balance between women's empowerment, traditional values, and the emergence of contemporary western values.

The above Figure 7.13 provides an idea of the various roles women play in different facets of life and the implications of role on brand/s.

Brand Imagery and Women

The New Age of social media, current happenings, quasi-westernized lifestyles, and cultural sensibilities have posed unique challenges to brand managers than ever before. They need to deal with the environment as efficiently as they deal with their brands.

The growing public outrage on the social issues concerned with women point to an important dimension that is associated with the management of brands – the portrayal of women in advertisements and the implications of such an approach on brand association. There are several complexities that are associated with branding decisions. Sensitivity to cultural beliefs, the extent to which psychological aspects of hedonism (internal pleasure) are to be used, and the changing environment are some of them.

The Rational and Emotional Parts of the Brain

Research has indicated that the emotional parts of the brain evolve before the rational (thinking part of the brain). The path through which sensory inputs reach the brain adopt a different path when emotional elements are involved. Emotions affect one's actions and consumer behavior associated with brands heavily relies on emotions, in general. "You have come a long way baby" was the advertisement tagline for Virginia Slims, the cigarette brand that had women as the target segment decades back in the US. It was one of the earliest advertisements that linked hedonism (sensual pleasure) with the emergent trends associated with women.

It is a well-known phenomenon that there is a biological need in human beings to attract the opposite gender. In an economy that has consumer lifestyles as its core, it is natural that gender-based appeals would be used by brands.

Freudian psychology explored the psyche that likes sensual pleasure by highlighting the fact that individuals have the "id" part. This part is a warehouse of primitive pleasures, especially the one that will not be accepted by society. These primitive pleasures can find outlets in a variety of ways like advertisements or brand associations. This is the reason why brands from several product categories ranging from coffee, deodorants, fashion wear, and personal accessories and hence, websites use the "baser" instincts (the id factor) while building their respective brand.

The Indian Context and Stereotypes of Women

The cultural aspects and its evolution in the Indian context have played a role in creating stereotypes for women. The well-entrenched imagery of mother–son/daughter relationship introduced decades back continues to exist even today (Raymond, Parachute, and Santoor). The other stereotype is the role of the wife who is sustaining and nurturing a happy family with "strong family connections". This can be seen across categories from detergents to dishwashers. The third kind of stereotype is the one associated with the modern and independent woman, the woman who is evolving and is capable of equaling any task in a male-dominated society. While these stereotypes have diffused themselves well (without creating controversies), the fourth stereotype is the one that brands need to be concerned about. This is the stereotype that is associated with the "id" aspect advocated by Freud. The cultural passage at this point in time is neither completely western nor does it subscribe to the traditional stereotype associated with women. The cumulative visual impact on the mind is phenomenal, especially given the fact that most of us are exposed to visual images more than any other form of image. Against the backdrop of recent incidents of violence, the ads that a brand rolls out need to be sensitive to women.

Indian Brands and Stereotyping of Women

Traditionally, there are only a few countries that have used the "mother" stereotype in the manner in which Indian advertising has used it. India, being an emerging economy, the stereotype of the "smart home-maker" is another traditional image that has been successfully used by marketers.

Such traditional stereotypes were cultivated even before the onset of television advertising. "Mummy, Mummy Modern bread" was one of the earliest radio jingles that reflected the child–mother relationship. Johnson & Johnson's motherly portrayal of woman in its ads is perhaps an excellent example of how care, warmth, and love of the motherly role had been transferred to the brand. One wonders if any "new mother" would use any other brand of baby care product for her child. Horlicks's promise of "taller, stronger and sharper" kid coupled with the "mother" image has been useful to the brand to extend itself to premium offerings like "Gold" and "Pro-mind". Vicks Vaporub's television ad reflected the warmth of the son–mother relationship when the son is being chided by his mother for getting drenched in the rain and then the son says he had gone out to get her birthday gift. Parachute hair oil had one of its ads involving the mother–daughter relationship. Clinic Plus for several years had been creating an image of the mother–daughter relationship and this continues to be reinforced by the brand till date. Pears soap ad uses the mother–child relationship to convey the brand's purity. Kent water purifier has used a well-known celebrity as a mother to herald its proposition. Pepsodent toothpaste had an ad that portrayed the mother scolding her son for snacking and spoiling his teeth. Dettol's ad showed a housewife who is caring towards the family. Wheel detergent uses an ad that portrays the smart housewife. None can forget Lalithaji, a character introduced by Surf, who was smart, hard-bargaining, and demanded the maximum value for anything she bought. The ad showed her using half the quantity of detergent (Surf) against the usual quantity of a competing detergent to effectively show the superiority of Surf. Dabur Real Life uses a young mother who is attached to her son. Knorr soup used a celebrity mother to popularize the brand. The "Mother" stereotype will not cease to exist as it is an ingrained part of the Indian psyche, however modern the consumers may become in the years to come.

In today's world, with fashion and grooming being a priority among women and girls, brands have been successful in developing trendy stereotypes. Titan Raga has introduced a watch for women by creating an image of ethnic sensuality (reference to the early ads involving a well-known celebrity). Pleasure scooters have featured the "independent, non-conformist" image of the modern girl with the caption – "Why should boys have all the fun?" One of the earliest portrayal of a modern girl was the cinema ad by toothpaste brand, Close up, that showed a boy–girl relationship while portraying its "Close up" smile. Scooty Streak has also showed a "modern, fun-loving" girl in its ad. In the eatables category, an ad by Tripthi *atta* showed the multiple roles played by today's women. And IFB dishwasher showed a young women executive who could presumably find more time to relax by using the brand's dishwasher.

Over the years, Fair & Lovely have created a "Middle-class dream" by building an aspiration-oriented image of a girl.

The Challenge for Brand Managers

Besides the ethical considerations, there are "down-to-earth" implications for brand managers who are associated with the management of brand associations. What should brands that have had "id"-based associations do? This is an important question that would affect not only the consumer perception of these brands; it would also have implications on the brands themselves if such brand associations are removed overnight. Should the brand downplay such associations henceforth? Should these brands shift to other related associations that may not be perceived as controversial? Should they establish sub-brands that may herald new associations to protect the parent brand? What should be done with the target segment that has not only grown but become loyal to such brand associations?

India is a land of diverse culture and lifestyles. This diversity has only increased manifold with the onslaught of westernization that triggers feelings of "coolness and independence". When dealing with women imagery, brand managers certainly have a tricky job on their hands trying to balance permissiveness and tradition.

Competing brands need not initiate brand wars; the environment can pose enough battles, least expected by the brand managers of this age.

Brand Communication, Brand Relationships, and Lifestyle Appeals

The digital area is likely to see a radical shift in brand communication. There are two aspects, as reflected by research. Lifestyle aspects seem to proliferate across product categories and hence, all of them will compete for the "share of identity"[47] associated with consumers. This may lead to limitations of using lifestyle appeals. The other aspect is the range of relationships that brands are likely to have with consumers. Brands can have several kinds of relationships with consumers and brands need to take them in to account. The following are some types [48] of relationships brands may have with consumers:

- Does the brand not treat the consumer well? – Abusive relationship.
- Is the consumer committed to use a brand for an extended periodtime (perhaps a brand like Lifebuoy)? – Committed relationship.
- Can the consumer not do without his/her morning cup of coffee brand or his/her mobile brand? –Dependent relationship
- Does the consumer feel that he has to ("forced to") buy from the nearest retail store due to sheer location of the outlet? – Master – Slave relationship
- Does the consumer refuse to buy a brand of durable because it let him/her down in its after-sales service? – Adversarial relationship
- Does the consumer go out of the way to support a brand like Coke or Ferrero Rocher (fans have created websites)? – Communal relationship
- Does the consumer buy a brand simply because it is value for money? – Exchange relationships
- Does the consumer enjoy shifting towards a set of *kirana* stores in his/her local traditional market, but feels that others should not know about it? – Secret Affair relationship

Summary

Learning Objective 1: To understand the elements and persuasive capabilities of communication, as well as the barriers to effective communication.

Communication is the transmission of a message from a sender to a receiver via a medium (or channel) of transmission. In addition to four basic components—sender, receiver, medium, and message—the fifth essential component of communication is feedback, which alerts the sender as to whether the intended message was, in fact, received. Senders encode their messages by using words, pictures, symbols, spokespersons, and persuasive appeals, and then the receivers decode them. If the messages are to be persuasive, the receivers must decode them as the senders intended. Communications can be either impersonal or interpersonal. Impersonal communications consist of messages that companies transmit through their marketing departments, advertising or public relations agencies, and spokespersons. The senders of interpersonal communications can be either formal sources (e.g., a salesperson in a physical or virtual retail location) or informal sources (e.g., peers with whom the consumer communicates face-to-face or via electronic means). The key factor underlying the persuasive impact of a personal or interpersonal message received from either a formal or informal source is the extent to which the receiver trusts and believes the source sending the message.

Media are the channels for transmitting communications. Traditional media are the original communications channels that advertisers have used, and are generally classified as print (newspapers, magazines, billboards) and broadcast (radio, television). New media are online channels, social networks, and mobile electronic devices. These media are drastically more advanced than traditional media because they allow marketers to send personalized messages to individual consumers who can respond to the messages immediately.

The two most important barriers that affect the accuracy with which consumers interpret messages are selective exposure and psychological noise. Selective exposure refers to consumers' selectivity in paying attention to advertising messages. Psychological noise, in the form of competing advertising messages or distracting thoughts, can affect the reception of a promotional message.

Learning Objective 2: To understand the distinctions between broadcasting and narrowcasting.

The term traditional media is synonymous with broadcast media (or mass media) and consists of channels where all receivers get the same one-way messages from marketers (i.e., they cannot send direct responses to the source of the messages). New media are channels of narrowcasting, defined as channels that permit marketers to send addressable, customized messages, based on data gathered from tracing consumers' surfing and clicks online, in combination with other information, to either small groups or individual consumers. Addressable advertising consists of customized messages sent to particular consumers. These messages are based mostly on the consumers' prior shopping behavior, which marketers have observed and analyzed.

Learning Objective 3: To understand how to design persuasive messages effectively.

Some of the decisions that marketers must make in designing a message include selecting images, creating advertising copy, using positive or negative message framing, choosing between one-sided or two-sided messages, and determining the order of presentation. Messages that depict images are often more effective that those with text only. Positive message framing stresses the benefits to be gained by using a specific product. Negative message framing stresses the benefits to be lost by not using the product. A one-sided message pretends that the product advertised is the only one in existence. Two-sided messages acknowledge competing products. The primacy effect indicates that material presented first is more noticeable and persuasive than subsequent materials. The recency effect holds that the material presented last is more noticeable and persuasive than preceding materials.

Learning Objective 4: To understand the effectiveness and limitations of prominent advertising appeals.

Marketers have many options to choose from when selecting promotional appeals, but the ones most widely used are comparative advertising, humor, fear or sexual appeals, and well-timed ads. Comparative advertising is a very common marketing strategy in which a marketer claims product superiority for its brand over one or more explicitly named or implicitly identified competitors, either on an overall basis or on selected product attributes. Though some critics of the technique maintain that comparative ads often assist recall of the competitor's brand at the expense of the advertised brand, the wide use of comparative advertising indicates that marketers are confident that comparative ads exert positive effects on brand attitudes, purchase intentions, and actual purchases. Fear is an effective appeal often used in marketing communications. Some researchers have found a negative relationship between the intensity of fear appeals and their ability to persuade, in that strong fear appeals tend to be less effective than mild fear appeals.

Humor is the most widely used approach because many marketers believe that humor will increase the persuasiveness of their communications. Humor attracts attention, enhances liking of the product advertised, and also enhances consumer comprehension of the ads. Humor that is relevant to the product is more effective than humor unrelated to the product. Humor is more effective in ads of existing products than in ads of new products, and more effective in targeting consumers who already have a positive attitude toward the product. Punning is wordplay, often consisting of a humorous double meaning.

Sexual appeals have attention-getting value, but studies show that they rarely encourage actual consumption behavior. Often, sexual advertising appeals detract from the message content and tend to interfere with message comprehension, particularly when there is substantial information to be processed. When using sex to promote a product, the advertiser must be sure that the product, the ad, the target audience, and the use of sexual themes and elements all work together. Timely appeals are exemplified by the many ads that appeared during and following the financial crisis of September 2008, which contained messages designed specifically for tough economic times.

Learning Objective 5: To understand how to measure the effectiveness of advertising messages.

Marketers measure their communications' persuasion effects (whether the message was received, understood, and interpreted correctly) and their sales effects (whether the messages of a given campaign have generated the sales level defined in the campaign objectives). Advertisers also gauge the exposure and persuasion effects of their messages by buying data from firms that monitor media audiences and conduct audience research to find out which media are read, which television programs are viewed, and which advertisements are remembered by their target audience(s).

Physiological measures track bodily responses to stimuli. Attitudinal measures gauge consumers' cognitive responses to messages, including their levels of engagement and involvement with the messages tested. Semantic differential and Likert scales are used in testing ad copy to assess whether respondents like the message, understand it correctly, and regard it as effective and persuasive. Researchers also use day-after recall tests, in which viewers of TV shows or listeners to radio broadcasts are interviewed a day after watching or listening to a given program and asked to describe the commercials they recall.

Review and Discussion Questions

7.1. Explain the differences between feedback from interpersonal communications and feedback from impersonal communications. How can the marketer obtain and use each kind of feedback?

7.2. List and discuss the effects of psychological noise on the communications process. What strategies can a marketer use to overcome psychological noise?

7.3. Discuss the strategic differences between traditional media channels and new media.

7.4. Compare broadcasting and narrowcasting and explain why are marketers moving away from using broadcasting and into narrowcasting and addressable marketing.

7.5. How can marketers construct and transmit addressable ads? Illustrate with a promotion of a product or service of your choice.

7.6. Should marketers use more verbal copy than artwork in print ads? Explain your answer.

7.7. For what kinds of audiences would you consider using comparative advertising? Why?

7.8. What are the advantages and disadvantages of using humor in advertising?

7.9. Why must marketers use fear appeals in advertising cautiously? How can they do so?

7.10. Do sexual appeals work better than other appeals? Explain your answer and illustrate with examples.

7.11. How is communications feedback related to the measurement of persuasion and sales effects?

7.12. A marketer of a new car model launched through commercials during the Super Bowl intends to use attitudinal measures, as well as day-after recall tests, to estimate the commercials' effectiveness. How should the company do so?

Hands-on Assignments

7.13. Find two print advertisements: One illustrating a one-sided message and the other a two-sided message. Which of the measures discussed in this chapter would you use to evaluate the effectiveness of each ad? Explain your answers.

7.14. Find print ads using each of the following advertising appeals: Fear, sex, and humor. Discuss their effectiveness and persuasive value in class.

7.15. Watch an hour-long TV program and its commercials, without writing any notes. A day later, list all the commercials you can recall seeing. For each commercial, identify: (a) The message framing approach used, and (b) Whether the message was one-sided or two-sided. Discuss what you had remembered in the context of selective exposure and psychological noise.

Key Terms

- addressable advertising *210*
- ambush marketing *208*
- attitudinal measures *221*
- cognitive learning *211*
- communication *204*
- communication feedback *204*
- comparative advertising *214*
- consumer involvement *214*
- customer satisfaction *220*
- data aggregators *210*
- day-after recall test *221*
- encoding *204*
- formal source *206*
- impersonal communications *206*
- informal source *206*
- interpersonal communications *206*
- Likert scale *221*
- media *207*
- media exposure effects *221*
- message *211*
- narrowcasting *209*
- need for cognition *214*
- need for humor *217*
- negative message framing *212*
- new media *207*
- one-sided message *213*
- persuasion effects *221*
- physiological measures *221*
- positioning *208*
- positive message framing *212*
- primacy effect *213*
- psychological noise *208*
- recall test *221*
- recency effect *213*
- recognition test *221*
- sales effects *221*
- selective exposure *207*
- semantic differential scales *221*
- sensation seeking *215*
- Starch Ad Readership Study *221*
- time shift *207*
- traditional media *207*
- two-sided message *213*
- word-of-mouth *207*

8

From Print and Broadcast Advertising to Social and Mobile Media

Learning Objectives

1. To understand the strategic superiority of impression-based (eyeballs) targeting over segment-based targeting.
2. To understand Google's targeting and advertising capabilities and its value to both consumers and marketers.
3. To understand the dynamics of social media and its strategic and promotional advantages over other media.
4. To understand how consumers use mobile media and their reactions to mobile advertising.
5. To understand how to measure the effectiveness of advertising in traditional and social media.
6. To understand the advancement of print and broadcast media into electronic communications.

Targeting Segments versus Eyeballs

The most important strategic impact of technology on marketing has been the ability to target consumers more precisely and effectively. Technology enables **impression-based targeting**—illustrated in Figure 8.1—through which advertisers specify the criteria describing the persons they wish to reach online and then bid in real time for the opportunities to reach them. A person reached is termed an "eyeball" or "impression." Impression-based targeting is implemented through **real-time bidding**, which is a technique that allows advertisers to reach the right user, in the right place, at the right time, and also sets the price that advertisers pay for each "eyeball" or "impression" (i.e., for each person reached). Specialized companies—generally known as "data aggregators"—enable advertisers to place bids on the opportunities to reach specific users, who meet a given criteria, on an impression-by-impression basis.

Before the arrival of the new targeting technologies, since the emergence of traditional advertising media (i.e., newspapers, magazines, radio, and television), TV networks, magazines, and newspapers have sold advertising space by offering marketers the opportunity to reach audiences (or segments) whose demographics and psychographics (lifestyles) matched those of the marketers' target markets. **Segment-based targeting** occurs when advertisers *prenegotiate* prices for advertising space in media (e.g., magazines or TV shows) whose audiences largely (but never completely) match the profiles of the consumers the advertisers wish to target. However, the audiences marketers reache via these media are larger and more diverse than their target markets and nearly always include many people who have no interest in the products advertised. For decades, after paying prenegotiated prices, marketers of competing (and often similar) products have been placing their ads within the same TV shows and magazines. Under

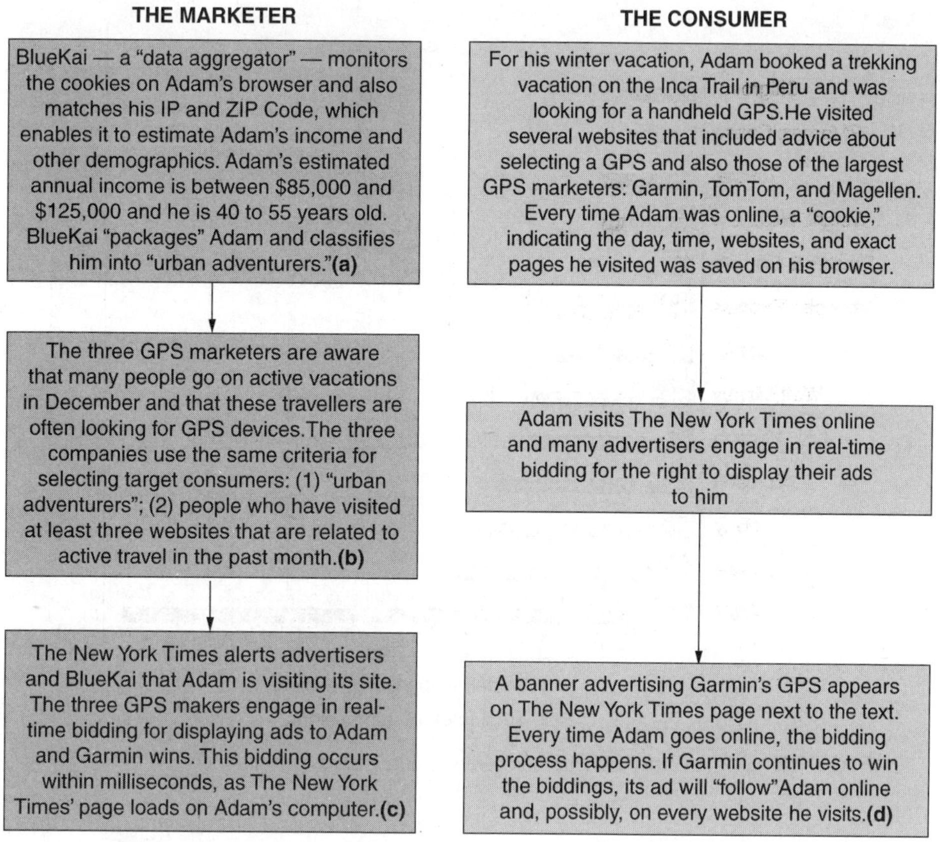

FIGURE 8.1 Impression-Based Targeting

Notes:

a. BlueKai has thousands of profiles, and sells many different services and delivery methods. There are scores of data aggregators, and the services they offer to advertisers and their data models vary greatly. BlueKai does not provide advertisers with *named* customers, but with the *browsers* of *anonymous* individuals who meet certain criteria at a given time.

b. It is unlikely that all three companies will set the exact same profiles. The profiles set are often broader and allow thousands of advertisers to bid on the impressions.

c. In reality, thousands of advertisers bid for the impression (i.e., Adam's "eyeballs"), not just GPS marketers. The bids are in small amounts of cents and typically are quoted in CPM—cost per thousand impressions.

d. The "following" may occur for a long or short time after the initial ad is displayed, depending on the degree of competition among advertisers to reach consumers like Adam.

Learning Objective

1 To understand the strategic superiority of impression-based (eyeballs) targeting over segment-based targeting.

this model, advertisers viewed the *creativity* of the ads, rather than the media where they *appeared*, as the key to the ads' persuasive effectiveness.

In contrast, **data aggregators** construct consumer profiles—based on cookies documenting people's online surfing (and other applicable information about them)—and identify prospective customers for specific products. Advertisers then compete for reaching the right "eyeballs" online by placing monetary bids. Because cookies are embedded in users' browsers, the data aggregators do not know the *names* of the consumers they "offer for sale," but recognize them as represented by their *browsers*. Thus, they offer advertisers browsers, and each browser represents an "impression." As illustrated in Figure 8.2, Facebook leads the way in the number of impressions created on the Internet.[1]

The Advantages of Impression-Based Targeting

Impression-based targeting offers several advantages over segment-based marketing:

1. Advertisers employing segment-based promotion invariably pay for reaching people who are neither inclined to buy their products when they see the ads nor likely to become future customers. Additionally, these persons also tune out

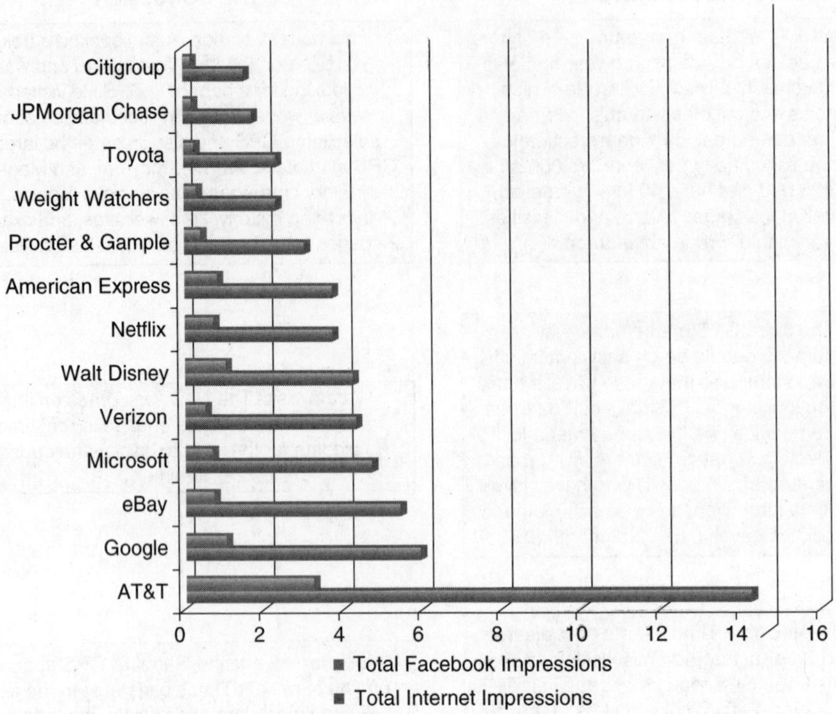

FIGURE 8.2 Internet and Facebook Impressions

advertisements for products they are not interested in. Recognizing this shortcoming early on, John Wanamaker (1838–1922)—one of the pioneers of buying advertising space—stated: "Half the money I spend on advertising is wasted; the trouble is I don't know which half." Impression-based targeting enables marketers to identify which "halves" of their advertising expenditures are wasted and design messages that reach primarily those who are likely to become customers.

2. In addition to being mostly "one-size-fits-all," messages sent via traditional media are one-way communications, and the consumers who receive them cannot interact with their contents. In contrast, receivers of impression-based ads can view and rotate images, click on links for detailed information about the products, compare brands, and much more.
3. According to the communications model, consumers' responses to ads represent feedback or measures of the ads' effectiveness. Feedback from ads placed in traditional media is delayed and often of limited use. For example, it is impossible to determine the impact of a very expensive Pepsi ad shown during the Super Bowl. The advertiser has no way of knowing how many consumers have reached for a Pepsi upon seeing the ad or purchased a Pepsi shortly after seeing it. In contrast, receivers' interest in impression-based ads can be determined immediately by observing the elements they click on within the ads, how long they stay at the website, and how often they return, among other measures (discussed later in this chapter).
4. Consumers can easily escape TV ads by **time shifting**, which involves starting to watch a show about fifteen minutes after it begins and using devices that allow them to skip commercials easily. In fact, advertisers have been fighting advanced ad-skipping features, and some TV channels rejected ads promoting electronics with such devices.[2] Researchers have also discovered "binge viewers," people who record an entire season of a TV series and then watch all the episodes consecutively and without the commercials.[3]

Impression-based ads often "follow" consumers online and keep reminding them about the products they were interested in. **Retargeting** occurs when ads for specific products that consumers have already pursued online "follow" them and show up repeatedly whenever they go online using the same computer. For example, when a consumer looks at, say, hiking boots at Amazon.com, a cookie is placed into that person's browser, linking it with the boots. When that consumer (or another person using the same computer) visits other sites, he or she still sees an ad for the boots on the screen.[4]

Learning Objective

2 To understand Google's targeting and advertising capabilities and its value to both consumers and marketers.

Google's Consumer Tracking and Targeting

Google is the most widely used search engine online and a prominent advertising medium. Across browsers, most online surfers use Google to find answers to questions, locate websites and sources for products and services, track down information, and much more. Google is the largest provider of the data and targeting tools that advertisers need for impression-based targeting, as well as the major supplier of real-time bidding to advertisers seeking impressions among consumers who fit certain criteria.

Google reaches consumers by using:

1. **Web-search ads**, which are ads generated by consumers' searches.
2. **Online display ads**, which are fixed banners that do not vary according to users' profiles or search patterns, posted on websites.
3. **Mobile advertising**, which are ads that appear on mobile devices in Google search results, on content websites, and in apps.

Google's most prominent use is as a search engine. After online users type in queries, two areas appear on the screen. The "organic results" are the links directing users to sites and resources that are applicable to their Google searches. The "sponsored space"—typically appearing on the right side or the top—consists of advertising banners that Google has sold to advertisers or "sponsors." For example, customers looking to buy flowers for Mother's Day and typing the word "flowers" into the search line will be directed to places where they can buy flowers (these links appear below the search line). Most likely, links to flower outlets close by will appear on the first search page, because Google identifies searchers' Zip Codes via their IP addresses. But, on the right side or top of the screen, consumers will see the banners of flower outlets that bid on these advertising spaces and won. Because Mother's Day generates more flower sales than any other occasion, it is likely that these banners will advertise major flower distributors, such as 1-800-FLOWERS. That is because only major outlets in the flower industry would have placed highly competitive bids on advertising space that is particularly expensive on Mother's Day.

Each time a potential customer clicks on a sponsored banner ad, the advertiser pays Google a fee. The fees can range from a few cents for terms that very few (if any) users are likely to enter in the search engine, to several dollars (and up) for words that

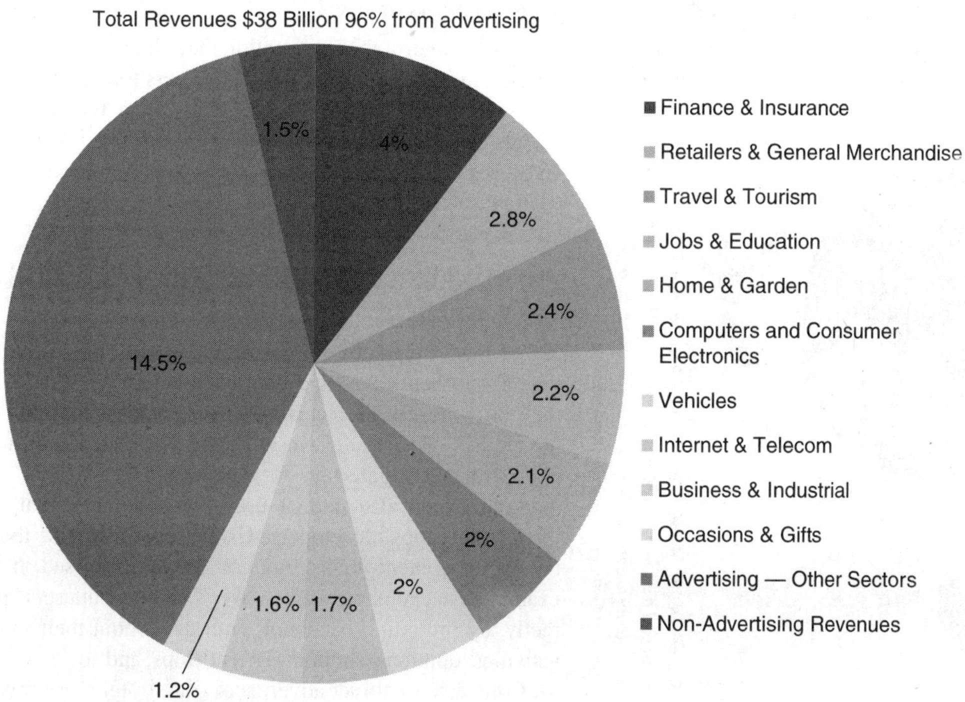

FIGURE 8.3 Google's Advertising Revenues

many users are likely to type in; the latter are what bring up ads sponsored by large marketers. The advertisers' costs-per-click also vary according to whether or not the same user has clicked on the ad previously (measuring the effectiveness of online ads is discussed later in this chapter).

Another source of revenue for Google is graphical and video ads posted on YouTube, which is owned by Google, and on thousands of non-Google sites. Google also runs a shopping site where retailers pay for being displayed in Google's product-search engine.[5] Figure 8.3 depicts the sources of Google's advertising revenues; as shown, most of the revenues come from the marketers of consumer goods.

Consumers and Social Media

Learning Objective

3 To understand the dynamics of social media and its strategic and promotional advantages over other media.

Social media refers to means of interactions among people in which they create, share, and exchange information and ideas in virtual communities and networks. Social media depend on mobile and Web-based technologies to create highly interactive platforms through which individuals and communities share, co-create, discuss, and modify user-generated content.[6] However, even in the "new" and "non-traditional" social media, marketing symbols that have been around for decades are used. For instance, marketers are increasingly featuring their "mascots" online, because they feel that customers will bond with mascots featured in social media just like they did when the mascots appeared in other media. Figure 8.4 features the M&M'S® "person"—a beloved American icon, who has appeared in social media in recent years, as well as in print and broadcast media for decades.

The structure of social media includes the following elements:

1. Profiles are the ways by which consumers tell others about themselves (i.e., their age, personality, and interests).
2. Friends are trusted members of the social network used. They are allowed to post comments that designated members of the network can read. The networks allow users to keep tabs on what their friends are doing online (e.g., posting new pictures or updating their profiles).
3. Groups within social networks help users find people with similar interests.
4. Social networks create interactions among group members via "discussion boards" and by allowing members to post pictures, music, video clips, and other tidbits for the groups' members to view.
5. Consumers must have opt-ins and opt-outs that allow them to control the information they share with friends and the information they receive from others. A Nielsen study indicated that about one-third of consumers found ads on social networks annoying. However, 26% were more open to ads recommended by friends, another 26% said that they did not mind being identified based on their social media profiles, and 17% felt connected to brands advertised on social networking platforms.[7]

Source: DOVE, M&M'S, the M&M'S Character and SNICKERS are registered trademarks of Mars, Incorporated. These trademarks and advertisements are used with permission. Mars, Incorporated is not associated with Pearson Education, Inc.

FIGURE 8.4 Red M&M'S®

Permissions to Collect Personal and Social Information

Social media marketing is enabled by the information consumers provide about themselves and their social contacts, mostly via "apps" that they buy cheaply or receive for free. **Apps** (short for "applications") are chunks of software—installed on one's computer, tablet, or smartphone—that are gateways to games, online resources, and social networking. Apps also collect users' personal information and provide them to the apps' developers. Using apps illustrates the importance of the "free" content-for-information model discussed in Chapter 1. For example, Facebook provides a "free" service, but users "pay" for it, indirectly, by providing Facebook with data about their interests, hobbies, activities, opinions, shopping, friendships, and social contacts. Facebook uses this data to attract advertisers who, in turn, use this information to develop highly targeted and sophisticated promotional messages.[8]

Like all entities on the Internet, Facebook is required to ask users for permission to use the data they provide. A survey conducted by The Wall Street Journal identified the most widely used apps on Facebook and the number of permissions for information each app asks from users (see Figure 8.5). Then, the study identified the number and type of permissions sought by the most popular apps. As illustrated in Figure 8.6, users are asked to provide four kinds of information:

1. ***Basic permissions*** include name, identification, gender, photo, personal demographics, and list of friends.
2. ***User permissions*** are requests to allow the installation of the applications on the users' computers.
3. ***Friends permissions*** include requests to share information the users have about friends using the same app.
4. ***Sensitive information requests*** include questions about users' highly personal lives and opinions, such as political or religious affiliation and even sexual orientation. For instance, an app entitled "Between You and Me" asked questions about users' and their friends' sexual orientations; other quiz-type apps often pose provocative questions, such as "Is your friend's butt cute?"[9] (The ethics of the mechanics used to secure permissions are discussed in Chapter 15.)

Social Advertising's Best Practices

Marketers listen to the interactions, or social conversations, and use the information gathered to generate more buzz for their products within social networks. For example, Dr. Pepper broadcasted two messages daily on its Facebook fan page. The company

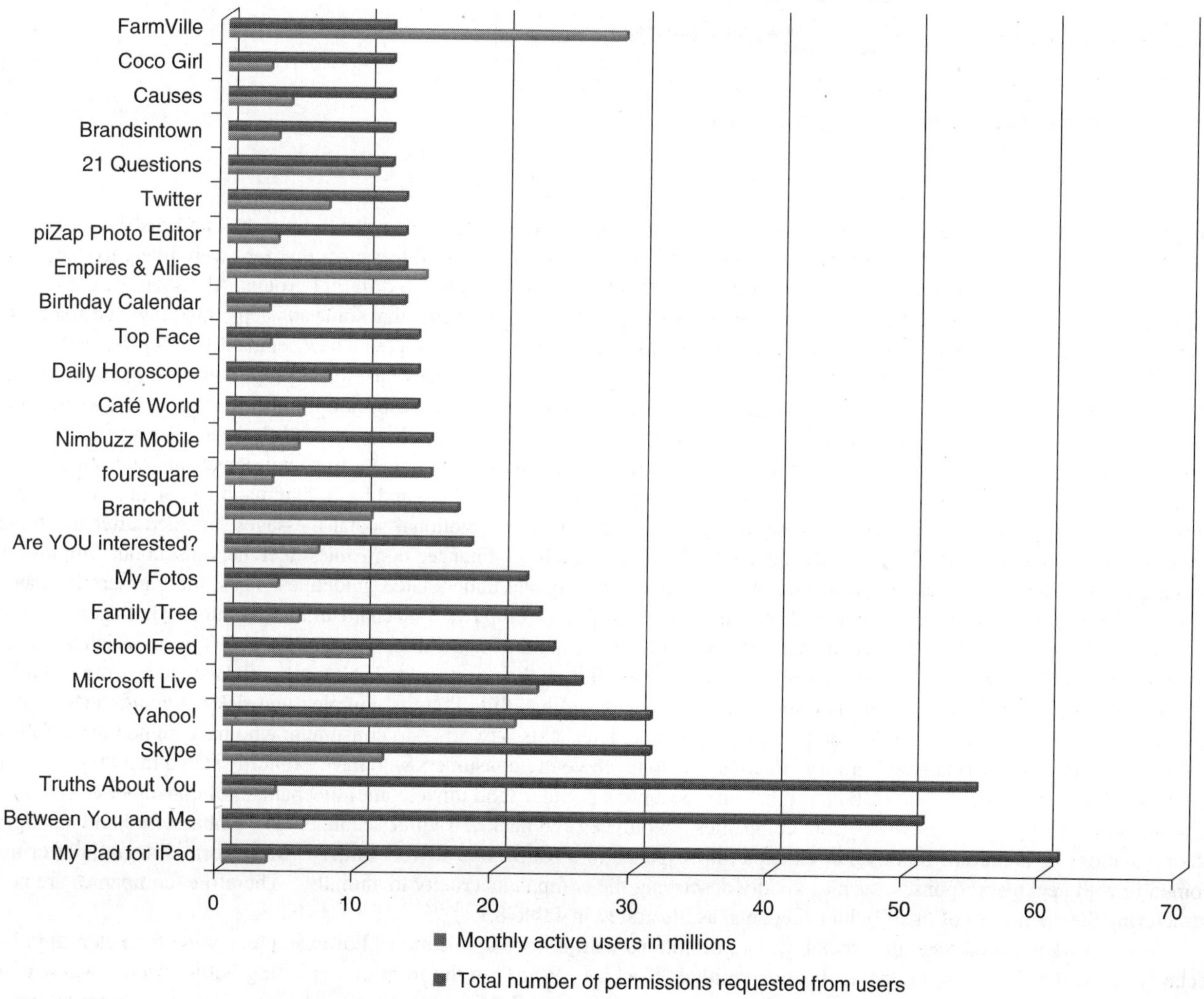

FIGURE 8.5 Numbers of Permissions Sought by Prominent Apps

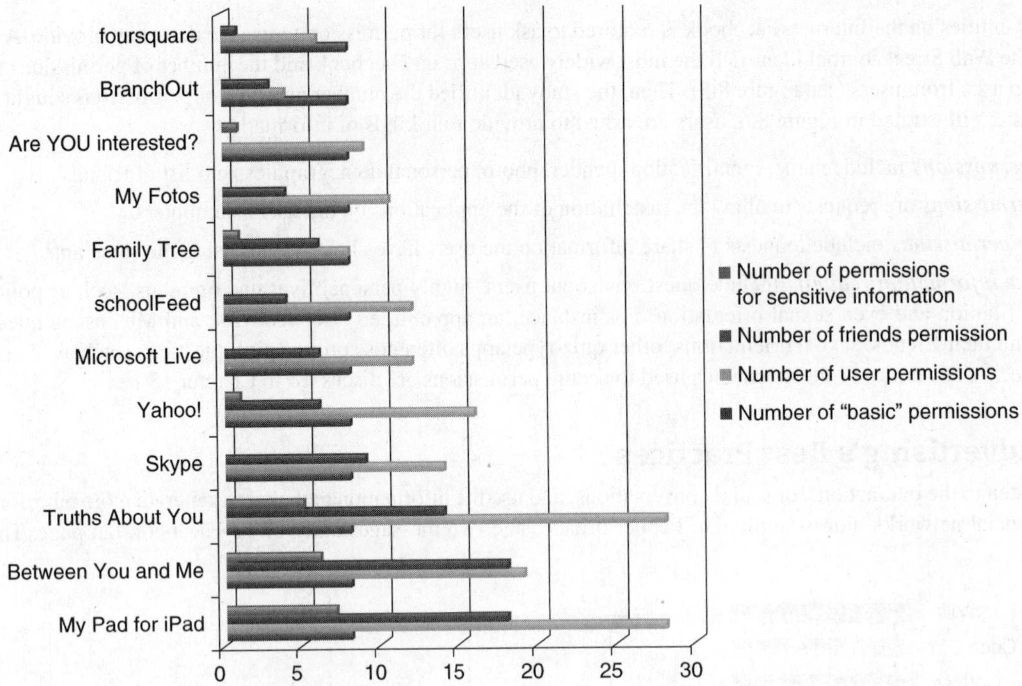

FIGURE 8.6 Types of Permissions Sought

discovered that fans liked edgy one-liners, such as "If liking you is wrong, we don't want to be right," and disliked messages focused on prices and special offers. Based on this discovery, the company developed messages that fans were likely to share with each other. Rosetta Stone tried alternative messages on its Facebook page, targeted to different groups. Although the company's main target market is travelers who need to study other languages, Rosetta discovered that some ads depicting language study as a form of mental fitness received high response rates. Thus, Rosetta accidentally discovered a new segment for its products.

Most brands now have official Twitter handles and Facebook pages. Companies have discovered that customers are highly enthused about and more responsive to Twitter messages from the corporate bosses, especially if such messages encourage consumers to tell the senders about their experiences with the brands. Some companies have decided that centralizing social media communications is impractical, so they train and empower their employees to participate in social conversations with customers, within defined guidelines. Dell opened a social media university for employees and has a command center that scans social conversations. Dell uses what it "hears" to improve products and create promotional social messages modeled after the social conversations it has monitored. In highly regulated industries, such as finance, companies feel nervous about employees' social conversations, even if the employees have been trained and operate under stated guidelines. Thus, the Farmers Insurance Group, where agents initially ran their own Facebook pages freely, now employs a mechanism that monitors what agents say on Facebook for compliance. For example, if an agent talks about noninsurance financial services in a Facebook page, which is against company policy, Farmers' compliance department immediately contacts the agent and tells him or her to take the posting down.[10]

Companies' Twitter accounts are key social media devices and handling them is complex and risky. A marketer's Twitter account lets users, who represent the company, send 140-character texts—tweets—to consumers who have signed up to follow these users. Although this channel is a very effective way to reach young consumers who have explicitly stated that they are willing to receive messages from the marketer, it has also become a popular (and unwelcome) mechanism of consumer complaints. Furthermore, inappropriate responses from companies' employees and hacked Twitter accounts have embarrassed and damaged the reputations of numerous brands. For example, in response to a McDonald's tweet under "#McDStories," legions of critics joined in with negative responses, such as vividly describing the company's cruelty to animals.[11] Therefore, companies are now structuring the operations of their Twitter accounts, as illustrated in Table 8.1.[12]

Savvy marketers combine their social media promotions with iPhone applications. For example, a wine marketer targeting echo boomers developed an iPhone application entitled "Rock My Whirl" in the form of a spinning-bottle game.[13] Many marketers allow consumers to interact with their brands' designs. For example, Cosmopolitan magazine allows consumers to star in

TABLE 8.1 Effective Tweeting Illustrations

TWEETS' SENDERS	NUMBER OF FOLLOWERS AND TWEETS' CONTENTS	TWEETS' WRITERS
Whole Foods Supermarkets	More than two million consumers receive recipes and answers to questions. A weekly Twitter chat among followers addresses such issues as holiday menu planning.	One writer from the company's main account, as well as individual accounts created and handled by different stores.
Southwest Airlines	More than one million travelers receive promotional messages and stranded ones receive help. Complaints are answered quickly. Tweets reflect the company's casual and humorous culture, but not always; a social media crisis plan takes over the account during emergencies.	A team of about 10 people from the company's customer relations department handles the account.
Best Buy	The account has about 40,000 followers. Qualified employees answer technological questions.	Several thousand employees, who have studied specific guidelines and enrolled via a site that verified their employment status, respond to customers' questions.

photo shoots for an advertising campaign; consumers can share these photos and video clips with friends via YouTube and some of these materials also appeared on digital boards in New York's Time Square.[14] InStyle.com enables consumers to apply celebrity hairstyles to their photos, and another site invites consumers to design their own handbags. Many movies use social networks to tell consumers that their friends have seen the movie and ask them whether they are going to see it as well. Another successful practice is encouraging buzz. For example, some websites notify consumers that their friends viewed a clothing collection at a department store and suggest that they should check it out also. After they click on links to the collection, their friends are notified. Most likely, these back-and-forth notifications generate discussions among friends about the clothes they saw.

Numerous sites ask consumers to take polls. For example, an airline's website asked consumers to vote on their favorite in-flight technological feature (e.g., Wi-Fi) and then informed them how many consumers, in total, voted and how many of their friends had done so. Several upper-end watchmakers teamed up and created a very expensive, experimental watch that was designed primarily to create buzz about very pricy watches. The only promotion for the product was getting watch enthusiasts to write about this unusual watch in their blogs.[15] However, aggressive advertising on social media can backfire. For example, when Walmart purchased 50 million ads on Facebook, which were placed on users' Facebook pages, many consumers who resent Walmart's labor practices demanded the removal of these ads.[16]

Most companies selling consumer goods have integrated social media into their advertising campaigns. Established brands—such as Coca-Cola, Volkswagen, AT&T, Ritz Crackers, and Men's Fitness magazine—are directing viewers of their ads to their Twitter messages or Facebook pages, sometimes with sophisticated, cloud-based ad platforms. For example, an ad for a cleaning product read: "Clean should smell better" and instructed users to "Hover to expand." When users hovered, they reached the company's Facebook page.[17] Small and unknown brands, which do not have the resources to advertise nationally, have been using social media aggressively to widen their exposure.[18] The growth of social media has also changed long-standing practices. To generate advanced excitement about Super Bowl ads—which are always eagerly anticipated—many advertisers released limited versions of the ads and other "teasers" during Christmas, two months before the game.[19] In the not-for-profit sector, during one of the most destructive hurricanes in history, transit agencies used social media extensively to calm irate riders and keep them informed.[20]

One of the myths regarding social media has been that it reaches only young consumers. However, the age gap on social networks has been narrowing rapidly. In one year, only 9% of Internet users 55 to 64 years old used social networking, but 43% of this age group reported doing so two years later.[21]

The characteristics of effective social media campaigns are:

1. Social media campaigns must be planned together with advertising in traditional media.
2. Marketers must consider the fact that social media simultaneously reaches several audiences (i.e., consumers, retailers, and other parties with whom the company does business), which justifies larger advertising budgets.
3. Executives should closely examine consumers' clicks on the "like" buttons and "mine" and use data from their Facebook pages to develop new niches for their products (sometimes with partners in other product categories).

4. Bosses who tweet personally strengthen the connections between their brands and customers.
5. Employees should be encouraged to tweet, but guidelines for such communications must be set and monitored for compliance.[22] However, research suggests than many CEOs resent (and even fear) using Twitter.[23]

Social Media Communication Channels

There are several types of social media channels:[24]

1. **Owned social media**, which consist of messages sent by marketers to consumers via channels that the marketers control.
2. **Paid social media**, which consist of messages sent via channels that are not owned by the marketers, who pay for using the channels.
3. **Earned social media**, which are channels where consumers pass along messages about brands to one another.

Commonly, when using paid social media, an advertiser (e.g., Walmart) pays the social network (e.g., Facebook) only after users click on its ads. However, more and more advertisers prepay for large blocks of ads placed on social media users' pages or sent to them via live news feeds.

The most widely used platforms to transmit social message are:

1. Branded blogs and micro-blogging platforms (e.g., Twitter) that encourage interactions among consumers; these messages resemble conversations.
2. Social networks such as Facebook and Myspace.
3. Widgets, gaming, and other applications that users can download.
4. Mobile phones (discussed in the following section).

Most companies use several platforms simultaneously.[25]

Box 8.1 Social Media and Reinforcing Attitudes

Kit Kat is a chocolate brand that used the popular theme of "Have a break, Have a KitKat". The target segment was in the range of 17–25 years and had a prominent social media presence. Research done in a few countries had revealed that the target segment was under social peer pressure to keep up with the updates and comments on social media.[26] Essentially, this aspect can be related to the concept of normative pressure among groups to conform to their norms and such expression of interaction is a part of the lifestyle of the target segment. This can be related to the value-expressive function of the Katz's theory on attitudes. KitKat responded with perhaps, the first automatic answering mechanism on the social media (KitKat social media answering machine). The user can download the social media widget and ensure that it automatically posts, likes favorable comments without any involvement from the user when he/she is having a "break". The result was in consonance with their "Have a Break" tagline. The user could have a break and still appear to comment on the posts without being under pressure to do so. And the widget can be customized, too. KitKat had revitalized and reinforced itself in a contemporary manner using social media. Classical concepts associated with attitudes and reference groups had anchored the strategy. It is no surprise that the widget was downloaded in 100 countries.

Consumers and Mobile Advertising

Learning Objective

4 To understand how consumers use mobile media and their reactions to mobile advertising.

Mobile advertising consists of sending promotional messages to consumers' cell phones, iPads, electronic readers, and other devices that people carry while on the go. Initially, the extent of mobile advertising in other countries, especially in Europe and even more so in Southeast Asia, was far greater than in the United States. However, one report indicated that U.S. companies have spent more on mobile advertising than any other country, including Japan, which had been the leader in mobile advertising. During a recent year, advertisers spent more than $6.43 billion globally on mobile media, with the United States contributing $2.3 billion and Japan following with $1.7 billion. Nevertheless, mobile advertising still accounts for just 1% of the total advertising spending in the United States and worldwide. The primary reason for the growth of mobile advertising is that more and more people are using smartphones and other mobile Internet devices such as tablets and e-readers.[27] Mobile advertising should be distinguished from mobile-advertising campaigns on social networks, which consist of ads that pop up on, for example, Facebook mobile news feeds to its users after marketers have purchased this advertising space from Facebook.[28]

Consumer Response to Mobile Advertising

Because mobile advertising is a new medium, it is important to understand how and why consumers use mobile devices and their reactions to such ads. One study discovered that mobile devices provide four types of value to users:

1. ***Monetary value:*** The device provides good value for the money that also exceeds the value consumers receive from using nonmobile communication devices.
2. ***Convenience value:*** Saving time and money, improving efficiency, and making life easier.
3. ***Emotional value:*** Feeling good and relaxed when using the device.
4. ***Social value:*** Being accepted by others and impressing them.

The results indicated that the higher the values consumers receive from mobile devices, the more likely they are to use the devices to purchase products and engage in word-of-mouth about what they bought.[29]

Studies have identified cross-cultural differences among consumers' responses to mobile ads. A study of Japanese men showed that mobile ads generated effective word-of-mouth. A study of European consumers showed that cross-cultural differences impact the effectiveness of mobile advertising. Research on Korean shoppers indicated that their attitudes toward mobile advertising depended mainly on the convenience of the interface and their ability to control content. Research of Chinese consumers showed that ease of use, perceived usefulness, and trust were the key factors in receptivity to mobile advertising. Researchers also found that the adoption of mobile "broadcasting" in Japan, Germany, and Korea was positively related to the extent of access to mobile devices and the entertainment and social interaction they provide.[30]

One study investigated the influence of the language and source of text advertisements on attitudes toward and purchase intentions regarding products advertised on mobile devices. The researchers found that reputable companies with highly perceived credibility can use *entertaining* language, but companies with less credibility and poorer reputations should create *serious*, clear, and concise mobile ads.[31]

The Advantages and Shortcomings of Mobile Advertising

An analysis of a large sample of mobile ads indicated that:

1. Mobile marketers are still spending most of their money on search ads. **Search advertising** is placing online advertisements on Web pages that show results from search engine queries.
2. Marketers have been creating mobile ads that are fun, pay rewards, and help customers find useful information (e.g., referrals).
3. As smartphone screens became larger, marketers began using mobile ads that take over the entire screen.
4. Some mobile marketers have been experimenting with inserting ads in places where consumers do not expect to see any, in an effort to overcome consumers' tuning-out of promotional messages. For example, Facebook and Twitter have slipped ads into the flow of digital conversations. Some models of the Kindle e-reader display messages for local services, regardless of whether users use the device or let it "go to sleep."
5. Many advertisers use banner ads on mobile devices' screens because such ads are cheap, although most recognize that consumers find banners annoying.[32]

Another practice that is becoming increasingly popular is developing technologies that enable advertisers to link what consumers do on their computers with their cell phones. For example, Google can send consumers cell phone ads that are congruent with their searches on home computers.[33] At the same time, mobile advertising has its limitations: First, smartphones' screens are rather small. Secondly, it is technically impossible to use cookies with apps the way it is with browsers. Thus, marketers cannot track actions and optimize their ads the way they do in response to customers' computer surfing.[34] Marketers also recognize that most consumers are reluctant to receive ads when using their cell phones.

In spite of its limitations, mobile advertising has one outstanding capability: It can identify users' geographic locations and deliver contextually relevant offers. For example, consider a consumer driving with a GPS navigation device (on a smartphone) who receives an ad for a sale in a store located near a highway exit several miles away. The consumer reacts to the message, stops by the store, purchases the item, and pays by credit card. The data about the purchase are immediately entered into a database that includes demographic information about the consumer, as well as the person's usage of mobile devices. Later on, the consumer receives an email thanking her for the purchase and asking her to subscribe to "alerts" about future sales. Probably immediately, the data about the entire shopping encounter are integrated with the data of thousands of persons who responded to such mobile ads, allowing marketers to create profiles of the types of buyers who respond to mobile ads. Another example is a recent joint venture between iPhone and Amazon.com. iPhone or iPad users can now use special software that enables them to browse through products offered by Amazon.com (and other large retailers) and purchase the products. Furthermore, users of the iPhone can use the device to take photos of any products they see in stores or outside and transmit them to Amazon.com. Amazon then matches these photos with available products and sends its recommendations to the customers.[35] Yet another example of the selling power of online and mobile media—stemming largely from buyers' ability to customize their purchases—is a large music label that reported selling more than half of its total U.S. music via paid digital downloads, where buyers purchased individual songs (e.g., via iTunes) instead of CD albums.[36] Taxis in New York City are now equipped with TV screens that display commercials for the stores that they pass, which the vehicles' GPS devices pinpoint.[37] As yet another example, one company distributed mobile phones to college students and offered them discounted calling rates in exchange for agreeing to receive ads.[38]

There are several mobile advertising platforms. For example, Google and Apple provide advertising space on applications supported by their mobile devices.[39] Some TV ads feature bar codes that consumers can scan using their cell phones and obtain immediate information about products.[40] Because searching for items, as well as entering credit card numbers, can be cumbersome given most cell phones' small screens, many retailers are now simplifying the search engines on their mobile sites.[41] Google even offers an application (named "Google Goggles") that enables consumers to take pictures of an object, say a movie poster, and find out more about the movie without typing anything into a search engine.[42] Other retailers are experimenting with applications that allow consumers to find products in the store and even scan them for payment. In some subway stations in London and South Korea, consumers can scan bar codes of products displayed on posters, buy them, and have the products delivered to their homes shortly afterwards.[43] One marketer of tennis wear enables attendees of a tennis event to order customized shirts from their mobile phones and pick them up at the stadium immediately after the match.[44] Another example of creative mobile promotion is a restaurant that enables "culinary voyeurism" via a live video feed from its kitchen to the mobile phones of diners or customers with reservations.[45]

What's in Store for Consumers?

Predicting the future is tricky and often inaccurate. However, it is obvious that social media is increasingly integrating with mobile devices and that more and more of our interactions with people, products, and information occur digitally and not physically. For example, "near field communications" is a new technology that allows smartphones to communicate with each other wirelessly and without Wi-Fi. Clearly, this will make exchanges of content among friends and marketers and consumers faster and more prominent. Some even predict the emergence of a "Smobile (social+mobile) Web." Because online search results are increasingly driving purchase decisions, companies will compete increasingly and aggressively in transmitting relevant, timely, and creative content daily to consumers' stationary and mobile communication devices. Gadgets that provide us with timely promotions, such as glasses embedded with maps featuring commercial outlets that we are passing on the street, will become progressively cheaper and popular (a prototype of such "Google Glasses" already exists).[46] In summary, we will be receiving constant access to our social lives, information, and buying opportunities, at any time, via our mobile devices.

Measuring Media's Advertising Effectiveness

Learning Objective

5 To understand how to measure the effectiveness of advertising in traditional and social media.

Effective advertising is the result of careful and systematic planning. Therefore, advertisers should use the following steps in designing social media campaigns:[47]

1. Define the campaign's objectives and strategic approaches.
2. Examine the platforms available and determine which ones to use so as to achieve the objectives.
3. Produce the campaign's content using internal or external resources.

4. Examine the pricing models for securing access to social media, which, unlike pricing for advertising space on traditional print and broadcast communication channels, vary greatly. Then, set the expenditures needed to achieve the campaign objectives.
5. Measure the campaign's effectiveness.

The measures discussed in Chapter 7 assess the extent to which consumers noticed, paid attention to, liked, and remembered promotional messages, but not whether exposure to a given ad induced an *actual* purchase. For the most part, marketers *infer* the purchase behaviors triggered by ads from broad sets of sales data, as it is rarely possible to identify a cause-and-effect relationship between a given message and the resulting purchase behavior. In contrast, promotions placed in social media employ "electronic cookies," which are digital tracking devices that enable senders to monitor the receivers' responses precisely and often immediately. However, even with electronic tracking, some advertisers have removed their Facebook ads because they had trouble measuring whether the ads led to sales.[48]

The most widely used measures of the effectiveness of online promotions are analyses of website visits, users' influence within social networks, and the audiences' demographics.[49] More sophisticated measures include Google Analytics and Nielsen's cross-platform measurement.

Analyzing Website Visits

Marketers who analyze website visits usually track the following metrics:

1. ***Unique visitors.*** The number of visitors to the website that have accessed its content. User profiles (based on their Web addresses) are also monitored.
2. ***Cost per unique visitor.*** The total cost of placing the application or ad divided by the number of unique visitors.
3. ***Return visits.*** The average number of times a user returns to the site within a specific period.
4. ***Time spent.*** The average amount of time from the start of the visit until the end of the last activity on the page.
5. ***Page views.*** The average number of pages that users have clicked through.
6. ***Interaction rate.*** The proportion of viewers who interact with an ad or application.
7. ***Actions.*** The actions taken during visits, such as entering contests, responding to poll questions, redeeming coupons, playing games, posting comments, sending messages, inviting friends, and downloading or uploading materials and applications.
8. ***Conversation-related measures.*** Data including the number of unique visitors participating, the number of related links that participants reach during the conversation and the duration between the first and last posts, and the average time between posts.
9. ***Visitor demographics.*** (a) Examining how the target audience navigates around the site and which demographic profiles have the most engagement; (b) Evaluating whether the content created is a good match with the users and whether it converts many into buyers; and (c) Determining how to improve the sell rate and reduce the cost per impression.[50]

Gauging Influence within Social Network

As an example, one's degree of influence on Twitter is measured as follows: The person's number of followers, the number of people following the followers, the frequency of updating tweets, and the extent to which his or her tweets are referenced or cited.

Twitter also identified several types of users: *Celebrities* have many followers but follow very few, if any, users. *Conversationalists* follow about the same number of users as follow them. *Spammers* "collect" users with the intent to push content to as many people as possible.

Google Analytics

Google Analytics is a service offered by Google that evaluates the effectiveness of websites and profiles their users by collecting and analyzing the following data:

1. Tracking where visitors come from: Referrals, search engines, display advertising, pay-per-click networks, email campaigns, and other digital links (e.g., clicks within PDF documents).
2. Customers' actions after they "land" at the initial page: Viewing other pages, downloading files, registering with the site, and other actions.

3. Website visitors' geographic location and their visits' lengths. This method also assigns websites' users into profiles and segments them.

Google Analytics enables marketers to measure the effectiveness of their websites and promotional efforts and, to an extent, predict the impact of planned advertising campaigns on customers' behavior. In addition, Google Analytics' e-commerce service tracks sales activity and performance and provides marketers with their sites' transactions, revenue, and many other commerce-related metrics. Marketers can also identify pages, links, and promotional efforts that perform poorly and do not achieve the sites' objectives (e.g., "converting" visitors to users, generating repeat visits, and getting users to register).

Media Exposure Measures

Since advertising in mass media started (initially in newspapers and magazines) approximately in the middle of the nineteenth century, advertisers have recognized that many messages were reaching consumers who had no interest in the products advertised and that accurately gauging the persuasive effectiveness of ads placed in mass media was impossible. **Media exposure effects** measure how many consumers were exposed to the message and their characteristics. Consumer research companies assess *how many* consumers received the message and construct a profile of the receivers. The largest syndicated company that collects such data and sells it to advertisers is Nielsen. Originally, Nielsen monitored TV viewing, but it now maintains many panels of consumers who have consented to the monitoring of certain aspects of their media exposure and consumption.

There are many other companies that monitor consumers' media and advertising exposure. For example, comScore monitors online traffic and Web visits and also tracks mobile advertising on cell phones. Mediamark Research Inc. (MRI) provides magazines with data on their *circulations* as well as a descriptive *audience profiles* (breakdowns of readers by gender, median age, and household income). Arbitron measures the audiences of radio broadcasts.

Broadcasters, publishers, and owners of websites use media exposure measures to determine the size of their audiences and set the rates that they charge advertisers for placing promotional messages in their media. However, disputes regarding the results of audience measurements are common. For example, for years advertisers argued that Nielsen's panels did not adequately represent minorities, and media companies claimed that the company failed to properly measure viewers who use time-shifting devices. More recently, one website's estimate of its monthly number of visitors was 1.8 million, whereas comScore's estimate of the same audience was only 421,000. The major sources of such discrepancies are uncertainties about how to measure Internet use in the workplace and consumers who delete the cookies (small identifying files placed on a computer's hard drive) that are essential in counting website visits. Many believe that a better tracking system is crucial for the growth of online advertising.[51]

Nielsen's Cross-Platform Measurement

Media exposure measures assess *how many* consumers received the message, and also profiles them. The largest syndicated companies that collect such data and sell it to marketers are Nielsen and Arbitron. Nielsen now has many consumer panels who provide continuous data about media exposure and consumption. Arbitron is known primarily for monitoring radio broadcast audiences and, more recently, for developing **portable people meters**, which are small devices, equipped with GPS, that the consumers clip onto their belts and wear all day (in exchange for monetary incentives). The devices monitor codes embedded in the audio streams of media that consumers receive (e.g., TV and radio programs and in-store announcements) and also have the capacity to capture visual images of the screens and written materials that consumers are exposed to (e.g., billboards and other out-of-home media, magazines and newspapers, and online surfing). At night, the devices are plugged into cradles and transmit the data collected to Arbitron. Recently, Nielsen bought Arbitron and integrated the PPM technologies into cross-platform effectiveness measures that compete with newer companies that have been developing similar techniques (e.g., comScore).[52]

Traditional Media's Electronic Evolution

Learning Objective

6 To understand the advancement of print and broadcast media into electronic communications.

Print and broadcast media are one-way communications where all the members of a given audience receive the same one-way messages from marketers. Newspapers, magazines, TV, and radio use segment-based targeting. Because each individual has his or her own traits, characteristics, interests, needs, experience, and knowledge, senders of advertising messages segment their audiences into groups that are homogeneous in terms of relevant characteristics, including media exposure patterns. Segmentation enables senders to create specific messages for each target group and to run them in specific media that are seen, heard, or read by the relevant target group. It is unlikely that a marketer could develop a single message that would appeal simultaneously to its total audience. A cost-effective media choice has been closely matching the *advertiser's consumer profile* to a *medium's audience profile.* Rather than selecting one media category to the exclusion of others, most advertisers use a multimedia campaign strategy, with one primary media category carrying the major burden of the campaign and other categories providing supplemental support.

Newspapers and Magazines

Newspapers provide access to large audiences and are effective for reaching large audiences. However, they are generally inadequate when it comes to reaching consumers with specific demographics. Newspaper ads can be designed and published quickly, but they have a short life. There is considerable clutter because many messages, particularly for local services and research outlets, compete for attention. Nevertheless, because of redemptions of specific promotions and timely measurement of sales volume after the ads are published, feedback can be collected quickly. Advertising costs are determined by size of ad and the medium's circulation. Newspaper ads are affordable for local businesses and enable joint advertising by national manufacturers and local sellers. However, online advertising enables mom-and-pop firms, which have never had the funds for traditional advertising, to promote their businesses, and major players in the digital adverting business, such as Facebook and Groupon, are competing for small businesses.[53] By some estimates, in 2014, local business will spend about 10% of their total advertising expenditures on online promotions (i.e., \$3.1 billion out of \$35 billion).[54]

Magazines reach specific geographic, demographic, and interest-focused groups and enable more precise targeting than newspapers, with visually high-quality ads. Special-interest magazines are highly credible. Magazines offer long message life and increased exposure to ads because of pass-along readership. At the same time, ads require longer lead time for production, and numerous magazines do not guarantee ad placement in a particular position within the magazine. Feedback from magazine ads is often delayed and is measured via Starch scores (see Chapter 5). Advertising rates are determined by cost of page, which is a function of the magazines' circulation, and top magazines charge very high rates. In recent years, magazine advertising has declined rapidly. As shown in Figure 8.7, magazine ad pages during a recent year have declined considerably, as they did in prior years.[55] Figure 8.8 depicts the decline in advertising in popular magazines.[56]

Although most magazines and newspapers are still printed on paper, almost all now offer online editions and many are planning to phase out their paper editions. Online, both magazines and newspapers can flourish by offering readers customized editions that are based on the readers' interests. For example, readers of The New York Times or The Wall Street Journal no longer have to flip pages to find the stories that they wish to read. They can subscribe to online versions where the stories that they are interested in appear immediately and include links to previous articles about the topics covered and other relevant information. For example, a Sports Illustrated story about soccer might include electronically linked references to past matches. In addition, advertisers can customize the messages sent to readers.

The prices of magazines' online editions are nearly always bundled with subscriptions to the print editions, but their costs have been going up. For example, Condé Nast, publisher of high-end titles like Vogue and The New Yorker, raised prices on its bundled print and electronic subscriptions, effectively making print subscribers pay more for online versions that they previously received for free. However, it appears that consumers are willing to pay the higher prices: Condé Nast subscribers who chose to sign up for digital subscriptions renewed at a 25% higher rate than those who did not.[57]

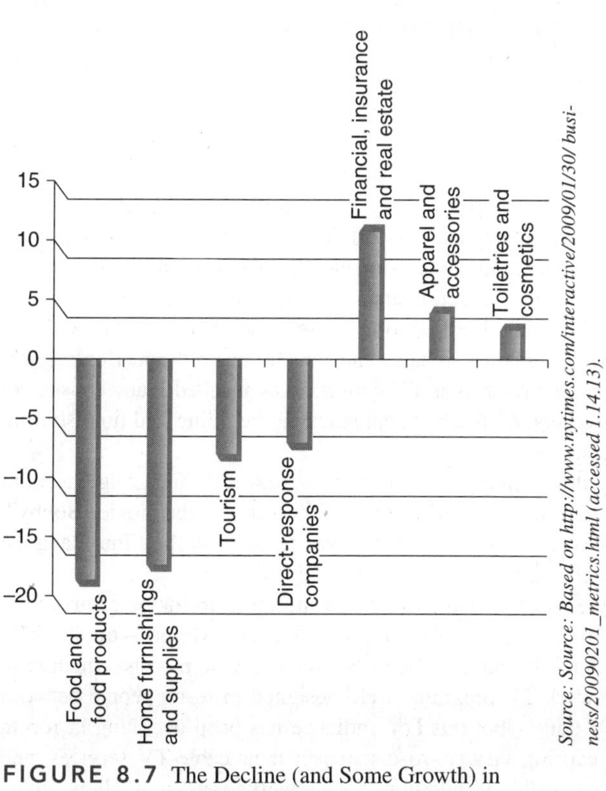

FIGURE 8.7 The Decline (and Some Growth) in the Number of Magazine Ad Pages for Major Industries during 2011 (percentages)

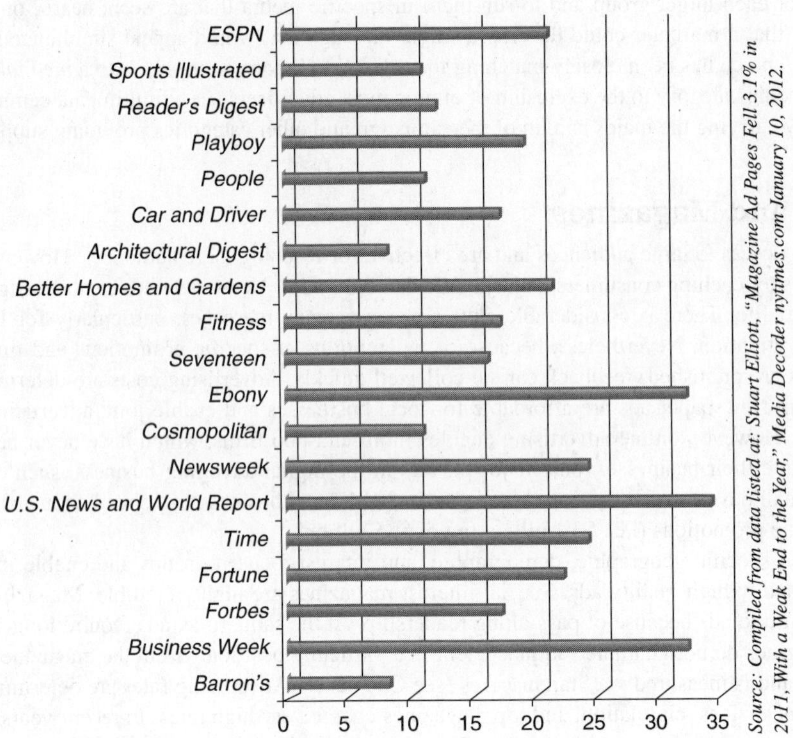

FIGURE 8.8 The Decline in Ad Pages in Popular Magazines over Three Years (percentages)

Television and Radio

Network and cable TV reach very large audiences. However, many programs, particularly on network TV, reach audiences that are heterogeneous in their demographics, spending power, interests, and lifestyles. Network TV (and later cable TV) has been the most desirable (and expensive) advertising medium for many decades because television enables marketers to send messages that draw attention and generate emotion. However, with many TV ads for competing and often similar brands creating clutter, marketers had to design short-duration messages and repeat them frequently. Furthermore, the feedback from TV ads has been imprecise and did not enable marketers to effectively determine which ads led to sales and which ones did not. Because TV reaches large and diverse audiences, marketers have been aware that many of their TV commercials reached many consumers that neither had interest in the products advertised nor became customers. Also, more sophisticated recording and time-shifting devices have been allowing viewers to avoid seeing TV commercials altogether.

Product Placement is not new to the Indian context. During the sixties the Hindi movie "Arzoo"[58] (featuring Rajendra Kumar and Sadhna) positioned an Indian airlines image. Rajdoot"s motorcycle brand Bobby was featured in the movie "Bobby", in the eighties, during the seventies. The movie "Hero" featured Yamaha motorcycle. Coke was featured in the film "Rang De Basanti". "Dhoom 2" had Coke, Pennzoil, Pepe, Sony, Disney channel, Sugar Free, and McDonalds.[59]

Both the production and broadcast of television ads are very expensive and, with more and more forms of communications emerging, some major TV advertisers are changing course. For example, during one year, General Motors—traditionally one of the largest advertisers at the Super Bowl—discontinued such ads because of the broadcast's very high costs, which have reached about $3.8 million for a 30-second spot.[60] Also, most network TV programs were designed to reach people between 18 and 49 years of age, of whom about 25.1 million watched TV daily—but this key audience has been declining in recent years.[61] Furthermore, the lure of YouTube and Netflix has been causing viewers to disconnect their cable-TV services, and the numbers of pay-TV subscribers have been steadily declining as well.[62] In addition, TV networks must now allow online streaming in real time of programs that are scheduled to be shown later on, during prime viewing time, such as Olympic Games held in other time zones, although such streaming can cannibalize the scheduled broadcast and reduce exposure to paid commercials.[63]

Radio's advantages are its high geographic and demographic audience selectivity, as well as the short lead time needed for producing and placing commercials. Presently, almost all radio broadcasts, globally, are available online.

Interactive TV

Interactive TV (iTV) combines TVs' broadcasting capabilities and the interactivity of the Internet. iTV can be delivered to one's TV, computer, or mobile device in the form of a *two-way* communication between subscribers and providers of cable or satellite TV. Viewing on iTV is much more engaging, personal, and dynamic than watching one-way TV programs. For example, using remote controls or smartphones, viewers of Top Chef can vote on contestants, immediately see the results of the votes, download recipes, see behind-the-scenes segments, and even buy products featured on the show. Viewers of sports programs can view scores, statistics, and alerts of the results of other sporting events held at the same time. Consumers can also access highly targeted content, customize the advertising they wish to receive, and click on links with additional information during a commercial.[64] One study showed that interactive banners superimposed on TV commercials significantly reduced the rate at which viewers changed channels during ad breaks.[65]

Several cable companies are now using targeting technology to route ads to specific households based on data about income, ethnicity, gender, and whether the homeowner has children or pets. Compared to regular television, iTV enables marketers to send *addressable ads*, deploy *interactivity* between the sender and the receiver (which increases the receiver's level of engagement with the content), and *measure the persuasive impact* of their messages quickly and effectively.

Out-of-Home Media

Out-of-home media consist of communications that target consumers in captive and less cluttered environments outside of their homes. This category consists of new promotional tools as well as some older means that were significantly updated with new technology. For instance, **captive advertising screens** are placed in locations where consumers spend time, such as elevators, cinemas, retail stores, restaurants, bars, fitness clubs, college campuses, and transit. Digital billboards and displays, with interactive capabilities, are placed in transit locations, events, and stores. A billboard promoting a show on citizen surveillance used a built-in camera to take pictures of passersby with the notification "Person of Interest Identified." Those individuals then received access to their "classified files" to send to their friends or post online.[66]

Ambient advertising (experiential advertising) consists of constructing sensory environments that simulate an actual experience with the product. For example, during the cold holiday season, Kraft Foods built and maintained heated bus shelters (in Chicago and other northern cities), designed to convey to consumers the warm feeling they would get if they ate Kraft stuffing.[67] By some estimates, spending on digital out-of-home media during a recent year was $2 billion and expected to rise 12.5% during the next one.[68]

Fiama Di Wills, for its soap offering for men, used experiential advertising to describe the "refreshing and indulgent" experience associated with the offering.

Branded Entertainment

Branded entertainment (product placement) consists of featuring products within the contents of entertainment, such as TV, movies, video games, among others. When TV emerged as an advertising medium (in the early 1950s), companies sponsored the most popular TV shows and featured their products prominently within the broadcasts. Over the years, paid-for *embeds* of products and brands have appeared in most films and TV shows. Due to consumers' ability to avoid viewing commercials, advertisers' expenditures on branded entertainment have increased significantly. Apparently, marketers believe that they can build and increase product awareness by integrating brands into the content of entertainment programs, where consumers cannot avoid them (the forms of such integration were discussed in Chapter 4).

Many programs that are billed as "entertainment" are, in fact, showcases for prominently featuring products and forming emotional connections between brands and consumers (e.g., The Apprentice, Top Chef, Survivor, and various "makeover" programs). Products have also appeared on the sets on news broadcasts and within the dialogues of programs. Legislators have increasingly criticized overly aggressive product placements (the ethical aspects of product placement are discussed in Chapter 15).[69] By some estimates, globally, companies have been spending between $25 and $30 billion annually on branded entertainment, with American companies spending the most.

In addition to embedding brands in films and TV programs, many marketers have developed **webisodes** (i.e., short videos shown online featuring entertainment centered around a brand) and **advergames**, which are video games with embedded brands. A study showed that, overall, advergames enhanced brand recall. However, repeatedly playing the same game had no effect on brand recall, but did have a negative impact on brand attitude, indicating viewer wear-out.[70]

More Applications of Social Media in Consumer Behavior

The following instances and Figures 8.9 and 8.10 show the nature of social media and its proliferation in the Indian psyche. Social media not only affects our interactions with others but also, on a very large scale, determines our economic behavior.

Application 1: Post-Purchase Satisfaction and Social Networking

Several brands cited in the social marketing context[71] use social media tools to enhance customer satisfaction. Cleartrip.com, the online travel portal, redressed the grievance of a consumer when he Tweeted about his problem. Ching's Secret, maker of packaged food, used the networking to clarify that it is not using genetically-modified food in its range. Parle used social networking to track where its brand Hippo was out of stock and replenish it in such areas. E-zone encourages interaction among its consumers on its Facebook page for product usage and it also uses the social network for obtaining consumer insights. Barista Coffee, after observing reactions on the social media, advanced its chocolate merchandise on the occasion of Raksha Banadhan. Café Coffee Day used feedback from social media to introduce certain merchandise on Friendship Day. It targets 14–19 year olds who spend considerable time on social networks. Cadbury launched virtual gifting of chocolates on Facebook.

Application 2: Facebook and Indian Brands

Facebook, the revolutionary online social media with a billion users, is a hugely popular advertising portal for Indian companies.[72] The objective of using such an online social media may not be just to sell the brand but to engage with the brand in a variety of ways. Pepsi launched a context for cricket lovers during the 2011 ICC Cricket World Cup; Vodafone created apps and posts to create conversations among its 3.2 million fans. Mahindra & Mahindra has built up a community of five million fans and P&G had about 6.9 lakhs fans for its "Thank you, Mom" campaign. While there are various dilemmas and skepticism about how Facebook can be used by brands, social media usage is almost a habit for most consumers who have been a part of it. The classical reference group concept seems to have come alive with the exponential growth of Facebook.

As brands get strengthened in an emerging market like India, brand managers need to make the social media a part of their integrated marketing communications plan. This would also enable a brand to synergize its offline and online communications.

Application 3: Social Media and User Generated Associations

Orabrush, the tongue cleaner priced at $US 5 a piece, sold one million worth of brushes by advertising through YouTube and Facebook. Its giant tongue called Morgan was advertised as a clip on YouTube that received 24 million views. 40,000 consumers signed to receive updates of the brand. In a viral outcome that followed, several YouTube celebrities have made their own videos for the brand.[73]

The example reflects the importance of strengthening the need for an offering that may generally not attract significant involvement levels among consumers (though there is a functional benefit that such an offering may be more effective than a tooth brush for removing bacteria that creates bad breath). Such a conceptual approach is supplemented by social networking sites and hence, triggering a need for the category. Soon we may have Indian brands using such approaches (incidentally tongue cleaner is almost a new category in the Indian context). The category may not be all together new; branding such a category will be a challenge.

Also, these branding strategies can be associated with "user-generated branding associations".[74]

Application 4: Brands, Social Media, and the Mere Exposure Effect

Mere exposure to brands is likely to make them likeable.[75] Brands use this effect under a variety of situations. Kissan ketchup brand was losing market share and hence, introduced the Kissanpur campaign that motivated kids and involved mothers in growing tomatoes at home.[76] With the help of a website and a social media initiative, the brand had kept the interest of the children for three months, the period required to grow a tomato plant. Its market share had increased by seven percent! Puma is set to uncork after-hour parties with the launch of its first ever stand-alone food-and-beverage club, Puma Social, in Bangalore.[77] The brand is one of the foremost players in the Indian market and this launch may be perceived as an attempt to further its youth-connect proposition.

Application 5: The Power of Reference Groups and Digital Media

Hindustan Unilever's "Gang of Girls" online promotional initiative in 2006 [78] provides a an interesting combination of reference groups and online community interaction that was very successful. The company felt a need to revitalize Sunsilk shampoo as it was being perceived as staid and old. The "Gang of Girls" initiative was a result of a research showing that young girls were interested in communicating with one another "sharing personalization of beauty, fun, and advice", something much more than just hair care. The website not only had provisions for free-flowing interaction among "gangs", but also threw open a contest and created a provision for consumers to have access to Hair Care Bars that were linked to salons for expert advice on looks. The website had 61,400 registered users with 37,154 "gangs".[79] Sunsilk's market share grew from 18 % in 2002 to 40 % in 2006 and the brand was also ranked high on "modernity".

Application 6: Can Virtual Self On Social Media Diffuse Brands Faster?

Internet and social media seem to have a profound impact on several product categories and brands among consumers. A scientist from Oxford had reported that consumers will become more obsessed with their self, be concerned about becoming "mini celebrities", and want instant gratification if they are addicted to social media.[80] The virtual self-concept, with the focus on socially conspicuous brands, is likely to diffuse faster with the proliferation of virtual media. For instance, a consumer using a variety of perfumes and other cosmetic products is likely to be conscious about her self-image as perceived by her interaction on Facebook.

Application 7: Mobile Media and Brand Perception*

Wheel brand of detergent introduced an initiative by which the missed calls of consumers who had called from their cell phones were returned by the company, leading to three million unique engagements. Red Label introduced a promotion in which one film celebrity asked consumers to convince another celebrity that it was the best brand of tea. 2.8 million people called the number! Ceat tyres introduced an app "Ceat Tire Assist" that provided monsoon and road assistance for bikers with tips on safety and tire usage. While Wheel and Red Label's initiatives would reinforce the mere exposure to these brands (strengthening the perception of these brands), Ceat app would create a perception of relevance among the consumers.

*Inputs from Ravi Radhakrishnan, "SMS Mob to Win" and Amit Bapna , "Tyred of Idiots," *The Economic Times*, June 19,2013.

Application 8: The Digital Route to Differentiation

In the skin care category, there are not only too many brands, but there are also a multitude of offerings from each brand and the consumer is likely to be confused about what would fit with their needs. While ads create general awareness about the brands and their latest offerings, differentiation at the individual level of the consumer is a challenge for all brands. Neutrogena introduced the "Healthy Skin Advisor App" at the point of purchase at its outlets.[81] This promotion involved the Healthy Skin Advisor (sales person at the outlet) taking pictures of the consumer at the outlet on a tablet and pointing problem areas on like acne marks, pimples, patchy skin, dark circles, tanned skin, etc. The consumer was also asked questions about her skin type. After this, the "skin analysis" was emailed to the consumer with solutions involving Neutrogena's offerings. The campaign proved success for the brand.[82]

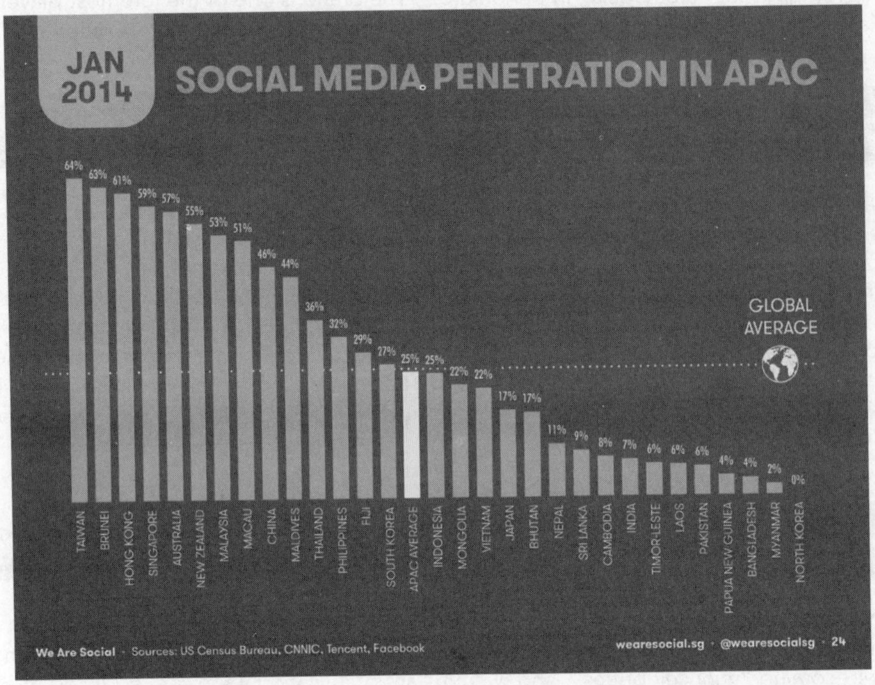

Source: We Are Social[83]

FIGURE 8.9 An Analysis Showing the Range of Social Media Penetration in the Countries of the Asia-Pacific Region

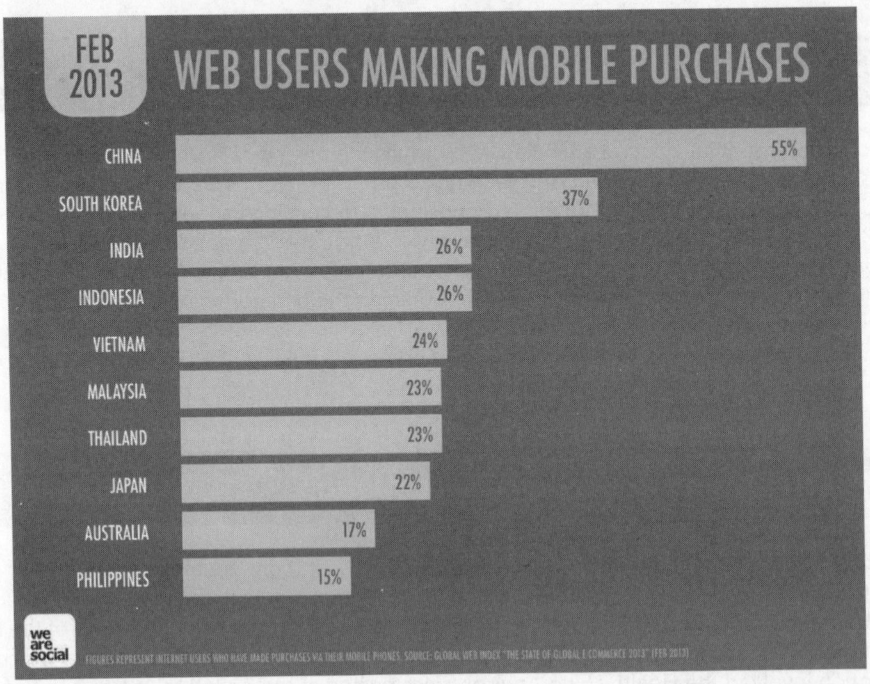

Source: We Are Social[84]

FIGURE 8.10 Represents Internet Users Who Have Made Purchases through Their Mobile Phones

Summary

Learning Objective 1: To understand the strategic superiority of impression-based (eyeballs) targeting over segment-based targeting.

Since the emergence of traditional advertising media (newspapers, magazines, radio, and television), TV networks, magazines, and newspapers have sold advertising space by offering marketers the opportunity to reach audiences whose demographics and psychographics (lifestyles) match those of the marketers' target markets. However, the audiences marketers reached via these media were larger and more diverse than their target markets and almost always included many people who had no interest in the products advertised. In contrast, today's sophisticated tracking of consumers enables data aggregators to construct consumer profiles—based on cookies documenting people's online surfing (and other applicable information about them)—and identify prospective customers for specific products. Advertisers then compete to reach the right "eyeballs" online by placing monetary bids.

Segment-based targeting occurs when advertisers prenegotiate prices for advertising space in media (e.g., magazines or TV shows) whose audiences largely (but never completely) match the profiles of the consumers the advertisers wish to target. Impression-based targeting occurs when advertisers specify the criteria describing the persons they wish to reach online and then bid in real time for the opportunities to reach such people. A person reached is termed an "eyeball" or "impression." Impression-based ads often "follow" consumers online and thus keep reminding them about the products they were interested in. Retargeting occurs when ads for specific products that consumers have pursued online "follow" them and show up repeatedly whenever they go online using the same computer.

Learning Objective 2: To understand Google's targeting and advertising capabilities and its value to both consumers and marketers.

Google is the most widely used search engine online and a prominent advertising medium. Consumers using Google are reached by three types of ads: (1) Web-search ads (generated by consumers' searches); (2) Online display ads (fixed banners that do not vary according to users' profiles or search patterns, posted on websites); and (3) Mobile ads (ads that appear on mobile devices in Google search results, on content websites, and in apps).

Google's most prominent use is as a search engine. After an online user types a query, two areas appear on the screen. The "organic results" are the links directing users to sites and resources that are applicable to their Google searches. The "sponsored space"—typically appearing on the right side or the top—consists of advertising banners that Google has sold to advertisers or "sponsors." Each time a potential customer clicks on a sponsored banner ad, the advertiser pays Google a fee. The fees can range from a few cents for terms that very few users are likely to enter in the search engine, to several dollars (and up) for words that many users are likely to type in.

Learning Objective 3: To understand the dynamics of social media and its strategic and promotional advantages over other media.

Social media refers to means of interactions among people in which they create, share, and exchange information and ideas in virtual communities and networks. Social media depend on mobile and Web-based technologies to create highly interactive platforms through which individuals and communities share, co-create, discuss, and modify user-generated content. The structure of social media includes consumers' profiles, friends and groups within social networks, interactions among group members, and opt-ins and opt-outs that people use to control the information they post or receive online.

Social media marketing is enabled by the information consumers provide about themselves and their social contacts, mostly via apps that they buy cheaply or receive for free. Apps (short for "applications") are chunks of software—installed on one's computer, tablet, or smartphone—that are gateways to games, online resources, and social networking. Apps also collect users' personal information and provide them to the apps' developers. There are several types of media channels: Owned social media, paid social media, and earned social media.

Social media campaigns must be planned together with advertising in traditional media. Marketers must consider the fact that social media simultaneously reaches several audiences (i.e., consumers, retailers, and other parties with whom the company does business), which justifies larger advertising budgets. Executives should closely examine consumers' clicks on the "like" buttons and mine data from their Facebook pages to develop new niches for their products.

Learning Objective 4: To understand how consumers use mobile media and their reactions to mobile advertising.

Mobile advertising refers to sending promotional messages to consumers' cell phones, iPads, electronic readers, and other devices that people carry while on the go. Mobile advertising can identify users' geographic locations and deliver contextually relevant offers. As smartphone screens become larger, marketers are increasingly using mobile ads that take over the entire screen. Some mobile marketers have been experimenting with inserting ads in places where consumers do not expect to see any, in an effort to overcome consumers' tuning-out of promotional messages. Social media is increasingly integrating with mobile devices as more and more of our interactions with people, products, and information occur digitally rather than physically.

Learning Objective 5: To understand how to measure the effectiveness of advertising in traditional and social media.

A widely used measure of effectiveness is analysis of websites' visits, including the number of unique visitors, cost per unique visitor, return visits, visit length, pages viewed and links clicked, actions taken during visits, and visitors' demographics. There are also measures of users' influence within social networks.

Google Analytics is a service offered by Google that evaluates the effectiveness of websites and profiles their users. It enables marketers to measure the effectiveness of their websites and promotional efforts and, to an extent, predict the impact of planned advertising campaigns on customers' behavior. Marketers can also identify pages, links, and promotional efforts that perform poorly and do not achieve the sites' objectives.

Media exposure effects measure how many consumers were exposed to the message, as well as their characteristics. Broadcasters, publishers, and owners of websites use media exposure measures to determine the size of their audiences and set the rates they charge advertisers for placing promotional messages in their media. Services that sell media exposure data to marketers have developed portable people meters (PPMs), which are small devices, equipped with GPS, that consumers clip onto their belts and wear all day (in exchange for monetary incentives). The devices monitor codes embedded into the audio streams of media that consumers receive, and also have the capacity to capture visual images of the screens and written materials that consumers are exposed to.

Learning Objective 6: To understand the advancement of print and broadcast media into electronic communications.

Traditional print and broadcast media have been evolving into more sophisticated forms. Newspapers provide access to large audiences and are effective for reaching large audiences. However, they are generally inadequate when it comes to reaching consumers with specific demographics. Newspaper ads can be designed and published quickly, but they have a short life. Newspaper ads are affordable for local businesses and enable joint advertising by national manufacturers and local sellers. Magazines reach specific geographic, demographic, and interest-focused groups and enable more precise targeting than newspapers, with ads of high visual quality. Special-interest magazines are highly credible. Magazines offer long message life and increased exposure to ads because of pass-along readership. Although most magazines and newspapers are still printed on paper, almost all now offer online editions, and many are planning to phase out their paper editions. Online, both magazines and newspapers offer readers customized editions that are based on the readers' interests. In addition, advertisers can customize the messages sent to readers.

Network and cable TV reach very large audiences. However, many programs, particularly on network TV, reach audiences that are heterogeneous in their demographics, spending power, interests, and lifestyles. In addition, more sophisticated recording and time-shifting devices have been allowing viewers to avoid seeing TV commercials. Interactive TV (iTV) combines TV broadcasts and the interactivity of the Internet. iTV can be delivered to a TV, computer, or mobile device in the form of a two-way communication between the subscriber and providers of cable or satellite TV.

Other forms of media are not genuinely new technologically, but are innovative and growing. Out-of-home media consist of communications vehicles that target consumers in captive and less cluttered environments outside of their homes. This category consists of new promotional tools as well as some older means that were significantly updated with new technology. Ambient advertising (also known as experiential advertising) consists of promotions designed to simulate an actual consumer experience with the product. Branded entertainment (product placement) is created by featuring products within the contents of entertainment, such as TV, movies, video games, and online sites, among others. Marketers have developed webisodes (short videos, shown online, that feature entertainment centered around brands) and advergaming (video games played at homes, arcades, or online with brand or brands embedded).

Review and Discussion Questions

8.1. Strategically speaking, why is impression-based targeting better than segment-based targeting?

8.2. Describe Google's role in advertising online.

8.3. List and describe four advantages of social media over traditional media.

8.4. Compare the advantages and disadvantages of the following measurement techniques: Google Analytics, media exposure effects, and Nielsen's cross-platform measures.

8.5. List and describe two advantages and two disadvantages of mobile advertising.

8.6. Why has advertising on network TV and in magazines been steadily declining?

Hands-on Assignments

8.7. Take pictures of two illustrations of out-of-home media, present them in class, and describe why are they effective or not.

8.8. List and describe five product placements that you have seen in TV shows and movies.

8.9. Join one of the apps in Figure 8.4 and categorize the permission you have been asked for according to the four permissions categories discussed in this chapter.

Key Terms

- advergames *243*
- ambient advertising (experiential advertising) *243*
- apps *232*
- branded entertainment (product placement) *243*
- captive advertising screens *243*
- data aggregators *229*
- earned social media *236*
- Google Analytics *239*
- impression-based targeting *228*
- interactive TV (iTV) *243*
- media exposure effects *240*
- mobile advertising *231*
- online display ads *231*
- out-of-home media *243*
- owned social media *236*
- paid social media *236*
- portable people meters *240*
- real-time bidding *228*
- retargeting *230*
- search advertising *237*
- segment-based targeting *228*
- social media *232*
- time shifting *230*
- webisodes *243*
- Web-search ads *231*

9

Reference Groups and Word-of-Mouth

Learning Objectives

1. To understand the credibility of reference groups and their influence on consumer behavior.
2. To understand the persuasive power and credibility of spokespersons, endorsers, celebrities, salespersons, vendors, and media.
3. To understand the dynamics and measurement of opinion leadership and word-of-mouth.
4. To understand the strategic applications, advantages, and potential perils of word-of-mouth.
5. To understand the process for diffusion of innovations, and adopter categories as distinct market segments.

REFERENCE GROUPS are groups that serve as sources of comparison, influence, and norms for peoples' opinions, values, and behaviors. Within any setting, including consumer behavior, people are strongly influenced by what others think and how they behave. The most important reference group is the **family** because it provides children with the skills, knowledge, attitudes, and experiences necessary to function as consumers, a process called **consumer socialization** (see Chapter 10). Other important reference groups are a person's **social class**, (see Chapter 10), **culture** (see Chapter 11), and **subculture** (see Chapter 12). The Campbell's ad in Figure 9.1 illustrates the how families influence young children's brand preferences.

Word-of-mouth consists of communications where satisfied customers tell other people how much they like a business, product, service, or event (although the information transmitted can also be negative). Word-of-mouth is one of the most credible forms of buying-related information because consumers view others who don't stand to gain personally by promoting something as highly credible. It can take place face to face or via electronic communications, and the exchangers of the information may know each other personally or only online. Word-of-mouth occurs often when neighbors talk across their lawns or over a cup of coffee; when friends and neighbors share stories about shops and products that they like (or dislike); and in texting, emailing, chat rooms, and online social communities, among other forms of communication. It has been said that "word-of-mouth is the best advertising" because reference groups, such as friends, neighbors, relatives, and other consumers a person meets online in social networks, chat rooms, and through Twitter, strongly influence one's consumption behavior. This influence is strong because people perceive others like themselves as having nothing to gain from their purchase recommendations. Consumers view reference groups with which they have personal contacts as more credible than advertisements and other promotions sent by marketers. The ad featured in Figure 9.2 encourages mothers to engage in word-of-mouth and rave about Campbell's soup.

Box 9.1 Word-of-Mouth and Referral Profitability

Word-of-mouth has several interesting dimensions if it is used among groups of consumers. Research has revealed that referrals (one consumer getting another prospective consumer known to him to buy the brand he/she had bought) have taken a challenging meaning in the light of customer lifetime value.

Can a brand (especially in services) introduce a referral program (pay a consumer for bringing other consumers to buy the brand) to get higher margins out of referred consumers or to make the referred consumers stay longer and to obtain greater customer lifetime value (generated by a consumer during his association with the brand/company).[1] Such an approach is applicable to the banking and mobile sectors in India. Significant volumes of business in the mobile sector come from the youth segment that socially networks (both online and offline). A brand like Airtel or Spice may be part of the consumer's lifestyle in that particular target segment. The challenge for such brands, other than pricing their services or using imagery-based positioning strategies, is to also incorporate referral schemes in their promotional mix. With the glamour associated with mobile sets and the symbolism reflected by the service provider brands, referrals could herald a creative kind of buzz, not witnessed earlier among youth.

We begin this chapter with a discussion of source credibility and the influences of selected reference groups. We then review several sources of information that are sponsored by marketers, such as spokespersons and endorsers. Next, we discuss the process of opinion leadership and conclude with an overview of the strategic applications of word-of-mouth.

Source: Courtesy Campbell's Soup Company

FIGURE 9.1 The Family Is a Reference Group: Campbell's Chunky Soup

Source: Campbell's

FIGURE 9.2 Stirring Up Word-of-Mouth Among Mothers: Campbell's Chicken Stars

Learning Objective

1 To understand the credibility of reference groups and their influence on consumer behavior.

Source Credibility and Reference Groups

Reference groups have a high degree of **source credibility**, defined as a source's persuasive impact, stemming from its perceived expertise, trustworthiness, and believability. When the source of communications about a product is well respected and highly thought of by the intended audience, the message is much more likely to be believed. Conversely, a message from a source considered unreliable or untrustworthy is likely to be received with skepticism and probably rejected. In discussing credibility, we must distinguish between formal and informal sources of information. A **formal source** is either a person or medium providing consumption-related information and hired and paid by an organization. An **informal source** is a person whom the message receiver knows personally, such as a parent or friend who gives product information or advice, or an individual met and respected online.

Reference Group Influence

Many hotel bathrooms feature "standardized" signs urging guests to reuse their towels in order to help save the environment. One hotel used a message stating that: "Most of your fellow guests reused their towels. Please help us save the environment and reuse yours." This "social norm" message persuaded about 25% more people to reuse towels. Subsequently, a more detailed social norm message stated that: "Most of the guests who have stayed in this room reused their towels. Please help us save the environment and reuse yours." Responding to this message, even more guests reused their towels.[2] From a communication perspective, the "social norm" messages were more persuasive than the "standard" message because they were credible and believable, whereas most guests perceived the standard messages, at least partially, as efforts by hotels to cut down on expenses. In contrast, messages stating that *others* have acted responsibly were convincing because most people adhere to social norms. People can be persuaded by various sources, such as consumers like themselves, the media, and salespeople, only if they trust these sources. People readily reject messages from sources that they do not trust and perceive as biased and not credible.

Reference groups serve as comparative and normative frames of reference for a person's values and behaviors. **Normative influence** consists of learning and adopting a group's norms, values, and behaviors. The most pertinent normative influence comes from groups to which people naturally belong, such as family, peers, and members of one's community. Generally, normative influence occurs among members of the same socioeconomic group. For example, families have a large normative influence on children because they mold young children's initial consumption-related values. Such as which foods to select for good nutrition, appropriate ways to dress for specific occasions, how and where to shop, or what constitutes "good value". **Comparative influence** arises when people compare themselves to others whom they respect and admire, and then adopt some of those people's values or imitate their behaviors. For example, when a recently-graduated student who holds a "start of the ladder" position in a corporation admires her boss and aspires to live like the boss and have similar possessions, the boss exerts comparative influence on the lower-level employee.

The concept of reference group can be also used metaphorically. Ads for the Art of Shaving—a line of upscale shaving products—have appeared under the tagline "Welcome to the brotherhood of shaving." The idea behind this theme is to make men feel that they belong to a select group of metrosexuals who care greatly about personal grooming and shaving and are trusted experts to each other. The campaign's ads have appeared only in magazines, unlike ads for other shaving products that appear on TV and in print, because a TV campaign may "dilute" the "insider mystique of the brand."[3]

Types of Reference Groups

A group to which a person belongs to, or realistically can join, is called a **membership group**. For example, the group of men with whom a young executive plays poker weekly would be considered his membership group. A **symbolic group** is a group to which an individual is unlikely to belong, but whose values and behaviors that person adopts. For instance, professional tennis players may constitute a symbolic group for an amateur tennis player, who identifies with certain players and imitates their behavior (e.g., by purchasing a specific brand of tennis racquet or tennis shoe). However, the amateur tennis player does not (and probably never will) qualify for membership as a professional tennis player because she has neither the skills nor the opportunity to compete professionally. Table 9.1 illustrates the relationship between group membership and the type of group influence.

TABLE 9.1 Group Membership and Type of Influence

	NORMATIVE INFLUENCE	COMPARATIVE INFLUENCE
Membership Group	High level of conformity to the standards of immediate membership groups, such as family and peers. The influencer and influenced belong to same socio-economic group and are both aware of the influence.	Conformity to the standards of groups that the influenced aspires to join, and probably will. The two parties are one or two socioeconomic groups apart. The influenced and influencer probably know each other and are aware of the influence.
Symbolic Group	No significant influence. The influencer is outside the influenced reference group. The influenced are unaware of the unlikely influencers' norms.	High degree of influence, although the influenced know that they will never join the influencers. Socially, the parties are far apart, but the influencers recognize the degree of their influence.

Box 9.2 Examples of Symbolic Reference Groups

Kurkure, a ₹1000 crore brand, offered an interesting example of how symbolic reference groups (imaginary membership associated with consumers) could be combined with primary membership (face to face membership of consumers) in its advertisement. The finding states that for Indians, food, snacking, and family are interlinked[4]; this was perhaps the driving factor for the creation of fictitious family of celebrities in Kurkure's ad.

Reference Groups among Youngsters and Examples of Associated Categories/Brands

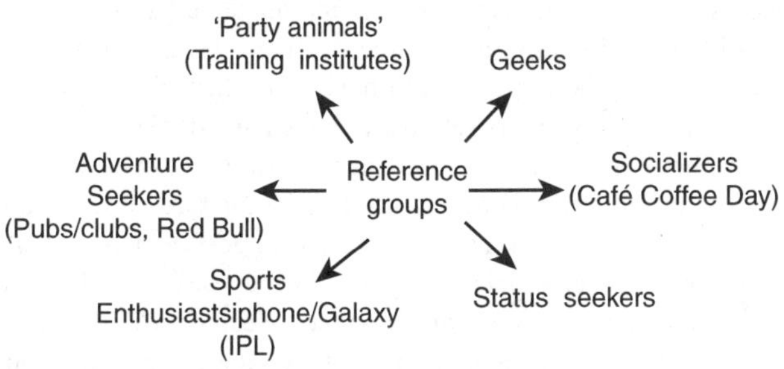

FIGURE 9.3 Reference Groups

Figure 9.3 illustrates how different reference groups can be formed among youngsters in an environment of changing lifestyles. Opinion leaders and role models are associated with each of these reference groups. Different channels like Facebook and Twitter can be used with the categorization of reference groups if the idea is to spread the word-of-mouth (WOM). For example, re-tweeting in Twitter is important to ensure a message is carried through the respective reference group. Identification of re-tweeters or participants in Twitter who are known to take 'social authority'[5] is important from the viewpoint of a brand that uses reference group-based strategies. Reference groups can also be applied to apps in mobiles. "My heritage" is an app that was launched by iPlay and iTunes had a database of 4000 celebrities and the user can match his image with the content of the database (face recognition technology) and load it up on social networking sites.[6] The classical concept of reference group associated with celebrities is still very much applicable to the digital era.

Consumption-Related Reference Group

The consumption-related groups that influence consumers' attitudes and behavior include friendship groups, shopping groups, virtual communities, and advocacy groups.

Friendship Groups

Seeking and maintaining friendships is a basic drive for most people. Friends fulfill a wide range of needs: They provide companionship, security, and opportunities to discuss problems that an individual may be reluctant to discuss with family members. Friendships are also a sign of maturity and independence, for they represent a breaking away from the family and the forming of social ties with the outside world. Often, friendships are formed at work. People who work together often get to know, respect, and become credible sources of information for one another regarding purchases.

Shopping Groups

People may shop together just to enjoy shopping or to reduce their perceived risk; that is, they may bring someone along whose expertise regarding a particular product category will reduce their chances of making incorrect purchases. In instances where none of the members of the shopping group knows much about the product under consideration (such as an expensive home entertainment center), members may feel more confident with a collective decision. Referral programs are an important element of shopping groups. For example, a warehouse membership club (e.g., Costco or Sam's Club) might offer rewards to current members who convince others to join. Such programs may reward only the current customer (member) for finding a new customer, may reward only the new customer, or may reward both parties (either equally or unequally). A study found that although both current and potential members preferred getting entire rewards (100% each), current members found a 50/50 distribution to be more appropriate if the member they recruited had to make a financial investment to join (e.g., pay a membership fee).[7]

Another example of a shopping group is the shared experience of waiting in line. Retail experts say that by standing in a crowd, shoppers see themselves as making the right buying decision—a concept known as "social proof." Retailers also recognize the value of keeping shoppers waiting, because waiting crowds create attention and generate sales even after the initial frenzy has died down.[8]

Virtual Communities

Many websites encourage consumers to leave comments and have others respond to them. Most young adults have extensive "buddy lists" and regularly communicate with people whom they have met online but never in person. Online, it does not matter if you are tall or short, thin or fat, handsome or average looking, and many feel free to express their thoughts and even be intimate with those they have never met face to face. The anonymity of the online environment allows people the freedom to express their views and benefit from others' views. One study investigated "foodies," an online group dedicated to the preparation and consumption of food and drinks, whether at home or in restaurants. The groups' members post recommendations for restaurants and foods across the world. The findings showed that the "foodies" paid great attention to the accuracy of their postings and took great care in not posting potentially misleading information.[9]

The fact that people can share their interests, hobbies, and opinions with thousands of peers online has benefited marketers. For example, for more than 60 years, American TV producers have broadcasted entertainment programs supported by advertising fees. Much like a book or a movie, the contents of these programs were designed without significant input from the audiences. Generally, Nielsen ratings have been used to gauge the success of TV programs and determine the advertising rates on various broadcasts. After watching them, many viewers frequently discussed TV programs at their offices' water coolers, and some may have even talked back to their televisions while watching. However, the writers and producers of these programs had no reliable way to listen to what viewers were saying. Several years ago, avid TV viewers set up a website named televisionwithoutpity.com, which provides TV viewers with a forum to discuss, complain about, or compliment popular TV shows. Visitors to the website share their opinions about programs' plotlines—often with a humorous touch—and make guesses about future developments; some even make suggestions regarding the content of future episodes. Because viewers who post their comments are very involved with the programs they watch, the producers of the shows can read their postings and get a sense of audiences' reactions to plotlines and dialogues. Then, the writers can incorporate such feedback into future episodes. Because TV shows are filmed several weeks prior to a broadcast, writers can also change future episodes in ways that reflect the viewers' postings. For example, if viewers indicate that they are bored with or irritated by a particular story line, it can be revised or even concluded sooner than planned.

Box 9.3 Crowd Sourcing and Building Reference Groups for Brands

Crowd sourcing refers to the idea of obtaining ideas related to several brand initiatives (ranging from new product introduction to customer satisfaction initiatives) through the social/digital media to attract the attention of marketers and consumers. Brands like P&G (new product offerings), Dell (ideas), Lay's (new flavor), Samsung (using Galaxy phone's art applications), Hero (uploading videos for an ad campaign)[10] are using crowd sourcing for various purposes. A possible application of crowd sourcing would be the construction of demographic and psychographic profiles of different consumers who respond to crowd sourcing. There is a possibility for the development of psychographic profiles that may be associated with specific reference groups. For instance, a regional manufacturer of readymade apparel that is into crowd sourcing may find that a specific reference group has a symbolic need that is not being satisfied by any of the major national brands and this could be an important off-shoot of crowd sourcing.

Advocacy Groups

The objective of consumption-focused advocacy groups is to assist consumers in making decisions and support consumers' rights. There are two types of advocacy groups: Entities organized to correct a specific consumer abuse and then disband, and groups whose purpose is to address broader, more pervasive problem areas and operate over an extended period of time. A group of irate parents who join together to protest the opening of an adult X-rated video rental store in their neighborhood, or a group of neighbors who attend a meeting of the local highway department to demand that additional stop signs be placed on specific corners, are examples of temporary, cause-specific consumer-action groups. An example of an enduring consumer-action group is Mothers Against Drunk Driving (MADD), a group founded in 1980 and operating today throughout the United States in the form of local chapters in all major cities and all state capitals. MADD representatives serve on numerous public advisory boards and help establish local task forces to reduce drunk driving. Additionally, the organization supports laws that restrict alcoholic beverage advertising and is opposed to any advertising that may have a negative impact on young people.

Application 1: Reference Groups and Rural Marketing Initiatives

[11]Shaktiman initiative from Unilever India aims to cover 150,000 villages that have a population of less than 2000. Shaktiman involves appointing a male member of a family who would distribute the products of the company in the village. 45% of Unilever's turnover comes from rural areas. Earlier the company had initiated a similar exercise a few years back with self-support groups involving women entrepreneurs to distribute its products. Such reference groups will motivate prospective members to join the group and it is useful to the company as well as the member joining the self-support group.

Application 2: Social Media and Reference Groups

Social media played a significant role in the diffusion of e-retailers (online sellers) like Shoppers Shop, travel sites like Yatra and Make My Trip, and Deal trailers like Fashion and You (daily and discounted offerings on a daily basis with regard to branded items). Besides, group buying was also reflected through such online social interactions.[12]

Factors Affecting Reference Group Influence

The degree of influence that a reference group exerts on an individual's behavior depends on the individual, product, and social factors. These factors include conformity, the group's power and expertise, the individual's experience and personality, and the conspicuousness of the product.

Conformity

The objective of some marketers, especially market leaders, is to enhance consumer conformity. They often do so by portraying reference group influences in their promotions. In contrast, marketers of new brands or brands that are not market leaders often try to convince consumers to be different and not follow the crowd. To influence its members, a reference group must:

1. Inform or make members aware that the brand or product exists.
2. Provide the individual with the opportunity to compare his or her own thinking with the attitudes and behavior of the group.
3. Influence the individual to adopt attitudes and behavior that are consistent with the group's norms.
4. Legitimize the member's decision to use the same products as other members.

The MADD ad in Figure 9.4 discourages a reckless conduct—drunk driving—that young people (especially males) often engage in because they want to be liked by their "buddies" and, especially when intoxicated, participate in risky and often tragic behaviors encouraged in party-like "macho" settings. The ad implies that driving with drunken buddies legitimizes one's drunk driving, because peers are an important reference group. Young adults will respond to this message because it is credible. The ad portrays reference group influence that ended up tragically and is likely to persuade young men not to make the same mistake that

FIGURE 9.4 Discouraging Conformity to Group Influence

the dead driver did. Table 9.2 lists several characteristics of individuals who are likely to conform to groups' behaviors and established practices.

TABLE 9.2 Characteristics of Conformists

1. They feel that if someone is behaving in a certain way in a group, that is the right way to behave.
2. They prefer wearing stylish clothing and pay attention to what others are wearing.
3. They try to fit in during social gatherings so as not to be out of place.
4. They are guided by others' behavior if they feel unsure how to behave in a situation.
5. They often behave in a manner they feel others want them to behave.
6. They change their mannerisms and approaches if they feel that someone they are interacting with disapproves of them.
7. They often pick up slang expressions from others and start using them.
8. They always pay close attention to others' reactions to their behaviors.

Groups' Power and Expertise

Different reference groups may influence the beliefs, attitudes, and behaviors of individuals at different times or under different circumstances. For example, the dress habits of a young staff member working for a conservative law firm may vary, depending on her place and role. She conforms to the dress code of her office by wearing conservative clothing and skirts or dresses that end below the knee by day, but may wear more trendy, flamboyant, revealing styles when she goes out with her friends.

Consumers who are primarily concerned with approval from others usually adopt the same products and brands as those group members who have status. When consumers are preoccupied with the power that a person or group can exert over them, they often purchase products that conform to the norms of that person or group in order to be complimented on their choices. However, unlike reference groups that are not power based, "power groups" may bring about behaviors, but not changes in attitudes. Individuals may conform to the behavior of powerful persons or groups, but probably will neither change their attitudes nor internalize their choices.

Relevant Information and Experience

Individuals who have firsthand experience with a product or service, or can easily obtain detailed information about it, are less likely to be influenced by the advice or example of others. In contrast, persons who have little or no experience with an item, and do not trust advertising messages, are more likely to seek out the advice or example of others. For instance, when a young corporate sales rep wants to impress his client, he may take her to a restaurant that he has visited before and liked or to one that has been highly recommended by a restaurant guide. If he has neither personal experience nor information, he may seek the advice of a friend, or imitate the behavior of others by taking the client to a restaurant that is frequented by executives whom he views as role models. One study examined how product and consumer characteristics moderate the influence of online consumer reviews on product sales using data from the video game industry. The findings indicated that online reviews were more influential for less popular games and games whose players had greater Internet experience.[13]

Source: United States Navy

FIGURE 9.5 A Credible Role Model

The ad for the U.S. Navy in Figure 9.5 shows a sailor, who, to young civilians, is a member of a symbolic reference group that, unlike most symbolic groups, they can potentially join. The ad's objective is to encourage young men and women become members of a select group—the Navy. The ad shows a sailor who has the information and experience to advocate joining the Navy. Potential recruits are likely to find him a credible role model and believe his statement that in addition to moving ships (by using propellers), the Navy has given him a promising career and "advanced" (or propelled) his future.

Product Conspicuousness

The degree of reference group influence on purchase decisions varies according to product conspicuousness. A conspicuous product is one that stands out and is noticed by others,

Source: Egmont Hjemmet Mortensen

FIGURE 9.6 A Conspicuous Product

such as an expensive watch or a newly released digital camera. Products that are especially conspicuous and status revealing (e.g., a large diamond ring) are most likely to be purchased with an eye to the reactions of relevant others. The ALT magazine ad in Figure 9.6 features a conspicuous product. Privately consumed products that are less conspicuous (shaving cream or bath soap) are less likely to be purchased with a reference group in mind. Table 9.3 depicts a framework illustrating that more-conspicuous products are subject to greater reference group influence, both in terms of owning the product to begin with and the brand or type owned. The opposite is true for less-conspicuous products. For example, a person's reference group will have strong influence on whether or not to have a tattoo or piercing, as well as on the type of piercing one gets or the design of a tattoo, because both are highly visible. Because some people wear jewelry and others do not, reference groups are likely to influence only the type of jewelry a person chooses to wear, but not whether or not to wear jewelry. In contrast, a reference group will influence neither one's decision to use or not use toothpaste (because everyone uses this product) nor the brand chosen (because the brand of toothpaste one uses is invisible to others).

Walk down any street in America and you will see someone wearing a hat, T-shirt, or jacket emblazoned with the logo of a famous sports team. Similarly, while driving, look at the license plates of passing cars. Very quickly, you will see license plates

TABLE 9.3 Product Conspicuousness, and Reference Group Influence[a]

	PRODUCTS	REFERENCE GROUP INFLUENCE ON BUYING OR NOT BUYING	REFERENCE GROUP INFLUENCE ON BRAND
Very Conspicuous	Piercing	+	+
	Tattoo	+	+
	Jewelry	=	+
	Baseball cap	=	+
	Smartphone and apps	=	+
	Magazine read online	=	+
	Dance clubs	=	+
	Hairspray	–	–
	Contact lenses	–	–
	Undergarments	–	–
Not Conspicuous At All	Toothpaste	–	–

[a] + considerable influence; = neutral; – no influence

containing variations of the names and logos of universities, favorite sports teams, environmental groups, and many other institutions and causes. Research has found that among those attending a sporting event, the more an individual identifies with a particular team, the more likely he is to purchase the products of the companies that sponsor that team.[14] Interestingly, technology has affected conspicuousness. Before e-readers, many women avoid reading printed erotica in public, because they were concerned that the books' titles, which were visible on the covers for others to see, would reflect badly on them and reinforce the "dumb blonde" stereotype. However, with e-readers, what one reads publicly is invisible and scores of erotica books have been written and rapidly sold; several even became best sellers.[15]

Personality Characteristics

Several personality traits affect the degree of a reference group's influence on its members. People who are compliant, have a tendency to conform need to be affiliated and liked by others, and are other-directed are more receptive to group influences. Competitive people who desire to control other people and events and are inner-directed are less likely to look for guidance from reference groups.

Reference Groups, Self Concepts, and Brand Associations

New age guru Deepak Chopra may be of the view that one should not look at others for identity to avoid stress.[16] But reference group concept in marketing examines how groups can influence the attitudes, behavior, and purchase of brands by individual consumers and how consumers respond to reference groups. Fastrack, Café Coffee Day, Red Bull, and Facebook are just some of the brand names that trigger group associations concerning groups of youngsters associated with the respective target segment. Reference groups play an important role in the diffusion of some brands associated with groups. Most of these brands have a strong element of self-concept and the combination of self-concepts with reference group concept generates a number of options to marketers.[17] There may be consumers who derive a part of their self-identity by using brands associated with the groups that they like (in-group) and avoid brands associated with the groups that they do not like. For instance, Fastrack's provocative digital campaign for its Tee range[18] may be associated with the 'id' part of Freudian theory on psychology. A consumer who likes the associations of the brand and the group that likes the brand may want to associate himself or herself with the group (in-group). However, some individuals who do not believe in such reflection of the 'id' factor in ads may not like to be associated with the brand or group that likes the brand (out-group for a consumer who does not like the brand). A consumer using Louis Phillipe formal brand of shirt may also like the LP brand of casual brand from the same company. The associations of both these brands from the same company may target the same consumer belonging to the same reference group. The situation of usage concerned with the usage of brands by the consumer may vary, but the associations may be acceptable to the same reference group. Some consumers even within the same group (in-group) may have a self-concept by which they are "independent" (meaning that even though they belong to the in-group, they would like to have a brand association that is different from the in-group members as a part of their self-concept). Such a situation may call for a brand association that offers a distinctive association but the one that does not negatively impact the others in the In-group. Special edition of Mont Blanc pens or other premium and luxury goods are examples that attract "independent" in-group consumers who have a self concept that is in tune with the in-group, but will still subtly get differentiated to convey a degree of individuality by possessing the limited edition versions of the brand. Several of the self concept-reference group connections may vary in strength and intensity. A brand, marketing to youngsters, may be able to split the entire market for the product category into possible in-groups and out- groups and map the brands associated with the respective groups.[19]

Learning Objective

2 To understand the persuasive power and credibility of spokespersons, endorsers, celebrities, salespersons, vendors, and media.

Credibility of Spokespersons, Endorsers, and Other Formal Sources

Source credibility is the believability of the endorser, spokesperson, or individual in an advertisement. The spokesperson can be an actual customer, a company employee, a celebrity, or a model. Researchers have identified the following dimensions in measuring the credibility of a person or organization: Expertise, trustworthiness, attractiveness, and likability. Consumers recognize that the intentions of commercial entities (e.g., manufacturers, service companies, financial institutions, retailers) are to generate profits and therefore view marketers as less credible than informal reference groups. Companies can convey credibility through solid past performance, good reputation, product quality, and good service. Their perceived credibility is also a function of the image and attractiveness of their spokespersons, the reputation of the retailers that carry their offerings, and the media where they advertise. One study of sponsorships of sporting teams showed that a clearly perceived fit between the sponsor and the entity being supported strongly enhanced the sponsor's credibility.[20]

Firms with well-established reputations have an easier time selling their products than firms with lesser reputations. Consumers perceive well-established and liked brands as credible and, therefore, these brands often introduce new items under the same brand name. Marketers also use **institutional advertising**, which consists of promoting a company's image without referring to any of its specific offerings.

Not-for-profit sources generally have more credibility than for-profit (commercial) sources. Formal sources that are perceived to be "neutral"—such as Consumer Reports (an American magazine published monthly since 1936), a consumption-related report, or an exposé in reputable media—have greater credibility than commercial sources, because they are viewed as more objective in their product assessments. That is why *publicity* is so valuable tc a manufacturer: Consumers believe citations of products in editorial contexts more than they do paid advertisements.

Endorsers and Spokespersons

Many studies have investigated the relationship between the effectiveness of the messages and the spokespersons or endorsers they feature. The key findings of this research are as follows:

1. The synergy between the endorser and the type of product or service advertised is very important. The greater the fit between the celebrity and the product endorsed, the higher the persuasiveness of the message. Therefore, for example, for personal grooming products, a physically attractive celebrity spokesperson is likely to enhance message credibility and generate a favorable and enduring attitude toward the brand. For products unrelated to physical appearance (e.g., detergents), an attractive endorser is unlikely to have an effect. A glamorous celebrity endorser is more likely to be perceived as a credible source, and positively affect attitudes toward the brand, if featured in an ad for a *hedonistic* product (e.g., a very expensive watch) than for a *utilitarian* one (e.g., an inexpensive, everyday watch).
2. Endorsers whose demographic characteristics (e.g., age and ethnicity) are similar to those of the target audiences are viewed as more credible and persuasive than those whose characteristics are not. For instance, consumers with strong ethnic identifications are more likely to be persuaded by endorsers of similar ethnicities than individuals with weaker ethnic identifications. A person's ethnic identification is the degree to which she identifies herself as a member of her ethnic group.
3. Although consumers may like an ad featuring a famous endorser, they will buy the product advertised only if they trust the marketer as well. Thus, when marketers measure the persuasiveness of advertising messages that feature famous endorsers, they must also measure consumers' attitudes toward the brands advertised, as well as consumers', purchase intentions.
4. Marketers who use celebrities in testimonials or endorsements must ensure that the message contents are congruent with spokespersons' qualifications. A tennis star can believably endorse a brand of an analgesic and comment about how it relieves sore muscle pain. However, a recitation of medical evidence supporting the brand's superiority over other brands is beyond his or her expected knowledge and expertise, and thus may reduce (rather than enhance) message credibility. One study indicated that both perceived expertise and trustworthiness might change consumers' attitudes favorably toward products, and that trustworthy sources did not alter attitudes without being perceived as experts.[21]

Thus, in selecting endorsers, marketers must ensure that there is a synergy among the celebrity's trustworthiness, expertise, physical attractiveness, and the product or brand endorsed. They must also take into account the celebrity's number of prior endorsements, because consumers perceive celebrities who appear in commercials too often as less credible than celebs with lesser commercial exposure.

Celebrities

Celebrities, particularly movie stars, TV personalities, popular entertainers, and sports icons, are a symbolic reference group because they are liked, admired, and often have a high degree of perceived credibility. Therefore, many marketers use them to promote their products and services; by some estimates, 25% of U.S. commercials include celebrity endorsers.[22] To their fans and much of the public, celebrities represent an idealization of a life that most people imagine that they would love to live. Advertisers spend enormous sums of money to have celebrities promote their products, with the expectation that the reading or viewing audience will react positively to the celebrity's association with their products.

The "pitchman" (or woman) who appears in a promotional message has enormous influence on the credibility of the message. Of all the benefits that a celebrity might contribute to a firm's advertising program—fame, talent, credibility, or charisma—credibility is the most important. By celebrity credibility, we mean the audience's perception of both the celebrity's *expertise* (how much the celebrity knows about the product area) and *trustworthiness* (how honest the celebrity is about what he or she says about the product).[23] To illustrate, when a celebrity endorses only one product, c1onsumers are likely to perceive the product in a highly favorable light and purchase it. In contrast, when a celebrity endorses a variety of products, his or her perceived credibility is reduced because then the economic motivation underlying the celebrity's endorsements becomes too pronounced.[24] A study that examined the impact of celebrity athlete endorsers on teens found that such endorsers generated favorable word-of-mouth and increased consumers' brand loyalties. This study also found that female teens provided more favorable word-of-mouth about products endorsed by their favorite celebrity athletes than did male teens.[25] Today's sophisticated consumers are seeking greater authenticity in marketing from the brands they like. Thus, PepsiCo had a hybrid project with Beyoncé that included her appearances in commercials, as well as a multimillion-dollar fund to support some of her creative projects. Pepsi's goal was to enhance its reputation with consumers by acting as an artistic patron instead of simply paying for celebrity endorsements.[26]

Marketers employ celebrities in promotion in the following ways:

1. **Celebrity testimonial**—Based on personal usage, the celebrity attests to the product's quality. A campaign for golf equipment featured Justin Timberlake—adored by millions of teens and young adults—in an attempt to make the game of golf more appealing and "sexy."[27] A TV ad for an advanced model of the iPhone featured Martin Scorsese—a legendary movie director—using the phone's Siri feature to schedule appointments and check traffic conditions.
2. **Celebrity endorsement**—Celebrities appear on behalf of products, with which they may or may not have direct experience or familiarity. For example, Chuck Norris—the martial art star—has been featured in social media ads for Era detergent. The campaign's theme is that Era is as tough on stains as Chuck Norris is on the "bad guys" (in movies). Figure 9.7 features "K.J." Noons—a kickboxing and martial arts champion—as a spokesperson for a not-for-profit organization named People for the Ethical Treatment of Animals (PETA). "K.J." is a tough fighter and he states that while he and his opponents in the ring are equally matched, animals often need protection from violence and abuse by bigger and stronger humans. The depiction of a strong, tough person protecting helpless animals makes the message credible.
3. **Celebrity actor**—The celebrity plays a part in a commercial for the product.
4. **Celebrity spokesperson**—The celebrity represents the brand or company over an extended period. For example, James Bond—one of the world's iconic superheroes—has become a spokesperson for the Omega watch and the exclusive Aston Martin luxury car.

Source: Egmont Hjemmet Mortensen

FIGURE 9.7 A Celebrity Endorsement

Not all companies feel that using celebrity endorsers is the best way to advertise. Some companies avoid celebrities because they fear that if the celebrity gets involved in some undesirable act or event (e.g., an ugly matrimonial problem, a scandal, or an arrest and criminal charges), the resulting press coverage will negatively affect sales of the endorsed brand. For example, after Rush Limbaugh—a conservative and often combative radio talk show host—called a young female student a "slut" and "prostitute" because she supported contraception, a lot of marketers stopped advertising on his show.[28] Similarly, after stories about John Travolta's gay sexual escapades appeared in the media, he was immediately replaced in ads for a very expensive watch, although he had appeared in those ads for years. Tiger Woods also lost many of his commercial endorsement gigs after it was revealed that he had cheated on his wife with strippers and was addicted to sex. Aflac Insurance fired a famous comedian, who supplied the voice of the company's duck mascot for more than a decade, after he posted jokes about the earthquake and tsunami in Japan.[29] Oscar Pistorius, a double amputee who races on carbon-fiber blades and competed in the Olympics, has been featured in many Nike campaigns; one ad showed him starting to sprint with the CAP: "I am the bullet in the chamber."* However, Nike dropped Pistorius from its ad campaigns after the South African sports star was charged with murder in the shooting death of his girlfriend.[30]

Many ads show everyday consumers endorsing products. For instance, TV commercials for Broadway shows often feature people raving about a musical as they are coming out of the theater. One study discovered that "slice-of-life commercials"—promotional messages showing typical consumers in everyday situations—were more effective than commercials featuring either a fantasy or emotional appeals. The ethnicity and gender of the model affected the customers' perceptions of credibility.[31]

Salesperson Credibility

Salespeople who engender confidence and who give the impression of honesty and integrity are most persuasive. A salesperson who "looks you in the eye" often is perceived as more honest than one who evades direct eye contact. For many products, a sales representative who dresses well and drives an expensive, late-model car may have more credibility than one without such outward signs of success. For other products, a salesperson may achieve more credibility by dressing in the role of an expert. For example, a person selling home improvement products is likely to be perceived as more credible if he looks like someone who has just climbed off a roof or out of a basement, rather than like a banker.

Vendor Credibility

The reputation of the retailer who sells the product has a major influence on message credibility. Products sold by well-known, quality stores carry the added endorsement (and implicit guarantee) of the store itself (e.g., "If Amazon.com recommends it, it must be a good book"). The aura of credibility generated by a reputable vendor reinforces the manufacturer's message as well. That is why so many ads for national brands often list the stores carrying the product.

The consumer's previous experience with the product or vendor has a major impact on the credibility of the message. Fulfilled product expectations increase the credibility accorded to future messages by the same advertiser; unfulfilled product claims or disappointing product experiences reduce the credibility of future messages. Thus, the key basis for message credibility is the ability of the product, service, or brand to deliver consistent quality, value, and satisfaction to consumers.

Medium Credibility

The reputation of the medium that carries the advertisement also enhances the credibility of the message. For example, the image of Vogue confers an added status on the products advertised in that magazine. Most consumers believe that a respectable medium would only advertise products that it "knows" to be of good quality. Because specialization implies knowledge and expertise, consumers regard advertising they see in special-interest magazines and websites as more credible than ads in general-interest sources.

A source's credibility may rapidly decline. For decades, Oprah Winfrey has been one of the most credible sources in America. However, her credibility declined sharply after her show hosted a writer who made up the supposedly personal accounts of hardships and other dramatic experiences that he published in a book about his life. Similarly, Dan Rather, a very famous journalist, was fired from his position on 60 Minutes—a highly respected TV news magazine created in 1968—after he cited erroneous facts in a broadcasted segment. Clearly, such negative events are likely to adversely affect the reputations of

* Associated Press, "Nike Makes No Plans for Pistorius in Future Ads," online.wsj.com, February 18, 2013.

products advertised during these TV shows; although the effects are mostly temporary, marketers must be prepared for these repercussions.

Effects of Time on Source Credibility

When information is transferred from the short-term memory to the cerebral cortex (where long-term memory is located), over time, it is separated from the context in which it was learned. For example, although you know that the nation's capital is Washington, D.C., you probably do not remember how you learned this piece of information. One's disassociation of the message from its source over time, and remembering only the message content but not its source, is called the **sleeper effect**. Thus, though a high-credibility source is initially more influential than a low-credibility source, studies show that both positive and negative credibility effects tend to disappear after six weeks or so. Furthermore, the theory of **differential decay** suggests that the memory of a negative cue (e.g., a low-credibility source) simply decays faster than the message itself, leaving behind the primary message content. However, reintroduction of the same or similar message by the source serves to jog the audience's memory, and the original effect remanifests itself; that is, the high-credibility source remains more persuasive than the low-credibility source. For marketers, the implication of the sleeper effect and differential decay is that messages featuring high-credibility spokespersons must be repeated regularly if they are to maintain high levels of persuasiveness.

Celebrity Appeals in the Indian Context

Celebrities are important elements of reference group concepts. They have been a part of the Indian culture for several decades and they inspire consumers (in the respective segment) in various ways using their expertise, credibility, and charisma.

How can celebrities add value to brand positioning aspects and brand associations when concepts of reference groups are applied?

There are several ways by which celebrities can add value to positioning strategies. The Indian context perhaps offers the most diverse examples in the world, both in terms of product categories that employ celebrities and the nature of the celebrities employed by them. SachinTendulkar, Amitabh Bachchan, and Shah Rukh Khan are celebrities who have represented diverse categories over the years and it would be interesting to research if there are such examples in the world.

The following are examples from the Indian context (the examples present historical and contemporary ones):

Palmolive shaving cream	:	Kapil Dev and Sunil Gavaskar's endorsement of its effectiveness (charisma of the celebrity endorses the brand; this is common even in the present day context).
Brylcreem	:	Farokh Engineer, the dashing opening batsman and wicketkeeper of the seventies, endorsed the brand to give it a racy, sporty touch.
Lux	:	Positioned as a luxury soap, topical celebrities are chosen time to time (Glamour, charisma, and endorsement add value).
Boost	:	Sachin Tendulkar (a sportsman's knowledgeable endorsement of a brand on its supply of energy).
Raga	:	Katrina Kaif's endorsement for a watch that was created for the ethnic woman to showcase her beauty and sensuality.
Reid and Taylor	:	Amitabh Bachchan replacing James Bond for the higher-end brand from S. Kumar (apparel brand).
Gold Café	:	Pataudi endorsed this classy, granular coffee brand.
Asian Paints	:	Saif Ali Khan endorsed its brand and associated with fun and surprise.
Junior Parker	:	Amitabh endorsed its class when Parker introduced a lower priced version.
XYLYZ	:	The luxury watch brand from Titan launched a campaign that had a sports celebrity, fashion celebrity and a technologist endorsing it (to create a new image of a luxury watch.
Guess	:	Priyanka Chopra was selected by this American denim brand because she resembled Sophia Lauren.
Fiama Di Wills	:	Deepika Padukone endorsed the brand's 'science with nature' proposition.
Thumps Up	:	Salman Khan's image provided the 'tough, rugged and adventurous' impression to the brand.
Pleasure	:	A two wheeler launched exclusively for women had Priyanka Chopra breaking cultural beliefs ('That stupid Village girl' TV ad) to provide an image of 'modern, independent, and self-assured' user imagery.

30 Plus	:	A tablet that was focused on energy had actor Jitendra (nineties) known for his 'energy-based' roles endorsing it.
Knorr Soup	:	Kajol endorsed the brand suggesting the fun involved serving it for kids. The ad shows the actress as a caring mother having fun with her kids.
Snickers	:	The brand of chocolate from Mars company had Rekha and positioned it as a Snack with the tag-line 'Hungry? Grab a Snickers.'
Cadbury	:	Amitabh was used to enhance the trustworthiness of (chocolate) the brand after there was a furore with worms being found in the chocolate offering of the brand.
Chinny Pickles	:	Used a regional celebrity in Tamilnadu to advocate for the regional delicacy.
Anacin	:	Used a regional celebrity to advocate the relieving (analgesic) action of the offering (observational learning is indicated in this example as viewers would observe the relief experienced by the model and by the tablet when required).
Van Heusen	:	The readymade apparel brand had Deepika Padukone to provide a modern and sophisticated fashion association among its target segment.
Nesfit	:	Had Sachin, Leander Paes, and Prakash Padukone to endorse the (Nestle) effectiveness of the offering.
Yamaha bikes	:	John Abraham to provide an youthful and modern association as the brand had not advertised as frequently as it competitors before.
Cinthol	:	Featured cricketer Imran Khan during the eighties when the he was at the peak of his career (perhaps to bring in a topical association).
Sun Feast	:	Featured Shah Rukh Khan in a playful sequence with children to cash in on the car's popularity with kids when the brand was launched.
Santro	:	Starring Shah Rukh Khan to endorse its brand and gain visibility in a market where the brand was completely new and competing brands were strongly positioned. The star was also used for its subsequent ilo launch.
Taj (tea)	:	The noted tabla player, Zakir Hussain, was used in the initial years to reflect the fine preference of the classical artist. Later Saif Ali Khan was introduced to make the brand connect with the target segment.

Note: The associations used in the explanation are based on the author's perception/analysis/interpretation of the ads and information. It was meant to provide academic understanding of the concepts involved; they may not reflect the perception of consumers.

Learning Objective

3 To understand the dynamics and measurement of opinion leadership and word-of-mouth.

Word-of-Mouth and Opinion Leadership

Originally, sociologists who studied the communications process among peers named it **opinion leadership**, defined as the process by which one person—the opinion leader—informally influences others, who might be either opinion seekers or recipients. This influence occurs between two or more people, neither of whom is or represents a commercial seller or would gain directly from providing advice or information. Opinion receivers view the intentions of opinion leaders as being in their best interests, because the opinion leaders receive no material gain for the advice they provide. Because opinion leaders often base their product comments on firsthand experience, their advice reduces the opinion receivers' perceived risk and anxiety in the course of buying new products. Furthermore, opinion leaders view any feedback they get about their prior recommendations from opinion receivers as credible and are likely to include it in the advice they provide to others in the future.

Opinion leaders provide both information and advice. They talk about their experiences with products and advise others whether or not to buy products or brands. The information that opinion leaders transmit includes advice on selecting the best brands, using the products correctly, where to buy the products, and other aspects. Opinion leaders are particularly important when it comes to recommending service providers with whom they have had personal relationships, such as doctors, lawyers, hairdressers, garage mechanics, restaurants, or travel companies, because small service businesses have very limited advertising resources, and the main way they can get new customers is via recommendations by existing clients.

Generally speaking, opinion leadership is *category specific*; that is, opinion leaders often specialize in certain product categories about which they offer information and advice. When other product categories are discussed, however, they are just as

TABLE 9.4 The Motivations of Opinion Leaders and Receivers

OPINION LEADERS	OPINION RECEIVERS
Self-Involvement	
• Reduce post-purchase dissonance	• Reduce perceived risk
• Gain attention from others	• Reduce search and shopping time
• Show off expertise	
• Experience "converting" others	
Product Involvement	
• Express satisfaction or complain about a product or service	• Learn additional and more efficient ways to use products
	• Learn about newly introduced products
Social Involvement	
• Express friendship by providing others with consumption-related information	• Buy products that have the approval of others

likely to reverse their roles and become opinion receivers. A person may be very knowledgeable about cars and a lot of people may ask for his advice when contemplating buying a new automobile. But, when he considers buying, say, a new iMac, he may seek advice from someone else whom he considers an opinion leader regarding technology; this might even be the same person who asked the iMac buyer for advice when buying a new car.

Getting the attention of trendsetters is crucial for most companies because a tweet or a Facebook post can generate great interest. New York's Comic Con—an annual gathering of comic-book and science-fiction fans—included representatives from Mattel, Disney, and Nintendo, among others. Marketers realize that attendees at such events are people who are setting trends. They are the early adopters of science-fiction-related items and the people who make them "hot" and immensely popular.[32]

Opinion leadership is a two-way street. A word-of-mouth encounter may start by one party offering advice or information about a product to another party. However, this opinion leader may become an opinion receiver later on. For example, a student going on her first job interview may seek information from other students who have already gone on several job interviews (i.e., opinion leaders). She might ask them about the questions posed, how they dressed, and which aspects of the interviews they found unexpected and stressful. However, after her own interview, she is likely to share her experiences with those who had advised her. At that point, those who previously advised her become opinion receivers and will probably share her insights about interviewing with others seeking their advice in the future. Indeed, the input from opinion receivers to opinion leaders becomes part of the opinion leaders' expertise. The motivations of opinion leaders and receivers are featured in Table 9.4.

Characteristics of Opinion Leaders

Just who are opinion leaders? Can they be recognized by any distinctive characteristics? Can they be reached through specific media? Marketers have long sought answers to these questions, for if they are able to identify the relevant opinion leaders for their products, they can design marketing messages that will inspire opinion leaders to communicate with and influence the consumption behavior of others. For this reason, consumer researchers have attempted to develop a profile of the opinion leader. This has not been easy to do, because opinion leaders often specialize in certain product categories about which they offer information and advice. When other product categories are at issue, they become opinion receivers. A person who is considered particularly knowledgeable about home electronics may be an opinion leader in terms of this subject, yet when it comes to purchasing a new washing machine, the same person may seek advice from someone else—perhaps even from someone who has sought his advice on home electronics.

Although it is difficult to construct a profile of the opinion leader without focusing on a particular product category, studies indicate that, in the context of consumer behavior, opinion leaders share the following characteristics, which are also

1. Opinion leaders are highly knowledgeable regarding a particular product category, follow new products that come into the markets, and are often consumer innovators in their area of expertise.
2. Opinion leaders are self-confident, outgoing, and sociable. They readily discuss products and consumption behaviors with others.

TABLE 9.5 Characteristics of Fashion Opinion Leaders

1. Their opinions on fashions count with others.
2. When it comes to fashionable clothing, people turn to them for advice.
3. People know that they know how to pick fashionable clothing.
4. They often persuade people to buy the fashions they like.
5. They influence people's opinions about clothing.
6. They find shopping stimulating and an adventure.
7. They enjoy shopping with friends and family.
8. They enjoy shopping when they try to find just the perfect gifts.
9. They often go shopping when they want to treat themselves to something special.
10. They shop to keep up with the new trends and fashions.

3. Opinion leaders read special-interest publications and regularly visit websites devoted to the specific topic or product category in which they specialize. They have specialized knowledge that enables them to make effective recommendations to relatives, friends, and neighbors.
4. Usually, opinion leaders and receivers belong to the same socioeconomic and age groups.

Word-of-mouth is highly important in the fashion industry where styles change frequently and "social approval" is a key factor in one's decision to adopt a particular fashion or not. Table 9.5 lists the most noted characteristics of fashion opinion leaders.

Measuring Opinion Leadership

Consumer researchers can measure the degree of opinion leadership and its impact on consumption behavior by using one of the following methods: (1) The self-designating method, (2) The sociometric method, and the (3) The key informant method. Additionally, Klout scores measure people's degree of influence online.

Self-Designating Method

The **self-designating method** employs a self-administered questionnaire that requires respondents to evaluate the extent to which they have provided others with information about a product category or specific brand or have otherwise influenced the purchase decisions of others. Table 9.6 lists sample questions that can be used in a study of technological opinion leaders. Marketers use the self-designating technique more often than other methods because it is self-administered and can be easily incorporated into marketing research questionnaires. However, this method relies on consumers' self-evaluations, and respondents often overestimate their roles as opinion leaders.

Sociometric Method

The **sociometric method** measures the person-to-person communications about a product or brand among members of a community where most people know each other by name (e.g., a college dormitory or sorority). Respondents are asked to identify:

1. The specific individuals (if any) to whom they provided advice or information about the product or brand under study.
2. The specific individuals (if any) who provided them with advice or information about the same product or brand.

TABLE 9.6 Sample Items Used in the Self-Designation of Opinion Leaders (responses on a "Strongly Agree" to "Strongly Disagree" Scale)

1. I am usually the first one in my circle of friends to know about new technologies.
2. I know more about technologies than most people.
3. My opinions about technologies count with other people.
4. When considering buying a new technological product, people turn to me for advice.
5. I often influence others' opinions about technologies.
6. People know that I use the same products that I recommend.
7. I often influence people to buy the same technological products that I like.

If respondents identify one or more individuals to whom they have provided some form of product information and those individuals confirm the respondents receive "opinion leadership points." Then, the people from whom the respondents received advice are interviewed and asked to confirm the respondents' reports. On the basis of these interviews, respondents receive "opinion receivership points." One's designation as an opinion leader or receiver is based on comparing the two sets of scores.

Sociometric questioning provides the most valid results for designating opinion leaders and receivers. However, the questioning is expensive and analyzing the results is complex. In addition, this method can be used only within populations where most members know each other by name and regularly interact; it is inapplicable for studies that use large samples.

Key Informant Method

Researchers can also study opinion leadership by using a **key informant**, that is, a person who is keenly knowledgeable about the nature of social communications among members of a specific group. Researchers ask the key informant to identify those individuals in the group who are opinion leaders. However, the key informant does not have to be a member of the group under study. For example, a professor can be a key informant and identify those among his students who are most likely to be opinion leaders about a particular product. This research method is relatively inexpensive because it involves collecting data from one person only, whereas the self-designating and sociometric methods require questioning many respondents. Marketers seldom employ the key informant method, though, because it is very difficult to find a single individual who can objectively identify opinion leaders within a given consumer group.

Klout Scores

The **Klout score** measures people's influence online based on their abilities to generate engagement and feedback to what they post. For example, if a person posts a picture of a new restaurant online and others respond, possibly by also visiting the restaurant and posting reviews, the person accumulates Klout points. Klout measures influence on a scale of 1 to 100 (the average Klout score is 40); the greater one's ability to drive conversations and inspire social actions such as likes, shares, and re-tweets, the higher one's score will be. The Klout score focuses on the amount of conversation and interactions that people generate, rather than the volume of their posts; that is, the score is designed to determine one's degree of influence and not merely activity. Klout sells the information it "mines" to customers like airlines and banks. Those companies then offer "secret" rewards or more responsive customer service to the people with high scores. For example, one airline began allowing people with Klout scores over 40 to visit its first-class airport lounge. Some hotels examine people's Klout scores as they check in and provide perks to guests with higher scores.[33]

As Klout scores became increasingly popular among businesses trying to identify and reach opinion leaders online, Klout broadened the sources from which it "mines" information. To measure real-world influence more accurately, Klout added Wikipedia to the mix. If a person has been featured on a Wikipedia page and that page has a high Google PageRank (a value indicating the importance of a particular page), the person's score will rise; if others link to that Wikipedia page, the score will climb even higher. Klout also added a feature called "moments," which are posts that generated action from the people in one's social networks, such as tweets that received a lot of re-tweets and replies, or a Facebook post that started a discussion among one's friends.

Learning Objective

4 To understand the strategic applications, advantages, and potential perils of word-of-mouth.

Strategic Applications of Word-of-Mouth

In marketing, word-of-mouth consists of transmitting advice and other types of information about products, brands, and shopping experiences. Until about 15 years ago, any consumption-related information transmitted by a consumer could reach relatively few people (e.g., the person's friends, family, work groups, and members of other organizations to which the person belonged). Today, one's review of a movie, book, product, university, professor, and even employer can be easily and quickly posted online and reach thousands of people. Furthermore, constantly emerging new technologies allow people to compile and post increasingly sophisticated and attention-getting materials online and vividly share their consumption experience with others, both visually and verbally.

Word-of-mouth taking place online is called **e-wom** and occurs in social networks, brand communities, blogs, chat rooms, and tweets.

Social Networks

Online, **social networks** are virtual communities where people share information about themselves with others, generally with similar interests, with whom they have established relationships that, for the most part, exist only in cyberspace. Because consumption and the products people buy are integral parts of their lives, their online profiles and discussions with others include a tremendous amount of purchase information and advice. The major social networks are Facebook, YouTube, Twitter, and Myspace.

One study identified three dimensions underlying consumers' engagement in e-wom:

1. ***Tie strength***—the degree of intimacy and frequency of contacts between the information seeker and the source.
2. ***Similarity*** among the group's members in terms of demographics and lifestyles.
3. ***Source credibility***—the information seeker's perceptions of the source's expertise.[34]

Another study investigated how consumers react to negative e-wom and found out that readers of negative reviews of *hedonic* products (i.e., products used mainly for pleasure) attributed the comments to the reviewers' internal and non-product-related reasons and did not consider them useful. However, readers of negative reviews for *utilitarian* products attributed the reviews to product-related reasons and found them more useful than positive reviews.[35] One study researched the impact of the type of e-wom on consumers' likelihood to transmit the information further. It discovered that highly involved consumers received and transmitted more *rational* product information (e.g., the tablet that has the highest-definition screen and fastest processor) than information appealing to *emotions* (e.g., "When I got it, I just 'bonded' with this tablet and other students looked at me when I used it in class").[36] One study investigated the impact of "social connectedness" on word-of-mouth. The results showed that *moderately* connected people (i.e., the majority of the sample) were as willing as *highly* connected persons to engage in word-of-mouth. The researchers attributed these findings to people's need to give advice and the enjoyment of sharing information with others.[37]

Brand Communities

A **brand community** is a specialized, nongeographically bound community formed on the basis of attachment to a product or brand. Generally, admirers of a particular item, often with nostalgic emotions and in possession of versions that are no longer made, find others with similar interests and form a community fostering a feeling of belonging across geographic, linguistic, and cultural barriers. Brands around which such networks have emerged include Harley-Davidson motorcycles, Barbie dolls, and PEZ candy. Although marketers may attempt to join communities centered on their brands, such efforts may be unwise, because the brand community's members join the forum to interact with other consumers and may view the marketer as an unwelcome outsider.

Weblogs

Scores of websites enable anyone post information on anything and everything quickly, for free, and from any location and at any time. Many sites also offer continuous access to chat rooms where discussions among many participants take place in real time. On these sites, consumers are free to express opinions, describe experiences with products and services, solicit purchase advice, and read others' testimonials about products and brands. Another medium for disseminating word-of-mouth is the blog (short for "Weblog"). A **blog** is a discussion or informational site published on the Internet and consisting of discrete entries ("posts"). At first, blogs were the works of single individuals or small groups, and most covered only a single topic. Today, most blogs have multiple authors and are often managed by media outlets, companies, and other interest groups. A **microblog** has less content than the traditional blog and allow users to exchange small elements of content, such as short sentences, individual images, and video links, mostly via Twitter. **Twitter** is an online social networking service and microblogging service that enables its users to send and read text-based messages of up to 140 characters, known as "tweets."

With millions of blogs online, and their readers' frequent tweets, blogs have become the most powerful platform for exchanging consumption-related information. For example, after a dissatisfied consumer posted information on a group discussion site that U-shaped Kryptonite bicycle locks could be picked with a Bic ballpoint pen, within a few days, a number of blogs posted videos demonstrating how this could be done. Four days after the original posting, Kryptonite issued a statement promising that their new line of bicycle locks would be tougher. However, bloggers kept up the pressure and shortly thereafter The New York Times and the Associated Press published articles about the problem. Over the following 10 days, about 1.8 million people read postings about Kryptonite, and the company announced that it would offer free exchange for unsecured locks.[38]

There is an interesting paradox in the dynamics of e-word-of-mouth: Although marketers have virtually no control over the information exchanged, online platforms are probably their most important sources of consumer information. The fact that the phrase "I Googled" a particular topic, person, or product is now part of America's language demonstrates the nearly universal use of the Web as a primary source of information. Additionally, digital platforms provide consumers with more comprehensive product information than advertising messages, and this information is often perceived as more credible than data provided in ads. Furthermore, all major sales' websites enable consumers to compare prices, outlets, and versions of products. Lastly, consumers can find scores of suggestions online regarding a variety of ways to use a product.

Monitoring word-of-mouth online has become very beneficial. The number of comments posted on Twitter and other social media websites about television shows has exploded, to the point where those comments now affecting the shows' plotlines. For example, writers of USA Network's drama Covert Affairs framed the final episode of the show's second season to respond to constant questions on Twitter about whether a lead character, Auggie Anderson, would regain his lost eyesight.[39]

Stimulating Word-of-Mouth

Marketers long ago realized the power of word-of-mouth communications between consumers, which it is almost always more effective than promotional messages paid for by advertisers, and they often encourage it in ads (see Figure 9.2). Long before the emergence of the Web, marketers portrayed word-of-mouth in advertisements, stimulated word-of-mouth among consumers through advertising slogans such as "tell your friends how much you like our product,"* and instituted referral programs through which customers were rewarded for bringing in new clients. For example, a campaign for Vaseline Clinical Therapy asked female consumers who received free samples of the product to "freely prescribe it to anyone they thought might need it."* The venue selected for the campaign was Kodiak Island—a remote location in Alaska known for its harsh weather.[40] One study seeded ads for mobile phones with prominent bloggers and followed them for several months. The study discovered that these bloggers, in an effort to build their individual reputations within social networks, enhanced the advertisers' promotional messages. The bloggers not only communicated the marketing messages, but also converted them—through language, substance, or tone—to conform to the norms and expectations of potential buyers.[41]

Commercials for Broadway shows often portray people exiting the theater, raving about the show they have just seen and telling others to come and see the performance. It is also widely recognized that the amount of word-of-mouth is positively related to movies' box office revenues, especially during the first week or so after the movies open. While stimulating interpersonal communications is not new, the emergence of e-wom resulted in a surge in the amount of money and creativity devoted to online campaigns and strategic initiatives centered on viral marketing and the use of buzz agents.

Viral Marketing

Viral marketing (viral advertising) is a marketing technique that uses pre-existing social networks and other technologies to produce increases in brand awareness or to achieve other marketing objectives through encouraging individuals to pass along email messages or other contents online. It uses self-replicating viral processes, analogous to the spread of computer viruses. Viral marketing may take the form of video clips, interactive Flash games, **advergames**, e-books, brandable software, images, text messages, and email messages. For example, a company marketing hair gel posted humorous audiovisual clips on the Web as part of a continued spoof and satire of hair products and encouraged viewers to pass along the clips' Web location to others.[42] In another example, Facebook "mined" members' postings about movies and then sent marketing messages to the members' friends with invitations to rent the same movies from Netflix.[43] A study discovered that consumers who found out about a new cell phone service through friends' posted recommendations were 24% more likely to view the cell phone service provider positively than people who found out about the service elsewhere.[44]

Email is the key tool of viral marketing because so many people routinely forward emails to others, and many have preset email groups for sharing different types of information (e.g., a "Joke list"). A study that investigated the motivations for passing along emails found that:[45]

1. People were receptive only to emails from people they knew. The kind of emails they received included jokes, virus alerts, inspirational stories, requests to vote on certain issues, video clips, and links to other websites.
2. The main reasons for not forwarding emails were outdated, dull, and inappropriate contents. About one-third of the forwarded emails included personalized notes from the forwarders, and most of the senders did not alter the emails' original subject lines.
3. The key reasons for forwarding emails were enjoyment (e.g., fun, entertaining, exciting) and helping others (i.e., let others know that the senders care about them). The forwarders also reported that they only passed along contents that they believed the receivers would find interesting and appropriate.

The findings of research studies indicate that marketers using viral campaigns must create relevant messages that the initial recipients will enjoy and find fun. Because forwarded emails are often sent with the original subject lines, these must be worded carefully. However, viral marketing campaigns viewed as too aggressive generated negative postings in blogs and chat forums, including accusations of invasion of privacy and spam generation.[46] A study of Chinese college students indicated that they were

* Stephanie Clifford, "Spreading the Word (and the Lotion) in Small-Town Alaska," nytimes.com, October 9, 2008.

more likely to pass along emails and text messages if their friend did so as well and if they believed the recipients would find the messages fun and interesting.[47]

Sometimes, though, viral marketing becomes problematic. For instance, a viral drinking game known as "icing" became highly popular among college students. The game consisted of fast and hazardous "competitive" consumption of Smirnoff's Ice malt beverage among friends. Thousands of videos depicting people "icing" each other, including during occasions such as weddings and graduations, rapidly appeared on scores of websites and focused on the "brothers icing each other" theme. Smirnoff was rumored to have started this viral campaign, but the company denied the accusation.

Marketers reward customers for "e-referrals." For example, eBay and Amazon always remind users to send notices of their purchases or auction winnings to their friends. It must be noted that referral programs existed long before the Internet and online commerce. For decades, marketers have been utilizing such promotions as "bring a friend and get one extra month when you renew your membership at the gym," and dentists have been giving reduced prices for teeth cleaning to patients who recommended them to their friends. Nevertheless, the Internet and social networks have enabled marketers to develop faster, broader-reaching, and more effective referral programs.

Buzz Agents

Many firms enlist typical consumers to serve as their **buzz agents**—consumers who promote products clandestinely and generally receive free product samples but not monetary payments. For example, buzz agents may bring a brand of barbeque sauce to a Fourth of July party, read books promoted by publishers on mass transit with the titles clearly visible, suggest to store owners who do not carry a given product that they should do so, and talk other consumers into trying certain products during shopping trips. Buzz agents are motivated by being called upon to serve as opinion leaders and get an ego boost by appearing knowledgeable to their peers and having access to new products before others do.[48]

Many technology start-ups with limited promotional budgets employ buzz agents by initiating "ambassador programs" on college campuses. For example, Foursquare, an app that allows friends to keep in touch constantly, used an ambassador to promote the use of the program among her fellow students, and even got the college newspaper to carry a story about the app. Another student became an ambassador for Stylitics, a new fashion-focused social networking site. She put up posters, distributed flyers, and featured the website on her Facebook page. In addition to their increased recognition on campus, the ambassadors gain internship-like work experience and some even receive "ambassador points" which they can redeem at retail outlets.[49] Another example is Samsung Nation, an online loyalty program, offers rewards to consumers who talk up Samsung. Participants play games on the website (where they learn more about Samsung's products), win virtual points, and get others to join. Those who are most active in posting online comments about Samsung earn "Twitterati" badges. The company carefully studies the profiles and behaviors of the most active members, because they are the ones most likely to become innovators when Samsung introduces new products.[50]

Several companies offer buzz-related services to marketers. For example, bzzagent.com recruits people to spread word-of-mouth and assists its clients in creating marketing buzz campaigns. Similarly, Procter and Gamble created a company known as Tremor specializing in targeting teens and their families. Tremor screens applicants for buzz agent positions and selects only those who are likely to be effective word-of-mouth communicators. Some marketers hire actors or fashion models to go out and simulate demand for their products. For instance, a campaign for a new brand of flavored vodka hired actors and models to visit bars and nightclubs and order martinis made with the new brand. The actors pretended that they were ordering a well-established cocktail, but the real objective of this effort was to *create* a *new* drink. Similarly, in a recent campaign for an online gambling site in London, cab drivers were asked to steer passengers to a discussion about poker, direct them to the gambling site, and even provide "free hand" coupons to passengers who expressed considerable interest.[51]

Managing Negative Rumors

Long ago, marketers realized that it is impossible to control word-of-mouth communications. Negative comments or untrue rumors can sweep through the marketplace and undermine products. Such rumors may suggest that a product was produced under unsanitary conditions or contains unwholesome or culturally unacceptable ingredients. Rumors may also suggest that the product has harmful effects, such as a medication being depressant or stimulant, or including ingredients that cause cancer. Another example of a harmful rumor is information suggesting that a firm is owned or influenced by an unfriendly or misguided foreign country, governmental agency, or religious cult.

The Internet is a prolific ground for spreading negative rumors. Digital technologies now enable disgruntled consumers to reach millions of people easily and describe their often-exaggerated negative experiences with products and services. Consider a disgruntled airline passenger, an unhappy retail customer, or even a student unhappy with a professor—all of whom can post their stories and opinions online for all to see and respond to. When two brothers in New York City found that Apple was charging $200 to replace a failed battery, they set up ipodsdirtysecret.com. Consumers critical of Starbucks can vent their anger at ihatestarbucks.com; in fact, there are hundreds of ihate.com websites.

Compared with positive or even neutral comments, negative comments are relatively uncommon. For this reason, consumers are especially likely to notice negative information and avoid the products or brands subjected to such criticism. In the entertainment sector, many films, musicals, and plays have quickly floundered because of negative buzz, as have quite a few newly introduced food products. Consumers, it turns out, share negative experiences with others much more readily than positive ones.

Marketers refer to persistent spreaders of negative word-of-mouth online as "determined detractors." Perhaps the best known determined detractor is the person who ate nothing but McDonald's food for 30 days and produced an extremely critical documentary about the experience, entitled Super Size Me. Furthermore, disgruntled buyers can reach very large audiences by posting exaggerated and overly dramatic clips featuring negative product and service encounters on YouTube. One study discovered that some consumers who posted unfavorable information wanted to vent negative feelings or warn others. Others sought exposure, self-enhancement, social benefits, and even economic rewards.[52]

Learning Objective

5 To understand the process for diffusion of innovations, and adopter categories as distinct market segments.

Diffusion of Innovations: Segmenting by Adopter Categories

Over time, positive word-of-mouth leads to the widespread adoption of products that fulfill needs, work well, are clearly differentiated, and provide value. However, not all consumers adopt new products or new versions of existing products simultaneously. The concept of **adopter categories** is a classification that depicts where consumers stand in relation to other consumers in terms of the first time they purchase an innovation (e.g., a new product or model). This classification, which was developed by sociologists who conceived a theory entitled the Diffusion of Innovations, consists of five categories of adopters: Innovators, early adopters, early majority, late majority, and laggards. In marketing terms, each category represents a distinct market segment, so marketers must study each group in order to target it effectively.

Because the adopter categories model was developed by sociologists, applying it to consumer behavior is not straightforward. Sociologically, the model assumes that *all* members of a given society would, eventually, adopt the innovation. Thus, the number of people belonging to each category was calculated in a manner resembling a statistical normal distribution: Innovators—the first 2.5% to adopt; Early adopters—the next 13.5%; Early majority—the next 34%; Late majority—the following 34%; and the Laggards—the last 15%.

However, marketers cannot assume that, for example, every consumer will eventually buy an e-book reader. Therefore, they define "society" as everyone assumed to be in the market for the product shortly, or at some future time, after the introduction of an innovation. Marketers generally define innovators as approximately the first 10% of the total potential adopters of a particular product. This figure stems from historical data collected from various industries where product innovations are common. Then, marketers estimate the percentages of consumers belonging to the remaining adopter categories. Figure 9.8 uses e-book readers to demonstrate the original diffusion of innovations model. The characteristics of each adopter category are described next.

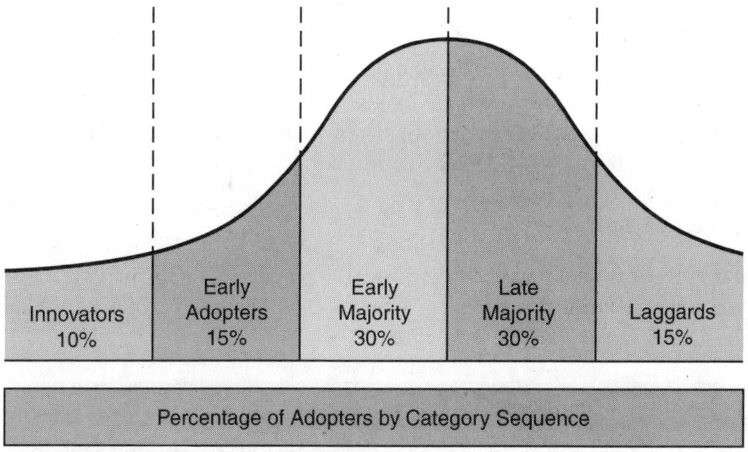

FIGURE 9.8 Hypothetical Adopter Categories of e-Book Readers

Innovators

The **innovators** are the earliest consumers to buy new products. They are prepared to take the risk that the product will not work well, become unavailable, or be quickly replaced by an improved model (i.e., they are broad categorizers). They are often willing to pay somewhat higher prices for newly introduced products, because they enjoy being the first to own gadgets and show

TABLE 9.7 Shopping Activities of Fashion Innovators

1. They are the first in their circles to know who are the latest "hot" designers and emerging fashion trends.
2. They shop much more for new fashions than their friends.
3. They are among the first in their circles to buy new outfits and fashions.
4. They know more about fashion than most people.
5. If they find out that new clothing is available in stores, they check them out.
6. They like to touch clothing and other products in stores for fun, even if they do not intend to buy them.
7. They are reluctant to buy clothes that they cannot touch.
8. They feel more confident about buying clothing and other products after touching them and examining them physically.

them off. When targeting innovators, ads should show them using new products conspicuously and being noticed and even asked questions by others (e.g., "Where did you get that?" "Do you like it?" "I have an older model, do you think I should switch to the one you are using?"). Many innovators like to shop with others; Table 9.7 details typical shopping patterns of fashion innovators.

Early Adopters

The **early adopters** are consumers who buy new products within a relatively short period following introduction, but not as early as the innovators. They are venturesome, likely to engage in word-of-mouth, and also likely to assist others who are considering adopting the new products. Ads targeting members of this segment should show them praising the new products.

Early Majority

The **early majority** consists of consumers who buy innovations after the early adopters have done so. This segment is larger than the preceding two groups combined. For example, when a new model of an e-reader was introduced, they waited for prices to decline and, after quite a few people purchased it (and its price declined), they decided to buy the new model. The ads targeting members of this group should assure them that the product has been successful and provide them with purchase incentives.

Risk aversion is defined as the reluctance to take risks and low tolerance of ambiguous situations, as illustrated by the consumption-related characteristics of risk-averse consumers in Table 9.8. Members of the early majority are somewhat risk averse, whereas the late majority and laggards are highly risk-averse consumers.

Late Majority

Members of the **late majority** are risk averse and slow to adopt innovation. They wait until most other consumers have adopted the new product before buying it. When they finally buy their first e-readers, they are likely to buy older models, which marketers sell at lower prices, and alway look for extensive guarantees. If these consumers are happy with their initial purchases, they are likely to become members of the early majority and likely to buy newly introduced e-readers.

Laggards

The **laggards** are the very last consumers to adopt innovations. By the time they get around to purchasing their first e-readers, the innovators and early adopters have already switched to the most advanced models. Laggards are high-risk perceivers and the last ones to recognize the value of innovative products.

TABLE 9.8 Characteristics of Risk-Averse Consumers

1. They always read and follow the manufacturers' warnings about removing products' tags and back plates and use products exactly as instructed by manufacturers.
2. When it comes to medications (including over-the-counter products), they always obey the instructions on how to take the medicines and carefully read the restrictions and potential side effects.
3. They feel reluctant to buy products that they have never used before.
4. If products come in assembled or unassembled forms, they buy the assembled versions even if these are a bit more expensive.
5. They do not improvise when they cook and follow recipes fully.

Non-Adopters

Marketers often "write off" non-adopters, but not all non-adopters are the same, and understanding nonusers is important. For instance, one study found two distinct segments among non-adopters of Internet banking:

1. ***Prospective adopters,*** who could potentially become customers.
2. ***Persistent non-adopters,*** who are very unlikely to become customers.

The study suggested that online banks should identify prospective customers among nonusers rather than lump all nonusers into a single category.[53]

Summary

Learning Objective 1: To understand the credibility of reference groups and their influence on consumer behavior.

Within any setting, including consumer behavior, people are strongly influenced by how others think and behave. Reference groups are groups that serve as sources of comparison, influence, and norms for people's opinions, values, and behaviors. Word-of-mouth consists of communications where satisfied customers tell other people how much they like a business, product, service, or event, although word-of-mouth can also be negative.

The perceived honesty, objectivity, expertise, and trustworthiness of reference groups make them highly credible sources. Consumers perceive people whom they know personally as more credible than paid-for promotional messages. People learn norms and values mostly from families and peers. They also imitate and adopt the values and habits of persons whom they respect or admire. The groups to which people belong, as well as groups that they aspire to join, influence their norms and behaviors. Consumption-related groups also influence consumers' attitudes and behavior. Sociocultural groups that determine people's behavior, norms, morals, and consumption patterns include family, social class, culture, subculture, and (for global consumers) cross-culture.

Learning Objective 2: To understand the persuasive power and credibility of spokespersons, endorsers, celebrities, salespersons, vendors, and media.

The perceived credibility of spokespersons, endorsers, and other sources that companies use in their advertising is the key to the ads' effectiveness. The spokesperson can be an actual customer, a company employee, a celebrity, or a model. Companies also convey their credibility through solid past performance, good reputation, high product quality, and good service. Their perceived credibility is also a function of the image and reputation of the retailers that carry their offerings and the media where they advertise. Marketers employ celebrities for product testimonials and endorsements, as well as spokespersons and actors in commercials.

Over time, consumers disassociate messages from their sources; they tend to remember only the messages' contents, but not their sources. Therefore, marketers must regularly repeat messages that feature high-credibility spokespersons in order to maintain the messages' persuasiveness.

Learning Objective 3: To understand the dynamics and measurement of opinion leadership and word-of-mouth.

Opinion leadership is the process by which one person—the opinion leader—informally influences others, who might be either opinion seekers or recipients. This influence occurs between two or more people, neither of whom represents a commercial seller nor would gain directly from providing advice or information. Opinion leaders who have expertise in a given product category provide advice and influence the consumption of others within the same category. They also follow any new items introduced closely, and are the first to buy new items. They tend to be self-confident, outgoing, and sociable. Several research methods are aimed at identifying opinion leaders.

Learning Objective 4: To understand the strategic applications, advantages, and potential perils of word-of-mouth.

Electronic word-of-mouth takes place online and occurs in social networks, brand communities, blogs, chat rooms, and tweets. Marketers hire buzz agents and initiate viral marketing to stimulate word-of-mouth in cyberspace. Buzz agents are consumers who promote products clandestinely and generally receive free product samples but not monetary payments. Viral marketing is a marketing technique that uses pre-existing social networks and other technologies to produce increases in brand awareness or to achieve other marketing objectives through encouraging individuals to pass along email messages or other contents online.

It is impossible to control word-of-mouth communications. Negative comments, frequently in the form of untrue rumors, can sweep through the marketplace and undermine a product. The Internet is a prolific ground for spreading negative rumors because disgruntled consumers can reach millions of people easily and exaggerate (or even lie about) their negative experiences with products and services.

Learning Objective 5: To understand the process for diffusion of innovations, and adopter categories as distinct market segments.

Over time, positive word-of-mouth leads to the widespread adoption of products. However, not all consumers adopt new products or new versions of existing products simultaneously. Sociologists who studied how innovations are adopted within societies identified five categories of adopters: Innovators, early adopters, early majority, late majority, and laggards. The concept of adopter categories is a classification scheme that depicts where consumers stand in relation to other consumers in terms of the first time they purchase an innovation (e.g., a new product). Each category represents a distinct market segment, so marketers must study each group in order to target it effectively.

Review and Discussion Questions

9.1. Why is an opinion leader a more credible source of product information than an advertisement for the product? Are there any circumstances in which information from advertisements is likely to be more influential than word-of-mouth?

9.2. What are reference groups? List and discuss at least four groups that influence your purchases. For each group, indicate whether its influence is comparative or normative (or, possibly, both) and explain your answers.

9.3. What is the difference between membership groups and symbolic groups? List one membership group and one symbolic group that influence your purchases. Explain which group influences you more and why.

9.4. How can companies strategically use buzz agents and viral marketing? Illustrate with examples.

9.5. Compare the advantages and disadvantages of the methods of measuring opinion leadership.

9.6. How can marketers use social networks, brand communities, and weblogs to locate new customers and target them?

9.7. List and discuss the factors that affect the credibility of formal communications sources of product information. What factors influence the perceived credibility of informal communications sources?

9.8. You are the marketing vice president of a large soft-drink company. Your company's advertising agency is in the process of negotiating a contract to employ a superstar female singer to promote its product. Discuss the reference group factors that you would consider before the celebrity is hired.

9.9. What are the implications of the sleeper effect for the selection of spokespersons and the scheduling of advertising messages?

9.10. Amazon has introduced a new e-book reader that is more expensive than previous models but has many more features. How can the company use the adopter categories in marketing this product?

Hands-on Assignments

9.11. With a paper and pencil, spend one hour watching a network television channel during prime time. Record the total number of commercials that aired. For each commercial that used a celebrity endorser, record the celebrity's name, the product or service advertised, and whether the celebrity was used in a testimonial, as an endorser, as an actor, or as a spokesperson.

9.12. Describe two situations in which you served as an opinion leader and two situations in which you sought consumption-related advice or information from an opinion leader. Indicate your relationship to the persons with whom you interacted. Are the circumstances during which you engaged in word-of-mouth communications consistent with those described in the text? Explain.

9.13. Find ads that encourage consumers to engage in word-of-mouth communications.

9.14. Prepare a list of negative rumors that you (or your friends) have heard recently about a company or a product.

9.15. Locate an online company that recruits buzz agents and register as one. Keep a diary of all your contacts with the organization for about one month. Summarize the diary and discuss whether the company was right to make you a buzz agent and explain why or why not.

Key Terms

- adopter categories *271*
- advergames *269*
- blog *268*
- brand community *268*
- buzz agent *270*
- celebrity actor *261*
- celebrity endorsement *261*
- celebrity spokesperson *261*
- celebrity testimonial *261*
- comparative influence *252*
- consumer socialization *250*
- culture *250*
- differential decay *263*
- early adopters *272*
- early majority *272*
- e-wom *267*
- family *250*
- formal source *252*
- informal source *252*
- innovators *271*
- institutional advertising *260*
- key informant *267*
- Klout score *267*
- laggards *272*
- late majority *272*
- membership group *252*
- microblog *268*
- normative influence *252*
- opinion leadership *264*
- reference groups *252*
- risk aversion *272*
- self-designating method *266*
- sleeper effect *263*
- social class *250*
- social network *267*
- sociometric method *266*
- source credibility *252*
- subculture *250*
- symbolic group *252*
- Twitter *268*
- viral marketing (viral advertising) *269*
- word-of-mouth *250*

Case Four: Keystone Light/MillerCoors

"Canhole"

Lead Agency: **Leo Burnett/Arc Worldwide**

Strategic Challenges

Summer is the season for beer: Billions of dollars are up for grabs; the competition for floor space, incremental displays, and "customer activation" is intense and hotly contested.

The big dogs rule: Miller Lite, Coors Light, Bud Light, Budweiser, and Corona rule the summer months, which makes it difficult for smaller, below-premium brands such as Keystone Light to get any attention from distributors or retailers. Typically, Keystone Light can only place statics stickers on in-store coolers to plead its case to shoppers.

Pricing challenges made it more difficult: Beer companies, including MillerCoors, have raised the price of the below-premium segment (closing the price gap) in an effort to get drinkers to trade up to the pricier premium brands—which is the companies' priority and vital to overall performance. However, this pricing strategy couldn't have happened at a worse time for Keystone Light. Its target consumers were being hit hard by the sagging economy and were looking for even more value while still trying to get out and have some summer fun with their buddies.

The overall challenge: In the sea of big-name brands during the summer, how does the company give a smaller, below-premium beer a reason to be featured at retail?

Objectives

1. **Stave off decline of the Keystone Light business in the convenience store channel** by stealing share, volume, and display opportunities from the company's key competitor: Anheuser-Busch's below-premium powerhouse, Natural Light.
2. **Increase overall Keystone Light brand engagement** to help establish a purpose and personality for Keystone Light's new brand character (Keith Stone), in order to increase interaction, acceptance, and sharing by consumers.

Insights

The company's target was a simple guy with simple needs, which was named "The Cruiser." He doesn't have a lot of money, so he's learned to be resourceful and inventive with things he has on hand in order to have a good time.

For him, a great meal is a frozen burrito, a bag of Doritos, and a warm hot dog right off the roller. He enjoys the occasional fart joke and ribbing his buddy because his sister can kick his butt at Halo (with one hand tied behind her back). He's comfortable with who he is and values friendship over all else. He has also built a fair number of beer pyramids in his day.

Once the company understood the Cruiser and how he behaves, it needed to know what he does during the summer. Using a combination of quantitative and qualitative research, the company discovered that the Cruiser's summer is all about "Bro-ments." He gets together with more friends, more often, during the summer. The Cruiser values impromptu, memorable experiences that are the outcome of ingenuity and inventive social occasions. In other words, he likes spending time with his buddies, telling jokes, and not acting his age—all while drinking beer. This is basic male bonding stuff termed "Bro-ments."

The Big Idea

Bro-ments in a Box

Questions

1. In order to give the Cruiser an incentive that appealed to his fun-loving ingenuity and inventiveness, every time he bought a pack of Keystone Light, he got a completely self-contained Cornhole game. The Cruiser had to punch out the perforated hole designed into the box and use his crushed empty cans of Keystone Light as "bags" during hours of summer party and sport Bro-ments with his buddies. The company named this fun activity "CANHOLE." How would this promotion help achieve any of the company's objectives?
2. How can Cruisers use Canhole to connect with others on the Internet and social networks? How can the company encourage the Cruisers to do so? How does Maslow's Hierarchy of needs applicable to this situation?
3. Apply the concept of product involvement to the Canhole promotion and the second objective.
4. Suggest "cross merchandising" opportunities for Canhole. That is, getting marketers of products that Cruisers might consume during Canhole games to participate in the promotion. Explain your choices.
5. List and discuss three likely personality traits of the Cruiser.
6. Develop a psychographic profile of the Cruiser.
7. Looking at the PRIZM groups' descriptions online, select three segments that are likely to include a large number of Cruisers. Explain your choices.

Source: Effie Worldwide, Effie Showcase Winners. Reprinted by permission. Keystone Light is a 2012 Silver Effie Winner. For information on Effie's programs for students, visit the Collegiate Effies at www.effie.org

10

The Family and Its Social Standing

Learning Objectives

1. To understand the family as a consumer socialization agent.
2. To understand family decision-making and its members' consumption-related roles.
3. To understand the role of the family life cycle in market segmentation and targeting.
4. To understand the consumption patterns of nontraditional families and non-family households.
5. To understand the impact of social stratification on consumer behavior.
6. To understand how to measure social class and segment consumers accordingly.

THIS CHAPTER describes two **reference groups** that have a powerful impact on consumer behavior: Family and social class. A **family** is defined as two or more persons related by blood, marriage, or adoption residing together. In Western societies, there are three types of families: Married couples, nuclear families, and extended families. A married couple and one or more children constitute a **nuclear family**. The nuclear family, together with at least one grandparent or other relation living within the household, is called an **extended family**.

The **family life cycle** is a composite variable that combines marital status, size of family, age of family members (focusing on the age of the oldest or youngest child), and employment status of the head of household, and then classifies the family into a "typical" stage. The four ads in Figure 10.1 feature Toyota models catering to different types of families. The Toyota Auris hatchback model is a sporty car. It features a "diffuser," with reflectors on each side, which gives it a stylish look. The Yaris subcompact is promoted as a car on which one can get a "great deal." The Verso is a seven-seater family car featuring elegant style and comfort. The Avensis is available as a sedan or wagon and features a refined design and touch-screen multimedia.

Each car model appeals to a different stage of the family life cycle. The sporty Auris is for bachelors or newly married couples who have no children and want to enjoy their new life together. As evident in the ad for the Yaris, a child is on the way. The young couple probably feels anxious about their finances (maybe because the mother has quit her job) and are therefore seeking a car at a reasonable price. Next, the couple has two young kids and, presumably, more financial resources (e.g., the father had advanced in his career and the mother might have gone back to work) and are likely to purchase the Verso—a stylish family car. Moving forward, the kids are growing up and thus (as with all young kids) must be in front of a screen at all times. Assuming that

Source: Andreas Ackerup, Saarti Sweden

(a) Bachelors or Honeymooners: Toyota Auris

(b) Newlyweds: Toyota Yaris

(c) Married with Small Children: Toyota Verso

(d) Large Family: Toyota Avensis

FIGURE 10.1 Toyota's Models Target Different Stages of the Family Life Cycle

the couple's disposable income went up (e.g., dual income), it's time for the Avensis, with its stylish design and built-in multimedia gear.

The first part of this chapter describes the influence of the family on its members' development as consumers, as well as how the family functions as a consumption unit and the dynamics of family decision-making. We explore households that fit into the family life cycle, as well as atypical and non-family living situations.

Each household, whether family or non-family, belongs to a social class. **Social class** is the division of members of a society into a hierarchy of distinct status classes, in which members of a class have relatively the same status and members of the other classes have either more or less status. The second part of this chapter examines the demographics and consumption patterns of America's social classes. It describes how to measure social class and segment and target consumers according to social standing. The chapter concludes with examples of how social-class membership affects consumption habits, tastes, and values.

Learning Objective

1 To understand the family as a consumer socialization agent.

The Family as a Socialization Agent

Socialization refers to the process of teaching people behave in a way that is acceptable to their society. In the context of marketing, the most important role of the family is the socialization of family members, ranging from young children to adults. This process includes

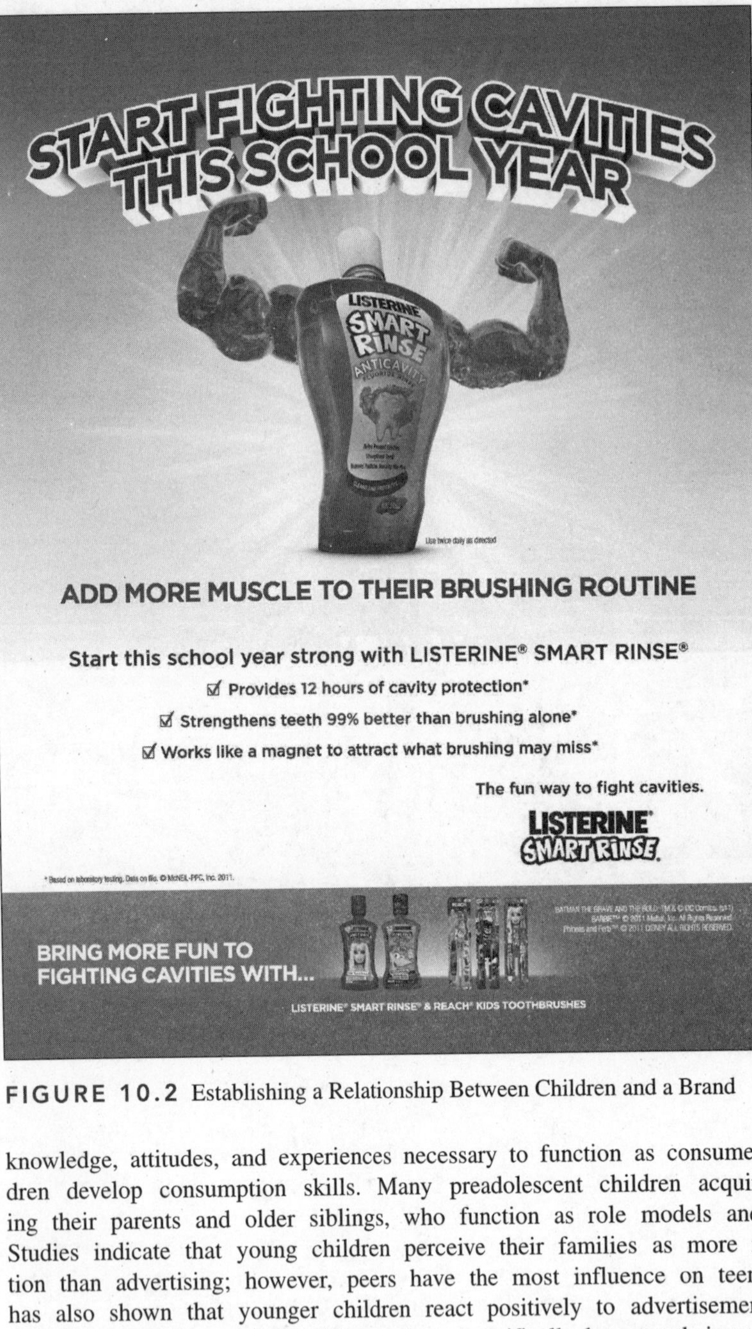

Source: LISTERINE® is a registered trademark of Johnson & Johnson. Used with permission

FIGURE 10.2 Establishing a Relationship Between Children and a Brand

imparting to children the basic values and modes of behavior consistent with their culture, including moral principles, interpersonal skills, dress and grooming standards, appropriate manners and speech, and the selection of suitable educational and occupational or career goals.

Parental socialization responsibilities have been expanding because it has become increasingly harder for young adults to find good jobs. Parents thus feel that their children must be ahead of others from a very young age—a competitive pressure that often results in demanding daily schedules for many children (e.g., daily preschool classes, after-school classes, play dates, weekend enrichment, and sports and arts programs). Some have argued that the barrage of structured activities and constant exposure to mass media and online social networks provide children with very little time to explore their own creativity.[1] Nevertheless, the socialization of young children provides marketers with opportunities to establish relationships between children and brands very early in the children's lives. Very often, such connections extend into a person's adolescence, teenage years, and adulthood. The ad for Listerine Smart Rinse in Figure 10.2 is an example of a marketer's initiative to establish a bond between a brand and very young children.

The aspect of childhood socialization that is particularly relevant to the study of consumer behavior is **consumer socialization**, which is defined as the process by which children acquire the skills, knowledge, attitudes, and experiences necessary to function as consumers. Numerous studies have researched how children develop consumption skills. Many preadolescent children acquire their consumer behavior norms by observing their parents and older siblings, who function as role models and provide cues for learning consumption skills. Studies indicate that young children perceive their families as more reliable sources of information about consumption than advertising; however, peers have the most influence on teenagers' and adolescents' consumption.[2] Research has also shown that younger children react positively to advertisements employing spokespersons featured in parental roles, whereas teens often like products specifically because their parents disapprove of their purchases.[3] Figure 10.3 illustrates the sources that influence children's socialization over time and indicates that socialization is a two-way process. The two-directional arrows indicate that a young person is both socialized and influences those who are doing the socializing.

A **socialization agent** is a person or organization involved in the socialization process "because of frequency of contact with the individual and control over the rewards and punishments given to the individual."[4] Mothers are generally considered to be stronger consumer socialization agents than their husbands, because they tend to be more involved with their children, and are more likely to mediate their children's exposure to commercial messages. Additionally, they provide instruction in the skills needed by consumers, and serve as gatekeepers to information and influence by regulating the money that their offspring can spend. When investigating how mothers interact and relate to marketplace influences, a recent study found six distinct segments

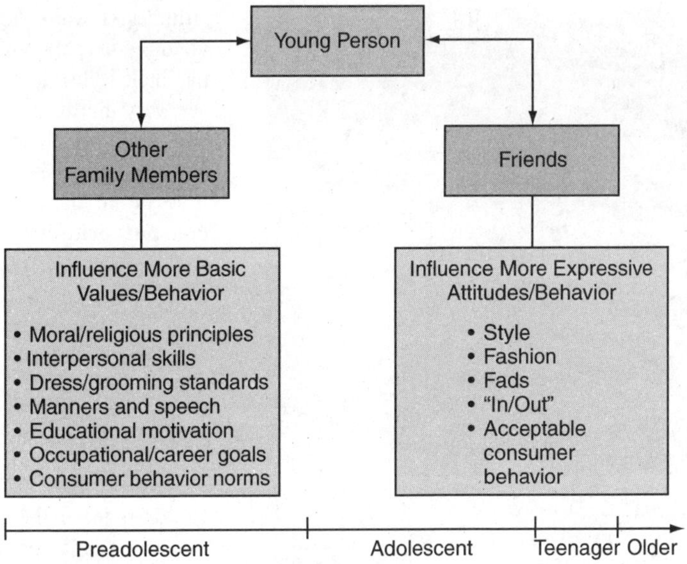

FIGURE 10.3 Socialization Sources

of mothers—three with a positive attitude toward marketing (marketing receptive) and three with a negative attitude (marketing resistant) The Indian context provides one of the best examples of marketers using the stereotype of the "mother/wife" in creating and nurturing brand associations. Despite changes in the environment and lifestyles in the last two decades, the "mother" in an Indian family continues to inspire brand associations across categories and socioeconomic classes. The mother is instrumental as a socialization agent in developing the tastes and preferences of children and this aspect can even have intergenerational impact. Normally, married daughters tend to follow rituals that their mothers have followed and this aspect of the culture provides scope for brands to use intergenerational marketing. For example, Surf or Horlicks are brands that have been a part of the Indian markets for decades, and with appropriate strategies marketers will be able to forge the "mother-daughter" linkages that may hold good for the second generation. Clinic Plus is an interesting example of the link being taken to contemporary dimensions in recent times and the mother–daughter/son association has been a part of the brand imagery for the last several years. Brands that have used these linkages in the Indian context are Vicks, Horlicks, Complan, and Bournvita (milk additives), Meera shampoo, Lifebuoy handwash, Dettol (both antiseptic lotion and floor cleaners—family association in the latter), Knorr soups, Johnson & Johnson baby care products, Pears soap, Kent water filter (with celebrity), and Pepsodent toothpaste. The lady of the house is also seen to provide care and comfort to her husband/family in many advertisements, including Saffola edible oil, Qaker Oats, Wheel detergent, and Kellogg's cornflakes.

Early socialization aspects that involve brands can also provide several opportunities for marketers. Someone who had grown up with Gems (chocolate from Cadbury) will appreciate the brand's communication that one is never too old to enjoy the brand. The market for nostalgia, too, can make use of family socialization. For example, several adults in the age group of 50–60 may have grown up with brands like Lux, Iodex, Dettol, and Titan watches during their twenties or even earlier. How can these brands trigger a sense of nostalgia among these consumer segments is an interesting proposition.

The ad for Mott's juice in Figure 10.4 depicts a mother as a socialization agent who is teaching her children that juices with less sugar are healthier. Researchers identified distinct socialization styles among mothers, based on mothers' attitudes toward marketing, which are described in Table 10.1.[5]

There is no universal model of how children develop their consumption skills; learn to understand the role of advertising in the formation of buying preferences; and master the relationship between monetary resources, value, and limits on buying. Next, we describe three aspects of consumer socialization.

Parental Styles and Consumer Socialization

Several decades ago, sociologists began to study the impact of parental styles on children's development, and later on marketers applied those findings to consumer socialization. Figure 10.5 features a classification of parental stules along two dimensions: *permissive* versus *restrictive* and *very nurturing* versus *non-nurturing*. The table identifies four parental styles and lists their respective

Source: Dr. Pepper Snapple Company

FIGURE 10.4 Socialization Agent

attitudes toward advertising, consumption, and yielding to children's buying requests. The four parental styles include: **indulgent parents**, who are very nurturing and highly permissive during consumer socialization; **neglecting parents**, who are very permissive, but provide their children with little or no nurturing during consumer socialization; **authoritative parents**, who are very nurturing and also very restrictive with respect to consumer socialization; and lastly, **authoritarian parents**, who are very restrictive and not nurturing during consumer socialization.

Consumer Socialization Is Learning

Children learn the importance of possessions at an early age, as demonstrated by a child seeing a commercial for a doll or action figure on television, pointing to the screen, and shouting "I want that!" A study conducted with school-aged children in Minnesota found that materialism increases from middle childhood (ages 8–9) to early adolescence (ages 12–13), and then declines from early to late adolescence (ages 16–18). The research also found an inverse relationship between self-esteem and materialism in children and adolescents (i.e., children with high self-esteem are more likely to express lower levels of materialism, and vice versa).[6] Furthermore, the study noted that rather than blaming the media for the materialism exhibited by children and adolescents, finding ways to increase their self-esteem is a more positive approach. Another study found that adolescents use ridicule as a mechanism to exchange

TABLE 10.1 Mothers' Socialization-related Attitudes

MARKETING RECEPTIVE	MARKETING RESISTANT
The Balancer:	The Protector:
Married and has a career. Multitasks and teaches her children how to become good consumers. Lets children learn from experience and make buying mistakes.	Highest income and education among all the segments. Rational and teaches her children to shop and spend responsibly. Resents the influence of the media on her children.
The Nurturer:	The Struggler:
Focused on her family and often sacrifices her own desires to meet the wants of her children. Trusts well-known companies and brands.	Does not have the money to indulge her children's requests. Very price- and value-conscious shopper. Views her life negatively.
The Diva:	The Stoic:
Self-focused and seeks acceptance and attention from others; is a conspicuous consumer. Views her children as a part of her image, and often gives in to children's requests to make her life easier.	Culturally and socially isolated. Views herself as a caretaker and homemaker. Loves her children but feels emotionally distanced from them. Deliberates regarding purchases.

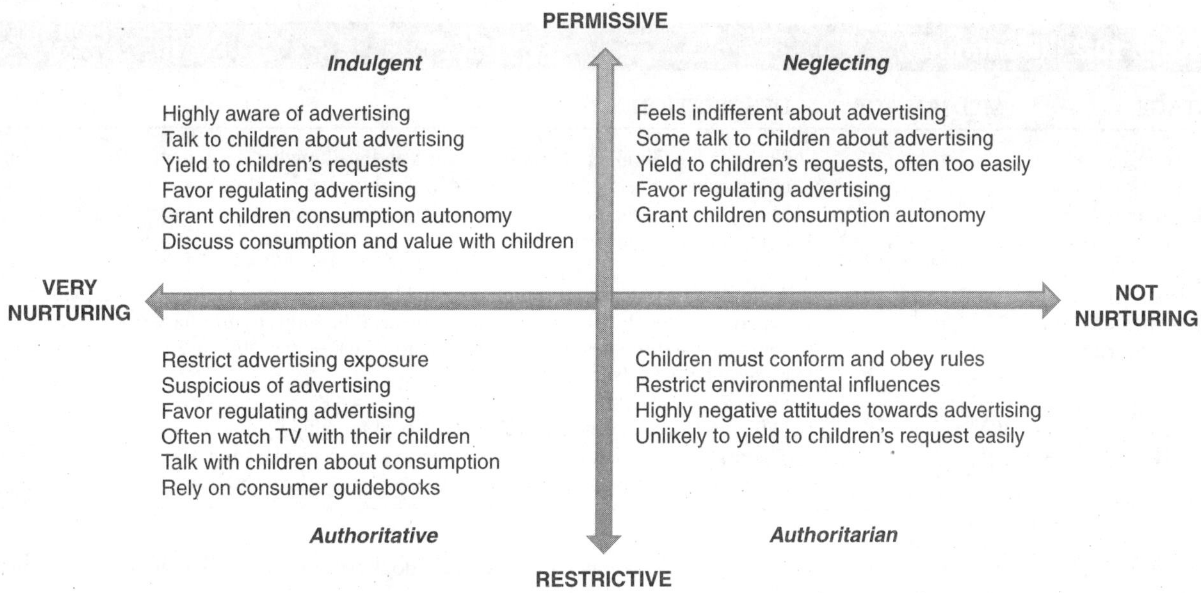

FIGURE 10.5 Parental Styles and Consumer Socialization

information about what should and should not be consumed and valued; ridicule is also a form of ostracizing peers who shop unlike most do.[7] A Canadian study of college students (with the majority being full-time students, and 85% living at home with parents) indicated that older college students were influenced by their parents, and less influenced by their peers and media.[8] The study also found that older college students were more competent consumers than their younger counterparts.

The model in Table 10.2 details stages that children go through in learning to function as consumers, and identifies their sources of information at each stage.

Adult and Intergenerational Consumer Socialization

The socialization process is ongoing, beginning in early childhood and extending throughout a person's life. After childhood, as teenagers and adolescents, young consumers continue learning about consumption and many become skeptical about some aspects of marketing. One study found that more socially affluent adolescents were less skeptical of advertising than their less affluent peers. Lower socioeconomic status adolescents, having less money than their wealthier peers, were more critical of advertising claims. Additionally, the study found that Internet usage was negatively related to skepticism, possibly because Internet surfers can skip ads and only visit websites that interest them.[9]

When newly married people establish their own households, adjusting to consuming as a couple is the continuation of socialization. Similarly, the adjustment of a soon-to-be-retired couple, perhaps moving to a warmer climate, is also part of ongoing socialization. Even a family that is welcoming a pet into its home faces the challenge of socializing the pet so that it fits into the family environment. Research found that pet owners treat their pets as full-fledged family members. For instance, 58% of

TABLE 10.2 Children's Development as Consumers

STAGE	MEDIAN AGE	DESCRIPTION
Shopping with parents and observing	12 to 15 months	Children notice all the items that are fun to eat and play with and begin to recall specific ones. They learn how shopping satisfies needs. Parents may buy some items to reward children for good behavior.
Making requests while shopping with parents	2 years	By age 2, children begin to connect advertising with items in the stores and delight parents with their cognitive development. They request items–mostly foods and toys–by pointing. Children also begin to pay more attention to advertising and some insist on watching more TV.

(Continued)

TABLE 10.2 (Continued)

STAGE	MEDIAN AGE	DESCRIPTION
Selecting with permission while shopping with parents	3 1/2 years	Children are climbing off shopping carts and walking besides parents. They recognize most brands of cereal, snacks, ice cream and frozen deserts and know their locations. Many have favorite brands and even stores, and parents begin to select brands and items that their children prefer.
Independent purchases while shopping with parent	5 1/2 years	A child's first independent purchase is likely to be in a supermarket, convenience or department store. Children begin to understand the limits of monetary resources and some may feel frustrated when denied items because they are too expensive or do not represent good value.
Shopping independently	8 years	Parents gradually, and often reluctantly, begin to allow children to go to stores alone. The first independent trip is likely to be to a convenience store. Children discover the wonders of shopping and having to decide among many choices.

those surveyed indicated that they have sent or received a holiday card from their dogs or cats, and 78% regularly talked in different voices ("I wuv you") to their pets and referred to them as family members.[10]

Many product preferences and brand loyalties are transferred from one generation to another, sometimes across three or four generations.[11] For instance, brand preferences for products such as peanut butter, mayonnaise, ketchup, coffee, and canned soup are frequently passed on from one generation to another. In some families—like Asian households—grandparents not only play an important role in teaching younger members consumption-related skills, but also participate in all major consumption decisions. Very often, Asian grandparents live with their children and grandchildren.

Box 10.1 Brands and the Reversal of Intergenerational Influence

Even a decade back quite a few consumers may have preferred Colgate or Surf or Red Label, primarily because these brands had been introduced to them by their parents. Intergenerational loyalty is worth exploring especially in a collectivist (collectivism as a dominant cultural dimension) country like India.

Changing lifestyles and fragmented preferences within the family may reverse the intergenerational influence. Godrej's Expert advanced hair dye is an example. The ad showed youngsters convincing their mother about using the brand and the youngsters get excited after seeing the 'face-lift' given to their mother by the brand. Brands may use the younger generation in the family to influence the older generation to try out categories that were not within the mindset of the latter.

The Family's Supportive Roles

The family has several supportive functions that are part of the socialization process and consumer behavior. These include economic well-being, emotional support, and suitable family lifestyles.

Economic Well-being

The most important economic function of the family is to provide financial resources to its members and allocate its income in a way that supports all members adequately. The data in Table 10.3 show how an "average" U.S. family spent its money over one year. The largest expenditures were on housing, transportation, food at home, pension and social security, health care, food away from home, and entertainment.[12]

Emotional Support

A core function of the family is providing its members with love, affection, and intimacy. When most women had no jobs outside the home, children received most of their emotional support from their mothers. However, as more and more women joined the labor

TABLE 10.3 How the "Average" Family Spends Its Money

EXPENDITURE CATEGORY	DOLLARS	PERCENT
Food at home	3,753	8.1
Food away from home	2,619	5.6
Alcoholic beverages	435	0.1
Housing	16,895	36.3
Apparel and services	1,725	3.7
Transportation	7,658	16.5
Health care	3,126	6.7
Entertainment	2,693	5.8
Reading	110	0.2
Tobacco products	380	0.7
Life and other personal insurance	309	0.8
Pensions and social security	5,471	11.7
Miscellaneous	1,320	2.8
Total of above	46,494	

Source: U.S. Census Bureau, "Average Annual Expenditures of All Consumer Units by Selected Major Types of Expenditures: 1990 to 2009,"Statistical Abstract of the United States: 2012, Table 684. http://www.census.gov/comendia/statab/2012/1250684.pdt. Accessed 6/20/2012

force—with some pursuing more demanding and lucrative careers than their husbands—men have played an increasingly important role in rearing children. If the family cannot provide adequate assistance when it is needed, it may turn to a counselor, psychologist, or other professionals. In most communities, there are educational and psychological centers designed to assist parents who want to help their children improve their learning and communication skills or better adjust to their environments. The Lever soap ad in Figure 10.6 shows how the family provides emotional support.

Suitable Family Lifestyles

What people view as a "suitable" lifestyle reflects their experiences while growing up. Their parents' priorities regarding learning and education, recreational activities, hobbies, setting of career goals, media exposure, and shopping habits are all part of the lifestyle that children imitate, at least to some degree, when they set up their own households. Changing family lifestyles are greatly influencing consumption patterns. For example, the growth of the demand for convenience foods and rising popularity of fast and takeout foods are the result of career moms having little if any time for household chores. With both spouses working, many parents are increasingly aware of the importance of spending quality time with their children.

Learning Objective

2 To understand family decision-making and its members' consumption-related roles.

Family Decision-making and Consumption-related Roles

Marketers recognize that families operate as units in terms of consumption behavior, and many researchers have studied the dynamics of family decision-making. Specifically, marketers focus on husband–wife decision-making, the relative influence each family member has regarding consumption, children's role in family decision-making, and the multiple roles that family members may assume regarding the purchase, use, and maintenance of their homes, products and services.

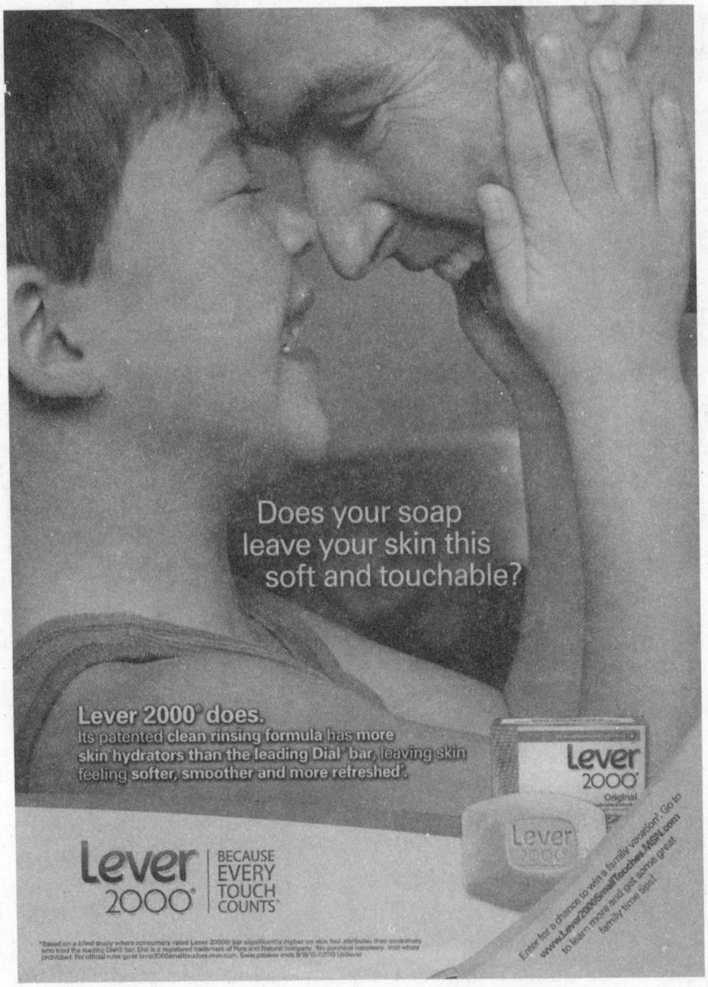

Source: Unilever

FIGURE 10.6 The Family Provides Emotional Support

Husband–Wife Decision-making

Marketers have studied each spouse's relative influence in consumption and identified four patterns of husband–wife decision-making:

1. **Husband-dominated decisions** are those where the husband's influence is greater than the wife's.
2. **Wife-dominated decisions** are those where the wife's influence is greater than the husband's..
3. **Joint decisions** are those where the husband's and wife's influences are equal.
4. **Autonomic decisions** are those where either the husband or the wife is the primary or only decision maker.

The relative influence of a husband and wife on a particular consumer decision depends mainly on the product or service category. For instance, during the 1950s, the purchase of a new automobile was strongly husband-dominated, whereas food and financial banking decisions were often wife-dominated, but these patterns are no longer the case. Some studies indicate that women influenced 85% of all decisions regarding car purchases and bought about 45% of all vehicles sold in the U.S. independently. More than half of female car buyers sought advice from expert sources before buying a new car, spent more time in the purchasing process than men (17 weeks versus 15), and, on average, visited three dealerships, seeking both the best price and polite treatment.[13]

Carmakers and automobile dealers have studied the specific needs of women drivers. For example, GM pays particular attention to details in trim, fabric, colors, compartments, and shapes and positioning of controls. In addition, storage is a big deal to women buyers, whether it's room for groceries, handbags, kids' toys, foldable seats, or car booster seats. Many car manufacturers have considered women's heights in the design of seating and steering columns, as well as designing door handles that women drivers with long fingernails can grab easily. Apparently, both men and women like "aggressive and elegant" lines in the form of "smoothness from one end to the other with no rough edges and a tight, flush design." Like men, women want performance and design, but they also want more features. Examples of features designed with women in mind include inside door handles that are individually illuminated with dim lights, concave consoles with attractive buttons and digital information displays, and entertainment system screens that can be raised and lowered by the push of a button.[14]

Traditionally, women have controlled their families' day-to-day household spending, but men were in charge of major decisions on banking and financial planning. However, one study indicated that British women are now more likely than their husbands to choose banks and make provisions for future savings and spending. The study showed that 91% of households where women were in charge of financial planning had significant savings, but only 82% of households had such savings when men had that responsibility. This was especially true among younger couples; in households with males over the age of 45, men tended to be in charge of money matters. The study predicted that a majority of women of all ages would be in charge of most households' financial decision by 2020. Furthermore, among couples under the age of 45, women were more likely than men to choose the family's bank (52% of households), take control of making detailed future plans for savings (52%), and pay day-to-day bills and keep track of spending (54%). Apparently, women are better savers; the results showed that 37% of single men had no savings, compared to 30% of single women. Greater control of families' finances by women will increase households' savings, as women tend to have a longer-term orientation to saving and also be more cautious savers in selecting where to hold and invest savings. This might also mean that mortgage repayments and consumer spending could become less vulnerable to turmoils in employment or financial markets in the future.[15]

Husband–wife decision-making is related to cultural influence. Research comparing husband–wife decision-making in the People's Republic of China and in the United States revealed that, among Chinese couples, there were substantially fewer joint decisions and more husband-dominated decisions for many household purchases than among American spouses.[16] However, when comparing urban and rural Chinese households, the research showed that in large cities, such as Beijing, married couples were more likely than rural couples to share equally in purchase decisions. Another study compared family decision-making among American and Singaporean families; that study discovered that joint decision-making was characteristic of American families, whereas Singaporean families' decisions were often husband dominant.[17]

Children's Influence on Family Decision-making

Over the past several decades, children have played a more active role in what the family buys, as well as in the family decision-making process. Children's growing influence is the result of families having fewer children (which increases the influence of each child), the existence of more dual-income couples who can afford to permit their children to make a greater number of the choices, and encouragement by the media to allow children to "express themselves." In addition, single-parent households often push their children toward household participation and self-reliance. For example, kids in supermarkets make an average of 15 requests, of which about half are typically granted.[18]

One study, which included interviews with both parents and their children, focused on the influence of children during family decisions regarding vacations. The researchers pointed out that although children believed that they had a large degree of influence on vacation-related decisions, their parents viewed the children's influence as merely moderate.[19] Another notable study investigated the tactics that children use when they want their parents to buy them something or to "get their way" during family decisions. The study identified the following tactics that children typically use:

1. ***Pressure:*** The child demands, threatens, and tries to intimidate the parents.
2. ***Exchange:*** The child promises something (e.g., to "be good" or clean his room) in exchange.
3. ***Rational:*** The child uses a logical arguments and factual evidence.
4. ***Consultation:*** The child seeks parents' involvement in the decision.
5. ***Ingratiation:*** The child tries to get the parent in a good mood first and then make the request.[20]

One study identified a group termed "teen Internet mavens"—teenagers who spend considerable time on the Internet and are very proficient in searching for information and responding to requests from others. The study showed that the mavens believed that they were more influential in researching and evaluating family purchases than their parents, which the parents confirmed.[21]

Children Are Three Markets

An expert on marketing to children pointed out that children should be divided into three separate markets, as described in Table 10.4. Many marketers can apply this framework to targeting different segments of the children's market. For example, when viewing children as influencers, marketers of food products and vacations should depict kids' involvement in these decisions, but must do so in a subtle way and not feature children pressuring their parents to buy products. In addition, recognizing that children form brand preferences early, marketers should show how thankful kids are when their parents buy certain brands.

TABLE 10.4 Children as Three Markets

ROLE	DESCRIPTION	EXAMPLES
Children as influencers	Children make requests when accompanying parents on shopping trips and also at home.	Items for themselves (toys, electronics, clothing). Items for homes (furniture, food and beverage preferences). Services for the entire family (vacations, restaurants).
Children as a primary market	Children who shop independently while shopping with their parents or buy things with their own money.	The most commonly purchased products are snacks/sweets, toys, games, clothes, movies, sport events, concerts and video games.
Children as future consumers	Children start contemplating future purchases: "When I grow up I will buy myself . . ."	The future consumers are fully aware of brands, and marketers should focus on building relationships with them.

Measuring Family Decision-making

Measuring family decision-making is complex, because family members may not agree with each other's perspective about their relative influence during purchase decisions, which also precludes interviewing them together. Nevertheless, Table 10.5 features an instrument designed to measure family decision-making.

TABLE 10.5 Measure of Family Decision-making Regarding Vacations

1. About your family and household:
   Two spouses _____
   One spouse or parent _____ Mother _____ Father
   Number of children 12 years old or younger _____
   Do any other adults live in your household? Please specify _____
2. How does your family make vacation-related decisions? The questionnaire below lists the typical decisions that must be made and we ask you to indicate how much influence each member(s) of your family has regarding each one. For example, if the wife is the most influential party in deciding on how to travel to the vacation's destination (e.g., fly or drive), please put a checkmark in the column entitled "wife" and the row entitled "most influential" next to "how to get to the destination" (listed in the first column on the left). Leave any boxes that are not applicable blank (e.g., the household includes no teenagers).

DECISIONS	DEGREE OF INFLUENCE	HUSBAND	WIFE	CHILDREN 12 YEARS OLD OR YOUNGER	TEENAGERS
Whether to go on vacation or not	Most influential				
	Very influential				
	Somewhat influential				
	Least influential				
	No influence at all				
How much to spend on the vacation	Most influential				
	Very influential				
	Somewhat influential				
	Least influential				
	No influence at all				
When to go on vacation	Most influential				
	Very influential				
	Somewhat influential				
	Least influential				
	No influence at all				
Type of vacation (e.g., Disney, national parks, biking, camping)	Most influential				
	Very influential				
	Somewhat influential				

(Continued)

TABLE 10.5 (Continued)

DECISIONS	DEGREE OF INFLUENCE	HUSBAND	WIFE	CHILDREN 12 YEARS OLD OR YOUNGER	TEENAGERS
	Least influential				
	No influence at all				
Destination(s)	Most influential				
	Very influential				
	Somewhat influential				
	Least influential				
	No influence at all				
How to get to the destination (e.g., drive or fly)	Most influential				
	Very influential				
	Somewhat influential				
	Least influential				
	No influence at all				

TABLE 10.6 Family Members' Consumption-related Roles

ROLE	DESCRIPTION
Influencers	Family member(s) who provide information to other members about a product or service.
Gatekeepers	Family member(s) who control the flow of information about products and services into the family.
Deciders	Family member(s) with the power to decide which product to buy and where.
Buyers	Family member(s) who make the actual purchase of a particular product or service
Preparers	Family member(s) who transform the product into a form suitable for consumption by other family members.
Users	Family member(s) who use the service or consume the product.
Maintainers	Family member(s) who service or repair the product so that it continues to function well.
Disposers	Family member(s) who initiate or carry out the disposition of a product or the discontinuation of the service.

Family Members' Roles

Table 10.6 shows another perspective on family decision-making which consists of identifying the roles that members play in buying decisions. For example, many parents are *gatekeepers*, who control the information that reaches the family's children by using the parental control features available on TVs, computers, and other communication devices. As described earlier, *indulgent* and *authoritative* parents are attentive gatekeepers. When targeting these parents, electronics makers should emphasize their products' sophisticated information-control features. Companies selling SUVs should recognize that children might be *influencers* in the family's purchase of a new model, although they are neither the *deciders* nor *buyers* of family cars. Children from dual-income households are often the *deciders*, *buyers*, and *preparers* of foods, so marketers of cuisine goods must study the roles of children in this area of the family's consumption. For example, children should be able to open packaging safely and easily, and understand measurement units and preparation instructions. Because children—in the role of *maintainers*—often perform housekeeping chores by themselves, makers of, say, vacuum cleaners should observe how children use their products and make sure that kids can do so safely.

Learning Objective

3 To understand the role of the family life cycle in market segmentation and targeting.

The Family Life Cycle

The **family life cycle** represents the life stages of a typical family. It is a composite variable that combines marital status, size of family, age of family members (focusing on the age of the oldest or youngest child), and employment status of the head of household, and then classifies the family into a "typical" stage. The ages of the parents and the relative amount of disposable income are inferred from the family's stage in the cycle. As illustrated in this chapter's opening, Toyota's car models were designed with the family life cycle in mind. Although it is no longer typical of American families, because of the emergence of non-family households and families that cannot be placed into a "typical" phase, the family life cycle remains a widely used form of segmentation, and is also used to analyze the consumption of households that do not fit neatly into it.

The family life cycle starts with bachelorhood and then moves on to marriage (and the creation of the family unit). Marriage usually leads to the growth of the family when children arrive, and later on to family contraction, as grown children leave the household. The cycle ends with the dissolution of the family unit due to the death of one spouse. The stages of the family life cycle are featured in the following sections.

Bachelorhood

The **bachelorhood** stage refers to young single men and women, mostly college educated, who have incomes that allow them to leave home and establish their own households. Increasingly, though, even employed college graduates continue to live at home and save toward setting up their own homes. Single persons spend considerable amounts on clothing, cars, and travel and entertainment. Marketers should differentiate between singles who live at home (with their parents) and those who have left it. The ads in Figures 10.7 and 10.8 target single and affluent women, who can afford expensive furniture and vacations.

Source: Ligne Roset

FIGURE 10.7 Targeting Women in the Bachelorhood Stage: High-Priced Furniture

Source: RockResorts, LLC.

FIGURE 10.8 Targeting Women in the Bachelorhood Stage: Exclusive Vacations

Honeymooners

The **honeymooners** stage refers to young and newly married couples. Educated, engaged couples have a combined discretionary income. If both establish career paths, their incomes grow steadily. A spouse going back to graduate school usually calls for curtailing spending and a more moderate lifestyle. People with considerable discretionary incomes are prime targeting prospects. Most couples overspend on their weddings (see the ad in Figure 10.9). Afterward, they are in the market for home furnishings, travel, and financial planning services. Because many young husbands and wives both work, these couples often have a combined income that permits them to purchase more indulgent possessions, as well as save and invest money.

Honeymooners have considerable start-up expenses when establishing a new home. They must find a place to live, buy furniture, and decorate and set up their households. They are the prime targets of marketers in many sectors, and of advisory magazines (e.g., Homes and Gardens), as well as decorators, designers, architects, and financial planners.

Parenthood

The **parenthood** stage designates married couples with at least one child living at home. This is the longest stage of the family life cycle. The ad for toys that help children's cognitive development in Figure 10.10 targets young parents (the ads in Figures 10.4 and 10.6 do the same).

Source: Bed, Bath & Beyond

FIGURE 10.9 Targeting Honeymooners

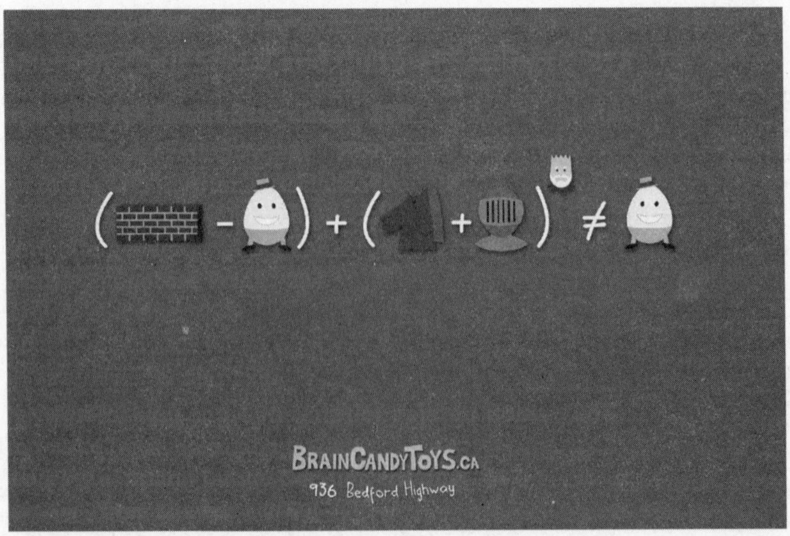

Source: Ads created by Revolve, CA for Brain Candy Toys, CA

FIGURE 10.10 Targeting Young Parents

Parenthood (also known as the "full-nest" stage) usually extends over more than a twenty-year period. Because of its long duration, this stage can be divided into shorter phases. The *preschool phase*, *elementary school phase*, *high school phase*, and *college phase*. Throughout these parenthood phases, the interrelationships of family members and the structure of the family gradually change. Furthermore, the financial resources of the family change significantly, as one (or both) parents progress in their careers and as child rearing and educational responsibilities gradually increase and then decrease as children become self-supporting.

Many magazines target parents and children of different ages, either together or separately. For example, there are many special-interest publications, such as Humpty Dumpty, designed for the young child who is just learning to read; Scholastic Magazine, for the elementary school pupil; Boy's Life, for young boys; and American Girl, Seventeen, and Glamour for teen and young adult girls interested in fashion. In addition, a relatively new magazine, Cookie, is targeting the parents in the more than 22 million U.S. homes with annual incomes in excess of $75,000 and children under 10 years of age.[22]

Post-parenthood

The **post-parenthood** stage refers to older married couples with no children living at home. Because parenthood extends over many years, the start of this stage (also known as "empty nest") is traumatic for some parents and liberating for others. For many parents, this stage represents the opportunity to do all the things they could not do or afford while their children lived home or went to college.

During this stage, most married couples are financially secure and have a lot of leisure time. They travel more frequently, take extended vacations, and are likely to purchase a second home in a warmer climate. They have higher disposable incomes because of savings and investments, and they have fewer expenses (no mortgage or college tuition bills). They look forward to being involved grandparents. Therefore, families in the post-parenthood stage are an important market for luxury goods, new automobiles, expensive furniture, and vacations to faraway places. Chapter 12 discusses postretirement consumer behavior.

Box 10.2 Potential in the Indian Context-'Empty Nest' Stage of Family Life Stage

"Empty Nest" is a family stage during which both the husband and wife go through the aging process without their children being with them. Financially, they may be comfortable; they may have more of leisure time and may also like to travel or even continue to work. The present generation of post–sixty years adults (generally regarded as senior citizens) have longevity of life that has both positives and negatives.

While the positives are obvious, the negatives include lifestyle diseases, a large sum of money or insurance required to meet such problems, and more importantly, the reliable manpower support required for both the husband and wife as they age and slowly become dependent (while their children are away). Some of them may have no affordability limits to face problems and some of them may depend on their children. Such a situation opens up several opportunities for marketers. Serene is a brand that has opened up senior citizen homes in several cities. Apollo Hospitals has opened up an evening clinic in Bangalore so that children may be able to accompany their parents. Most importantly, the demand for reliable 'in-house' services (like nursing and electronic surveillance) may have a huge potential in future in India. Online services may even provide customized services with constant interaction with children who are placed abroad and can pay for the services. There is a definite need for a reliable and trustworthy brand in the Indian context as perceived risk of consumers opting out for such services is likely to be high.

Dissolution

The **dissolution** stage refers to the family with one surviving spouse. If the surviving spouse is in good health, is working or has adequate savings, and has supportive family and friends, the adjustment is easier. The surviving spouse (women live longer than men) often tends to follow a more economical lifestyle. Many surviving spouses seek each other out for companionship; others enter into second (or third and even fourth) marriages (Chapter 12 describes the characteristics of older consumers).

Summary of the Family Life Cycle

The traditional family life cycle concept details the types of products and services that a household or family might be most interested in at each stage. In addition, it is also possible to trace how the family life cycle concept affects a single product or service over time. As an example, a qualitative study conducted in Denmark indicates that family life cycle stage influences the experiences that consumers seek during their vacations. For example, less "traditional" vacations when single, such as backpacking through Europe, and more "traditional" vacations when married with a young child, such as a week at a Caribbean island hotel.[23]

Family and Its Social Setting in the Indian Context

Traditionally, the Indian family was a joint family consisting of the husband and wife, parents of the husband, and his relatives. Religious stories and cultural mythologies that was once a part of one's childhood is giving away to computer games and fun on the YouTube. The onset of nuclear families has had a major impact on the lifestyle of families in the Indian context.

There are three kinds of social setting that can be identified in the Indian context– family with the traditional homemaker, the family with a 'quasi-progressive' wife, and the family with the contemporary wife in a typical urban nuclear family in which both the husband and the wife are highly qualified professionals. The traditional wife takes care of the children and attempts to balance the demands of the children with the implicit norms provided by the husband. She may not have the final say on discretionary expenditure concerned with computer games and fun foods for children (in some families, the affordability for indulgence is also a consideration). Contrary to the popular perception that the traditional homemaker can only be found in homes that are economically not very highly placed, there are traditional homemakers in every socio-economic stream. The 'quasi-progressive' families have a wife where she has the freedom to decide on day-to-day needs of the family and also provide inputs on obtaining durable categories for the family. Several brands of snack foods, detergents, floor cleaners, and milk additives are advertised to influence such homemakers. The third category of urban contemporary homemakers are those who would like to have an equal say in most decisions concerning the household – that could range from biscuits for children to buying a new home. Several jewelry, cosmetic brands, and real estate brands target this segment of homemakers who can open up avenues for discretionary spending. Such expenditures associated with aspiration-based lifestyles may include vacationing, buying furniture, and cars. In all the three categories, the well- being of children are the top priority for the homemakers. The stereotype of a homemaker is strongly associated with an Indian homemaker, regardless of the category they belong. Such a concern was reflected in the ads of brands like Lifebuoy, Dettol, Bournvita, and Horlicks. A distinguishing characteristic of Indian families (across socio-economic spectrum) is the "Family" shopping associated with wedding occasions (apparel, jewelry and furniture categories are examples). The family as well as other members of the extended family (close relatives) will join together and enjoy the shopping. Several Chennai-based retailers advertise in regional television channels to attract such segments of consumers.

Parents' interest in the choice of the best educational alternatives for their children is another contemporary area that has given rise to career counsellors and teaching institutes that prepare students for competitive entrance exams.

Learning Objective

4 To understand the consumption patterns of nontraditional families and non-family households.

Nontraditional Families and Non-family Households

When targeting segments that do not represent "typical" families or households, marketers must distinguish between two groups:

1. **Nontraditional families**, defined as families that do not readily fit into the family life cycle.
2. **Non-family households**, defined as living situations that are not legally defined as families (e.g., couples who live together but are not married).

The most common nontraditional family forms and non-family households are also described in Table 10.7. At one time, these forms of families and households were relatively rare and marketers ignored them. However, what is considered a "typical" family or household has changed considerably over time. For instance, traditional families represented 81% of all U.S. households in 1970, but only 66% in 2010. The number of households consisting of married couples with children under 18 decreased from 40% in 1970 to about 20% in 2010, and the number of "not married, no children" households (i.e., non-family households) rose from almost 19% in 1970 to 34% in 2010.[24] During this same time frame, the percentage of family households without a spouse present rose from 11% to almost 18%, and the number of people living alone grew from 17% in 1970 to almost 27% in 2010. Also, whereas in 1970, 65% of men and 60% of women age 18 and older were married, by 2010 these figures had declined to 53% of men and 50% of women.[25]

TABLE 10.7 Descriptions of Nontraditional Households

NONTRADITIONAL FAMILIES	
Childless couples	Many couples, especially those who delayed marrying in order to advance their careers at a young age, choose not to have children.
Couples who marry in their late 30s and later	Many career-oriented men and women may live together for years and, even if they get married eventually, are likely to have no more than one child.
Divorced single parents	More single-parent families because of high divorce rates.
"Nesters"—Children returning to their parents' homes	Young single-adult children who return home to avoid the expenses of living alone while establishing their careers. Divorced daughters or sons, sometimes with their children, return home to their parents. Frail elderly parents who move in with children. Newlyweds living with in-laws in order to save money before setting up their own households
NON-FAMILY HOUSEHOLDS	
Unmarried couples	People who choose to live together with or without children.
Single parents	Women (mostly) or man who choose to adopt children or have their own and raise them without the other biological parent.
Gay couples (married or not)	Several states allow gay marriages and many other recognize domestic partnerships. Many gay couples adopt or have their own children with heterosexuals, who may or may not be involved in rearing the children.

Source: Compiled from data at: U.S. Census Bureau, Census 2010 Summary File 1 counts shown in American Fact Finder. http://www.comsus.gov/prod/cen2010/briefs/c2010 br-14/ Accessed 6/21/12.

Figure 10.11 illustrates the significance of non-family household in the United States. As people get older, many more non-family households emerge, and, because of increased life expectancy, this segment has been growing and marketers must not ignore it. Figure 10.12 shows that, across age groups, there are significantly more women than men living in non-family households, and this ratio becomes even more pronounced as people age.[26]

Consumer Behavior of Nontraditional Families and Households

Several studies have focused on nontraditional families and non-family households. One study discovered that married couples make more purchase decisions separately, whereas cohabitating couples make their decisions together.[27] When

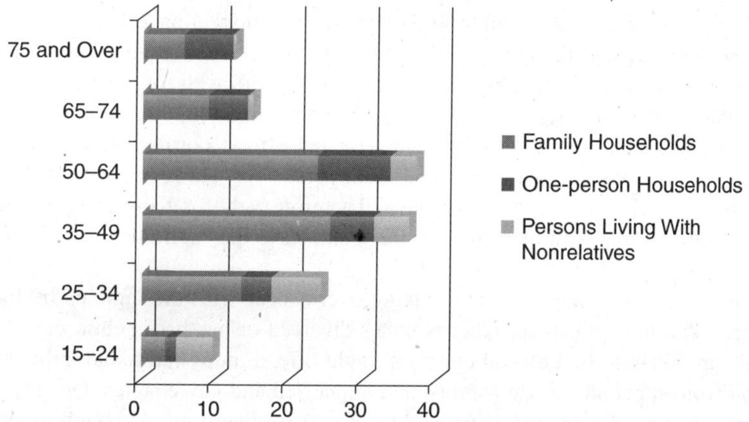

FIGURE 10.11 Number of Family and Non-family Households by Age (in millions)

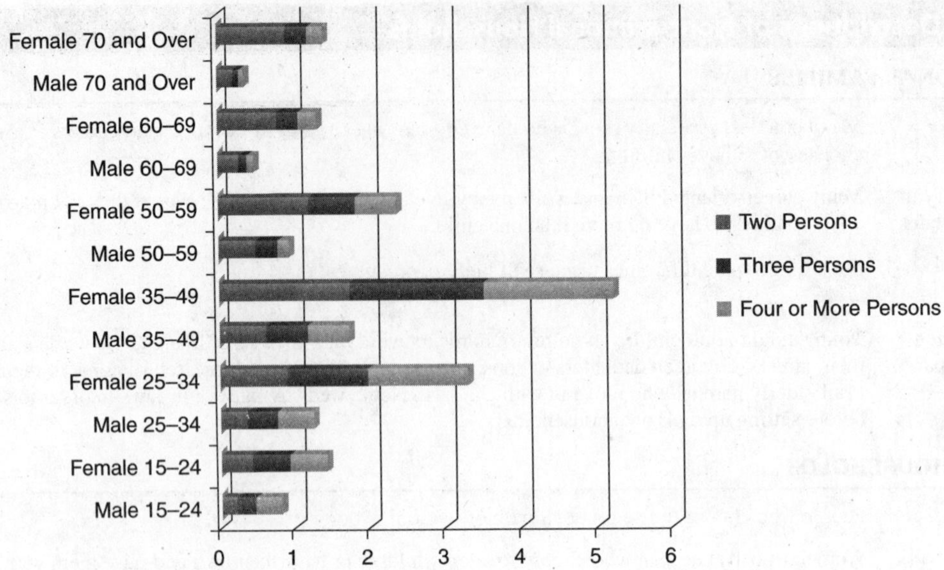

FIGURE 10.12 Number of Non-family Households: No Spouse Present by Gender, Age, and Household Size (in millions)

households undergo status changes (such as divorce, temporary retirement or job loss, a new person joining the household, or the death of a family member), their consumption patterns and preferences change. Sometimes, these households represent lucrative target markets. For example, divorce often requires that one (or both) of the former spouses find a new residence, buy new furniture, and perhaps find a job. Thus, divorced people are likely to contact real estate agents, visit furniture stores, and, sometimes, contact headhunters or seek professional career guidance. In addition, the residences and consumption patterns of newly divorced parents must accommodate the needs of visiting children, whose influence regarding buying may change following a divorce. One study pointed out that children in newly formed single-parent households have greater influence in the choice of the large items and holiday vacations than children from intact families.[28]

Advertising to Nontraditional Households

Targeting consumers like the ones featured in Table 10.7 represents a marketing dilemma. On the one hand, marketers of many products must now acknowledge the existence of segments that consist of nontraditional households. On the other hand, some members of traditional families might react negatively to portrayals of nontraditional households, because of religion and beliefs as to what is or is not "right." Marketers must come up with ads that appeal to both types of households without offending either one. For example, if advertisements for baby food portray only children being reared by young parents, unmarried, single, and older parents might not find them persuasive. However, some young parents rearing children might find ads showing single or divorced parents offensive. Therefore, ads for baby food should focus on the children's happiness, health, and warm relationship with those rearing them and leave the "definition" of the households shown up to the viewers.

An ad that shows two young professional women talking over a beer with the tagline "he likes my kid and he drinks brand X," implies, of course, that the woman speaking is either divorced or has had a child out of wedlock. Although many young and "with it" people are likely to find this ad clever, it might offend more traditional individuals. Over the years, more and more ads have shown divorced people, single parents, and unmarried and gay couples. On several occasions, conservative groups have publicly criticized such ads and even boycotted the products advertised. Although marketers can no longer ignore lucrative market segments that some might find objectionable, they must design ads that are persuasive but unlikely to be controversial.

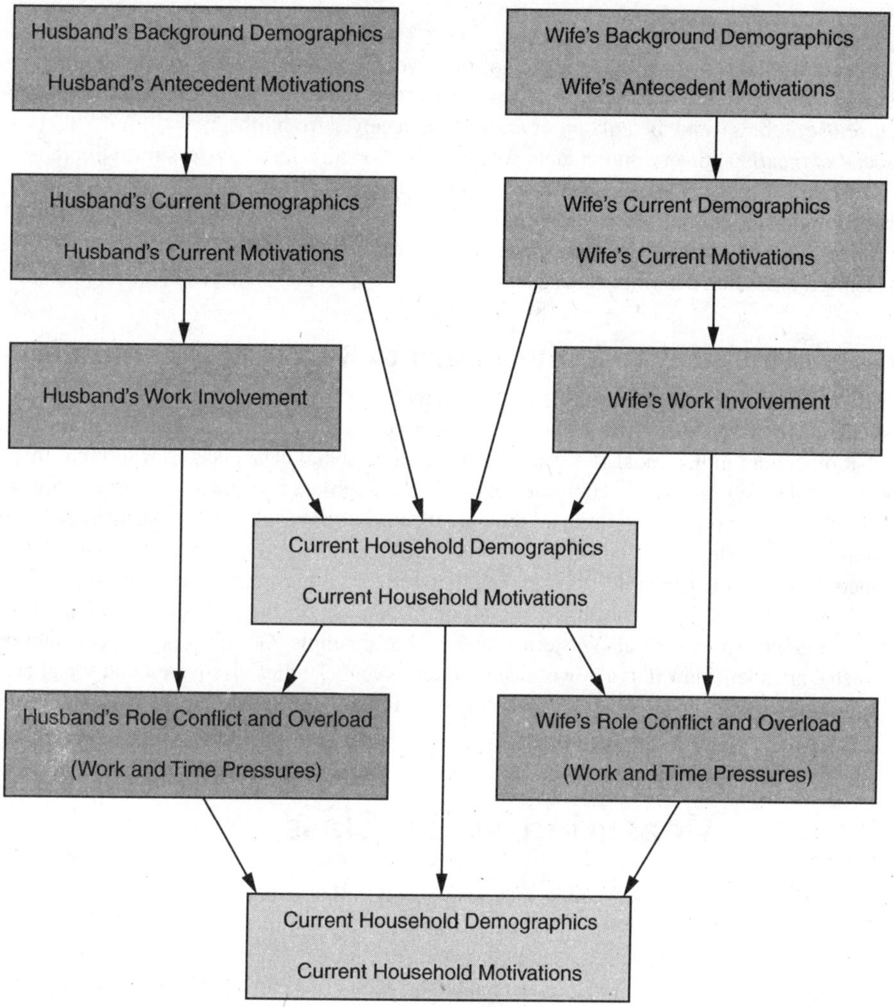

FIGURE 10.13 Dual Spousal Work Involvement

Dual Spousal Work Involvement Household Classification System

Figure 10.13 shows a classification system named "dual spousal work involvement," which consists of eight types of households based on combinations of occupations and "career-related motivations." The eight groups shown differ in consumption patterns. For example, dual low-occupation and nonworking wife and low-occupation husband households consumed a lot of fast and convenience foods but very few healthy and nutritious items. In contrast, dual, very high-occupation career couples consumed many healthful items and few convenience foods.[29]

Learning Objective

5 To understand the impact of social stratification on consumer behavior.

Social Standing and Consumer Behavior

Social class is the division of members of a society into a hierarchy of distinct status classes, so that members of each class have relatively the same status and members of all other classes have either more or less status. Some form of class structure (or social stratification) has existed in all societies throughout history. In contemporary societies, people who are better educated or have prestigious occupations have more status relative to other members of the same society. Belonging to a given social class also reflects the differences in the values, attitudes, and behaviors (including consumer behavior) among members of the different social classes. Social class is a continuum along which society's members—usually as households—are placed into one stratum; that is, "assigned" to a social class according to their relative prestige within that society.

Social Class and Social Status

Social class stems from **social status**, which is the degree of prestige the members of one social class have in comparison with members of other social classes. Status is composed of several factors, including *wealth* (amount of economic assets), *power* (the degree of influence over others), and the amount of *esteem* one receives from others.

According to social comparison theory, individuals compare their own material possessions with those owned by others in order to determine their relative social standing. This is especially apparent in a materialistic society, where status is often associated with consumers' purchasing power. Thus, people with more purchasing power (and more possessions) have more status and those with less money have less status. The more expensive and exclusive one's possessions are, the more status one has. In addition, two other demographics that determine social standing are occupational status and educational attainment.

Social Class Is Hierarchical and Often Used to Segment Consumers

Social-class categories are ranked in a hierarchy, ranging from low to high status. Members of a specific social class perceive members of other social classes as having either more or less status than they do. When it comes to consumption, people look for cues indicating that others are either equal to them (about the same social class), superior to them (higher social class), or inferior to them (lower social class). Marketers often use social class to segment consumers, because members of the same social class share values, attitudes, and priorities regarding all the aspects of their lives, including consumer behavior.

Social-class hierarchies are reflected in consumption patterns. Consumers purchase certain products because these products are favored by members of either their own or a higher social class (e.g., a high-priced Swiss wristwatch), but avoid products that they perceive as "lower-class" (e.g., a "no-name" brand of sneaker or off-the-rack suits). Relationships between product usage and social-class membership exist in all Western societies. For example, Germans perceive instant coffee as an upscale product, whereas French consumers view it as a downscale product.[30] Many studies discovered that social class often determined consumer attitudes toward adopting certain products or not, and strongly influenced their purchases of product types, services, and brands.

Learning Objective

6 To understand how to measure social class and segment consumers accordingly.

Measuring Social Class

The demographic factors that determine a person's social class include income (usually household income), wealth (savings and liquid assets), source of income or wealth (inherited or self-made), occupation, and educational attainment (number of years of formal education or the highest degree attained). Social class can be measured subjectively or objectively.

Subjective versus Objective Measures

Subjective measures consist of asking people to estimate their own social class. A typical subjective measure consists of the following question:

"*Which of the following four categories best describes your social class: Lower class, lower-middle class, upper-middle class, or upper class?*"

Lower class	[ ]
Lower-middle class	[ ]
Upper-middle class	[ ]
Upper class	[ ]
Do not know/no answer	[ ]

When researchers use subjective measures of social class, many people identify themselves, often incorrectly, as belonging to the middle class. In fact, most people, both in the United States and other countries and cultures, tend to classify themselves in the middle strata. For example, every year in Japan, a "Life of the Nation" survey asks citizens to place themselves into one of five social-class categories: upper, upper-middle, middle-middle, lower-middle, and lower class. Whereas in the late 1950s more than 70% of respondents placed themselves in one of the three middle-class categories, this percentage has increased, and in more recent surveys about 90% categorized themselves as middle class.[31]

Many researchers maintain that responses to subjective measures represent the participants' *self-perceptions* and sense of belonging or *identification* with others, rather than comparisons with others belonging to different social groups. Thus, subjective measures actually reflect one's **social-class consciousness**, defined as a person's level of identification with a given social class.

Objective measures consist of demographic variables and asking respondents factual questions about themselves, their families, or their places of residence. Objective measures of social class include one or more of the following variables: Occupation, amount of income, education, and other related factors (e.g., source of income). These data are often incorporated into geo-demographic clustering, where Zip Code and residence/neighborhood information are employed to locate consumers with certain incomes, levels of education, and other socio-demographic items (see Chapter 2).

Marketers and providers of geo-demographic data rely heavily on socioeconomic data from the U.S. Census Bureau. Social class consists of a person's education, occupation, and income, which are closely correlated variables in almost all households. In measuring a household's social standing, the occupation and education measured are those of the "head of household," as designated by the household's members. After we examine each of the three demographics separately, we discuss several social class indices that combine them.

Occupation

People's occupations reflect their social standing relative to other members of the same society. It is often considered to be the best gauge of social class and status, as is illustrated by the often-asked question "What do you do for a living?" We use the responses to this question to "size up" people upon meeting them for the first time and form our initial impressions. Occupational prestige reflects a society's priorities and morals. For example, within the Judeo-Christian tradition, human life is paramount; hence, in the Western world, medicine and nursing are prestigious occupations. In contrast, the communist system held collectivism in high regard; individualism was considered weak and undesirable. As a result, in the Soviet Union (which finally collapsed in 1992), the medical profession was not a prestigious occupation, and medical standards and facilities were far inferior to Western ones. Under communism, very large, uniform, unattractive, blocky, and mostly gray structures were expressions of the "collective will," and their engineers and builders were highly respected. Hence, under communism, it was easy to become a physician, but only a select few were admitted to engineering schools. In the Western world, it is very difficult to be admitted to medical school and become a physician, because we have great respect for life and health and want to ensure that those who treat us medically are truly skilled and thoroughly educated.

Unlike income or educational attainment, occupational prestige cannot be determined objectively (or numerically). Instead, occupational rankings are based on public opinion as measured by administering surveys to large national samples (sized between 1,000 and 3,000 people). One method of calculating job prestige—named the *ladder of social ranking*—consists of giving respondents index cards with about 100 or so jobs listed on them and asking them to arrange the cards from the most to the least prestigious. Another method consists of questioning respondents directly. For example, the results of the Harris Poll (featured in Figure 10.12) are based on responses to the following question: "*I am going to read off a number of different occupations. For each, would you tell me if you feel it is an occupation of very great prestige, considerable prestige, some prestige, or hardly any prestige at all?*"*

An **occupational prestige ranking** represents society's collective beliefs regarding the occupation's social worth and desirability, as stemming from the knowledge required to attain it (i.e., educational level) and the material rewards that occupants receive (i.e., income). Interestingly, prestige rankings reflect society's historical events and changing economics, as illustrated by the Harris Poll surveys of occupational prestige (2007 is the latest survey available), which are featured in Figure 10.14. As shown, the prestige of firefighters and police and military officers has increased steadily after the 9/11 terrorist attacks and the subsequent engagement of the American military in operations overseas. The prestige of business-related executives has been low, probably because of the insider-trading and accounting scandals of the past decade. Many surveys have shown that the occupational prestige of bankers and stockbrokers continued to plummet following the financial blowup of 2008 and the stagnant economy that followed. The prestige of doctors has steadily increased, despite the continuing debate over medical costs and the emergence of health insurance coverage as the most prominent social problem in the United States. In the Harris Poll study, occupations that more than one-quarter of respondents indicated had "hardly any prestige at all" included stockbrokers, union leaders, real estate brokers, and entertainers.

Another way to gauge an occupational prestige is the degree of ethics and honesty associated with it. As principles for our behavior, ethics and honesty are the most important behavioral guidelines within our culture. The Golden Rule, originating in biblical times and mandating that you "treat others as you would like others to treat you,"; George Washington's statement that "I cannot tell a lie"; and President Lincoln's fame as "Honest Abe" have been part of every child's education, and personal

* The Harris Poll #86, August 4, 2009 By Regina A. Corso, Director, The Harris Poll, Harris Interactive

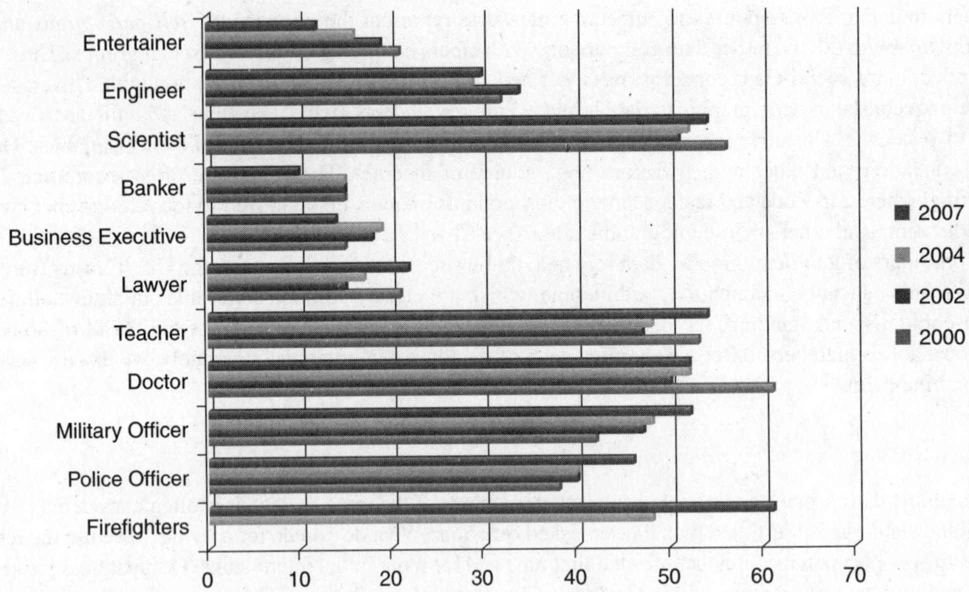

FIGURE 10.14 Occuptional Prestige Ranking: Percentage Responding that Occupation Has "Very Great Prestige"

Source: The Harris Poll #86, August 4, 2009 By Regina A. Corso, Director, The Harris Poll, Harris Interactive

honesty is regarded as a virtue. The Gallup Poll has continuously measured Americans' perceptions of the honesty and ethics associated with popular occupations by using the following question: "*Please tell me how you would rate the honesty and ethical standards of people in these fields—very high, high, average, low, or very low?*"* The professions perceived as *most* honest and ethical (by more than 50% of respondents) are featured in Figure 10.15A, and the ones viewed as the *least* honest and ethical (by 40% or more of respondents) are listed in Figure 10.15B.

Education

The more education people have, the more likely it is that they are well paid, have prestigious occupations, and therefore belong to higher social classes than the less educated. According to the latest estimates from the U.S. Census Bureau, there are

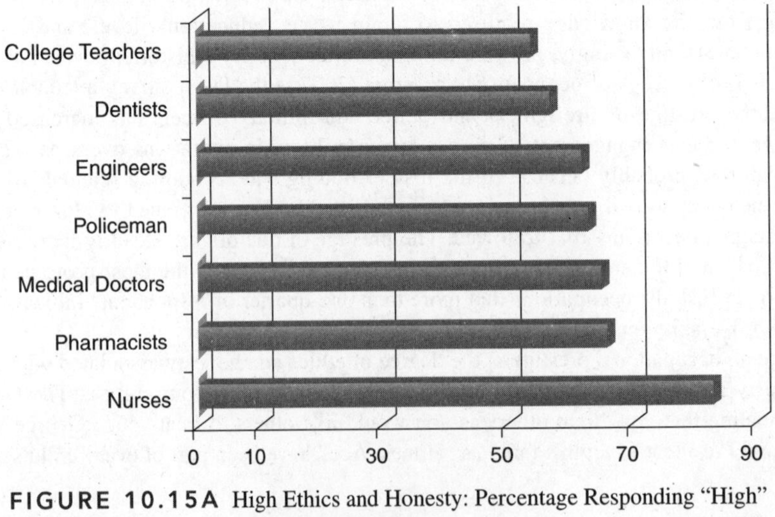

FIGURE 10.15A High Ethics and Honesty: Percentage Responding "High" or "Very High" Honesty

Source: Based on Gallup, Honest and Ethics Poll.

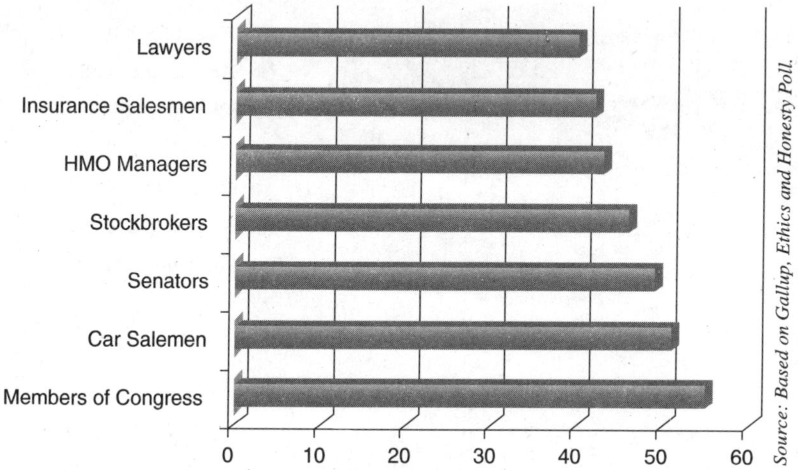

FIGURE 10.15B Low Ethics and Honesty: Percentage Responding "Low" or "Very Low" Honesty

now 114 million households in the United States, with an average of 2.59 persons per household. Figure 10.16 illustrates the correlation between educational attainment and the amount of household income.[32] The "pies" represent different educational attainment levels and the incomes associated with them. As education increases, so does income. For example, the size of the "slice" representing incomes between $25,000 and $34,999 is significantly larger among high school graduates (Figure 10.16D), as compared with those who went to high school but did not graduate (Figure 10.16C). The "slice" representing the $100,000 and over income group occupies about 45% in the "pie" of the "bachelor's degree and higher" group (Figure 10.16G), which illustrates that college education makes people more affluent.

Social-class membership is often mirrored in one's education. For example, students at the most selective universities in the country are often the sons and daughters of alumni and upper-class Americans, whereas lower-class children are often encouraged to "get a good job." In a series of articles on social class, a 50-year-old man, whose father was a factory worker, was quoted: "The whole concept of life was that you should get a good job in the factory . . . if I'd said I wanted to go to college, it would have been like saying I wanted to grow gills and breathe underwater."[33] Almost one in three Americans in their mid-twenties today is a college dropout (compared to one in five in the late 1960s), and most of those are members of poor and working-class families. In contrast, the children of the middle and upper classes generally graduate from college "because they can hardly imagine doing otherwise."[34]

Income

Individual or family income is frequently used to measure social standing. When using income as a measure, it is important to study the *source* of income, as well as its amount. It is also important to distinguish between *income* and *wealth*. Wealth is based on savings, may include inheritance, and is often the outcome of having network and alliances, some of which expand over generations. Income often represents only the ability to spend more, whereas net worth (i.e., wealth) can be used to create more financial resources. The distribution of net worth in the United States has become markedly unbalanced over the past few decades. In the year 2001, the richest 1% of households possessed almost 34% of all net worth; the bottom 90% of all households accounted for only 28.5% of all net worth. Since then, the rich have gotten richer, and the poor have gotten poorer.[35]

Although income is a commonly used estimate of social-class standing, many consumer researchers maintain that it is not a good measure. Some point out that a blue-collar electrician and a white-collar administrative assistant may both earn $87,000 a year, but will spend their incomes differently because of the difference between their educations and occupations. The same is true in the case of a prominent physician and a successful plumbing contractor, each earning $200,000. The amount of income represents the *ability* to spend money, but *how* the money is spent is determined by peoples' priorities, which are reflections of their education, occupation, and social contacts.

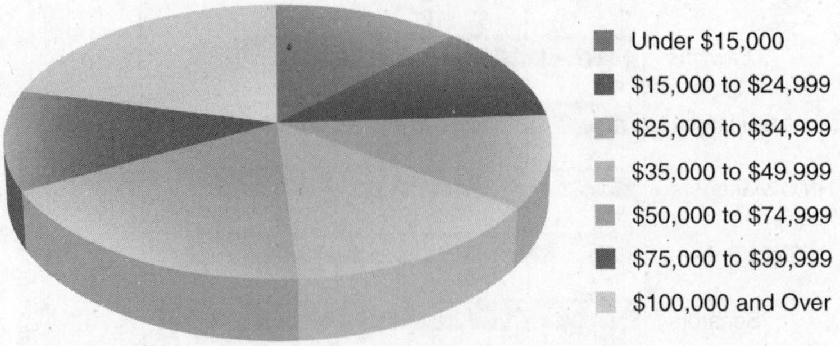

FIGURE 10.16A Twenty-Five or Older Americans' Incomes (Median $50,971)

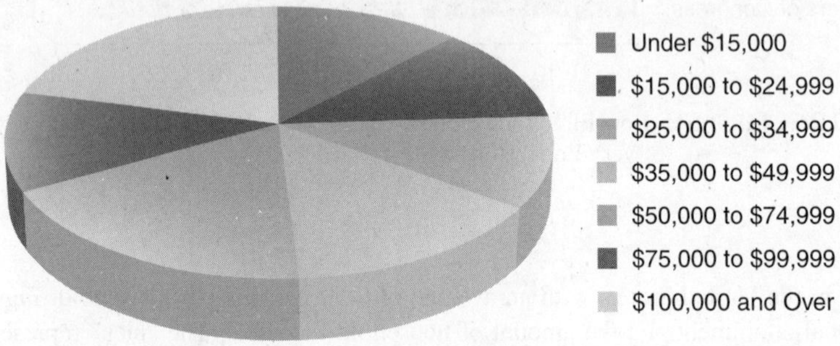

FIGURE 10.16B Incomes of 25 or Older with Less than Ninth-Grade Education (Median $21,635)

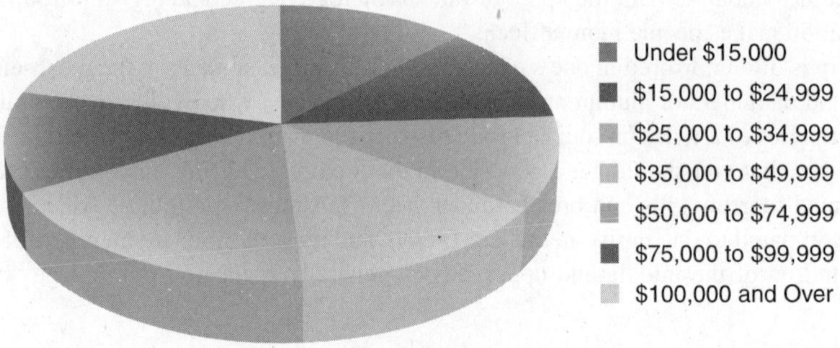

FIGURE 10.16C Incomes of 25 or Older with Some High School Education (Median $25,604)

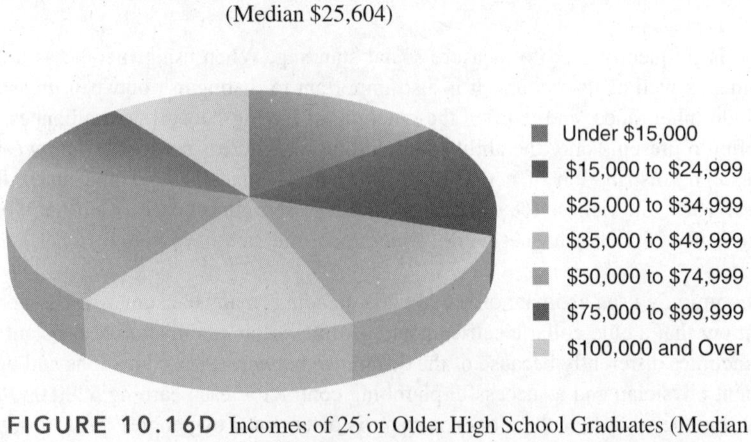

FIGURE 10.16D Incomes of 25 or Older High School Graduates (Median $39,647)

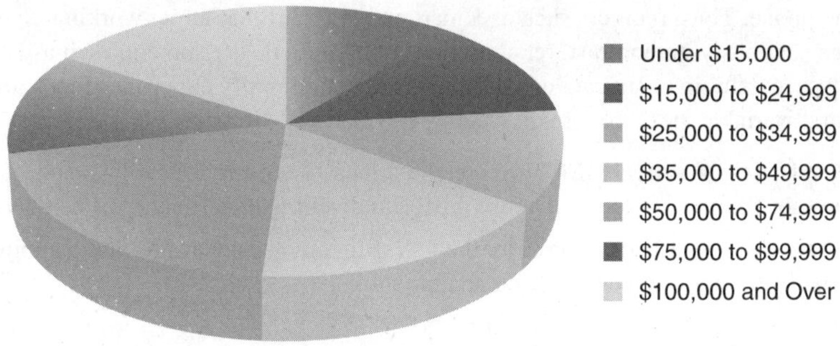

Source: (Figure 10.17A-E) U.S. Census Bureau, Statistical Abstract of the United States, 2012; census.gov/prod/2011pubs/12statab/income Accessed 6/21/2012.

FIGURE 10.16E Incomes of 25 or Older with Some College But without Degree Education (Median $44,301)

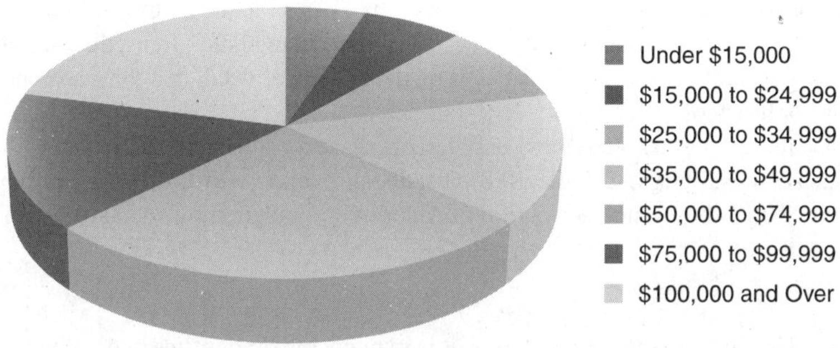

Source: (Figure 10.17F-G) U.S. Census Bureau, Statistical Abstract of the United States, 2012; census.gov/prod/2011pubs/12statab/income Accessed 6/21/2012.

FIGURE 10.16F Incomes of 25 or Older with Associate College Degree (Median $67,728)

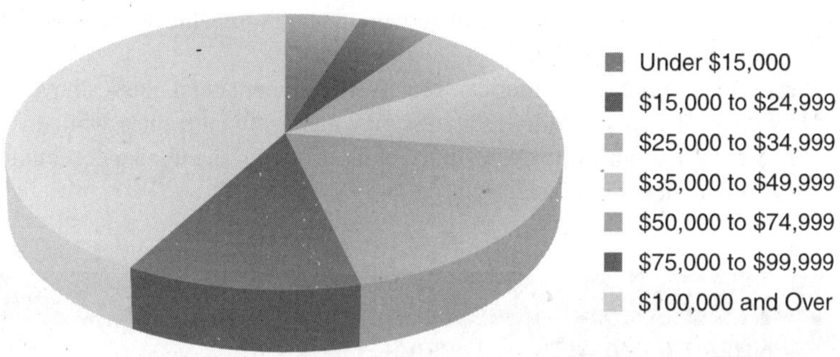

FIGURE 10.16G Incomes of 25 or Older with Bachelor's Degree or Higher (Median $82,722)

Magazines are an excellent medium because they reach selective consumer segments in terms of income, education, and occupation. For example, marketers who target upper-middle-class consumers should consider placing ads in Wine and Food magazine because most of its readers are young, educated, and hold managerial positions.[36]

Multivariable Measures

A **multivariable index** consists of more than one demographic variable and combines several socioeconomic factors to determine social-class standing. Many believe that these indices reflect the complexity of social class better than single-variable indexes. For instance, a research study that explored consumers' perceptions of mail and phone order shopping—using a composite of income, occupational status, and education—discovered that the consumers with higher social standing preferred buying by phone or mail over in-store shopping.[37] The same research also found that downscale consumers preferred in-store shopping to buying from catalogues or by phone. Thus, retailers such as Kmart and Walmart that target working-class consumers should use direct-marketing and catalogs cautiously. In contrast, retailers catering to upscale consumers, such as Neiman Marcus and Saks Fifth Avenue, have been very successful in using catalogs to sell even extraordinarily expensive goods to affluent consumers.

The most widely used multivariable measures are:

1. **Index of Status Characteristics (Warner's ISC)** is a weighted measure of the following socioeconomic variables: Occupation, source of income (not amount of income), house type, and dwelling area (quality of neighborhood).[38]
2. **Socioeconomic Status Score (SES)** was developed by the U.S. Bureau of the Census, and combines three socioeconomic variables: Occupation, family income, and educational attainment.[39]

Social Classes' Characteristics and Consumer Behavior

There is no uniform definition as to how many distinct classes depict the class structure of the U.S. population. Most early studies divided Americans into five or six social-class groups. Other researchers have found nine-, four-, three-, and even two-class schemas suitable. The choice of how many separate classes to use depends on the amount of detail that the researcher believes is necessary to adequately explain the attitudes or behavior under study.

Lifestyles, consumption patterns, leisure activities, hobbies, media exposure, and many other factors are homogeneous within and heterogeneous among social classes. Table 10.8 presents an overview of the American population as divided into seven social classes, and Figure 10.17 shows the distribution of America's population by social class.

Upward Mobility

Social-class membership in the United States is not as fixed as it is in many other countries and cultures (e.g., the UK and India). Americans have traditionally believed in **upward mobility**, defined as the opportunity to move from a lower social class to a higher one, because of the wide availability of educational resources (e.g., expensive top schools, but also inexpensive state and city universities providing high-quality education) and the opportunities produced by the free enterprise, capitalistic economy. Indeed, the classic Horatio Alger tale of a penniless young orphan who manages to achieve great success in business and in life is the central theme in many American novels and movies.

Because upward mobility has been attainable in American society, the higher social classes have been reference groups for ambitious men and women of lower social status. Examples are the new management trainee who strives to dress like the boss, the middle manager who aspires to belong to an exclusive country club, or the graduate of a community college who gives up necessities in order to save money to send her son to Yale.

TABLE 10.8 Social-Class Profiles of the United States

THE UPPER-UPPER CLASS—INHERITED WEALTH AND PRIVILEGE
• Also known as "upper crust," "WASPS," or "blue bloods"
• Less than 1% of the population together with the Nouveau Rich
• Inherited privilege, wealth, and trust funds
• Status and wealth are passed on from generation to generation (homes, trust funds)
• Multigenerational wealth and leadership positions (e.g., presidents, senators, judges)
• Serve as trustees and on boards of directors for universities, hospitals, charities
• Control and own significant portions of corporate America
• Heads of major financial institutions; owners of long-established firms
• Attended exclusive boarding schools and Ivy League universities
• Belong to exclusive clubs, "summer" together, marry people "like themselves"

(Continued)

TABLE 10.8 (Continued)

- Accustomed to wealth, so do not spend money conspicuously
- Consider "toys" bought to display wealth publicly (e.g., yachts) to be vulgar
- Hobbies: Shooting, sailing, parasailing, golf, horseback riding

THE NOUVEAU RICH—MONEY IS KING

- Also known as the "lower-uppers," "super rich," or "capitalist class"
- Less than 1% of the population together with the Upper-Upper
- Have millions and often billions of dollars but seldom inherited wealth
- Some have little or no college education (e.g., celebrities)
- Some are entrepreneurs (often in the technology sector) who attended top universities
- Often isolated from others because of bodyguards and large entourages
- Often featured in tabloids, gossip columns, and public scandals
- Strive to join the Upper-Uppers (e.g., by marriage), mostly unsuccessfully
- Highly conspicuous consumption—the more vulgar, the better
- Prime target for "hot" (and mostly short-lived) fashion and interior design trends
- Employ large staffs—chefs, nutritionists, maids, nannies, personal assistants

THE UPPER-MIDDLE CLASS—ACHIEVING PROFESSIONALS

- Key features are high educational attainment and professional achievement
- Approximately 15% of the population
- Career-oriented, highly educated professionals whose work is largely self-directed
- Corporate managers, business owners, doctors, lawyers, professors
- College graduates, many with advanced degrees
- Active in professional networks, community, and social activities
- Trendsetters in health, fitness, and environmental causes
- Have a keen interest in obtaining the "better things in life"
- Homes, cars, and travel symbolize their achievements
- Consumption is often conspicuous, but not vulgar
- Some are very child oriented

THE LOWER-MIDDLE CLASS—FAITHFUL FOLLOWERS

- Semi-professionals and craftspeople with an average standard of living
- About 30% of the population
- Primarily nonmanagerial white-collar workers and highly paid blue-collar workers
- Most have some college education and are white-collar
- Strive to achieve respectability and be good citizens
- Raise their children to be good and honest adults
- Value religion and are involved in its social activities
- Value and price conscious and avoid fads and "hot" styles

THE UPPER-LOWER CLASS—SECURITY-MINDED

- Also known as the "working class," solidly blue collar, no college education
- About 30% of the population
- High school education
- Clerical and mostly blue-collar workers whose work is highly routinized
- Adequate standard of living dependent on the number of income earners
- Strive for security (often gained from union membership)
- View work as a means to "buy" enjoyment
- Want children to behave properly
- High wage earners in this group may spend impulsively

(Continued)

TABLE 10.8 (Continued)

- Interested in items that enhance their leisure time (e.g., TV sets, hunting equipment)
- Males typically have a strongly "macho" self-image
- Males are sports fans, heavy smokers, beer drinkers

THE WORKING POOR—THE INSECURE

- Also known as the "lower class"
- About 13% of the population
- Service, clerical, and some blue-collar workers
- Low on the social ladder
- High economic insecurity and risk of poverty
- Some high school education

THE UNDERCLASS—ROCK BOTTOM

- Also known as the "lower-lower class"
- About 12% of the population
- Limited or no participation in the labor force; uneducated, unskilled laborers
- No political or social power and unable to improve their communities
- Reliant on the government, often unemployed and without health insurance
- Children are often treated poorly
- Live a day-to-day existence

Source: Based on MRI Spring 2012, www.fwmedia.com, accessed July 16, 2012

Marketers recognize that many people aspire to have the same lifestyles and possessions as the members of higher social classes. Therefore, they frequently depict products and symbols associated with higher classes when advertising to the middle or even lower class. For example, Ralph Lauren's flagship store in New York City, on Madison Avenue, is located in the Rhinelander Mansion—built in the French Renaissance style more than a century ago—and is decorated with dark, fine antique furnishing and dark carpets, resembling generations-old wealth. The Polo logo also references the upper class, because many members of this select group own polo ponies and belong to clubs that sponsor polo matches. Many of Lauren's clothing items carry crests resembling insignia designating European nobility.

About a century ago, a sociologist conceptualized the **trickle-down effect**. Originally applied to fashion, the concept stated that members of lower classes adopt the fashions of the upper class and maintain them even after the upper class has abandoned these fashions. Upper class persons abandon fashions adopted by "everyone" because they no longer reflect their exclusivity. To "restore" their exclusivity, members of the upper class adopt new fashions, which are subsequently copied by the lower classes, and the cycle is repeated. The trickle-down concept is also congruent with the model of adopter categories (see Chapter 9). Invariably, as more people adopt a fashion or product, its price declines because more providers emerge. For instance, plastic surgery was once affordable only for movie stars and other very wealthy consumers. Today, even members of lower social classes can easily find a plastic surgeon whose services they can afford.

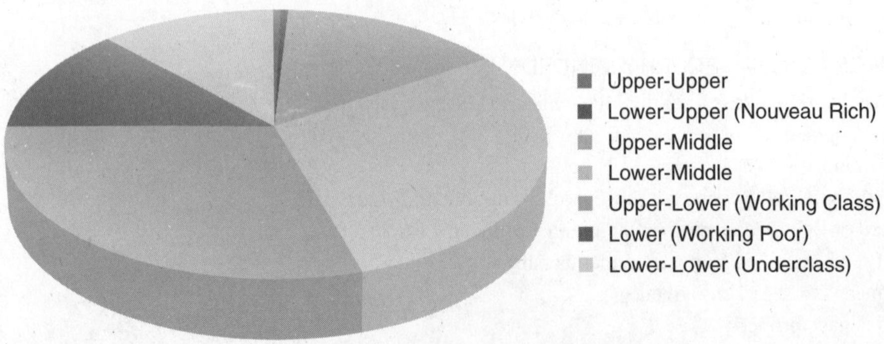

FIGURE 10.17 The Distribution of Social Classes in the United States

Affluent Consumers

Affluent households have large disposable incomes and are a lucrative target market for luxury cruises, foreign sports cars, ski resorts, second homes, fine jewelry, and art, among many other goods. Overall, the affluent are healthier, have higher life expectancies, and are more likely to become marketers' "customers for life" than the less wealthy.[40] However, some studies indicate that children of the affluent often have problems with substance abuse, anxiety, and depression, which are caused by excessive pressures to achieve and isolation from parents (both physically and emotionally).[41]

Americans' wealth grew dramatically during the 1990s, partially due to the longest bull stock market in U.S. history. From 2002 to 2004, the number of *high net worth individuals* (HNWIs) in North America, defined as individuals with a minimum net worth of $1 million, grew by 9.7% to 2.7 million. Between 2006 and 2007, this number grew from 2.9 million to more than 3 million, a gain of 3.7%.[42] Indeed, although North America has only 6% of the world adult population, it accounts for 34% of the world's household wealth.[43]

For more than 30 years, Ipsos Mendelsohn (a marketing research firm) has annually studied the **affluent market**, defined as households with annual incomes of $100,000 or more. The survey divided the affluent market into three segments:

1. ***Least affluent:*** Households with annual incomes of $100,000 to $149,000 (12% of American households, $1.7 trillion combined income).
2. ***Middle affluent:*** Households with annual incomes from $150,000 to $249,000 (6% of all households, $1.3 trillion combined income).
3. ***Most affluent:*** Household with annual incomes of $250,000 or more (2% of all households, $1.6 trillion estimated household income).

Although affluent households represent only 20% of total U.S. households, they account for more than half of the combined income of all the households in the United States. The average household income for the affluent is $195,600, with average household liquid assets of $500,900.[44] By some estimates, 9 million American households have a net worth of at least $1 million. The IPSOS/Mendelsohn Affluent Survey distinguishes between *affluence* and *wealth*; it defines wealthy household as having liquid assets of at least $1 million (e.g., cash or cash equivalents, such as CDs, mutual funds, stocks, bonds). According to this definition, out of the 23.3 million affluent households, about 3 million households are considered wealthy. In addition, more than 1 million households have both more than $1 million in wealth and annual household incomes of at least $250,000.[45]

The media habits of the affluent differ from those of the nonaffluent.[46] The members of households earning more than $100,000 a year watch less TV, read more newspapers and magazines, and listen to the radio more than less affluent persons. Table 10.9 lists magazines that cater to affluent consumers.[47]

Affluent consumers are not uniform; they can be divided according to their consumption habits and lifestyles. The "upper deck" consumers are the top 10% of the United States population in terms of annual income, and consist of several segments (see Table 10.10). Marketers can employ this segmentation in many ways. For instance, consumers belonging to the "no strings attached" segment are more interested in going to live theater performances; members of the "nanny's in charge" segment would rather attend a country music performance; and members of the "good life" segment are particularly interested in bird-watching.[48]

Middle-class Consumers

There is no standard definition of "middle class" and business people and sociologists often define it somewhat differently. Many sociologists divide the middle class into two strata: The "upper or professional middle class", which includes highly educated, salaried professionals and managers (about 15 to 20% of all Americans); and the "lower middle class", consisting mostly of semi-professionals, skilled craftspersons, and lower-level management (about one-third of the population). Sociologists describe middle-class persons as having comfortable living standards, economic security, and the expertise they need to maintain their lifestyles. To many, college education is a key indicator of middle-class status. Others focus on the nature of the occupations that are most commonly found among members of the middle class, which enable members to be independent, intrinsically motivated, nonconformist, and innovative.

Some define the middle class as 50% of the combined incomes of all American households, which amounts to about 57 million households earning between $25,000 and $85,000.[49] In contrast, some polls suggest that 90% or more of Americans consider themselves to be "middle class," "upper-middle class," or "working class."[50] Marketers generally consider middle class as

TABLE 10.9 Magazines That Cater to Households with Annual Incomes of $100,000 or More

MAGAZINE	READERSHIP (000)	MEDIAN AGE	MEDIAN HOUSEHOLD INCOME (00)	MEDIAN NET WORTH (00)
Allure	1,267	39.7	142.7	641.7
Architectural Digest	1,389	52.4	152.5	869.0
Barron's	414	53.7	163.3	1,015.0
Bicycling	685	44.0	148.6	636.4
Cigar Aficionado	276	48.8	168.5	613.0
Cosmopolitan	3,179	32.6	142.0	565.8
Essence	1,087	44.9	135.5	470.9
Men's Health	3,179	41.8	152.0	483.4
National Geographic	6,281	50.5	146.1	680.8
People	8,328	46.7	144.7	574.8
Robb Report	175	50.7	187.4	1,077.5
Rolling Stone	1,557	39.5	150.5	543.8
Scientific American	1,002	48.8	158.4	697.9
Time Magazine	4,904	51.5	149.3	850.1
Vanity Fair	1,602	48.0	155.8	768.8
Vogue	2,211	42.7	147.7	690.4

Source: Based on 2011 Survey Ipsos Mendelsolm.

TABLE 10.10 The Upper Deck Market Segments

NAME	SIZE	DESCRIPTION
Well-feathered nests	37.3% of Upper Deck	Households that have at least one high-income earner and children present
No strings attached	35.1% of Upper Deck	Households that have at least one high-income earner and no children
Nanny's in charge	8.3% of Upper Deck	Households that have two or more earners, none earning high incomes, and children present
Two careers	9.4% of Upper Deck	Households that have two or more earners, neither earning high incomes, and no children present
The good life	10.0% of Upper Deck	Households that have a high degree of affluence with no person employed or with the head of household not employed

households ranging from lower-middle to middle-middle class. Many researchers maintain that America's middle social class has been shrinking. They argue that some members of the middle class are moving upstream to the ranks of the upper-middle class, whereas others are losing ground and slipping backward to the working class.[51]

Procter and Gamble—the maker of virtually all brands of personal care and home maintenance products (globally)—defined middle class as the core of its business and as households with annual incomes between $50,000 and $140,000 (amounting to 40% of American households). As the stagnant economy, initiated by the financial crisis in fall 2008, has dragged on, the purchasing power of these households has steadily declined, and P & G discovered that its core customers were no longer willing to pay more for iconic, premium-priced brands (e.g., Pampers and Tide). In response, the company introduced lower-priced alternatives, such as Gain dish soap that goes for about half of what its Dawn Hand Renewal dish soap costs.[52]

Downscale Consumers

Working-class or blue-collar people—typically defined as households earning less than $40,000 annually—control somewhere near 30% of the total income in the United States and are an important market segment. Some studies have pointed out that these consumers are often more brand loyal than other groups because they cannot afford mistakes caused by switching to unfamiliar brands. Downscale consumers often spend higher percentages of their incomes on food than do middle-class shoppers.

Marketing to the working class can be tricky. For example, a study conducted in the UK showed that brands catering to blue-collar households often introduced "upmarket" makeovers, because research indicated that "working class" represents something to escape from, and to some is even a pejorative term. The study also showed that Pizza Express was among the most popular brands among the working class, presumably because its members are less likely to go to table-service restaurants.[53] To many working-class consumers, food represents an area of "indulgence," which may have undesirable outcomes. One British writer, reflecting on the growth of super-sized fast-food offerings in the United Kingdom, noted that "[i]t isn't the wealthy middle classes . . . that are generally obese—it's the under-class . . . with little budget [or] knowledge of diet . . . that is suffering."[54] Indeed, studies in the UK (and in the United States) confirmed that obesity among children from lower classes is significantly more common than among wealthier kids.[55]

Clothing, Fashion, and Shopping

A Greek philosopher once said, "Know, first, who you are; and then adorn yourself accordingly."[56] What is considered fashionable, tasteful, or elegant varies across social strata. For example, some working-class consumers often wear T-shirts, caps, and clothing that carry logos, trademarks, or names of celebrities or music group. In contrast, upscale consumers prefer clothing without conspicuous labels and in subtle colors and practical styles (e.g., L. L. Bean or Brooks Brothers).

America's upper social class has often been identified with the "preppy look" and often emulated by lower classes. Preppies (both males and females) prefer practical, comfortable, and timeless rather than trendy clothing. There are few designer labels and even fewer trends. Machine-washable khaki shorts and unisex dressing are very popular because khaki is to preppies what denim is to the lower classes: An everyday staple. Visors are a favorite for women—they keep the sun out of your eyes without messing up your hair, and they're excellent for tennis. Clothing embroidered with animals or sea creatures are always popular, like bathing trunks embroidered with crabs, as are shirts embroidered with club logos. Any excuse to wear themed clothing is embraced, and wearing red, white, and blue on the Fourth of July is expected at the holiday's parties. Polo shirts are an exception to the no-obvious-designer-labels rule; in fact, preps were wearing Polo long before it became a designer label. The preppy style originated among members of the upper class also known as WASPs (White Anglo-Saxon Protestant). WASPs are often irritated by shopping guides urging people—men in particular—to buy expensive designer clothes in order to "look like a WASP," such as ads for expensive, designer-label white buck shoes. Most preps have a pair of such shoes that, most likely, they purchased from Johnston & Murphy (for $130) years ago. Most importantly, preppies wear white bucks only for special occasions like weddings or cocktail parties, but not for running errands on a Saturday afternoon.[57]

A brand's social-class symbolism is a tricky issue. Although never publicly confirmed, some journalists have periodically reported that companies such as Timberland and L. L. Bean—perceived as the archetypal choices of upper-class Caucasians—were irritated after their products (particularly men's shoes) became popular among young members of minority groups residing in inner cities. Apparently, these marketers felt that such "undesirable" customers might blemish the images of their products. Ironically, some fashions originated among adolescents and teens residing in low-income neighborhoods. For example, several years ago, after observing lower-class kids, several designers began marketing pairs of men's shorts—one longer than the other—to be worn simultaneously, with one on top of the other; this new fashion was very successful. When shopping, consumers avoid stores that appeal to social classes significantly different from their own, but savvy marketers can cater to multiple social classes. For example, The Gap stores offer quality clothing to middle-class consumers. The Gap also introduced Old Navy clothing stores to sell good-value clothing to working-class families who usually purchased their casual and active wear clothing from general merchandise retailers such as Kmart, Walmart, or Target. The Gap also owns Banana Republic, originally a small retailer of safari-themed clothing that is now positioned as an upscale store.

Saving, Spending, and Credit Card Usage

The management of financial resources is closely related to social-class standing. Upper-class consumers are "future oriented" and confident of their financial acumen; they invest in insurance, stocks, and real estate. In comparison, lower-class consumers are generally concerned with "immediate gratification;" when they do save, they are primarily interested in safety and security. When it comes to bank credit card usage, members of the lower social classes use their bank credit cards for installment purchases, whereas members of the upper social classes pay their credit card bills in full each month. That is, lower-class purchasers use their credit cards to "buy now and pay later" for things they might not otherwise be able to afford, whereas upper-class purchasers use their credit cards as a convenient substitute for cash.

An Australian study focused on the differences in financial management and a "sense of empowerment" between working-class and young professionals (25–30 years of age). The study discovered that young professionals perceived themselves to be empowered in the sense that they could achieve whatever they set their minds to, and they were disciplined and results oriented. In contrast, working-class participants perceived themselves as being average and expressed frustration (e.g., "I can never finish things") and uncertainty about the future.[58]

Communications

When it comes to describing daily life, members of the lower class often portray it in personal and concrete terms, whereas members of the middle-class use different language, and upper-class members use their own lexicon. The following responses to the question "*Where do you usually purchase gas?*" illustrate such differences:

Upper-middle-class answer: "*At Exxon or Sunoco.*"

Lower-middle-class answer: "*At the station on Seventh Street and Post Avenue.*"

Lower-class answer: "*At Charlie's.*"

Sociologically, linguistics indicates that middle-class consumers have a broader or more general view of the world, whereas lower-class consumers have a narrow and personal perspective and see the world only through their immediate experiences. There are also regional differences in terminology. For instance, the children's game of hopscotch (where players toss a small object into the numbered spaces of a pattern of rectangles outlined on the ground and then hop or jump through the spaces to retrieve it) is called "potsy" in Manhattan, but "sky blue" in Chicago.

Exposure to mass media differs by social class. In watching TV, the members of higher social classes prefer current events and drama, whereas lower-class individuals prefer soap operas, quiz shows, and situation comedies. Higher-class consumers read more magazines and newspapers than do their lower-class counterparts. Lower-class consumers have greater exposure to publications that dramatize romance and the lifestyles of movie and television celebrities. For example, magazines such as True Story appeal heavily to blue-collar or working-class women, who enjoy reading about the problems, fame, and fortunes of others. Middle-class consumers read fact-based and informative magazines and newspapers, and watch more movies and late-night programs, than lower-class persons.[59]

Downward Mobility

Commonly, in America, each generation lived better than its predecessor. However, there are now signs that some **downward mobility**, defined as moving down, rather than up the social ladder, is taking place. In fact, many predict that today's youngest generation—the Eco Boomers—will experience lower living standards than their parents.

Specifically, researchers have found that the odds that young men's incomes will reach middle-class levels by the time they reach their thirtieth birthday have been slowly declining, regardless of ethnicity, education, or parents' income.[60] For example, while household income grew by $1,869 from 1969–1979, by $2,855 from 1979–1989, and by $3,888 from 1989–2000, from 2000–2007 the change in household income was a *negative* $324.[61]

Additionally, income inequality has been rising to levels not seen since the 1880s—known as the "Gilded Age"—and the gap between the rich and the poor has widened considerably since 1970. Although the income of households in the top fifth grew 70% between 1979 and 2000, the real income of households in the bottom fifth rose only 6.4%. Although most Americans find little wrong with income inequality as long as plenty of social mobility still exists, there are signs that social mobility is also failing. Some data show that 42% of the individuals born into the poorest fifth remained at the bottom and that another 24% moved from the bottom only slightly, to the next-to-bottom group. Only 10% of adult men born into the bottom quarter ever made it to the top quarter.[62]

Geo-demography and Social Class

Marketers use geo-demography to identify the geographic locations of consumers belonging to various social classes. The rationale for using geo-demographics is that "birds of a feather flock together"; that is, families with similar socioeconomic status reside in the same neighborhoods or communities. **Geo-demographic segments** are groups of households that have been identified, classified, and described according to Zip Codes and data from the U.S. Census and state and local governments.

The most sophisticated geo-demographic segmentation is Nielsen's **PRIZM®** (www.MyBestSegments.com), which combines socioeconomic and demographic factors—education, income, occupation, family life cycle, ethnicity, housing, and urbanization—with consumer buying and media exposure data, and which marketers use to locate concentrations of consumers with similar lifestyles and buying behaviors. This framework designates every household in the United States as belonging to one of 66 segments (see Table 2.3). PRIZM also classifies all U.S. households into eleven "life stages".

Many marketers have studied the product usage, media exposure, and other consumption factors of the PRIZM® segments that are likely to purchase their products and services. For example, investment services should identify the financial websites that "Affluentials" visit frequently and observe what kind of investment opportunities these consumers find attractive. Marketers of very expensive vacations and conspicuous luxury goods should study the spending habits of "Young Accumulators." However, these marketers should not target the "Accumulated Wealth" segment, because its members have "old money" and shy away from buying conspicuous luxury goods, which they regard as being "in poor taste" "and showing off" one's money.

Summary

Learning Objective 1: To understand the family as a consumer socialization agent.

The family is the primary reference group for many attitudes and behaviors. The family is also the prime target market for most products and product categories. As the most basic membership group, a family is defined as two or more persons related by blood, marriage, or adoption who reside together. Socialization is the process of making people behave in a way that is acceptable to their society. In the context of marketing, the most important role of the family is the socialization of family members, ranging from young children to adults. This process includes imparting to young children the basic values and modes of behavior consistent with their culture, including moral principles, interpersonal skills, acceptable dress and grooming standards, appropriate manners and speech, and the selection of suitable educational and occupational or career goals.

Learning Objective 2: To understand family decision-making and its members' consumption-related roles.

Marketers recognize that families operate as units in terms of consumption behavior, and many researchers have studied the dynamics of family decision-making. Specifically, marketers focus on husband–wife decision-making; the relative influence each family member has regarding consumption; children's role in family decision-making; and the multiple roles family members can assume in buying, using, and maintaining their possessions. Most consumer studies classify family consumption decisions as husband-dominated, wife-dominated, joint, or autonomic decisions. The relative influence of a husband and wife on a particular consumer decision depends mainly on the product or service category. Over the past several decades, there has been a trend toward children playing a more active role in what the family buys, as well as in the family decision-making process. Measuring family decision-making is complex, because marketing research questionnaires are designed to be administered to only one respondent at a time. Also, family members may not all agree with each other's perspective regarding the degree of relative influence during a purchase decision, which precludes interviewing all members together.

Learning Objective 3: To understand the role of the family life cycle in market segmentation and targeting.

The family life cycle represents the life stages of a typical family. It is a composite variable that combines marital status, size of family, age of family members (focusing on the age of the oldest or youngest child), and employment status of the head of household, and then classifies the family into a "typical" stage. The ages of the parents and the relative amount of disposable income are inferred from the family's stage in the cycle. The family life cycle starts with bachelorhood and then moves on to marriage (and creation of the family unit). Marriage usually leads to a growing family (with the birth of children) and later to family contraction (as grown children leave the household). The cycle ends with the dissolution of the family unit (due to the death of one spouse).

Learning Objective 4: To understand the consumption patterns of nontraditional families and non-family households.

There are living arrangements that are not "typical." Families that do not readily fit into the family life cycle include childless couples, people who marry late in life, young people who continue to live with their parents or return after having moved out, and divorced couples. Living situations that are not legally defined as families (e.g., couples who live together but are not married) include unmarried couples, single parents, and gay spouses. The number of non-family households has been on a rather steep rise, which represents a marketing dilemma: Marketers of many products must now acknowledge the existence of nontraditional household segments, but must do so without offending members of traditional families who might react negatively to portrayals of nontraditional households, because of religion and beliefs as to what is or is not "right."

Learning Objective 5: To understand the impact of social stratification on consumer behavior.

Social stratification (or social class) is the division of members of a society into a hierarchy of distinct status classes, so that members of each class have relatively the same status and members of all other classes have either more or less status. Some form of class structure (or social stratification) has existed in all societies throughout history. In contemporary societies, people who are better educated or have prestigious occupations have more status relative to other members of the same society. Belonging to a given social class is also reflected in differences in the values, attitudes, and behaviors (including consumer behavior) among members of different social classes. Social class is a continuum along which society's members—usually as households—are placed into one stratum; that is, "assigned" to a social class according to their relative prestige within that society.

Learning Objective 6: To understand how to measure social class and segment consumers accordingly.

The measurement of social class is concerned with classifying individuals into social-class groupings. These groupings are of particular value to marketers, who use social classification as an effective way to identify and segment target markets. There are two basic methods for measuring social class: Subjective measurement and objective measurement. Subjective measures rely on an individual's self-perception, whereas objective measures use specific socioeconomic measures, either alone (as a single-variable index) or in combination with others (as a composite-variable index). Composite-variable indexes, such as the Index of Status Characteristics and the Socioeconomic Status Score, combine a number of socioeconomic factors to form one overall measure of social-class standing.

Review and Discussion Questions

10.1. How does the family influence the consumer socialization of children? What role does television advertising play in consumer socialization?

10.2. As a marketing consultant, you have been retained by the Walt Disney Company to design a study investigating how families make vacation decisions. Among the family members, whom would you interview? What kind of questions would you ask? How would you assess the relative power of each family member in making vacation-related decisions?

10.3. Which of the five stages of the family life cycle constitutes the *most* lucrative segment for each of the following products and services: (a) TV cable subscriptions, (b) Club Med vacation, (c) Domino's Pizza, (d) iPods, (e) mutual funds, and (f) the fastest Internet access available in one's location? Explain your answers.

10.4. Why do marketing researchers use objective, rather than subjective, measures of social class?

10.5. Under what circumstances would you expect income to be a *better* predictor of consumer behavior than a composite measure of social class? When would you expect the composite social-class measure to be superior?

10.6. Which status-related variable—occupation, education, or income—is the *most* appropriate segmentation base for: (a) family vacations, (b) opera subscriptions, (c) subscribing to online.wsj.com, (d) shopping at Whole Foods supermarkets, (e) buying from freshdirect.com, (f) purchasing new models of the iPhone, and (g) becoming a member of a 24-hour fitness center?

10.7. Consider the Rolex watch, which has a retail price range starting at about $4,500 for a stainless-steel model to tens of thousands of dollars for a solid-gold model. How might Rolex use geo-demographic clustering in its marketing efforts?

10.8. You are the owner of two furniture stores, one catering to upper-middle-class consumers and the other to lower-class consumers. How do social-class differences influence each store's: (a) product lines and styles, (b) advertising media selection, (c) copy and communications style used in the ads, and (d) payment policies?

Hands-on Assignments

10.9. In this chapter, we have considered how parents and siblings play a role in the consumer socialization of their children and young brothers and sisters, and how adults continue to be socialized throughout their lives. However, we have not considered how children (especially teens and young adults) influence the socialization of their parents. Make a list of ten ways in which you have contributed to or influenced the ongoing socialization of your parents.

10.10. Identify one traditional family and one nontraditional household featured in a TV sitcom or series. Classify the traditional household according to the family life cycle stage and the other according to the living arrangements featured in Table 10.7. Compare the characteristics and consumer patterns of the two households.

10.11. Copy the list of occupations in Figure 10.15 and ask students majoring in areas other than marketing (both business and nonbusiness) to rank the relative prestige of these occupations. Do you believe that any differences in the rankings are related to the students' majors? Explain.

Key Terms

- affluent market *307*
- authoritarian parents *282*
- authoritative parents *282*
- autonomic decisions *286*
- bachelorhood *290*
- consumer socialization *280*
- dissolution *293*
- downward mobility *310*
- extended family *278*
- family *278*
- family life cycle *278*
- geo-demographic segments *311*
- honeymooners *291*
- husband-dominated decisions *286*
- index of status characteristics (Warner's ISC) *304*
- indulgent parents *282*
- joint decisions *286*
- least affluent *307*
- middle affluent *307*
- most affluent *307*
- multivariable index *303*
- neglecting parents *282*
- non-family households *294*
- nontraditional families *294*
- nuclear family *278*
- objective measures *299*
- occupational prestige ranking *299*
- parenthood *291*
- post-parenthood *293*
- PRIZM *311*
- reference group *278*
- social class *279*
- social status *298*
- social-class consciousness *299*
- socialization *279*
- socialization agent *280*
- socioeconomic status score (SES) *304*
- subjective measures *298*
- trickle-down effect *306*
- upward mobility *304*
- wife-dominated decisions *286*

11

Culture's Influence on Consumer Behavior

Learning Objectives

1 To understand culture's role, dynamics, evolution, and impact on consumers' priorities and behaviors.

2 To understand language, symbols, and rituals as expressions of a learned culture.

3 To understand how to measure the influence of culture on consumer behavior.

4 To Understand How Core Cultural Values Impact Indian Consumers.

5 To Understand the Cultural Aspects of Emerging Markets.

CULTURE is the collective values, customs, norms, arts, social institutions, and intellectual achievements of a particular society. Cultural values express the collective principles, standards, and priorities of a community. Most of the promotional messages across the world reflect, to some degree, the target audiences' cultural values. For instance, Americans value personal achievement and success and like to demonstrate their accomplishments by showing off prosperity and material possessions. The Dodge ad in Figure 11.1 recognizes this desire. By telling consumers that they will make a "bold statement" to other drivers by driving a Dodge brand vehicle, the ad reflects and reinforces the eagerness to show off one's wealth. Americans also greatly value efficiency and progress, especially when it comes to technological innovations. Dell's ad in Figure 11.2 promotes an Ultrabook, which is small and thin, yet strong, powerful, and durable. The ad's tagline—"Everything. And More."—appeals to Americans' beliefs that technological advances provide them with more productive ways to work and manage their lives.

This chapter describes the societal role and dynamics of culture, explains how cultural values satisfy needs, and investigates how they are learned, expressed, and measured.

Source: Courtesy of Chrysler Group LLC.

FIGURE 11.1 An Appeal Based on Personal Achievement and Prestige

Source: Copyright © 2013 Dell, Inc. Used with permission.

FIGURE 11.2 An Appeal Based on Progress, Efficiency, and Practicality

Learning Objective

1 To understand culture's role, dynamics, evolution, and impact on consumers' priorities and behaviors.

Culture's Role and Dynamics

We often refer to culture as an "invisible hand" that guides the actions of people of a particular society. When consumer researchers ask people why they do certain things, they frequently answer, "Because it's the right thing to do"—a response reflecting the ingrained influence of culture on our behavior. We can truly understand and appreciate the influence of our culture only after visiting other countries and observing the local values and behaviors. For instance, after visiting restaurants in France or Italy, many Americans may realize that they eat too much food and snack too often. Furthermore, if we travel within the United States, we will also observe differences in the norms and preferences of subcultures. For instance, whereas consumers living in the Northeastern section of the United States have historically preferred ketchup on their hamburgers, consumers living in other sections have liked mustard, or a mixture of mustard and ketchup (see Chapter 12).

Some researchers conceptualized different "levels" of cultural norms:

1. ***The supranational*** level reflects the underlying dimensions of culture that affect multiple societies (i.e., subcultural cross-national or cross-cultural boundaries). For instance, it might reflect regional character (e.g., people living in several nations in a particular region of South America), or racial and religious similarities or differences, or shared or different languages.
2. ***The national*** level reflects shared core values, customs, and personalities that represent the core of the "national character" of a particular country.
3. ***The group*** level reflects the subdivisions of a country or society, such as subcultures, and the influences of various reference groups.[1]

On the supranational level of culture, which crosses national boundaries, researchers have developed a lifestyle matrix for four segments of global youth aged 14 to 24:

1. ***In-crowd:*** It's all about privilege and reinforcement; members of this group seek approval from others and prefer classic brands like Nike and Abercrombie & Fitch to uphold tradition.
2. ***Pop Mavericks:*** Word-of-mouth spreads rapidly, and passion, individuality, and instant gratification are important; members prefer brands that they can personalize—brands like Diesel and Adidas.
3. ***Networked Intelligentsia:*** They are the hub of online social networks, and it's all about revolution, creativity, and deconstruction; members prefer cult brands, like Vespa (in America) and Vans, which add to their sense of obscurity.
4. ***Thrill Renegades:*** It's all about infamy, adrenaline, and anarchy (and pretending that law and order do not exist).[2]

When operating in India, marketers need to be aware of and sensitive to its cultural diversity. The cultural diversity is reflected in several aspects of life ranging from behavior/rituals to specific values. ISKCON (premises shown in Figure 11.3), is a religious subculture with followers all over the world. It adheres to the values of compassion towards all forms of life and "food for all." Its Akshaya Patra scheme feeds 13,94,757 children below the poverty line in Bengaluru and in 20 other locations in nine states of the country.

Culture's Continuous Evolution

Marketers must always monitor cultural changes to discover new opportunities and abandon markets that have "dried up" because of cultural changes. To this end, marketers should periodically reconsider *why* consumers are doing what they do, *who* are the purchasers and the users of their offerings, *when* they do their shopping, *how* and *where* they can be reached by the media, and *what* new product and service needs are emerging. For example, cultural changes in America have increasingly recognized the expanded career options open to women. Today, most women work outside the home, and frequently in careers that were once exclusively male oriented. Later in this chapter, we explain why achievement and personal success are two of America's core values and how marketers can use them in advertising. Although traditionally associated with men, especially male business executives, achievement has become important for women as well, as they increasingly enroll in undergraduate and graduate business (and other college) programs and often attain top-level business positions. Also, many women are now in professions previously dominated by males (e.g., medicine, engineering, science). Therefore, many ads that target women

Source: Courtesy of ISKCON

FIGURE 11.3 ISKCON, Bengaluru

now depict appeals that emphasize achievement and success, whereas some years ago the same kinds of promotions appealed to women's roles as mothers and housewives.

A longitudinal study examined how women have been depicted in advertising over the years, and discovered that changing gender roles were manifested in promotional messages. Specifically, there has been a fourfold increase in the number of women as the "figure" (i.e., the focal point of the print advertisement) compared to men, and a substantial increase in the number of ads portraying women as business professionals.[3]

Box 11.1 Formation of a Rare Subculture – The Indian Context with Culture's Continuous Evolution

India is a land of subcultures and an interesting example of this has been discovered in the north-eastern state of Manipur. The cultural activist organizations in the state have banned Bollywood movies (perceived by consumers as a reflection of the state of the art fashion associated with the masses). While Manipuri movies have got a fillip in the state, the youth are now looking up to Korean movies.[4] These movies have gained popularity in the state for their fashion and grooming practices. From the marketers point of view, this is an unusual situation of an eastern foreign culture (while the normal diffusion takes place with the western trends) diffusing into an Indian state.

Fastrack used "Move on" in its campaigns the reality among the youth[5] by using values that are very different from the conservative values associated with the Indian culture. The ads showed a girl dumping her boyfriend and another showed a girl referring to her boyfriend as luggage and flirting with a man at the check-in counter of an airport. It should be noted that such an orientation for a brand does not mean that such values have radically transformed the Indian context. It may be appropriate for a specific sub segment of consumers (in this case the target segment for the brand).

Cultural Beliefs Reflect Consumers' Needs

Culture expresses and satisfies the needs of societies. It offers order, direction, and guidance for problem solving by providing "tried-and-true" methods of satisfying physiological, personal, and social needs. For example, culture provides standards about when to eat ("not between meals"); where to eat ("most likely, the restaurant is busy because the food is good"); what is appropriate to eat for breakfast (pancakes), lunch (a sandwich), dinner ("something hot and good and healthy"), and snacks ("something with quick energy, but not too many calories"); and what to serve to guests at a dinner party ("a formal sit-down meal"), at a picnic (barbecued "franks and burgers"), or at a wedding (champagne). Culture also determines whether a product is a necessity or discretionary luxury. For example, whereas mobile phones (initially introduced as car phones) were once expensive and uncommon, today they are a necessity because fewer and fewer people have landlines and payphones are largely extinct.

Culture also dictates which clothes are suitable for different occasions (such as what to wear around the house, and what to wear to school, to work, to church, at a fast-food restaurant, or to a movie theater). In recent years, dress codes have changed drastically and Americans have been dressing casually for occasions that once required more formal attire. For example, in large cities, only a handful of restaurants and clubs still require men to wear jackets and ties. With the relaxed dress code in the corporate work environment, fewer men are wearing dress shirts, ties, and business suits, and fewer women are wearing dresses, suits, and pantyhose. Instead, employees wear casual slacks, sports shirts and blouses, and even neat jeans and polo shirts.

Some customs, however, are unlikely to change. For example, soft-drink companies would prefer that consumers receive their morning "jolts" of caffeine from one of their products, instead of coffee. Because most Americans do not consider soda a suitable breakfast beverage, soft-drink companies have faced a dual challenge: "overcoming" culture, as well as the competition among breakfast drinks. Teas, soft drinks, and even caffeinated water have challenged coffee as the traditional source of morning caffeine—mostly unsuccessfully. Indeed, coffee is entrenched in our culture not only as a breakfast beverage, but also as the core of the "coffee break." Wisely, coffee marketers have not relied on their cultural advantage, but have been preempting their competitors by introducing assortments of gourmet and flavored coffees and also by aggressively targeting young adults with such exotics as espresso, cappuccino, and café mocha.

When a specific standard no longer satisfies the members of a society or reflects its needs, it is modified or replaced. For example, once it was unheard of for restaurant servers to pose questions of a personal nature. Now, we commonly answer servers' questions about our food allergies and other medical, food-related limitations. At times, society's collective interest contradicts an emerging custom. For instance, because most young Americans are now electronically connected all the time and at almost any place, distracted driving because of texting or calling on mobile phones is causing more car accidents. The two ads shown in Figure 11.4 are part of a government initiative to discourage distracted driving.

Application 1: Culture and Business to Business Marketing

Tetra Pak, the packaging company in the B2B marketing domain, has used an interesting metaphor drawn from the Indian culture as an initiative to expand more into the beverages market. The television commercial (TVC)[6] depicts the over-protective nature of Indians by showing a baby fondly dotted with *kajal* (kohl) on his face and draws comparison to the six-layered protection offered by the brand towards food and its nutritional benefits. In India, kohl symbolizes protection from evil spirits.

Application 2: The Cultural Dimension to Ego-defensive Function

Complan, the health drink, has been around for about four decades. The brand has successfully repositioned itself as a health drink associated with height enhancement (from a drink that was prescribed for convalescing people). The sustainable core proposition of enhancing height has been around for about 25 years or so.

The current campaign reinforces the same proposition (despite the onslaught from Horlicks's "taller, stronger, and sharper" campaign).

Making fun of physical appearances of people is considered an appalling act, but it is a widely spread behavioral phenomena found across the globe. Cultural sophistication may inhibit such expressions in a few societies. Unfortunately, such jokes seem to be a part of the Indian culture (movie jokes in several regional movies).

Complan uses this cultural aspect with the ego-defensive function. The TVC shows a young boy asking a doctor for a diet that would increase his height as he is being made fun of in school. Complan comes into the picture putting an end to his low self-esteem; he drinks Complan and his height increases. Under such situations, it is to be noted that the ego-defensive function is equally associated with the mothers (and several brands use this aspect). This ad cuts across both the child and mother in terms of its appeal, without even showing the image of the mother (which is the normal practice).

Source: (Left & Right) National Highway Traffic Safety Administration

FIGURE 11.4 Discouraging Distracted Driving

Symbolism in the Indian Cultural Context

Mother-child relationship has a universal appeal and the Indian context probably typifies the portrayal of this relationship. This trend has been reflected in advertisements over the last five decades, including radio jingles and cinema ads. For almost a century Johnson & Johnson (J&J) has used this relationship as the symbol of love, warmth, and affection, thereby associating it with the unique relationship of mother and child all over the world. The brand's offerings range from wipes for the up-market consumer to a ₹10 soap for the middle-class consumer.[7] Its symbol of mother and child commands a high loyalty and J&J has taken care to ensure that its imagery is viewed consistently by all segments of consumers.[8] The mother–child relationship illustrates the values associated with the occasion of bathing, portrays the baby as the hero, suggests enjoyment to the mother who goes through the ritual of bathing the child, and it has become an eternal symbol of this unique relationship.

Hofstede's model fits well with this product context and explains how a brand has made of use of such an application. Wipro and Marico are firms that entered the baby soap segment and exited it[9], perhaps due to the strongly entrenched image of J&J developed over a period of time with cultural dimensions.

Cadbury's has been constantly using cultural aspects to become a part of the consumption ritual of the user.[10] It used the "sweet tooth" culture in India to expand its market; it also made an interesting point by positioning its Dairy Milk chocolate as a dessert in an attempt to compete with the Indian *mithai* (sweet dish).[11] In the ad, a bar of chocolate was depicted as something that a family could share (it is a custom among Indian families to share *mithai*).

ITC's Bingo had been making strides in the competitive snacks category. In this case, distribution too has played a role. The brand had an interesting ad – a gang of thieves loot a house (also becoming a part of the accepted culture?). While leaving, the leader tastes a pack of Bingo and suddenly asks his followers to release the inmates of the house and says, "I cannot do harm to a house hold whose salt I have eaten." Salt is a considered a symbol of gratitude in the Indian culture. This is a well- entrenched belief in several part so the country and it also serves to drum up the USP – Bingo *Salted* Potato chips!

Learning Objective

2 To understand language, symbols, and rituals as expressions of a learned culture.

Learning Cultural Values

To be considered a cultural value, a belief or custom must be shared by a significant portion of the society, because culture is essentially a series of norms that guide personal and group conduct and link individuals into a largely cohesive group. Generally, members of a society share their values and customs through a common language, although some cultures include more than one language.

Forms of Learning

We learn cultural norms and customs mostly from family and peers, and begin to understand at a very young age that some behaviors are appropriate and others are not. Anthropologists have identified three forms of cultural learning. **Formal learning** takes place when parents, older siblings, and other family members teach younger members "how to behave." **Informal learning** takes place when children imitate the behaviors of selected others, such as family, friends, or TV and movie heroes and characters. **Technical learning** happens when teachers instruct children, in educational environments, about what should be done, how it should be done, and why it should be done, in social as well as personal settings. Our ethical values (e.g., the importance of kindness, honesty, and responsibility) are also formed during childhood as we learn them from parents, teachers, and other significant adults.[12]

Enculturation and Acculturation

Anthropologists distinguish between the learning of one's own (or native) culture and the learning of new cultures. **Enculturation** is learning one's own culture. **Acculturation** is learning new or foreign cultures. In Chapter 13, we demonstrate that acculturation is important for marketers that sell products in multinational markets. When selling products overseas, marketers must study the culture(s) of their potential customers so as to determine whether their products will be acceptable and how to communicate the characteristics of their products effectively and persuade consumers to buy them.

Sometimes, consumers can be "foreigners" in their own countries. For example, one study traced a group of provincial women in Thailand as they enrolled at a university in Bangkok (Thailand's capital city). As their first semester began, the women quickly formed their own group; they kept to themselves and did not mix with students from Bangkok or participate in the city's social scene. Ironically, the longer the provincial women lived in Bangkok, the more they resisted adopting Bangkok's culture and strongly expressed their provincial values.[13]

Key components of one's enculturation are the family and the process of **consumer socialization** (see Chapter 10). This process consists of teaching children and young adults consumption-related values and skills, such as the meaning of money and value, how to judge product quality, styles and preferences, product usage, and the meaning and objectives of promotional messages.[14] In addition to the family unit, educational and religious institutions also convey cultural values to younger members. Educational institutions impart the knowledge of arts, sciences, civics, and professional and specialized skills. Religious institutions provide spiritual and moral guidance and values, which often have a substantial impact on behavior.

Marketing Influences on Cultural Learning

The contents of media, advertising, and marketing reflect cultural values and convey them to all members of society very effectively. Given Americans' extensive exposure to print, broadcast, and online media, promotional messages are powerful vehicles for imparting cultural values. Every day, at almost any time, we are exposed to hundreds of promotional cues and messages, many of which we hear and see more than once. The repetition of marketing messages both conveys and reinforces cultural beliefs and values. For example, in the highly competitive environment of cellular communications, providers have aggressively promoted such features as low rates of dropped calls, high extent of coverage, and flexible pricing plans. After years of seeing such ads, wireless phone users learned to expect extensive benefits from cellular gadgets, and their expectation levels have been going up steadily—further reinforced by the frequent introductions of more sophisticated mobile communications.

In advertisements, cultural values are not only depicted in the advertising copy, but are also coded in the visual imagery, colors, movements, music, and other nonverbal elements of an advertisement.[15] Many products became American icons and tangible expressions of the nation's cultural values. For example, Tea is a part of the Indian culture. Chai Point outlets in Bangalore have made use of this aspect. Likewise, festivals are a part of the Indian culture and Asian Paints had made use of them.

Marketers also transmit a lot of information that enables consumers to express shared cultural values. For example, advertising in sophisticated magazines such as Vogue, Bon Appetit, and Architectural Digest instructs readers how to dress, how to decorate their homes, and what foods and wines to serve guests. Online, people form virtual communities that are focused on products and enable consumers to exchange and learn product-related customs. Social media is rapidly becoming a key factor in conveying and sharing cultural values. People follow tweets of influential people and peers and write in blogs that are focused on their activities, interests, and opinions. As a result, for example, more people may get involved in civic groups and humanitarian causes. Their actions, respectively, express the importance of personal achievement and success and humanitarianism, which are two of our core values (discussed later in this chapter).

Box 11.2 Branding Communication and Cultural Intricacies

One of the aspects of culture, useful for brand managers, is the contextual differentiation between high-context and low-context cultures.[16] India is a high-context culture where communication between consumers or even individuals will have to be interpreted with the socio-cultural nuances that involve display of emotions, symbols, gestures, and even body language (as against a low-context country like US where communication conveys direct meaning). How does such high-context cultural backdrop be used in ads? The ad for Surf (Quick wash) detergent positions itself against stains. The proposition of the brand is not conveyed straight away as a "detergent that fights stains on clothes". There is a small story developed in the TVC that shows a happy family wherein the daughter-in-law uses the brand and wins the praise of her mother-in-law. Mother-in-law and daughter-in-law relationships have a traditional significance in India.

Another example is the TVC from Johnson & Johnson for its blood sugar monitoring meter, One Touch. "Ease of use" is the proposition of the brand. This proposition is conveyed by a "song and dance" kind of overtone with the middle-aged couple celebrating the brand's ease of use with the child in the context. Family orientation and an overt display of happiness – strongly entrenched in the Indian culture – were used by the brand.

Language and Symbols

Cultural values are reflected in the languages, symbols, communications, and artifacts of a society. A **symbol** is anything that represents something else, and symbols can be either verbal or nonverbal. Words are verbal symbols, so the text of any ad is a composition of symbols. Nonverbal symbols, such as figures, colors, shapes, and even textures, are cultural cues that appear within advertisements, trademarks, packaging, and product designs. Many symbols have linguistic as well as psychological meanings. For example, the word "hurricane" is defined as a particular type of severe weather condition, but often stirs feelings of danger and thoughts of finding protection and safety. Similarly, the word "Cadillac" has symbolic meaning: To some it suggests a fine luxury automobile; to others it implies wealth and status (e.g., the phrase "the Cadillac of refrigerators" indicates that a refrigerator is the best in its product category).

Symbols can have contradictory meanings. For example, the advertiser that uses a trademark depicting an old craftsman to symbolize careful workmanship may instead be communicating an image of outmoded methods and lack of style. Marketers who use slang in advertisements directed at teenagers must do so with great care; slang that is misused or outdated will symbolically date the marketer's firm and product, and may also be offensive to some.

Prices and channels of distribution are symbols and reflect cultural meanings of products. For instance, the stores where clothes are sold (and also the prices of the items) symbolize their quality. In fact, all the elements of the marketing mix—the product, its promotion, price, and the stores at which it is available—are symbols that communicate the item's quality, value, and image.

Rituals

In addition to language and symbols, cultures include ritualized behaviors. A **ritual** is a type of symbolic activity consisting of a series of steps occurring in a fixed sequence and repeated periodically.[17] Rituals can be public, elaborate, or ceremonial (e.g., weddings), or mundane routines (e.g., daily grooming). Typically, ritualized behavior is formal and often scripted (e.g., a religious service or proper conduct in a court of law), and occurs repeatedly (e.g., singing the national anthem before the start of a sports event).

Many rituals include artifacts, and some products are marketed specifically for certain rituals. For instance, turkey, stuffing, and cranberries are part of the ritual of Thanksgiving Day. Rituals such as graduations, weekly card games, or visits to beauty salons include artifacts. Table 11.1 lists culturally appropriate artifacts for various occasions.

Application 1: Rituals, Children, and Indian Brands

The Surf Excel cricket commercial had made use of several aspects of the Indian culture and had also linked some aspects of the Hofstede's model that may be applicable to the Indian context. The ad showed a boy being pushed into slushy waters by his playmates while playing cricket (in several middle class households, getting dirty while playing is a part of the sports ritual even in today's digital world). The boy who is the "victim" of the quarrel (the one who has been pushed down) makes use of the opportunity to get his clothes dirty and hugs his playmates as a symbol of belongingness (collectivism reflected in a country like India that places emphasis on belongingness). The brand proposition of clearing stains is conveyed through the tagline in the ad that suggests that "stains are good" (implying that they enhance belongingness). Pepsodent is another brand (incidentally from the same company, Hindustan Unilever) that used kinds habit of snacking on the way back home from school to convey its proposition of "anti-germ" protection (snacking among kids on their way back to home from school is yet another cultural ritual in India).

Application 2: Cultural Beliefs and Brands

Rituals are a part of all cultures. For several decades consumers in India have used talcum powders during sweaty summers as a well-entrenched ritual. Garnier Men's deodorant (though deodorant is not a part of the larger mass culture's grooming ritual), has introduced the proposition that it absorbs five times the sweat as compared to a talcum powder.[18] This proposition reflects the efforts of the brand to connect with the Indian consumer.

Application 3: The Ritual–brand Linkage

Ritual is an activity (either symbolic or functional) that is generally repeated over time with multiple fixed and episodic sequences that reflect seriousness, inner intensity, and formality. For example, eating and bathing are rituals that serve some kind of functional utility; grooming is another ritual that may reflect the some degree of symbolism about the self.[19] Marketers need to make brands part of a ritual appropriate for the consumer segment.

Sunsilk Natural Recharge is a brand of shampoo that has hair strength as its proposition and makes the brand a part of the "office going" ritual in its advertisement.

After-Shower was a brand of hair gel that targeted youngsters and had become a part of the grooming ritual. Marie biscuits are a part of the tea-drinking ritual. Ujala, a variant of liquid blue, became a part of the ritual of consumers adding drops of blue to their white clothes while washing them. Parachute Advansed coconut oil advocated that the consumer should apply the oil before bath. Using a hand wash (Lifebuoy, for instance) has become a part of our day-to-day ritual. 3 Roses tea advertisement featured a young wife caring for her husband's health, presumably by being a part of the "serving the tea" ritual.

TABLE 11.1 Selected Rituals and Associated Artifacts

RITUAL	ARTIFACTS
Wedding	White gown (something old, something new, something borrowed, something blue)
Birth of child	U.S. savings bond, silver baby spoon
Birthday	Card, present, cake with candles
Fiftieth wedding anniversary	Catered party, card and gift, display of photos of the couple's life together
Graduation	Pen, U.S. savings bond, card, wristwatch
Valentine's Day	Candy, card, flowers
New Year's Eve	Champagne, party, elegant formal dress
Thanksgiving	A turkey dinner served to family and friends
Going to the gym	Towel, exercise clothes, water, iPod
Sunday football	Beer, potato chips, pretzels
Super Bowl party	Same as Sunday football (but more)
Starting a new job	Get a haircut and buy new clothes
Getting a job promotion	Taken out to lunch by coworkers and receive token gift
Retirement	Company party, a watch, and a plaque
Death	Send a card, send flowers, donate money to charity in honor of the deceased

TABLE 11.2 Facial Beauty Ritual of a Young Advertising Executive

1. I pull my hair back with a headband.
2. I take off my makeup with L'Oréal makeup remover.
3. Next, I gently rub a Qtip with some moisturizer around my eyes to make sure all of my eye makeup is removed.
4. I wash my face with Noxzema facial wash.
5. I apply Clinique Dramatically Different Lotion to my face and neck.
6. If I have a blemish, I dry it out with Clearasil Treatment.
7. Once a week, using a wet and warm cloth, I apply Clinique Clarifying Lotion 2 to my face and neck to remove dead skin cells.
8. Every three months, I get a professional salon facial to clean my pores deeply.

Ritualistic behavior is an action or series of steps that have become a ritual. For example, golfers who take a few practice swings before actually hitting the ball display a ritualistic behavior. Personal-care activities are often ritualized; Table 11.2 describes the daily ritual of a woman's facial care.

Learning Objective

3 To understand how to measure the influence of culture on consumer behavior.

Measuring Cultural Values

Culture reflects a society's values, customs, and rituals, which in turn reflect how we live and communicate. The most widely used measurements of cultural values are content analysis, consumer field observation, and value measurement instruments.

Content Analysis

Content analysis, as the name implies, focuses on the content of societies' verbal, written, and pictorial communications, including promotional messages. Content analysis can be applied to marketing, gender and age issues, sociology and political science, psychological studies, and many other fields. Among other concepts, content analysis can:

1. Identify the intentions, focus, or communication trends of an individual, group, or institutions.
2. Describe attitudinal and behavioral responses to communications.
3. Determine psychological or emotional state of persons or groups.[20]

Content analysis can determine what social and cultural changes have occurred in a specific society or compare different cultures. Content analysis of more than 250 ads appearing in 8 issues of Seventeen Magazine—4 Japanese issues and 4 American issues—found that teenage girls are portrayed quite differently. Portrayals of American teen girls often reflected images of independence and determination, whereas those of Japanese teen girls portrayed happy, playful, childlike girlish images.[21] Another content analysis study compared American and Chinese television commercials targeted to children and revealed that 82% of the Chinese ads aimed at children were for food products, whereas 56% of the ads directed at American children were for toys.[22]

Field Observation

When examining a specific society, anthropologists frequently study cultures through **field observation**, which consists of observing the daily behavior of selected members of a society. Based on their observations, researchers draw conclusions about the values, beliefs, and customs of the society under investigation. For example, if researchers were interested in how women select jeans, they might position trained observers in department and clothing stores and note how many and which types of jeans buyers pick up, look at, and try on.

Field observation:

1. Takes place within a natural environment.
2. Generally, the subjects are not aware that they are being watched.
3. Focuses on observation of behavior.

Because the emphasis is on a natural environment and observable behavior, field observation of buying and consumption activities occurs in stores, and, less frequently, during in-home product usage.

In some cases, researchers become **participant-observers**; that is, they become active members of the environment that they are studying and engage in the same behaviors, rituals, and customs that they study. For example, if researchers were interested in examining how consumers select a washing machine, they might take a sales position in an appliance store and observe and interact with the customers. Researchers who specialize in field observation often videotape subjects at work, at home, in their cars, and in public places. For instance, if researchers ask teenagers directly why they are buying certain T-shirts, teenagers might give answers that they believe will make them look sensible to the researchers. Instead, watching teenagers as they shop and listening to their conversations with other shoppers or salespersons might reveal more about the kids' motivations for buying. As a classic example, when Nissan was designing its Infiniti automobiles in the 1990s, two individuals, posing as students, rented rooms in the suburban homes of two families in the Los Angeles area and observed the car-related behaviors and preferences of "typical" Americans, without the families' awareness. Among other findings, they discovered that the Japanese notion of luxury was very different from the American notion; whereas the Japanese crave simplicity, Americans crave visible opulence.[23]

In addition to fieldwork, marketers have used **depth interviews** and **focus groups** (see Chapter 16) to study social and cultural changes. In focus group discussions, consumers are apt to reveal attitudes and behaviors that signal shifts in values that may affect, for example, the acceptance of new products and services. Focus groups have been used to generate ideas for persuasive strategies designed to reinforce customer loyalty and retention. Studies showed that established customers, especially for services (such as investment and banking), expected marketers to acknowledge their loyalty by providing them with more personalized services. Subsequently, several companies instituted loyalty (or frequency) programs tailored to customers' specific needs.

Researchers exploring the symbolic meanings of foods conducted 30 in-depth interviews (lasting 1.5 to 2.5 hours) of females and males within the (very wide) age range of 22 to 71 years old. They found that, in the context of cultural settings, there are seven types of foods: *Symbolic* foods (e.g., homemade and comfort foods); *individual* foods (e.g., healthy foods); *social* foods (e.g., foods typically shared with family and others); *cultural* foods (e.g., foods eaten during sexual encounters and believed to enhance libido); *ritualistic* foods (e.g., foods associated with nostalgic events); *context* foods (e.g., date and coffee-break foods); and *experience* foods (e.g., unfamiliar foods from other cultures).[24]

Value Measurements

Anthropologists have traditionally observed the behavior of members of a specific society and inferred the underlying values of the society from the behaviors observed. However, there are also structured, self-administered questionnaires that measure individuals' cultural values, such as the Rokeach Value Survey, the Values and Lifestyles **VALS** (discussed in Chapter 2) measure, and Gordon's survey of personal and interpersonal values.

Rokeach Values Survey

The **Rokeach Value Survey** is a self-administered, two-part values inventory:

1. Eighteen **terminal values** that reflect goals and desirable states of existence and are defined as *ends* (e.g., happiness, pleasure, freedom, self-respect).
2. Eighteen **instrumental values**, defined as the *means* to achieve the ends (e.g., ambitious, honest, polite, responsible).

Respondents are asked how important each value is to them as "a guiding principle" in their lives.

Within each set of values, there are also two subsets: Some terminal values focus on *personal* aspects (e.g., a comfortable or exciting life, happiness, inner harmony) and the others on *interpersonal* ones (e.g., a world of peace and beauty, national security). The instrumental values are composed of *competence* (e.g., ambitious, intellectual, responsible) and *moral* values (e.g., forgiving, helpful, polite).

According to the Rokeach typology, in terms of cultural orientation, individuals can belong to one of four types. Table 11.3 describes the characteristics of each type and also lists applicable, illustrative promotional themes.

As an example, let's assume that a study employed the Rokeach Value Survey to categorize a given population. The members of one segment uncovered were mostly concerned with "world peace," followed by "inner harmony" and "true friendship." Members of this segment were involved in domestic-oriented activities (such as gardening, reading, and going out with the family to visit relatives); they were less materialistic, nonhedonistic, and reluctant to try new products. In contrast, the members of another segment were self-centered and concerned with values such as "self-respect," "a comfortable life," "pleasure," "exciting life," "accomplishment," and "social recognition." They were least concerned with values related to the family and other people, such as friendship, love, and equality. Because they were self-centered, achievement-oriented, and pleasure seekers, they preferred provocative and highly fashionable clothes, enjoyed adventurous lifestyles, and were willing to try new products.

Gordon's Surveys of Personal and Interpersonal Values

Gordon's Survey of Personal and Interpersonal Values measures values that determine how people cope with their daily lives.[25] There are two surveys—one for **personal values** and one for **interpersonal values**—that are partially described in Table 11.4, together with the illustrative characteritics that exemplify each value. As expected, Gordon's values are strongly reflected in Americans' core values, which are discussed next.

TABLE 11.3 The Rokeach Typology and Illustrative Promotional Themes

		TERMINAL VALUES: GOALS AND DESIRED STATES OF EXISTENCE	
		PERSONAL VALUES: PERSONAL FOCUS	**SOCIAL VALUES: INTERPERSONAL FOCUS**
INSTRUMENTAL VALUES: Preferable behaviors and means for achieving terminal values.	COMPETENCE VALUES: Being ambitious, capable, and responsible. When violated, the person feels ashamed and inadequate.	Promotional messages should reflect consumers' sense of accomplishment, self-respect, and striving for a comfortable life and independence.	Rather than depicting merely concern, messages should show helping others and the role of one's skills in doing so.
	MORAL VALUES: Being cheerful, helpful, and honest. When violated, the person feels guilty.	Promotions should stress concern for societal issues and intense conviction to advance such causes.	The majority of Americans. Promotions should stress conformity, caring for others, and social consciousness.

TABLE 11.4 Marketing-Applicable Values from Gordon's Inventory

PERSONAL VALUES	INTERPERSONAL VALUES
ACHIEVEMENT Enjoying challenge, growth, and accomplishment. Knowing what one wants to accomplish and doing so in an outstanding manner.	**LEADERSHIP** Being in charge and having authority and power. Not having to follow orders. Leading groups. Having others work under one's direction.
GOAL ORIENTATION Prefer having well-defined objectives and completing tasks. Knowing exactly what one is aiming for.	**RECOGNITION** Being looked up to, considered important, and admired. Having people make favorable remarks. Being noticed.
VARIETY Disliking routines and preferring new experiences. Visiting new places. Trying new and different things. Being able to have a variety of experiences and travel a lot.	**CONFORMITY** Doing the correct thing and following regulation. Doing what's accepted and proper. Conforming strictly to rules and moral standards.

Learning Objective

4 To Understand How Core Cultural Values Impact Indian Consumers.

Indian Core Values*

Indian society is driven by a set of **core values**, though these may vary in the urban and rural contexts. These values remain basic to Indian culture and are strongly embedded in most subcultures. The variation in the urban milieu may be attributed to changing lifestyles, the impact of Westernization, and the diffusion of technology. Even within the urban context, these values may have further variations or contradictions. Young couples working with high-technology firms may lead a typically Western lifestyle (cars, fast food and weekend holidays) but still hold on to or practice certain religious beliefs and customs that are totally ethnic in nature. In general, Indian consumers are culture-conscious in the sense that they conform to the cultural expectations of society. Core values of a society are adopted by a significant number of people; are enduring, or followed by people for a long time; and enable marketers to understand the behavior of consumers. The following are some of the core values of Indians.

Family Orientation

Family for an average Indian not only includes one's own family (spouse and children) but also the extended family—parents, siblings, grandparents, etc. The commitment of the male consumer (in some cases, the female consumer, too) to the family is such that he, as the chief wage earner, supports the entire joint family. This has several marketing implications. First, the disposable income of such a consumer gets radically reduced and he (or she, since the wife makes most of the daily purchase) is always looking for value-based brands at a lower price point. This logic works equally for purchases concerning oneself and one's immediate family members. The brands at the lower end of the market in a number of product categories like tea, soap, toothpaste, and shampoo typically cater to these kinds of consumers. This type of consumer also mixes brands and products from the unorganized sector to balance his/her expenditure on such consumption needs. In fact, low-end brands attempt to upgrade the consumer from the products of the unorganized sector (unbranded and local products, which may be marketed in an unstructured and haphazard manner). A consumer may buy a branded detergent powder like Surf to wash his/her "special" clothes and may buy low-end washing soaps (branded but cheaper) for washing ordinary clothes. Once in a while, he/she may buy shampoo sachets that are offered for around ₹2 to ₹2.50 (Chik shampoo was introduced at 50 paise). Such implications in terms of "value" offerings (₹1 is less than 5% of a US dollar) will not be felt in developed countries.

As the consumer feels the need to economize, he/she may also down-trade—or buy less expensive brands after using higher-priced ones. Down-trading occurs as the consumer's response to price increases across product categories; and also when the cost of essential services like electricity, water, or cooking fuel goes up. This behavior of consumers is important for marketers as there have been constant efforts by companies to upgrade consumers in several categories. For example, Unilever India Limited has a number of price points in almost all its product lines. Colgate has also a number of brands at different price points—Colgate

* This section is an adapted version of the text in S. Ramesh Kumar, *Consumer Behaviour and Branding: Concepts, Readings, and Cases, The Indian Context* (Delhi: Pearson Education, 2009).

Herbal, Colgate, Colgate Gel, and Colgate Total brands. Consumers may down-trade at any price point in the product-line and not necessarily at the lower end of the market (though brands at the upper end may experience a degree of price insensitivity).

Savings Orientation

Saving is still an inherent value of Indians; given the uncertainty in income generation (a majority of the population depends on agriculture and about 24% lives in urban areas, monthly salary as a regular source of income being available only to a small cross-section of the population). Unlike in developed countries, community medical services or assured pension after retirement are not available to most consumers. Most Indian families have to depend on personal savings for their living after retirement and for their medical expenses all through their lives. Therefore, saving up for old age is a major concern for Indians. Consumers fall back on their savings to celebrate festivities—very specifically, weddings in the family—and spend as lavishly as possible. Recently, consumers have begun spending on durable products after the basic needs have been taken care of. Bicycles, watches, and TVs are perhaps popular "entry-level" purchases for the average Indian who is able to take care of the basic necessities. Savings as a habit pervades all sections of the society. Consumers belonging to all socio-economic classes are interested in jewelry and for most of them it may mean investing a considerable amount of their savings. Traditionally, jewelry is more associated with women. Families with girl children are more likely to spend their savings on jewelry. Mostly, consumers buy their jewelry from family jewelers who have been associated with them for several generations. Branded jewelry like Tanishq and Carbon cater to just about 2% of the jewelry market and target an up-market niche. The popularity of installment payments for a number of products ranging from bicycles to computers can be attributed to consumers splitting savings between traditional purchases like jewelry and appliances required for a convenient living.

Festivities

Celebrating festivals is very much a part of India's culture in all the states. The subculture within a state (territory) determines the type of festival that is to be actively celebrated. For example, Pongal is not quite popular except in Tamil Nadu. Like most festivals in this country, Pongal has a special association with the farmers of the state. Durga Puja in West Bengal is celebrated with a great deal of enthusiasm every year. But it is not popular in all states even though its variations are celebrated in other parts. Similarly, Onam in Kerala is another example of a regional festival. Such festivals are a huge opportunity for marketers. Given that 76% of Indians live in rural areas, a number of companies step up their advertising campaigns and logistics during the festive months. Several brands in a number of product categories offer sales promotional programs during festive seasons and hundreds of thousands of consumers make use of "value-based" deals during these times. A number of consumers postpone their purchases, especially durables, in the hope of getting such deals. Even a niche jewelry brand like Tanishq came out with rakhis (fraternal friendship bonds tied by girls to boys they consider to be their brothers) in gold on Raksha Bandhan. Gold coins with images of gods (a sign of financial prosperity) are given away as gifts by marketers of durable brands, normally through specified outlets in a city.

Shopping as a Ritual

Shopping is a ritual of sorts, among both urban and rural Indians. The type of buyers, the shops they buy from, and the products they purchase vary across geographical territories and the economic spectrum of consumers. Retail outlets may range from a roadside shop selling vegetables to departmental stores like Big Bazaar or Croma or Shoppers Stop, which promise ambience, variety, and service over other conventional outlets. The fact that only about 5% of products (in value terms) are retailed through departmental stores is a reflection of the fragmented nature of retailing in India, quite the reverse of what happens in developed countries. Housewives shop almost regularly for basic commodities and vegetables even though the trend may be changing in the urban context. Bargaining, especially in the case of commodities and vegetables, is an unwritten rule in the transaction process. The popular departmental stores cater to the middle class and have a sales promotion strategy for all the year across product categories. In the case of durable products like TVs, refrigerators, or two-wheelers, the average Indian consumer is oriented toward the "extended problem-solving" kind of decision making. As part of the great shopping ritual, members of a family visit outlets with the objective of comparing prices and arriving at the best deal in a product category. The shopping of durables by typical Indian consumers can be associated with the compensatory style of decision making, with buyers analyzing one brand after another (especially when sales promotions are advertised). It is extremely difficult to find retailers (durable categories) who refuse to sell the brand below the marked retail price in order to clinch the deal with the consumer. This has been true of FMCG products in recent times and such shops use signboards that say something like "Buy and Save" to achieve big volumes.

The rural Indian scenario (a rural area is defined as a geographical region with a population of around 5,000 people and where 75% of the male population is engaged in agriculture) presents a unique characteristic, which marketers have used. In a number of villages and towns (there are around 635,000 villages in India), flea markets are held every week and people buy the basic necessities (sometimes even durables like bicycles and watches) from there. These are generally held one specific day in a week and retailers spread their "product-mix" in makeshift stalls. Most of them stock fast-moving units across product categories that they buy from wholesalers near their place of trade. A number of companies make use of video-vans that arrange some kind of entertainment (most commonly, a movie) and end with a brand message. Not every village or town, of course, has this makeshift market that attracts consumers from a number of neighboring villages. Most consumers in semi-urban and rural areas visit the closest market in the town/city for their purchases. Given the nature of the potential of durables (upper-end ones like refrigerators and color television sets), brands are not in a position to have a network of outlets reaching out to most parts of the country (like FMCG companies that reach millions of outlets in rural areas). There are potential markets in villages where higher-end durable categories may be consumed, but the rural households in such categories, unlike their urban counterparts, are spread out while the latter are concentrated in specific pockets. Some of them, however, may be concentrated in a specific state (Punjab, for instance, has a number of such households in rural areas). Marketers of durables can adopt specialized channel strategies. A brand can identify such customers, have a company-owned outlet (depending on its feasibility), and start a direct marketing exercise to reach out to these households. Company-owned outlets are preferred becausethe company establishes contact with these consumers and can, at a later stage, attempt up-selling and cross-selling of its products. LG, the brand that has a leading share in several categories of durable products, opened up sales offices in semi-urban markets in an effort to reach out to consumers in the hinterland.

Mythology

Mythological stories, scriptures, and music are an inherent part of the Indian culture. Apart from creating a brand experience in a service like tourism, toys, and souvenirs, and artifacts can also be drawn from the Indian cultural milieu. Such products are marketed in places of tourist interest but the products are not branded. Most of these may not even have good quality in terms of product finish and durability. Tourism, largely promoted by government enterprises, has received considerable impetus in the form of infrastructure and service support. But there is a vast potential for creating a brand in this industry—among both foreign and domestic travelers. A value-based branding experience can create a huge market in tourism, which seems to have taken off in a big way only in the upper social crust. Local toy manufacturers cater to specific markets and a large chunk of the industry is in the unorganized sector. Branded toys with Indian cultural themes (with several elements of the marketing mix brought together) can open up attractive avenues for a brand. Even multinational brands like Leo and Mattel can develop ethnic products and make them affordable to the masses considering the potential that exists in this sector.

Food Habits

As in most Asian countries, hot, spicy delicacies are popular in India too. It may be worthwhile to note that food habits have a strong link with culture and are difficult to change. With the exception of Maggi noodles during the 1980s, there has not been a single "foreign" food item that has become as popular. Bread, which has been around for several decades, is still not popular barring certain urban and some semi-urban markets. But it is interesting to note that several variants of wheat flour are popular throughout India. The consumption of biscuits with tea, too, has almost become part of the eating culture of million of Indians both in urban and rural markets. The success of Tiger biscuits, with its low-priced packs, reflects the strength of such a habit.

Changing Cultural Trends In Indian Urban Markets

The urban setting is very different from the rural or semi-urban market setting. There are tar-get segments in cities comprising professionally qualified, high-salaried people who are into the fast track of life. The cultural values of this segment reflect the trends in the urban markets (trends with regard to niche consumers that do not cover the majority of the population). This segment is strongly influenced by the lifestyle and aspirations of the West. The following values can be associated with this niche.

Achievement Orientation

These aspects contribute to the intrinsic and extrinsic motivational levels and are reflected in the consumption of products and brands. Possessing a middle-end car (like Opel or Honda City), membership of prestigious clubs, and holidaying in a foreign resort are some products and services these consumers are interested in procuring. These products/brands reinforce a feeling of accomplishment in individuals and are perceived as rewards. Cielo positioned itself as a brand for "those who have arrived" when it entered India. Though the brand is no longer in the market, it is a typical example of how a brand positioned the car, a status symbol, as an aspirational product in an appropriate context.

Work Ethic

As a logical extension of the previous value, contemporary consumers are breaking away from traditional work practices and are involved in high-tension, fast-paced jobs. They experience time pressure and hence prefer time-compression or convenience products. A variety of retail outlets across product categories have emerged in the context (ordering of groceries online, direct marketing of brands, one-stop shops, fast-food restaurants like McDonald's or Pizza Hut, and grocery shops in petrol pumps are some examples). There is a growing need for servicesthat offer high levels of satisfaction. On-call services like plumbing, bill payment, laundry services, and home delivery of grocery and food are some of them.

Material Success

Young professionals between 25 and 30 years, who are extremely conscious of their materialistic success, have emerged in the last decade. This segment is significantly and markedly different from its equivalent counterparts (in terms of education and status) two decades ago. Present-day young adults have tremendous exposure to the environment through education or work experience abroad. They belong to cutting-edge professions like software or are high-profile entrepreneurs. The education, intelligence, and aspirations of these consumers have resulted in their acquiring substantial wealth at a relatively young age. The wealth is spent on essential products, which have contributed to the service economy—health, amusement, timecompression, and convenience. Besides, this segment chooses products and brands with a symbolic overtone; probably to tell the society that they have "arrived." There is great demand for quality-oriented, branded services like laundry services, in-home delivery of food, baby-sitters, pet-care people and, in a small way, online marketing of essentials.

Middle-of-the-Road Approach to Tradition

A niche segment of consumers, who are urban, highly educated, and in the upper end of the socio-economic strata, adopt a middle-of-the-road approach toward rituals and other cultural practices. Most are neither too permissive nor too traditional in their approach toward tradition. In the food segment, Indians have traditionally preferred home-cooked food, with eating out being reserved for very special occasions. In urban India, however, as more and more women are working outside the home, eating out on a regular basis, especially among young professionals, has become a part of the culture. Figure 11.5 illustrates how a brand like Ashirwad, from ITC, will appeal to consumers who enjoy traditional dishes with the added proposition of convenience.

Source: ITC

FIGURE 11.5 ITC Ready-To-Eat Meals

Impulse Gratification

While a number of consumers may be using credit cards, neo-urban young adults exhibit a compulsive need to buy products and services through credit cards. This niche segment may possess multiple credit cards. Some banks even attempt to get into the consideration set of such consumers by offering discounts to students of premier institutions, in the hope that they are prospective consumers interested in banking with them.

Use of Hi-Tech Products

High-profile consumers use products like iPods, iPhones, iPads, computers, and hi-tech products in the categories of household appliances and entertainment systems. This lifestyle aspect may be of interest to marketers of high-end products like fuzzy-logic washing machines, plasma television sets and, perhaps, products using bluetooth technology (a company with a rich database of consumers belonging to this segment can have several variations of permission marketing (which essentially deals with getting the consumer involved in the brand's messages that suits his/her interests rather than bombard the consumer with a barrage of direct mailings). This segment is oriented toward information, is independent and involved in its search and has the potential and willingness to spend. A number of brands may address this segment through a media-mix. The penetration of PCs is high among members of this segment as is online information processing, even though these consumers may eventually transact at a retail outlet. Several brands are positioned to this segment with lifestyle and symbolic appeals. Symbolic positioning can be backed up with a strong cognitive (information-oriented) copy on the Internet. Interactivity can be put to good use if the Web site can customize the information provided to the consumer. Queries are likely to be diverse in nature and TV commercials can be supplemented by the Internet. There is also a possibility for the brand to develop a brand community on the net. The urban, niche segment is ideal for the marketers interested in one-to-one marketing or relationship marketing.

A recent research study[26] published by S. Ramesh Kumar with his co-authors identified 32 Indian values that are relevant to marketing. These values include traditional and contemporary ones:

1. Power distance (social hierarchy emerging from different aspects of living)
2. Uncertainty avoidance (dealing with the unfamiliar)
3. Forward-looking (futuristic orientation of the individual)
4. Conservatism (not wanting to lead a fashionable lifestyle)
5. Need for affiliation (a sense of belongingness with others)
6. Family bonding (a close and a bonded relationship with family)
7. Utilitarianism (buying products that have sheer utility value)
8. Fatalism (resigned to destiny)
9. Nominalism (following rituals with regard to one's culture)
10. Achievement seeking (a strong desire to be successful)
11. Respect for age (respecting old people)
12. Cooperation (providing support to others in group work)
13. Nuclear family (one's immediate family consisting of spouse and children without one's parents or a joint family with other relatives)
14. Group emphasis (a tendency to be in groups both for formal and informal gatherings)
15. Respect for work (commitment and involvement with one's work)
16. Seeking prosperity (desire to acquire materialistic possessions as a way of living)
17. Hospitality (being cordial with friends and relatives)
18. Social orientation (choosing a lifestyle that will reflect one's personality)
19. Self-esteem (one's beliefs about one's self-worth)
20. Honor (not overspending as a matter of honor and prestige to ensure that one does not get into debt)
21. Innovation (one's desire to experiment with brands and products)
22. Conspicuous Western symbols (use of brands and products that symbolize Westernization)

23. Gifting trends (a desire to gift others on various social occasions)
24. Personal grooming (desire to groom oneself for social purposes)
25. Family hierarchy orientation (accepting that the main salary earner, generally men, influence the family purchases)
26. Ethnocentrism (desire to buy brands made in one's own country)
27. Individualism (desire to be identified as an individual)
28. Thriftiness (desire to save money by being price sensitive)
29. Celebrity orientation (a desire to get influenced by celebrities in advertisements with regard to purchase decisions)
30. Time orientation (a desire to be nostalgic about the days gone by)
31. Emotional decision making (a desire to make purchase decisions based on emotions)
32. Neo-mindset orientation (a desire to be break conventions and be rebellious)

Learning Objective

5 To Understand the Cultural Aspects of Emerging Markets.

Cultural Aspects of Emerging Markets*

Hofstede[27] defined culture as the mental programming of people in an environment. He called culture a combination of symbols (women wearing abundant 22 karat gold jewelry are perceived as prosperous in several parts of India), heroes (celebrities are widely used in Indian advertising), rituals (wedding rituals in India), and values (it is unusual to find even educated and Westernized women smoking in public places in India). This combination of factors is useful in differentiating between one marketing scenario and another. Kenichi Ohmae[28] defined an emerging economy as a country with a per capita income of less than US$10,000. India has a per capita income of around US$700 and as an emerging economy has a complex set of factors associated with its demographic and cultural dimensions. The explosion of mass media and the aspirations of young consumers (about 40% of the Indian population is below the age of 21 years) in a country with a strong traditional culture have resulted in advertisements innovatively using both traditional and contemporary cultural dimensions to influence consumers.

Several facets of culture are overtly and covertly used in marketing communications. In addition to cultural overtones finding a place in advertising, there are some product categories that are culturally oriented (meaning that these product categories are a part of the Indian culture in terms of the habits and lifestyles of consumers). Advertising appeals for these product categories too need to be formulated with the cultural factors and target segment of consumers taken into consideration.

The Indian Context

India has a population of about one billion and it is a country of contrasts with regard to lifestyles at different levels of its socio-economic structure. About 74% of the population lives in villages or hamlets. A village is a rural area that has a population below 5,000, has a population density of less than 400 per sq. km and where 75% of the males are engaged in agriculture. There are about 635,000 villages in the country and 63% of villages have a population of between 1,000 and 5,000. The population can be categorized into different kinds of households with regard to economic criteria. There are 100.1 million households classified as "deprived,"[29] earning less than US$ 1,969, 91.3 million households known as "aspirers," earning US$ 1,969–4,376, 10.9 million households of "seekers," earning US$ 4,376–10,941, 2.4 million households of "strivers," earning US$ 10,941–21,882, and 1.2 million households of "global Indians" who earn over US$ 21,882. While lifestyles of each of these clusters differ in terms of product and services categories purchased, there are also cultural differences between these clusters, and consumers within each of these segments may belong to different subcultures as these households are spread throughout the country in metropolitan areas as well as rural areas.

Brands have national advertising campaigns in English and in Hindi, the official language of the country. But there are states that do not have Hindi-speaking people and hence many brands also come out with advertisements in regional languages and sometimes with regional content, too. Soap operas in regional languages are very popular in the respective states and brands use these soap opera slots to advertise appropriate brands and product categories depending on the type of target segment. For example, Coke may carry a TV commercial in several states (sometimes in regional languages) during the summer and textile and TV brands may advertise during the months of October and November, the religious and festive season, during which most

* Parts of this section were first published in the *Journal of Integrated Marketing Communication*, 2009. Reproduced with permission. .

states will have festivities. Durable purchases peak during this season. For instance, Cadbury, the multinational brand of chocolates, introduces special packs during the festival seasons. Ethnic wear for women is a category that has regional brands, which advertise during these seasons in their regions. Quite a few advertisements in the Indian context have "storytelling" themes, and brand and cultural dimensions (both traditional and modern) get interwoven in these themes.

The changing lifestyles of consumers after the globalization of the Indian economy are also frequently reflected through advertisements. Though India still has a male-dominated culture, women in select "pockets" of the country have made rapid strides with regard to education and employment. Some advertisements also reflect these changes, especially ones that are aimed at urban target segments. Several millions of consumers in rural markets derive their aspirations from urban-oriented advertisements. The advertisements for a soft drink, Thums up (owned by Coca-Cola in India), had a macho appeal that was very urban, but the brand was advertised nationally in both urban and rural areas of the country. There are also brands that were very rural some decades back but have acquired an urban imagery to attract urban target segments. For instance, Lifebuoy (from Unilever India limited) was launched several decades back as a rural brand of soap with a strong carbolic scent and its cinema hall commercials showed football players (a popular rural sport at that time). The brand was popular throughout the country with its "germ-killing" proposition, especially in rural areas. Recently, however, the brand repositioned itself as an urban, family soap with a change in its fragrance with the same "germkilling" proposition. The concept of "family soap" is also a popular in India, where several members of the family use the same bar of soap.

Almost every product category also has up-market branding associations. Jewelry has been a part of the Indian culture for centuries. Most of the jewelry demand is in the unorganized sector (small traders dealing with unbranded offerings limited to specific geographical areas). Customers also develop a relationship with these traders and several families in the country may have intergenerational links with these jewelers and their family members (the buyer–seller relationships transcend generations). Even in such a category, there are regional and national brands that are advertised with contemporary appeals for urban women. Some of the brands combine traditional appeals with modernity. For instance, a national brand, Tanishq, launched diamonds (traditionally supposed to denote higher status of the wearer in India). The television commercial shows a husband and wife in traditional clothes, with the husband admiring the diamonds on his wife and finally an elderly lady (likely to be perceived to be the mother-in-law who normally stays with the son even after his marriage as per the culture of the country) seeing the husband falling at the feet of the wife. In Indian culture, prostrating implies a request for blessings from someone who is of a higher social rank or is older. Traditionally, wives are supposed to seek blessings from their husbands. The Tanishq advertisement also has a song from a popular south Indian movie of the 1960s. Nostalgic linkages with traditional culture, traditional roles in the culture, and the changing role of women in the society, are well captured in the advertisement for a product (in this case also a brand) that has been a part of the culture for centuries.

Frequently Used Product Categories In India

An analysis of the advertisements of FMCGs was made using the 32 values identified earlier and the concept of ritual setting.[30] A product is a ritual artifact. When the product is used in a specific setting (created by brand communication), the consumer derives meaning from the communication. The ritual setting is the context portrayed by a brand's communication and it creates a specific perception in the mind of the consumer. For instance, a brand of Titan watches is positioned as a gift across several categories involving relationships of romance and warmth. The "gift-giving ritual setting" creates the "gifting-brand" association. FMCG brands were chosen as they are a part of the everyday life of consumers, and the communication of brands across categories indicates strong cultural values. The advertisements of brands chosen have cultural values that are dominant in the marketing communication context. We have presented some of the brand analyses here.

Hamam (Soap)

This brand from Unilever India has been in the country for decades and was advertised as the "family soap" a few decades back. The brand's proposition during the 1990s was a "natural" soap using the association of an innocent child. The brand launched herbal variants. In recent times, its advertisements have centered on portraying women who can be perceived as beautiful while still being traditional (identified from their apparel, looks, presence of elderly family members). Some of the advertisements also project a child with traditional apparel and a ritual known as *kolam*—traditional artwork with a white powder drawn at the entrance of the house that symbolizes prosperity and good omen. Advertisements show a family that values traditional beauty. The traditional beauty is also portrayed in a way such that the woman is also a stereotype of conservative middle-class households.

Values identified: family bonding, seeking prosperity

Ritual setting: middle class, traditional family, ritual associated with culture, appreciation of tra-ditional beauty with regard to women, happiness

Lux (Soap)

It is interesting to note that Unilever India that also has Lux under its portfolio of soaps uses another approach to distinguish this product (Lux) using other cultural dimensions. Lux has a history of using topical (reigning) celebrities from films for the last several decades. The brand has introduced different variants for different kinds of applications concerned with skin. The advertisement shows a celebrity from films (frequently someone who is also a Miss India or a Miss World), usually dressed in Western clothes, who is the center of attention for her beauty and class. The advertisement projects the brand as being associated with contemporary beauty—someone who is modern and not conscious of her beauty.

Values identified: Social orientation, conspicuous Westernized symbols, celebrity orientation, neo-mindset orientation
Ritual setting: very urban, Westernized, fitness and health culture (the "in-thing" among urbanites), international association of the celebrity, "state-of-the-art," charm as associated with beauty contests

Sunrise (Coffee)

This brand is from another multinational (Nestlé) and it is aimed at urban youth, particularly couples. The TV commercial shows a young couple shopping in a departmental store when thehusband gets a phone call and informs his wife that his elderly uncle and aunt, who were unable to make it for their wedding (implying that they are recently wedded), have come to their home to visit them. It is customary for the wife to treat the relatives of her husband with reverence, especially if the couple is newly married. The wife is in a Western outfit and signals to the husband to go ahead and receive the traditional, elderly visitors. The wife enters through the window of the house (unseen by the visitors), quickly changes into ethnic clothing and presents herself to the visitors. She serves Sunrise, which is well appreciated by her visitors and then accepts their blessings by prostrating before them. Prostrating before elders is strongly valued in India, especially by Hindus.

Values identified: Respect for elders, family bonding, family hierarchy, emotional decision-making
Ritual setting: urban, young couple, traditional apparel, Western apparel, comfortable urban home, preparation of traditional coffee

Coke (Cola)

A well-known brand name throughout the world, Coke has been in the country since the mid-1990s (Coke was earlier withdrawn from the country during the mid-1970s). Coke has used several celebrities from films and a recent ad shows a group of youngsters on a bike longing for some food during a night out. Finally, they find the drink and the signature tune of the jingle ends with the theme that it is better to celebrate the day without waiting for the next day. The ad uses a celebrity.

Values identified: need for affiliation, group emphasis, celebrity orientation and social orientation
Ritual setting: urban youth enjoying themselves as a group

It may be interesting to note that the same brand used a different celebrity to position the brand as *thanda* (meaning, cold) and to popularize it in rural areas. The ritual setting was rural.

Pepsi (Cola)

A strong competitor to Coke in the cola market, Pepsi has used a number of cricket celebrities over a period of time with themes conveying group fun and "mischief." A recent TV commercial has three reigning film celebrities enacting a humorous theme.

Values identified: celebrity orientation, social orientation, group emphasis
Ritual setting: urban setting

Colgate (Toothpaste)

Colgate has several variants in the country. Colgate Strong Teeth positions itself as a toothpaste for strong teeth. The advertisement shows the father and son painting the fence of the house. The father asks the son to paint the spaces in between the fence's cross design and the son replies that the dentist too told him that he should brush the space between his teeth using Colgate.

Values identified: family bonding and family hierarchy orientation, utilitarianism
Ritual setting: advice of father to son and brushing of teeth as a ritual (using the brand)

Closeup (Toothpaste)

This was a brand launched in the 1970s as a toothpaste-cum-mouthwash, with the advertisement focusing on "the close-up smile" of urban young teenagers and getting "close" to unleash the "close-up" smile. A recent advertisement for the brand shows a group of youngsters chatting in a restaurant and one youngster who cannot laugh aloud at a joke because of "bad" teeth. The other table has another youngster (using the brand) who is all smiles, with his whiteteeth shown while laughing. The setting and the laughter assume special significance because of girl companions.

Values identified: social orientation, self-esteem, group affiliation, utilitarianism
Ritual setting: romantic, need for good teeth to impress members of the opposite sex

Using similar analyses, the following were extracted for various brands:

Gillette (Razors and Blades)

Values identified: Conservatism, thriftiness, personal grooming, innovativeness, utilitarianism
Ritual setting: excitement of using a new product form at a lower price, durability of offering, ethnic orientation (as compared to the other up-market products of the company, utilitarianism

Red Label (Tea)

Values identified: family bonding (especially with the mother-in-law included in the emotional bonding), emotional decision-making, and a variant of family hierarchy orientation
Ritual setting: urban, family that is not too stringent on traditions, unusual companionship, domestic happiness with the brand being a part of it

Surf Excel (Detergent Bar)

Values identified: social orientation, need for affiliation, utilitarianism
Ritual setting: difficult stains, stains that may occur in the everyday lives of a majority of users of bar detergent, strong cultural orientation

Dettol (Floor Cleaner)

Values identified: family hierarchy orientation, family orientation, utilitarianism
Ritual setting: middle-class housewife, homemaker, group (family) affiliation

Cadbury (Chocolates)

Values identified: celebrity orientation, social orientation, group affiliation
Ritual setting: Celebrity looking not very urban (showing the popularity of the celebrity in rural areas too), middle-class neighborhood, common-man orientation of the group and occasion identified, celebration, humor

Horlicks (Milk Additive)

Values identified: group affiliation, indirect family orientation as the "mother" segment is influenced by the advertisement, indirectly seeking prosperity through success
Ritual setting: urban groups of school children, Westernized jingle, "showcasing" of achievement

Head & Shoulders (Shampoo)

Values identified: celebrity orientation, utilitarianism, social orientation and group affiliation
Ritual setting: urban, embarrassing problem, fun orientation

Parry's (Sugar)

Values identified: family orientation, family hierarchy, utilitarianism
Ritual setting: mother-child interaction, highlighting a specific practice in the culture

Inferences with Regard to Cultural Values in Advertisements

1. In an emerging market like India, *integrated marketing communications* (IMC) should be formulated taking into consideration the values that are associated with the culture, especially when they have been an important part of the advertising scenario for several decades.
2. The analysis of advertisements of several categories/brands clearly shows that there are specific cultural values that are used by most advertisements. Celebrity orientation, family orientation, family hierarchy orientation, utilitarianism, and group affiliation are some of the cultural values that are common to several advertisements. These values may be called "cultural interface values" as they serve to integrate marketing communication with the prevalent culture in the market.
3. The ritual setting adds meaning to the perception of the advertisements containing cultural values. The ritual setting can vary from brand to brand and category to category. It needs to be formulated based on the type of target segment for the respective brand.
4. The ritual setting is also important in identifying the extent to which cultural values are portrayed in the advertisement. There are categories where utilitarianism is not very explicit (like soft drinks and chocolates). Such brands are driven by hedonic motivation rather than by utilitarianism. Hence, the ritual setting may be more pronounced to project the cultural values in the advertisement to a greater extent than compared to categories that offer tangible benefits.

Adapting IMC to Emerging Markets

An IMC should project a consistent image of the brand through synergized communication through various media channels. This is more important in the digital era where connectivity (telecommunication developments), digitalization (content in the digital mode), convergence (mobile-cum-computer), and social networking (groups that bond together quickly over Internet groups) have an impact on consumers who are able to participate in the digital era. The challenge for IMC with regard to a particular brand is to have the right balance not only with regard to cultural values and ritual setting but also with regard to how "cultural interface values" and ritual setting are conveyed across channels like TV commercials, print advertisements, the Internet, mobile advertisements, point-of-purchase advertisements, hoardings, cinema advertisements and even wall paintings (quite popular in rural areas in India) to convey a consistent and coherent brand image over a period of time.

An example will be useful to illustrate the process of using cultural values for formulating the IMC for a brand in an emerging market. Iced green tea is a category that is quite new to an emerging market like India. A brand of iced green tea can advertise to the urban, young group (group affiliation) and use a popular celebrity (celebrity orientation). The proposition can be health (utilitarianism based on the positive aspects of green tea) through the group fun route. The product can be launched in a few urban areas with the celebrity and several media impressions will be generated (publicity). The brand's Web site can run a promotional campaign on how its benefits (utilitarianism) could have contributed to the characteristics of a particular celebrity (celebrity orientation) and have several rounds of filtering before deciding on a group, the "Green Tea Group," to meet the celebrity. This meeting can be covered through television channels that run youth programs (group affiliation). The company can start a blog to identify several other green tea groups (who would interface with the celebrity under different ritual settings) by encouraging bloggers to compare the brand with regular soft drinks. Some criteria can be used to identify the groups. Regular TV and print advertisements can also be used to convey the benefits of the brand (utilitarianism with an appropriate ritual setting).

After the first phase of advertisements, the second phase can have a set of advertisements on how the group fun of green tea groups can spread into their respective families (with a different ritual setting). The print advertisements can also publish specific benefits of green based on well known research sources. This will be associated with both family orientation and group affiliation values. Point-of-purchase advertisements can portray photographs of the "Green Tea Group," with a ritual setting highlighting group fun and the brand name. After a few months, the brand can introduce monthly meetings of the groups, presided over by a lo-cal youth icon (group affiliation and a variant of celebrity association). Sales promotion in the form of free sampling can be done in colleges and software companies (as these are places with urban youth population). An innovative SMS contest that involves group fun, nutritional aspects of the brand, and a film of the celebrity initially elected for the launch will also associate the brand with the mobile mania among the young sweeping across the country.

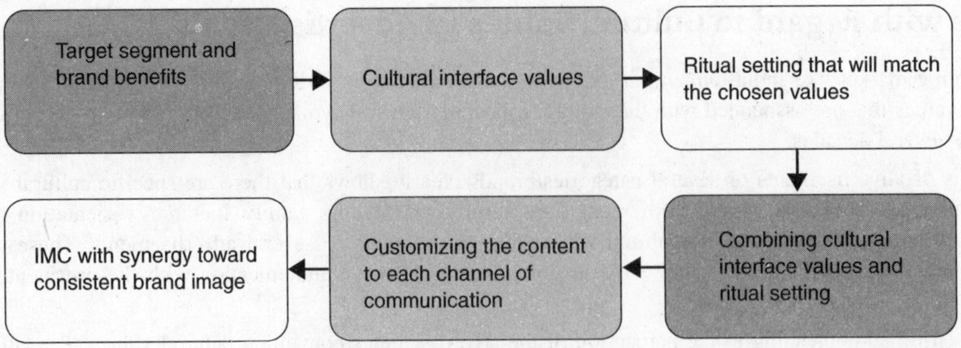

FIGURE 11.6 IMC and Cultural Dimensions: Emerging Markets

An IMC of this kind (see Figure 11.6), covering all channels of communication, planned on cultural values and differentiated ritual settings, will strengthen the brand with consistent messages across channels. Such an approach will also create the buzz factor necessary for the brand.

Cultural values are important brand differentiators in emerging markets with heterogeneous consumer groups. A combination of cultural aspects and IMC will result in a pioneering marketing exercise for any brand attempting the approach in an emerging market.

Summary

Learning Objective 1: To understand culture's role, dynamics, evolution, and impact on consumers' priorities and behaviors.

Culture is the collective values, customs, norms, arts, social institutions, and intellectual achievements of a particular society. Cultural values express the collective principles, standards, and priorities of a community. Most of the promotional messages across the world reflect, to some degree, the cultural values of the target audiences. Cultures always evolve, so marketers must monitor the sociocultural environment so as to market existing products more effectively and develop new products that are congruent with changing cultural trends. Understanding cultural changes is not an easy task, because many factors produce cultural changes within a given society, including new technologies, population shifts, resource shortages, and customs from other cultures.

Learning Objective 2: To understand language, symbols, and rituals as expressions of a learned culture.

To be considered a cultural value, a belief or custom must be shared by a significant portion of the society, because culture is essentially a series of norms that guide personal and group conduct and link together individuals into a largely cohesive group. Generally, society's members share their values and customs through a common language, although some cultures include more than one language. We learn cultural norms and customs mostly from family and peers, and begin at a very young age to understand that some behaviors are appropriate and others are not. Anthropologists have identified three forms of cultural learning: Formal learning, informal learning, and technical learning. Our ethical values are also formed during childhood, as we learn them from parents, teachers, and other significant adults. Anthropologists distinguish between enculturation (learning one's own culture) and acculturation (learning a new or foreign cultures). The contents of media, advertising, and marketing reflect cultural values and convey them to all members of society very effectively. Given Americans' extensive exposure to print, broadcast, and online media, as well as the easily ingested and entertaining presentation formats of their contents, media and advertising are powerful vehicles for imparting cultural values.

Cultural values are reflected in societies' languages, symbols, communications, and artifacts. A symbol is anything that represents something else; symbols can be either verbal or nonverbal. Words are verbal symbols and the text of any ad is a composition of symbols. In addition to language and symbols, cultures include ritualized behaviors. A ritual is a type of symbolic activity consisting of a series of steps (multiple behaviors) occurring in a fixed sequence and repeated periodically.

Learning Objective 3: To understand how to measure the influence of culture on consumer behavior.

The most widely used measurements of cultural values are content analysis, consumer field observation, and value measurement instruments. Content analysis focuses on the content of societies' verbal, written, and pictorial communications, including promotional messages. When examining a specific society, anthropologists frequently study cultures through field observation, which consists of observing the daily behavior of selected members of a society. Based on their observations, researchers draw conclusions about the values, beliefs, and customs of the society under investigation. There are also structured, self-administered questionnaires that measure individuals' cultural values, such as the Rokeach Value Survey, the Values and Lifestyles instrument, and Gordon's Survey of Personal and Interpersonal Values.

Review and Discussion Questions

11.1. Distinguish among beliefs, values, and customs. Illustrate how the clothing a person wears at different times or for different occasions is influenced by customs.

11.2. A manufacturer of fat-free granola bars is considering targeting school-age children by positioning its product as a healthy, nutritious snack food. How can the three forms of cultural learning be used in developing applicable marketing strategies?

11.3. The Citrus Growers of America is designing an advertising campaign aimed at getting consumers to switch to orange and grapefruit juices instead of soft drinks, as a "sugar jolt" in the late afternoon. Describe how the organization can use the Rokeach and the Gordon measures in planning its campaign.

11.4. For each of the following products and activities:

a. List two relevant core values and explain your choices.

b. Describe how each value either encourages or discourages buying the product or engaging in the activity.

The products and activities are:

1. Donating blood
2. Visiting tanning salons
3. Buying an e-reader
4. Buying a GPS device
5. Drinking diet beverages
6. Travelling overseas
7. Using sun protection products regularly
8. Buying a convection oven
9. Buying a pair of sneakers online
10. Following the latest fashions

11.5. Why are companies increasingly introducing green products and engaging in ecologically friendly practices?

11.6. How did consumers react to green products?

Hands-on Assignments

11.7. Identify a singer or singing group whose music you like and discuss the symbolic function of the clothes that person (or group) wears.

11.8. Thinking of your daily routines, identify one routine that you consider a ritual. Describe it and explain why it is a ritual. Assume that you allow a marketing researcher come to your house and observe your entire ritual. Explain how the marketer of a product that you use during your routine can employ the observation to design an ad aimed at getting you to switch brands.

11.9. a. Summarize an episode of a TV or online series that you watch regularly. Describe how the episode transmitted cultural beliefs, values, and customs.

b. Select three commercials that were broadcast during the episode and describe how each reflects a cultural value(s).

11.10. a. Find advertisements for two brands of deodorants. Do a content analysis of the written and pictorial aspects of each ad. Identify any core values portrayed in each ad and explain your choices.

b. Describe how the symbols in each ad convey the deodorant's characteristics and brand image.

11.11. Find five ads promoting green products or activities and explain whether you believe each one is effective or not.

Key Terms

- acculturation *320*
- Americans' core values *325*
- consumer socialization *320*
- content analysis *324*
- culture *314*
- depth interview *324*
- enculturation *320*
- field observation *324*
- focus group *324*
- formal learning *320*
- Gordon Survey of Personal and Interpersonal Values *325*
- informal learning *320*
- instrumental values *325*
- interpersonal values *325*
- participant-observers *324*
- personal values *325*
- ritual *327*
- ritualistic behavior *323*
- Rokeach Value Survey *325*
- symbol *321*
- technical learning *320*
- terminal values *325*
- VALS *325*

12

Cross-Cultural Consumer Behavior: An International Perspective

Learning Objectives

1. To understand how to study the values and customs of different cultures in order to develop effective marketing strategies.
2. To understand how to decide whether to customize products for global markets or to sell standardized ones.
3. To understand how to identify global marketing opportunities.
4. To understand how to apply psychographics to segmenting multinational markets.

PATEK PHILIPPE is one of the world's best Swiss timepiece makers. Its prices range from \$15,000 to more than \$1 million, and one of its 1928 models sold for \$3.6 million. Patek Philippe is a **world brand** because its watches are manufactured, packaged, and positioned in exactly the same way regardless of the country in which they are sold. As the ads in Figure 12.1 illustrate, Patek Philippe created a global campaign, where the advertising copy is in different languages, but the message the ads communicate is the same: Patek Philippe is not only a unique watch, but also an heirloom. It is a timeless artifact passed on from one generation to the next. It is exclusive, indispensible, and represents parents' deep and forever lasting bonds with their children, which are universal and cross-cultural truths. Like all of Patek Philippe's ad campaigns, the tagline "Begin your own tradition" originates from the brand's foundation: "You never really own a Patek Philippe. You merely look after it for the next generation."

Not all products, or services, or firms lend themselves to a global marketing strategy. Indeed, Table 12.1 identifies four marketing strategies that are available to firms that sell consumer products across nations and cultures. A **global marketing strategy** consists of selling the same product using the same positioning approach and communications globally. A **local marketing strategy** consists of customizing both the product and the communications program for each unique market. Within this continuum are two **hybrid marketing strategies**, which consist of standardizing either the product or advertising message, while customizing the other one.

The four cells in Table 12.1 represent market growth opportunities. Marketers must conduct cross-cultural consumer analysis to obtain consumer reactions to alternative product and promotional themes, in order to choose the best strategy. For example, Frito-Lay, the U.S. snack-food giant, has been standardizing the promotional messages for its potato chips across the world, but created different flavors for

Source: Photograph by Peter Lindbergh for Patek Phillipe

Source: Photograph by Peter Lindbergh for Patek Phillipe

Source: Photograph by Peter Lindbergh for Patek Phillipe

FIGURE 12.1 Patek Philippe Globally

TABLE 12.1 Global Marketing Strategies

PRODUCT STRATEGY	COMMUNICATION STRATEGY	
	STANDARDIZED COMMUNICATIONS	CUSTOMIZED COMMUNICATIONS
STANDARDIZED PRODUCT	**Global strategy:** Uniform product/uniform message	**Hybrid strategy:** Uniform product/customized message
CUSTOMIZED PRODUCT	**Hybrid strategy:** Customized product/uniform message	**Local strategy:** Customized product/customized message

This chapter explores consumer behavior across cultures and effective strategies for appealing to consumers around the globe.

various markets. Thus, across nations and cultures, the top flavors of potato chips are:

1. Lay's Sour Cream & Onion (popular across the world)
2. Dill Pickle (Canada and North America)
3. Mushroom (UK), Garden Tomato & Basil (children across the world)
4. Pepper Relish (Mexico, Central America, Germany, and Western Europe)
5. Classic Potato Chips, Hot and Sour (Asian nations)
6. India's Mint Mischief, Limón (sprinkled with lemon juice and liked by kids)
7. Ruffles Mayonnaise Chips

Learning Objective

1 To understand how to study the values and customs of different cultures in order to develop effective marketing strategies.

Cross-Cultural Analysis and Acculturation

Within the scope of consumer behavior, **cross-cultural analysis** is defined as determining to what extent the consumers of two or more nations are similar or different. Such analyses can provide marketers with an understanding of the psychological, social, and cultural characteristics of the non-Americans they wish to target, so that they can design effective marketing strategies for the specific markets. Table 12.2 lists the research issues that should be considered in cross-cultural analysis. Cross-cultural consumer analysis might also include a comparison of subcultural groups (see online) within a single country (such as English and French Canadians, Cuban Americans and Mexican Americans in the United States, or Protestants and Catholics in Northern Ireland).

The objective of cross-cultural consumer analysis is to determine how consumers in two or more societies are similar and how they are different. For instance, Table 12.3 presents the differences between Chinese and American cultural traits.[1] Countries like China and Mexico are "collectivistic" ("we") cultures, whereas the United States and the United Kingdom are "individualistic" ("I") cultures. A study of "I" versus "we" consumers in Montreal, Canada, found that collectivists rely more on word-of-mouth, preferring information from trusted, familiar sources when forming their expectations regarding airline travel. Individualists, in contrast, rely on unambiguous verbal or written communication, and attach more importance to explicit and implicit promises and third parties.[2] A study of consumers in Australia (an individualist nation) and Singapore (a collectivist country), found that Singaporean consumers were more responsive to social influence in a hypothetical buying situation than Australian consumers. Moreover, Australian subjects were more internally oriented, whereas Singaporean subjects were more externally oriented. This resulted in Australians attributing more responsibility to themselves for good or bad outcomes of their buying decisions.[3]

TABLE 12.2 Cross-Cultural Analysis

FACTORS	EXAMPLES
Differences in language and meaning	Words or concepts (e.g., "personal checking account") may not mean the same in two different countries.
Differences in market segmentation opportunities	The income, social class, age, and sex of target customers may differ dramatically between two different countries.
Differences in consumption patterns	Two countries may differ substantially in the level of consumption or use of products or services (e.g., mail-order catalogs).

(Continued)

TABLE 12.2 (Continued)

FACTORS	EXAMPLES
Differences in the perceived benefits of products and services	Two nations may use or consume the same product (e.g., yogurt) in very different ways.
Differences in the criteria for evaluating products and services	The benefits sought from a service (e.g., bank cards) may differ from country to country.
Differences in economic and social conditions and family structure	The "style" of family decision making may vary significantly from country to country.
Differences in marketing research and conditions	The types and quality of retail outlets and direct-mail lists may vary greatly among countries.
Differences in marketing research possibilities	The availability of professional consumer researchers may vary considerably from country to country.

TABLE 12.3 A Comparison of Chinese and American Cultures

CHINESE CULTURAL TRAITS	AMERICAN CULTURAL TRAITS
• Centered on a set of relationships defined by Confucian doctrine	• Centered on the individual
• Submissive to authority	• Greater emphasis on self-reliance
• Ancestor worship	• Resents class-based distinctions
• Passive acceptance of fate by seeking harmony with nature	• Active mastery in the person–nature relationship
• Emphasizes inner experiences of meaning and feeling	• Concerned with external experiences and the world of things
• A closed worldview, prizing stability and harmony	• An open view of the world, emphasizing change and movement
• Culture rests on kinship ties and tradition with a historical orientation	• Places primary faith in rationalism and is oriented toward the future
• Places weight on vertical interpersonal relationships	• Places weight on horizontal dimensions of interpersonal relationships
• Values a person's duties to family, clan, and state	• Values the individual personality

Source: Alexander Josiassen, "Consumer Disidentification and Its Effects on Domestic Product Purchases: An Empirical Investigation in the Netherlands," Journal of Marketing, Vol. 75 (March 2011): 124–140.

An understanding of the similarities and differences that exist between nations is critical to the multinational marketer who must devise appropriate strategies to reach consumers in specific foreign markets. The greater the similarity between nations, the more feasible it is to use relatively similar marketing strategies in each nation. However, when the cultural beliefs, values, and customs of specific target countries are found to differ widely, then a highly individualized marketing strategy is indicated for each country. As another illustration, in addition to the IKEA furniture company's generic global website that uses English, the firm also offers a series of localized websites (in selected languages) and other mini-sites (in more languages) that only provide contact information.

A study in four Central European nations (Croatia, the Czech Republic, Hungary, and Poland) found that although these nations are in the same geographic region, national differences would make it unwise to employ the same advertising content and imagery in all four countries.[4] However, in contrast to these results, other consumer research examining the notion of an Asian regional brand has found that some marketers have been able to create a "multicultural mosaic" for their brand that can "appeal across national boundaries". They have done this by creating the image of an Asian consumer that is "urban, modern, and multicultural."[5]

A firm's success in marketing a product or service in a number of foreign countries is likely to be influenced by how similar the beliefs, values, and customs are that govern the use of the product in the various countries. For example, the worldwide TV commercials and magazine ads of major international airlines (American Airlines, British Airways, Continental Airlines, Air France, Lufthansa, Qantas, Swissair, United Airlines) all depict the luxury and pampering offered to their business-class and first-class international travelers. The reason for their general cross-cultural appeal is that these commercials speak to the same types of individual worldwide—upscale international business travelers—who have much in common.

TABLE 12.4 "Consumer Styles" in Four Nations

GERMAN CONSUMERS:

- Less brand loyal
- More price-sensitive
- Least likely to seek variety in products
- Most likely to consider themselves impulsive shoppers
- Least likely to say they dislike shopping

U.S. CONSUMERS:

- More likely to seek new and different products than French and German consumers
- See advertising as more informative than do French and German consumers

UNITED KINGDOM CONSUMERS:

- More likely to seek new and different products than French and German consumers
- See advertising as more informative than do French and German consumers
- See advertising as insulting

FRENCH CONSUMERS:

- Believe shopping is no fun
- Claim to engage in comparison shopping, but are not the most likely to purchase products on sale

TABLE 12.5 Consumer Clusters (Segments) in Four Nations

CLUSTER	FRANCE	GERMANY	UNITED KINGDOM	UNITED STATES
Price-Sensitive Consumers	27.5	38.7	19.3	21.0
Variety-Seeking Consumers	22.0	19.4	22.4	23.3
Brand-Loyal Consumers	30.4	20.0	36.2	22.2
Information-Seeking Consumers	20.1	21.9	22.1	33.5

A study in four countries (United States, United Kingdom, France, and Germany) examined whether there were differences in terms of "consumer style" (i.e., how a consumer approaches the purchase and consumption experience, including attitudes, beliefs, and decision rules about price, value, etc.) in the four nations.[6] Table 12.4 presents some of the differences among subject participants from the four countries. Based on consumer style, the researchers were able to segment these consumers into four clusters: (1) Price-sensitive consumers, (2) variety-seeking consumers, (3) brand-loyal consumers, and (4) information-seeking consumers, which are described in Table 12.5. Because German consumers, for example, tend to be less brand loyal and more price sensitive than their counterparts from the other three nations in the study, it is not surprising that German participants are underrepresented in the brand-loyal consumer cluster and overrepresented in the price-sensitive cluster.[7]

Measures of Cross-Cultural Aspects

There are several frameworks for assessing consumption-related cultural differences. One study identified the dimensions that cross-cultural studies should address:[8]

1. Judgments regarding the quality of a country's products.
2. Willingness to buy a country's products.
3. Ethnocentrism—willingness to buy foreign-made products (see Chapter 3).
4. Perceptions of a country's consumption culture.
5. Acculturation—identification with a country's culture.
6. Ethnic self-identification.
7. National self-identification.

Another study investigated the interrelationship between consumers' attitudes toward local and global products and identified the following relevant dimensions for measuring such attitudes (sample statements for "agree"/"disagree" scales are shown for each item):[9]

1. ***Entertainment:*** "I enjoy entertainment that is popular in many countries around the world more than traditional entertainment that is popular in my own country."
   "I enjoy traditional entertainment that is popular in my own country as well as entertainment that is popular in many countries around the world."
2. ***Furnishings:*** "I prefer to have home furnishings that are traditional in my country rather than furnishings that are popular in many countries around the world."
   "I don't really like my own country's traditional home furnishings or furnishings that are popular in many countries around the world."
3. ***Food:*** "I enjoy foods that are popular in many countries around the world more than my own country's traditional foods."
   "I enjoy my own country's traditional foods as well as foods that are popular in many countries around the world."
4. ***Lifestyles:*** "I prefer to have a lifestyle that is traditional in my own country rather than one that is similar to the lifestyle of consumers in many countries around the world."
   "To be honest, I don't find the traditional lifestyle in my own country or the consumer lifestyle that is similar in many countries around the world very interesting."
5. ***Brands:*** "I prefer to buy brands that are bought by consumers in many countries around the world rather than local brands that are sold only in my country."
   "I prefer to buy both local brands that are sold only in my country and brands that are bought by consumers in many countries around the world."

Acculturation

Acculturation is the process by which marketers learn—via cross-cultural analysis—about the values, beliefs, and customs of other cultures and then apply this knowledge to marketing products internationally. In fact, acculturation is a dual learning process: First, marketers must learn everything that is relevant to the product and product category in the society in which they plan to market; then they must persuade, or "teach," the members of that society to break with their traditional ways of doing things and adopt the new product. To gain acceptance for a culturally new product in a foreign society, marketers must develop a strategy that encourages members of that society to modify or even break with their own traditions (to change their attitudes and possibly alter their behavior). To illustrate the point, a social marketing effort designed to encourage consumers in developing nations to secure polio vaccinations for their children would require a two-step acculturation process. First, the marketer must obtain an in-depth picture of a society's present attitudes and customs with regard to preventive medicine and related concepts. Then the marketer must devise promotional strategies that will convince the members of a target market to have their children vaccinated, even if doing so requires a change in current attitudes.

Too many marketers contemplating international expansion believe that if their products are successful domestically, they will also succeed overseas. This biased viewpoint increases the likelihood of marketing failures abroad. It reflects a lack of appreciation of the unique psychological, social, cultural, and environmental characteristics of distinctly different cultures. To overcome such a narrow and culturally myopic view, marketers must learn everything that is relevant about the usage or potential usage of their products and product categories in the foreign countries in which they plan to operate. Take the Chinese culture, for example. For Western marketers to succeed in China, it is important for them to take into consideration *guo qing* (pronounced "gwor ching"), which means "to consider the special situation or character of China." An example of *guo qing* for Western marketers is the Chinese policy of limiting families to one child. An appreciation of this policy means that foreign businesses will understand that Chinese families are open to particularly high-quality baby products for their single child ("the little emperor").

Consumer Research Difficulties

Conducting consumer research studies in other foreign countries is often difficult. For instance, it is hard to conduct Western-style market research in the Islamic countries of the Middle East. In Saudi Arabia, for instance, it is illegal to stop people on the streets, and focus groups are impractical because most gatherings of four or more people (with the exception of family and religious gatherings) are outlawed. American firms desiring to do business in Russia have found a limited amount of information regarding consumer and market statistics. Similarly, marketing research information on China is generally inadequate, and surveys that ask personal questions arouse suspicion. Marketers have tried other ways to elicit the data they need. For example, Grey Advertising has given cameras to Chinese children so they can take pictures of what they like and do not like, rather than asking them to explain their preferences to a stranger. Moreover, ACNielsen conducts focus groups in pubs and children's playrooms rather than in conference rooms; and Leo Burnett has sent researchers to China to "hang out" with consumers.

Another issue in international marketing research concerns scales of measurement. In the United States, a 5- or 7-point scale may be adequate, but in other countries, a 10- or even 20-point scale may be needed. Still further, research facilities, such as telephone interviewing services, may or may not be available in particular countries or areas of the world. To avoid such problems, consumer researchers must familiarize themselves with the availability of research services in the countries they are evaluating as potential markets, and must learn how to design marketing research studies that will yield useful data. Researchers must also keep in mind that cultural differences may make "standard" research methodologies inappropriate.

Learning Objective

2 To understand how to decide whether to customize products for global markets or to sell standardized ones.

Localization versus Standardization

As illustrated in the chapter opener, American companies marketing overseas can adapt their offerings in other nations or market them the same way they do at home. For example, McDonald's is an example of a firm that tries to localize its advertising and other marketing communications to consumers in each of the cultural markets in which it operates.

Product and Service Customization for Local Cultures

The Ronald McDonald that we all know has been renamed Donald McDonald in Japan, because the Japanese language does not contain the *R* sound. Additionally, the McDonald's menu in Japan has been localized to include corn soup and green tea milkshakes.[10] In Sweden, McDonald's developed a new package using woodcut illustrations and a softer design to appeal to the consumers' interest in food value and the outdoors. Each French person eats about 150 grams of bread a day, or roughly 55 kilograms a year. The French eat some form of bread with all meals, viewing bread as an extension of the knife and fork for pushing food around on the plate. In France, McDonald's introduced McBaguette, a traditional French bread with a burger made from France's famed Charolais beef and topped with French-made Emmental cheese and mustard.[11] Filipinos like their dried chicken with either rice or spaghetti, and both KFC and McDonald's are serving them such dishes.

In contrast, when rival Pizza Hut ventured into China, parent company Yum Brands Inc. opted to introduce Pizza Hut Casual Dining, a chain that more closely resembles a Cheesecake Factory in terms of menu and motif, with a vast selection of American fare, including ribs, spaghetti, and steak, as well as café latte. However, Domino's was not interested in offering table service, even if that was what locals were used to. The company entered the new market with a tried-and-true business model of delivery and carryout pizza that it deploys around the world. In contrast, the chain's U.S. competitor, Pizza Hut, has reinvented itself for China, India, and other emerging markets, in order to mesh with the strikingly different consumer trends there.[12]

Starbucks adjusted its offering in several European countries. For instance, the British like to drink takeaway coffee, so Starbucks is planning hundreds of drive-through locations in Britain. Many Britons consider the Starbucks version too watery, so baristas in Britain recently began adding a free extra shot of espresso. Sixty percent of French people like espresso, but many complained that Starbucks' espresso tasted charred. In response, Starbucks introduced a lighter "blonde" espresso roast in Paris. In London, the company experimented with taking customers' names with their orders and then addressing them by name when filling it. Participating patrons got a free coffee, but, using Twitter, many others had complaints about bogus, American-style "chumminess". In Amsterdam, the company opened a striking space with local woods and avant-garde architecture, including a stage for poetry readings, designed to make Starbucks feel more like a trendy neighborhood shop.[13]

The maker of sunglasses bearing such brands as Ray-Ban, Ralph Lauren, and Prada has started making glasses in China specifically tailored for the Chinese. Part of their strategy included making technical tweaks to better suit Asian facial characteristics, such as a lower nose saddle, where glasses rest on the face, and prominent cheekbones. Ray-Ban, Oakley, and Vogue have also rolled out special Asian collections.[14] In contrast, Mattel shut its Barbie stores in China after learning that Chinese parents wanted their girls to model themselves after studious children, not flirts. Consequently, Mattel decided to market mostly educational toys in China. Home Depot Inc. closed about half its stores in China, finding scant interest among Chinese for do-it-yourself renovation, and decided to come up with a new strategy for the Chinese market.[15]

Linguistic Barriers

Many American brand names and slogans must be revised or changed altogether in non-English-speaking countries. Linguistic differences are probably the most challenging factor facing companies that are expanding globally, as illustrated by the following examples:

1. The slogan "Chevy Runs Deep" did not translate well in some languages. The company replaced it with the slogan "Find New Roads" because the car represents different things to different people, and the new theme resonates with consumers around the world.[16]
2. When General Motors introduced the Chevy Nova in South America, it was apparently unaware that "no va" means "it won't go." After the company figured out why it was not selling any cars, it renamed the car in its Spanish markets and called it Caribe.
3. When Parker Pen marketed a ballpoint pen in Mexico, its ads were supposed to say "It won't leak in your pocket and embarrass you." However, the company mistakenly thought the Spanish word "embarazar" meant "embarrass." Instead the ads said that "It won't leak in your pocket and make you pregnant."
4. When Vicks first introduced its cough drops on the German market, it was chagrined to learn that the German pronunciation of "v" is f—making its name in German the guttural equivalent of "sexual penetration."
5. In Taiwan, the translation of the Pepsi slogan "Come alive with the Pepsi Generation" came out as "Pepsi will bring your ancestors back from the dead."

The rapidly growing Chinese market represents an enormously difficult cultural and linguistic challenge. The name *Coca-Cola* in China was first rendered as *Ke-kou-ke-la*. Unfortunately, the Coke company did not discover until after thousands of signs had been printed that the phrase means "bite the wax tadpole" or "female horse stuffed with wax" (depending on the dialect). Coke then researched 40,000 Chinese characters and found a close phonetic equivalent, *ko-kou-ko-le*, which can be loosely translated as "happiness in the mouth." Some brands, like Cadillac (*Ka di la ke*), or Hilton (*Xi er dun*), are phonetic translations that mean nothing in Chinese. Nevertheless, a genuine Chinese name can say a lot about the product's characteristics and result in consumer attachment to the brand. For example:[17]

1. Snickers' Chinese name is *Shi Li Jia*, which literally means "honorary powerful support."
2. Tide detergent is called *Tai Zi*, which, in addition to resembling the name *Tide* phonetically, also means "gets rid of dirt."
3. Colgate is *Gao Lu Jie*, meaning "revealing superior cleanliness."
4. Mr. Muscle is *Wei Meng Xian Sheng*, which literally means "Mr. Powerful."
5. Citibank is *Hua Qi Yinhang*, which literally means "star-spangled banner bank."
6. Lay's is called *Le Shi*, meaning "happy things."

Promotional Appeals

Promotional appeals must reflect the local culture's values and priorities. For example, after surveys indicated that, globally, Coke was regarded as more "daring" and "energetic" than Pepsi, the Pepsi company came up with a new ad push with the tagline: "Live for Now," and then changed it to "People Who Define the Now" and its ads featured well-known disc jockeys, celebrities, and artists. Pepsi has a long history of using groundbreaking pop culture artists in its ads (e.g., Madonna, Michael Jackson).[18] A study revealed that there are significant differences between UK and Greek humorous advertising. Compared with the U.S., in the UK, riskier, more aggressive, and affective humorous advertisements are used. In contrast, Greeks preferred neutral humorous advertisements whose appeal was not perceived as very offensive. Additionally, in Greece, there was a lower percentage of print ads using humor, compared with the UK.[19] Another study showed that many fragrance ads shown in Western countries featured overt sexual appeals. However, in Asian countries, particularly those that are predominately Muslim or Buddhist, advertisers should not portray women in sexual poses.[20]

Regarding South Asian cultures, one study discovered that Australian, Chinese, and U.S. consumers form significantly different attitudes regarding the same ad. However, buying intentions toward the advertised brand are not significantly different. Despite the general assumption that Chinese consumers might react least favorably to sex-appeal ads, the study found that they hold similar attitudes toward such ads as U.S. consumers and even more favorable attitudes than Australian consumers.[21] A study of Chinese Generation X consumers, aged 18 to 35, with high incomes and education, found that they were equally persuaded by individualistic and collectivistic ad appeals, whereas their older counterparts were more persuaded by collectivistic rather than individualistic ad appeals.[22] A study focused on Chinese wine consumers discovered that some mixed red wine with lemonade and preferred corked (rather than twist-off or screw-cap) wine bottles. The study also uncovered a link between wine consumption and beliefs in traditional Chinese medicine. Interestingly, some Western medicine maintains that red wine consumption reduces cholesterol.[23]

Comparative advertising has been used more in the United States than in other countries. However, one study of American and Thai consumers discovered that the persuasive ability of comparative ads among both groups was related to the two personality traits: **Self-construal**, which refers to how individuals perceive, comprehend, and interpret the world around them, particularly the behavior or action of others towards themselves, and **need for cognition** (Chapter 3).[24] Another study compared American and Korean consumers and demonstrated that cultural values were more important in influencing reactions to comparative ads than reactions to noncomparative ads, and that need for cognition had an impact on the persuasiveness of comparative ads among consumers in both nations.[25] These studies and many others support the view that, if used properly and in the right context, comparative marketing is a highly effective positioning strategy.

Legal Barriers

At times, local laws force American marketers to alter their offerings. Here are a few examples:

1. Australia's parliament passed a law restricting logos, branding, colors, and promotional text on tobacco packets. Brand names have to appear in standard colors and positions in a plain font and size on packets colored a dark olive-brown, which government research has found holds the lowest appeal to smokers. Health warnings with graphic images of the harmful effects of smoking make up 75% of the front of the packaging.[26]
2. Singapore tightened its rules on casino advertising as part of efforts to limit the social impact of resort hotels on urbanites. Casinos must obtain government approval for all casino advertising and promotions, media-related activities, and sponsorships.[27]
3. The UK's Advertising Standards Authority said that it has referred Groupon Inc.—the Internet daily-deals company—to the Office of Fair Trading for breaches of the nation's advertising code. Apparently, Groupon failed to conduct promotions fairly, by not making significant terms and conditions clear, failing to provide evidence that offers are available, and exaggerating savings claims.[28]
4. China's regulators banned advertising during television dramas, dealing a blow to marketers who had ramped up ad spending to reach the nation's growing consumer class. The new rules restrict commercials from interrupting the plots of TV dramas, allowing showing ads only back-to back between programs.[29]
5. Chinese trademark laws are very "fluid." For instance, Michael Jordan sued Qiaodan Sports because, phonetically, the company's name resembles "Jordan." However, the company said that it had the exclusive right to the Qiaodan trademark and was operating "in accordance with Chinese laws."[30]

World Brands versus Local Brands

Marketers of products with a wide or almost mass-market appeal have also embraced a world branding strategy. For instance, multinational companies and their brands, such as General Motors, Gillette, Estée Lauder, Unilever, and Fiat, have each moved from a local strategy of nation-by-nation advertising to a global advertising strategy. Researchers examining more than 2,500 Taiwanese advertisements, in terms of the use of Western models and English brand names, found that less than half of ads were "global-looking."[31] The Lauder Company—marketer of popular brands like Estée Lauder, Clinique, and Bobbi Brown—introduced a hybrid East-Meets-West beauty line called Osiao (pronounced O-Shao). Osiao's specialized formulas contain Chinese plants like ginseng. To communicate the brand's imported status to consumers, the product names on the bottles appeared in English.[32]

A 12-nation consumer research project found that global brands tend to be viewed differently than local brands, and that consumers worldwide associate global brands with three characteristics:

1. ***Quality Signal:*** Consumers believe that the more people who purchase a brand, the higher the brand's quality (which often results in a global brand being able to command a premium price). Furthermore, consumers worldwide believe that global brands develop new products and breakthrough technologies at a faster pace than local brands.
2. ***Global Myth:*** Consumers view global brands as a kind of "cultural ideal"; their purchase and use make consumers feel like citizens of the world, and give them an identity (i.e., *"Local brands show what we are; global brands show what we want to be"*).
3. ***Social Responsibility:*** Global companies are held to a higher level of corporate social responsibility than local brands, and are expected to respond to social problems associated with what they sell.

In this 12-nation study, the importance of these three dimensions was consistent, and the insights revealed by the research accounted for more than 60% of the variation in the overall brand preferences. The study also identified intracountry segments with respect to how a country's citizens view global brands:[33]

1. ***Global Citizens*** (55% of the total respondents) use a company's global success as an indication of product quality and innovativeness, and are concerned that the firm acts in a socially responsible manner.
2. ***Global Dreamers*** (23%) view global brands as quality products, and are not particularly concerned about social responsibility issues.
3. ***Antiglobals*** (13%) feel that global brands are higher quality than local brands, but dislike brands that preach U.S. values and do not trust global companies to act responsibly. Generally, they try to avoid purchasing global brands.
4. ***Global Agnostics*** (8%) evaluate global brands in the same way they evaluate local brands.[34]

A study of consumers from eight countries discovered that the following two means of presenting brands were perceived most favorably. First, *self-enhancement* advertisement stressing that the brand conveys one's status and exquisite taste. Second was advertising that stressed *openness* in terms of allowing people to pursue their goals in exciting ways.[35] A study comparing U.S. and South Korean adolescents found that Americans considered the availability of well-known brands significantly more important than the South Koreans did, and the Americans were more willing to pay high prices for clothes with a well-known brand name than their counterparts. However, one of the reasons may have been that well-known brands are very expensive in South Korea, and most adolescents there cannot afford them. Interestingly, American adolescents were motivated primarily by social approval and recognition, whereas their counterparts' main motive was self-expressions through the fashions they adopted.[36]

Distribution of consumer goods in other nations can sometimes seem nearly impossible. For example, a Nestlé sales agent in South Africa ventured into one of Johannesburg's high-crime neighborhoods—where most sales agents would not go—with just taxi money, two cell phones, and a briefcase with order forms. His objective was to distribute Nestlé products, such as baby food and non-dairy creamers, in tiny shops and single-serving packages. Apparently, many South African customers are very price-sensitive and buy food items in smaller packages and in small stores, instead of supermarkets.[37]

Figure 12.2 shows four ads for the Patek Philippe watch illustrating a global brand. The ads express the same theme, but in different languages. Table 12.6 lists the most prominent global brands and Table 12.7 describes the global appeals of several brands.[38]

Source: Patek Philippe

Source: Patek Philippe

FIGURE 12.2 Patek Philippe Is a Global Brand

Source: Patek Philippe

Source: Patek Philippe

FIGURE 12.2 *(Continued)*

TABLE 12.6 The 20 Most Valuable Global Brands

RANK	BRAND	2012 BRAND VALUE ($BILLIONS)
1	Coca-Cola	77.8
2	Apple	76.6
3	IBM	75.5
4	Google	69.8
5	Microsoft	57.9
6	GE	43.7
7	McDonald's	40.1
8	Intel	39.4
9	Samsung	32.9
10	Toyota	30.3
11	Mercedes-Benz	30.1
12	BMW	29.1
13	Disney	27.4
14	Cisco	27.1

TABLE 12.6 (Continued)

RANK	BRAND	2012 BRAND VALUE ($BILLIONS)
15	Hewlett-Packard	26.1
16	Gillette	24.9
17	Louis Vuitton	23.6
18	Oracle	22.1
19	Nokia	21.0
20	Amazon	18.6

Source: Both tables are based on: "Best Global Brands 2012," Interbrand Report, http://www.Interbrand.com/en/news-room/press-releases/2012-10-02-7543da7.aspx

TABLE 12.7 Profiles of Several Global Brands

BRAND	PROFILE AND GLOBAL APPEAL
Coca-Cola	Universally recognized more than any other in the world because it makes people experience fun, freedom, and refreshment. The brand maintains a powerful sense of nostalgia that unites generations of Coke lovers and reinforces consumers' deep connections to the brand. Its edgy campaigns continue to push boundaries, and Coca-Cola reinforced its values through celebratory promotions relating to its 125th-year anniversary ("Sharing Happiness") and the London Olympics ("Move to the beat").
McDonald's	McDonald's stands out because of its exceptional brand management, significant global presence, and delivery of consistent quality and affordability. The company is also working to respond to critics by increasing the number of healthful menu options and effectively communicating its sustainability efforts to both customers and employees, building energy saving and waste reduction into staff incentives.
Louis Vuitton	Louis Vuitton's continued success can be attributed to consistently upholding its core values and remaining loyal to its travel-centric heritage. Louis Vuitton has also improved its digital presence—from charting its history on Facebook to launching an app that enables customers to share travel experiences. The brand expanded to new markets and became a top gift brand in China.
Amazon	Amazon aims to be a place where consumers can find anything they want to buy—online. It delivers by regularly expanding its products and services and, in doing so, has remained a leader in customer service. Amazon sustained the success of its Kindle brand, stretching it beyond its e-reader origins into a legitimate iPad alternative, introducing both the Kindle Touch and Kindle Fire in 175 countries.
H&M	With an ever-increasing number of competitors gaining traction globally and more big retailers stepping into low-cost fast fashion, H&M has been finding new ways to maintain industry leadership. It continues to partner with big-name designers, celebrities, and high-profile supermodels, and this strategy clearly resonates with the aspirations of its fashion-savvy, pop-culture-following target customers.
Disney	It is heritage rich, meaningful, and worthwhile to millions of people of all ages and backgrounds around the world. The world of entertainment has been steadily transforming as audience behaviors evolve, content consumption habits change, and the old gives way to the new. Disney has demonstrated an ability to remain resilient over the years in the face of change.
Apple	While many assume it's the products that define Apple, it's really a certain kind of thinking, a certain set of values, and an unmistakable human touch that pervades everything Apple does—which is why our connections to the brand transcend commerce.
Google	With minimal room for growth in search engine market share, Google continues to transform itself into a broader IT company. New products and services include the Project Glass augmented-reality head-mounted display, Google TV, and Google Drive—a cloud computing service.

(*Continued*)

TABLE 12.7 (Continued)

BRAND	PROFILE AND GLOBAL APPEAL
Microsoft	Microsoft also pushed into the hardware market with its own Surface tablets and into the competitive fray—the global market for converged software/hardware ecosystems. This move will likely define the brand's future.
Toyota	In addition to showing solid numbers with repeat customers, Toyota is strengthening its appeal with younger consumers. The brand has intensified its incentives push and reduced its fleet sales. This helps customers find a good deal while also holding the line on the resale value of their vehicles. Toyota's Prius customers continue to deepen their connection to the Toyota portfolio and the Prius lineup is creating an influx of new customers.
eBay	Most of eBay's growth has come from mobile retailing and PayPal, not its core e-commerce business. More than 90 million users have downloaded eBay's mobile app, and the brand is on track to double volume over both mobile and PayPal. However, eBay is not alone in its mobile e-commerce prowess. Amazon's customers have also embraced its mobile app, and the competition in this sector continues to intensify.
Nike	Nike continually increases the power of its brand through innovation. Slyly, as an "ambush marketer" rather than an official Olympic sponsor in London, the brand attracted publicity, spotlighted new products, and managed, as always, to link world-renowned athletes to its latest offerings. As part of its long-term growth strategy, Nike announced its intention to divest its Cole Haan and Umbro businesses, which will allow it to focus its resources on driving growth in the Nike, Jordan, Converse, and Hurley brands. Nike is also using social media skillfully to generate awareness and buzz, while continuing to engage the public through events and contests.

Source: Both tables are based on: "Best Global Brands 2012," Interbrand Report, http://www.Interbrand.com/en/news-room/press-releases/2012-10-02-7543da7.aspx

Brand Shares and Extensions

All companies continuously monitor their brand shares in domestic and foreign markets. Euromonitor International is the most prominent database of brand shares in virtually all product categories around the world. For example, Table 12.8 illustrates that Procter & Gamble and Unilever have successfully penetrated four important shampoo markets. In both the United States and China—the world's largest markets—Head & Shoulders dominates the shampoo sector, and other Procter & Gamble brands have significant presence. In contrast, in Germany, a local brand has the largest market share and Procter and Gamble's shampoo has had limited success. Interestingly, in each of the four countries, a large portion of the market represents lesser-known brands.

Local brands can sometime overtake well-established American offerings. China is P&G's second-largest market, with $6 billion in sales. However, while P&G's market share in diapers, laundry care, and hair care has risen in China, its share of oral care, bath and shower, and skin care has been slipping. Although Chinese herbal toothpaste for sensitive gums sells for double

TABLE 12.8 The Top Ten Shampoo Brands in Four Global Markets

RANK	UNITED STATES		CHINA		GERMANY		BRAZIL	
	MARKETER	BRAND	MARKETER	BRAND	MARKETER	BRAND	MARKETER	BRAND
1	Procter & Gamble	Head & Shoulders *(14.8%)*	Procter & Gamble	Head & Shoulders *(18.5%)*	Henkel AG & Co KGaA	Schwarzkopf *(17.9%)*	Unilever	Sunsilk *(19.9%)*
2	P&G	Pantene *(12.2%)*	P&G	Rejoice *(13.5%)*	P&G	Pantene *(9.6%)*	Unilever	Clear *(10.2%)*
3	Unilever	Suave *(12%)*	P&G	Pantene *(9%)*	L'Oréal	L'Oréal Paris *(7.4%)*	L'Oréal	L'Oréal Paris *(8%)*
4	L'Oréal	Garnier *(7.6%)*	Unilever	Clear *(6.6%)*	Unilever	Dove *(6.7%)*	L'Oréal	Garnier *(8%)*

(Continued)

TABLE 12.8 *(Continued)*

RANK	UNITED STATES		CHINA		GERMANY		BRAZIL	
5	P&G	Clairol *(6.7%)*	Unilever	Lux *(5.6%)*	Beiersdorf AG	Nivea *(6.5%)*	Colgate-Palmolive Co.	Palmolive *(7.4%)*
6	Unilever	TRESemmé	Beiersdorf AG	Slek	Kao Corp	Guhl	P&G	Pantene
7	Unilever	Dove	Jiangsu Longliqi	Longliqi	P&G	Head & Shoulders	Unilever	TRESemmé
8	Johnson & Johnson	Neutrogena	Unilever	Dove	L'Oréal	Garnier	Unilever	Dove
9	Vogue	Organix	La Fang International	La Fang	Johnson & Johnson	Terzolin	Niely do Brasil	Niely Gold
10	L'Oréal	L'Oréal Paris	Henkel AG & Co KGaA	Syoss	P&G	Clairol	Natura Cosméticos SA	Natura

Note: Brands' market shares (in percentages) from Euromonitor International are available for the top five brands (to lower-tier subsciptions to the service).

the price of a similar product by Procter & Gamble, Chinese consumers apparently prefer their local product. Although local Chinese brands are closing the perceived quality gap with foreign products, for some items consumers no longer readily distinguish between the two. A study of Chinese consumers in the country's smaller cities, where shoppers are sharply increasing their spending on home and personal care goods, indicated that 70% of consumers thought P&G's Ariel laundry detergent was a local brand.[39]

Just because a brand may be global in character does not mean that consumers around the world will necessarily respond similarly to a brand extension. One study examined reactions to brand extensions among Western culture (U.S.) and Eastern culture (India) consumers. It hypothesized that the Eastern holistic way of thinking (which focuses on the relationships between objects), rather than the Western analytic style of thinking (which focuses on the attributes or parts of objects), would affect the manner in which consumers judged the "fit" of a brand extension. The research results confirmed this hypothesis: Low-fit extensions (McDonald's chocolate bar and Coke popcorn) received positive evaluations from the Eastern culture subjects. In contrast, moderate-fit extensions (Kodak greeting cards and Mercedes-Benz watches) received equal responses from both cultural groups. For the Eastern culture participants, liking Coke products, and the fact that Coke and popcorn are complementary products, in that they can be consumed together, were enough to make the brand extension acceptable. The American subjects, in contrast, saw little product-class similarity between Coke and popcorn.[40] As a follow-up, these same researchers replicated their earlier study, and went on to determine that American Indians were significantly more holistic in their thinking than Caucasian Americans; they reported that certain factors, such as corporate reputation, may be used more frequently by Easterners than by Westerners as a basis for judging the "fit" of a brand extension.[41]

Perhaps because of the dominance of English-language pages on the Internet, non-English-speaking European nations wish to distinguish themselves and their cultures by designing websites that reflect their countries and specific cultures. Thus, German websites might employ bright colors and a geometrical layout to give them a "German feel"; a French website might have a black "chic" background; and a Scandinavian website might provide a variety of images of nature. A study of global American brands examined how they standardize their websites in Europe (United Kingdom, France, Germany, and Spain). The study found that although the manufacturers' websites did have a minimal level of uniformity with respect to color, logo, and layout, the textual information and visual images were dissimilar from one market to the next. Still further, as with traditional advertising media, standardization for durable goods was higher than for nondurables.[42]

An interesting example of brand extension is DreamWorks Animation's China film project: Tibet Code, an Indiana Jones–type adventure story based on a wildly popular series of recent Chinese novels set in ninth-century Tibet. Although China's policies on Tibet are a persistent target of Western human-rights critics, and a constant challenge to its international image, the company dismissed suggestions that Tibet Code served any political purpose.[43]

Learning Objective

3 To understand how to identify global marketing opportunities.

Global Marketing Opportunities

Firms are increasingly selling their products worldwide, for a variety of reasons. First, there has been an ongoing buildup of "multinational fever," and the general attractiveness of multinational markets, products, or services originating in one country means that they are increasingly being sought out by consumers in countries in other parts of the world. Second, many American firms have realized that overseas markets represent an important opportunity for their future growth when their home markets reach maturity. This realization is propelling them to expand their horizons and seek consumers in markets all over the world. Moreover, consumers around the globe are eager to try "foreign" products that are popular in different and far-off places.

Global markets are dynamic, and new marketing opportunities emerge continuously. For example, Chinese shoppers have been shying away from conspicuous luxury goods, such as fancy watches and designer handbags, because luxury goods have become symbols of corruption and of the country's widening wealth gap.[44] As the country's disposable income has risen, Russia has become a lucrative market for American fast-food chains. McDonald's opened its first restaurant on Pushkin Square in 1990 and now operates 279 restaurants in Russia. Burger King has opened 22 restaurants, mostly in mall food courts, in 2 years. Carl's Jr. has 17 restaurants in St. Petersburg and Novosibirsk. Wendy's has opened 2 restaurants and plans 180 throughout Russia by 2020. The Subway sandwich chain has opened about 200 shops in Russia. Yum Brands, which owns KFC, Pizza Hut, and Taco Bell, operates a co-branded chicken restaurant chain in Russia, called Rostik's-KFC, and Il Patio in the Italian food segment, and has about 350 restaurants in Russia.[45]

Young Europeans are now embracing American fashions. After watching such U.S. television series as Gossip Girl, Glee, and Vampire Diaries, European teenagers are replacing Chanel jackets and knotted scarves with American casual tailored sweatpants and frayed oxfords. Abercrombie & Fitch now has a store on the Champs Élysées in Paris and other American fashions are following the trend.[46] Although formerly unthinkable within Japan's strong national culture, because of declining incomes, as well as fears about radiation from a nuclear disaster in Fukushima, a growing number of Japanese consumers have been abandoning their loyalty to expensive, premium-grade homegrown rice. Instead, they have been seeking out cheaper alternatives from China, Australia, and the United States.[47] During Christmas, Printemps, a high-end Paris department store whose stylish Christmas window displays are eagerly awaited every year, showed figures of Asian male and female dancers because a large portion of the store's shoppers are now Asians. Molson Coors, an originally American beer company, introduced more new products in Canada in 18 months than it did in the United States for the previous 15 years. Apparently, Canadians have been increasingly receptive to niche products and shunning mass-marketed goods. The company introduced Molson Canadian 67 Sublime, a lemon- and lime-infused version of the low-calorie beer. This and other products have been positioned as sophisticated and easy to drink. The company also discovered that the new products lured wine and spirits drinkers to the beer market.[48]

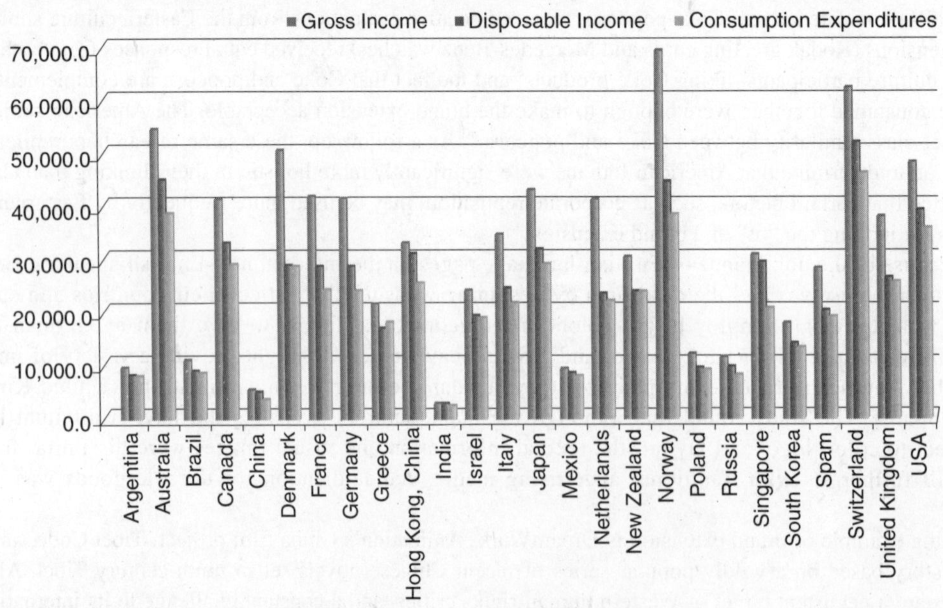

FIGURE 12.3 Spending Power and Consumer Expenditures

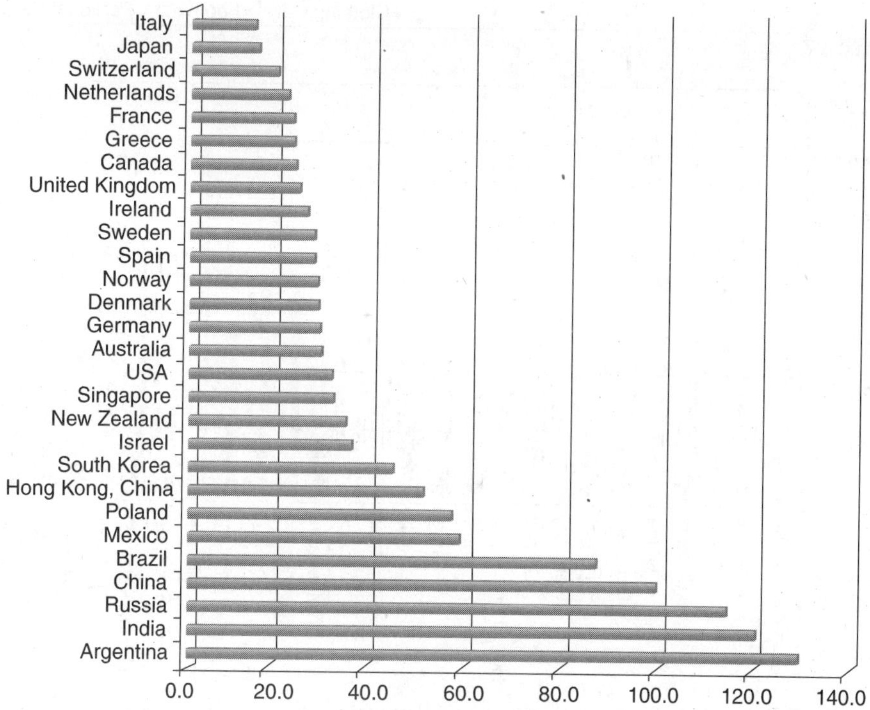

FIGURE 12.4 Forecasted Growth in Consumer Expenditures Between 2012 and 2020 (percentages)

Spending Power and Consumption Patterns

The most important criterion for identifying global marketing opportunities is a country's consumer spending and its growth prospects. Figure 12.3 shows consumer gross income, disposable income, and consumer expenditures in numerous countries. Although Norway had the highest gross income, Norwegians' disposable income is not that much higher than that of Americans, because Norway's tax rates are much higher than those in the United States. The small gap between disposable income and consumer expenditures in the United States reflects the nation's modest savings rate. In Greece, consumer expenditures are slightly higher than disposable income, which indicates that Greeks have been "living beyond their means," which is probably a function of uncertainty regarding the future of the euro in Greece. Figure 12.4 shows the percentages of anticipated growth in consumer expenditures through the end of the decade. Clearly, the most growth is expected in Asia and South America, with only modest growth rates in Europe.

The five charts in Figure 12.5 depict the percentages of their disposable incomes that consumers in prominent nations spend on necessities. Figure 12.5A illustrates that clothing is a major expenditure for Russians and Hong Kong's Chinese. The Swiss and Norwegians—citizens of the world's two most affluent nations—spend a great deal on personal care products, which are expensive in these countries because of import taxes (the two nations are not members of the EU, where most import and export barriers have been greatly reduced or eliminated). The Russians and Polish are heavy consumers of meat, whereas Japan and Chinese in Hong Kong like seafood and fish (Figure 12.5B). Very few nations, such as people in New Zealand, France, and Germany, consume more fruit than vegetables, because these countries are known for their fresh produce. On the other hand, people in Brazil, Mexico, India an Israel eat mostly vegetables. The data in Figure 12.5D—showing that India is the world's top consumer of breads and cereals—deserve further explanation. Consumers in India start the day with daily breads called chapatti, parantas, and dosas. The Indian breakfast is heavy and there is a feeling of fullness at the end. Kellogg introduced its cereals in India in the 1990s and positioned them as an alternative to the regularly consumed breakfast, but a Kellogg's Corn Flakes breakfast does not give that feeling of fullness. Additionally, the Indian breakfast is known for its variety (e.g., depending on the region, there can be 30 types of dosas), and often an item that is eaten one day will not be consumed during the following two or three weeks. Offering Indians the same type of corn-flake-based breakfast each day contradicts their culture. Indians have spicy and hot food for breakfast and find corn flakes in cold milk too sweet. Indians have been taught from childhood that milk has to

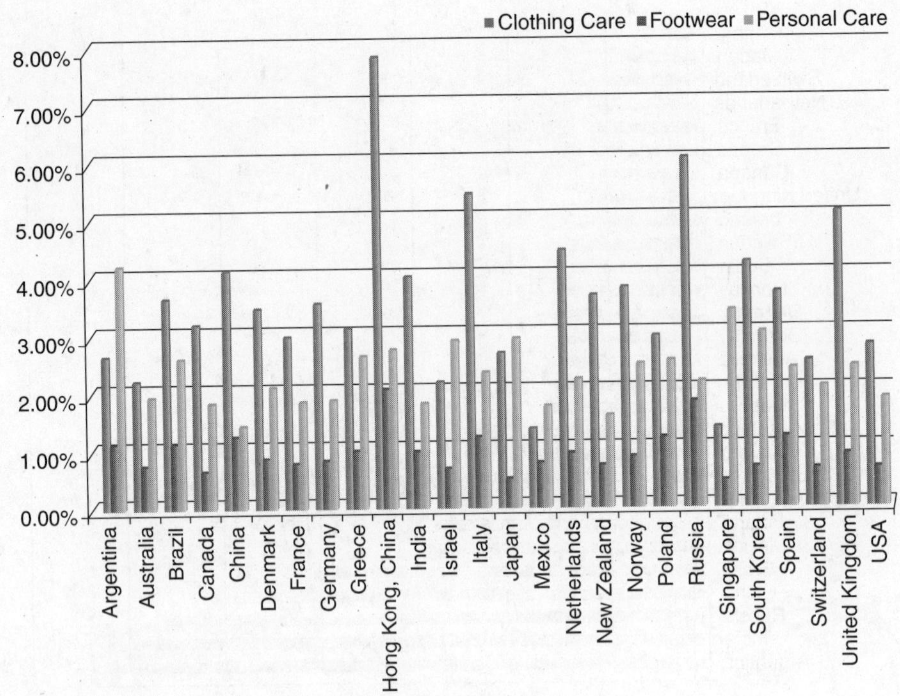

FIGURE 12.5A Clothing, Footwear, and Personal Care

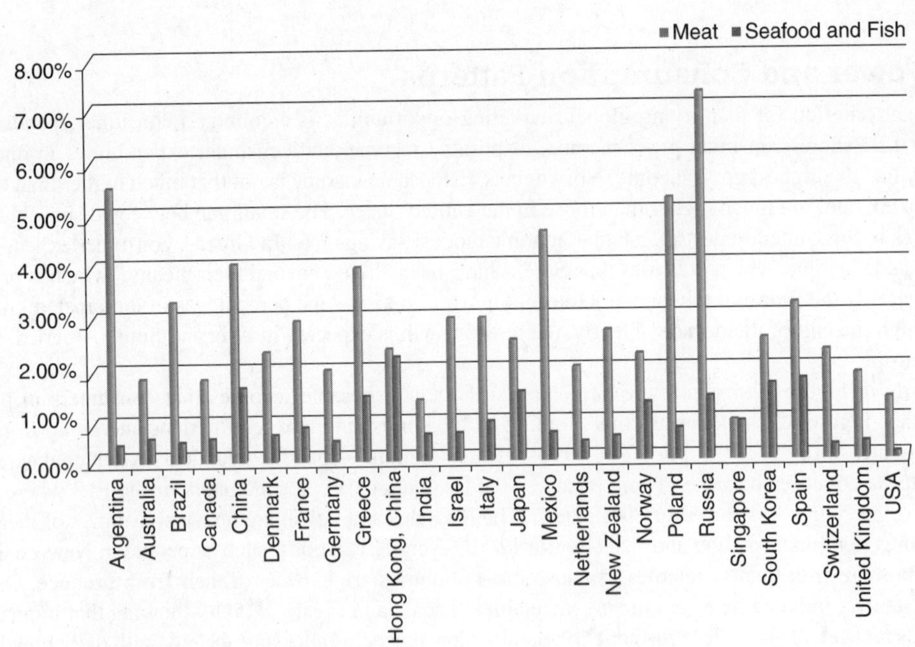

FIGURE 12.5B Meat, Seafood, and Fish

be consumed every day and that milk should always be consumed hot. Therefore, the data in Figure 12.5D reflect Indians' love of various breads, but not cereals. Figure 12.5E shows that Mexico, India, and Brazil are the world's heaviest buyers of bottled water, because clean, fresh water is scarce in these countries.

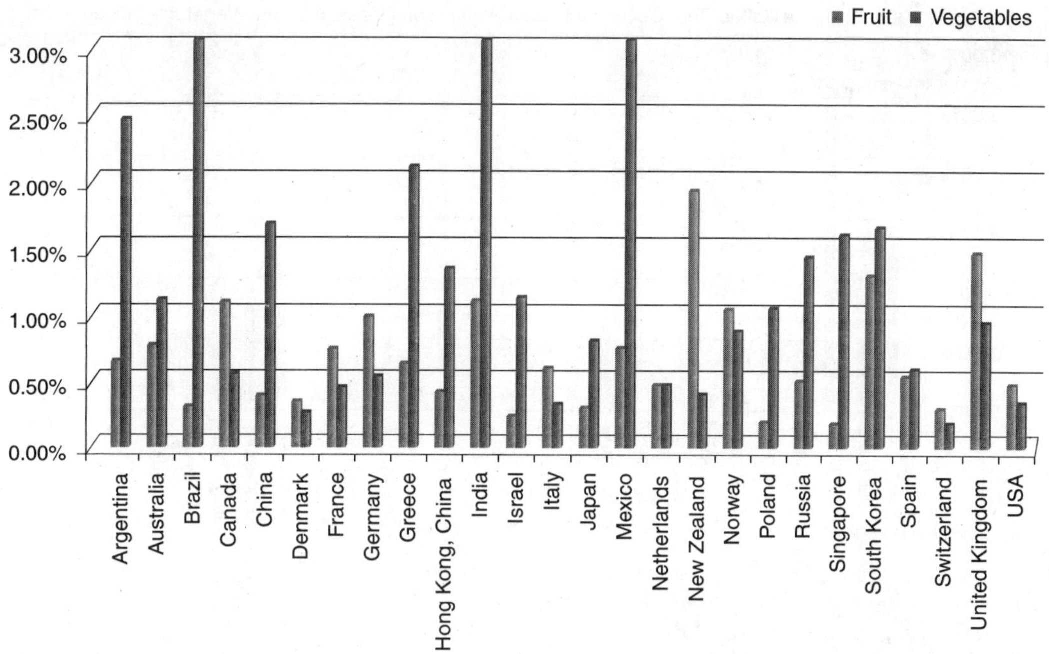

FIGURE 12.5C Fruit and Vegetables

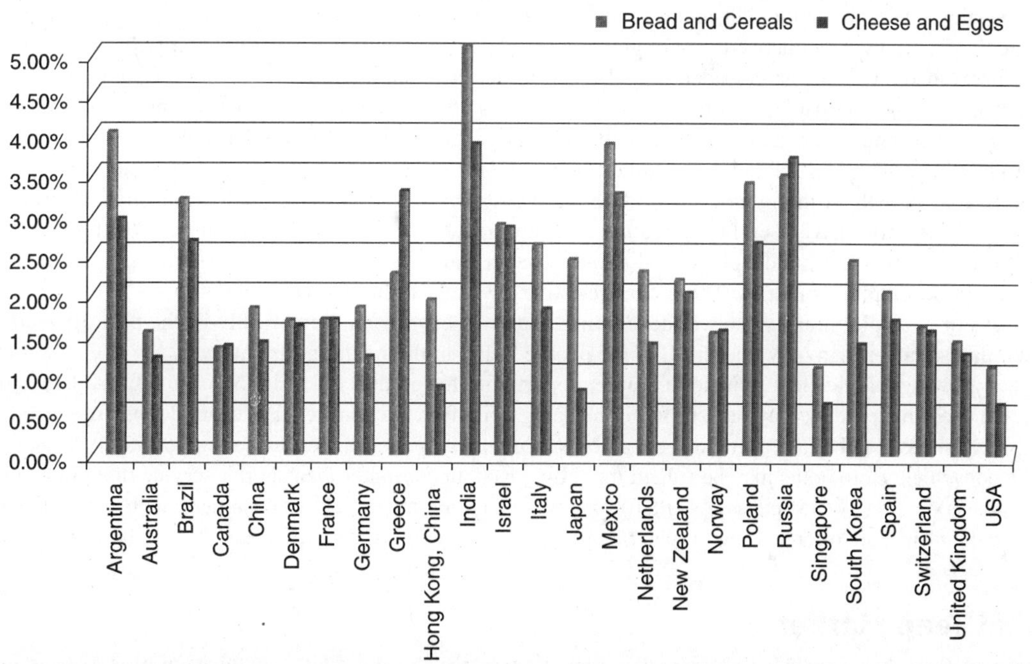

FIGURE 12.5D Bread, Cereals, Cheese, and Eggs

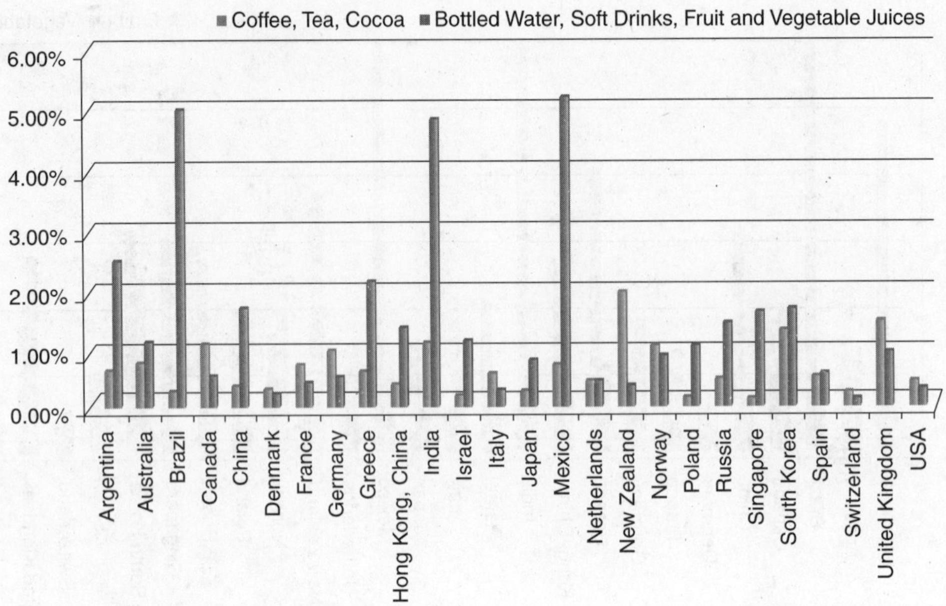

FIGURE 12.5E Drinks and Beverages

The Growing Global Middle Class

Recent projections state that the middle class will increase by 1.8 billion people over the next decade, of which 600 million will be in China. Within a decade, the middle class will grow from 30% to 52% of the world's population. By 2025, China will have the world's largest middle class, and India's middle class will be 10 times larger than it currently is.[49] The growing middle class in developing countries is a very attractive target to global marketers, who are always eager to identify more customers for their products. The news media have given considerable coverage to the idea that the rapid expansion of the middle class is based on the reality that, although per capita income may be low, there is nevertheless considerable buying power in a country such as China, where most income is largely discretionary (because of government subsidies of basic necessities). Indeed, this same general pattern of a growing middle class is taking place in many parts of South America, Asia, and Eastern Europe.

The rather rapid growth in the number of middle-class overseas has attracted the attention of many well-established marketing powerhouses, who have been facing mature and saturated domestic markets with little growth potential. Whereas in 1960 two-thirds of the world's middle class lived in industrialized nations, by the year 2000 some 83% of middle-class citizens were living in developing countries. These changes strongly suggest that more people are now living longer, healthier, and better lives. For example, literacy rates in developing countries have risen dramatically in the past 50 years, and today more than two-thirds, rather than only one-third, of the people living in these nations are literate.[50]

Although a growing middle class provides a market opportunity for products like Big Macs and fries, it should always be remembered that the same product may have different meanings in different countries. For example, whereas a U.S. consumer wants his or her "fast food" to be fast, a Korean consumer is more likely to view a meal as a social or family-related experience. Consequently, convenient store hours may be valued more by a Korean consumer than shorter service time. In China, despite a traditional emphasis on "fresh" (just picked or killed) food, the emerging middle-class consumers, with rising incomes and rising demands on their time, are often willing to spend money to save time, in the form of alternatives to home-cooked meals.[51]

The Global Teen Market

Overall, teenagers (and their somewhat older brothers and sisters, the "young adult" segment) appear to have quite similar interests, desires, and consumption behavior no matter where they live. Therefore, in response to this perspective, consumer researchers have explored the makeup, composition, and behavior of this segment. One study considered the fashion consciousness of teenagers in the United States, Japan, and China.[52] The research revealed that American and Japanese teens were highly similar, differing only in that the Japanese teens were more likely than American teens to choose style over comfort (most likely because of the importance, in the Japanese Confucian society, of meeting the expectations of group members). In contrast,

TABLE 12.9 Teenage Creatives' Values

CREATIVES' TOP VALUES			CREATIVES' BOTTOM VALUES		
	ALL TEENS	CREATIVES		ALL TEENS	CREATIVES
Freedom	55%	66%	Public image	30%	17%
Honesty	49%	61%	Status	22%	12%
Equality	39%	50%	Wealth	23%	11%
Learning	37%	47%	Looking good	25%	9%
Preserving the environment	31%	45%	Traditional gender roles	13%	1%
Curiosity	34%	40%	Faith	19%	2%
Creativity	29%	36%			

Chinese teens were less fashion conscious than either the American or the Japanese teens, which supports the idea that differences exist between highly developed and less highly developed nations with respect to teen fashion consciousness.[53]

A famous advertising agency conducted a World Global Teen Study that reported changing trends among the world's teenagers.[54] During the 1990s, according to the BBDO research, the "coolest" teens were found in the United States. Currently, though, the "coolest" teens, the Creatives, can be found in all of the 13 countries examined. The Creatives represent about 30% of all teenagers, and are especially numerous in Western Europe (some 23% of U.S. teens are Creatives). Table 12.9 presents the top values and bottom values of both Creatives and all teenagers. Notice, for example, that while 13% of all teens value traditional gender roles, only 1% of Creatives do.[55]

Learning Objective

4 To understand how to apply psychographics to segmenting multinational markets.

Cross-Cultural Segmentation

As the world became more integrated—largely because of shared communication media—a global marketplace has emerged. For example, as you read this you may be sitting on an IKEA chair or sofa (made in Sweden), drinking Earl Grey tea (England), wearing a Swatch watch (Switzerland), Nike sneakers (China), a Polo golf shirt (Mexico), and Dockers pants (Dominican Republic). Some global market segments, such as teenagers, appear to want the same types of products, regardless of which nation they call home: They desire products that are trendy, entertaining, and image oriented. This global "sameness" allows, for example, a sneaker marketer to launch styles appealing to segments in different countries using the same global advertising campaign. However, cross-cultural differences also force marketers to adapt products for overseas markets. As an illustration, the core benefit that McDonald's provides is consistency and value by having a standardized, almost identical menu in each of its U.S. outlets. McDonald's had to adapt its uniform offerings to the needs and cultures of global consumers. Thus, in India, McDonald's does not serve beef products, and in Saudi Arabia, McDonald's outlets include separate dining sections for men and women.

In Chapter 2, we discussed the VALS framework, which is the most prominent lifestyle segmentation system in the United States (see Figure 2.5 and Table 2.7). Several other countries created their own VALS. For example, in Japan, businesses use the Japan-VALS framework to monitor Japan's consumer environment; generate new product ideas; segment Japanese consumers into potential target markets; differentiate brands; and develop effective pricing, distribution, and promotional strategies. The Japan-VALS segments stem from consumers' *primary motivations* and *degree of innovativeness*, where innovativeness is measured as attitudes toward social change. Primary motivations include tradition, achievement, and self-expression. As illustrated in Figure 12.6, Japanese consumers are classified according to their degree of innovativeness, where Integrators are the most innovative and Sustainers the least.

Research studies have identified many cross-cultural differences that enable marketers to segment overseas markets. For example, although more than 50% of Japanese and American women work outside the home (which enhances the need for many convenience and time-saving products), Japanese women have been slower to embrace the liberated attitudes of working women in the United States. Seen in this light, the determination of whether or not to market a time-saving cleaning device as a world

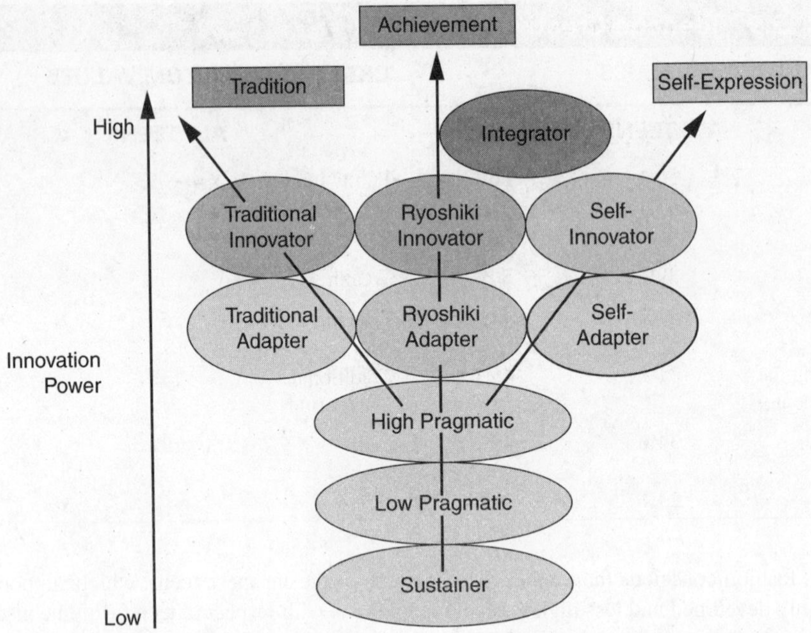

FIGURE 12.6 Japan's VALS

brand is a critical strategic decision. Some firms might attempt to establish a global branding strategy, whereas others would design an individual or local marketing strategy—one that treats Japanese and American working women differently.

Global psychographic research often reveals cultural differences of great importance to marketers. For example, Roper Starch Worldwide, a major multinational marketing research company, interviewed 35,000 consumers in 35 countries in order to identify shared values, irrespective of national borders. The research sought to uncover the bedrock values in peoples' lives so as to understand the motivations that drive both attitudes and behavior. After completing the interviews in North and South America, Asia, and Europe, six global value groups were uncovered:

1. ***Strivers***—ambitious and materialistic.
2. ***Devouts***—responsible, respectful, and conservative.
3. ***Altruists***—unselfish in their concern for others, society, and the future.
4. ***Intimates***—focus on social relationships and family.
5. ***Fun Seekers***—young in age and outlook, value adventure and good times.
6. ***Creatives***—seek knowledge and insight, and have a keen interest in books and new media.

Global *Desi*: International Brands and India

International brands adapt themselves to the Indian context in a variety of ways. There are different kinds of Indian consumers – someone buying a Harley Davidson motorbike in India can expect the same version as the one sold in the US, whereas a consumer in the domain of a FMCG may expect several ethnic variations. Kellogg's introduced mango and *pudina* (mint) variants of cornflakes. Coke and Thumps up (both from Coca-Cola) have been promoted in different ways. Coke, in particular, has more of an ethnic association with its various campaigns. In the category of washing machines and refrigerators, leading brands like Samsung, LG, and Whirlpool have incorporated India-specific features. Gillette pioneered Vector Plus and Guard to encourage consumers to switch over to contemporary blades from the traditional ones. Gillette also has a shaving gel, but with a shaving brush (gel is used as a brushless alternative in developed markets). Kurkure, from the makers of Pepsi, is a widely popular substitute for several kinds of Indian snacks. Philips introduced an appliance called "Air Fryer", as shown in Figure 12.7, for cooking healthy food without deep frying in a lot of oil (this is a strong cultural practice in India). The brand also conducted a sales promotion to demonstrate how food prepared in this appliance is not only healthy, but is tasty as well.

Source: Philips

FIGURE 12.7 Air Fryer from Philips

Coke had introduced a stock keeping unit at ₹5 (both in terms of its price and its glass bottle container) as an India-specific initiative. Parker pens introduced Junior Parker pen at a low-price point (as compared to its original version) with Amitabh Bachchan as the brand ambassador. Keeping in tune with the Indian culture, Colgate has an herbal toothpaste offering; the brand also has a toothpaste offering with salt as it is considered appropriate for oral cleanliness. Sunsilk shampoo has a "Recharge" variant that is targeted towards women who ride two-wheelers and who would like to have their hair intact under the helmet. Tropicana had introduced several local flavors in India. McDonald does not have a beef or pork offering in India as it is not in tune with Indian religious values. Subway and Pizza Hut, the US brands of fast food, opened an exclusive vegetarian restaurant in Ahmedabad. Unilever has detergent bars in India (Rin, Surf Excel) as millions of consumers prefer these over detergent powders for washing clothes. Apple's iPhone introduced its gold-colored variant. Indian culture has a strong liking towards gold as it symbolizes richness and status.

Subsequently, we can expect several global brands to create a fine balance between global and local strategies when it comes to placing their product in the Indian market,

Summary

Learning Objective 1: To understand how to study the values and customs of different cultures in order to develop effective marketing strategies.

Within the scope of consumer behavior, cross-cultural analysis is defined as determining to what extent the consumers of two or more nations are similar or different. Such analyses provides marketers with an understanding of the psychological, social, and cultural characteristics of the foreign consumers they wish to target, so that they can design effective marketing strategies for the specific national markets involved. An understanding of the similarities and differences that exist between nations is critical to the multinational marketer who must devise appropriate strategies to reach consumers in specific foreign markets. Some of the problems involved in cross-cultural analysis include differences in language, consumption patterns, needs, product usage, economic and social conditions, marketing conditions, and market research opportunities. Acculturation is the process by which marketers learn—via cross-cultural analysis—about the values, beliefs, and customs of other cultures and apply this knowledge to marketing products internationally.

Learning Objective 2: To understand how to decide whether to customize products for global markets or to sell standardized ones.

The greater the similarity between nations, the more feasible it is to use relatively similar marketing strategies in each nation. When the cultural beliefs, values, and customs of specific target countries are found to differ widely, then a highly individualized marketing strategy is indicated for each country. In deciding whether or not to customize products to local cultures, marketers must consider local values, linguistic barriers, and legal issues.

Learning Objective 3: To understand how to identify global marketing opportunities.

Firms are increasingly selling their products worldwide, for a variety of reasons. Many firms have learned that overseas markets represent an important opportunity for their future growth when their home markets reach maturity. This realization is propelling them to expand their horizons and seek consumers in markets all over the world. Moreover, consumers around the globe are eager to try "foreign" products that are popular in different and far-off places. As increasing numbers of consumers come in contact with the material goods and lifestyles of people living in other countries, and as the number of middle-class consumers grows in developing countries, marketers are eager to locate these new customers and offer them the products.

Learning Objective 4: To understand how to apply psychographics to segmenting multinational markets.

Global psychographic research often reveals cultural differences of great importance to marketers. Psychographics identifies shared values, irrespective of national borders. Much of this research has sought to uncover the bedrock values in peoples' lives, in order to understand the motivations that drive both attitudes and behavior. The VALS research methodology has been used to identify psychographic segments in other countries.

Review and Discussion Questions

12.1. With all the problems facing companies that go global, why are so many companies choosing to expand internationally? What are the advantages of expanding beyond the domestic market?

12.2. In terms of consumer behavior, are the world's countries and their cultures becoming more similar or more different? Discuss.

12.3. What is cross-cultural consumer analysis? How can a multinational company use cross-cultural research to design each factor in its marketing mix for a non-domestic market? Illustrate your answer with examples.

12.4. What are the advantages and disadvantages of global promotional strategies?

12.5. What are the advantages and disadvantages of localized promotional strategies?

12.6. Give three examples of linguistic problems that companies have faced during marketing in global markets and describe how these problems could have been avoided.

12.7. Give three examples of product problems that companies have faced during marketing in global markets and describe how these problems could have been avoided.

12.8. An American company is considering introducing yogurt in Japan. What cultural aspects should the company study before deciding whether or not to do so?

12.9. Coca-Cola is considering introducing very small bottles of its product in Brazil. These would cost *less* than bottled water. Discuss whether or not the company should do so.

12.10. As shown earlier, Hong Kong's Chinese spend more on clothing than any other nation. Research Hong Kong's culture and geographic location and explain why they do so.

12.11. Looking at the charts presented earlier in this chapter, select a product that members of a particular nation consume heavily. Research the country's culture and geographic location and describe why they are heavy consumers of the product selected.

12.12. Looking at the charts presented earlier in this chapter, select a product that members of a particular nation consume very lightly. Research the country's culture and geographic location and describe why they are light users of the product selected.

Hands-on Assignments

12.13. Have you ever traveled outside the United States? If you have, identify some of the differences in values, behavior, and consumption patterns that you noted between people in a country you visited and Americans.

12.14. Interview a student from another culture about his or her use of: (a) credit cards, (b) fast-food restaurants, (c) shampoo, and (d) sneakers. Compare your consumption behavior to that of the person you interviewed and discuss the similarities and differences you discovered.

12.15. Select one of the following countries: Mexico, Brazil, Germany, Italy, Israel, Kuwait, Japan, or Australia. Assume that a significant number of people in the country you chose would like to visit the United States and have the financial means to do so. Now, imagine that you are a consultant for your state's tourism agency and that you have been charged with developing a promotional strategy to attract tourists from the country you chose. Conduct a computerized literature search of the databases in your school's library and select and read several articles about the lifestyles, customs, and consumption behavior of the people in the country you chose. Prepare an analysis of the articles and, on the basis of what you read, develop a promotional strategy designed to persuade tourists from that country to visit the U.S.

Key Terms

- acculturation *345*
- cross-cultural analysis *342*
- global marketing strategy *340*
- hybrid marketing strategies *340*
- local marketing strategy *340*
- need for cognition *348*
- self-construal *348*
- world brand *340*

Case Five: LG Mobile/LG Electronics MobileComm USA

"Before you text, give it a ponder"

Primary Agency: Young & Rubicam/VML
Contributing Agencies: TRU, MindShare, Smith & Jones

Strategic Challenge

Mobile textual harassment is no joke

For teens, texting is like talking; it's intertwined with the way they communicate and socialize. LG's research revealed that what adults and the media think of as "mobile bullying" is a behavior so ingrained in everyday teenage life that it is seen as a normal and expected part of communicating. But mobile textual harassment is in truth an enormous problem affecting millions of tweens and teens. Forty-one% admit they have sent, received or forwarded a text with rumors about someone that were untrue. Four million say they've received a threatening text, while more than 10 million teens also report having sent a "SEXT" message. Five million confess they have been pressured by a boyfriend or girlfriend to send a text with a naked photo. And an alarming 60% of kids who say they have been bullied electronically have never told their parents about the incident.

An opportunity to deliver the LG brand promise by shifting teens' attitudes

Cell phone misuse is expected to escalate as more kids get phones with web access and data plans become more affordable. While today the issue has garnered a lot of media attention, at the time of this effort no cell phone carrier, manufacturer or other commercial voice in the U.S. had become an advocate against the behavior.

At the heart of the LG brand essence "Life's Good" is an overt commitment to make a positive impact on the world. Encouraging teens to text responsibly was an ideal opportunity to continue delivering this promise, and most important, the right thing for LG to do as a technology leader. Although LG had a noble goal to help reduce mobile bullying, the advertising agency realized that it could never expect to stop the behavior, given its prevalence among youth. But, an effective campaign could change kids' attitudes about the seriousness and importance of the issue. The campaign's objective became to raise consciousness about a behavior that was unconscious.

The Adverising Agency—team agreed that if the campaign successfully changed attitudes, attitudes, it would have a positive impact on LG's business.

Strategic challenge: How could LG Mobile help change teens' attitudes about mean texting?

Objectives

The goal was to create a campaign whose positive impact on teens' attitudes about mobile bullying would also drive LG Mobile's brand perceptions, relevance and consideration among the target audience.

Taking into account that LG had never developed this type of campaign before, it was difficult to set benchmarks, benchmarks, but LG agreed that success would be changing attitudes by 15% and brand relevance and consideration by 10%. LG also aimed to increase brand equity and engagement and generate earned media.

The campaign had two types of objectives:

I. **Benchmark-Based**
- **Attitudinal Shift**—Change teens' attitudes and perceptions about mean texting. Grow +15% based on pre-campaign in-market survey benchmark.
- **Brand Relevance and consideration**—Increase by 10% based on pre-campaign in-market survey benchmark.

II. **Other performance indicators**
- **Brand Value (equity)**—Increase equity of LG Mobile among teens as a socially responsible company.
- **Brand Engagement**—Motivate teens to interact with the LG brand.
- **Earned Media (and press coverage)**—Given that the effort would have minimal media investment ($1.7MM), LG wanted to generate unpaid media to achieve greater awareness of the issue and momentum around LG Mobile.

The Big Idea

Motivate teens to think about the personal consequences of sending a mean text.

Teens won't stop texting

LG's research . . . research (July 2009) revealed teens felt it was "ok" to share gossip because when they took a photo of a popular kid in a compromised position they were simply reporting on a truth, just like journalists. They were not able to consider the victim's feelings but all could describe a situation where they had sent a text they wished they hadn't. A time when sharing a text had personal consequences for them. Maybe it backfired. A girl wants to please her boyfriend and sends him a topless picture of herself but the guy then decides to pass it around to his friends when they break up. This they understood and wanted to avoid.

For the campaign . . . campaign to be successful, successful, it had to raise . . . to raise awareness about the personal consequences of mobile misuse. misuse. The big idea was to . . . to motivate teens to think of the personal consequences of sending a mean text, which text, which the advertising agency articulated . . . articulated strategically as "think before you text."

[1]TRU/LG Texting Education Survey, 2010

[2]LG Family Texting Study, 2009

[3]TRU/LG Texting Education Survey, 2010

[4]LG Family Texting Study, 2009

[5]I-Safe America Cyber Bullying Survey 2003–2004

13

Consumer Decision-Making and Diffusion of Innovations

Learning Objectives

1 To understand the consumer's decision-making process.

2 To understand the dynamics of buying gifts.

3 To understand how innovative offerings gain acceptance within market segments and how individual consumers adopt or reject new products and services.

THIS CHAPTER integrates the concepts discussed so far into a framework that illustrates how consumers make buying decisions. Consumption decisions vary. For example, the ad featured in Figure 13.1 is by the Gemological Institute of America (GIA), a nonprofit educational institute of the jewelry industry. The tag line "Understand what you're buying" is directed at consumers seeking to buy diamonds. In consumer decision-making terms, purchasing a diamond represents **extensive problem solving** because consumers buy diamonds infrequently and have no established criteria for evaluating them. The GIA ad tells buyers what to look for in a diamond: Carat weight, clarity, color, cutting style, and other features. In contrast, the Advil ad in Figure 13.2 represents **routinized response behavior**, because consumers have experience with over-the-counter pain relievers and do not need to establish the criteria for evaluating them. More importantly, diamonds are not branded, whereas the Advil brand has a quality reputation and is instantly recognized by millions of consumers around the world. In stores, consumers reach for Advil without much thought. The ad also shows that Advil's reputation enables the brand to use **family branding**, which is marketing different versions of a product under the same brand (see Chapter 5).

When consumers have already have established the basic criteria for evaluating a product or service but still need additional information to understand the differences among brands, they engage in **limited problem solving**. This type of decision occurs when consumers purchase updated versions of products they have bought before, which often have additional features: For example, buying a new laptop computer with multiple input devices, some of which did not exist previously (e.g., a mini disk slot or a faster USB port).

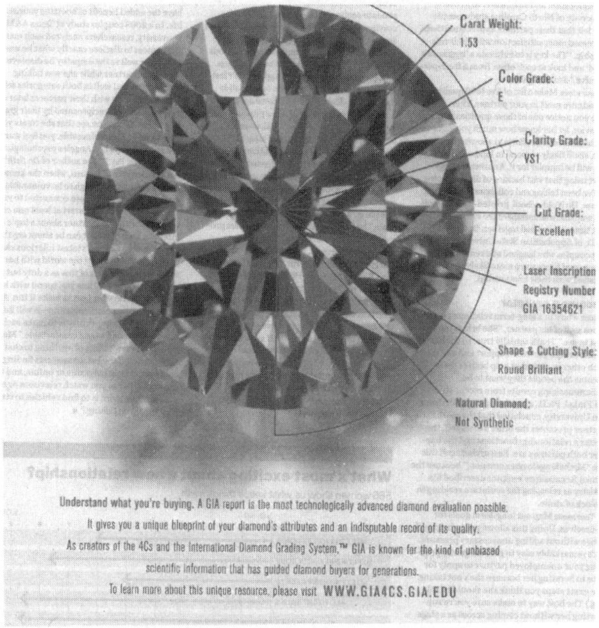

Source: Gemological Institute of America

FIGURE 13.1 Purchase Decision: Extensive Problem Solving

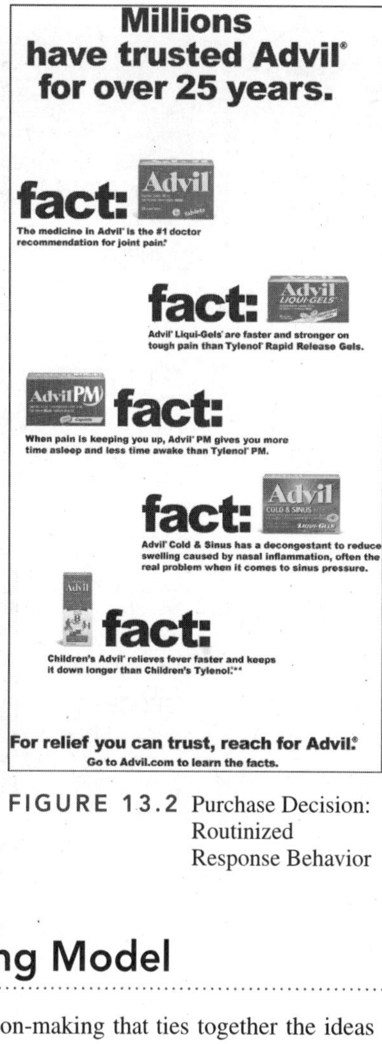

Source: Pfizer, Inc.

FIGURE 13.2 Purchase Decision: Routinized Response Behavior

Learning Objective

1 To understand the consumer's decision-making process.

Consumer Decision-Making Model

Figure 13.3 presents a model of consumer decision-making that ties together the ideas on consumer decision-making and consumption behavior discussed throughout this book. It does not presume to provide an exhaustive picture of the complexities of consumer decision-making. Rather, it is designed to synthesize and coordinate relevant concepts into a significant whole. The model includes three components: input, process, and output.

Decision-Making: Input

The input component of the consumer decision-making model includes three types of external influences:

1. The marketing mix consists of strategies designed to reach, inform, and persuade consumers to buy the marketer's products repeatedly. They include the product, advertising and other promotional efforts, pricing policy, and the distribution channels that move the product from the manufacturer to the consumer.
2. The sociocultural influences include the consumer's family, peers, social class, reference groups, culture, and, if applicable, subculture, which are discussed in Chapter 9 and Part Four.
3. The input also includes communications, which are the mechanisms that deliver the marketing mix and sociocultural influences to consumers and are described in Part Three.

The impact of the marketing mix and sociocultural influences is the input that determines what consumers purchase and how they use what they buy. Because these influences may be directed to the individual or actively sought by the individual, a two-headed arrow is therefore used to link the *input* and *process* segments of the model (see Figure 13.3).

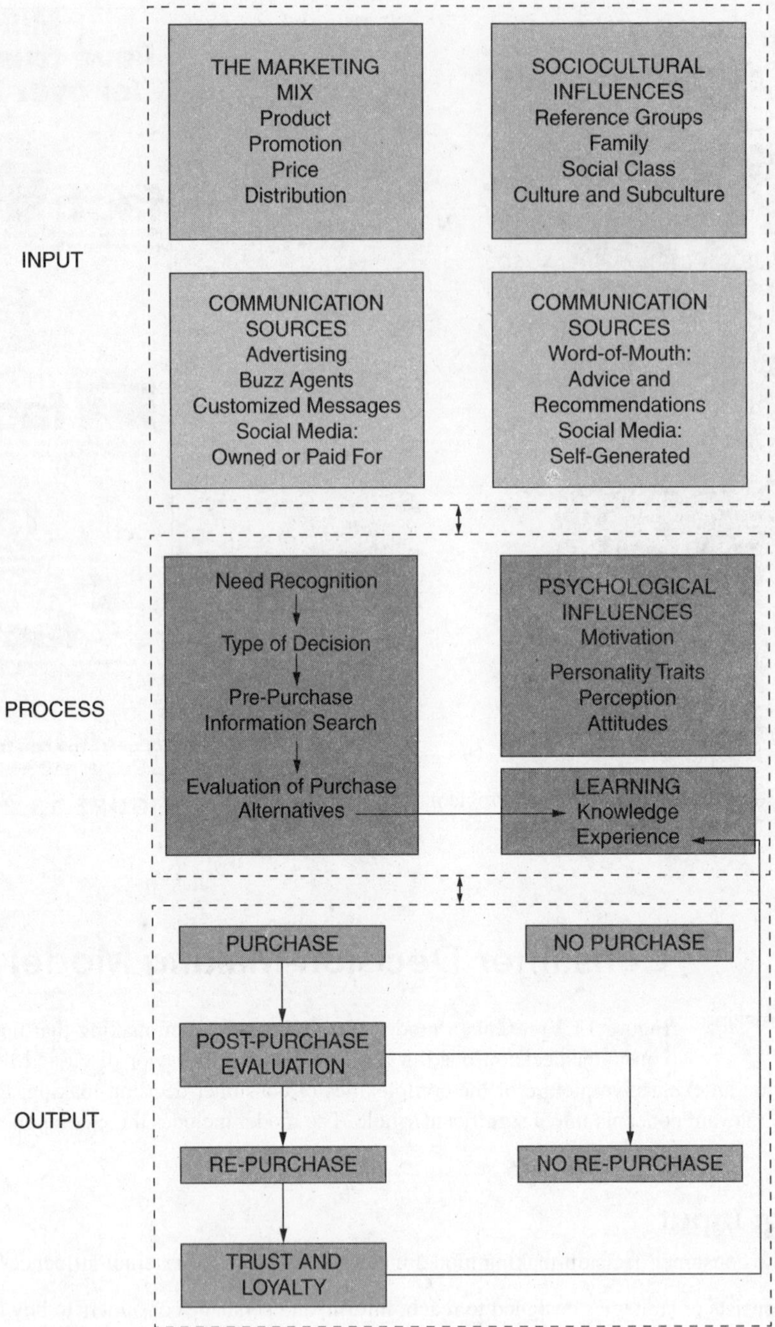

FIGURE 13.3 Consumer Decision-Making Model

Box 13.1 The Changing Nature of Consumer Decision-Making (CDM)

Consumers in the digital era consider three stages of consumer decision-making – the initial consideration stage, the elaboration stage, and the moment of purchase stage.[1] All these stages have important implications for marketers. Contrary to the traditional CDM model, consumers add or subtract brands when they consider the elaboration stage. This is in contrary to the traditional assumption that the number of brands would decrease when the consumers close in on their purchase. Aquaguard water purifier may want to concentrate more on the moment of purchase than the initial two stages. Kent, a similar product, has also made inroads into the market and may get accommodated in the elaboration stage without being present in the initial consideration stage. A new brand of organic vegetables in a city like Bangalore may use customized information to target consumers through digital channels and break into the elaboration stage. Research published in McKinsey Quarterly shows that these stages – besides having implications on purchase – may also affect the loyalty pattern.

Decision-Making: Process

The process component of the model is concerned with how consumers make decisions. To understand this process, we must consider the influence of the psychological concepts examined in Part Two of this book. The model's *psychological field* consists of the internal influences (motivation, perception, learning, personality, and attitudes) that affect consumers' decision-making processes (what they need or want, their awareness of various product choices, their information-gathering activities, and their evaluation of alternatives).

Need Recognition

Need recognition occurs when a consumer is faced with a "problem." For instance, take a young executive who decides to purchase a new cell phone with a high-quality digital camera. He imagines that he would benefit from having a high-quality digital camera built into his phone because it would make it easier and more convenient to take more vivid and realistic photos, without having to lug around a separate digital camera. This executive has recognized a need and identified a suitable response.

There are two types of need recognition. Some consumers are *actual state* types, who perceive that they have a problem when a product fails to perform satisfactorily (e.g., a cordless telephone that develops constant static). In contrast, other consumers are *desired state* types, for whom the desire for something new may trigger the decision process.[2]

Pre-Purchase Search

Pre-purchase search begins when a consumer perceives a need that might be satisfied by the purchase and consumption of a product. Sometimes, recalling past purchases provides the consumer with adequate information to make the present choice. However, when the consumer has had no prior experience, he or she may have to engage in an extensive search for useful information on which to base a choice.

The consumer usually searches his or her memory (the *psychological field*) before seeking *external* sources of information regarding a given consumption-related need. Past experience is considered an *internal* source of information. The greater the relevant past experience, the less external information the consumer is likely to need to reach a decision. Many consumer decisions are based on a combination of previous experience (internal sources) and marketing and noncommercial information (external sources). The degree of perceived risk can also influence this stage of the decision process (see Chapter 4). In high-risk situations, consumers are likely to engage in complex and extensive information search and evaluation; in low-risk situations, they are likely to use very simple or limited search and evaluation.

The act of shopping is an important form of external information. According to consumer research, there is a big difference between men and women in terms of their response to shopping. Whereas most men do not like to shop, most women claim to like the experience of shopping; and although the majority of women found shopping to be relaxing and enjoyable, the majority of men did not feel that way.[3]

An examination of the external search effort associated with the purchase of different product categories found that, as the amount of total search effort increased, consumer attitudes toward shopping became more positive, and more time was made available for shopping. Not surprisingly, the external search effort was greatest for consumers who had the least amount of product category knowledge.[4] It follows that the less consumers know about a product category and the more important the purchase is to them, the more extensive their pre-purchase search is likely to be. Conversely, consumers high in subjective knowledge (a self-assessment of how much they feel that they know about the product category) will rely more on their own evaluations rather than on others' recommendations.

It is also important to point out that the Internet has had a great impact on pre-purchase search. Rather than visiting a store to find out about a product, or calling the manufacturer and asking for a brochure, consumers can go to manufacturers' websites to find much of the information they need about the products and services they are considering. For example, many automobile websites provide product specifications, prices, and dealer cost information; reviews; and even comparisons with competing vehicles. Volvo's website, for example, lets you "build" your own car, and see how it would look, for example, in different colors. Some auto company websites will even list a particular auto dealer's new and used car inventory. There are also websites that allow women to customize a large number of cosmetic products.

With respect to surfing the Internet for information, consider one consumer's comments drawn from a research study: "I like to use the Web because it's so easy to find information, and it's really easy to use. The information is at my finger-tips and I don't have to search books in libraries."[5] However, a Roper Starch Survey found that an individual searching the Internet gets frustrated in about 12 minutes, on average; other research suggested that although the Internet may reduce physical effort, there is nevertheless a "cognitive challenge" that limits consumers' online information searches.[6]

What happens if a search is a failure? According to a study of "search regret," consumers' post-purchase dissonance results from an unsuccessful pre-purchase search.[7] Furthermore, the same research revealed that failure can also have a damaging effect on retailers. However, retailers can help eliminate or reduce search regret by providing ample information, trying to reduce out-of-stock situations, and giving salespeople proper training.[8]

How much information a consumer will gather also depends on various situational factors. Table 13.1 lists several factors that increase consumers' pre-purchase information search. For some products and services, the consumer may have ongoing experience on which to draw (such as a golfer purchasing a "better" set of golf clubs), or the purchase may essentially be discretionary in nature (rather than a necessity), so there is no rush to make a decision.

Online versus Traditional Information Search

For a while now, researchers have been examining how the Internet has affected the way consumers make decisions. It is often thought that because consumers have limited information-processing capacity, they must develop a strategy for searching for information online. The strategy is based on both individual (e.g., knowledge, personality traits, demographics) and contextual

TABLE 13.1 Factors That Increase Pre-Purchase Information Search

PRODUCT FACTORS

Long periods of time between successive purchases
Frequent changes in product styling
Frequent price changes
Volume purchasing (large number of units)
High price
Many alternative brands
Much variation in features

SITUATIONAL FACTORS

Experience: First-time purchase; No past experience because the product is new; Unsatisfactory past experience within the product category.
Social Acceptability: The purchase is for a gift; The product is socially visible.
Value-Related Considerations: The purchase is discretionary rather than necessary; All alternatives have both desirable and undesirable consequences; Family members disagree on product requirements or evaluation of alternatives; Product usage deviates from important reference groups; The purchase involves ecological considerations; Many sources of conflicting information.

CONSUMER FACTORS

Demographics: Education, income, occupation, age, wealth, and marital status.
Personality Traits: One's degree of dogmatism, willingness to accept risk, product involvement, and novelty seeking.

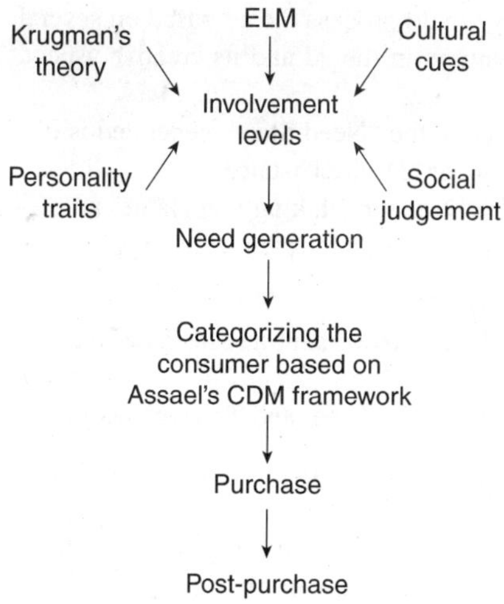

FIGURE 13.4 Explaining the Consumer Decision-Making Aspects

factors (characteristics of the decision tasks). The three major contextual factors that have been researched are:[9]

1. ***Task Complexity*** – the number of alternatives and amount of information available for each alternative.
2. ***Information Organization*** – the presentation, format, and content.
3. ***Time Constraint*** – the amount of time the consumer has to decide.

Consumer Decision-Making - The "Need" Stage and Its Linkages with Classical Theories

- Ashirwad is a brand of *atta* (wheat flour) that has been very successful.
- Sonata is a brand of watch that has been successful.
- Fair&Lovely is a successful brand.
- Reynold pens were successful when it was introduced in the eighties.

Unlike the conventional decision-making strategies associated with consumer behavior, there is another perspective to consider in CDM process. The approach suggested, uses the conventional decision-making stages, but offers a different perspective on CDM. Specifically, the model takes into account certain theories and addresses the importance of formation of needs. The suggested CDM process can be conceptualized as shown in Figure 13.4.

Conventional CDM process starts with the "Need" stage. But it is the involvement level is that is responsible for generating and articulating the need associated with the individual consumer. Henry Assael proposed that the involvement levels are associated with

a) Krugman's involvement theory
b) Social Judgment Theory
c) Elaboration Likelihood Model (ELM)

This proposed model has added "Personality Traits" as the fourth factor to these theories.[10]

How Does the CDM Process of the Model Work?

Let us assume that one of the brands of fairness creams for men is interested in analyzing the CDM process to formulate a strategy for the brand. How can consumer behavior support such a strategy?

Social Judgment theory[11,12] mentions that an individual (in this case, the consumer of fairness cream) will have a latitude of acceptance (a mental state to accept beliefs that are in line with his thinking on fairness cream), "latitude of rejection" (to reject the beliefs that are not in tune with his thinking). There can also be a possibility that a consumer is indifferent with regard to the issue (non-committal kind). It is clear that a consumer who believes that the fairness cream (any brand) lays the foundation for his confidence and success in life (relevance) is different from a consumer who believes that fairness cream is a waste of money. In between these two extremes, there may be a consumer who may believe in using fairness creams for "moderate social purposes" (lower degree of involvement) or another consumer who have to use it only for specific situations (situational involvement), for instance, in a run-up to a special event at the office. Let's assume Mohan, a high-involvement consumer (Krugman)[13], thinks that the fairness cream has a high degree of relevance for him; he is most likely to pursue the following steps:

- He actively searches for information across brands (Fair & Lovely, Fair & Handsome, Nivea, etc.)
- He may use several attributes to compare the brands
- He may think that his social esteem among his reference group is based on his fairness.
- He may look for an optimal solution for his fairness need and may have certain personality traits (like being a high-monitor, achievement orientation, and self-fulfillment) that creates a strong state of need.

This state emphasizes the difference between the consumer's actual needs and desired need.

Additionally, as per the ELM model, a consumer who has a high degree of motivation will process the attributes and benefits associated with the brand (central route) when they perceive an advertisement.[14] This high degree of involvement is perhaps due to the relevance of the category to him and also because of the perceived risk associated with his self-esteem.

The consumers who are (relatively) involved to a very low degree with the category would process the ad based on several aspects that are peripheral to the ad itself. These aspects could include the celebrity featured in the ad and its creative aspect. Also, a consumer could process an ad through the central as well as the peripheral route.

The major implication of the "Involvement Levels" at the beginning of the model is that the "Need State" generated is different for different segments (involvement-based segment) and there is no generic "Actual" or "Desired" state.

After the need state, Assael's framework combines Low and High involvement with Decision-Making and Habit and creates an excellent continuity with regard to the CDM model. For the same category of fairness cream for men, consumers can be categorized under:

i) Complex decision-makers (highly involved consumers who have a combination of high involvement and decision-making with in-depth aspects)

This is a segment that will use TV ads, websites of the brands as well as Facebook, YouTube, and Twitter to compare Fair & Handsome, Fair & Lovely and Nivea on several attributes.

ii) Loyal Consumers

This segment may prefer a brand for a variety of reasons and form a habit of buying the brand. The brand may become a part of their ritual or event through habits. Habits can be created by contextual cues like time (day or night).

Location (home), social setting (friendly), and preceding or ensuing events ("After-shower", for instance) are some of the reasons why occasion-based positioning is effective. When contextual cues are maintained, the habit is triggered within the consumer. Hence, brand loyalty can exist due to the attitude towards the brand and habit. The habit, viewed in this context, is different from the conventional treatment of the term "habit" in the literature that is generally associated with inertia buying.

iii) Variety-seeking Consumers

This segment of consumers will have a low degree of involvement with the category and may experiment with many brands in the category based on some more information or simply for the sake of change.

iv) Consumers who reflect inertia

A segment of consumers (who are involved to a very small degree) may pick up a brand (Fair & Lovely, for instance) simply because it is widely advertised or because they link up the advertising with the brand at the point of purchase. They are "inertia" consumers (little commitment to the brand).

Depending on their involvement, the "purchase" stage requires different marketing strategies for different types of consumer segments. In fact, unlike the conventional CDM process where the purchase stage triggers operational aspects of purchase, this stage (as per this model) can trigger several aspects of product line development and researching consumer segments.[15]

Should there be an exclusive brand (with several additional benefits – functional, social or psychological) for the "complex buying behavior" segment?

Are there adequate retail outlets that provide an "experiential" touch to the "complex- buying behavior" segment?

Should a retail outlet located in a specific area carry both the lower-end brand and the higher-end brand? Should there be a middle brand (in terms of price) that can upgrade the "variety seeking" consumer?

What is the percentage of "inertia" consumers who buy the brand? Can enhancing the brand involvement ("slice of life" appeal of solving a problem with the cream rather than aspiration-based appeal) through ads make the consumer more involved with the brand though he may not be involved in the category?

Finally, the post-purchase stage has to take into the involvement levels of the consumer. Will a highly involved consumer participate in a "Reality Show"? (Media aspects). Will he or she be prepared for a customized set of services with regard to personal care? (brand extension). As consumers of the brand, will "inertia" consumers be prepared for a sales promotional deal when they consider buying the brand at the point of purchase? Can variety-seeking consumers be consumers for some other related category associated with the brand? (skin lotion as these consumers may be inclined towards trying out brands).

Several of the important aspects that are associated with the conventional CDM process like compensatory rule (where the consumer compensates for the negative aspects of a brand with its positive aspects) or non-compensatory rule (where a consumer rejects a brand because it fails to match up on a specific dimension) can be related to the process of CDM model, as discussed.

Also, will CDM process work for all categories of products or services?

A brand like IFB launching dish-washing machines targets young and married professionals (a new concept product in the Indian context). Given the time constraints and the demands of multiple roles, the target segment is likely to be highly involved with such an offering.

A brand like Kaya offers personal care or beauty services. Consumers at different levels of involvement are likely to approach the service.

A brand of smart phone like Galaxy or iPhone that has both utilitarian benefits and status benefits and is likely to attract consumers who reflect a high sense of personal relevance towards such brand.

A brand like Reliance Fresh that is high on sales-promotional deals and "Value for money" offers or Big Bazaar with its low prices on several categories is likely to appeal less to consumers who would like to have variety in every category and high degree of sales support and ambience at the store.

The CDM model discussed highlights the important levels of different segments. Every stage in the CDM model is likely to draw insights from the "need" stage.

Brand-Sets and Attributes Considered During Evaluation

Within the context of consumer decision-making, the **evoked set (consideration set)** refers to the specific brands (or models) a consumer considers in making a purchase within a particular product category. An **inept set** consists of brands (or models) that the consumer excludes from purchase consideration because they are unacceptable or seen as inferior. An **inert set** consists of brands (or models) the consumer is indifferent toward because they are perceived as not having any particular advantages. Regardless of the total number of brands (or models) in a product category, a consumer's evoked set tends to be quite small on average, often consisting of only three to five brands or models.

The evoked set consists of the small number of brands the consumer is familiar with, remembers, and finds acceptable. Figure 13.5 shows the evoked set as a subset of all available brands in a product category. Marketers must ensure that their products become a part of a consumer's evoked set if they are to be considered at all. Excluded products include:

1. Unknown brands or models because of the consumer's selective exposure to advertising media and selective perception of advertising stimuli.
2. Unacceptable brands of poor quality or not having specific features or attributes or inappropriate positioning in either advertising or product characteristics.
3. Brands that are perceived as not having any special benefits.
4. Overlooked brands that have not been clearly positioned.
5. Brands that are not selected because they do not satisfy perceived needs.

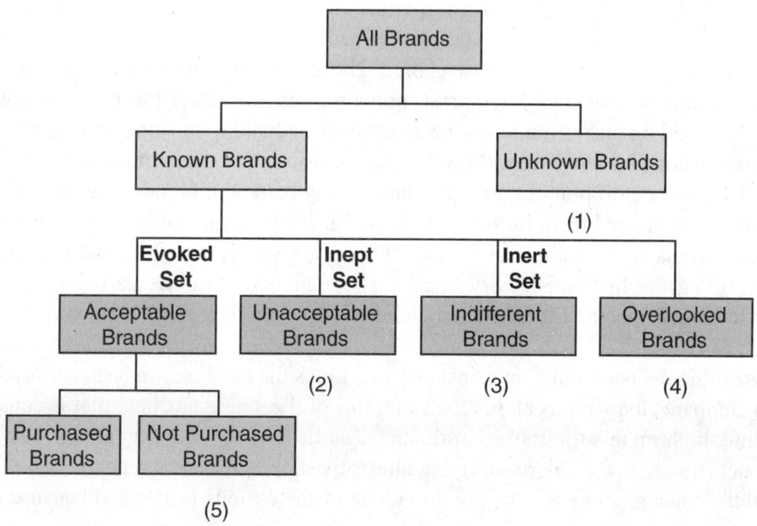

FIGURE 13.5 Brand-Sets Considered During Evaluation

In each of these instances, the implication for marketers is that promotional techniques should be designed to impart a more favorable and relevant, product image to the target consumer. This may also require a change in product features or attributes (more or better features). An alternative strategy is to get consumers in a particular target segment to consider a specific offering and possibly put it in their evoked set.

Research also suggests that the use of white space and choice of typeface in advertisements may influence the consumer's image of the product. For example, quality, prestige, trust, attitude toward the brand, and purchase intention have been shown to be positively conveyed by white space, and typefaces were perceived as being attractive, warm, and liked when they were simple, more natural, and included serifs.[16] It has also been suggested that consumers may not, all at once, incorporate the entire number of possible choices into their evoked set, but instead may make several decisions within a single decision process. Consumers screen their options and eliminate unsuitable alternatives before they start the information search process, which makes reaching a final decision more manageable.[17]

In reality, the criteria consumers use to evaluate the products within their evoked sets are in the form of important product attributes. In addition to price, examples of product attributes that consumers have used while evaluating product are:

1. ***E-Book readers***: Size, weight, touch screen, battery life, memory size, and the compatibility with a cell phone signal.
2. ***Orange juice***: Amount of pulp, degree of sweetness, weakness or strength of flavor, color, and packaging.
3. ***Wristwatches***: Alarm features, water resistance, quartz movement, and size of dial.

When a company knows that consumers will be evaluating alternatives, it sometimes advertises in a way that recommends the criteria consumers should use in assessing product or service options. We have probably all had the experience of comparing or evaluating different brands or models of a product and finding the one that just feels, looks, and/or performs "just right." Interestingly, research shows that when consumers discuss such "right" products, there is little or no mention of price; items often reflect personality characteristics or childhood experiences; and it is often "love at first sight." In one study, the products claimed to "just feel right" included Big Bertha golf clubs, old leather briefcases, Post-it notes, and the Honda Accord.[18]

Research has explored the influence of brand credibility (which consists of trustworthiness and expertise) on brand choice, and has found that it improves the chances that a brand will be included in the consumer's evoked set. Three factors that affect a brand's credibility are: The perceived quality of the brand, the perceived risk associated with the brand, and the information costs saved by deciding to buy the brand and end the search for information.[19] Furthermore, the study indicated that trustworthiness is more important than expertise when it comes to making a choice.

Consumer Decision Rules

Decision rules are procedures that consumers use to facilitate brands and other consumption-related choices. These rules reduce the burden of making complex decisions by providing guidelines or routines that make the process less taxing. There are two types of consumer decision rules. **Compensatory decision rules** come into play when a consumer evaluates brand or model options in terms of each relevant attribute and computes a weighted or summated score for each brand. The computed score reflects the brand's relative merit as a potential purchase choice. The assumption is that the consumer will select the brand that scores highest among the alternatives evaluated. In contrast, **noncompensatory decision rules** do not allow consumers to balance positive evaluations of a brand on one attribute against a negative evaluation on some other attribute.

There are three types of noncompensatory rules. In following a **conjunctive decision rule**, the consumer establishes a separate, minimally acceptable level as a cutoff point for each attribute. If any particular brand or model falls below the cutoff point on any one attribute, that option is eliminated from further consideration. Because the conjunctive rule can result in several acceptable alternatives, it becomes necessary in such cases for the consumer to apply an additional decision rule to arrive at a final selection (for example, accepting the first satisfactory brand). The conjunctive rule is particularly useful in quickly reducing the number of alternatives to be considered. The consumer can then apply another, more refined decision rule to arrive at a final choice.

In following a **lexicographic decision rule**, the consumer first ranks the attributes in terms of perceived relevance or importance. The consumer then compares the various alternatives in terms of the single attribute that is considered most important. If one option scores sufficiently high on this top-ranked attribute (regardless of the score on any of other attributes), it is selected and the process ends. When there are two or more surviving alternatives, the process is repeated with the second highest-ranked attribute (and so on), until the consumer reaches the point that one of the options is selected because it exceeds the others on a particular attribute.

With the lexicographic rule, the highest-ranked attribute (the one applied first) may reveal something about the individual's basic consumer (or shopping) orientation. For instance, a "buy the best" rule might indicate that the consumer is *quality oriented*; a "buy the most prestigious brand" rule might indicate that the consumer is *status oriented*; a "buy the least expensive" rule might reveal that the consumer is *economy minded*.

A variety of decision rules appear quite commonplace. According to a consumer survey, nine out of ten shoppers who go to the store for frequently purchased items possess a specific shopping strategy for saving money:[20]

1. **Practical Loyalists**—those who look for ways to save on the brands and products they would buy anyway.
2. **Bottom-Line Price Shoppers**—those who buy the lowest-priced item with little or no regard for brand.
3. **Opportunistic Switchers**—those who use coupons or sales to decide among brands and products that fall within their evoked set.
4. **Deal Hunters**—those who look for the best bargain and are not brand loyal.

We have considered only the basic consumer decision rules. Most of the decision rules described here can be combined to form new variations, such as conjunctive-compensatory, conjunctive-disjunctive, and disjunctive-conjunctive rules. It is likely that, for many purchase decisions, consumers maintain in long-term memory overall evaluations of the brands in their evoked sets. This would make assessment by individual attributes unnecessary. Instead, using the **affect referral decision rule**, the consumer selects the brand with the highest perceived overall rating. This type of synthesized decision rule represents the simplest of all rules.

Table 13.2 applies the decision rules to purchasing an e-book reader.

Decision Rules and Marketing Strategy

An understanding of which decision rules consumers apply in selecting a particular product or service is useful for marketers in developing promotional programs. A marketer who is familiar with the prevailing decision rule can prepare a promotional message in a format that will facilitate consumer information processing. The promotional message might even suggest how potential consumers should make a decision. For instance, an advertisement for the latest cell phone might tell potential consumers "what to look for in a new feature-rich cell phone." The ad might advise consumers to consider the attributes of long battery life, high-resolution screen, high-resolution video recording, and a particularly high-quality digital camera.

Incomplete Information and Noncomparable Alternatives

In many decision-related situations, consumers have incomplete information on which to base decisions and must use alternative strategies to compensate for the missing elements. Missing information may result from advertisements or packaging that mention only certain attributes, the consumer's own imperfect memory of attributes for no present alternatives, or because some attributes are experiential and can only be evaluated after product use. There are four ways in which consumers can cope with missing information:

1. Consumers may delay the decision until the missing information is obtained.
2. Consumers may ignore missing information and decide to continue with the decision process using only the available information.

TABLE 13.2 Applying the Decision Rules to Purchasing an E-Book Reader

DECISION RULE	RATIONALE
Compensatory	"I selected the e-book reader that came out as the best when I balanced the good ratings against the bad ratings."
Conjunctive	"I selected the e-book reader netbook that had no bad features."
Disjunctive	"I picked the e-book reader that excelled in at least one attribute."
Lexicographic	"I chose the e-book reader that scored the best on the attribute that I consider to be the most important."
Affect referral	"I bought the brand with the highest overall rating."

3. Consumers may change the decision strategy to one that better accommodates missing information.
4. Consumers may infer ("construct") the missing information.

In discussing consumer decision rules, we have assumed that a choice is made from among the brands (or models) evaluated. Of course, a consumer may also conclude that none of the alternatives offers sufficient benefits to warrant purchase. If this were to occur with a necessity, such as a home water heater, the consumer would probably either lower his or her expectations and settle for the best of the available alternatives or seek information about additional brands, hoping to find one that more closely met predetermined criteria. In contrast, if the purchase is more discretionary (e.g., a new pair of shoes), the consumer probably would postpone the purchase. In this case, information gained from the search up to that point would be transferred to long-term storage and retrieved and reintroduced as input when the consumer regained interest in making such a purchase (see Chapter 5).

Decision-Making: Output

The output portion of the consumer decision-making model consists of purchase behaviors and post-purchase evaluation of the purchases. Consumers make three types of purchases. When a consumer purchases a product (or brand) for the first time and buys a smaller quantity than usual, the purchase is a trial. Thus, a trial is the exploratory phase of purchase behavior in which consumers attempt to evaluate a product through direct use. For instance, when consumers purchase a new brand of laundry detergent about which they may be uncertain, they are likely to purchase a smaller quantity than if it were a familiar brand. Consumers can also be encouraged to try a new product through such promotional tactics as free samples, coupons, and/or sale prices.

When a new brand in an established product category (cookies, cold cereal, yogurt) is found by trial to be more satisfactory or better than other brands, consumers are likely to repeat the purchase. Repeat purchase behavior represents **brand loyalty**. Unlike a trial, in which the consumer uses the product on a small scale and without any commitment, a repeat purchase usually signifies that the product meets with the consumer's approval and that he or she is willing to use it again and in larger quantities.

Trial purchases are not always feasible. For example, with most durable goods (e.g., refrigerators, washing machines, electric ranges), a consumer usually moves directly from evaluation to a purchase and long-term commitment without an actual trial. While purchasers of a new Volkswagen Beetle were awaiting delivery of their just-purchased cars, they were kept "warm" by receiving a mailing that included a psychographic tool called "Total Visual Imagery" that was personalized to the point that it showed them the precise model and color they had ordered.[21]

Still further, post-purchase evaluation occurs after consumers have used the product, and in the context of their expectations. When a product's performance matches expectations, consumers feel neutral. **Positive disconfirmation of expectations** occurs when the product's performance exceeds expectations and the consumer is satisfied. **Negative disconfirmation of expectations** occurs when performance is below expectations and the consumer is dissatisfied.

Cognitive dissonance (see Chapter 6) occurs when consumers try to reassure themselves that they made wise choices. In doing so, they may rationalize the decision as being wise; seek advertisements that support their choice and avoid those of competitive brands; attempt to persuade friends or neighbors to buy the same brand (and thereby confirm their own choice); or turn to other satisfied purchasers for reassurance.

The degree of post-purchase analysis that consumers undertake depends on the importance of the product decision and the experience acquired in using the product. When the product lives up to expectations, the consumers probably will buy it again. When the product performance is disappointing or does not meet expectations, they will search for better alternatives. Thus, the consumer's post-purchase evaluation "feeds back" to the consumer's psychological field and influences similar decisions in the future. In Figure 13.6, Royal Challengers Bangalore (RCB) highlights the important of consumer engagement even during off-season; in this case, RCB used a contest in the digital media to keep its fans engaged during the off-season. Studies show that customer retention is often an outcome of the brand's reputation—especially for products that consumers find difficult to evaluate.[22] Research also found that younger customers have more involvement and higher expectations of service offerings and often experience cognitive dissonance after purchasing services.[23]

Satisfied customers feel that they receive "value for their money." As an outcome of an evaluative judgment (i.e., the consumer purchases one of the brands or models in his or her evoked set), value implies the notion of a trade-off of benefits—the features of the purchased item—versus the sacrifice necessary to purchase it (the price of the product).[24] As early as 1911, researchers suggested that one should view consumption as "voting." Just as a consumer influences a political election by the act of voting, that same consumer influences the environment and society by his or her purchases.[25]

Source: United Spirits

FIGURE 13.6 Consumer Engagement

Learning Objective

2 To understand the dynamics of buying gifts.

Consumer Gifting Behavior

Gifts are a particularly interesting part of consumer decision-making. Gifts represent more than ordinary, "everyday" purchases, because they are symbolic, and mostly associated with important events (e.g., Mother's Day, births and birthdays, engagements, weddings, graduations, and many other accomplishments and milestones). **Gifting behavior** is a gift exchange that takes place between a giver and a recipient. The definition is broad in nature and embraces gifts given voluntarily ("Just to let you know I'm thinking of you"), as well as gifts that are an obligation ("I had to get him a gift").[26] It includes gifts given to (and received from) others and gifts to oneself ("self-gifts"). Moreover, the majority of products that we refer to as "gifts" are in fact items that we purchase for ourselves.

Gifting represents symbolic communication, with meanings ranging from congratulations, love, and regret to obligation and dominance. The nature of the relationship between gift giver and gift receiver determines the gift chosen, but can also have an impact on the subsequent relationship between the giver and the recipient.[27] There are several types of gifts:[28]

1. ***Intergroup Gifting*** occurs whenever one group exchanges gifts with another group (such as one family with another). Similarly, gifts given to families will be different than those given to individual family members. For example, a "common sense" wedding gift may include products for setting up a household rather than a gift that would be used personally by either the bride or the groom.
2. ***Intercategory Gifting*** takes place when either an individual is giving a gift to a group (a single friend is giving a couple an anniversary gift) or a group is giving an individual a gift (friends chip in and give another friend a joint birthday gift). The gift selection strategies "buy for joint recipients" or "buy with someone" are especially useful when it comes to a difficult recipient situation (when "nothing seems to satisfy her"). These strategies can also be applied to reduce some of the time pressure associated with shopping for the great number of gifts exchanged during the American Christmas-season gift-giving ritual. For example, a consumer may choose to purchase five intercategory gifts for five aunt-and-uncle pairs (intercategory gifting), instead of buying ten personal gifts for five aunts and five uncles (interpersonal gifting). In this way, less time, money, and effort may be expended.[29]
3. ***Intragroup Gifting*** is characterized by the sentiment "we gave this to ourselves"; that is, a group gives a gift to itself or its members. For example, a dual-income couple may find that their demanding work schedules limit leisure time spent together as husband and wife. Therefore, an anniversary gift ("to us") of a long weekend in Las Vegas would be an example of an intragroup gift. It would also remedy the couple's problem of not spending enough time together. In contrast, interpersonal gifting occurs between just two individuals: the gift giver and the gift receiver. By their very nature, interpersonal gifts are intimate because they provide an opportunity for a gift giver to reveal what he or she thinks of the gift receiver. Successful

gifts communicate that the giver knows and understands the receiver and their relationship. For example, a pair of "just the right" cufflinks given to a friend is viewed by the receiver as "she really knows me." In contrast, an electric can opener given as a Valentine's Day gift, when the recipient is expecting a more intimate gift, can mean the deterioration of a relationship.

Researchers have discovered that both male and female gift givers feel more comfortable in giving gifts to the same sex. However, they also experienced more intense feeling with respect to gifts given to members of the opposite sex.[30] Additionally, although females get more pleasure than males from giving gifts, and generally play the dominant role in gift exchanges, both sexes are strongly motivated by feelings of obligation. Still further, everyone knows that selecting and giving a gift often causes "gifting anxiety" on the part of the givers, the recipients, and the gifting situations. Knowledge of gender differences is therefore useful for marketers, because it implies that additional support might be appreciated at the point of purchase (while in a store) when a consumer is considering a gift for an opposite-sex recipient.

One study of gifts purchased online found that **variety-seeking** (see Chapter 5) extends to gifting, as subjects with this trait considered a wider range of product categories when buying gifts for others.[31] A Hong Kong study identified a continuum of gift receivers: "romantic other," "close friend," and "just friends." For example, a gift given to a "romantic other" involves a high emotional expectation, but one given to a friend has a low emotional expectation.[32]

Intrapersonal gifting, or a self-gift, occurs when the giver and the receiver are the same individual.[33] A self-gift is a state of mind. If a consumer sees a purchase as the "buying of something I need," then it is simply a purchase. In contrast, if the same consumer sees the same purchase as a "self-gift," then it is something special, with special meaning. Consumers may treat themselves to self-gifts that are products (clothing, compact disks, or jewelry), services (hairstyling, restaurant meals, spa membership), or experiences (socializing with friends). For example, while purchasing holiday gifts for others, some consumers find themselves in stores that they might not otherwise visit or find themselves looking at merchandise (such as a scarf) that they want but would not ordinarily buy.

The gifting process starts with the question: "Should I give a gift to X?" The answer can be yes or no depending on a variety of factors (e.g., relationship, occasion). If the answer is yes, the gift giver continues by asking: "What shall I give X as a gift?" This leads to the next question: "Do I want to give X something that X desires (i.e., do I want to put in some real effort researching the gift)?" If the answer is yes, the gift giver is then faced with the question: "How do I learn what X desires as a gift?" Here there are two choices: predicting the preferences of the recipient or asking the recipient what he or she desires. If the consumer answers no to the question, "Do I want to give X something that X desires?" then the gift giver has two choices (according to the model): (1) to give a gift that he or she would like (i.e., "To you for me"), or (2) to give a gift that attempts to alter or improve the gift receiver to the gift giver's liking (i.e., "Identify imposition"). The symbolic messages associated with these gifts tend to be less valued by the recipient. If preference prediction rather than direct questioning of the recipient for a gift idea is chosen, then there will be an element of surprise. In addition, if the giver does not bother to learn the recipient's preferences, then the outcome can also be a surprise—but maybe not a good surprise.[34]

Box 13.2 Segments, Lifestyles, and CDM

Mittal, et al.[35] mentions specific situations that trigger CDM. Replenishment of stocks, availability of variants, or introduction of new products are important situations in low-involvement categories. These situations are also affected by the level of information searched, place of information search (in-store), duration involved in decision-making, and sources of information used in the decision-making. A college student may be taken in by the buzz created by a chocolate advertisement that is offered in a new form (Cadbury Bournville). A middle-aged urban lady who is interested in health and fitness may look for the nutritional details of Kellog's Special K Cereal when she visits a modern retail outlet like Nilgiris. A rural consumer may be interested in the low-priced stock-keeping unit of the pain balm Moov, which he or she may occasionally use and would want to avoid buying a more expensive pack.

There are several ways in which a brand can get into the consideration set of consumers. The consumer segment and their respective lifestyle provide directions to the marketer. In the case of consumer durables, Mittal and his colleagues suggest that the need can be triggered by a new environment, a consumer experiencing a problem for the first time, a replacement phase, and life-cycle changes. These are important aspects for consumers in an

(Contiuned)

Box 13.2 (Continued)

emerging market. With about 50% of the Indian population below 25 years of age, the demands for cell phones are high. They are highly involved in searching information from various sources like friends and advertisements. Several models have been introduced by Nokia, Samsung, Micromax, and Karbonn for these segments. Peter England introduced suits for young professionals or people who were entering the job market. Hyundai launched its Santro Xing version – i10, i20, and Grand after being successful with its standard Santro. The brand's success may have created a favorable set-up for the new version i10 and the Xing offering may motivate repeat purchases. Flatscreen and LCD TV sets from brands like Samsung and LG may get into the consideration set of repeat buyers who can purchase at the higher end of the television market. Several years back Akai had a strategy that was in tune with an emerging market like India. There was a huge demand for color televisions in rural markets and there was a replacement market in urban areas. Akai introduced an exchange scheme that may have strategically linked both the urban and rural markets.

Perceived risk (discussed in Chapter 4 and in the next section on diffusions) experienced by consumers when they are new to the environment is also useful in certain situations. Healthcare is a promising market in India and millions of consumers require value-based healthcare services in different geographical areas. Brands like Apollo (with franchisee arrangements in several locations) have the opportunity to address the perceived risk of consumers, especially when they relocate from the region. Pharmacy chains like Mediplus or Religare also reduce the perceived risk of consumers by the proposition of genuine medicines in a market that has a significant presence of fake supplements.

The target and nature of the segment also decide how brand associations are developed over a range of price points. Titan has several sub-brands to cover a range of price points. Hindustan Unilever has a number of brands covering a price range in tea, detergent, shampoo, and soap categories. Nokia and LG are examples in cell phone and television categories, respectively.

Application 1: Cyber Groups, Brands, and CDM

There are professional tweeters for brands and these kinds of tweets have a loyal following. Kurkure, Figo, Royal Challenge, and Nano have been a part of micro-blogging in Twitter with about four million Indian users.[36] The cyber groups may have links with other groups who in turn may lead themselves to more groups. This interlinking across groups – ranging from strong to weak links – is likely to have an impact of attitude formation towards brands that are tweeted and also on the various stages of consumer decision-making.

Application 2: Related Services, Digital Inputs, and CDM

Trip Advisor, the world's largest travel website, has concentrated itself on hotel bookings rather than travel bookings because consumers are increasingly booking tickets from websites of airlines rather than online travel booking sites. 10% of its traffic comes from mobiles, 25% from smart phones,[37] and it also gets user reviews from 200 countries.

These aspects present a very interesting situation for managers analyzing CDM. Consumers expect more value from hotel bookings than travel bookings by using these websites .

Would this also hold good for any level of spending or just for the lower end of the travel market? How do these consumers search for information and what actually constitutes value. How can such a company integrate social media with its other promotional strategies? How does loyalty develop after the purchase is over (post-purchase)? How should these companies work with airlines to bundle their services? (Trip Advisor has such collaborations).

Application 3: Nurturing the Category and the Brand

Luxor Nano Clean introduced a new product that was intended for cleaning and protecting surfaces. With the launch, Luxor Group became the first company to bring Nano technology into the Indian markets, which is a widely accepted technology globally.[38] The price points were ₹100 and ₹150. It was available in nine variants and Amitabh Bachchan was its brand ambassador. While the market may be growing significantly, the challenge for the brand is to grow the category itself. It was a difficult ask, especially when it was in competition with brands that were launched by multinationals with greater distribution power. How can the CDM be applied by such a brand by using different psychological concepts to market both the category and strengthen itself ?

Hence, it is not just enough to inform the consumers about the "actual" and "desired" state ; consumers need to recognize the difference and act on it.

Application 4: Involvement Levels and CDM

Mahindra & Mahindra introduced a TVC that appealed to consumers to wait for the launch of the bikes of the company (that has an Italian origin) before finalizing on their festive purchases.[39]

The advertisement takes into account the pre-purchase involvement levels of consumers and brings the offering within the consideration set of the consumers. This happens before the final purchase is being considered by consumers who have had well-entrenched brands in the considerations set. The pre-purchase involvement level is important as it covers consumers who may also reflect situational involvement that may be associated with purchase of the product.

Application 5: Culture and CDM

In the context of consumer behavior, rituals, and festivities in India lend themselves amenable to a greater degree than "culture-based religious beliefs". It may be difficult to find branded offerings that cater to superstitions, but several categories can be associated with superstitious beliefs when people visit temples in several parts of India.

Candles dolls, bangles, lamps, and grains (as appropriate) are sold to devotees who believe that these, if offered to the respective God, will help them realize their prayers. Superstitions are rife in India and hence, these offerings are also made to ward off the "evil eye". Lack of distribution network, presence of local offerings, scattered geographical coverage, and opportunity costs keep major brands away. (ITC had entered the incense stick market probably due to its distribution strengths). Temples being associated with superstitious aspects, buildings in rural parts of India have dolls in front of them. These are made by families and sold to shops though the volume may not be very high.

Regional retailers in Chennai advertise their gemstones provide customized offerings for individuals who believe that their destiny or fortune revolves around these gems. Such offerings have opened up a market that may have been dormant in the past. Buoyed by the television ads of these retailers, smaller towns are also getting attracted to "gemology-based fortune". Interestingly, this phenomenon may not have an Indian origin!

Application 6: Need Stage to Purchase Stage

While brands compete with one another on a various dimensions, the digital route to branding offers interesting pointers for brands to engage consumers right from the need stage to the purchase stage.[40] Toyota and Google together announced the Toyota Collaborator, a social media-based car shopping tool. Buyers of Corolla can discuss with family and friends in real-time through Google Hangout on several customizable features. And, these prospective buyers can use Google Street View to drive around their block for a virtual drive.

Brand Equity and Consumer Decision-Making Process: Emerging Markets

Kevin Lane Keller pioneered the well-known Customer Based Brand Equity Model (CBBE) in his widely published text book, *Strategic Brand Management*. When considered with the CDM model, it can provide useful insights for an emerging market like India. The "Need" state in the CDM process is the one that sets the backdrop for the interpretation of the model. The following aspects need to be considered when CBBE model is used with the process.

i) How is "Awareness" created in the mind of the consumer?

ii) How is the imagery created in the mind of the consumer?

iii) How are performance, feelings, and judgments mentioned in the model formed? Are they formed before the purchase stage or after the purchase stage?

The "Resonance" stage of the model is associated with the various aspects mentioned in i), ii) and iii). The combination of CBBE and CDM process is especially important for durable brands. The following exhibits will establish the linkages between CBBE and CDM. Such linkages will also emphasize the importance of point of purchase.

Brands from the mobile category are provided as an illustrative example. Several stages in the brand equity model are associated with the "consideration and purchase" phases of consumer decision-making.

These brands namely Samsung Galaxy Note 3, Nokia Lumia 1020, and Sony Xperia Z1 that are in the same price range of ₹44,000 to ₹48,000 were selected to indicate that these models may compete with one another in the consideration set of consumers. Exhibits 1 and 2 reflect the awareness, features, and imagery created through the respective advertisements. Exhibit 3 reflects a combination of features associated with the three brands.

Keller's model CBBE is associated with awareness and imagery as its initial steps. It can be seen from the exhibits that

a) Awareness created by ad is limited.

b) Not all features and benefits can be combined by ads.

c) Consumers may differ in terms of the features/benefits sought by them.

d) The Word of Mouth (WOM) is not within the control of brands and hence, applying CBBE model becomes more critical when brands uses it along with advertisements.

e) Ads of brands were focusing only on one aspect of creating an attitude towards the reflective brand.

Awareness and imagery is created by the ad of the respective brand (online and/or offline brand communication). The consumer's "need" state may depend on the benefits expected from a consumer. Also, awareness (other than that created by ads) will depend on the extent to which the consumer is educated about the "need-match" (how attributes and benefits of a brand match the need of the consumer) at the point of purchase. It is only after this stage that the feelings, judgments, and performance associated with the respective brand can be judged well by the consumer.

Table 1 and 2 explains the extent to which mobile phones have penetrated into the Indian market. India has proved to be a very lucrative market for mobile phones and coupled with the diverse needs of any consumer, it is important that a brand makes a significant investment at the point of purchase to (dealer or retailer points) to attract his or her attention. Moreover, such a strategy will also strengthen the cognitive and affective aspects of the respective brand, resulting in a stronger attitude towards the brand – a prerequisite for brand resonance to be achieved.

EXHIBIT 1

ADVERTISEMENT OF THE BRANDS	FEATURES INDICATED IN THE ADVERTISEMENT
Ad on Samsung Galaxy Note 3	Galaxy Note 3 and Gear Smart watch, My Magazine, Action Memo, Smart Relay.
Ad on Nokia Lumia 1020	41 mega pixel camera.
Ad on Sony Experia Z1	Water proof metallic design, 21 mega pixel camera, Triluminos display, Touch screen, Music player.

(**Unpublished work of S. Ramesh Kumar and Sanjay Kumar Jena*)

EXHIBIT 2

BRANDS	IMAGERY (CREATED THROUGH THE AD)
Samsung Galaxy Note 3	The protagonist in the advertisement realizes the problems of the old toy store (Gustavo) that her grandfather had founded in 1911. The old store is important not only to attract customers, but also to pay its debts. She plans to do something for the betterment of the store. She then finds a dance competition to be held at Langham Theater. With the help of Samsung Galaxy Note 3 and Gear smart watch, she creates a short film known as "Dreams" to showcase the old toy store during the dance competition. Everybody is amazed by looking at the creativity reflected in her creation. The ad ends with the line "Design your life". This commercial reveals how Samsung Galaxy can help anyone achieve their dreams.
Nokia Lumia 1020	The commercial largely focuses on the specific features of its 41 mega pixel camera. It exhibits how the camera, with pure motion and high-definition technology, shoots very high-resolution images.
Sony Xperia Z1	Film star Katrina Kaif is the protagonist in this advertisement. Sony Xperia Z1 helps her in various circumstances, be it capturing different moments, sharing information on social media, listening music, etc. This commercial reveals the different features of the phone like water-proof metallic design, 21 mega pixel camera, Triluminos display, touch screen, music player, etc. With the line "the best of Sony for the best of you", it communicates the integration of Sony's Walkman, Cyber Shot and Bravia into Xperia Z1.

EXHIBIT 3

FEATURES	SAMSUNG GALAXY NOTE 3	NOKIA LUMIA 1020	SONY XPERIA Z1
Color	Black, Classic White, Blush Pink	White, Black, Yellow	White, Purple, Black
Display	5.7-inch Full-HD Super AMOLED display	4.5-inch AMOLED display	5-inch LED
Camera	13 megapixel	41 megapixel	20.7 megapixel
Operating System	Android 4.3 Jelly Bean	Windows Phone 8 Amber update	Android 4.2.2 Jelly Bean
Memory	3GB RAM, 32GB 32 GB of expandable storage	2GB RAM, 32GB of non expandable storage	2GB RAM, 16GB expandable to 64GB via a micro SD card
Processor	Exynos 5 Octa 5420 processor	1.5GHz dual-core Qualcomm Snapdragon S4	2.2GHz quad-core Qualcomm Snapdragon 800
Battery Capacity	3200 mAh	1020 mAh	3000 mAh
FM radio	Absence	Presence	Presence
Additional features	S Pen Air Command (Action Memo, Scrapbooker, Screen Write, S Finder and Pen Window options)	Clear Black technology	Water and dust resistant

(*Continued*)

EXHIBIT 3 (Continued)

FEATURES	SAMSUNG GALAXY NOTE 3	NOKIA LUMIA 1020	SONY XPERIA Z1
	S Planner	Recording full-HD videos at 30 frames per second	LED flash,
	Voice Recorder	Xenon flash	Self-timer
	ChatOn messaging app	High resolution images	Smile Shutter
	Samsung Apps app store	Backside illuminated sensor	Preview
	Samsung Hub content store	Six elements lens array	Timeshift Burst mode
			Face detection
			Geotagging
			Shutter sound for still and self-timer
			Steady Shot
			Microphone for video

References:

1. Based on https://samsungindiaestore.com/product/Mobiles/Smart_Phon (accessed on November 24, 2013).
2. Based on http://www.sony.co.in/productcategory/mob-phone (accessed on November 24, 2013).
3. Based http://www.nokia.com/inen/phones/phone/lumia1020/offers/ (accessed on November 24, 2013).
4. Based on http://www.youtube.com/watch?v=m4sTLfTKOGo (accessed on November 24, 2013).
5. Based on http://www.youtube.com/watch?v=eEyuXuzB1rw (accessed on November 24, 2013).
6. Based on http://www.youtube.com/watch?v=eqA0i_1Xy5g (accessed on November 24, 2013).
7. Based on http://gadgets.ndtv.com/mobiles/reviews/samsung-galaxy-note-3-review-435534 (accessed on November 25, 2013).
8. Based on http://gadgets.ndtv.com/mobiles/reviews/sony-xperia-z1-review-426248 (accessed on November 25, 2013
9. Based on http://gadgets.ndtv.com/mobiles/reviews/nokia-lumia-1020-review-433854 (accessed on November 25, 2013).

Learning Objective

3 To understand how innovative offerings gain acceptance within market segments and how individual consumers adopt or reject new products and services.

Diffusion and Adoption of Innovations

Diffusion of innovations is the macro process by which the acceptance of an innovation (i.e., a new product, new service, new idea, or new practice) takes place among members of a social system (or market segments), over time. This process includes four elements:

1. ***The Innovation***: new product, model, or service.
2. ***The Channels of Communication***: informal or formal, impersonal or personal groups.
3. ***The social system***: a market segment.
4. ***Time***.

In contrast, the **innovation adoption process** is a micro process that focuses on the stages through which an individual consumer passes when deciding to accept or reject a new product.

Box 13.3 Diffusion of Brands and Consumer Involvement with the Characteristics of Diffusion

As shown in Figure 13.7, diffusion characteristics of compatibility, "trialability", and consumer lifestyle have been combined well in Café Coffee Day's FiltaFresh, "brew your own coffee swiftly", offering. The offering has a coffee

(Continued)

Box 13.3 (Continued)

bag arrangement that does away with the need of storing coffee, having a coffee filter and cleaning it, and also a container to store coffee. The compatibility is the fact that serious coffee drinkers who prefer traditional filter coffee can use the bag to brew pure coffee quickly. This offering is compatible with the changing lifestyle where a consumer has little time for an elaborate ritual. The offering is also compatible with the typical filter coffee consumption ritual that is still in practice in the southern parts of India.

Source: Cafe Coffee Day

FIGURE 13.7 Diffusion Characteristics

The Meaning of "New" Products

Marketers need to differentiate between emerging markets and developed markets on what consumers perceive as "new." A touch of reality is required when conventional definitions of new products are applied to an emerging market like India, especially mass markets in several product categories. Value, convenience, and cultural associations are factors that may, in combination, work in the Indian context. If branding examples are considered from the last three decades, these three aspects appear to be important in several categories. Good Night's mosquito coils have an association with the cultural practice of smoking away insects. Vatika's hair oil with a combination of lime and coconut ingredients can be associated with the cultural practice of using such ingredients for hair care. The value of one-time use packs (sachets) has "revolutionized" the shampoo category in which more than 50% of the sale is associated with such packs.

Decades back Frooti had introduced the first tetra-packed juice drink with a mango flavor (mango is a fruit with a strong cultural association). Adding a tinge of blue to white clothes is a cultural practice in several parts of India and the dye brand Ujala became a major success when it introduced the additive in liquid form (Robin Blue from Reckitt & Benkiser in the powdered form was a part of households for several decades). PepsiCo's Kurkure and ITC's Bingo snacks have strong cultural associations in terms of their taste. In India, Nokia introduced a mobile phone model at a lower price point with features that included a torch and FM radio. In rural areas, carrying a torch is a cultural practice and India is also

Source: CavinKare

FIGURE 13.8 A Chik Shampoo Sachet

one of the major music markets in the world. Chik shampoo introduced the jasmine variant (jasmine flower is a part of the hair grooming ritual in south India). As shown in Figure 13.8, a cultural connotation, wherever applicable, is useful to a brand. Godrej's No. 1 soap brand (an 87-year-old brand) created value with several popular variants at a lower price point (compared to competitive brands). Wipro Santoor and Manjal soap brands use turmeric as their ingredient (turmeric's association with beauty or facial care is wellknown all over India). The Himalaya brand of over-the-counter medicines and personal care products makes use of the traditional ayurvedic system of medicine in a contemporary manner. During the 1980s Maruti's no-frill model (and Nano in recent times) in the passenger car market redefined the values associated with cars in India. There are many other examples of newness among Indian brands that have three factors: convenience, cultural associations, and value (to a lesser extent). These examples reflect the importance of such dimensions when marketers consider newness in the Indian context.

Types of Innovations

The definition of what is a "new product" varies among product developers and marketing strategists. From a consumer perspective, an **innovation** represents any item that the consumer perceives as new. Many marketers maintain that new products should be classified into three categories reflecting the extent to which they require consumers to change existing consumption behavior or buying patterns.

1. A **continuous innovation** has the least disruptive influence on established behavior. It involves the introduction of a modified product rather than a totally new product. Examples include the newly redesigned Apple MacBook, the latest version of Microsoft Office, reduced-fat Oreo cookies, Hershey Cacao (i.e., a form of dark) chocolate bars, American Express gift cards, Band-Aid Tough-Strips, and the Oral-B® Advantage Glide. Figure 13.2 is an example of continuous innovation.
2. A **dynamically continuous innovation** is somewhat more disruptive than a continuous innovation but still does not alter established behavior. It may involve the creation of a new product or the modification of an existing product. Examples include digital cameras, digital video recorders, MP3 players, DVRs, USB flash drives, and disposable diapers.
3. A **discontinuous innovation** requires consumers to adopt new behavior. Examples include airplanes, radios, TVs, automobiles, fax machines, PCs, videocassette recorders, medical self-test kits, and the Internet.

Box 13.4 New Products, New Markets, and Success

Diffusion of new products requires to be monitored by companies. There seems to an "inflection point" at which there is a proliferation of segments and offerings within the category (shampoo in sachets, ball pens, and watches are examples that diffused themselves with a rapid pace during the late eighties and nineties). Health-based offerings like Max, the no-sugar cola from Pepsi, and Monaco Smart Chips (baked) from Parle were withdrawn from the market due to low consumer receptivity.[35] Despite the demand for flat panel television sets, the plasma television market did not grow due to lack of screen sizes that consumers preferred.[35]

Product Features That Affect Adoption

Not all new products are equally likely to be adopted by consumers. Some products catch on very quickly (e.g., affordable cell phones), whereas others take a very long time to gain acceptance or never seem to achieve widespread consumer acceptance (e.g., electric cars). Diffusion researchers have identified five product characteristics that influence consumer acceptance of new products, which are detailed next.[41]

Source: Hindustan Unilever Limited

FIGURE 13.9 Relative Advantage

Relative advantage is the degree to which potential customers perceive a new product as superior to existing substitutes. For example, cellular telephones enable users to be in communication with the world and allows users to both receive and place calls and text messages. The fax machine offers users a significant relative advantage in terms of ability to communicate. A document can be transmitted in as little as 15 to 18 seconds at perhaps one-tenth the cost of an overnight express service, which will not deliver the document until the following day. (Of course, sending the document as an attachment to an email entails no cost and, like a fax, gets delivered in seconds.)

Figure 13.9 illustrates why machine wash detergents like Surf Excel Matic are designed to work efficaciously in high water environments present in washing machine to provide ideal stain removal. This is the reason why top machine manufacturers recommend Surf Excel Matic. Brands need to focus on relative advantage as a dynamic aspect in a changing environment.

Compatibility is the degree to which potential consumers feel a new product is consistent with their present needs, values, and practices. For instance, an advantage of 3M's Scotch Pop-up Tape Strips is that they are easier to use than roll tape for certain tasks (such as wrapping gifts), yet they represent no new learning for the user. Similarly, in the realm of shaving products, it is not too difficult to imagine that a few years ago, when Gillette introduced the Fusion razor, some men made the transition from inexpensive disposable razors and other men shifted from competitive nondisposable razors (including Gillette's own MACH3 razors) to using the new product. This newer product is fully compatible with the established wet-shaving rituals of many men. However, it is difficult to imagine male shavers shifting to a new depilatory cream designed to remove facial hair. Although potentially simpler to use, such a cream is incompatible with most men's current values regarding daily shaving practices.

Compatibility varies across cultures. For example, although shelf-stable milk (milk that does not require refrigeration unless it has been opened) has been successfully sold for years in Europe, Americans thus far have generally resisted the aseptic milk package.

Complexity—the degree to which a new product is difficult to understand or use—affects product acceptance. Clearly, the easier it is to understand and use a product, the more likely that product is to be accepted. For example, the acceptance of such convenience foods as frozen french fries, instant puddings, and microwave dinners is generally due to their ease of preparation and use. Interestingly, although DVD players can be found in most American homes, many adults require the help of their children to use the devices to record particular television programs. The introduction of cable boxes with built-in DVRs has helped to reduce the ongoing challenge involved in easily recording a TV program. A study of the adoption of mobile commerce transactions conducted via a mobile device or wireless telecommunication found that "perceived ease of use" had a positive effect on the intention to adopt.[42]

The issue of complexity is especially important when attempting to gain market acceptance for high-tech consumer products. Four predominant types of "technological fear" act as barriers to new-product acceptance: (1) Fear of technical complexity,

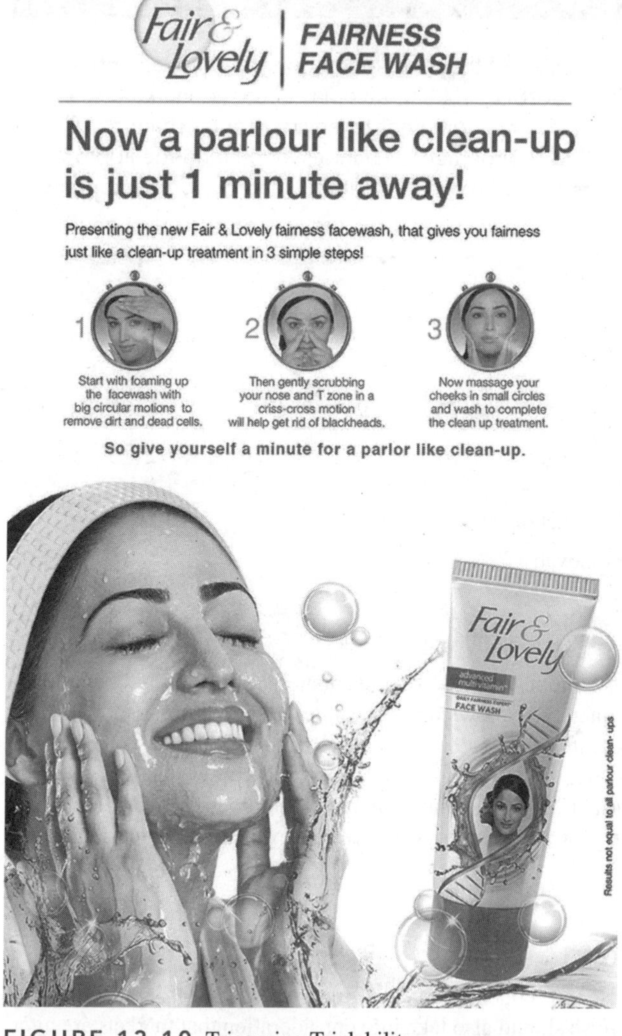

Source: Hindustan Unilever Limited

FIGURE 13.10 Triggering Trialability

(2) fear of rapid obsolescence, (3) fear of social rejection, and (4) fear of physical harm. Of the four, technological complexity was the most widespread concern of consumer innovators.[43]

Trialability refers to the degree to which a new product can be tried on a limited basis. The greater the opportunity to try a new product, the easier it is for consumers to evaluate the product and ultimately adopt it. In general, frequently purchased household products tend to have qualities that make trial relatively easy, such as the ability to purchase a small or "trial" size. Because a computer program cannot be packaged in a smaller size, many computer software companies offer free working models (demo versions) of their latest software to encourage computer users to try the program and subsequently buy the program.

After firmly establishing fairness as its benefit, Fair and Lovely's extension into face wash, as illustrated in Figure 13.10, is likely to trigger trialability among consumers, especially when the category is growing at a fast pace.

Aware of the importance of trial, marketers of new supermarket products commonly use substantial cents-off coupons or free samples to provide consumers with direct product experience. In contrast, durable items, such as refrigerators or ovens, are difficult to try without making a major commitment. This may explain why publications such as Consumer Reports are so widely consulted for their ratings of infrequently purchased durable goods.

Observability (communicability) is the ease with which a product's benefits or attributes can be observed, imagined, or described to potential consumers. Products that have a high degree of social visibility, such as fashion items, are more easily diffused than products that are used in private, such as a new type of deodorant. Similarly, a tangible product is promoted more easily than an intangible product (such as a service).

Box 13.5 Brand Features and Diffusion of Innovation in the Indian Context

In the category of mobile phones, Nokia's market share has fallen in the recent times, despite the brand's efforts to diffuse itself in the country through various marketing strategies.

The brand's 1100 model, introduced a few years back, was very Indian in its design with a mobile, radio, and a torch rolled into one. But, its competitors were more aware and sensitive to the evolving needs of the consumer, for example, introduction of dual SIM phones and this may caused the brand's decline in market share.[35] Micromax, a competing brand, has not only built up a strong rural distribution, but it also offers a model that doubles up as a remote for television and air-conditioners.

Spice offered an ultra-violet feature in one of its models that can detect false currency. Samsung introduced Marine model that runs on solar energy. Nokia, in line with its global strategy of providing services, is offering four

(Continued)

Box 13.5 (Continued)

million songs as free downloads from its Ovi store (about one million of them are Indian songs). There are interesting implications for diffusion of innovation concepts. Theodore Levitt's marketing myopia cautioned marketers from being "over prone" to the features of products, especially while being indifferent to environmental changes. The mobile category points out the need for a brand to adapt itself to environmental changes (of offering the appropriate services, entertainment or any other) while also updating its product-line with features that may be appropriate to "everyday-lifestyle" interface of the target segment.

The Adoption Process

The innovation adoption process consists of five stages through which potential consumers pass in attempting to arrive at a decision to try or not to try a new or innovative product. The five stages are:

1. **Awareness**: The consumer becomes aware that an innovation exists.
2. **Interest**: The consumer becomes interested in the innovative product or service.
3. **Evaluation**: The consumer undertakes a "mental trial" of the innovation.
4. **Trial**: The consumer tries the innovation.
5. **Adoption**: If satisfied, the consumer decides to use the innovation repeatedly.

Although the traditional adoption process model is insightful in its simplicity, it does not adequately reflect the full complexity of the consumer adoption process. For one thing, it does not adequately acknowledge that quite often, consumers face a need or problem-recognition stage before acquiring an awareness of potential options or solutions (a need recognition preceding the awareness stage). Moreover, the adoption process model does not adequately provide for the possibility of evaluation and rejection of a new product or service after each stage, especially after trial (i.e., a consumer may reject the product after trial or never use the product on a continuous basis). Finally, it does not include post-adoption or post-purchase evaluation, which can lead to a strengthened commitment or to discontinued use.

Diffusion of Innovation in the Indian context

The characteristics of diffusion are important both for new and existing products in an emerging market. Emerging markets have low penetration of product categories and a brand that needs to diffuse should also take into consideration that markets are unorganized, and that there are non-price factors and category development factors that are important.

At the bottom of the oral care category, Colgate toothpowder attempts to upgrade consumers who may be using substitutes like coal powder or *neemsticks*. Reynolds did not price its pens low; in fact, it followed the skimming strategy to price it above the unbranded offerings and became a pen of preference for its many consumers because of its relative advantage. On the other hand, Chik shampoo introduced a 50 p sachet to create a relative advantage. It is essentially the value perception that matters, along with the product attributes or benefits. But a brand also needs to be careful about the manner in which a category is perceived. Ariel detergent powder was launched with the proposition that consumers need not use a washing bar in a context where rubbing clothes with a washing bar is a ritual. But it introduced a washing bar soon afterwards. In this example, it is the compatibility of consumer habits with the product that mattered. Gillette Vector introduced a low-priced razor that helps to get rid of even hard stubble. This was compatible with the shaving practice in India, where electric shavers have not become diffused. Besides reasons of pricing, consumers had to alter their regular shaving practice and this may have created barriers in diffusion. The perception of consumers about dishwashers may be influenced by compatibility aspects, perceived risk, and complexity aspects associated with diffusion. Baby powder, over-the-counter medicines, and electrical appliances are categories that may be associated with high-perceived risk. As one of the earliest brands in the Indian market, Johnson & Johnson has established trust among its consumers (mothers) for baby products. Himalaya, the brand that has products based on the alterative system of medicine (ayurveda), has built its trust through a scientific system of testing, as reported in its Web site. It is interesting to note that "triability", complexity perceived risks, and "observability" are together useful in the cell phone category in India with millions of users. Nokia has a number of products at several price points for different segments. Some of its models have several features and serve benefits that include Web surfing, emails, and video streaming. Consumers observe brands being used by others and the category's diffusion can be associated with several diffusion characteristics. Hair creams, liquid detergents, hair dyes or colorants and contact lenses are categories that have been a part of the Indian context for decades and not developed.

Parachute Aftershower used several diffusion characteristics to develop the hair care market. L'Oréal and Garnier timed their promotional aspects to increase visibility among target segments in urban markets where there is increasing focus on personal grooming. Moov pain balm, by positioning itself as a backache specialist, created relative advantage associated with the proposition. Dove used the moisturizer route to diffuse itself in the soap category (existing category). Sometimes an attitude needs to be created through cognitive beliefs to convey the relative advantage. Frozen vegetables and soya-based foods are categories where this approach needs to beapplied, taking into consideration the taste sensitivity of consumers in India. A brand like Threptin (a meal supplement in the form of biscuits which has been around in India for about five decades) has created associations as a food supplement in-between meals among the young and overworked urban population. The brand can position itself in line with the belief among this target segment that overeating and eating unhealthy food are bad.

Diffusion of innovation in the Indian context has an interesting trail of history. Category development, timing of the brand's introduction and cultural aspects are some of the important aspects that affect the diffusion of brands. The following are some examples with comments associated with the respective brand/category:

BRAND/CATEGORY	COMMENTS ON DIFFUSION OF THE CATEGORY/BRAND
Ezee, Genteel liquid detergents	Available in the market for several decades. How should the brands in this category get into the ritual of consumer's washing of clothes?
Cadbury Drinking Chocolate	Available in the market for decades. Does cultural aspects of taste act as a barrier for greater diffusion of the category?
Detergent bars (Surf Excel, Rin)	Continues to be a popular choice by Indian consumers, perhaps due to habits.
After-shower hair cream	Brylcreem was a pioneering brand in the category. Did after shower brand diffuse fast as it became a part of the dressing ritual among youngsters?
Tea bags (Taj Mahal)	The brand created awareness about tea bags during the mid-eighties. Have tea bags diffused adequately among consumers? Are taste and the ritual of making tea (cultural aspects) proving to be barriers?
Hima Peas (packaged green peas)	The brand was introduced during the sixties. Was it ahead of its time? Even today would packaged vegetables (frozen) be acceptable to consumers?
Videocon's Karoke music	Targeted youngsters a few decades back. Was it ahead of its time? Would such a concept succeed in the era of digital music?
Café culture	Socializing over coffee was pioneered by Indian Coffee House-ICH (Indian Coffee Board) in a few cities and towns during the sixties. Consumers of the bygone era would have nostalgic memories of ICH. Contemporary versions of ICH are the cafes we find today (Café Coffee Day and Barista, for example)

The Diffusion of Innovations and Perceived Risk in an Emerging Market

Perceived risk is an important consideration that affects the diffusion of innovations in both new and existing categories. Its influence on existing categories is important to emerging markets like India that has a low penetration of branded offerings across categories. Consumers may be willing to pay more if they are convinced that a branded offering is better (in terms of convenience or utility or safety).

Despite different brands having introduced talcum powder for children, Johnson & Johnson holds a major chunk of this market. Branded butter has been in the market for years. Amul Lite and Nutralite are brands that target consumers who are health conscious. Consumers may perhaps like to be convinced that these offerings are free from chemicals. The Himalaya brand of herbal products has the proposition of "herbs" that appeals to consumers who associate perceived risk with regular allopathic, "English" medicines that are used for commonplace ailments. Reva is a well-known brand of electric car that is also exported. Consumers who are in the process of buying their first car may have apprehensions about the functional performance of the product, especially given the situation that this product is priced higher than regular entry level passenger cars. While smartphones from iPhone or Samsung Galaxy may appeal to consumers, given the complex attributes of the products, a cross-section of them may have perceived risks associated with technological obsolescence and even functional performance.

An urban youth would probably end up using a Chinese make of an MP4 player instead of the latest iPod (social risk). Consumers who would like to color their hair may initially visit a beautician for some time before they venture to do it themselves (social risk) in a market like India where such products are being popularized by multinational brands. These aspects have implications on several aspects of the marketing mix – advertising, distribution, and even packaging – associated with stock-keeping units. Several brands of regular hair dyes are available in small packs. Regular hair dyes have been available in the market (Godrej was one of the earliest brands) for several decades, but the products have been getting diffused to higher levels only recently. Consumers have recognized the need for personal grooming in a changing environment. Environmental changes, too, dilute perceived social risks associated with a category. (Several years back, applying hair color may not have been a social ritual and people would only color their hair to hide gray hairs, but these days it is common for even young people to color their hair.) Contact lens and non-stick cookware have been a part of Indian context, but have a long way to get diffused among the mass markets. Physical risks and performance risks may have to be addressed by brands.

Summary

Learning Objective 1: To understand the consumer's decision-making process.

Not all consumer decision-making situations require the same degree of information research. Extensive problem solving occurs when consumers have no established criteria for evaluating an item within a product category. Limited problem solving occurs when consumers have established the basic criteria for evaluating the product category, but need more information to decide among the brands and product models available. Routinized response behavior occurs when consumers have experience with the product category and the brands offered and buy items often and almost instinctively. A model of consumer decision-making ties together the consumption behavior discussed throughout this book. It includes three components: Input, process, and output.

Learning Objective 2: To understand the dynamics of buying gifts.

Gifts represent more than ordinary, everyday purchases, because they are symbolic, and mostly associated with important events. Gifting behavior is a gift exchange that takes place between a giver and a recipient. The definition is broad in nature and embraces gifts given voluntarily, as well as gifts that are an obligation. It includes gifts given to (and received from) others and gifts to oneself (self-gifts). Moreover, the majority of products that we refer to as "gifts" are in fact items that we purchase for ourselves.

Learning Objective 3: To understand how innovative offerings gain acceptance within market segments and how individual consumers adopt or reject new products and services.

Diffusion of innovations is the macro process by which the acceptance of an innovation (i.e., a new product, service, idea, or practice) takes place among members of a social system (or market segments), over time. This process includes four elements: (1) The innovation (new product, model, service); (2)the channels of communication (informal or formal, impersonal or personal groups); (3)the social system (a market segment); and (4)time.

In contrast, the innovation adoption process is a micro process that focuses on the stages through which an individual consumer passes when deciding to accept or reject a new product.

Review and Discussion Questions

13.1. What kinds of marketing and sociocultural inputs would influence the purchase of: (a) HDTV set, (b) Concentrated liquid laundry detergent, and (c) Fat-free ice cream? Explain your answers.

13.2. What are the differences among the three problem-solving decision-making approaches? What type of decision process would you expect most consumers to follow in their first purchase of a new product or brand in each of the following areas: (a) Chewing gum, (b) Sugar, (c) Men's aftershave lotion, (d) Carpeting, (e) Paper towels, (f) Smartphone, and (g) Luxury car? Explain your answers.

13.3. Assume that this coming summer you are planning to spend a month touring Europe and looking for an advanced digital camera. (a) Develop a list of product attributes that you will use as the purchase criteria in evaluating various digital cameras. (b) Distinguish the differences that would occur in your decision process if you were to use compensatory versus noncompensatory decision rules.

13.4. How can Apple use its knowledge of customers' expectations in designing a marketing strategy for a new iPad?

13.5. How do consumers reduce post-purchase dissonance? How can marketers provide positive reinforcement to consumers after the purchase to reduce dissonance?

13.6. Sony is introducing a 65" Ultra HD TV that has a higher screen resolution than other TVs and advanced signal processing. The TV's introductory price is $10,000.

a. Who should be Sony's initial target market? What are the target consumers' demographics and psychographics?

b. How would you identify the innovators for this product?

c. Is the new model a continuous, dynamically continuous, or discontinuous innovation? Explain your answer.

13.7. Describe how Sony can use the five product features that affect adoption in order to speed up the diffusion of its new TV model.

Hands-on Assignments

13.8. Identify a product, service, or style that was recently adopted by you and/or some of your friends. Identify what type of innovation it is and describe its diffusion process up to this point in time. What are the characteristics of the people who adopted it first? What types of people did not adopt it? What features of the product, service, or style are likely to determine its eventual success or failure?

13.9. Identify five friends who have recently purchased a new smartphone (with some features that they consider to be "new"). Interview each person and ask him or her:

a. Why did you select this phone over other smartphones that you were looking at or considering?

b. Do you currently like the phone for the same reasons that caused you to purchase it, or have you found additional reasons?

c. What improvements would you recommend for the next model?

d. After you are finished, get together with other students and discuss what you have found. Look for similarities and differences.

13.10. Describe the need recognition process that took place before you purchased your last can of soft drink. How did it differ from the process that preceded the purchase of a new pair of sneakers? What role, if any, did advertising play in your need recognition?

13.11. List three colleges that you considered when choosing which college or university to attend and the criteria that you used to evaluate them. Describe how you acquired information on the different colleges along the different attributes that were important to you and how you made your decision. Be sure to specify whether you used compensatory or noncompensatory decision rules.

13.12. Select a newspaper or magazine advertisement that attempts to provide the consumer with a decision strategy to follow in making a purchase decision. Evaluate the effectiveness of the ad you selected.

Key Terms

- adoption *383*
- affect referral decision rule *375*
- awareness *388*
- cognitive dissonance *376*
- compatibility *386*
- compensatory decision rules *374*

- complexity *386*
- conjunctive decision rule *374*
- continuous innovation *385*
- diffusion of innovations *383*
- discontinuous innovation *385*
- dynamically continuous innovation *385*
- evaluation *388*
- evoked set *373*
- extensive problem solving *366*
- family branding *366*
- gifting behavior *377*
- inept set *373*
- inert set *373*
- innovation adoption process *383*
- innovation *383*
- interest *388*
- lexicographic decision rule *374*
- limited problem solving *366*
- need recognition *369*
- negative disconfirmation of expectations *376*
- noncompensatory decision rules *374*
- observability *387*
- positive disconfirmation of expectations *376*
- pre-purchase search *369*
- relative advantage *386*
- routinized response behavior *366*
- trial *388*
- trialability *387*
- variety-seeking *378*

14

Marketing Ethics and Social Responsibility

Learning Objectives

1. To understand the meaning and importance of marketing ethics and social responsibility.
2. To understand how marketers can exploit consumers by targeting children and encouraging over-eating and other forms of irresponsible buying.
3. To understand ethically questionable practices such as covert marketing, manipulative exposure to advertising, and truth-in-advertising issues.
4. To understand the nature and consequences of provocative advertisements.
5. To understand how marketers abuse consumers' privacy and the measures that can stop such practices.
6. To understand how marketers can advance society's interests by advocating socially beneficial conduct and discouraging adverse behavior.

MARKETING ETHICS are moral principles that govern marketers' behavior. On the personal level, these principles express the differences between right and wrong behavior and the goodness or badness of human character. The objective of most not-for-profit organizations and consumer advocacy groups is to promote good and socially beneficial behaviors such as contributing to charity, using energy responsibly, and reducing bad behaviors such as using drugs, discrimination, and driving while texting or drunk. For example, for decades, PETA (People for the Ethical Treatment of Animals) has campaigned against furriers and fashion designers that use fur and leather, discouraged consumers from using cosmetics manufactured with animal testing, and asked people to choose humane, solutions when they find mice, squirrels, raccoons, and other wild animals in their yards and homes. Figure 14.1 portrays two PETA ads promoting humans' loving coexistence with animals.

Why should marketers, whose objective is to make money, be concerned about ethics? After all, there are many federal consumer protection laws and scores of laws and regulations established by states and local governments. These laws dictate what marketers can and cannot do, and often regulate the manner in which they advertise, price and distribute their products and services. For example, some town and cities forbid placing vending machines for cigarettes and junk foods in public areas and near schools. As another example, New York City's government has been considering laws that will force all restaurants to post caloric information next to each item served and banning the sales of super-size sodas in restaurants. Furthermore, some cities no longer allow cigarette machines in bars (or anywhere else) and require retailers to ask for proof of age from young adults who try to buy cigarettes. Speaking of exploiting children, there are laws that limit the amount of advertisements that can be shown during children's TV programs. In all of these examples, marketers' actions are regulated. Thus, why should marketers worry about what is

FIGURE 14.1 PeTA Advocates Animals' Rights

Source: (Left & Right) People for the Ethical Treatment of Animals (PeTA)

morally right? After all, doesn't a widely quoted legal standard for engaging in a given practice state: "All that is not forbidden is allowed?"

Marketers must be concerned with ethics because not all that is allowed is in the best interest of society or, for that matter, marketers' goals. Marketing practices that overtly contradict societal interests end up with embarrassment, loss of consumers, and, more often than not, increased regulation. In short, such practices lead to lost customers, decreased profits, and diminished consumer confidence in promotional messages and products. In this chapter, we will be straightforward and critical of amoral marketing strategies. We are proud of and enthusiastic about our field and experts in marketing and consumer behavior, and in no way antimarketing. In the following discussions, we follow the saying of Spencer Johnson, a famous contemporary writer: "Integrity is telling myself the truth. And honesty is telling the truth to other people."

Learning Objective

1 To understand the meaning and importance of marketing ethics and social responsibility.

The Societal Marketing Concept: Utopia or Reality?

As stated at the very beginning of this book, the essence of marketing is fulfilling the needs of consumers more effectively than competitors. Nevertheless, sometimes this concept is at odds with society's best interests. For example, products such as tobacco and alcohol "satisfy" consumer "needs" but are harmful, and many products that are convenient to use (and thus "satisfy needs") significantly contribute to environmental deterioration and climate change (e.g., products packaged in convenient but not reusable packaging, such as single-usage protective coverings used by dry cleaners). We must also consider the cumulative persuasive impact of advertising on consumer behavior. For example, depicting perfectly tanned people is likely to result in excessive sun bathing or tanning via ultraviolet light, despite undeniable documentation that such practices significantly increase the chances of developing cancer. Many studies have shown that repeated exposure to very thin "ideal" figures in promotional messages leads to negative self-perceptions (particularly in women) and is largely responsible for the increase in eating-related disorders. More Americans with eating disorders and cancer means higher public health expenditures, which lead to a decline in our living standards. Marketers know that ads focused on beauty and attractiveness, especially if they stress the importance of these attributes over other personal characteristics, are likely to be scrutinized by the media, consumer advocacy groups. Therefore, many advertisements now portray more realistic-looking models and beauty product ads stress that although a person's physical appearance is important, one's self-worth or "true beauty" comes from "within." A study of the sexual objectification of women in advertising showed that although the number of ads containing such portrayals has been increasing, females became less offended by these images, and that such ads had little impact on women's purchase intentions.[1]

Given the fact that all companies prosper when society prospers, companies should integrate social responsibility into every marketing decision. Thus, a more appropriate conceptualization of the traditional marketing concept is the **societal marketing concept**, which advocates balancing society's interests with the needs of consumers and marketers. This concept calls upon marketers to satisfy the needs and wants of their target markets in ways that preserve and enhance the well-being of consumers and society as a whole, while also fulfilling the profit objectives of their organizations. According to the societal marketing concept, fast-food restaurants should serve foods that contain less fat and sugar, but more nutrients. In addition, marketers should not advertise foods to young people in ways that encourage overeating. Furthermore, companies should not use professional athletes in liquor or tobacco advertisements, because celebrities often serve as role models for the young and using them in ads may result in underage youngsters' use of these products.

A serious deterrent to implementation of the societal marketing concept is the short-term orientation of many business executives, which stems from the fact that managerial performance is evaluated on the basis of short-term results. Thus, a young and ambitious advertising executive may create a striking advertising campaign, using unreasonably slim females with pale faces and withdrawn expressions, in order to increase the sales of the advertised product, without considering the negative impact of the campaign, such as an increase in eating disorders among young women. The societal marketing concept maintains that companies would be better off in a stronger, healthier society, and that companies that incorporate ethical behavior and social responsibility in their business dealings attract and maintain loyal consumer support over the long term.

The purpose of studying consumer behavior is to understand why and how consumers make their purchase decisions. These insights enable marketers to design more effective marketing strategies, especially when advanced technologies allow them to collect more data about consumers and target customers more precisely. Some maintain that an in-depth understanding of consumer behavior makes it possible for unethical marketers to exploit human vulnerabilities in the marketplace and engage in other unethical marketing practices to achieve corporate business objectives.

In response to public criticisms and concerns, many trade associations representing marketers of consumer goods have developed industry-wide codes of ethics. They recognize that industry-wide self-regulation is in marketers' best interests, in that it deters government from imposing its own regulations on industries. A number of companies have incorporated specific social goals into their mission statements, and include programs in support of these goals as integral components of their strategic planning. Most companies also recognize that socially responsible activities improve their image among consumers, stockholders, the financial community, and other relevant publics. They have found that ethical and socially responsible practices are simply good business, resulting not only in a favorable image, but also ultimately in increased sales. The converse is also true: Perceptions of a company's lack of social responsibility or unethical marketing strategies negatively affect consumer purchase decisions. Figure 14.2 contains a letter from a consumer advocacy group to McDonald's. The letter accuses McDonald's of failing to keep a promise it made to eliminate trans fats from its cooking oil, and clearly illustrates the damage that socially irresponsible actions can inflict on a company's image.

Although some companies have taken steps toward more responsible marketing, others have not. For example, Coca-Cola broadened the distribution of its low-calorie drinks and said it would put calorie counts on the front of its packaging around the world as part of its global efforts to counter accusations that its sugary drinks are fueling obesity. The company also promised to sponsor physical activity and committed to not marketing its drinks to children under 12 years of age—but it did not specify exactly how it plans to do so.[2] Other companies engage in practices that are, intuitively, against society's interests. For example, the FDA discovered that food makers have been adding caffeine to candy, potato chips, waffles, and a range of other items. For instance, A pack of Wrigley's Alert Energy Caffeine Gum can deliver the equivalent of four cups of coffee, or about 320 milligrams of caffeine. Although the package contain a warning that it is "not recommended for children or persons sensitive to caffeine," the FDA would like food companies to agree to voluntary limits for caffeine.[3]

In this chapter, we describe several unethical forms of marketing and suggest what can be done to prevent them. The topics covered here are exploitive marketing, crafty (i.e., less than honest) marketing communications, provocative marketing, and abuses of consumers' privacy. On the positive side, we discuss forms of marketing focused on social responsibility.

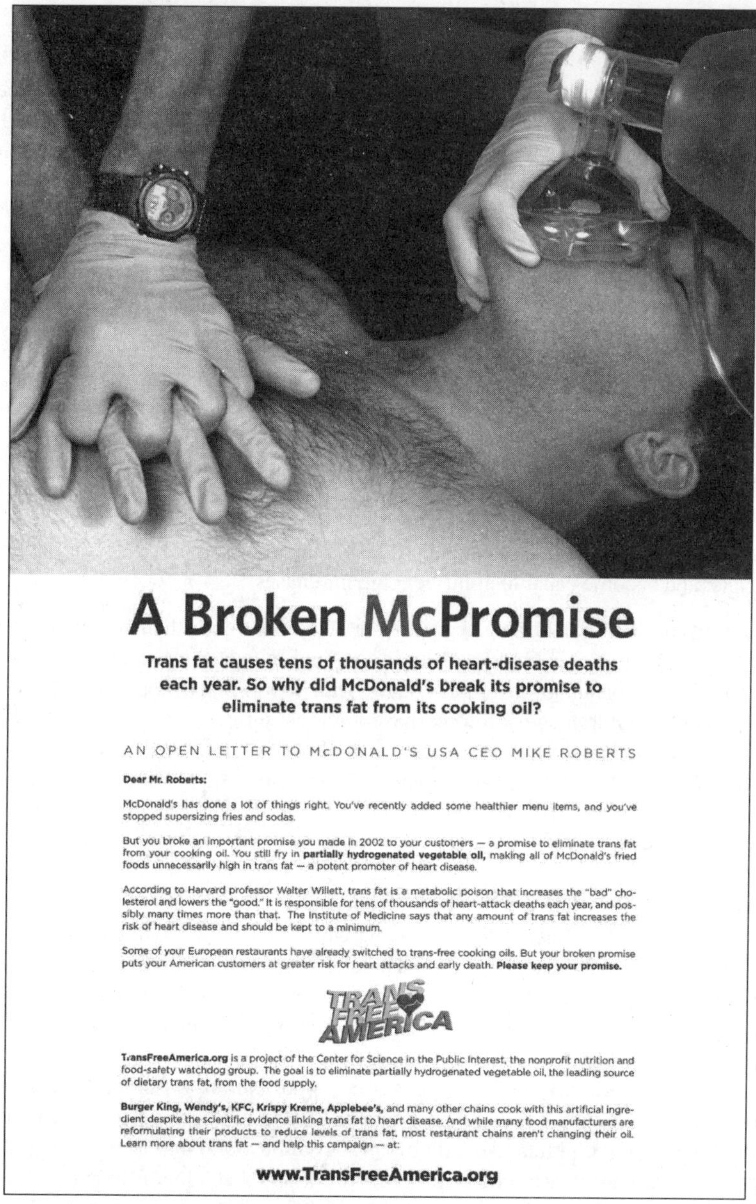

Source: Center for Science in the Public Interest

FIGURE 14.2 Irresponsible Marketing Can Damage a Company's Image

Box 14.1 Brands and Social Initiatives

In a study associated with corporate social responsibility (CSR)[4], Indian buyers had reflected intent to buy a product that has a social or environmental benefit. Several companies and brands were involved with social initiatives.[5] Lifebuoy launched a campaign that emphasized the role of hand washing to reduce the mortality rate among children. Coca-Cola launched an initiative with Sachin Tendulkar to provide assistance to 273 schools; Procter and Gamble's *Shiksha* was an initiative to provide education for all. Toyota's Greenathon Aircel's Save the Tiger, and Killer Jeans water saver initiatives were associated with environmental causes.

Learning Objective

2 To understand how marketers can exploit consumers by targeting children and encouraging overeating and other forms of irresponsible buying.

Exploitive Marketing

There are many targetable segments that can be easily exploited because they are more vulnerable than most other consumers, because of less education, old age, low income, and no political power. Next, we examine two particular forms of exploitive marketing: Targeting children and encouraging overeating and irresponsible buying.

Marketing to Children

Consumer socialization is the processes by which young people acquire skills, knowledge, and attitudes relevant to their functioning as consumers in the marketplace. A comprehensive review of twenty-five years of research on consumer socialization identified three stages:

1. ***Perceptual*** (3–7 years old), during which children begin to distinguish ads from programs, associate brand names with product categories, and understand the basic script of consumption.
2. ***Analytical*** (7–11 years), during which children capture the persuasive intent of ads, begin to process functional cues regarding products, and develop purchase influence and negotiation strategies.
3. ***Reflective*** (11–16 years), when children understand advertising tactics and appeals, become skeptical about ads, understand complex shopping scripts, and become capable at influencing purchases.[6]

Children become brand aware as they age and begin to prefer brands more than nonbranded items.[7] Brand knowledge starts with child-oriented product categories such as toys and food, and by age 8 children can name multiple products in categories targeted to them. Children's consumption requests start with food-related items and grow to include toys, clothing, sporting goods, and video games as children age. Children have the most influence over child-related items and children from higher socioeconomic classes influence parents more than those of lower socioeconomic status.[8] Overall, the older the child, the more influence he or she has on a parent's purchase behavior. Older children are better negotiators and learn strategies such as bargaining and persuasion that are more effective with parents than emotional strategies such as begging and crying.[9] Some children perceive themselves as having more influence over purchases, particularly with regard to food items, than do their parents.[10]

The growth of the Internet and electronic technology resulted in a significant increase in the amount of time children spend with various forms of media. A study reported that, among children aged 8 to 18, the time spent with electronic devices increased by 1 hour and 17 minutes from 2004 to 2010. Some studies showed that children spend a total of 7 hours and 38 minutes a day in front of televisions, computers, iPods, mobile phones, or video games. Including multitasking, children are exposed to 10 hours and 45 minutes of media content during that time. Furthermore, fewer than half of the children studied reported having parental rules regarding media viewing.[11]

More media consumption provides marketers with increased opportunities to target children with marketing messages designed to influence their purchase behavior. Food and beverage marketing has been a particular public policy concern because of its influence on the diets and health of children. A study by the Committee on Food Marketing and the Diets of Children and Youth found that television advertising influences children aged 2 to 11, and that a lot of these promotions were for high-calorie, low-nutrient foods associated with adiposity.[12] Research sponsored by the Center for Science in the Public Interest discovered that marketing of high-calorie, low-nutrition foods to children has been increasing dramatically and becoming more aggressive and sophisticated.[13] The report concluded that such marketing has undermined parental authority regarding food consumption and called for restrictions on the marketing of foods to children. In the absence of regulation, parents play a mediational role in children's consumption and media exposure and may welcome intervention by public policy makers.

Self-regulation versus Laws

Advertising to children is subject to self-regulation, according to guidelines developed by the Children's Advertising Review Unit (CARU) of the Council of Better Business Bureaus. Among others, the CARU guidelines state that product presentations or claims must not mislead children about the product's performance or benefits, that presentations must not exploit the child's imagination or create unrealistic expectations, that products must be shown in safe situations, and that ads must refrain from encouraging behavior that is inappropriate for children. Because, according to stimulus–response theory, children can easily form associations between stimuli and outcomes, the guidelines also direct marketers to avoid ads that: (1) Encourage children to pressure their parents to buy the products advertised, and (2) make children feel that ownership of a given product will make them more accepted by peers. Regarding loyalty-building measures such as kid's clubs, premiums, and sweepstakes, the CARU guidelines acknowledge that children do not always understand the true purpose of such measures, and direct marketers to ensure that loyalty programs do not exploit children.[14]

CARU's news releases illustrate many possible misuses in advertising to children. For example, in response to CARU's routine monitoring of children's advertising and its subsequent request, a marketer of cotton candy machines agreed to modify a TV commercial that featured children operating an electrical candy machine without parental supervision and while dancing or talking on the phone. In another case, after viewing a commercial showing Oreo cookies going into a toaster and popping out as KoolStuf pastries, a 4-year-old child inserted Oreos into a toaster and, when they did not pop out, tried to retrieve them with a pair of scissors. The child's mother complained to CARU, which brought the incident to the attention of Oreo's marketer, who subsequently agreed to modify the commercial. Procter & Gamble agreed to modify a TV spot for Pringles that CARU believed encouraged excessive consumption of the snack food.[15]

A major concern is that food marketers "teach" children to eat more than they should and thereby cause the surging obesity and health problems among young consumers. Marketers spend at least $10 billion annually on promoting foods and beverages to America's children. At the same time, the number of obese or overweight children has at least doubled over the past 15 years and keeps going up steadily and alarmingly. Over the past few years, lawmakers have called for legislation regulating food advertising to children; presumably to avoid such regulation, several companies have voluntarily modified their marketing practices. For example, Kraft Foods stopped TV advertising of certain products to children, and increased its advertising of sugar-free drinks and smaller packages of cookies. McDonald's, a company frequently accused of selling junk foods with too much fat and poor nutritional quality, eliminated some of its "super-sized" offerings and began selling more salads. It even offers apples as a dessert alternative to calorie-laden pies. More recently, McDonald's had a program that awarded food prizes to small kids who got good grades on their report cards; the program was advertised on book jackets and discontinued after McDonald's was criticized by parents and consumer advocacy groups and even ridiculed by some media.[16]

Rules proposed by the Obama administration, which would take effect in 2016, would only allow foods that contain no trans fat, have and not more than 1 gram of saturated fat and 13 grams of added sugar per "eating occasion" to be marketed to children. Also, the foods could not contain more than 210 milligrams of sodium per serving. The sodium restrictions would tighten by 2021. Additionally, the foods must provide a "meaningful contribution to a healthful diet," including ingredient from at least one major healthy food group such as fruit, vegetables, whole grain, fish, eggs, and beans. The proposed guidelines also expand the traditional definition of "children" from kids under the age of 12 to children aged 2 through 17, although the final rules for teenagers will likely be "narrower in scope and possibly limited to in-school marketing activities and social media." While some experts say that the guidelines do not go far enough, advertisers have been fighting them aggressively and it is unlikely that all will be mandated legally.[17]

Nevertheless, the rate of self-regulation has accelerated. In an effort to stop the spread of anti-soda measures in city halls after New York City moved to limit portion sizes and other cities levied taxes on sugary beverages, soda makers will start displaying the calorie contents of their drinks on vending machines and point consumers toward less sugary versions.[18] McDonald's began posting calorie counts on all its menus—a move that could put pressure on other fast-food restaurants to do the same. The company also unveiled several menu additions aimed at making its offerings more healthful. They include an egg-white McMuffin, a grilled chicken option for the Happy Meal, and seasonal fruits and vegetables like blueberries and cucumbers. The Walt Disney Company announced that all products advertised on its child-focused television channels, radio stations, and websites must comply with a strict new set of nutritional standards. Several years earlier, Disney sharply curtailed the use of its name and characters with foods high in sugar, salt, and fat. Mickey Mouse stopped appearing on boxes of Pop-Tarts, and Buzz Lightyear and his Toy Story pals disappeared from McDonald's Happy Meals. Nickelodeon and Discovery Kids instituted similar restrictions shortly thereafter.[19]

Trying to be more socially responsible is not always possible or easy. General Mills reduced the sugar in most of its kids' cereals to 10 grams per serving from levels as high as 15 grams. However, surveys showed that to get kids to like the cereals, not only do the cereal's frosted oats need to taste sweet enough, but they also have to float in milk for at least 3 minutes. The company knew that 9 grams of sugar per serving was the point where the sweetness is not enough for a kid to eat regularly. The company has been reducing the sugar amounts in its cereals gradually, so that consumers get used to a lower sweetness level a little at a time (see discussion of the **JND** in Chapter 4).[20]

California passed a state law that banned the sale or rental of violent video games to minors. However, the Supreme Court overturned this law because it is unconstitutional, even if it is designed to protect children.[21] Side by side with overeating, children's lack of physical activity greatly contributes to children's high rates of overweight and obesity.

Clearly, there are merits to the argument that, ultimately, any consumption behavior, including excessive eating, is the responsibility of the adults who consume overly rich foods or allow their children to consume them and not of the marketers who produced the foods. However, children are a vulnerable population. In addressing this issue and fearing that "McDonald's-made-me-fat" lawsuits will gain momentum, the food companies have pursued legislation that will not allow obese persons to sue them for personal damages.[22]

Regarding advertising to children, there is a consensus that even if children understand the purpose of promotional messages, marketers must take special care in advertising to them because of the amount of time kids spend viewing TV and online. Generally, advertising to children in the United States is less regulated than in European countries. Regulating marketing to children does not always work. Table 14.1 indicates that numerous practices generally forbidden in marketing to children online are widely employed by websites targeting children.[23] As yet another example of abusing children's privacy, a study of 40 popular and free child-friendly apps, conducted by The Wall Street Journal, discovered that nearly half transmitted a device ID number, which is a major tracking tool. Some 70% passed along information about how the apps were used, and, in some cases, specified which buttons were clicked and in which order. Although the FTC regulations do not allow gathering information from apps and online services "directed to children" under 13 without parental knowledge, the FTC has no strict definition of this regulation.[24]

TABLE 14.1 Regulating Online Marketing to Children

PART A: COMMON PRACTICES IN MARKETING FOODS TO CHILDREN ONLINE THAT ARE GENERALLY FORBIDDEN UNDER FEDERAL OR SELF-REGULATION

1. Promoting foods of low nutritional quality; not providing enough nutritional labeling; misleading nutritional claims.
2. Embedding food ads in games and facilitating children's learning to consume the foods advertised.
3. Creating "buzz" about the products and encouraging children to send ads to their friends (i.e., viral marketing).
4. Offering children brand-related items that they can use after leaving the Web sites and tying the online advertising with other exposures to the brands.
5. Not including "ad breaks" and reminders that the content watched is advertising.
6. Offering children that may be too young opportunities and prizes if they register at the Web site.
7. Offering direct inducements to purchase (e.g., access to a secret site).

PART B: AN ILLUSTRATION OF THE LIMITED SUCCESS OF SELF AND FEDERAL REGULATION REGARDING WEB SITES TARGETING CHILDREN

CONTENT ANALYSIS FINDINGS	CURRENT GUIDE AND REGULATORY EFFORTS
64% of Web sites encouraged children to send email greetings or invitations to visit the Web site to their friends.	Advertising should not urge children to ask parents or others to buy products. (CARU)
53% of Web sites offered unlimited viewing of television advertisements.	Advertisements are limited to 10.5–12 minutes per hour. (Children's Television Act of 1990 [47 U.S.C. § 303])
76% of Web sites offered at least one brand "extra," and 52% offered two or more: 43% offered sweepstakes: and 31% offered premiums to stimulate sales.	Advertisers should take special care in using these kinds of promotions to guard against exploiting children's immaturity. (CARU)
39% of Web sites offered specific purchase incentives, such as game rewards.	Advertisers should avoid using sales pressures in advertising to children. (CARU)
18% of the Web sites provided ad break reminders that the content was advertising.	The Federal Communications Commission requires ad breaks for children's television programming.
47% of the Web sites offered a tie-in to movie or television shows and characters.	Television advertising should not use program personalities (live or animated) adjacent to their shows. (CARU and Federal Communications Commission)

Source: Part A. Journal of Public Policy and Marketing. Elizabeth S. Moore, American Marketing Association, 2007. Part B: Journal of Public Policy and Marketing. Kathryn Seiders, American Marketing Association, 2007.

Inspiring Overeating and Irresponsible Spending

Marketing is a form of persuasion. In order to learn how to convince consumers to adopt a product or induce consumption, marketers have carefully studied the situational factors surrounding the buying decision. For example, people become hungrier in cold environments, so it is always cold in supermarkets (some nutritionists advise consumers to go food shopping directly after a filling meal). Marketers know that the longer consumers stay in the store and wander around, the more they buy. Therefore, in supermarkets and other stores, the displays are moved around systematically; that's why you often discover that the cereal aisle has been moved since you last visited the supermarket. Men are much more likely than women to deviate from shopping lists and prior consumption plans. That's why supermarket personnel are instructed to approach any men they see just standing around and offer help. Fairly recently, many Web retailers noticed that their online sales peak between 6:30 and 10:30 p.m., across time zones. Apparently, consumers who are drinking alcohol have fewer inhibitions and are likely to spend more freely. Thus, many online retailers started offering special sales and sending promotional emails during this time period.[25]

Designing foods that encourage overeating is a scientific process. For example, marketers know that some processed foods actually make people feel hungrier after eating them. Research has identified the "bliss point" at which consumers like, say, sweetness, the most; at lower and higher levels of sweetnes, consumers dislike the product's taste. Marketers have been using their knowledge of humans' responses to taste to design foods that produce the highest levels of craving. The cardinal rule in processed foods is "when in doubt, add sugar." Oscar Mayer introduced a desert Lunchable in the form of Fun Pack, which, in addition to bologna and white bread, includes a Snickers bar, a package of M&M's (or a Reese's Butter Cup), and a sugary drink.[26]

A report based on data from the Center for Disease Control and Prevention (CDC) projected that obesity rates, across states, would reach at least 44% by 2030, and in 13 states that number would exceed 60%. Obesity raises the risk of numerous diseases, from type 2 diabetes to endometrial cancer, meaning more sick people and higher medical costs in the future. The increasing burden of illness will add $66 billion in annual obesity-related medical costs over and above today's $147 billion to $210 billion. Another study found that by 2030, 42% of U.S. adults could be obese, adding $550 billion to healthcare costs over that period.[27]

Marketers are directly responsible for Americans' decreasing physical activity and their consumption of unreasonably large quantities of unhealthy and non-nutritious foods. One study demonstrated that consumers believe that foods that are *less* healthy taste *better*, are enjoyed *more*, and are preferred when a hedonic meal takes place.[28] In the course of getting us to eat more, marketers have studied our eating habits in detail and used the results in packaging and determination of portion sizes. Marketers have also used their knowledge of perception to increase the quantities of foods consumers eat by the way these items are packaged or presented. For example, studies showed that:[29]

1. Both children and adults consume more juice when the product is presented in short, wide glasses than in tall slender glasses.
2. Candies placed in clear jars were eaten much quicker than those presented in opaque jars.
3. Sandwiches in transparent wrap generated more consumption than those in opaque wraps.
4. The visibility and aroma of tempting foods generated greater consumption.
5. Presenting foods in an organized manner, such as mixed assortments in bowls (or "grab bags"), buffets, potlucks, or dinner-table settings leads to more eating.
6. Assortment size or duplication, in forms such as multiple product tastings, multiple offerings of party snacks, duplicate buffet lines, and family dinners with multiple dishes, stimulate eating.
7. Minimal variations in the size of serving bowls whenever multiple options and sizes are present lead to eating more.
8. People generally do not keep track of how much food they consume. When told, they are often surprised at how much they have consumed.
9. Large inventories of foods at home increase the quantity believed to be appropriate for a given meal.
10. Small packages do not necessarily decrease consumption and can sometimes actually increase it. Responsible companies should sell small packages individually, rather than bundling them together in a larger container, because the availability of multiple small packages leads to overconsumption.

Another form of encouraging irresponsible consumption is banks' targeting of teenagers and college students and providing them with too much easy credit, which puts them into financial difficulties for years. For example, because of very aggressive marketing of credit cards to college students, college loan debt has been rising: The average graduate leaves college with more than $18,000 in credit card debt, often coupled with a low credit rating.[30] One study showed that, on average, students received their first credit card at age 18 (some did so when they were as young as 15). More than 10% owned more than 5 cards. Most of these young people did not keep credit card receipts, did not check their monthly statements against their purchases, and were unaware of the interest rates they were charged; about 10% paid only the minimum required payment every month.[31] Recognizing that the marketing of credit cards to college students has become far too aggressive and against society's best interests, many states have passed, or are in the process of passing, strict rules limiting the marketing that banks and credit card companies can do on college campuses. In response to criticism, several banks began limiting the promotion of credit cards directed at students.[32]

One study identified several personality traits that contribute to students' misuse of credit cards and outlined promotional appeals that marketers can use in encouraging more responsible credit card usage among students.[33] Interestingly, two important personality traits were impulsiveness and materialism, which have also been linked to compulsive buying and addictive tendencies.[34] The study proposed that both marketers and public policymakers must educate younger customers about avoiding the trap of credit card misuse.

Manipulative or Uninformative Nutritional Labeling

Nutritional labels are placed on all packaged food items sold in the United States. Nevertheless, many critiques have pointed out that the current format of such labels is unclear and somewhat manipulative. For example, the labels list information on a "per-serving" basis. However, the Food and Drug Administration regulations allow manufacturers some discretion in setting serving sizes. For example, Kellogg's Frosted Flakes uses a serving size of 3/4 cup. Healthy Choice Chicken Tortilla Soup (microwaveable bowl) has a serving size of one cup, and Ritz Crackers have a serving size of five crackers. According to its label, a pint of Häagen-Dazs ice cream contains four servings. However, do most consumers eat only a fourth of a container of Cookies & Cream, then put the rest away for another day? A large package of Cool Ranch Doritos lists a single serving as one ounce, or roughly 12 chips, but consumers are highly unlikely to keep a chip count as they dig into bags. Although 160 calories and 2 grams of saturated fat sounds like a small price to pay for enjoying a serving of Oreo cookies, technically speaking, a serving is only 3 cookies.[35] Listing smaller serving sizes enables marketers to reduce the reported calories, fat, sugar, and carbohydrates in a product serving, and encourage consumers to consume more calories than they think they do. A study indicated that consumer attention to nutrition information focuses on calorie information but not serving size. In addition, manipulating service sizes reduces consumers' consumption-related "guilt."[36]

Under mounting criticism, the Food and Drug Administration has been under pressure to force marketers to list realistic serving sizes on packaged food labels. According to the Center for Science in the Public Interest (CSPI), a consumer advocacy group, the worst manipulators of the serving sizes ratios are labels for canned soups, ice cream, coffee creamers, and nonstick cooking sprays—all of which grossly understate the calories, sodium, and saturated fat the average person typically consumes when eating these foods. For instance, on its label, a single serving of Campbell's Chunky Classic Chicken Noodle soup is one cup—just under half a can—and contains about 790 milligrams of sodium. In a national survey of 1,000 consumers, only 10% of people said they would eat a one-cup portion. About 64% said they would eat an entire can at one time, taking in 1,840 milligrams of sodium in a sitting. That is roughly 80% of the 2,300 milligrams recommended as the upper limit for daily salt intake, and well above the 1,500 milligrams that health officials have said may cause hypertension. Sixty-one percent said they would also eat the entire can of a condensed soup, like Campbell's Chicken Noodle, which lists 2.5 servings per can. A single serving contains 890 milligrams of sodium, and the full can has 2,390 milligrams. About 27% of respondents said they would eat just half a can in one sitting. The Healthy Request line that Campbell's has introduced consists of soups that contain less than 480 milligrams of sodium per serving. Nevertheless, the amount of sodium that people actually end up consuming when they eat an entire can is enormous, according to the CSPI.[37]

The design in Figure 14.3 replaces serving size calories with total calories per package or bottle. It represents food ingredients using bold, colorful rectangles showing how much of which ingredients are in the food. A green, yellow, and red color-coding system denotes reasonable, questionable, or unhealthy amounts of carbohydrates or fat. The label is very attractive, but probably requires too much space on the food package.[38]

The definitions used in nutritional labeling are not always logical. For example, food labeled "organic" must meet verifiable standards set by the federal government, while that labeled "natural" is subject to no such requirements. Ironically, although sales of both "organic" and "natural" foods, which cost more than other foods, have been growing, surveys found that consumers prefer foods described as "natural" to those labeled "organic." In one case, a line of Nature Valley food products claims they are

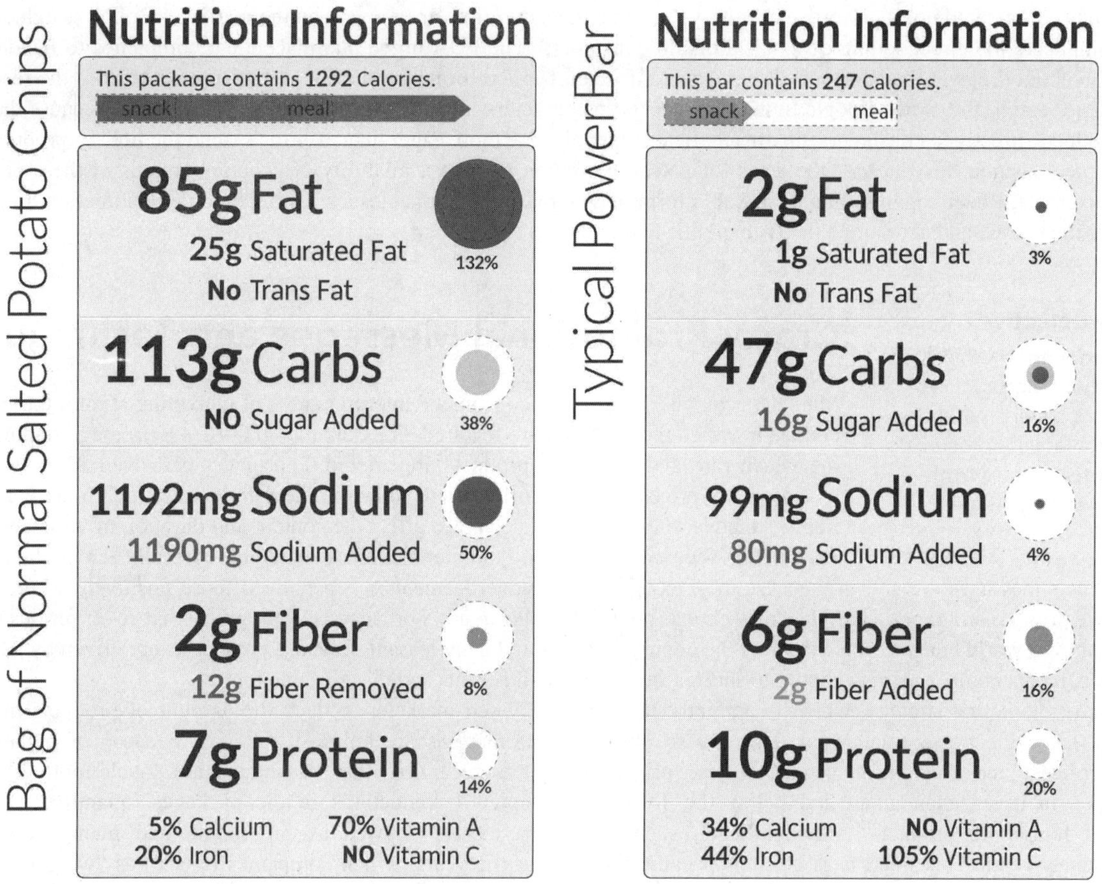

Source: Creator: Joe Brunelle. Project managers: Lily Mihalik and Diana Jou, University of California, Berkeley School of Journalism.

FIGURE 14.3 Total Instead of Serving Size Calories

"natural," although the items include high fructose corn syrup, high maltose corn syrup, and maltodextrin (a thickener than can also impart a slight sweetness to food). These ingredients are highly processed, do not exist in nature, and cannot be considered natural even under a very lenient definition. According to some studies, these ingredients cause hyperactivity and attention deficit among young children. Realizing the negative connotation associated with "high fructose corn syrup," the Corn Refiners Association asked the FDA to allow it to change the ingredient name to "corn sugar" on nutrition labels, but the FDA denied permission.[39]

Another interesting labeling battle revolves around bioengineering companies like Monsanto and DuPont, which have spent millions of dollars to fight a California ballot initiative aimed at requiring the labeling of genetically modified foods. Strangely, marketers of the biggest organic brands in the country—Kashi, Cascadian Farm, Horizon Organic—also have joined the antilabeling effort and contributed a lot of money to the effort to defeat the initiative. In contrast, the smaller, independent businesses and farms that most shoppers envision when they buy an organic peach or shampoo—companies like Nature's Path, one of Kashi's largest competitors—have been strongly supporting the labeling initiative.[40]

Direct-to-consumer Pharmaceutical Advertising

The promotion of pharmaceutical products directly to consumers has been permitted since 1997—and has increased the consumption of numerous categories of medications. In studies, consumers confirmed that they obtained most of the information about these medications from TV commercials rather than from their physicians.[41] Recognizing that direct-to-consumer advertising has become too aggressive, the pharmaceutical industry has developed voluntary restrictions regarding this marketing method. The Senate has called for a temporary moratorium on advertising new drugs to consumers, and a major pharmaceutical company has volunteered not to advertise new drugs to consumers during their first year on the market.[42] Online search engines further complicate the direct selling of medications to consumers. The FDA urged pharmaceutical companies to include risk information about drugs in the companies' search advertisements in the form of a short text that appears besides the results of one's Google search. But, since Google limits such ads to 95 characters, it is unclear how this can be done.[43] Because they can market products directly to consumers, pharmaceutical companies are more eager than ever to "extend the life" of products that have become consumer favorites, as the dates for patent expiration and the availability of generic versions of these products near. For example, Pfizer began selling a chewable form of Viagra; other companies are testing erectile dysfunction drugs that melt under the tongue and act more quickly than pills that are swallowed.[44]

Learning Objective

3 To understand ethically questionable practices such as covert marketing, manipulative exposure to advertising, and truth-in-advertising issues.

Crafty Promotional Messages and Techniques

Marketers can also manipulate consumers' interpretations of marketing stimuli through the context in which those stimuli are featured. For example, in QVC's Extreme Shopping, during which rare and expensive products are offered, consumers perceived $200 art prints as reasonably priced when the prints were shown immediately after much more expensive items.[45] Inadvertently, marketers can also affect the content and duration of news and other information-focused broadcasts. For example, many marketers carefully screen the context in which their messages are shown, because they recognize that advertisements are perceived more positively when placed within more positive programs. Thus, they may choose not to place ads in news broadcasts or programs that cover serious issues, such as wars and world hunger, where some of the content is bound to be unpleasant. Because broadcasts are driven by advertising revenue, media companies may choose to shorten the coverage of serious and disagreeable topics.

A crafty marketing strategy, which is perfectly legal, occurs when marketers reduce the amount of products in packaging, but leave the prices unchanged. They do so because their margins are going down (e.g., because of higher raw-materials prices) and they are reluctant to raise prices. Marketers recognize that consumers are much more likely to notice price increases than small and below the JND (see Chapter 4) reductions in the packages' quantities of food, drink, and household products. Although legal, such reductions can be viewed as misleading and manipulative. For example, many cereal boxes and bags of chips became lighter over the years, which companies refer to as "weight outs." A Snickers bar was reduced from 2.07 ounces to 1.86 ounces (Mars said this was done to reduce calories to 250 per bar), and the bottle size of Tropicana Pure Premium orange juice declined from 64 to 59 ounces. Kimberly-Clark introduced a box of Kleenex that has 13% fewer sheets, a measure referred to as "desheeting." The company said that the new Kleenex tissues are 15% "bulkier" and fewer tissues are needed to get the job done. Similarly, the number of sheets in various Cottonelle toilet paper roles declined from 176 to 230 sheets to between 166 and 216 sheets per role.[46]

Covert Marketing

Covert marketing (masked or stealth marketing) consists of marketing messages and promotional materials that appear to come from independent parties when, in fact, they are sent by marketers. Some maintain that covert marketing strategies often violate the FTC's definition of deceptive advertising, endorsement guidelines, and other regulations pertaining to marketing, and believe that the FTC should establish clearer rules to reduce the use of masked advertising.[47] Others argue that the widespread use of covert advertising abuses consumers' efforts to avoid advertising and will result in increased consumer distrust of product information; of particular concern here is the increased number of communications that are created by marketers but made to resemble genuine word-of-mouth.[48]

Popular methods of covert marketing include:

1. Actors posing as customers telling people the product benefits and giving them a chance to examine or try the product.
2. Paying bartenders for praising brands of alcoholic beverages and recommending them to customers.
3. Employees posing as customers online—in chat-rooms, blogs, etc.—and spreading positive word-of-mouth about the product and even providing samples. They also encourage people to tell others about the samples they have received.
4. Emails disguised as "urgent" messages or personal thank-you notes.
5. As discussed in Chapter 4 (on consumer perception), inserting advertising messages into the content of programs and disguising advertising messages as entertainment.

Product Placement: Advertising Embedded within Entertainment

Marketers increasingly use techniques that blur the distinctions between **figure and ground** and make it difficult for consumers to clearly distinguish advertising from entertainment content (see Chapter 4). For example, to combat fast-forwarding by consumers who wish to avoid TV commercials, marketers are increasingly turning to **product placements**, where the line between television shows and ads is virtually nonexistent. Six-packs of Mountain Dew were given to the winners of personal challenge contests on Survivor, and the judges of American Idol always have a Coca-Cola within easy reach. A new product developed by Burger King went on sale the day after it was featured on The Apprentice, and another show of this series focused on developing an ad for Dove Cool Moisture Body Wash. In addition, some news programs contain embedded ads, and promotional messages were also inserted into the dialogue of entertainment programs. While forecasts indicate that companies are going to steadily increase expenditures on branded entertainment, a newly formed consumer advocacy group, Commercial Alert, is lobbying for legislation that will require advertisers to disclose upfront ads that are designed as product placements.

Marketers also blend promotion and program content by positioning a TV commercial so close to the storyline of a program that viewers are unaware they are watching an advertisement until they are well into it. Because this was an important factor in advertising to children, the Federal Trade Commission has strictly limited the use of this technique. TV stars or cartoon characters are now prohibited from promoting products during the children's shows in which they appear. An **advertorial** is another potential misuse of figure-and-ground and occurs in print ads that closely resemble editorial matter. In broadcast media, **infomercials**, are 30-minute (or even longer) commercials that appear to the average viewer to be documentaries, and thus command more attentive viewing than obvious commercials would receive.

Many surveys have examined the impact of product placements in films on brand awareness, attitudes, and purchase intent. However, there is no evidence that firms' investments in film product placements are worthwhile.[49] Some studies showed that prominent placements, though more memorable, do not have much influence on consumption, whereas subtle placements, though less memorable, nonetheless have a greater impact on consumption. Thus, if they intend to continue using this tactic, marketers must design placements that have strong effect on memory as well as behavior.[50]

False or Misleading Advertising

The ethical issues related to advertising focus on the accuracy of the information provided and the potential misuse of promotional messages' persuasive abilities. Regarding accuracy, a toothpaste ad stating that "brand A is the best" is considered an acceptable form of advertising "puffery" because consumers generally understand that there is no credible way to determine what "best" means. A toothpaste ad stating that the brand is "endorsed by the American Dental Association" is an objective statement of fact that includes easily verifiable information. However, is an ad stating that the brand "provides more cavity protection than any other toothpaste" permissible advertising puffery, or is it false or misleading? The answer depends on how most reasonable consumers are likely to interpret the ad. Do they believe that there is a scientific way to measure the degree of cavity protection and that the maker of the brand has conducted a scientific study of all brands of toothpaste on the market and that the study proved the ad's claim? It is clear that determining how most reasonable consumers are likely to interpret an ad is a complex undertaking, and therefore there is no definitive answer to the question: At what point does puffery become deceptive? As discussed in Chapter 7, humor is the most popular advertising appeal. Regrettably, one study discovered that deceptive claims were found in about three-quarters of humorous ads, and that humor was often used to mask deceptive claims.[51]

Truth-in-advertising laws protect consumers from false advertisements. Over time, the FTC has developed guidelines as to what constitutes **deceptive advertising**, and it holds marketers responsible for determining their ads' potential to mislead consumers. However, although the FTC is responsible for stopping false or misleading ads, it is apparent that such ads continue to exist. For example, the FTC's website featured a "Red Flag" button alerting consumers that "misleading weight loss advertising is everywhere" and warning them against weight-loss claims that are too good to be true. Sample claims include that the product causes "substantial weight loss no matter how much you eat" or promises of "a weight loss of two pounds or more a week for a month or more without dieting or exercise."[52] The FTC encourages and investigates complaints by consumers and companies regarding false or misleading ads, but its public advice for consumers regarding weight-loss products illustrates that it cannot stop all misleading ads. The FTC can also require companies that have misled consumers to run **corrective advertising**. For example, years ago Listerine's maker was forced to correct the claim that the product prevents colds. A study indicated that corrective advertising sometimes resulted in consumer distrust toward other products sold by the company, and also toward similar products sold by unrelated marketers; this result suggested that corrective promotional messages may often not achieve their desired objectives.[53]

In addition to the FTC, there is the National Advertising Review Council (NARC), a self-regulatory group that monitors complaints from companies and consumers regarding truth in advertising and often determines what ads can or cannot state. For example, NARC determined that Colgate-Palmolive provided supportive evidence for the claim that its Oxy-Plus product "blasts away grease faster" than P&G's Ultra Dawn, but decided that there was no evidence supporting GlaxoSmithKline's claim that Super PoliGrip provides the "strongest hold ever"—a claim that the company subsequently withdrew. NARC also supported a challenge to promotions for cancer treatment which claimed that "Chemotherapy doesn't work for everyone."[54] In some cases, powerful companies can persuade media to stop running ads they deem deceptive. For example, Anheuser-Busch persuaded ABC, CBS, and NBC to stop running Miller Beer ads depicting consumers comparing beers and saying that the Miller beers have more flavor.[55] Table 14.2 gives examples of false or deceptive promotions.[56]

Apparently, a large number of promotional violations occur in the marketing of medications. One study identified the three major categories of violations:[57]

1. Unsubstantiated effectiveness claims: Representing the drug as more effective than the evidence available suggests; representing the drug as useful in a broader scope than the research evidence indicates.
2. Omitted risk information: Failure to reveal risks resulting from using the drug correctly; failure to present information on side effects; stating the risks in unclear language.
3. Unsubstantiated superiority claims: Presenting the drug as more effective or safer than others in spite of the fact that there is no evidence supporting such a claim.

What Is "Deceptive"?

It is often difficult to determine what constitutes "misleading" or "deceptive" advertising. For example, Sterling, a jewelry marketer, took legal action to stop Zale, its competitor, from advertising its product line as the "most brilliant diamonds in the world." Advertising can include *subjective* claims, such as "our wine has the most unique taste among red wines." However, Sterling claimed that the brilliance of a diamond *can* be systematically, reliably, and scientifically measured, and therefore the claim "most brilliant diamonds" is not a subjective claim. The court sided with Zale because there are no objective standards by which to measure a diamond's "cut" or "brilliance." Other subjective claims in the jewelry sector—that are perfectly legal ads—include "the first

TABLE 14.2 Deceptive or False Promotional Claims

PRODUCT	ISSUE	DESCRIPTION
Dannon Yogurt	Claimed health benefit	In response to consumer demand for products containing certain strains of live bacteria, Dannon's promotions for its probiotic dairy drinks—Activia and DanActive—claimed that bacterial cultures will help prevent colds or alleviate digestive problems. The FTC forced Dannon to drop the ad because it could not claim that the product will relieve digestive issues unless it also mentioned that a person has to eat at least three servings daily to get this benefit. The FTC allowed Dannon to state that Activia helps regulate the digestive system and DanActive helps to support the immune system.
Nestlé	Claimed health benefit	The FTC stopped Nestlé's advertising claiming that its Boost Kids Essential beverages help kids avoid colds and reduce school absences.
Pom Wonderful	Claimed health benefit	The marketer of this pricy pomegranate juice advertised that the product reduces the risk of heart disease, prostate cancer, and impotence. The FTC charged the marketer with making false and unsubstantiated claims.
Procter & Gamble Nyquil	Forbidden product attributes	Procter and Gamble wanted to add Vitamin C to its Vicks cold formulas. The FDA does not allow the addition of dietary supplements to drugs, because that may give consumers the impression that these drugs were evaluated and approved by the FDA.
Skechers Toning Shoes	False claim	The company claimed that its shoes help consumers tone muscles and lose weight. One of the taglines said: "Get in shape without setting a foot in the gym." The FTC fined the company $50 million.

(*Continued*)

TABLE 14.2 (Continued)

PRODUCT	ISSUE	DESCRIPTION
Ab Circle Pro	False claim	Ads for the Ab Circle Pro, a circular disk on which people swing back and forth, said that a 3-minute daily workout was equivalent to 100 sit-ups and would allow consumers to lose 10 pounds in 2 weeks. The FTC forced the company to give customers refunds.
Lancôme	Questionable claim	L'Oréal's Lancôme claimed that one of its products "boosts the activity of genes and stimulates the production of youth proteins." This implies that the product affects the way the human body works, which is a standard used to classify new drugs, not cosmetics. The FDA rebuked the company.
Twitter	Full disclosure	The FTC said that Twitter ads should include full disclosure, just like TV and print ads. For example, ads should include the average effectiveness of a weight-loss shake or note that a celebrity was paid to push a product. Making room for this kind of text in a 140-character tweet on Twitter is unrealistic, but other ways to include full disclosure are being considered.

Source: Amy Schatz and Ilan Brat, "Dannon Settles Complaints Over Yogurt Ads," December 16, 2010 online.wsj.com; Edward Eyatt, "Regulators Call Health Claims in Pom Juice Ads Deceptive," nytimes.com September 27, 2010; Associated Press, "FDA Warns P&G for Adding Vitamin C to Nyquil," nytimes.com October 14, 2009; Brent Kendall, "Sketvhers Settles With FTC Over Deceptive-Advertising of Toning Shoes," online.wsj.com May 16, 2012; Anemona Hartocollis, "Dispute Over City's Ads Against Sodas," nytimes.com October 28, 2010.

diamond ever to be certified visibly brighter" and "the world's most perfectly cut diamond."[58] The New York City Health Department put together a media campaign about how drinking a can of soda a day "can make you 10 pounds fatter a year." Although few would argue that soda is nutritious, and there is a body of evidence showing a high correlation between rising obesity and the consumption of sugary drinks, some health experts question the scientific validity of directly linking sugar consumption to gaining weight, because the reasons behind weight gain vary widely.[59] Organix is a manufacturer of hair-care products. Although the company has never claimed that its products are organic, critics maintain that the name in misleading. Furthermore, when Vogue—the company owning Organix—became available for sale, potential buyers expressed concerns regarding its Organix brand.[60]

Learning Objective

4 To understand the nature and consequences of provocative advertisements.

Provocative Marketing

Regrettably, too many marketing messages convey socially undesirable stereotypes and images. Some years ago, the makers of an American icon—G.I. Joe—introduced a substantially more muscular version of the doll and were subsequently accused of sanctioning the use of muscle-building drugs by teenagers. Similarly, the makers of Barbie—a doll that has gradually become thinner and bustier—were accused of conveying an unrealistic body image to young girls. Some objectionable ads can be the result of good intentions. For example, a not-for-profit organization in New York City ran an ad campaign aimed at raising public awareness of such children's disorders as autism, depression, and eating-related illnesses. The ads featured "Ransom Notes" depicting how the diseases held the families of the sick children captive by taking over their lives. Although many agreed that this advertising approach was effective in the context of the campaign's objectives, some parents of children afflicted with the illnesses featured found the ads too emotional and personal, and the campaign was discontinued. With social media outlets such as Twitter and Facebook making it even easier for complaints about provocative ads to go viral, many marketers began testing their Super Bowl commercials on audiences in advance of the big game. A research firm that specializes in **neuromarketing**, the study of advertising's effect on brain activity, worked with several Super Bowl advertisers. The firm strapped electrodes to focus group participants to see how different parts of their brains reacted to the commercials. While some experts question the validity of this research, marketers have been increasingly using the techniques.[61]

In trying to illustrate that some ads may bring about undesirable, although unintended, behavior, a New Jersey professor showed his students a magazine ad featuring a fit, smiling young man on a sidewalk in New York City with yellow cabs, pedestrians, and buildings in the background. The bright-red headline read, "Just once a day!" All other copy elements of the ad were concealed to disguise the actual product advertised. When the professor asked his students to guess what kind of product the ad was promoting, the consensus of the guesses was that the ad was for some kind of a pill, probably a vitamin. In fact, the ad was for a medication that is used as part of an HIV therapy regimen by persons who are HIV positive. Because visual images are very persuasive, is it possible that the fit young man and the bright-red "Just once a day!" caption could convey to young adults that being HIV positive is an easily manageable condition, and that one can therefore engage in unsafe sex with impunity? However, marketers have limited options, even if some misperceive the ads. Clearly, featuring an individual who looks unhealthy in an ad for a pharmaceutical designed to control a serious medical condition will not be effective. The Food and Drug Administration has alerted marketers of HIV medications to the fact that some of their ads, which often show healthy-looking persons involved in rigorous physical activity, may be conveying the notion that because the drugs can restore or maintain one's health, they implicitly encourage unsafe sex.

Many studies have focused on the use of objectionable themes in advertising. For example, one study of TV commercials directed at children discovered that diverse ethnicities were underrepresented compared to Caucasians and pointed out the need for more diverse ethnic representation in children's TV advertising. This is an important recommendation because children are generally deeply engaged in TV viewing and advertising's portrayals influence their views of social ethnicity.[62] A study of promotional elements found that images and words unsuitable for children produced the most consumer complaints, followed by bad language. The study also discovered that consumers felt more insulted by offensive themes than by the products, services, or ideas featured in the ads, and that consumers viewed ads delivered via intrusive media as more offensive than those delivered via other media.[63] Table 14.3 includes examples of provocative marketing.[64]

Although marketers continuously sponsor ads portraying values or behaviors that some (or many) consumers find distasteful or wrong, the importance of public scrutiny must not be underestimated. For example, one broadcast of the Super Bowl included many ads portraying crude humor and gags that were later criticized by many (and also amplified by the coincidental "wardrobe malfunction" of a female entertainer during the half-time show). As a result, advertisers during the following year's Super Bowl broadcast took special care to develop ads that were more mainstream and traditional—not an easy task, as Super Bowl ads (expected to be creative and unique) —are the most analyzed group of ads in American broadcasting.[65] In recent years, marketers have been testing Super Bowl commercials well in advance, with different publics, and changing any elements that appeared controversial.

TABLE 14.3 Examples of Provocative Marketing

PRODUCT	PROVOCATION	DESCRIPTION
Blast by Colt 45	Appealing to underage drinkers	Blast by Colt 45—a fruit-flavored beverage—was endorsed by the rapper Snoop Dogg, who also mentioned the brand in one of his songs. Sweetened alcoholic beverages are sometimes called "cocktails on training wheels" and young drinkers call them "alcopops."
Four Loko	Deadly combination masked as "an energy drink"	A company marketing a fruit-flavored malt beverage with 12% alcohol content and caffeine targeted college students. Some drinkers ended up in hospitals. While under FDA investigation, the company took the caffeine out of the product.
Adidas	Selling the same product for different prices in two countries	The shirts of New Zealand's premier rugby team—marketed by Adidas—were being sold online in the United States for approximately 50% less that their New Zealand price.
Nivea skincare	Despicable advertising	An ad for the product featured a black man holding a decapitated head with an afro and beard. The ad's tagline was: "Re-civilize yourself."
Groupon	Insensitive humor	One ad made fun of the people of Tibet, who are abused under Chinese rule; another ad made fun of endangered species.
A vodka named Wodka	Tasteless and negative stereotypical portrayals in advertising	An ad for Wodka—a very cheap vodka brand sold in Brooklyn, N.Y.—read: "Christmas quality, Hanukah pricing," and also featured one dog wearing a yarmulke and another one wearing a Santa hat. Another ad read: "Escort quality, hooker prices."
Benetton	Creative but objectionable	Benetton—made famous by creative but highly explicit advertising—came up with an "UNHATE" campaign featuring world leaders kissing other leaders whom they oppose, such as President Obama kissing Venezuela's leader and the prime minister of Israel kissing the Palestinian leader.

Sources: WSJ Staff, "Oh, Benetton. You and Your Controversial Ad Campaigns," online.wsj.com November 16, 2011; Jonathan Hutchinson, "The Price of a Jersey Sets Rugby Fans Against Adidas," NYTIMES.com August 24, 2011; Andrew Newman, "A Line of Brews Draws a Star Endorser," nytimes.com April 17, 2011; Abby Goodnough, "Caffeine and Alcohol Drink Is Potent Mix for Young," nytimes.com October 26, 2010; Sarah Nir, "Nivea Pulls Ads After Online Outcry," nytimes.com August 12, 2011.

Learning Objective

5 To understand how marketers abuse consumers' privacy and the measures that can stop such practices.

Abusing Consumers' Privacy

Consumers' loss of privacy is an increasingly problematic ethical issue, as marketers identify and reach out to increasingly smaller audiences through innovative media and more sophisticated tracking. The collection and dissemination of this information raises many privacy issues and various governmental bodies have proposed measures to ensure consumers' privacy. For example, some senators proposed a Commercial Privacy Bill of Rights, but the proposal fails to require businesses to provide consumers with data about themselves, which they can do very easily.[66]

Some retailers started testing new technology that allowed them to track customers' movements by following the Wi-Fi signals from customers' smartphones. The retailers gather data about in-store shoppers' behavior, using video surveillance and signals from their cellphones and apps to identify customers' genders, how many minutes they spend in the candy aisle and how long they look at merchandise before buying it. Retailers can also identify returning shoppers, because mobile devices send unique identification codes when they search for networks. Thus, stores can tell how repeat customers behave and the average time between visits. When customers found out about being tracked, many complained and said that they felt "stalked" and "creepy" while shopping under surveillance.[67]

The **e-score** is a digital calculation that evaluates people's buying power and value as consumers. However, these scores are largely invisible to the public. Fueled by Google Analytics, this digital ranking of American society is unlike anything that came before it. Nevertheless, unlike personal credit reports, consumers cannot find out what their e-scores are.[68]

The Federal Trade Commission recommended a "do not track" mechanism that is similar to the national "do not call" registry. It also proposed legislation regulating so-called data brokers, which compile and trade a wide range of personal and financial data about millions of consumers from online and offline sources. The suggested legislation would give consumers access to information collected about them and allow them to correct and update such data. Another proposal is to let consumers choose whether they want their Internet browsing and buying habits monitored.[69] The Digital Advertising Alliance—a group of digital advertising trade organizations—designed a turquoise triangle in the upper right-hand corner of banner ads. The AdChoices icon allows users who click on the turquoise triangle to opt out of having their behavior tracked online. The group's website has received about 100,000 inquiries about the icon. Facing several bills introduced in Congress calling for tighter regulation of mobile and digital privacy, as well as more control over online advertising to children, the group launched a campaign educating consumers about the turquoise triangle.[70]

Online marketers monitor and track consumers more closely and accurately than most people realize or would probably allow. For example, Facebook had a program called "beacon," which traced where users were going and sent their friends alerts about the goods that the users who were monitored bought or viewed online. After a public outcry, Facebook incorporated into the program a feature allowing users to opt out of it easily.[71] More recently, Facebook—which has 500 million users globally—unveiled a set of controls that it said would help people understand what they were sharing online, and with whom, and would simplify its opt out system.[72] Radically, newer versions of several browsers come with the don't-track-me option automatically enabled. During installation, a notice appears in a customization menu giving users the choice to keep that preselected don't-track-me preference as is, or switch it off.[73] Adlock is the name of software that, presumably, allows consumers to surf online and block some ads, but without ever missing the advertising that they were meant to see.[74] A survey presented at the Amsterdam Privacy Conference indicated that most Americans surveyed did not want any information at all collected about which websites they visit, and that they did not find online advertisements useful. Nearly 90% said they had never heard of a proposal by the Federal Trade Commission, known as a "do not track" mechanism, that would let users opt out of having their personal data collected for serving tailored advertisements.[75]

We must also note that the popularity of "do not track" threatens the barter system wherein consumers allow sites and third-party ad networks to collect information about their online activities in exchange for open access to maps, email, games, music, social networks, and much more. Marketers have been fighting to preserve this arrangement, saying that collecting consumer data powers effective advertising tailored to a user's tastes. In turn, according to this argument, those tailored ads enable smaller sites to thrive and provide rich content. A general council for the Interactive Advertising Bureau—an industry group—said that eliminating relevant advertising would make the Internet less diverse, less economically successful, and significantly less interesting.[76] Furthermore, although consumers lose a lot of privacy online, such is not always the case. In websites using "first party" behavioral advertising, the site collects consumer information to deliver targeted advertising at its site, but does not share any of that information with third parties. Additionally, **contextual advertising**, which targets advertisements based on the Web page a consumer is viewing or a search query the consumer has made, involves little or no data storage.

Finding and reading websites' privacy policies is difficult. Buried deep within the legalese used in privacy policies is information on how Web publishers collect and handle the data they use to show ads to their visitors. PrivacyChoice—a company that has analyzed and indexed the data in hundreds of privacy policies across the Web—has developed a scale ranking websites from 0 to 100, based on how a site collects and uses personal data. Websites and their users can easily compare privacy practices across the Internet and make smarter decisions about their own data. This tool would also result in more protective privacy practices by sites and tracking companies.[77]

Little-known software installed on millions of smartphones is raising even more questions about what data are being collected from mobile devices, where the data are going, and what they are being used for. The package—from a company namevd Carrier IQ Inc.—collected information on one carrier's smartphone with Google Inc.'s Android operating system. The software, which was not transparently visible to consumers, tracks actions such as when buttons are pressed and collects personal data such as the content of text messages. Google said that it is not affiliated with Carrier IQ.[78]

Even without special software, cell phones undermine privacy. Marketers can learn not only *who* you are (e.g., your personal characteristics) and *what* specific purchases you make, but can also learn *where* you are at any given moment because your cell phone, mobile email device, and the GPS integrated into your car or sports watch are "electronic bracelets" that monitor your movements. If you travel abroad with a roaming cell phone, upon landing at your destination, you may quickly receive a text welcoming you to that destination and offering you additional services designed for travelers. Clearly, in the not-too-distant future, when you drive a car equipped with a GPS with the radio on, the commercial that you will hear may alert you to, say, a McDonald's two exits down the highway. Another driver in a different location and listening to the same radio station would hear a different ad. In several large cities, advertisers use cabs equipped with GPS and advertising billboards on their roofs to create ever-changing advertising messages; the changing ad displays corresponded to the businesses the cabs pass as they travel (in some cabs, screens inside the cabs also display ads).

In one futuristic movie thriller set in 2054, the hero passes a billboard featuring the American Express card, which, after scanning his retina, becomes a hologram (presumably visible only to him) portraying his picture and personal data and urging him to use the card. He then enters a Gap store, where he is met by voices greeting him by name, asking how he liked his previous purchases, and suggesting items that he may like based on his past purchases. New types of coupons, printed from the Internet or sent to mobile phones, are packed with information about the customers who use them, and follow the customers to malls. The coupons look standard, but their bar codes often include identification information about the customer, his or her Internet address, Facebook page information, and even the search terms the customer used to find the coupon in the first place. In the mall, if a man walks into a Filene's Basement to buy a suit for his wedding and shows a coupon he retrieved online, the company's marketing agency can figure out whether he used the search terms "Hugo Boss suit" or "discount wedding clothes" before his purchase. The coupons can, in some cases, be tracked not just to an anonymous shopper but to an identifiable person: A retailer could know that Amy Smith printed a 15%-off coupon after searching for appliance discounts at Ebates.com on Friday at 1:30 p.m. and redeemed it later that afternoon at the store.[79]

In summary, experts point out that given the vast flow of information that consumers entrust to the Internet every day, it is hard to believe there is no general law to protect people's privacy online. Companies harvest data about people as they surf the Net, assemble it into detailed profiles, and sell it to advertisers or others without ever asking permission. Because there are no uniform international laws to deal with violations of online privacy, and because no one specifically monitors for potential violations of consumers' rights to privacy online, there is no consensus as to whether government regulation or voluntary measures could alleviate this concern.[80]

Learning Objective

6 To understand how marketers can advance society's interests by advocating socially beneficial conduct and discouraging adverse behavior.

Promoting Social Causes

Many not-for-profit organizations, including consumer advocacy groups, exist primarily to promote socially beneficial behaviors such as contributing to charity or using energy responsibly, and reducing such negative behaviors as abusing drugs, discriminating on the basis of race or sexual orientation, and driving while texting or drunk. Many companies try to increase their credibility by being "good corporate citizens" and integrating socially desirable practices into their operations. For example, Disney agreed not to feature any smoking in Disney-branded films.[81] One study indicated that a societal marketing program had a powerful impact on creating positive consumer attitudes toward the sponsoring company.[82] Another study found that a solid perceptual fit between the sponsoring organization and the cause(s) promoted enhances both consumers' involvement in the causes and their purchase intentions.[83]

Advocating Beneficial and Discouraging Detrimental Conduct

The primary objective of many not-for-profit organizations is to promote socially desirable behaviors and discourage ones that produce negative outcomes. For example, The Advertising Council—a group founded during World War II and dedicated to the advancement of socially worthy causes through advertising—ran a campaign that discouraged the use of derogatory phrases regarding a person's sexual orientation. The campaign's title was "Think Before You Speak," and its objective was to reduce the harassment and bullying of teenagers who are gay, lesbian, bisexual, or transgender (see Figure 14.4).[84] With the alarming increase of

Source: Courtesy of GLSEN, the Gay, Lesbian & Straight Network and the Ad Council's "Think Before You Speak" campaign

FIGURE 14.4 Using Derogatory Terms: "Think Before You Speak"

"digital harassment" among teenagers, The Advertising Council initiated a campaign entitled "That's Not Cool," alerting young adults that excessive and unwelcome sending of text messages can quickly become illegal stalking.[85] The Christopher Reeve Foundation is a not-for-profit group dedicated to raising money for treating people who live with spinal impairment and finding a cure for spinal injury; the group ran an ad campaign under its new slogan: "Today's Care. Tomorrow's Cure."[86]

Sometimes, even government organizations try to induce public behavior that they see fit. For example, because many TV series and films are shot on the streets of New York City, some hurried New Yorkers have grown increasingly annoyed at the delays and inconveniences caused by film crews, who must often close and obstruct city blocks and sidewalks during filming. The New York City mayor's office ran a campaign asking New Yorkers to play host to film crews even if they are reluctant to do so; the ads featured New Yorkers who work in the film industry and stressed the economic benefits of the industry's strong presence in the city.[87] The ad by New York City's Office of Emergency Management (shown in Figure 14.5) encourages the city's residents to become more aware of the city's vulnerability to hurricanes and be prepared for such weather.

Source: "Ready New York Advertisement" ©2004. New York City Office of Emergency Management. All Rights Reserved

FIGURE 14.5 New York City's Government Promotes Hurricane Preparedness

Source: Ad Council

FIGURE 14.6 Discouraging Texting While Driving

One of the most heavily discouraged detrimental behaviors in the past few years has been texting or using mobile phones while driving. Cellular carriers have even been working on technologies that would automatically disable mobile phones in moving cars.[88] Scores of not-for-profit organizations, companies, and local governments have been campaigning against this highly dangerous and often fatal practice using such ads as the one featured in Figure 14.6.

The list of worthy social causes has been increasing steadily. Table 14.4 includes a list of recent promotions of lesser-known socially beneficial causes.

Cause-related Marketing

Some firms engage in **cause-related marketing**, where they contribute a portion of the revenues they receive from selling certain products to causes that are socially desirable and supported by the American public. The Hertz ad in Figure 14.7 is an excellent example of such marketing. The ad welcomes soldiers returning home from combat overseas and asks consumers to rent Hertz cars so that the company can offer free rentals to returning troops. Fashion designers such as Armani and Ralph Lauren have donated selected portions of their sales to AIDS research and other charities. To acknowledge National Breast Cancer Awareness Month in October, many beauty and cosmetics companies earmarked a portion of the price of their "pink-ribbon" products to breast cancer charities. A few years ago, following a tsunami in Southeast Asia, several designers sold tsunami-relief T-shirts; many others encouraged consumers to make donations to a fund that was set up to help the storm's victims, and even included links to this fund on their websites. Other kinds of corporate-sponsored special events include marching bands, fireworks displays, parades, laser shows, and traveling art exhibits.

These sponsorships convey a subtle message to consumers: "We're a great (kind, good-natured, socially responsible) company; we deserve your business." One study demonstrated the importance of the fit between the sponsored cause and the company's positioning strategy, and showed that a low fit can harm the company's image.[89] In another study, an ad with a cause-related message elicited more favorable consumer attitudes than a similar ad without a cause-related message.[90] Yet another study showed that cause-related advertising is more effective among consumers who are more involved.[91]

TABLE 14.4 Promoting Socially Worthy Causes

ORGANIZATION	CAUSE	CAMPAIGN'S DESCRIPTION
Soprano's actor Joe Pantoliano	Mental illness awareness	Established a foundation and raised money by selling a DVD of a documentary he directed and fees from personal appearances.
Blood Center of Central Texas	Donating blood	Humorously suggest that the good deed of donating blood could offset everyday bad behavior.
United Methodist Church in Nashville	Eliminating Malaria	"A world of people united in the fight against a needless killer."
Keep California (not-for-profit group)	Keeping California's beaches clean	Using humor and filmed on the same beach where "beach blanket" movies were shot in the 1960s, the commercial satirizes the teenagers who appeared in those films.
The Advertising Council	Encouraging parents to read with their children	"Read to your child today and inspire a lifelong love of reading." The campaign features Curious George—an iconic monkey character—featured in a series of children's books.
American Heart Association	Using hands-only CPR	A "hands symphony" theme in TV spots. The campaign's website lets users create their own hand symphonies and an instructional application of the CPR is offered to users of smartphones.
Advertising Council	Greater involvement of fathers in their children's lives	Targeting American-Indian, Asian-American, and Hispanic fathers, the tagline is "Take time to be a dad today." Studies have shown that children of "absent fathers" do poorly in school and have lower levels of self-esteem.

Box 14.2 Social Causes and Indian Brands

In India, as part of their corporate social responsibility programs, companies tie up with NGOs or government agencies either for specific projects or as a long-term association. At the end of 2009, Rediff stated that India ranks fourth in Asia on CSR disclosure, though its performance in comparison to Western Europe and the USA is still generally poor.[92] As an example of short-term tie-ups, Novartis India donated 2% of its sales value of Ovaltine Plus to the NGO CRY (Child Relief and You) toward its Gujarat rehabilitation operations. When the tsunami hit India and Southeast Asia in 2004, along with many other companies, Procter & Gamble India donated $3.2 mn to the Prime Minister's Relief Fund.

Examples of long-term associations include ITC's nationwide campaign for water conservation called "Aashirvaad—Boond se Sagar," which is supposed to have put into place over 30,000 acres of life-saving irrigation system benefiting more than 40,000 people. Consumers buying Aashirvaad products (*atta*, spices, and salt) were made aware that a worthy contribution was being made to water conservation efforts from the proceeds of the sale of these products.[93] ITC's Choupal Pradarshan Khet program also brings the benefits of agricultural best practices to small and marginal farmers. This service covers over 70,000 hectares and reaches out to 1.6 million farmers. Canon India has also taken steps to manage e-waste. The Smile Foundation (for children's health and education, **www.smilefoundationindia.org**) receives support from companies like the Bank of America, HP, HIFC, IDBI, Microsoft, Tata Chemicals Ltd. and the Times Foundation. Coca-Cola has taken initiatives in rainwater harvesting, restoring groundwater resources, and sustainable packaging and recycling (**www.icmrindia.org**). SAP Labs India (**www.sap.com**) contributes towards children's education and sustainability, while Infosys supports activities concerned with healthcare, education, and community development through social welfare. Wipro has a social welfare organization, the Azim Premji Foundation, which actively promotes education for children. The nature and quality of these sponsorships constitute a subtle message to the consumer: "We're a great (kind, good-natured, socially responsible) company; we deserve your business."

A recent study demonstrated the importance of the fit between the sponsored cause and the company's positioning strategy and that a low fit can harm the company's image.[94] In another study, an ad with a cause-related message elicited more favorable consumer attitudes than a similar ad without a cause-related message.[95] Also, another study showed that cause-related advertising is more effective among more involved consumers.[96]

Consumer Ethics

Marketers implement ethical strategies in order "to do the right thing," to improve their image in the eyes of their constituencies, to reduce scrutiny, and as an alternative to government legislation. A study focused on measuring consumers' views and perceptions of companies that have been accused of such practices as exploitation of the Third World, animal testing, damage to the environment, and recycling. The researchers developed a scale that measures consumers' views regarding ethical business issues and companies that adopt morally "right" strategies. It includes questions about the personal, social, and money aspects of adopting ethical views, as well as potential positive and negative outcomes (see Table 14.5).[97]

Another facet of consumer ethics is *buyers'* dishonest behavior in the marketplace. For example, many stores started charging restocking fees, limiting return policies, and tracking abnormal return patterns because of buyers who bought items, used them, and then returned them for a refund (some stores encountered shoplifters who tried to return stolen merchandise). Also, in the digital world, software piracy is a major problem. One study that focused on ways to reduce consumers' software theft discovered that increasing the risk of getting caught is unlikely to reduce this practice and may actually increase piracy levels. The study also found that consumers were less likely to pirate and more willing to pay for software if the websites involved offered them extra value, such as downloadable ringtones and videos.[98]

Airlines enable and inadvertently encourage many forms of "creative"—possibly unethical—customer behavior. For instance, to avoid checked luggage fees, some passengers use vacuum-seal bags inside carry-on bags. The bags, which shrink down to a compact package when air is pulled out by a vacuum cleaner, allow them to fit considerably more items in a carry-on than would normally be possible. Others buy special trench coats, vests, and other garments made with large built-in pockets that allow people to carry everything from folded shirts to an iPad. When flights are cancelled because of weather, some passengers stay with friends and then present the airlines with bills from expensive hotels. Some passengers whose bags were lost claimed

Source: The Hertz Corporation

FIGURE 14.7 Hertz's Cause-Related Marketing

that their bags were filled with furs, computers, and lots of couture clothing. Some fliers who travel with wheelchairs or motorized scooters claim that their devices were damaged in the cargo hold during the flight.[99]

TABLE 14.5 A Scale Measuring Ethical Awareness and Concerns towards Marketing-Related Issues

Respondents used a 7-point scale ranging from "strongly agree" to "strongly disagree."
PERSONAL POSITIVES
My friends are concerned with this issue.
People who matter to me would respect me for being concerned about this issue.
This is an issue that I like to be associated with.
I feel better about myself if I take some form of action against firms that violate this issue.

(*Continued*)

TABLE 14.5 *(Continued)*

SOCIAL POSITIVES
It would be better for everyone in the long run if people favoured products that address this issue.
It would help if people bought from firms that address this issue.
Society would benefit from the removal of products that violate this issue.
People could make fairer choices if they were aware of which companies had high ethical principles regarding this issue.
PERSONAL NEGATIVES
It would be too much hassle to buy only from businesses that do not violate this issue.
It is not my responsibility to punish firms that ignore this issue.
It would take the pleasure out of shopping if I had to choose only from products that support this issue.
It would make shopping less convenient if I had to choose only from products that support this issue.
SOCIAL NEGATIVES
People would be annoyed if they were pressured into being concerned with this issue.
People are too busy today to be concerned with this issue.
People might think it was a waste of time to try to influence big business over this issue.
Having to take account of this issue would make shopping less convenient for people.
MONEY ISSUES
It does not cost me any more money to take this issue into account when shopping *(item reversed for these analyses)*.
It costs more to take account of this issue when shopping.

Source: With kind permission from Springer Science+Business Media: "Motivations of the Ethical Consumer", *Journal of Business Ethics*, 79 (2008):, Oliver M. Freedstone and Peter J. McGoldrick.

Box 14.3 Marketing Ethics and Its Awareness in the Indian Context

Greater awareness about the health hazards and claims of brands, emergence of monitoring agencies, and the need for ethical governance regarding consumerism are making an impact on the ethical considerations that marketers need to take into account in an emerging market like India. CONCERT Trust, with the funding of the department of consumer affairs, had conducted a study in India[100] that included 34 brands of biscuits and 25 brands of pickles. It was revealed that many of the biscuits had lesser amount of fiber, honey, and calcium that what they had promised on the label. Most of the pickles tested contained high levels of sodium and sweet pickles were high on sugars.

In an effort to curb false claims associated with celebrity ads, All India Radio FM channel[101] came out with an ad that asked companies not to waste money on celebrities and requested consumers not to believe them. The ad was made in a format that had two friends in a conversation. Central Consumer Protection Council had decided to set up a sub committee to crack down on false promises that are made through these ads featuring celebrities.

Summary

Learning Objective 1: To understand the meaning and importance of marketing ethics and social responsibility.

The marketing concept is sometimes incompatible with society's best interests. The societal marketing concept requires that all marketers adhere to principles of social responsibility in the marketing of their goods and services. Since all companies prosper when society prospers, companies must integrate social responsibility into all marketing decisions, and many have adopted the societal marketing concept. A serious deterrent to more widespread implementation of the societal marketing concept is the short-term orientation of most business executives and corporate boards in their drive to quickly increase market share and profits.

Learning Objective 2: To understand how marketers can exploit consumers by targeting children and encouraging overeating and other forms of irresponsible buying.

The study of consumer behavior allows marketers to understand why and how consumers make their purchase decisions, but it also enables unethical marketers to exploit human vulnerabilities in the marketplace and engage in other unethical marketing practices. Such practices include targeting vulnerable consumers such as children, teenagers, the elderly, and less-educated consumers, who may not have the knowledge or experience to evaluate the products or services being promoted and the potential negative consequences of using them.

Learning Objective 3: To understand ethically questionable practices such as covert marketing, manipulative exposure to advertising, and truth-in-advertising issues.

Marketers can manipulate consumers' interpretations of marketing stimuli through the context in which those stimuli are featured. Covert marketing consists of marketing messages and promotional materials that appear to come from independent parties but are, in fact, sent by marketers. Some maintain that covert marketing strategies often violate the FTC's definition of deceptive advertising, endorsement guidelines, and other regulations of marketing, and believe that the FTC should establish clearer rules to reduce the use of masked advertising. The FTC has developed guidelines as to what constitutes deceptive advertising, and it holds marketers responsible for determining their ads' potential to mislead consumers. Although the FTC is responsible for stopping false or misleading ads, and the agency encourages and investigates complaints by consumers and companies regarding false or misleading ads, it cannot locate and stop all misleading ads. The FTC can also require companies that have misled consumers through their advertising to run corrective advertising.

Learning Objective 4: To understand the nature and consequences of provocative advertisements.

Too many marketing messages convey socially undesirable stereotypes and images, some of which tend to encourage risky or illegal behavior or create unrealistic perceptions. Many studies have focused on the use of objectionable themes in advertising and discovered that negative portrayals of certain people or objects affect consumers' perceptions.

Learning Objective 5: To understand how marketers abuse consumers' privacy and the measures that can stop such practices.

Consumers' loss of privacy is an increasingly problematic ethical issue as marketers identify and reach out to increasingly smaller audiences through innovative media and more sophisticated tracking. The collection and dissemination of this information raises many privacy issues and various governmental bodies have proposed measures to ensure consumers' privacy. "Do not track" and opt-out mechanisms, regulation of data brokers and harvesters, and increased consumer access to the information collected about them are options for combatting the invisible tracking that is being done via Internet, cell phone, and coupon use.

Learning Objective 6: To understand how marketers can advance society's interests by advocating socially beneficial conduct and discouraging adverse behavior.

Many not-for-profit organizations, including consumer advocacy groups, exist primarily to promote socially beneficial behaviors. Many companies try to increase their credibility by being "good corporate citizens" and integrating socially desirable practices into their operations. Some firms engage in cause-related marketing, where they contribute a portion of the revenues they receive from selling certain products to causes which are socially desirable and supported by the American public. A good fit between the company and the cause appears to be crucial to the effectiveness of these campaigns.

Review and Discussion Questions

14.1. Some say that targeting *any* group of consumers who are willing and able to purchase a product is simply good marketing. For example, advertising sweet and fatty foods to young children is perfectly okay because children like sweets, and when parents buy these products at their children's request, the needs of both the kids and their parents are met and satisfied. What is your reaction to this view?

14.2. A soft-drink company distributed cell phones to preadolescents in low-income areas. The phones routinely received advertising messages for the drink. Following criticism, the company said that the benefits to the disadvantaged children from having the cell phones (e.g., safety) outweighed any "exploitive targeting" considerations. Do you agree or disagree with the company's position? Explain your answer.

14.3. At a time when many consumers can avoid advertising messages via time shifting devices, marketers increasingly use product placements (also known as branded entertainment). In your view, is this a wise strategy or not? Explain your answer.

14.4. Is it right to advertise prescription medications *directly* to consumers? Why or why not?

14.5. Why is it important to study consumer ethics?

14.6. What are the privacy implications of companies' increasingly widespread monitoring of online consumers?

Hands-on Assignments

14.7. Find, and discuss ads that depict each of the following:

a. Exploitive targeting of children

b. Overaggressive advertising

c. Direct-to-consumer advertising of pharmaceuticals

d. Cause-related marketing

e. Societal marketing by a not-for-profit group

f. Societal marketing by a for-profit company

g. Socially undesirable representation

14.8. Online, find three examples of advertising embedded within entertainment content and discuss them.

14.9. Compile a list of consumption behaviors that *you* consider unethical. For each behavior listed, explain why you view it as wrong. Also, for each behavior listed, discuss the possible reasons a person engaging in that practice may use to justify it.

14.10. Visit the news section at www.caru.org. Select three of the press releases featured there (other than those discussed in this chapter) and illustrate how they depict the unethical applications of learning or perception (see Chapters 4 and 5) in targeting children.

Key Terms

- advertorial *405*
- cause-related marketing *412*
- consumer socialization *398*
- contextual advertising *409*
- corrective advertising *406*
- covert marketing (masked or stealth marketing) *404*
- deceptive advertising *405*
- e-score *409*
- figure and ground *405*
- infomercials *405*
- JND *399*
- marketing ethics *394*
- neuromarketing *407*
- product placements *405*
- societal marketing concept *396*
- truth-in-advertising laws *405*

15

Consumer Research

Learning Objectives

1. To understand how to develop research objectives
2. To understand how to collect secondary data
3. To understand qualitative and quantitative research methods
4. To understand how to combine qualitative and quantitative research
5. To understand how to analyze data and report research findings

DISNEY'S CINDERELLA is one of the best-known characters in the world. Like any company, Disney needs to come up with new ideas and offerings to expand its markets, especially when the company is rapidly transmitting its contents to children via many forms of media, and not only through movies and theme parks, as was the case when Cinderella was first introduced. Besides, the elements of the Cinderella story originated in ancient Greece and the character no longer reflects modern role models. Therefore, for five years, a team of child psychologists, sociologists, and storytelling experts worked to create a new royal girl: Sofia the First.

Sofia is the product of years of research involving interviews and observations of children playing with toys, discussing role models with parents, and testing storylines as the new princess was coming to life. This effort represents **consumer research**, which is the process and tools used to study consumer behavior (see Figure 15.1). As the research progressed, Disney uncovered the traits that today's children aged 2 to 5 expect in a modern princess, which, in many ways, is an "anti-Cinderella." Sophia could not be a young woman looking for a man, in order to avoid the stereotype of girls needing a prince to save them. Evil stepmothers too could not be present. Sophia is the daughter of Miranda, an unmarried shoe-cobbler, living in a village in the kingdom of Enchancia. Miranda meets and marries Enchancia's King Roland. Sophia has to adjust to a royal way of life, new school, and two stepsiblings.

The development team tested the plotlines on preschoolers before writing the scripts. While testing one storyline, the researchers found out that kids did not understand the phrase "slumber party," and renamed the episode "The Big Sleepover." As the children listened to the story, the researchers filmed them and took

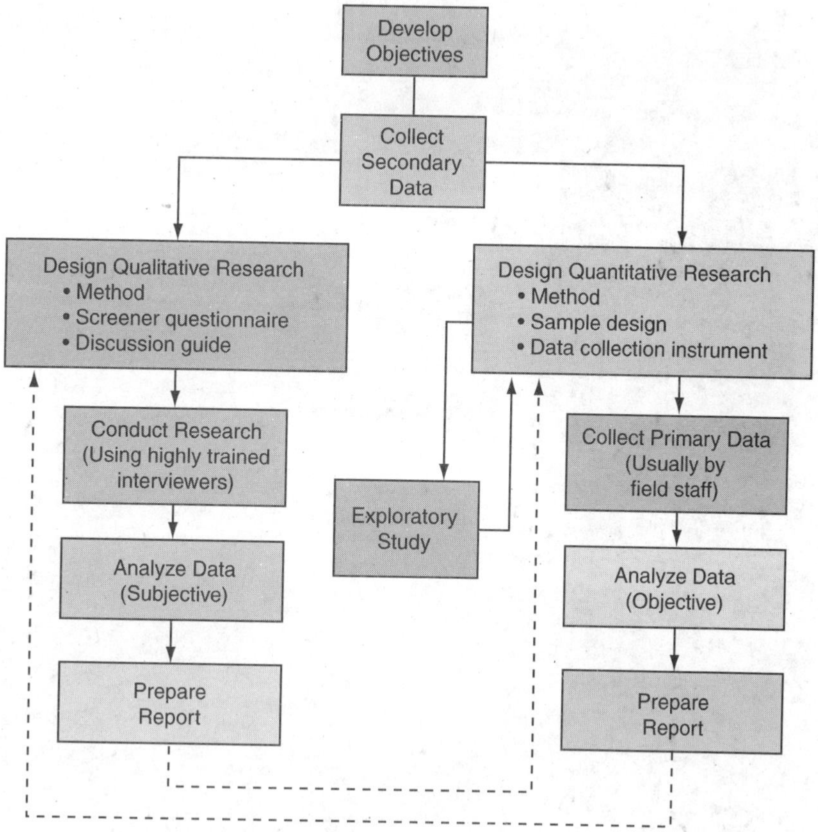

FIGURE 15.1 The Consumer Research Process

notes, which they later on used in developing the plots. The show's producers made Sofia the child of a single mother because doing so offered an easy way to explore themes of kids adapting to new living arrangements, which many young children can identify with. In addition, the writers introduced multicultural family dynamics: Although Miranda was not born in Enchancia, she married its king. Nevertheless, Sophia is still a Disney princess. She's pretty, lives in a castle, wears gowns, and even got advice from Cinderella, who visited her in the first episode.[1]

Consumer researchers regularly carry-out many different kinds of consumer research projects. For instance, they might conduct consumer depth interviews and focus groups to identify which benefits consumers seek from using their products or services. Also, they might conduct telephone surveys or mall intercept research to determine consumers' recall or recognition about their current advertising messages. To illustrate, Figure 15.2 presents a magazine ad for the Gillette Complete Skincare product. It is quite common to develop ad copies and supporting visual materials (be they for a magazine, newspaper, TV, radio, or Internet ad message) that marketers test the impact of the message before spending the often huge amount of money it takes to reach the targeted consumers with the right message. To this end, marketers might conduct a variety of different types of consumer research studies as they go through the process of developing their marketing messages, or to establish which product features are most important to consumers who make up the target market for a newly developed product.

This chapter begins with an examination of exploratory research and secondary data. Then, we describe **primary research**, defined as new research especially designed and collected for purposes of a current research problem. The two categories of primary consumer research are: **Qualitative research**, which consists primarily of focus groups and depth interviews, and projective methods; and **quantitative research**, which includes observational research, experimentation, and survey research.

FIGURE 15.2 Testing Print ads

Learning Objective
1 To understand how to develop research objectives

Developing Research Objectives

The first and most difficult step in the consumer research process is to accurately define the objectives of the research. Is it to segment the market for electronic readers? Is it to examine consumer attitudes about the experience of online shopping? What percentage of households shop for food online? Whatever the key research question, it is important for the marketing manager and the research manager to agree at the outset as to the specific purposes and objectives of the proposed consumer study. A clearly written statement of research objectives ensures that the information needed is indeed collected and costly errors are avoided.

If the purpose of a study is to come up with new ideas for products or promotional themes, the researchers use qualitative research. Qualitative studies consist of focus groups and/or one-on-one depth interviews, in which sampled consumers are individually interviewed by professionally trained interviewers. Alternatively, for example, if the purpose of the study is to find out how many consumers match the demographics or psychographics of the target market, or the characteristics of consumers who buy given brands and whether or not they are brand loyal, marketers conduct quantitative research.

Commonly, marketers use qualitative research before conducting large quantitative studies, because their results enable marketers to define the research objectives the large and expensive studies more precisely.

Learning Objective
2 To understand how to collect secondary data.

Collecting Secondary Data

The second step in the consumer research process is to search **secondary data**, defined as existing information that was originally gathered for a research purpose other than the present research. The rationale for secondary data searches is simply that it makes good sense to investigate whether currently available information will answer—in part or even in full—the research question at hand. It seems unwise to expend the effort and money, and rush into collecting new information before determining if there is any available information that would provide at least a good starting point. In other words, if secondary data can in part or full answer the question, new primary research can either be cut back or even avoided altogether. Secondary consumer-related data can be secured from internal sources within the company or organization, or external sources for free or at a cost. The following subsections explore secondary data.

Internal Secondary Data

Internal information or data could consist of previously collected in-house information that was originally used for some other purpose. It might have originally been gathered as part of a sales audit, or from past customer service calls, or letters of inquiry from customers, or collected via warranty cards. Increasingly, companies use internal secondary data to compute **customer lifetime value profiles** for various customer segments. These profiles include customer acquisition costs (the resources needed to establish a relationship with the customer), the profits generated from individual sales to each customer, the costs of handling customers and their orders (some customers may place more complex and variable orders that cost more to handle), and the expected duration of the relationship.

External Secondary Data

External secondary data come from sources outside of the firm or organization. They take many different forms. Some are free and can be found in a public library, other information is available for only a nominal fee, and still other data or information are quite expensive to secure. The following sections discusses some of the specific types of consumer behavior secondary information available from outside of the firm.

Government Secondary Data

Much data are collected by government bodies or their agencies, and are generally made available for a very nominal cost. For instance, within the United States, a major source of these data is the federal government, which publishes information collected by scores of government agencies about the economy, business, and virtually all demographics of the U.S. population. The best depositories of marketing-applicable information are FedStats, the U.S. Census Bureau, and the CIA's World Factbook. State and local governments, as well as studies prepared by the United Nations and various foreign governments, are also very useful for examining selective consumer behavior topics.

Periodicals and Articles Available from Online Search Services

Business-relevant secondary data from periodicals, newspapers, and books are readily accessible via online search engines. Two quite popular examples are ProQuest and LexisNexis. These two engines provide access to major newspapers such as The Wall Street Journal and The New York Times; business magazines such as Business Week, Forbes, Fortune, and Harvard Business Review; and marketing journals and applied publications focused specifically on marketing, such as Advertising Age, Brandweek, Marketing News, Journal of Marketing, Journal of Marketing Research, Journal of Consumer Research, and European Journal of Marketing. These materials are available in public and private libraries, especially business specialty libraries.

Syndicated Commercial Marketing and Media Research Services

Commercially available information about consumers is collected by syndicated research services that sell it to subscribing marketers. For example, Nielsen's MyBestSegment provides demographic and lifestyle profiles of the consumers residing in each U.S. Zip Code, Ipsos Mendelsohn offers its Affluent Media Survey to advertisers and their ad agencies, and Mediamark collects information on magazine audience profiles. Future research into consumers' exposure to media will consist of monitoring consumers via digital cable set-top boxes. Presently, digital cable boxes are primarily used to send signals to consumers' TVs to enable them to watch movies on demand and expanded channel lineups. However, the boxes can easily record all the programs that consumers tune into, channel surfing, avoiding commercial breaks, and recordings for later viewing, using digital video recorders that cable companies increasingly offer to subscribers. So far, cable companies have been reluctant to monitor consumers' viewing closely due to privacy concerns. However, some companies are exploring methods that will transform data from digital cable boxes into information that can be used for precise targeting of consumers while still protecting their privacy.[2]

Consumer Panels

For decades, marketers have purchased information from secondary data providers who collected consumer behavior data from household or family **consumer panels**. The members of these panels were paid for recording their purchases and media viewing habits in diaries. The diaries' data were then combined with additional information about households collected by, say, the U.S. Census. Marketers and advertising agencies paid the panel providers a subscription fee for their findings. Often the information not only told marketers about the families, purchases of the marketers' products, but also included the same information about competitors' brands.

Today, online technology enables panel research companies to collect increasingly sophisticated data from respondents. For example, a manufacturer of customized snowboards discovered that 10,000 snowboarding fans used its site's discussion forum to chat about their hobbies and buying habits, and also to rate different designs of snowboards. The snowboard marketer then started selling the data it collected from this online panel to other marketers interested in targeting the young, mostly male, respondents who so enthusiastically revealed so much about themselves while discussing snowboards online. Similarly, automobile manufacturers purchase consumer behavior panel data about recent car purchases from independent panel companies. Again, information about a marketer's own brands and competitors' brands, as well as information about the demographic differences among households that purchase various brands, gives the data buyers' insights for creating an effective marketing campaigns.

Obtaining secondary data before engaging in primary research offers several advantages. First, secondary data may provide a solution to the research problem and eliminate the need for primary research altogether. Even if this is not the case, secondary data used in exploratory research may help to clarify and refine the objectives of the primary study and provide ideas about selecting research tools and the difficulties that may occur during the full-scale study.

Although secondary information can be obtained more cheaply and quickly than primary data, it has some limitations. First, information may be categorized in units that are different from those that the researcher seeks (e.g., clustering consumers into the 15–20 and 21–25 age groups is useless to a researcher interested in consumers 17–24 years old). Some secondary data may not be accurate because of errors in gathering or analyzing it, or because the data were collected in a biased fashion to support a particular point of view. Also, secondary data may be outdated.

Learning Objective

3 To understand qualitative and quantitative research methods.

Designing Primary Research

Figure 15.1 shows that after considering the collection of secondary research, the diagram splits into two paths, with the left-side route taking a path of qualitative research, and the right-side route taking a path of quantitative research. The split reflects the purpose of the research objectives. If the purpose is to get new ideas (e.g., for positioning or repositioning a product), a qualitative study is often undertaken; alternatively, if descriptive and quantitative information is sought, some form of a quantitative study should be undertaken. The merits of using the different measurement instruments of qualitative and quantitative research are described in the two following subsections.

Qualitative Research

Contemporary qualitative consumer research is the result of understanding that consumers are not rational decision makers who objectively evaluate the goods and services available to them and select those that give them the highest utility (satisfaction) at the lowest cost. Qualitative consumer researchers are also known as **motivational researchers**. The central tenet of their orientation was that consumers were not always consciously aware of why they made the decisions they did. Even when they were aware of their basic motivations, consumers were not always willing to reveal those reasons to others, or even to themselves.

The leader of the motivational research movement was the Viennese psychoanalyst Dr. Ernest Dichter, who, after arriving in New York in the late 1930s, began to apply qualitative Freudian psychoanalytic techniques to uncover the hidden or unconscious motivations of consumers.[3] By the late 1950s and early 1960s, this research orientation became quite popular, and focus groups and depth interviews were used by many advertising agencies and consumer products companies in order to better understand consumer needs and motivations. Today, focus groups and depth interviews are very well-established research tools that are regularly used not only to secure insights about consumers' underlying needs and motivations, but also to gain consumer input for new product development efforts (including the creation of new products and even future advertising messages).[4] Because sample sizes are necessarily often small, findings cannot be generalized to larger populations. Nevertheless, qualitative research contributes extensively to the initial identification and development of new promotional campaigns and new product development that can eventually be further refined through a variety of quantitative research methods.

In designing and implementing an appropriate research strategy for conducting a qualitative study, the researcher must consider the purpose of the study, the type of interviews that are likely to be most appropriate given the purpose of the research, and the types of data instruments most suitable for securing the information needed. Although the specific research methods used may differ in composition, most forms of qualitative research questioning have their roots in psychoanalytic and clinical aspects of psychology. Specifically, they feature open-ended and free-response types of questioning and use of visual materials to stimulate respondents to reveal their innermost thoughts and beliefs.

The key methods used in qualitative studies are depth interviews and/or focus group sessions.

Depth Interviews

A **depth interview**, also frequently referred to as a "one-on-one" interview, is a lengthy, nonstructured interview (often 20 to 60 minutes in duration) between a single respondent and a highly trained researcher (often the same person who moderates focus group sessions). Commonly, the interviewer's strategy is to minimize his or her own talking time and provide as much time as possible for the consumer being interviewed to express his or her thoughts and behaviors, and respond to specific verbal and visual materials (e.g., mock-up of a potential print ad campaign). The researcher also must establish an atmosphere that encourages the consumer respondent to relax and open up in order to provide valuable insights. In many cases, the researcher's role is to probe the respondent by encouraging the person to talk freely about the product category and/or brand under study.

Generally, a series of the depth interviews takes place in a professionally set up interviewing room. These rooms are designed to provide audio and video recording equipment, and a one-way mirror for clients to view the interview without disrupting it (the researcher tells the participants that they are being observed).

Depth interview studies provide marketers with valuable ideas about product design or redesign, as well as insights for positioning or repositioning products. As already suggested, as part of a depth interview research project, a variety of stimulus materials is developed to enhance the discussion between the researcher and the respondent. They may take the form of written concept statements (describing a new product idea), drawings, or photos of new products, actual product samples, or rough renditions or videotapes of print ads or TV commercials. The purpose of such "stimulus materials," is to assist the respondent in expressing his or her inner thoughts and to encourage a more precise or accurate response to what is being investigated. Over the course of a day of conducting depth interviews, a researcher is likely to be able to complete about five to eight hours of interviews, depending on the length of each interview. Examples of probing questions for depth interviews are listed in Figure 15.3.

Request for elaboration: "Tell me more about that." "Give me an example of. . . ."

Request for definition: "What do you mean by . . . ?" "What does the term _____ mean to you?"

Request for word associations: "What other word(s) do you link with _____?" "Give me some synonyms that also describe _____."

Request for clarification: "How does that differ from . . . ?" "In what circumstances do you . . . ?"

Request for comparison: "How is _____ similar to _____?" "Which costs more, X or Y?"

Request for classification: "Where does _____ fit?" "What else is in the category of _____?"

"Silent" probe: This is a non-verbal probe and is characterized by such actions as raised eyebrows or hand gestures such as moving the right hand in a rolling motion that signifies "Tell me more."

Source: Naomi R. Henderson, "The Power of Probing," Marketing Research (Winter 2007): 39.

FIGURE 15.3 Examples of Probing Questions for Focus Groups and Depth Interviews

Focus Groups

A "discussion group" or **focus group** often consists of 8 to 10 participants who meet with a moderator-researcher-analyst to "focus on" or "explore" a particular product or product category (or any other topic or subject of research interest). During a focus group session (often two hours in duration), participants are encouraged to discuss their reactions to product and service concepts, or new advertising or marketing communications campaigns.

Because a focus group generally takes about two hours to complete (sometimes they can last for three or more hours), a researcher can generally conduct two or three focus groups (with a total of about thirty respondents) in one day; in contrast, it might take that same researcher five or six days to conduct 30 individual depth interviews. Analysis of responses from both depth interviews and focus groups requires a great deal of skill on the part of the researcher. Like depth interviews, focus group sessions are invariably audiotaped and videotaped, to assist in the analysis and to provide the client with a record of the sessions. Like depth interviews, focus groups are usually held in specially designed conference rooms with one-way mirrors that enable marketers and advertising agency staff to observe the sessions without disrupting or inhibiting the respondents.

For focus groups (and also depth interviews), respondents are recruited on the basis of a carefully drawn consumer profile that is detailed in a form called a **screener questionnaire**. The purpose of the "screener" is to ensure that the appropriate individuals are invited to participate in the research study, and that those who are not in the target market are not invited. An appropriate respondent is often paid $100 or more for his or her participation in the research process. In organizing focus group sessions, sometimes users of the company's brands are clustered in one or more groups, and their responses are compared to those of nonusers interviewed in separate sessions. Figure 15.4 presents a screener questionnaire that was used to recruit participants for focus groups for a study that dealt with introducing a premium line of canned vegetable soups. The screener questionnaire is designed to identify target consumers to be invited to participate in either an all-male or all-female focus group session. Individuals who are "screened out" (called "terminated" in research terminology) are those who do not meet the specifications for participation.

Some marketers prefer focus groups because they feel that the dynamic interaction between participants that takes place in focus groups tends to yield a greater number of new ideas and insights than depth interviews. Also, timing is sometimes very critical. In such cases, again, focus groups might be selected because it generally takes less time to complete a series of focus groups than a project of individual depth interviews. Other marketers (and in particular advertising agency professionals) prefer individual or depth interviews because they believe that individually interviewed respondents are free of group pressures and are less likely to give socially acceptable (and not necessarily truthful) responses. Moreover, the single participant is more likely to remain attentive during the entire interview, and—because of the greater personal attention received—is more likely to reveal private thoughts.

FOOD PREFERENCE STUDY SCREENER

ASK TO SPEAK WITH A FEMALE OR MALE HOUSEHOLD MEMBER WHO IS BETWEEN 18 AND 35 YEARS OF AGE. WHEN THE CORRECT PERSON IS LOCATED INTRODUCE YOURSELF.

Hello, I'm ________, from ________. We are involved in a research project that is interested in knowing more about people's feeling and preferences with regard to food products. I want to assure you that this is research and not a "sales pitch." May I ask you a few questions?

1. CHECK ONE:
   Female .... [ ]-POTENTIAL FOR GROUP 1
   Male .... [ ]-POTENTIAL FOR GROUP 2

RECRUITER: Q1. RECRUIT 12 FEMALES AND 12 MALES.

2. In which of the following age groups are you? (READ CHOICES)
   Under 18 years of age .... [ ]-TERMINATE
   18 to 24 years of age .... [ ]
   25 to 29 years of age .... [ ]
   30 to 35 years of age .... [ ]
   Over 35 years of age .... [ ]-TERMINATE

RECRUITER: Q2. SECURE A GOOD MIX ACROSS THE AGE SPAN INDICATED.

3. Do you or anyone else in your household work for any of the following types of businesses? (READ CHOICES)

	No	Yes
A market research firm or agency	[ ]	[ ]-TERMINATE
An advertising or public relations firm or agency	[ ]	[ ]-TERMINATE
A company that sells, manufactures, or distributes any type of food products	[ ]	[ ]-TERMINATE

4. a. Have you ever participated in a depth interview, focus group, or discussion group?
   Yes .... [ ]-ASK Q4b.
   No .... [ ]-SKIP TO Q5.
   b. When was the last time you participated in a depth interview, focus group, or discussion group?
   Within the past 6 months .... [ ]-TERMINATE
   More than 6 months ago .... [ ]-CONTINUE

5. For classification purposes, please tell me how much formal education you have completed. (DO NOT READ CHOICES)
   Less than a college graduate .... [ ]-TERMINATE
   At least a college graduate .... [ ]

RECRUITER: Q5 ALL RESPONDENTS ARE TO BE COLLEGE GRADUATES.

6. Also, for classification purposes, please tell me into which of the following categories your total family's or personal income falls. (READ CHOICES)
   Under $25,000 .... [ ]-TERMINATE
   $25,000 to $49,999 .... [ ]
   $50,000 or more .... [ ]

RECRUITER: Q6 ALL PARTICIPANTS MUST HAVE INCOMES OF AT LEAST $25,000.

7. Which of the following food products have you eaten within the past 5 days? READ FULL LIST.

	Yes	No
Frozen pizzas	[ ]	[ ]
Prepackaged cold cuts	[ ]	[ ]
Pre-sliced packaged cheeses	[ ]	[ ]
Canned soup	[ ]	[ ]
Potato chips	[ ]	[ ]
Canned fruit	[ ]	[ ]
Peanut butter	[ ]	[ ]
Frozen vegetables	[ ]	[ ]

RECRUITER: Q7. RESPONDENT MUST SAY "YES" TO *CANNED SOUP*; OTHERWISE TERMINATE.

FIGURE 15.4 Screener Questionnaire for Recruiting Respondents for a Consumer Study

8. **FOR SOUP AND ANY ONE OTHER FOOD ITEMS ANSWERED "YES" ("EATEN") IN Q7, ASK:**
   a. During the course of one week how often do you eat_____?
      Number of time_____
   b. During the course of one week how often do you have soup_____?
      Number of time_____

RECRUITER: Q8b. MUST SAY "AT LEAST TWO TIMES," OTHERWISE TERMINATE.

9. Now, I would like you to use your imagination. If you could serve dinner to a famous person from the past, who would it be? What would you serve for dinner?

RECRUITER: Q9 IS AN ARTICULATION QUESTION. THE RESPONDENTS SHOULD SHOW "CREATIVITY/GOOD IMAGINATION," AND BE ABLE TO ADD TO THE GROUP DISCUSSION.

10. As part of our current research we are conducting a discussion with 8 to 10 individuals. The discussion is called a "focus group." During the interview, you will have an opportunity to express your views and interact with the other participants on a variety of lifestyle and food consumption topics.

    The focus group will last for a full **2 hours.** You will receive $100.00 to help defray the cost of your time and travel.

    We would like to invite you to participate in the focus group session. It should prove to be an interesting and enjoyable session. The focus group will be held at (NAME OF FACILITY), which is located at (GIVE ADDRESS). It will take place on (DATE) at (GIVE CHOICE OF TIME). Can we count on having you attend?

    Yes .... [ ]-RECORD PARTICIPANT INFORMATION. REPEAT DAY, DATE, TIME, AND GIVE DIRECTIONS TO LOCATION.

    No .... [ ]-TERMINATE

THANK YOU FOR AGREEING TO PARTICIPATE, WE WILL CALL YOU THE DAY BEFORE THE RESEARCH TO REMIND YOU.

Record: A **female** participant, recruited for the 6:00 PM focus group _____
A **male** participant, recruited for the 8:00 PM focus group _____

FIGURE 15.4 (Continued)

Discussion Guides

A **discussion guide** is a step-by-step outline that sets out the line of questioning the researcher needs to cover with the respondent in a depth interview, or a group of respondents during a focus group session. Some moderator-researchers prefer to closely follow (question by question) the order set out in a discussion guide; other moderator-researchers "go with the flow" and allow the single respondent or focus group participants to go in the direction of what turns out to be particularly important to them. Surprisingly, a good researcher, following either the "question-by-question" or "go-with-the-flow" approach, will tend to finish with more information than was originally anticipated by the client. Indeed, it is common for qualitative research to produce strategically important insights that were not anticipated or even sought before the actual qualitative research was conducted. Such "extra" insights are a special benefit of both depth interviews and focus groups: namely, that they can provide extremely valuable and unanticipated information. Figure 15.5 shows a discussion guide created for a focus group used in a study of creating the new line of premium vegetable soups. Whereas the screener questionnaire was designed to recruit a sample of the target consumer participants for the focus group sessions on the proposed premium line of vegetable soups, the discussion guide was created to help the moderator lead the discussion and manage the flow of the key themes or "lines of questioning."

It is extremely rare for a moderator-researcher to conduct depth interviews or focus group sessions without the aid of a discussion guide. A discussion guide is a kind of "agenda" of topics and issues to be covered over the course of each depth interview or focus group session. However, qualitative research is much like jazz music: The expertise lies in the ability to improvise depending on the circumstance of the interview or the makeup of the group session.

Projective Techniques

When it comes to tapping into the underlying motives of individuals, **projective techniques** are a useful tool, borrowed from psychoanalytic theory and practice and adapted for studying the unconscious associations of consumers who may be concealing or suppressing some of their thoughts or reactions. Thus, projective exercises consist of a variety of disguised "tests" that contain

FOCUS GROUP:
CREATING A SUPERIOR LINE OF VEGETABLE SOUPS
Discussion Guide

I. INTRODUCTION

A. Introduce myself and my role
B. Tell participants about their roles
C. Identify session video-sound recording system and one-way mirror
D. Have each participant introduce him/herself—briefly talking about work, about household composition and interests/hobbies
E. Describe the "basic" purpose of the focus group discussion—TO CREATE A LINE OF SUPERIOR VEGETABLE SOUPS

II. SOUP BACKGROUND: *EARLIEST MEMORIES*

A. As you were growing up, what were your early memories of eating soup? Anything else?
B. In particular, what do you think of vegetable soup? In the "world of soup," where does "vegetable soup" fit in comparison to other soups? What do you think?
C. When you think of a "line of vegetable soups," what comes to mind? Are there six or more different vegetable soups?
D. Right now, what is your favorite vegetable soup?
E. Over the years, has your favorite vegetable soup been changing? In what ways?
F. How has your favorite vegetable changed from childhood to adulthood? Any other changes?
G. How would you characterize the difference between a really good restaurant vegetable soup, and a "homemade" vegetable soup? Which do you prefer? Why?

III. SOUP CONSUMPTION CIRCUMSTANCES

A. For you, is vegetable soup "a meal" or is it "a part of a meal"? Why is it this way for you?
B. What is the difference between vegetable soup as a "meal" and as "part of meal"? Anything else?
C. Is there such a person as a "soup person"? Describe such a person. Give me a profile of a "soup person." How do "soup people" tend to differ from non-soup people? Any other thoughts?

IV. SOUP SELECTION AND DECISION MAKING

A. In your household, how is the decision made as to which brand of soup is purchased and eaten? (Probe for various aspects of family choice and influence.)
B. Is there a single brand of soup that your family all agrees on? Which brand? Why?
C. How do you approach the selection of soup? Would you consider yourself to be: A specialist? An experimenter? A habitual purchaser?
D. What is your idea of a "soup connoisseur"? Describe such a person. Tell me more.
E. When it comes to food store soups, which is your favorite? Why?
F. In your mind's eye, what is a perfect vegetable soup?

V. SOUP TASTING EXERCISE
INTRODUCTION: "WE HAVE FIVE DIFFERENT VEGETABLE SOUPS FOR EACH OF YOU TO TRY, TONIGHT."

AFTER TRYING EACH ONE, I WANT YOU TO WRITE ON YOUR PADS YOUR THOUGHTS ABOUT THE PARTICULAR VEGETABLE SOUP.

A. What is your reaction to the ***first*** (repeat for each) vegetable soup that I gave you to try? Any other thoughts or feelings?
B. How would you describe it to a person who has not tasted it?
C. If this soup was available in a retail store, would you buy it? Why/Why not?
D. Any ideas as to how to make the soup taste even better?
E. **REPEAT FOR THE NEXT VEGETABLE SOUP, UNTIL EACH OF THE FIVE ARE SAMPLED.**
F. [**WRITE ON YOUR PAD**] Which of the five soups did you like the best? Which soup did you like the least? Again, write your answers down on your pad.
G. [**AROUND THE ROOM**] So, which one was the best?
H. Let's reflect on your reactions to the five soups.
I. [**WRITE ON YOUR PAD**] Considering the five vegetable soups, are there any other distinctive vegetables that need to be featured to make the overall selection better?

VI. ANY FINAL FEELINGS/THOUGHTS

A. Any final ideals or thoughts about the line of premium vegetable soups?
B. What would make it better? Anything else?
C. Where would you expect to purchase such a line of vegetable soups?

FIGURE 15.5 Focus Group Discussion Guide

TABLE 15.1 Projective Techniques

	DESCRIPTION	APPLICATIONS
Word Associations	The researcher has a list of words, some of them to be studied and some just as "filler." The researcher asks the respondent(s) to react, one-at-a-time, to each word by stating or (in a focus group setting) writing on a pad the first word that comes to mind, and to explain the link.	The word association exercise tends to be used when marketers seek to know what certain words (or a phrase) mean to consumers. The exercise is used to determine if a word or words have a sufficiently positive meaning or relevance to a product, or even a proposed product's name or description.
Sentence Completions	The researcher has a series of incomplete sentences that the respondent(s) needs to complete with a word or phrase.	The sentence completion exercise is an alternative to the word association exercise (it is used for the same purpose). In reality, it is easier to use and generally provides for more useable consumer insights than the word association exercise.
Photo/Visual for Storytelling	The researcher creates/selects a series of photos of consumers, different brands or products, range of print ads, etc., to serve as stimuli. The respondents are asked to discuss or tell a story based on their response to a photo or some other visual stimulus.	The product or consumer ideas secured from responding to the photos/visuals, in the form of "free association" or "storytelling" reveals how the participants feel about a topic, brands, or consumer within the context of the photos or other visual forms (e.g., cartoons). Ideas for new products or communication themes are possible outcomes.
Role-Playing	Is quite similar to storytelling; however, instead of telling a story, the participant(s) will be given a situation and asked to "act out" the role(s), often with regard to a product or brand, or particular selling situation.	Role-playing is appropriate in a focus group environment where different participants can be asked to role play and to act out different interacting roles.

ambiguous stimuli, such as incomplete sentences, untitled pictures or cartoons, word-association tests, and other-person characterizations. They are all designed to make it easier for consumers to express themselves and reveal their inner motivations. Projective techniques are sometimes administered as part of focus group research, but more often are used during depth interviews. Some of the most commonly used projective methods are featured in Table 15.1.

Online Focus Groups

Over the past 5 to 10 years, there has been a substantial amount of interest in, trial of, and acceptance of online focus groups and depth interviews. However, what is being called an "online focus group" can vary greatly. On the one hand, they can be very similar in nature and quality to a traditional focus group (i.e., sessions held in a local focus group facility, with moderator and participants interacting together). In such cases, they are often real focus group sessions that are "broadcasted" to individual client's laptops, or to a "sister" research facility in the client's hometown, and viewed by a gathering of clients. On the other hand, there is the option to select an online specialty research company, such as Harris Interactive, that provides focus group recruiting services from its very large panel of online consumers ready to participate. In addition, Harris Interactive has the capability of offering clients access to a "virtual version" of traditional focus groups. Specifically, it can provide a "virtual focus group room" environment: one where consumer participants and a moderator can log on to participate in an online focus group session. In certain ways, it can be similar to a regular offline focus group session.

The Scope of Quantitative Research

Marketers use quantitative research to understand the acceptance of various products or specific brands, as well as the impact of promotional messages on consumers. In other cases, the objectives are to assist marketers in pinpointing consumers' level of satisfaction with a product, service, distributor, or retailer, or possibly to attempt to identify areas in which the consumer has unmet needs, or even to attempt to better "predict" future consumer needs or behavior. The broad category of quantitative research includes experimentation, survey techniques, and observation. The findings are descriptive and empirical, and, if collected using appropriate sampling, can be generalized to larger populations. Because the data collected are quantitative, they lend themselves to sophisticated statistical analysis. Next, we consider three basic research designs: observational research, experimentation (in a laboratory or in the field, such as in a retail store), and surveys.

Observational Research

Watching or carefully observing consumers' actions of purchasing and consuming, especially in realistic surroundings (e.g., in stores, in malls, watching TV, and even in their home environments), is an extremely insightful way to learn what is valuable or meaningful to consumers. Indeed, **observational research** is an important research tool because marketers recognize that often the best way to gain an in-depth understanding of the relationship between people and products is by watching them in the process of buying and/or using the products.[5] Observing consumers in action enables researchers to comprehend what the product symbolizes to a consumer and provides greater insight into the bond between people and products that is the essence of brand loyalty. It is also important in uncovering issues or problems with a product. Many large corporations and advertising agencies use trained researchers/observers to watch, note, and sometimes videotape consumers in stores, malls, or even (with permission) in their own homes. For example, in studying responses to a new mint-flavored Listerine, the marketers hired a research firm that paid 37 New York City families to let it install cameras in their bathrooms to videotape mouthwash usage. The study found that consumers who used Scope gave the product a swish and spit it out. In contrast, users of the new Listerine kept the mouthwash in their mouths for much longer (one subject even held the mouthwash in his mouth as he left home and got into the car, and only spit it out after driving a couple of blocks).[6] Procter & Gamble (P&G) sent video crews to scores of households around the world, which enabled P&G executives in Cincinnati to watch a mother in Thailand feed her baby. They discovered that the mother was multitasking while feeding her baby and even glanced at her TV from time to time. Understanding such behavior can lead to the development of products and packages that will give P&G a strong competitive advantage in the marketplace.[7]

As an alternative to having trained observers view consumers, some firms prefer to use mechanical or electronic devices, such as counting or video-recording devices to capture customers' behaviors or responses to a particular marketing stimulus. For example, when Duane Reade—a large chain of drugstores in and around New York City—considers a location for a new store, the company uses electronic beams or hand counters to count the numbers of passersby at different times and under different weather conditions.[8] Government planners use data collected from electronic E-ZPass devices in passenger cars to decide which roads should be expanded, and banks use security cameras to observe problems customers may have in using ATMs.

Increasingly, consumers use automated systems in their purchases because these instruments make purchases easier and often provide rewards for using them. For example, consumers who use supermarket frequent shopper cards often receive special offers for promotional discounts tailored for them at checkout counters. Moviegoers who order tickets online can pick them up at ATM-like devices at movie theaters and avoid waiting in line at the box office. As consumers use more and more highly convenient technologies, such as credit and ATM cards, EZ-Passes, frequent shopper cards, cellular phones, and most of all online shopping, there are more and more electronic records of their consumption patterns. Consequently, observation of consumer behavior via electronic means has grown significantly and, as illustrated in the earlier discussion of portable people meters and two-way digital cable boxes, electronic observation of consumption behavior will become increasingly sophisticated.

Gambling casinos have been in the forefront of developing systems that track individual customer data collected during the various stages of a customer's visit, and cross-matching them with data collected during previous visits by that customer (including spending usage). They use this data to classify visitors into categories based on their "loyalty levels," and implement corresponding rewards that are delivered almost immediately. For example, normally about 50,000 people a day visit the Foxwoods Resort Casino in Connecticut. Most of them use magnetic cards called "frequent player cards." Sophisticated electronic network systems monitor the gaming patterns, eating habits, and room preferences of all visitors. Within seconds of a player taking a seat at a table, the casino's manager can read the guest's history on the screen, including alcoholic beverages preferred and gaming habits. Because there are electronic tags in the chips issued to each player, when a player leaves the table, his or her record is updated instantly and made available at any contact point for that customer throughout the entire casino complex. Thus, the casino can instantly reward customers who are good for business by giving free meals and room upgrades and inviting them to gamble in designated VIP lounges. The customers love the frequent player cards because the cards enable them to keep track of their spending, and the casinos benefit from each swipe of the card because it provides more information about each customer. The casino has two identical computer systems and, if needed, can switch to a backup immediately and thus avoid the loss of many thousands of dollars incurred during an even brief period of operating without computers.[9] More casinos are employing increasingly sophisticated software to create real-time and personal rewards to day-trippers who bet relatively small amounts of money—$50 to $100 per visit—but visit the casinos frequently. Casinos have recognized that although these consumers wager little money per trip, they view gaming as their primary entertainment, and observing their behavior and immediately using the data to encourage them to spend more money is likely to increase profits greatly over time.[10]

Another form of mechanical observation that entails monitoring the sales of products. A key component of Walmart's competitive advantage is the retailing giant's use of technology in its product audits. At any given moment, the company knows what is selling, how fast, and how much of the product remains in its inventory. Maintaining small inventories and moving products quickly enable the company to lower its prices and attract more customers. Walmart's record profits are derived from low per-item profits multiplied by selling billions of products quickly, and also moving products rapidly to where consumers are likely to buy them. For example, after observing that the sales of strawberry Pop-Tarts increased dramatically before a hurricane and that the top preseller before a hurricane was beer, the company quickly transports large quantities of these items to the locations a storm is set to hit.[11]

Marketers also use **physiological observation** devices that monitor respondents' patterns of information processing. For example, an electronic eye camera may be used to monitor the eye movements of subjects looking at a series of advertisements for various products, and electronic sensors placed on the subjects' heads can monitor their brain activity and attentiveness levels involved in viewing each advertisement. Neuroscientists monitoring cognitive functions in 12 different regions of the brain while consumers watched commercials for different products claimed that the data collected show the respondents' levels of attention and the decoding and recall of the promotional messages.[12]

Experimentation

Experiments (causal research) identify cause-and-effect relationships among factors. For instance, it is possible to test the relative sales appeal of many types of variables, such as package designs, alternative price points, or different promotional offers, by experiments designed to identify cause and effect. In the simplest form of such experiments, only one variable is manipulated (called the *independent variable*), while all other elements are kept constant. A **controlled experiment** ensures that any difference in the outcome (the *dependent variable*, which is most often sales) is due to different treatments of the variable under study and not to extraneous factors. For example, one study tested the effectiveness of using an attractive versus unattractive endorser in promoting two types of products: products that are used to enhance one's attractiveness (e.g., a men's cologne) and products that are not (e.g., a pen). The endorser used was a fictitious character named Phil Johnson who was described as a member of the U.S. Olympic water polo team. The photograph depicting the attractive endorser was a scanned image of an attractive athletic man, whereas the picture depicting the unattractive endorser was the same image graphically modified to reduce attractiveness. The subjects viewed each endorser-product combination for 15 seconds (simulating the viewing of an actual print ad) and then filled out a questionnaire that measured their attitudes and purchase intentions toward the products advertised. In this study, the combinations of the product (i.e., used/not used to enhance one's attractiveness) and the endorser's attractiveness (i.e., attractive or not attractive endorser) were the "manipulated treatments" (i.e., the independent variables), and the combination of the attitudes and purchase intentions toward the product was the dependent variable. The study discovered that the attractive endorser was more effective in promoting both types of products.[13]

A major application of causal research is **test marketing**. Sometimes, even after conducting depth interviews, focus groups, and survey research, the marketing firm realizes that it still needs to secure additional real-world feedback for a new product, service, or marketing communications program that it is considering, before it commits itself to a full-scale marketing rollout. In such situations, test marketing is a logical next step. Test marketing typically includes the selection of a representative single market area and then the conduct of a market introduction (only in that market) to test actual consumer response to the marketing effort under actual marketing conditions. From the test-marketing effort, the marketing firm hopes to be able to project how the entire market may respond to its marketing effort, without the full risks associated with skipping a test-marketing stage. Still further, some research firms carry out small-scale experiments that test consumer responses to alternative marketing strategies. This can be done prior to selecting a new product, redesigning a package, changing the price of a product, or trying out a new marketing campaign—all of these are marketing actions that can benefit from small-scale experimentation that manipulates variables in a controlled setting in order to predict sales or gauge the possible responses to the product.

Unlike a test market, which is usually in the real world, many experiments are conducted in a lab environment. Today some researchers employ "virtual reality methods." For example, in a market test, respondents can view, on a computer screen, supermarket shelves that are stocked with many products, including different versions of the same product; they can "pick up" an item by touching the image, examine it by rotating the image with a track ball, and place it in a shopping cart if they decide to buy it. The researchers observe how long the respondents spend in looking at the product, the time spent in examining each side of the package, the products purchased, and the order of the purchases. In general terms, it is quite important for marketers to continuously experiment and test-market their products and services.[14]

Survey Research

If researchers wish to ask consumers about their purchase preferences and consumption experiences, they can do so in person, by mail, by telephone, or online. Each of these survey methods has certain advantages and certain disadvantages that the researcher must weigh when selecting the method of contact.

TABLE 15.2 The Advantages and Disadvantages of Mail, Telephone, Personal Interview, and Online Surveys

	MAIL	TELEPHONE	PERSONAL INTERVIEW	ONLINE
Cost	Low	Moderate	High	Low
Speed	Slow	Immediate	Slow	Fast
Response Rate	Low	Moderate	High	Self-selected
Geographic Flexibility	Excellent	Good	Difficult	Excellent
Interviewer Bias	N/A	Moderate	Problematic	N/A
Interviewer Supervision	N/A	Easy	Difficult	N/A

Personal interview surveys (that are face-to-face) most often take place in a public space or a retail shopping area, such as within the public area of a mall, or a rented space within an office located in a mall. The latter, referred to as "mall intercepts," are used more frequently, as a replacement for the in-home interviews that used to be commonplace, because of the high incidence of not-at-home working women and the reluctance of many people today to allow a stranger into their homes.

Telephone interview surveys are also used to collect consumer data; however, evenings and weekends are often the only times to reach telephone respondents, who tend to be less responsive—if not actively hostile—to calls that interrupt dinner, television viewing, or general relaxation. Other problems arise, however, from the increased use of answering machines, telephone company voice-mail systems, and caller ID to screen calls. Some market research companies have tried to automate telephone surveys, but many respondents are even less willing to interact with an electronic voice than with a live interviewer. Table 15.2 compares the survey contact methods.

Mail surveys are conducted by sending questionnaires directly to individuals at their homes. One of the major problems of mail questionnaires is a low response rate, but researchers have developed a number of techniques to increase returns, such as enclosing a stamped, self-addressed envelope, using a provocative questionnaire, and sending notifications in advance as well as follow-up letters. Also, to deal with the ongoing problems of low response rates to unsolicited mail surveys, some consumer marketing companies are establishing their own ongoing consumer panels and periodically mail or email a questionnaire to consumer panel participants to fill out. As a motivation to complete the task, and ensure a satisfactory response rate, it is commonplace to pay respondents a prearranged participation fee for each round of completed surveys. Sometimes panel members are also asked to keep diaries of their purchases.[15]

Email surveys are an increasingly popular alternative to using the postal service as a means of distributing questionnaires to target consumers. One of the key attractions of using email is that it is as easy and quick to distribute a survey around the world as it is to distribute it down the block. Moreover, with an accurate list of email addresses, it is very inexpensive to distribute even a large number of questionnaires. We can expect that as the world increasingly turns to the Web for many types of social communications, we will see continued growth of emailing as a way to distribute surveys.[16]

Furthermore, there has been a rapid increase in the number of consumers who are interested in participating in **Internet surveys**. Potential respondents are directed to the marketer's (or researcher company's) website by online ads or targeted email invitations. Often, responses to online surveys are from consumer respondents who are self-selected, and therefore the results cannot be projected to the larger population. Most computer polls ask respondents to complete a profile consisting of demographic questions that enable the researchers to classify the responses to the substantive product or service questions.

Quantitative Research Data Collection Instruments

Data collection instruments are developed as part of a study's total research design to systematize the collection of data and to ensure that all respondents are asked the same questions in the same order. Data collection instruments include questionnaires, personal inventories, and attitude scales. These instruments are usually pretested and "debugged" to assure the validity and reliability of the research study. A study is said to have **validity** if it does, in fact, collect appropriate data needed to answer the questions or objectives stated in the first (objectives) stage of the research process. A study is said to have **reliability** if the same questions, asked of a similar sample, produce the same findings. Often a sample is systematically divided in two, and each half is given the same questionnaire to complete. If the results from each half are similar, the questionnaire is said to be reliable.

Questionnaires

For quantitative research, the primary data collection instrument is the questionnaire, which can be sent through the mail or online to selected respondents for self-administration or can be administered by field interviewers in person or by telephone. To motivate respondents to take the time to respond to surveys, researchers have found that questionnaires must be interesting, objective, unambiguous, easy to complete, and generally not burdensome. To enhance the analysis and facilitate the classification of responses into meaningful categories, questionnaires include both substantive questions that are relevant to the purposes of the study and pertinent demographic questions. Questionnaires consist of two types of questions:

1. **Open-ended questions** require answers in the respondent's own words (e.g., essay type questions).
2. **Closed-ended questions** require respondents to check the appropriate answer from a list of options (e.g., multiple-choice and true or false questions).

Open-ended questions yield more insightful information but are more difficult to code and to analyze; closed-ended questions are relatively simple to tabulate and analyze, but the answers are limited to the alternative responses provided (i.e., to the existing insights of the questionnaire designer).

Wording of the questions represents the biggest challenge in constructing questionnaires; Table 15.3 includes guidelines for writing clear and effective questions. The sequence of questions is also important: The opening questions must be interesting enough to "draw" the respondent into participating; the questions must proceed in a logical order; and demographic (classification) questions should be placed at the end, where they are more likely to be answered. The format of the questionnaire and the wording and sequence of the questions affect the validity of the responses and, in the case of mail questionnaires, the number (rate) of responses received.

There are many types of questionnaires that are commonly used in carrying out consumer research studies. In the real world of consumer research, one form of consumer survey is a **magazine readership survey**, like the one for *EARTH* (a fictitious magazine) that is presented in Figure 15.6. Such surveys are conducted to provide the publisher, editors, and circulation directors with reader feedback, as well as to provide the marketing and sales staff with information that would enable them to create a more convincing marketing package for selling adverting pages to potential advertisers and their advertising agencies. In particular, a standard use of the data secured from magazine readership surveys is preparation of a profile of a publication's readers so that potential advertisers can determine whether the publication delivers the audience that is most likely to respond positively to their advertising.

Attitude Scales

Researchers often present respondents with a list of products or product attributes, toward which they are asked to indicate their relative feelings or evaluations. The instruments most frequently used to capture this evaluative data are called **attitude scales**. The most frequently used attitude scales are Likert scales, semantic differential scales, behavior intention scales, and rank-order scales.

TABLE 15.3 Guidelines for Wording Questions

1. *Avoid leading questions.* For example, questions such as "Do you often shop at such cost-saving stores as Staples?" or "Weren't you satisfied with the service you received at Staples today?" introduce bias into the survey.
2. *Avoid two questions in one.* For example, "In your view, did you save money and receive good service when you last visited Staples?" is really two questions combined; they should be stated separately.
3. *Questions must be clear.* For example, "Where do you usually shop for your home office supplies?" is unclear because the term usually is vague.
4. *Use words that consumers routinely use.* For example, do not use the verb to rectify; use the verb to correct.
5. *Ensure that respondents are able to answer the question.* For example, it is unlikely that any respondent can accurately answer a question such as "How many newspaper or TV ads for Staples did you read or see during the past month?"
6. *Make sure that respondents are willing to answer the question.* Questions about money, health issues, personal hygiene, or sexual preferences can embarrass respondents and cause them not to answer. Sometimes asking the question in a less personal fashion can help generate more responses. For example, rather than asking older consumers whether they experience incontinence, the researcher should ask, "Millions of Americans experience some level of incontinence. Do you or anyone you know experience this difficulty?"

EARTH Magazine: IPSOS MENDELSOHN READERSHIP SURVEY

ABOUT YOU AND *EARTH MAGAZINE*

1. Where did you purchase this issue of *EARTH Magazine?*
   Local newsstand . . . . ☐1
   Airport terminal newsstand . . . . ☐2
   Bookstore (e.g., Borders, Barnes & Noble) . . . . ☐3
   Other . . . . ☐4

2. Why did you buy this issue of *EARTH Magazine? (Please 'X' all that apply.)*
   Intrigued by headlines on cover wrap . . . . ☐1
   Attracted by the cover art . . . . ☐2
   Curious about a specific article . . . . ☐3

   Heard about issue through:
   Word-of-mouth . . . . ☐4
   Print medium . . . . ☐5
   Broadcast medium . . . . ☐6
   Internet . . . . ☐7

   For a regular feature:
   Index . . . . ☐1
   Notebook . . . . ☐2
   Readings . . . . ☐3
   Puzzle . . . . ☐4
   Findings . . . . ☐5
   Annotation . . . . ☐6
   Reviews . . . . ☐7
   Forum . . . . ☐8

   For a regular feature (Cont'd):
   Photo essay . . . . ☐1
   Fiction . . . . ☐2
   Political reporting . . . . ☐3
   Overseas reporting . . . . ☐4
   Narrative non-fiction . . . . ☐5
   Personal essays . . . . ☐6

3. How many issues of *EARTH Magazine* did you buy on the newsstand/bookstore in the last 12 months?
   1 issue . . . . ☐1
   2–3 issues . . . . ☐2
   4–5 issues . . . . ☐3
   6–7 issues . . . . ☐4
   8–9 issues . . . . ☐5
   10–11 issues . . . . ☐6
   12 issues . . . . ☐7
   None . . . . ☐8

4. How long have you been a reader of *EARTH Magazine?*
   Less than 6 months . . . . ☐1
   7–12 months . . . . ☐2
   1 to under 2 years . . . . ☐3
   2 years or more . . . . ☐4

5. How many of the last 4 issues of *EARTH Magazine* have you read or looked into?
   4 out of the last 4 . . . . ☐1
   3 out of the last 4 . . . . ☐2
   2 out of the last 4 . . . . ☐3
   1 out of the last 4 . . . . ☐4
   None out of the last 4 . . . . ☐5

6. On average, how much time do you spend reading or looking into a typical issue of *EARTH Magazine?*
   Less than 1 hour . . . . ☐1
   1 hour to less than 2 hours . . . . ☐2
   2 hours to less than 3 hours . . . . ☐3
   3 hours to less than 4 hours . . . . ☐4
   4 hours or more . . . . ☐5

7. Have you ever made a purchase as a result of advertising you saw in *EARTH Magazine?*
   Yes . . . . ☐1
   No . . . . ☐2

8. How do you rate *EARTH Magazine* overall compared to other publications you read?
   One of my favorites . . . . ☐1
   Very good . . . . ☐2
   Good . . . . ☐3
   Average . . . . ☐4
   Poor . . . . ☐5

EARTH MAGAZINE WEBSITE

1. Have you visited the *EARTH Magazine*website in the past 12 months?
   Yes . . . . ☐1
   No . . . . ☐2 *Please go to Question 4*

2. How often do you visit the *EARTH Magazine* website?
   Once a month . . . . ☐1
   Less than once a week . . . . ☐2
   Once a week . . . . ☐3
   2–3 times a week . . . . ☐4
   4–5 times a week . . . . ☐5
   More than 5 times a week . . . . ☐6

3. On average, how much time do you spend on the *EARTH Magazine* website per visit?
   Less than 5 minutes . . . . ☐1
   5–9 minutes . . . . ☐2
   10–19 minutes . . . . ☐3
   20–29 minutes . . . . ☐4
   30–59 minutes . . . . ☐5
   One hour or more . . . . ☐6

4. Would you be willing to pay for archived issues of *EARTH Magazine* going back to 1950 if they were available on the *EARTH Magazine* website?
   Yes . . . . ☐1
   No . . . . ☐2 *Please go to "About You" section below*

5. *(If yes)* How much would you be willing to pay per year for archived issues of *EARTH Magazine?*
   \$1–\$9 . . . . ☐1
   \$10–\$19 . . . . ☐2
   \$20–\$29 . . . . ☐3
   \$30–\$39 . . . . ☐4
   \$40–\$49 . . . . ☐5
   \$50 or more . . . . ☐6

FIGURE 15.6 Magazine Readership Survey

Source: EARTH Magazine Readership Survey (New York, Ipsos Mendelsohn, 2008).

ABOUT YOU

1. Are you: a man ....☐1 a woman ....☐2
2. Please 'X' your age group.
   Under 21 ....☐1 35 to 44 ....☐3 55 to 64..........................☐5
   21 to 34 ....☐2 45 to 54 ....☐4 65 or older.........................☐6
3. Are you . . .
   Married........................☐1 Single ....☐3 Separated..........................☐5
   Partnered ....☐2 Widowed ....☐4 Divorced ....☐6
4. Please 'X' the highest level of education you have attained.
   Some high school or less ....☐1 Some college ....☐3 Postgraduate study ....☐5
   High school graduate ....☐2 College degree ....☐4 Postgraduate degree ....☐6
5. Please indicate your employment status.
   Employed full time (35 hrs or more per week) ....☐1 Not currently employed ....☐3 Please skip to Question 6
   Employed part time (less than 35 hrs per week) ....☐2 Retired ....☐4
   What is your job title, position, or rank?
   (Please be specific: e.g., partner, CEO, president, vice president, etc.) ______________
   What do you do for a living? (Please be specific: e.g., accountant, bookkeeper, lawyer, architect, etc.) ______________
6. What was your total estimated household income, before taxes, for last year? (Please include income for all household members and from all sources, including salaries or wages, profits, capital gains, rentals, social security, etc.)
   Less than $50,000 ....☐1 $500,000 to $749,999 ......☐1 $2,500,000 to $2,999,999............☐1
   $50,000 to $99,999 ....☐2 $750,000 to $999,999 ....☐2 $3,000,000 to $3,999,999............☐2
   $100,000 to $199,999 ....☐3 $1,000,000 to $1,499,999 ....☐3 $4,000,000 to $4,999,999............☐3
   $200,000 to $299,999 ....☐4 $1,500,000 to $1,999,999 ....☐4 $5,000,000 or more..................☐4
   $300,000 to $499,999 ....☐5 $2,000,000 to $2,499,999 ....☐5

Please join us! The *EARTH Magazine* **Reader Advisory Panel** is an exclusive panel made up of *EARTH Magazine* readers. Through future surveys, your perspective on consumer trends — from tech innovations, culture, and travel — will have a direct impact on what you see and read in the pages of *EARTH Magazine.* If you would like to join our Reader Advisory Panel, please print your e-mail address below:

Your e-mail address:______________________@______________________

THANK YOU VERY MUCH

Please mail the completed survey in the reply envelope *(no postage necessary).*

FIGURE 15.6 *(Continued)*

The **Likert scale** is the most popular form of attitude scale because it is easy for researchers to prepare and to interpret, and simple for consumers to answer. They check or write the number corresponding to their level of "agreement" or "disagreement" with a series of statements, each referring to the object under investigation. The scale consists of an equal number of agreement/disagreement choices on either side of a neutral choice. A principal benefit of the Likert scale is that it gives the researcher the option of considering the responses to each statement separately or of combining the responses to produce an overall score.

The **semantic differential scale**, like the Likert scale, is relatively easy to construct and administer. The scale typically consists of a series of bipolar adjectives (such as "good/bad," "hot/cold," "like/dislike," or "expensive/inexpensive") anchored at the ends of an odd-numbered (e.g., five- or seven-point) continuum. Respondents are asked to evaluate a concept (or a product or company) on the basis of each attribute by checking the point on the continuum that best reflects their feelings or beliefs. Care must be taken to vary the location of positive and negative terms from the left side of the continuum to the right side to avoid consumer response bias. Sometimes an even-numbered scale is used to eliminate the option of a neutral answer. An important feature of the semantic differential scale is that it can be used to develop graphic consumer profiles of the concept under study. Semantic differential profiles are also used to compare consumer perceptions of competitive products and to indicate areas for product improvement when perceptions of the existing product are measured against perceptions of the "ideal" product.

The **behavior intention scale** measures the likelihood that consumers will act in a certain way in the future, such as buying the product again or recommending it to a friend. These scales are easy to construct, and consumers are asked to make subjective judgments regarding their future behavior.

With **rank-order scales**, subjects are asked to rank items such as products (or retail stores or websites) in order of preference in terms of some criterion, such as overall quality or value for the money. Rank-order scaling procedures provide important competitive information and enable marketers to identify areas where improvement is needed in product design and product positioning. Figure 15.7 provides examples of the attitude scales described.

LIKERT SCALE

Next to each of the following statements, please record the number that best describes the extent to which you agree or disagree with each statement.

1. Strongly Agree	2. Somewhat Agree	3. Neither Agree nor Disagree	4. Somewhat Disagree	5. Strongly Disagree

______ It's fun to shop online.
______ I am afraid to give my credit card number online.

CUSTOMER SATISFACTION GUIDE

Overall, how satisfied are you with Bank X's online banking? ______

1. Very Satisfied	2. Somewhat Satisfied	3. Neither Satisfied nor Dissatisfied	4. Somewhat Dissatisfie d	5. Very Dissatisfie d

IMPORTANCE SCALE

The following list of features is associated with shopping on the Internet. Next to each feature, please record the number that best expresses how important or unimportant that feature is to you.

1. Extremely Important	2. Somewhat Important	3. Neither Important nor Unimportant	4. Somewhat Unimportant	5. Not at all Important

______ Speed of downloading the order form
______ Being able to register with the site

SEMANTIC DIFFERENTIAL SCALE

For each of the following features, please check one alternative that best expresses your impression of how that feature applies to online banking:

Competitive rates |—|—|—|—|—|—|—| Noncompetitive rates
Reliable |—|—|—|—|—|—|—| Unreliable

Note: The same semantic differential scale can be applied to two competitive offerings, such as online banking and regular banking, and a graphic representation of the profiles of the two alternatives, along with the bipolar adjectives included in the scale, can be easily constructed.

BEHAVIOR INTENTION SCALES

How likely are you to continue using Bank X's online banking for the next six months? ______

1. Definitely Will Continue	2. Probably Will Continue	3. Might or Might Not Continue	4. Probably Will Not Continue	5. Definitely Will Not Continue

How likely are you to recommend Bank X's online banking to a friend? ______

1. Definitely Will Recommend	2. Probably Will Recommend	3. Might or Might Not Recommend	4. Probably Will Not Recommend	5. Definitely Will Not Recommend

RANK-ORDER SCALE

We would like to find out about your preferences regarding banking methods. Please rank the following banking methods by placing a "1" in front of the method that you prefer most, a "2" next to your second preference, and continuing until you have ranked all of the methods.

______ Inside the bank ______ Online banking ______ Banking by telephone
______ ATM ______ Banking by mail

FIGURE 15.7 Attitude Scales

Customer Satisfaction Measurement

Gauging the level of customer satisfaction and its determinants is critical for every company. Marketers can use such data to retain customers, sell more products and services, improve the quality and value of their offerings, and operate more effectively and efficiently. **Customer satisfaction measurement** includes quantitative and qualitative measures, as well as a variety of contact methods with customers.

Customer satisfaction surveys measure how satisfied the customers are with relevant attributes of the product or service, and the relative importance of these attributes (using an importance scale). Generally, these surveys use five-point semantic differential scales, ranging from "very dissatisfied" to "very satisfied." Research shows that customers who indicate they are "very satisfied" (typically a score of 5 on the satisfaction scale) are much more profitable and loyal than customers who indicate that they are "satisfied" (a score of 4). Therefore, companies that merely strive to have "satisfied" customers are making a crucial error.[17] Some marketers maintain that customers' satisfaction or dissatisfaction is a function of the difference between what they had *expected* to get from the product or service purchased and their perceptions of what they *received*. A group of researchers developed a scale that measures the performance of the service received against two expectation levels: *adequate* service and *desired* service, and also measures the customers' future intentions regarding purchase of the service.[18] This approach is more sophisticated than standard customer satisfaction surveys and more likely to yield results that can be used to develop corrective measures for products and services that fall short of customers' expectations.

Mystery shoppers are professional observers who pose as customers and interact with and provide unbiased evaluations of the company's service personnel in order to identify opportunities for improving productivity and efficiency. For example, one bank used mystery shoppers who, while dealing with a bank employee on another matter, dropped hints about buying a house or seeking to borrow college funds. Employees were scored on how quickly and effectively they provided information about the bank's pertinent products or services. A company that requires sales clerks to check youthful customers' IDs when they seek to buy video games with violent content may employ mystery shoppers to see whether their employees are actually doing so.

Analyzing customer complaints is crucial for improving products and customer service. Research indicates that only a few unsatisfied customers actually complain. Most unsatisfied customers say nothing but switch to competitors. A good **complaint analysis** system should encourage customers to:

1. Complain about an unsatisfactory product or service.
2. Provide suggestions for improvements by completing forms asking specific questions beyond the routine "how was everything?"
3. Establish "listening posts" such as hotlines where specially designated employees either listen to customers' comments or actively solicit input from them (e.g., in a hotel lobby or on checkout lines).

Because each complaint, by itself, provides little information, the company must have a system in which complaints are categorized and analyzed so that the results may be used to improve its operations.

Analyzing customer defections consists of finding out why customers leave the company. Customer loyalty rates are important because it is generally much cheaper to retain customers than to get new ones. Therefore, finding out why customers defect, and intervening when customers' behaviors show that they may be considering leaving, is crucial. For example, one bank that was losing about 20% of its customers every year compared 500 transaction records of loyal customers with 500 transaction records of defectors, using such dimensions as number of transactions, frequency of transactions, and fluctuations in average balances. The bank then identified transaction patterns that tended to indicate future defection and started targeting potential defectors and encouraging them to stay.[19]

Sampling and Data Collection

Because it is almost always impossible to obtain information from *every* member of the population or universe being studied, researchers use samples. A **sample** is a subset of the population that is used to estimate the characteristics of the entire population. Therefore, the sample must be representative of the universe under study. As the well-established Nielsen Media Research company recently found out, suspicions that a sample may not be representative of its universe endanger the credibility of all the data collected, and therefore must be addressed promptly. Although Nielsen's TV ratings have been used to estimate TV audiences and calculate advertising rates for many decades, its clients recently charged that the Nielsen sample was no longer representative of the U.S. population, because it did not reflect accurately America's changing demographics and the large numbers of consumers who use devices such as TiVo to "time shift" and to avoid commercials during both live and recorded programs. In response to these criticisms, Nielsen redesigned its sample to include significantly more ethnic groupings and to reflect the changes in TV viewing habits.[20]

TABLE 15.4 Types of Samples

PROBABILITY SAMPLE	
Simple Random Sample	Every member of the population has a known and equal chance of being selected.
Systematic Random Sample	A member of the population is selected at random and then every *n*th person is selected.
Stratified Random Sample	The population is divided into mutually exclusive groups (such as age groups), and random samples are drawn from each group.
Cluster (Area) Sample	The population is divided into mutually exclusive groups (such as blocks), and the researcher draws a sample of the groups to interview.
NONPROBABILITY SAMPLE	
Convenience Sample	The researcher selects the most accessible population members from whom to obtain information (e.g., students in a classroom).
Judgment Sample	The researcher uses his or her judgment to select population members who are good sources of accurate information (e.g., experts in the relevant field of study).
Quota Sample	The researcher interviews a prescribed number of people in each of several categories (e.g., 50 men and 50 women).

An integral component of a research design is the **sampling plan**. Specifically, the sampling plan addresses three questions: whom to survey (the sampling unit), how many to survey (the sample size), and how to select them (the sampling procedure). Deciding whom to survey requires explicit definition of the universe or boundaries of the market from which data are sought, so that an appropriate sample can be selected (such as working mothers). The size of the sample is dependent on both the size of the budget and the degree of confidence that the marketer wants to place in the findings. The larger the sample, the more likely the responses will reflect the total universe under study. It is interesting to note, however, that a small sample can often provide highly reliable findings, depending on the sampling procedure adopted.

There are two types of samples. In a **probability sample**, respondents are selected in such a way that every member of the population studied has a known, nonzero chance of being selected. In a **nonprobability sample**, the population under study has been predetermined in a nonrandom fashion on the basis of the researcher's judgment or decision to select a given number of respondents from a particular group. Table 15.4 summarizes the features of various types of probability and nonprobability designs.

Data Collection

The step following sample selection is data collection. As indicated earlier, qualitative studies usually require highly trained social scientists to collect data. A quantitative study generally uses a field staff that is either recruited and trained directly by the researcher or contracted from a company that specializes in conducting field interviews. Completed questionnaires are reviewed on a regular basis as the research study progresses to ensure that the recorded responses are clear, complete, and legible.

Learning Objective

4 To understand how to combine qualitative and quantitative research.

Combining Qualitative and Quantitative Research

Researchers adapt the research processes to the special needs of the study. For example, if a researcher is told that the purpose of the study is to develop a segmentation strategy for a new online dating service, he or she would first collect secondary data, such as population statistics (e.g., the number of men and women online in selected metropolitan areas within a certain age range, their marital status, and occupations). Then, together with the marketing manager, the researcher would specify the parameters (i.e., define the sampling unit) of the population to be studied (e.g., single, college-educated men and women between the ages of 18 and 45 who live or work within the Boston metropolitan area). A qualitative study (e.g., focus groups) might be undertaken first to gather information about the target population's attitudes and concerns about meeting people online, their special interests, and the specific services and precautions they would like an online dating service to provide. This phase of the research should result in tentative generalizations about the specific age group(s) to target and the services to offer.

The marketing manager then might instruct the researcher to conduct a quantitative study to confirm and attach "hard" numbers (percentages) to the findings that emerged from the focus groups. The first-phase study should have provided sufficient insights to develop a research design and to launch directly into a large-scale survey. If, however, there is still doubt about any element of the research design, such as question wording or format, the marketing manager and the researcher might decide first to do a small-scale exploratory study. Then, after refining the questionnaire and any other needed elements of the research design, they would launch a full-scale quantitative survey, using a probability sample that would allow them to project the findings to the total population of singles (as originally defined). The analysis should cluster prospective consumers of the online dating service into segments based on relevant sociocultural or lifestyle characteristics and on media habits, attitudes, perceptions, and geodemographic characteristics.

Marketers frequently conduct research projects that include qualitative and a quantitative components. For example, they use qualitative research findings to discover new ideas and develop promotional strategies, and quantitative research findings to estimate the extent or amount of consumers who react in a particular way (i.e., positive or negative) to various promotional inputs. Frequently, ideas stemming from qualitative research are tested empirically through quantitative studies. The predictions made possible by quantitative research and the understanding provided by qualitative research together produce a richer and more robust profile of consumer behavior than either research approach used alone.

In reality, many consumer research studies carry out—concurrently or in sequence—a series of interrelated qualitative and quantitative studies, or move back and forth between one or more rounds of qualitative research and one or more rounds of quantitative research. In the many studies that the lead author of this book conducted for AT&T, it was quite common for him to undertake a number of focus groups or depth interview research studies that were followed by a quantitative stage using a very large internal consumer database, or the services of survey research companies that specialized in mail or telephone questionnaire surveys. The main point to keep in mind is that among marketing-oriented firms, consumer research is not commonly composed of a single study, but rather consists of a series of studies, often composed of a mix of qualitative research (most commonly focus groups and/or depth interviews) and quantitative research (most commonly some form of survey research, consumer panel data, or possibly an experiment). Commonly, the insights secured from a particular round of research are evaluated to determine whether more research is required, and if so, what should be the purpose and type of additional research. The combined findings enable marketers to design more meaningful and effective marketing strategies. Table 15.5 compares the quantitative and qualitative research designs.

TABLE 15.5 A Comparison of the Elements of Quantitative and Qualitative Research Designs

	QUALITATIVE RESEARCH	QUANTITATIVE RESEARCH (QUAN)
Study purpose	Studies are designed to provide insights about new product ideas and identify positioning strategies aimed at a target market. Ideas uncovered should be tested via quantitative studies. QUAL studies are also often used to refine the objectives and wording of QUAN studies.	QUAN studies are aimed at describing a target market—its characteristics and possible reactions of various segments to the elements of the marketing mix. Results are used for making strategic marketing decisions.
Types of questions and data collection methods	Open-ended, unstructured questions, stressing probing by the moderator or highly skilled interviewer. QUAL research also uses projective techniques, including disguised questions and response to pictures or prototypes.	QUAN research often consists of closed-ended questions with predefined response choices and limited numbers of open-ended questions that have to be coded.
Main methods	Focus groups and depth interviews.	Survey questionnaires, including attitude scales and questions that are not disguised. QUAN questioning often consists of surveys that are self-administered, or conducted in person, by phone or mail, or online. Observation of consumers, experimentation, and consumer panels are other QUAN data collection methods.

(Continued)

TABLE 15.5 (Continued)

	QUALITATIVE RESEARCH	QUANTITATIVE RESEARCH (QUAN)
Sampling methods	Small, nonprobability samples; findings are generally not representative of the universe under study.	Large probability samples. If the data collection instruments are valid and reliable, the results can be viewed as representative of the universe.
Data analysis	Data consist of transcripts or tapes of the verbal responses. The analysis is performed by skilled behavioral science researchers. Researchers seek to identify reoccurring "themes" of responses coming from participants.	After data are collected, they are coded and entered in the database. The researcher analyzes the data, using a variety of statistical methods of analysis, and estimates the extent to which the results represent the universe.

Learning Objective

5 To understand how to analyze data and report research findings

Data Analysis and Reporting Research Findings

In qualitative research, the moderator-researcher usually analyzes the responses received. In quantitative research, the researcher supervises the analysis: Open-ended responses are first coded and quantified (i.e., converted into numerical scores); then all the responses are tabulated and analyzed using sophisticated analytical programs that correlate the data by selected variables and cluster the data by selected demographic characteristics.

In both qualitative and quantitative research, the research report includes a brief executive summary of the findings and recommendations for marketing action. The body of the report includes a full description of the methodology used and, for quantitative research, also includes tables and graphics to support the findings.

Himalaya Face Wash: Brand Associations and Lifestyles

Dr. S. Ramesh Kumar and Eric Minj wrote this case solely to provide material for class discussion. The authors do not intend to illustrate either effective or ineffective handling of a managerial situation. The authors may have disguised certain names and other identifying information to protect confidentiality.

India was one of the emerging markets that had witnessed a radical change in the lifestyles of consumers in the last decade. About 60% of the country's population was below the age of 35, and youth comprised a significant proportion of the population. Professional personal grooming and the use of branded personal care products had become almost an everyday requirement for the urban population. The face wash category was one that had attracted several brands, which consumers were trying out both for their benefits as well as for the experience. The Himalaya Drug Company (Himalaya), which had the Himalaya brand of face wash, was interested in obtaining insights into how the lifestyle of consumers was associated with the use of this category. Several brands had positioned themselves according to various attributes and benefits. Himalaya wanted to understand the impact of values and lifestyles both on the category and on the brands in this category. They made use of a consumer survey — which was conducted in July and August 2011 — that investigated the lifestyle of consumers and connected it to various brands through the concept of laddering. Were the attributes and benefits of the brands associated with the lifestyles of the consumers? How were values related to brand association? Himalaya hoped to obtain insights through these questions that were part of a case study by Professor Ramesh Kumar, who was interested in connecting concepts with practice and who looked forward to exploring various aspects of consumer behaviour and brand associations.

INTRODUCTION

The Indian population had experienced a radical shift with regard to lifestyle changes and consumer preferences over the last two decades. Significantly, brand associations and marketing communication had played an important role in shaping the culture of consumers as they were offered more choices for consumption.[21] One of the important motivational factors for consumers was to let their values guide them in several facets of life.[22] Consumer behaviour and preferences made up one of the important facets through which consumers bought, consumed and developed attachments to brands.[23] Thus, brand associations were linked to the values of consumers.[24]

The face wash category had recently drawn in several brands. The target segment was youth in the age group of 18 to 25 years. Given the newness of the category and its potential in a market such as India where about 60% of the population was below the age of 35,[25] Himalaya was interested in understanding the psyche of consumers by analyzing their values. A value in this context referred to a preferred mode of existence as compared to other modes from which a consumer could choose. Aspiration through professional success, orientation towards the future, choosing symbols as a mode of expression and having a fun-filled life were some of the values that could be associated with the face wash category as well as with several other personal care categories that had been advertised in India for the last five decades or so.

METHODOLOGY

The purpose of the case study was to help Himalaya expand the existing user base for its face wash brand by using insights from the examination of brand associations and lifestyles. An extensive literature review was carried out to understand how to narrow down the values relevant to the category from the study of psychographics (that is, looking at activities, interests and opinions).

For the purpose of the study, a sample of 53 female respondents (within the age group of 22 to 30 years) was chosen. The data was collected in July and August 2011 in the city of Bangalore through questionnaires that were personally administered. The sample of female respondents in this particular age group was chosen because of the similarities in the target segments for the three face wash brands (EverYuth, Clean & Clear and Himalaya) that were considered for this study. Their profile was inferred by studying the relevant advertisements of these brands. A description of the brands' advertisements is provided in Exhibit 1.

The authors wanted to use a research methodology that involved the study of the lifestyles of consumers to assess their values, instead of using the concept of laddering[26] (which does not involve the lifestyles of consumers extensively). The authors felt that a detailed understanding of lifestyles could be obtained, and that such details would be useful in the analysis.

The objective of the methodology was to convert the lifestyle statements into values. After the ads of the three brands were analyzed for the values they reflected,[27] 72 lifestyle statements were constructed. The association of these lifestyle statements with values was also tested, initially with five respondents. The lifestyle statements were constructed around 24 values that were identified as being relevant to the target profile of face wash users.

The responses from the 53 respondents who used a face wash (Clean & Clear, Himalaya or EverYuth; (see Exhibit 2) were used to establish the relevance of a set of values for face wash users, taking into consideration the lifestyle indicators reflected in the survey. The challenge for Himalaya was to convert these lifestyle statements into values.

The authors arrived at the attributes and important aspects associated with the face wash category based on their analysis of the three brands and their own perception of the benefits that a face wash should offer. The category-level attributes and benefits were important as the brands needed to take them into consideration regardless of the theme they might have for their marketing communication.

POPULAR FACE WASH BRANDS

Clean & Clear

The Clean & Clear face wash brand from Johnson & Johnson was positioned as a teenage girl's "skin's best friend" and as ideal for all skin types.[28] The product was available in three variants: the Daily Care range for regular facial cleansing and for removing oil, dirt, and other pollutants; the Oil Control range for maintaining oil balance and for refreshing the skin; and the Acne Clearing range for pimple control. Clean & Clear's proposition was to derive confidence by means of a clean and clear skin.[29] The face wash also contained antibacterial ingredients. The advertisements for the brand focused on teenage girls as well as middle-aged women and highlighted the need to look trendy and cool. The advertisements showed several activities associated with the lifestyle of teenagers.[30] The product's proposition was a solution for maintaining the oil balance of the skin and for controlling pimples.[31]

EverYuth

EverYuth's Naturals brand of face wash was positioned as an anytime solution for refreshing face cleansing.[32] This face wash was advertised as providing purity, freshness and beauty.[33] It was available in four variants, which were advertised as being made from natural fruit extracts. The Lemon face wash, the Neem variant, the Cream variant and the Fruit face wash covered a wide range of skin care benefits. The advertisements for the brand communicated its proposition as a time-saving solution that offered instant beauty.[34] The commercials created the favourable associations of satisfaction, appreciation and confidence that were enjoyed by the user because of the instant beauty offered and highlighted the ingredients of the product.[35]

Himalaya Herbal

Himalaya's face wash ranges were positioned as natural and herbal products that were soap free.[36] Its ads made use of the idea of a friend as a "problem solver" to convey positive emotions about the brand and to provide assurances about the effectiveness of using it.[37] The Neem face wash was positioned as the solution for common skin problems and offered hassle-free and convenient skin care.[38] The advertisements also depicted men appreciating and admiring the user's beauty (implicitly suggesting that the user would appear attractive to the opposite sex).[38]

Exhibit 2 provides data on the lifestyle of the target segment, and Exhibit 3 the benefits of the face wash category. Exhibit 4 shows an advertisement for the Himalaya face wash brand that reflects its herbal proposition of oil-free skin.

The Challenge for Himalaya

Himalaya's challenge was to link the various aspects of the advertisements, the consumer values derived from the lifestyle data and the category attributes and benefits in order to enhance its brand associations, taking into consideration its competitors (EverYuth and Clean & Clear).

The authors would like to thank Antaash Sheikh, manager, marketing communication, Himalaya Drug Company, and Professor Dinesh Kumar, chairperson, research and publications, Indian Institute of Management, Bangalore, for all the support provided

EXHIBIT 1 Description of the Advertisements of the Three Face Wash Brands

Himalaya Face Wash

Central Character	A teenage girl or a middle-aged woman who is attractive, fashionable, and socially active; is focused on her career or education; and is concerned about the way she looks.
Setting	Problem-solving approach.
Influencer	Friend, narrator.
Analysis of Ads (Television)	The ad centers on urban girls who are particular about their looks. The ad for Himalaya Oil Balancing Face Wash associates excessive facial oil with stickiness and depicts this as an issue causing inconvenience and social rejection. The product is recommended by a friend who describes the benefits of its herbal ingredients, which guarantee an oil-free face leading to soft facial skin. The association of social acceptance of the user's looks after using the brand is also conveyed.
Inferred Consumer Segment	Targeted at women between the ages of 16 to 25 who have oily skin or skin-related problems and are concerned about their looks.
Inferred Benefit Segment	Himalaya's Oil Balancing Face Wash claims to reduce excess facial oil and to keep the skin soft, providing confidence; the Neem Face Wash claims to help in removing acne and in keeping the skin clear.
Tri Components	Affective components such as the feel-good factor, self-acceptance, embarrassment, panic and confusion can be observed in the ad. The cognitive components in the ad relate to the description of the ingredients and beliefs about their benefits.
Motivation Function	The ad focuses on the importance of self-image and the benefits of the products. (Ego: Defensive and Utilitarian)

(*Continued*)

EXHIBIT 1 (Continued)

Clean & Clear Face Wash

Central Character	A teenage girl who is attractive, fashionable and socially active; is concerned about the way she looks; is open to trying out the latest products and trends in fashion; and is independent in nature.
Setting	Problem-solving approach.
Influencer	Friend, narrator.
Analysis of Ad (Television)	The ad focuses on urban girls who face the problem of oily facial skin. The product promises to keep the skin oil free for eight hours. The characters are young, attractive and trendy females who are keen on keeping themselves abreast with changes in fashion. They seek social praise by being well groomed. The ads also portray the concern, nervousness and lack of confidence among women due to skin problems. They show that care should be given so that the hectic lifestyle of the consumers does not cause oily skin and pimple problems. The helpful nature associated with the friend who recommends the brand to the main character creates an emotional appeal.
Inferred Consumer Segment	Targeted at women between the ages of 16 to 25 who have oily skin or face skin-related problems and who want to maintain a good appearance despite their busy schedules.
Inferred Benefit Segment	Clean & Clear Deep Action Cleanser claims to reduce excess facial oil, keeping the skin oil free for the next eight hours and providing confidence. Clean & Clear Foaming Face Wash claims to help in removing acne and in keeping facial skin oil free.
Tri Components	Affective components such as the feel-good factor, self-image, concern, nervousness, individualism and confusion can be observed in the advertisement. Cognitive components consist of the price, the ingredients and the benefits related to the product's usage.
Motivation Function	The ad focuses on the importance for the target segment to boost their self-image through the benefits of the brand. (Ego: Defensive and Utilitarian, Value Expressive)

Everyuth Face Wash

Central Character	Young women who are conscious about their looks and concerned about their health, who are involved in a lot of social activities and who want to have an identity of their own.
Setting	Problem-solving approach.
Influencer	Narrator.
Analysis of Ad (Television)	The advertisement shows urban women who have a busy lifestyle. The ad depicts the anxiety women face when they need to get prepared for a social interaction. The brand is positioned as the quickest solution for refreshed, clean, fair and soft skin. The ad also shows the opposite sex appreciating the user's beauty, thus highlighting the enhanced self-image resulting from the use of the brand. The ad also highlights the natural ingredients of the product and their benefits.
Inferred Consumer Segment	Targeted at women between the ages of 19 to 30 who have a busy lifestyle.
Inferred Benefit Segment	Refreshed and soft skin after using the brand and its quick application.
Tri Components	Affective components such as the feel-good factor, individualistic feeling and confidence are observed in the advertisement. Cognitive components include the natural ingredients and the benefits related to the product's use.
Motivation Function	The ad focuses on the importance of boosting the user's self-image and the benefits of the product. (Ego: Defensive and Utilitarian, Value Expressive)

Source: Authors' analysis of the advertisements of the three brands.

EXHIBIT 2 Lifestyle statements — Activities (A), Interests (I) and Opinions (O) of the Targeted Consumers for the Face Wash Category

AIO	STATEMENTS	MEAN
A	I get upset when I don't see the products that I want in a store.	2.87
I	I like to read the stories of people who I aspire to be like.	3.38
O	People like to travel to a lot of places for sightseeing and for memorable experiences.	4.04
A	I feel confident after I choose and use my brand of personal care products.	3.75
I	I like to watch movies that are intelligent and have female protagonists.	3.75
O	I take pride in performing even the smallest activities.	3.7
A	I only eat at certain restaurants.	2.77
I	I like to have maids do the cooking all the time.	2.26
O	Certain kinds of brands show that you are not elegant and classy.	3.15
A	I particularly enjoy shopping or visiting malls/retail stores.	3.81
I	I spend more time shopping for goods I fancy than for goods that I need.	3.36
O	Shopping is more a source of entertainment for me than a necessity.	3.09
A	I go out in the evening for drinks and entertainment.	3.64
I	I like to party on weekends or whenever I get time.	3.57
O	Malls/pubs/discotheques are the places to hang out for enjoyment and fun.	3.34
A	I often take advice from my parents about what I should buy.	2.68
I	I respect all traditions and often try to conform to them.	3.74
O	Traditions are contemporary and relevant in the present day.	3.68
A	I do purchase products out of emotional attachment.	3.49
I	Purchasing my favourite brand makes me happy.	3.89
O	I have a sort of emotional bonding with the product I use.	3.55
A	I find clothes made of khadi (homespun cloth) comfortable to wear.	3.32
I	Ayurvedic products appeal to me.	3.13
O	I love my country.	4.28
A	I purchase a lot of personal grooming products.	3.38
I	I prefer going to a beauty salon than shopping for beauty and grooming products.	3.28
O	I tend to form opinions about people who are poorly or too casually dressed.	2.72
A	I generally buy brands that reflect my uniqueness.	3.47
I	I like to be stand out from the crowd at times.	3.72
O	It's important that people respect one's individuality.	4.09
A	I often buy personal care product with friends.	2.94
I	I prefer to watch TV alone rather than to watch a movie with a group of friends.	2.34
O	Talking over the telephone is better than meeting people for communication.	2.38
A	I love to cook for my friends and family.	3.34
I	I feel upset when my friends don't call me to go shopping with them.	2.79

(Continued)

EXHIBIT 2 (Continued)

AIO	STATEMENTS	MEAN
O	Shops should have seating arrangements to accommodate family and friends while one is shopping.	3.57
A	I usually eat out for fun after shopping.	3.96
I	I find searching for remedies for beauty-related problems satisfying.	3.36
O	Finding the right product for me and/or for others gives me a sense of achievement.	3.55
A	I often advise my friends/colleagues/relatives about the products they should buy.	3.23
I	I like to tell my friends/colleagues/ relatives what would be right for them.	3.28
O	I take initiatives at work/college that showcase my talents.	3.58
A	I often try new brands before my friends/colleagues do.	2.85
I	I like to try a new product to see what it has to offer.	2.89
O	There are always better products available.	3.58
A	Sometimes, I buy cosmetics/beauty care products that were not on my shopping list.	3.62
I	I buy products simply because I liked the advertisements.	2.51
O	Free offers and promotions cannot sell products that are very rarely useful.	3.38
A	I only buy products that are popular/common with my friends/colleagues.	2.64
I	I like to be in touch with all the people I know through social networking.	3.28
O	Using similar brands strengthens my bonds with others.	2.7
A	I purchase brands/products that suit my personality and not what others are buying.	3.64
I	I think my lifestyle is an actual reflection of my personality.	3.53
O	My image is based on the things that I own.	2.91
A	I enjoy bargaining while shopping.	3.13
I	Price promotions in shops often attract me.	3.51
O	Low cost personal care products may be of good quality.	2.41
A	I use only tried and tested products.	3.49
I	I like to use my credit/debit card for purchase through the Internet.	3.47
O	I feel that only a few products are genuinely useful.	3.49
A	I enjoy joy rides and roller coaster rides.	3.47
I	I do not visit the cinema without finalizing what movie I should watch.	3.13
O	I do not like surprises.	2.17
A	I only shop for brands that have celebrity endorsements.	1.96
I	I like to read fashion magazines and other articles that inform me about the latest trends.	3
O	I trust the products that celebrities use.	2.32
A	I don't mind smoking at social gatherings.	2.02
I	I like to be up-to-date with the latest trends.	3.32
O	I am often influenced by some of the latest trends.	3.11
A	I often buy foreign brands.	3.25
I	I like to party regularly.	2.85
O	I think social drinking is acceptable and, at times, necessary.	2.98

Source: The data was obtained from the consumer survey conducted by the authors at Bangalore in July—August 2011.

EXHIBIT 3 List of Attributes and Benefits of the Brands in the Face Wash Category

ATTRIBUTES/IMPORTANT ASPECTS	CATEGORY BENEFITS
Many variants	Groomed looks
Moisturizer/pH neutral	Refreshed looks
Natural/herbal ingredients	Beauty maintenance
Antibacterial/germ protection	Complexion enhancement
Value for money	Feeling of being benefited
Unique/special component	Spotless beauty
Certification	Security of the offering

Source: The attributes/important aspects at the category level were obtained from the authors' analysis of the brands in the category.

EXHIBIT 4 An Advertisement for the Himalaya Brand of Face Wash

Source: The Himalaya Drug Company (reproduced with permission from the Himalaya Drug Company).

Note: Instructors teaching *Consumer Behavior* in institutions can have access to the solution note subject to verification of their professional affiliation.

Summary

Learning Objective 1: To understand how to develop research objectives

The first and most difficult step in the consumer research process is to accurately define the objectives of the research. Is it to segment the market for electronic readers? Is it to examine consumer attitudes about the experience of online shopping? What percentage of households shop for food online? Whatever the key research question, it is important for the marketing manager and the research manager to agree at the outset as to the specific purposes and objectives of the proposed consumer study. A clearly written statement of research objectives ensures that the information needed is indeed collected and costly errors are avoided.

Learning Objective 2: To understand how to collect secondary data

Secondary data is existing information that was originally gathered for a research purpose other than the present research. The rationale for secondary data searches is simply that it makes good sense to investigate whether currently available information will answer—in part or even in full—the research question at hand. It seems unwise to expend the effort and money, and rush into collecting new information before determining if there is any available information that would provide at least a good starting point.

The first source of secondary data is previously collected in-house information that was originally used for some other purpose. It might have originally been gathered as part of a sales audit, or from past customer service calls, or letters of inquiry from customers, or collected via warranty cards.

The second source of secondary data is information from sources outside of the firm or organization. They take many different forms. Some are free and can be found in a public library, other information is available for only a nominal fee, and still other data or information are quite expensive to secure. The major sources of external secondary data are: the government, articles from popular, professional, and academic publications, and syndicated commercial sources.

Learning Objective 3: To understand qualitative and quantitative research methods

If the purpose of a study is to come up with new ideas for products or promotional themes, the researchers use qualitative research. Qualitative studies consist of focus groups, depth interviews, and projective techniques.

If the purpose of the study is to find out how many consumers match the demographics or psychographics of the target market, or the characteristics of consumers who buy given brands and whether or not they are brand loyal, marketers conduct quantitative research. Quantitative research includes observation, experiments, and surveys.

Learning Objective 4: To understand how to combine qualitative and quantitative research

Marketers frequently conduct research projects that combine both a qualitative component (often composed of focus groups and/or depth interviews) and a quantitative component (often consisting of a survey research). For example, they use qualitative research findings to discover new ideas and develop promotional strategies, and quantitative research findings to estimate the extent or amount of consumers who react in a particular way (i.e., positive or negative) to various promotional inputs. Frequently, ideas stemming from qualitative research are tested empirically through quantitative studies. The predictions made possible by quantitative research and the understanding provided by qualitative research together produce a richer and more robust profile of consumer behavior than either research approach used alone.

Learning Objective 5: To understand how to analyze data and report research findings

In qualitative research, the moderator-researcher usually analyzes the responses received. In quantitative research, the responses are coded and analyzed statistically.

In both qualitative and quantitative research, the research report includes an executive summary of the findings, description of the methodology used, and recommendations for marketing actions.

Review and Discussion Questions

15.1. Have you ever been selected as a respondent in a marketing research survey? If yes, how were you contacted and where were you interviewed? Why do you think you, in particular, were selected? Did you know or could you guess the purpose of the survey? Do you know the name of the company or brand involved in the survey?

15.2. What is the difference between primary and secondary research? Under what circumstances might the availability of secondary data make primary research unnecessary? What are some major sources of secondary data?

15.3. What are the advantages and limitations of secondary data?

15.4. A manufacturer of a new product for whitening teeth would like to investigate the effects of package design and label information on consumers' perceptions of the product and their intentions to buy it. Would you advise the manufacturer to use observational research, experimentation, or a survey? Explain your choice.

15.5. Why might a researcher prefer to use focus groups rather than depth interviews? When might depth interviews be preferable?

15.6. How would the interpretation of survey results change if the researcher used a probability sample rather than a nonprobability sample? Explain your answer.

15.7. Why is observation becoming a more important component of consumer research? Describe two new technologies that can be used to observe consumption behavior and explain why they are better to use than questioning consumers about the same behavior.

Hands-on Assignments

15.8. Neutrogena is a manufacturer of personal care products for young adults. The company would like to extend its facial cleansers product line. Design (1) a qualitative and (2) a quantitative research design for the company focused on this objective.

15.9. Based on the discussion of focus groups and depth interviews (including Figures 15.3 and 15.4), develop a discussion guide for studying college students' reactions to their brand and model of cell phone.

15.10. Using one of the attitude scales in Figure 15.7, construct an instrument to assess your fellow students' opinions regarding the technological support services provided by your university.

15.11. Using the scales in Figure 15.7, develop a questionnaire to measure students' attitudes toward the instructor in this course according to the following guidelines:

a. Prepare five statements measuring students' attitudes via a Likert scale.

b. Prepare five semantic differential scales measuring students' attitudes.

c. Can the same dimensions be measured by using either scaling technique? Explain your answer.

Key Terms

- attitude scales *432*
- behavior intention scale *434*
- closed-ended questions *432*
- cluster (area) sample *437*
- complaint analysis *436*
- consumer panels *422*
- consumer research *418*
- controlled experiment *430*
- convenience sample *437*
- customer lifetime value profiles *421*
- customer satisfaction measurement *436*
- customer satisfaction surveys *436*
- depth interview *423*
- discussion guide *426*
- email surveys *431*
- experiments (causal research) *430*
- exploratory study *419*
- focus group *424*
- Internet surveys *431*
- judgment sample *437*
- Likert scale *434*
- magazine readership survey *432*
- mail surveys *431*
- motivational researchers *423*
- mystery shoppers *436*
- nonprobability sample *437*
- observational research *429*
- open-ended questions *432*
- personal interview surveys *431*
- physiological observation *430*
- primary research *419*
- probability sample *437*
- projective techniques *426*
- qualitative research *419*
- quantitative research *419*
- quota sample *437*
- rank-order scales *435*
- reliability *431*
- sample *436*
- sampling plan *437*
- screener questionnaire *424*
- secondary data *421*
- semantic differential scale *434*
- simple random sample *437*
- stratified random sample *437*
- systematic random sample *437*
- telephone interview surveys *431*
- test marketing *430*
- validity *431*

Case Six: *Pima Air and Space Museum*

"The Great Paper Airplane Project"

Lead Agency: BBDO San Francisco
Contributing Agency: Hunter Public Relations

Strategic Challenges

Hidden in the vast Arizona desert near Tucson, the Pima Air and Space Museum showcases over 300 aircraft and 125,000 artifacts. The purpose of the museum is to showcase and explain aerospace history. In July 2011, more than 50% of the museum's visitors were over 60 years of age and passionate fans of aerospace history. The museum recognized that it had to attract a new generation in order to give the museum a robust future. Management knew that because of the nature of the content, they would naturally capture parents and their children.

Objectives

1. To put Pima "on the map." Pima is a world-class destination literally hidden in a desert. In order to increase attendance, the museum had to get media exposure beyond Tucson.
2. To shift audience demographics by attracting younger visitors. Ideally, young parents between 25 and 50 years old.

Insights

Interviews with moms of young kids revealed that many moms saw Pima not as a showcase of heroic feats, but rather a sad reminder of "over-militarization." Many of Pima's airplanes were icons of military history, but a lot of the items demonstrated that aviation originates in applied mathematics, physics, engineering, design, and environmental science.

Pima's greatest attraction is a Lockheed SR-71 "Blackbird." The plane is an advanced, long-range, Mach 31 strategic reconnaissance aircraft built in the 1960s. During reconnaissance missions, the SR-71 operated at high speeds and altitudes to allow it to outrace threats. If the pilot detected a surface-to-air missile, he accelerated and outflew it. The SR-71 served with the U.S. Air Force from 1964 to 1998. Thirty-two aircraft were built; 12 were lost in accidents, but none lost to enemy action.

The Big Idea

Pima wanted to create a new generation of aviation fans by giving them a hands-on lesson in designing, building and flying the world's largest paper airplane

Bringing the Idea to Life

The museum engaged local schools—teachers and their students—in a paper-airplane competition. It sent out invitations to 390 local teachers, along with a custom-built lesson plan that showed how to fold a paper airplane and how to teach lessons about airspeed, lift, and force. Two hundred local school kids participated in the competition and the winner's plane flew a distance of 90 feet.

Working with a team of experts, the winner's plane was transformed into the world's largest paper airplane. Then, the 45 foot long plane was hoisted by helicopter 3,000 feet over the Arizona desert, and released for its first—and only—flight. After a short free fall, the plane leveled off for a flight of almost (0.93) a mile at a top speed of 98 mph. Following a less than graceful landing, the world's largest paper airplane was then put on display for all to see in the museum, along with a documentary of the contest and building it.

Questions

1. What are the psychological, socio-cultural and communication factors that played a role in designing the paper airplane competition?

2. Discuss the issue that the museum was facing from a positioning standpoint.
3. The building and launch of the world's largest airplane was a one-time event. How can it be the basis for further and more extensive media exposure for the museum?
4. How would you measures whether or not the museum has achieved its objectives?
5. Assuming that the museum attracted new visitors, how can it retain them and make them visit repeatedly?

Source: Effie Worldwide, Effie Showcase Winners. Reprinted by permission. Pima Air and Space Museum is a 2013 Gold Effie Winner. For information on Effie's programs for students, visit the Collegiate Effies at www.effie.org

Endnotes

Chapter 1

1. American Marketing Association, 2007.
2. Davis Hounshell, *From the American System to Mass Production 1800–1932* (Baltimore/London: John Hopkins University Press, 1984), 224.
3. www.gm.com/company/corp_info/history
4. Harminder Sahni, "Disrupt, and Rule," *Business Standard*, May 27, 2013.
5. Ibid
6. A.G. Lafley, "Every Market Needs a Winning Strategy," Interview by Kamini Banga, *The Economic Times*, May 27, 2013.
7. Julie Jason, "New Ad Targets McDonald's," online.wsj.com, September 14, 2010.
8. Erica Phillips, "Music Fan Sites to Pay Privacy Fine," online.wsj.com, October 3, 2012.
9. David Streitfeld, "Google Is Faulted for Impeding U.S. Inquiry on Data Collection," nytimes.com, April 14, 2012.
10. Leslie Kaufman and Tanzina Vega, "Media Giants Chase Online Ads with Original Shows," nytimes.com, May 5, 2013.
11. http://www.msi.org/video/how-dell-is-using-social-media-to-deepen-relationships-,and-build-trust/ (accessed on Oct 23, 2013).
12. http://blogs.hbr.org/2013/10/research-the-emotions-that-make-marketing-campaigns-go-viral/ (accessed on Oct 25, 2013).
13. Preethi Chamikutty, "Sap Changing Its Stripes, asap," *The Economic Times*, April 6, 2012.
14. "Check in for rewards," *Business India*, April 15, 2012.
15. Sujit John, "Ads on the move," *The Times of India*, September 12, 2012.
16. Suzanne Vranica, "Ads Let Viewers Be Mad Men," online.wsj.com, February 2, 2013; Suzanne Vranica, "Tweets Spawn Ad Campaigns," online.wsj.com, October 21, 2012.
17. Suzanne Vranica, "MTV Aims for Multitasker," online.wsj.com, September 5, 2012.
18. Shephali Bhatt, "The Dark Horse Rides Online," *The Economic Times*, August 21, 2013
19. "Boiling over," *Business India*, August 19–September 1, 2013.
20. "Luxury Car Markers Go Online To Net in Buyers," *Financial Times*, August 19, 2012
21. Ibid
22. Nikolaus Franke, Peter Keinz, and Christoph J. Steger, "Testing the Value of Customization: When Do Customers Really Prefer Products Tailored to Their Preferences?" *Journal of Marketing*, Vol. 73 (September 2009): 103–121.
23. Ann Zimmerman and Elizabeth Holmes, "Target to Match Online Prices, Following Best Buy," online.wsj.com, October 16, 2012.
24. Stephanie Clifford," "Retailers Add Gadgets for Shoppers at Ease with Technology," nytimes.com, November 23, 2012.
25. Jessica Vascellaro and Shara Tibken, "Apple Jumps into Textbooks," online.wsj.com, January 20, 2012.
26. Ellen Byron, "In-Store Sales Begin at Home," online.wsj.com, April 25, 2011.
27. Greg Bensinger, "Amazon's New Secret Weapon: Delivery Lockers," online.wsj.com, August 7, 2012.
28. Robin Sidel, "Retailers Join Payment Chase," online.wsj.com, March 2, 2012.
29. Christine Haughney, "Guided by *Lucky* Magazine, Shopping Will Soon Require Less Clicking," nytimes.com, August 5, 2012.
30. Daniella Zalcman, "Online Ingredients for Success," online.wsj.com, May 24, 2011.
31. Stephanie Clifford, "Shopper Alert: Price May Drop for You Alone," nytimes.com, August 9, 2012.
32. Frederick F. Reichheld and W. Earl Sasser, Jr., "Zero Defections: Quality Comes to Services," *Harvard Business Review* (September–October 1990): 105–111; Michael Treacy and Fred Wiersema, "Customer Intimacy and Other Value Disciplines," *Harvard Business Review* (January–February 1993): 84–93.
33. Andrew Adam Newman, "Marketers Promoting a Granola Bar Hit the Trails in National Parks," nytimes.com, March 7, 2012.
34. R. B. Zajonc, "Attitudinal effects of mere exposure," *Journal of Personality and Social Psychology*, Vol. 9 (2, Pt.2) (June 1968): 1–27
35. Delshad Irani, "Insta Reach," *The Economic Times*, August 28, 2013.
36. Ibid

37. Ibid
38. Ibid
39. Ravi Balakrishnan, "SMS MOB to Win," *The Economic Times*, June 19, 2013.
40. Ibid
41. Beryl Menezes, "Google Counters Microsoft-Noika With Kitkat," *DNA*, September 5, 2013.
42. Suzanne Vranica, "Ads Let Viewers Be Mad Men," online.wsj.com, February 2, 2013; Suzanne Vranica, "Tweets Spawn Ad Campaigns," online.wsj.com, October 21, 2012.
43. Stephanie Clifford, "Social Media Are Giving a Voice to Taste Buds," nytimes.com, July 30, 2012.
44. David Benedy, "Seven Sins of Content Marketing," *The Economic Times*, March 28, 2012.
45. Ibid
46. Sarah Jacob and Rahul Sachitanand, "Stirred, Not Shaken," *The Economic Times*, March 28, 2012.
47. Amit Bapna, "The First Screen," *The Economic Times*, September 12, 2012.
48. "*Dove Real Beauty Sketches*," YouTube video, 3.00, posted by "Doveunitedstates." April 14, 2013, http://www.youtube.com/watch?v=XpaOjMXyJGk (accessed on September 5, 2013).
49. David Aaker, "A Beauty of a Brand Builder," *Marketing News*, Vol. 47 (August 8, 2013): 12
50. Rolph E. Anderson and Srinivasan Swaminathan, "Customer Satisfaction and Loyalty in E-Markets: A PLS Path Modeling Approach," *Journal of Marketing Theory & Practice,* Vol. 19 (2) (Spring 2011): 221–234.
51. C. M. Sashi, "Customer Engagement, Buyer-Seller Relationships, and Social Media," *Management Decision*, Vol. 50 (2) (2012): 253–272.
52. Based on Thomas O. Jones and W. Earl Sasser, Jr., "Why Satisfied Customers Defect," *Harvard Business Review*, (November–December 1995): 88–99.
53. Zeithami, Valerie A. et. al. "The Customer Pyramid: Creating and Serving Profitable Customers," *in California Management Review*, vol. 43, no. 4, Summer 2001. © 2001 by the Regents of the University of California. Published by the University of California Press.
54. Susanne Craig, "What Restaurants Know (About You)," nytimes.com, September 4, 2012.
55. Shalini Ramachandran, "Pay-TV Providers Get Picky about Their Customers," online.wsj.com, May 9, 2013.
56. Tillmann Wagner, Thorsten Hennig-Thurau, and Thomas Rudolph, "Does Customer Demotion Jeopardize Loyalty?" *Journal of Marketing*, Vol. 73 (May 2009): 69–85.
57. "Q&A: Paco Underhill, Author, Founder, Envirosell," '*Business Standard*, December 12, 2011.
58. Madusree Chatterjee, "Mills &Boon's Desi Romance with Indian Faces," *The Economic Times*, December 19, 2011.
59. Chitra Narayanan, "Parachuting into Innovation," *The Hindu Business Line*, March 29, 2012.
60. Kala Vijayaraghavan and Rahul Sachitanand, "The Fortune Just Above the Bottom," *The Economic Times*, March 6, 2012.
61. Narmata Singh, "FMCG Cos Clean growth rides on Middle India," *The Times of India*, December 26, 2011.
62. Raviteja Sharma, "Luxury Providers Woo Rich with Chic Shindigs," *The Economic Times*, September 12, 2012

Chapter 2

1. Information from the publications' websites (June 2012).
2. Mini Joseph Tejaswi, "We Use Tech To Know Customers Better", Interview with Ms Amrita Gangotra, *The Times of India*, October 5, 2010.
3. Based on selected data from MyBestSegments at claritas.com (May 2012).
4. Sreeradha D. Basu, Writankar Mukherjee and Lijee Philip, "Retail's Small Wonder," *The Economic Times*, September 20, 2010.
5. Bhupesh Bhandari, "Earning Its Credits," *Business Standard*, September 20, 2010.
6. Arindam Bhattacharjee, "A Brew for the Young," *Business Standard*, October 4, 2010.
7. Brian Stelter, "MTV Is Looking Beyond 'Jersey Shore' to Build a Wider Audience," nytimes.com, October 24, 2010; Tanzina Vega, "A Campaign to Introduce Keds to a New Generation," nytimes.com, February 22, 2011.
8. Michelle Kung, "Movie Studios Smell Out Teen Spirits," online.wsj.com, April 25, 2011.
9. Based on selected portions of a report issued by Pew Internet (accessed May 2012).
10. Stuart Elliott, "Vodka Brand Goes Edgy as It Reaches Out to Women," nytimes.com, August 9, 2010.
11. Stephanie Clifford, "Frito-Lay Tries to Enter the Minds (and Lunch Bags) of Women," nytimes.com, February 25, 2009.
12. Lauren A. E. Schuker, "VH1 Cultivates Its Female Side," online.wsj.com, April 17, 2011.
13. Elizabeth Holmes, "Dude, Pass the Exfoliator," online.wsj.com, April 26, 2012.
14. Anil Mathur, Lee Euehun, and George P. Moschis, "Life-Changing Events and Marketing Opportunities," *Journal of Targeting, Measurement & Analysis for Marketing,* Vol. 14 (2) (January 2006): 115–128.
15. Ellen Byron, "As Middle Class Shrinks, P&G Aims High and Low," online.wsj.com, September 12, 2011.
16. Stephanie Clifford, "Even Marked Up, Luxury Goods Fly Off Shelves," nytimes.com, August 3, 2011.

17. Tanzina Vega, "Marketers, and Media Companies, Set Their Sights on Latin Women," nytimes.com, December 8, 2011.
18. Stuart Elliott, "Pretty as (Census) Picture," nytimes.com, March 28, 2011.
19. Writankar Mukherjee and Sreeradha D. Basu, "Brands Now Tweak Products to Suit Regions, communities," *The Economic Times*, October 10, 2010.
20. Stowe Shoemaker and Dina Marie V. Zemke, "The 'Locals' Market: An Emerging Gaming Segment," *Journal of Gambling Studies,* Vol. 21 (4) (Winter 2005): 379–407.
21. Namrata Singh, "Unilever Picks India to Craft Brands for Life," *The Times of India*, February 9, 2013.
22. Times Network, "Low Cost Mobiles to Run on Android," *The Times of India*, October 19, 2010.
23. Steve Brooks, "The Green Consumers," *Restaurant Business* (September 2009): 20–22.
24. Tara McBride Mintz, "Profiling Green Consumers: A Descriptive Study," MBA Thesis, Appalachian State University, North Carolina, May 2011.
25. Colgate's website (May 2012).
26. Paul G. Patterson, "Demographic Correlates of Loyalty in a Service Context," *Journal of Services Marketing*, Vol. 21 (2) (2007): 112–125.
27. Carlos Flavian and Raquel Gurrea, "The Role of Readers' Motivations in the Choice of Digital versus Traditional Newspapers," *Journal of Targeting, Measurement & Analysis for Marketing,* Vol. 14 (4) (2006): 325–335.
28. Brian T. Ratchford, Debabrata Talukdar, and Myung-Soo Lee, "The Impact of the Internet on Consumers' Use of Information Sources for Automobiles: A Re-Inquiry," *Journal of Consumer Research*, Vol. 34 (June 2007): 111–119.
29. Gillian Sullivan Mort and Judy Drennan, "Marketing M-Services: Establishing a Usage Benefit Typology Related to Mobile User Characteristics," *Database Marketing & Consumer Strategy Management*, Vol. 12 (4) (2005): 327–341.
30. Muhammad Alijukhadar and Sylvain Senecal, "Segmenting the Online Consumer Market," *Marketing Intelligence & Planning*, Vol. 29 (4) (2011): 421–435.
31. Arunima Mishra, "Against All Odds," *Business Standard*, September 27, 2010.
32. Jaime R. S. Fonseca and Margarida G. M. S. Cardoso, "Supermarket Customers Segments Stability," *Journal of Targeting, Measurement and Analysis for Marketing,* Vol. 15 (4) (2007): 210–221.
33. Carmen Rodriguez Santos, Miguel Cervantes Blanco, and Ana Gonzalez Fernandez, "Segmenting Wine Consumers According to Their Involvement with Appellations of Origin," *Brand Management,* Vol. 13 (4/5) (April–June 2006): 300–312.
34. Stuart Elliott, "A Push to Promote Familiar Brands Online," nytimes.com, November 17, 2011.
35. Sayantani Kar, "Consumers Lead the way," *Business Standard*, January 10, 2011.
36. Dana Mattioli and Miguel Bustillo, "Can Texting Save Stores?" online.wsj.com, May 8, 2012.
37. Charles Duhigg, "How Companies Learn Your Secrets," nytimes.com, February 16, 2012.
38. Elizabeth Olson, "Marketing goes mobile," *Deccan Herald*, August 10, 2011.
39. Keller K.L, Stenthal B, and Tybout Alice, "Three Questions You Need to Ask about Your Brand" *Harvard Business Review*, 80 (September 2002): 80–89.
40. Helen Edwards, "Multiple Personality Order," *The Economic Times*, October 20, 2010.
41. Christina Passariello and Max Colchester, "L'Oreal Slogan Must Be Proved Anew," online.wsj.com, November 15, 2011.
42. Stuart Elliott, "Bounty Now Promises a Competent Clean," nytimes.com, June 28, 2010.
43. www.crest.com
44. Anjali Prayag, "Indulgence over 25 years," *The Hindu Business Line*, April 25, 2012.
45. Ibid
46. Louise Story, "Home Equity Frenzy Was a Bank Ad Come True," nytimes.com, August 15, 2008.
47. Bobby Kurian and Samidha Sharma, "Nisa Godrej backs e-tailer for infants," *The Times of India*, February 25, 2014.

Chapter 3

1. Elizabeth Olson, "Brands Using Virtual Goods For Real Gains," *The Economic Times*, September 8, 2010.
2. Preeti Khicha"s interview with Dr Andreas Schaaf, BMW India President, Business Standard, Jan17, 2011.
3. Chung-Yao Huang, Yong-Zheng Shen, Hong-Xiang Lin, and Shin-Shin Chang, "Bloggers' Motivations and Behavior: A Model," *Journal of Advertising Research*, 47 (4) (December 2007): 472–483.
4. Adapted from Kanghui Baek, Avery Holton, Dustin Harp, and Carolyn Yaschur, "The Links That Bind: Uncovering Novel Motivations for Linking on Facebook," *Computers in Human Behavior,* 27 (2011): 2245–2267.
5. Craig Martin, "Consumption Motivation and Perceptions of Malls: A Comparison of Mothers and Daughters," *Journal of Marketing Theory & Practice*, 17 (Winter 2009): 49–61.
6. See Tillmann Wagner and Thomas Rudolph, "Toward a Hierarchy of Shopping Motivations," *Journal*

of Retailing & Consumer Services, 17 (2010): 415–429.

7. See Abraham H. Maslow, "A Theory of Human Motivation," *Psychological Review*, 50 (1943): 370–396; Abraham H. Maslow, *Motivation and Personality* (New York: Harper & Row, 1954); Abraham H. Maslow, *Toward a Psychology of Being* (New York: Van Nostrand Reinhold, 1968): 189–215.
8. Maslow 1954, 1968.
9. Abraham H. Maslow, Motivation and Personality (New York: Harper & Row, 1954); and Abraham H. Maslow, Toward a Psychology of Being(New York: Van Nostrand Reinhold, 1968): 189–215.
10. Matthew Jelavic and Kristie Oglilvie, "Maslow and Management: Universally Applicable or Idiosyncratic?" *Canadian Manager* (Winter 2010): 16–17.
11. Sylvia Miller, M. Clinton, and John Camey, "The Relationship of Motivation, Needs, and Involvement Factors to Preferences for Military Recruitment Slogans," *Journal of Advertising Research*, 47 (1) (March 2007): 66–78.
12. "India's annual per capita income rose to Rs 61, 564 in 2011-12," Zeenews.com, January 31, 2013, http://zeenews.india.com/business/news/economy/indias-annual-per-capita-income-rose-to-rs-61-564-in-2011-12_69231.html (accessed on February 12, 2014).
13. Wann-Yih Wu and Badri Munir Sukoco, "Why Should I Share? Examining Consumers' Motives and Trust on Knowledge Sharing," *Journal of Computer Information Systems* (Summer 2010): 11–19.
14. *Sources:* Emily Eakin, "Penetrating the Mind by Metaphor," *New York Times*, February 23, 2002, B9, Bl-1; Ronald B. Leiber, "Storytelling: A New Way to Get Close to Your Customer," *Fortune*, February 3, 1997; Bernice Kramer, "Mind Games," *New York*, May 8, 1989, 33–40.
15. Neale Martin and Kyle Morich, "Consumer Choice: Toward a New Model of Consumer Behavior," *Journal of Brand Management*, 18 (March 2011): 483–505.
16. Delshad Irani, "Advertising Viagra," *The Economic Times*, March 21,2012.
17. Shephali Bhatt, "Spice Boys," *The Economic Times*, October 23, 2013.
18. Homi Bhabha"s interview with Srijana Mitra Das, "Sans humanities the centre of Indian education doesn't hold" *The Times of India*, April 6, 2012.
19. For example, see Karen Horney, *The Neurotic Personality of Our Time* (New York: Norton, 1937).
20. Joel B. Cohen, "An Interpersonal Orientation to the Study of Consumer Behavior," *Journal of Marketing Research*, 6 (August 1967): 270–278; Arch G. Woodside and Ruth Andress, "CAD Eight Years Later," *Journal of the Academy of Marketing Science* 3 (Summer–Fall 1975): 309–313; see also Jon P. Noerager, "An Assessment of CAD: A Personality Instrument Developed Specifically for Marketing Research," *Journal of Marketing Research*, 16 (February 1979): 53–59.
21. Stefan Soyez and Kat Soyez, "A Cognitive Model to Predict Domain-Specific Consumer Innovativeness," *Journal of Business Research*, 63 (2010): 778–785.
22. Bert Vandecasteele and Maggie Geuens, "Motivated Consumer Innovativeness: Concept, Measurement, and Validation," *International Journal of Research in Marketing*, 27 (2010): 308–318.
23. Tanawat Hirunyawipada and Audhesh K. Paswan, "Consumer Innovativeness and Perceived Risk: Implications for High Technology Product Adoption," *Journal of Consumer Marketing*, 23 (7) (2006): 197; Ji Eun Park, Jun Yu, and Joyce Xin Zhou, "Consumer Innovativeness and Shopping Styles," *Journal of Consumer Marketing*, 27 (5) (2010): 437–446.
24. Gilles Roehrich, "Consumer Innovativeness," and Angela D'Auria Stanton and Wilbur W. Stanton, "To Click or Not to Click: Personality Characteristics of Internet versus Non-Internet Purchasers," in *2001 AMA Winter Educators' Conference*, 12, edited by Ram Krishnan and Madhu Viswanathan (Chicago: American Marketing Association, 2001): 161–162.
25. Walfried M. Lassar, Chris Manolis, and Sharon S. Lassar, "The Relationship Between Consumer Innovativeness, Personal Characteristics, and Online Banking Adoption," *International Journal of Bank Marketing*, 23 (2) (2005): 190–201.
26. Isita Lahiri and Amitava Gupta, "Brand Extensions in Consumer Non-durables, Durables and Services: A Comparative Study," *South Asian Journal of Management*, 12 (4) (October–December 2005): 34–42.
27. Byoungho Jin and Yong Gu Suh, "Integrating Effect of Consumer Perception Factors in Predicting Private Brand Purchase in a Korean Discount Store Context," *Journal of Consumer Marketing*, 22 (2) (2005): 62–77.
28. Milton Rokeach, *The Open and Closed Mind* (New York: Basic Books, 1960).
29. Kurt Matzler, Sonja Bidmon, and Sonja Grabner-Kräuter, "Individual Determinants of Brand Affect: The Role of Personality Traits of Extraversion and Openness to Experience," *Journal of Product & Brand Management*, 15 (7) (2006): 434–451.
30. Ann Marie Fiore, Hyun-Jeong Jin, and Jihyun Kim, "For Fun and Profit: Hedonic Value from Image Interactivity and Responses Toward an Online Store," *Psychology & Marketing*, 22 (8) (2005): 675–686.
31. Ann Marie Fiore, Leung-Eun Lee, and Grace Kunz, "Individual Differences, Motivations, and

Willingness to Use a Mass Customization Option for Fashion Products," *European Journal of Marketing*, 38 (7) (2004): 835–849.

32. Walter Wymer. Donald Self, and Carolyn Sara Findley, "Sensation Seekers as a Target Market for Volunteer Tourism," *Service Marketing Quarterly*, 31 (2010): 348–362.
33. Elizabeth C. Hirschman, "Innovativeness, Novelty Seeking and Consumer Creativity," *Journal of Consumer Research*, 7 (1980): 283–295; Piyush Sharma, Bharadhwaj Sivakumaran, and Roger Marshall, "Impulse Buying and Variety Seeking: A Trait-Correlates Perspective," *Journal of Business Research*, 63 (2010): 276–283.
34. Chingching Chang, "Diagnostic Advertising Content and Individual Differences," *Journal of Advertising*, 36 (3) (Fall 2007): 79–87.
35. Chien-Huang Lin and Pei-Hsun Wu, "The Effect of Variety on Consumer Preferences: The Role of Need for Cognition and Recommended Alternatives," *Social Behavior & Personality*, 34 (7) (2006): 874–889.
36. Tracy L. Tuten and Michael Bosnjak, "Understanding Differences in Web Usage: The Role of Need for Cognition and the Five Factor Model of Personality," *Social Behavior & Personality*, 29 (4) (2001): 391–398.
37. Dahui Li and Glenn J. Browne, "The Role of Need for Cognition and Mood in Online Flow Experience," *Journal of Computer Information Systems*, 46 (3) (Spring 2006): 15–28; Maria Sicilia, Salvador Ruiz, and Jose L. Munuera, "Effects of Interactivity in a Web Site," *Journal of Advertising*, 34 (3) (Fall 2005): 40–53.
38. Maria Kozhevnikov, Stephen Kosslyn, and Jeffifer Shepard, "Spatial versus Object Visualizers: A New Characterization of Visual Cognitive Style," *Memory & Cognition*, 33 (4) (2005): 710–722.
39. Elaine Sherman, Leon Schiffman, and Yong Zhang, "A Cross-Cultural Investigation of Consumer Frugality: The Case of the United States and China," *Global Business & Technology Conference Proceedings*, Istanbul, Turkey (July 2011); Jeffrey Podoshen, Lu Li, and Junfeng Zhang, "Materialism and Conspicuous Consumption in China: A Cross-Cultural Examination," *International Journal of Consumer Studies*, 35 (2011): 17–25; Srinivas Durvasula and Steven Lysonski, "Money, Money, Money—How Do Attitudes Toward Money Impact Young Chinese Consumers?" *Journal of Consumer Marketing*, 27 (2) (2010): 169–179.
40. Marsha L. Richins and Scott Dawson, "A Consumer Values Orientation for Materialism and Its Measurement: Scale Development and Validation," *Journal of Consumer Research*, 19 (December 1992): 303–316; Jeff Tanner and Jim Roberts, "Materialism Cometh," *Baylor Business* Review (Fall 2000): 8–9.
41. Scott I. Rick, Cynthia E. Cryder, and George Loewenstein, "Tightwads and Spendthrifts," *Journal of Consumer Research*, 34 (April 2008): 767–782.
42. Alain d'Astous and Jonathan Deschenes, "Consuming in One's Mind: An Exploration," *Psychology & Marketing*, 22 (1) (January 2005): 1–30.
43. Helga Dittmar, "A New Look at 'Compulsive Buying': Self-Discrepancies and Materialistic Values as Predictors of Compulsive Buying Tendency," *Journal of Social & Clinical Psychology*, 24 (6) (September 2005): 832–859. Also see Laurence Claes et al., "Emotional Reactivity and Self-Regulation in Relation to Compulsive Buying," *Personality & Individual Differences*, 49 (2010): 526–530.
44. Hui-Yi Lo and Nigel Harvey, "Shopping Without Pain: Compulsive Buying and the Effects of Credit Card Availability in Europe and the Far East," *Journal of Economic Psychology*, 32 (2011): 79–92; Kay Palan, Paula Morrow, Allan Trapp, and Virginia Blackburn, "Compulsive Buying Behavior in College Students: The Mediating Role of Credit Card Misuse," *Journal of Marketing Theory & Practice*, 19 (1) (2011): 81–96.
45. Banwari Mittal, Holbrook Morris, Beatty Sharon, Raghubir Priya and Arch Woodside, *Consumer Behavior: How Humans Think, Feel, and Act in the Marketplace* (Cincinnati: Open Mentis, 2008).
46. Sagar Malviya, "Liquor Companies Serve Old Wine in Small 60 Ml Bottle; Sales Double," *The Economic Times*, December 13, 2013.
47. Olaf Werder and Marilyn S. Roberts, "Generation Y's Consumer Ethnocentrism: Implications for Advertisers in a Post September 11th World," *American Academy of Advertising Conference Proceedings* (2005): 185; Gregory S. Black and Leon F. Dube, "Implications of Collective Trauma on Consumer Purchase Attitudes," *Atlantic Economic Journal* (published online), December 20, 2006.
48. Osman Mohamad, Zafar U. Ahmed, Earl D. Honeycutt, Jr., and Taizoon Hyder Tyebkhan, "Does 'Made In...' Matter to Consumers? A Malaysian Study of Country of Origin Effect," *Multinational Business Review* (Fall 2000): 69–73; Irvin Clarke, Mahesh N. Shankarmahesh, and John B. Ford, "Consumer Ethnocentrism, Materialism and Values: A Four Country Study," in *2000 AMA Winter Educators' Conference*, 11, edited by John P. Workman and William D. Perreault (Chicago: American Marketing Association, 2000): 102–103.
49. Subhash Sharma, Terence A. Shimp, and Jeongshin Shin, "Consumer Ethnocentrism: A Test of Antecedents and Moderators," *Journal of the Academy of Marketing Science*, 23 (1995): 27.

50. Hamin Elliott and Greg Elliott, "A Less-Developed Country Perspective of Consumer Ethnocentrism and 'Country of Origin' Effects: Indonesian Evidence," *Asia Pacific Journal of Marketing & Logistics,* 18 (2) (2006): 79–92.
51. George Balabanis and Adamantios Diamantopoulos, "Domestic Country Bias, Country-of-Origin Effects, and Consumer Ethnocentrism: A Multidimensional Unfolding Approach," *Journal of the Academy of Marketing Science,* 32 (Winter 2004): 80–95.
52. Byeong-Joon Moon, "Effects of Consumer Ethnocentrism and Product Knowledge on Consumers' Utilization of Country-of-Origin Information," *Advances in Consumer Research,* 31 (2004): 667–673.
53. Fang Liu, Jamie Murphy, Jianyao Li, and Xiangping Liu, "English and Chinese? The Role of Consumer Ethnocentrism and Country of Origin in Chinese Attitudes Towards Store Signs," *Australasian Marketing Journal*, 14 (2) (2006): 5–16.
54. Jufei Kao, "Is It a Foreign Product? A Scale to Classify Products in an Era of Globalization," *Advances in Consumer Research,* 31 (2004): 674–682.
55. Marieke de Mooji, *Consumer behavior and Culture: Consequences for Global Marketing and Advertising* (New Delhi: Sage Publications, 2004).
56. Kamini Mathai, "Fair Play," *The Times of India*, January 14, 2012.
57. Marieke de Mooji, *Consumer behavior and Culture: Consequences for Global Marketing and Advertising* (New Delhi: Sage Publications, 2004).
58. Shintaro Okazaki, "Excitement or Sophistication? A Preliminary Exploration of Online Brand Personality," *International Marketing Review*, 23 (3) (2006): 279–303.
59. Pankaj Aggarwal and Ann L. McGill, "Is That Car Smiling at Me? Schema Congruity as a Basis for Evaluating Anthropomorphized Products," *Journal of Consumer Research*, 34 (December 2007): 468–479.
60. Vanitha Swaminathan, Karen M. Stilley, and Rohini Ahluwalia, "When Brand Personality Matters: The Moderating Role of Attachment Styles," *Journal of Consumer Research*, 35 (April 2009): 567–579.
61. Didier Louis and Cindy Lombart, "Impact of Brand Personality on Three Major Relational Consequences (Trust, Attachment, and Commitment to the Brand)," *Journal of Product & Brand Management*, 19 (2) (2010): 114–130.
62. S. Ramesh Kumar, "Is it Love, Actually," *The Hindu Business Line*, May 17, 2012.
63. P. C. M. Govers and J. P. L. Schoormans, " Product Personality and Its Influence on Consumer Preference, " *Journal of Consumer Marketing*, 22, 189–197.
64. "Reinventing Cadbury," *ICMR*, "http://www.icmrindia.org/casestudies/catalogue/Marketing/Reinventingpercent20Cadburypercent20-percent20Marketingpercent20Case.html" (accessed on August 15, 2011).
65. Gokul Krishnamurthy, "Pushing a dual premium strategy," *The Hindu Business Line*, December 1, 2011.
66. Ibid
67. Scarlett C. Wesley, Deborah C. Fowler, and Maria Elena Vazquez, "Retail Personality and the Hispanic Consumer: An Exploration of American Retailers," *Managing Service Quality,* 16 (2) (2006): 177–180.
68. Qimei Chen and Shelly Rodgers, "Development of an Instrument to Measure Web Site Personality," *Journal of Interactive Advertising*, 7 (1) (Fall 2006). Retrieved from http://jiad.org/article86.
69. Tara Parker-Pope, "Are Most People in Denial about Their Weight?" nytimes.com, April 18, 2012.
70. Russell W. Belk, "Possessions and the Extended Self," *Journal of Consumer Research*, 15 (September 1988): 139–168; Amy J. Morgan, "The Evolving Self in Consumer Behavior: Exploring Possible Selves," in *Advances in Consumer Research*, 20, edited by Leigh McAlister and Michael L. Rothschild (Provo, UT: Association for Consumer Research, 1992): 429–432.
71. Richard G. Netemeyer, Scot Burton, and Donald R. Lichtenstein, "Trait Aspects of Vanity: Measurement and Relevance to Consumer Behavior," *Journal of Consumer Research*, 21 (March 1995): 613–627.
72. Neha Dewan, "Clones of Brand Ambassadors Rage with Advertisers," *The Economic Times*, July 20, 2011.
73. Elizabeth C. Hirschman and Morris B. Holbrook, "Hedonic Consumption: Emerging Concepts, Methods and Propositions," *Journal of Marketing*, Vol.46 (3) (1982): 92–101.
74. Kardes, Cline and Cronley, *Consumer Behavior: Science and Practice*, (Independence: South-Western Cengage Learning, 2011)
75. Ibid
76. Rahul Sachitanand, "The Fasting and the Furious," *The Economic Times*, January 23, 2012.
77. Kardes, Cline and Cronley, *Consumer Behavior: Science and Practice*,(Independence: South-Western Cengage Learning, 2011)
78. "*Dove Real Beauty Sketches*," YouTube video, 3.00, posted by "Doveunitedstates." April 14,2013, http://www.youtube.com/watch?v=XpaOjMXyJGk (accessed on September 5, 2011).
79. Sovon Manna, "India became a men oriented market over the last decade," *The Times of India*, April 27, 2013.

Chapter 4

1. "Motorola, Lenova sign on Intel Smartphones," *The Economic Times*, January 12, 2012.
2. Serena Ng, "Pet-Food Brand's Image Bites Back at Colgate," online.wsj.com, February 5, 2013.
3. Samar Singh Sheikhawat, "We came to be seen as a young and technology savvy brand," *Business Standard*, December 9, 2013.
4. Jeff Bennett, "Chevrolet Ads Take 'New Road,'" online.wsj.com, January 8, 2013.
5. Swaraj Baggonkar, "Life without Bajaj," *Business Standard*, January 24, 2011.
6. Ravi Balakrishnan, "Social Climbers," *The Economic Times*, December 18, 2013.
7. "Sheena on The Art of Choosing." Vivek Kaul's interview with Sheena Iyengar, *The Economic Times*, November 4, 2011.
8. Reported in the health supplement of "The Week," May, 2011.
9. Aradhna Krishna, *Customer Sense*: *How the 5 Senses Influence Buying Behavior* (New Delhi: Palgrave Macmillan, 2013).
10. "Audio Advertisement in TOI creates a huge Buzz," *The Times of India*, September 22, 2010.
11. Masoom Gupte, "Learn to stretch success," *Business Standard*, December 10, 2012.
12. Daniel Milotic, "The Impact of Fragrance on Consumer Choice," *Journal of Consumer Behaviour,* (December 2003): 179; Lawrence K. Altman, "Unraveling Enigma of Smell Wins Nobel for 2 Americans," *New York Times*, December 5, 2004, A18.
13. Aradhna Krishna, May O. Lwin, and Maureen Morrin, "Product Scent and Memory," *Journal of Consumer Research,* Vol. 37 (June 2010): 57–67.
14. For example, Joann Peck and Jennifer Wiggins, "It Just Feels Good: Customers' Affective Response to Touch and Its Influence on Persuasion," *Journal of Marketing*, Vol. 70 (October 2006): 59–69.
15. Stephanie Clifford, "Stuff Piled in the Aisle? It's There to Get You to Spend More," nytimes.com, April 7, 2011.
16. WSJ Video, "When a Sound Is Worth a Thousand Words," online.wsj.com, October 23, 2012.
17. Amy Schatz, "FCC Turns Down Volume of TV Commercials," online.wsj.com, December 13, 2011.
18. Catherine Saint Louis, "Fragrance Spritzers Hold Their Fire," nytimes.com, April 15, 2011.
19. Sources: Louise Story, "Times Sq. Ads Spread via Tourists' Cameras," nytimes.com, December 11, 2006; Stuart Elliott, "Show and Tell Moves into Living Room," nytimes.com, April 4, 2008; Stuart Elliott, "Joint Promotion Adds Stickers to Sweet Smell of Marketing," nytimes.com, April 2, 2007; Louise Story, "Anywhere the Eye Can See, It's Likely to See an Ad," nytimes.com, January 15, 2007; Stuart Elliott, "Brainy Brand Names Where They're Least Expected," nytimes.com, October 3, 2008; Stuart Elliott, "You Are Here (and Probably Seeing an Ad)," nytimes.com, August 14, 2008; Elizabeth Olson, "Practicing the Subtle Sell of Placing Products on Webisodes," nytimes.com, January 3, 2008; Stephanie Clifford, "More Bells, Whistles and Packets of All Sorts," nytimes.com, April 22, 2008.
20. Sheri J. Broyles, "Subliminal Advertising and the Perpetual Popularity of Playing to People's Paranoia," *Journal of Consumer Affairs*, Vol. 40 (2) (Winter 2006): 392–406.
21. Rob Walker, "Subconscious Warm-Up: Can a Brand Make You Perform Better?" *New York Times Magazine*, October 5, 2008, 22; Grainne M. Fitzsimons, Tanya L. Chartrand, and Gavan J. Fitzsimons, "Automatic Effects of Brand Exposure on Motivated Behavior: How Apple Makes You 'Think Different,'" *Journal of Consumer Research,* Vol. 35 (1) (June 2008): 21–35.
22. Jane Levere, "3 Ads about Budget Cuts for Children's Programs," nytimes.com, August 6, 2012.
23. Sigurd Villads Troye and Magne Supphellen, "Consumer Participation in Coproduction: 'I Made It Myself' Effects on Consumers' Sensory Perceptions and Evaluations of Outcome and Input Product," *Journal of Marketing*, Vol. 76 (33) (March 2012): 33–46.
24. Harish Bhat, "Many a slip between lip and lip," *The Hindu Business Line*, December1, 2011.
25. Ibid
26. Ibid
27. Linyun W. Yang, Keisha M. Cutright, Tanya L. Chartrand, and Gavan J. Fitzsimons, "Distinctively Different: Exposure to Multiple Brands in Low-Elaboration Settings," *Journal of Consumer Research*, Vol.40 (5) (February 2014): 973–992, http://belkcollegeofbusiness.uncc.edu/lyang27/research/Yangper cent20etper cent20al.per cent20-per cent20Multipleper cent20brandsper cent20JCR.pdf (accessed on November 1, 2013).
28. Stephanie Clifford, "Product Placements Acquire a Life of Their Own on Shows," nytimes.com, July 14, 2008.
29. Elizabeth Cowley and Chris Barron, "When Product Placement Goes Wrong: The Effects of Program Liking and Placement Prominence," *Journal of Advertising,* Vol. 37 (1) (Spring 2008): 89–99.
30. Andrew Adam Newman, "Taking Pickles Out of the Afterthought Aisle," nytimes.com, April 25, 2011.
31. S. Ramesh Kumar, *Consumer Behavior and Branding*, (New Delhi: Pearson Education, 2009).
32. Sarah Jacob, "Innovation Focus at Heart of Lifebuoy Variant," *The Economic Times*, April 12, 2012.
33. Delshad Irani, "Breaking New Ground," *The Economic Times*, March 20, 2013.

34. Joandrea Hoegg and Joseph W. Alba, "Taste Perception: More Than Meets the Tongue," *Journal of Consumer Research*, Vol. 33 (March 2007): 490–498.
35. Linda M. Scott and Patrick Vargas, "Writing with Pictures: Toward a Unifying Theory of Consumer Response to Images," *Journal of Consumer Research*, Vol. 34 (October 2007): 341–356.
36. Leonard L. Berry, Edwin F. Lefkowith, and Terry Clark, "In Services, What's in a Name?" *Harvard Business Review* (September–October 1988): 28–30.
37. Aysen Bakir, Jeffrey G. Blodgett, and Gregory M. Rose, "Children's Response to Gender-Role Stereotyped Advertisements," *Journal of Advertising Research*, Vol. 48 (2) (June 2008): 255–266.
38. Karl Kunkel, "Making Mattresses Tick: Manufacturers Rely on Distinctive Colors and Textures to Create Products That Entice Consumers with a Great First Impression," *HFN: The Weekly Newspaper for the Home Furnishings Network* (December 12, 2005): 33.
39. Joe Sharkey, "Hotels Learn the Importance of Expectations Built into a Brand Name," *New York Times*, June 18, 2002, C12.
40. Devina Joshi, "When The Going Gets Tough", *Business Standard*, January 6, 2014
41. Ibid
42. Some parts of the contents were first published by S. Ramesh Kumar in Knowledge Today website of Wharton. http://knowledgetoday.wharton.upenn.edu/2012/08/why-are-indian-brands-adopting-foreign-names/(accessed on August 17, 2012).
43. Phred Dvorak, Suzanne Vranica, and Spencer E. Ante, "BlackBerry Maker's Issue: Gadgets for Work or Play?" online.wsj.com, September 30, 2011.
44. Based on the descriptions in the brands' respective websites (accessed June 16, 2012).
45. Mark Hachman, "Dell's 'More You' Ads Mean a Renewed Consumer Push," online.wsj.com, July 5, 2011; Stuart Elliott, "Google Remixes Old Campaigns, Adding a Dash of Digital Tools," nytimes.com, March 8, 2012; Stuart Elliott, "In New Ads, Stirring Memories of Commercials Past," nytimes.com, January 12, 2012; Stuart Elliott, "Sit Under the Apple Tree With Me, Juice Brand Asks," nytimes.com, June 7, 2010; Stuart Elliott, "Promoting a Potato Chip Using Many Farmers, and Less Salt," nytimes.com, May 25, 2010; Stuart Elliott, "So, Virginia, What's the Story," nytimes.com, February 1, 2010.
46. Sravanthi Challapalli, "How commercial is your social media?" *The Hindu Business Line*, December 22, 2011.
47. Ibid
48. Ulrich R. Orth and Keven Malkewitz, "Holistic Package Designs and Consumer Brand Impressions," *Journal of Marketing*, Vol. 72 (May 2008): 64–81.
49. Jochen Wirtz, Anna S. Mattila, and Rachel L. P. Tan, "The Role of Arousal Congruency in Influencing Consumers' Satisfaction Evaluations and In-Store Behaviors," *International Journal of Service Industry Management*, Vol. 18 (1) (2007): 6–24.
50. Andreas Herrmann, Lan Xia, Kent B. Monroe, and Frank Huber, "The Influence of Price Fairness on Customer Satisfaction: An Empirical Test in the Context of Automobile Purchases," *Journal of Product & Brand Management*, Vol. 16 (1) (2007): 49–58.
51. Ben Lowe and Frank Alpert, "Measuring Reference Price Perceptions for New Product Categories: Which Measure Is Best?" *Journal of Product & Brand Management*, Vol. 16 (2) (2007): 132–141.
52. Daniel J. Howard and Roger A. Kerin, "Broadening the Scope of Reference Price Advertising Research: A Field Study of Consumer Shopping Involvement," *Journal of Marketing*, Vol. 70 (October 2006): 185–204.
53. Keith S. Coulter and Robin A. Coulter, "Distortion of Price Discount Perceptions: The Right Digit Effect," *Journal of Consumer Research*, Vol. 34 (August 2007): 162–173.
54. Sara Campo and Maria J. Yague, "Effects of Price Promotions on the Perceived Price," *International Journal of Service Industry Management*, Vol. 18 (3) (2007): 269–286.
55. Ritesh Saini, Raghunath Singh Rao, and Ashwani Monga, "Is That Deal Worth My Time? The Interactive Effect of Relative and Referent Thinking on Willingness to Seek a Bargain," *Journal of Marketing*, Vol. 74 (January 2010): 34–48.
56. Joan Lindsey-Mullikin, "Beyond Reference Price: Understanding Consumers' Encounters with Unexpected Prices," *Journal of Product & Brand Management*, Vol. 12 (2/3) (2003): 140–154.
57. Sarah Nassauer, "Marketing Decoder: Sandwich Meat," online.wsj.com, March 19, 2013.
58. Brian Wansink and SeaBum Park, "At the Movies: How External Cues and Perceived Taste Impact Consumption Volume," *Food Quality & Preference*, 12 (2001): 69–74.
59. Celina Gonzalez Mieres, Ana Maria Diaz Martin, and J. A. T. Gutierrez, "Antecedents of the Difference in Perceived Risk Between Store Brands and National Brands," *European Journal of Marketing*, Vol. 40 (1/2) (2006): 61–82.
60. Torben Hansen, "Understanding Consumer Perception of Food Quality: The Cases of Shrimp and Cheeses," *British Food Journal*, Vol. 107 (7) (2005): 500–525.
61. Ray Johnson and Johan Bruwer, "Regional Brand Image and Perceived Wine Quality: The Consumer Perspective," *International Journal of Wine Business Research*, Vol. 19 (4) (2007): 276–297.

62. Jeana H. Frost, Zoe Chance, Michael I. Norton, and Dan Ariely, "People Are Experience Goods: Improving Online Dating with Virtual Dates," *Journal of Interactive Marketing,* Vol. 22 (1) (Winter 2008): 51–61.
63. The research on expected versus perceived service quality and SERVQUAL appears in Valarie A. Zeithaml, A. Parasuraman, and Leonard L. Berry, *Delivering Quality Service: Balancing Customer Perceptions and Expectations* (New York: The Free Press, 1990); Valarie A. Zeithaml, Leonard L. Berry, and A. Parasuraman, "The Nature and Determinants of Customer Expectation of Service," *Journal of the Academy of Marketing Science* (Winter 1993): 1–12; A. Parasuraman, Leonard L. Berry, and Valerie A. Zeithaml, "Refinement and Reassessment of the SERVQUAL Scale," *Journal of Retailing,* Vol. 67 (4) (Winter 1991): 420–450; A. Parasuraman, Leonard L. Berry, and Valerie A. Zeithaml, "Understanding Customer Expectations of Service," *Sloan Management Review* (Spring 1991): 39–48.
64. Ibid.
65. By shirt number: (1) sold at Bloomingdale's, designed by Donatella; (2) sold at Macy's, designed by Polonimo; (3) sold at Camicia (a store in NYC's Soho district), designed by Bertoliani; (4) sold by street vendors in NYC, made in China; (5) sold at Barney's under the store's name; (6) sold at H&M, designed by Xaas.
66. After looking at the shirt photos and the names of the stores and designers, the most expensive shirt is the one you believe to be so. The photos in Figure 4.1 are generic, and the information regarding the stores and designers is fictitious, used here only as illustration.
67. Benedict Carey, "$2.50 Placebo Gives More Relief Than a 10 Cents One," nytimes.com, March 5, 2008.
68. Shibin Sheng, Andrew M. Parker, and Kent Nakamoto, "The Effects of Price Discounts and Product Complimentarity on Consumer Evaluations of Bundle Components," *Journal of Marketing Theory & Practice,* Vol. 15 (1) (Winter 2007): 53–64.
69. John Tierney, "Calculating Consumer Happiness at Any Price," nytimes.com, June 30, 2009.
70. Thomas E. DeCarlo, Russell N. Laczniak, Carol M. Motley, and Sridhar Ramaswamy, "Influence of Image and Familiarity on Consumer Response to Negative Word-of-Mouth Communications about Retail Entities," *Journal of Marketing Theory & Practice,* Vol. 15 (1) (Winter 2007): 41–51.
71. Annie Gasparro, "Whole Foods Aims to Alter 'Price Perception' as It Expands," online.wsj.com, February 15, 2012.
72. Nat Ives, "Wal-Mart Turns to Ads to Address Its Critics," nytimes.com, January 14, 2005; Stuart Elliott, "Wal-Mart's New Realm: Reality TV," nytimes.com, June 3, 2005.
73. Kevin Coupe, "The Halo Effect, Revisited," *Chain Store Age* (February 2006): 36–37.
74. Louise Story, "In Ads, Banks Try the Warm, Cozy Approach," nytimes.com, June 9, 2009.
75. Erik Holm, "Progressive's # Fails in Social Media May Be Warning to Insurers," online.wsj.com, August 21, 2012.
76. Anthony D. Cox, Dena Cox, and Susan Powell Mantel, "Consumer Response to Drug Risk Information: The Role of Positive Affect," *Journal of Marketing*, Vol. 31 (74) (July 2010): 31–44.
77. Fang He and Peter P. Mykytyn, "Decision Factors for the Adoption of an Online Payment System by Customers," *International Journal of E-Business Research,* Vol. 3 (4) (October–December 2007): 1–32.
78. Tibert Verhagen, Sellmar Meents, and Yao-Hua Tan, "Perceived Risk and Trust Associated with Purchasing at Electronic Marketplaces," *European Journal of Information Systems* (2006): 542–555; Sally Harridge-March, "Can Building of Trust Overcome Consumer Perceived Risk?" *Marketing Intelligence & Planning,* Vol. 24 (7) (2006): 747–761.
79. Jung-Hwan Kim and Sharron J. Lennon, "Information Available on a Web Site: Effects on Consumers' Shop-ping Outcomes," *Journal of Fashion Marketing & Management*, Vol. 14 (2) (2010): 247–262; Man-Ling Chang and Wann-Yih Wu, "Revisiting Perceived Risk in the Context of Online Shopping: An Alternative Perspective of Decision-Making Styles," *Psychology & Marketing*, Vol. 29 (5) (May 2012): 378–400.

Chapter 5

1. http://www.unilever.com/brands-in-action/detail/Dove/292077/ (accessed on November 15, 2013).
2. http://www.hul.co.in/ (accessed on November 15, 2013).
3. Sujit John, 'On Customer Trail,' *The Times of India*, August 31, 2011.
4. Ibid
5. Vivek Kaul,'Winner Takes All,' *The Economic Times*, February 2, 2012.
6. S. Sadagopan, 'Not being digital, Kodak gets out of Kodak moment,' *The Times of India*, February 6, 2012
7. Ibid
8. Charles Duhigg, "How Companies Learn Your Secrets," nytimes.com, February 16, 2012.
9. Vinod Mahanta, 'The Contrarian,' *The Economic Times*, October 19, 2012.

10. Masoom Gupte, 'One versus many,' *Business Standard*, January 28, 2013.
11. Abilasha Ohja, ' License to grow,' *Business Standard*, June 18, 2013.
12. Sayantani Kar, 'Boroplus More,' *Business Standard*, November 29, 2010.
13. Verolien Cauberghe and Patrick De Pelsmacher, "The Impact of Brand Prominence and Game Repetition on Brand Responses," *Journal of Advertising*, Vol. 39 (1) (Spring 2010): 5–18; Andrea L. Micheaux, "Managing E-Mail Advertising Frequency from the Consumer Perspective," *Journal of Advertising,* Vol. 40 (4) (Winter 2011): 45–65.
14. Marciej Szymanowski and Els Gijsbrechts, "Consumption-Based Cross-Brand Learning: Are Private Labels Really Private?" *Journal of Marketing Research*, (April 2012): 231–246; Zain-ul-Abideen and Abdul Latif, "Do Brand Extensions Affect Consumer Attitude: An Empirical Experience with Reference to Pakistani Consumers," *The Clute Institute*, Vol. 27 (2) (March/April 2011): 19–36.
15. Deepak Khaitan, ' Our Growth will come from buyouts,' *The Economic Times*, November 26, 2010.
16. Shobha G. Iyer, Bibek Banerjee, and Lawrence L. Garber, "Determinants of Consumer Attitudes Toward Brand Extensions: An Experimental Study," *International Journal of Management*, Vol. 28 (3) (September 2011): 809–821.
17. Tsan-Ming Choi, "Fast Brand Extensions: An Empirical Study of Consumer Preferences," *Brand Management*, Vol. 17 (7) (2010): 472–487.
18. Tom Meyvis and Chris Janiszewski, "When Are Broader Brands Stronger Brands? An Accessibility Perspective on the Success of Brand Extensions," *Journal of Consumer Research,* (September 2004): 346–358; Eva Martinez and Jose M. Pina, "Consumer Responses to Brand Extensions: A Comprehensive Model," *European Journal of Marketing,* Vol. 44 (7) (2010): 1182–1206.
19. Yuping Liu-Thompkins & Leona Tam, 'Not All Repeat Customers Are the Same: Designing Effective Cross-Selling Promotion on the Basis of Attitudinal Loyalty and Habit,' *Journal of Marketing*, Vol. 77 (September 2013): 21–36
20. Neale Martin, Habit: The 95 per cent of Behavior Marketers Ignore' (Pearson Education, 2009).
21. Ibid
22. Wayne D. Hoyer, Deborah J. MacInnis, *Consumer Behavior* (Stamford: Cengage Learning, 1999).
23. S. Ramesh Kumar, 'When Old Habits Die Hard,' *The Hindu Business Line*, May 26, 2011.
24. App Helps Viewers Shop While Watching TV', *The Economic Times*, December 5, 2011.
25. Alexei Oreskovic, 'Google + Struggles to Win Over Brands, Businesses,' *The Economic Times*, May 14, 2013.
26. Charles Duhigg, The Power of Habit-Why we do and What we do in life and Business, (New York: Random House, 2012).
27. Interview with Paul Poleman- Vinay Kamath and K.Giriprakash,' Using the right levers for Emerging markets '*The Hindu Business line*, Nov 30, 2012.
28. Preeti Khicha, 'Can Axe Retain its Effect,' *Business Standard*, November 22, 2010
29. Ibid
30. Uri Gneezy and Aldo Rustichini, "A Fine Is a Price," *Journal of Legal Studies,* Vol. 29 (1, part 1) (2000): 1–18.
31. Gangseog Ryu and Lawrence Feick, "A Penny for Your Thoughts: Referral Reward Programs and Referral Likelihood," *Journal of Marketing,* Vol. 71 (January 2007): 84–94.
32. Anne Martensen, "Tweens' Satisfaction and Brand Loyalty in the Mobile Phone Market," *Young Consumers,* Vol. 8 (2) (2007): 108–116.
33. Jolie M. Martin and Michael I. Norton, "Shaping Online Consumer Choice by Partitioning the Web," *Psychology & Marketing*, Vol. 26 (10) (2009): 908–926.
34. Ratna Bhushan, "GSK Consumer inks deal with GSK Pharma to Widen Market," *The Economic Times*, May 7, 2013.
35. John Tierney, "How Many Memories Fit in Your Brain?" nytimes.com, June 22, 2007.
36. Kathryn A. Braun-LaTour, Michael S. LaTour, and George M. Zinkhan, "Using Childhood Memories to Gain Insight into Brand Meaning," *Journal of Marketing,* Vol. 71 (April 2007): 45–60.
37. Susan Fournier, (1998), "Consumers and their brands; Developing Branding Theory in Consumer Research," *Journal of Consumer Research*, Vol. 24 (4): 343–353.
38. Rajeev Batra, Aaron Ahuvia, and Richard P. Bagozzi. (2012), 'Brand Love,' *Journal of Marketing*, Vol 76(2) (2012).
39. Ratna Bhushan, ''Little' Cans of Joy,' *The Economic Times*, July 18, 2011.
40. Sagar Malviya, 'Brand Push by HUL. Hindustan Unilever plans to launch Dove Hair oil as super premium brand,' *The Economic Times*, September 4, 2012.
41. Class discussion by Aruna Divya, FPM student at Indian Institute of Management, Bangalore.
42. Rik Pieters and Michel Wedel, "Goal Control of Attention to Advertising: The Yarbus Implication," *Journal of Consumer Research,* Vol. 34 (August 2007): 224–233.
43. Hyun Seung Jin, Jaebeom Suh, and Todd Donovan, "Salient Effects of Publicity in Advertised Brand Recall and Recognition: The List-Stretch Paradigm," *Journal of Advertising,* Vol. 37 (1) (Spring 2008): 45–58.

44. William E. Baker, "Does Brand Imprinting in Memory Increase Brand Information Retention?" *Psychology & Marketing* (December 2003): 1119+.
45. Tina M. Lowery, L. J. Shrum, and Tony M. Dubitsky, "The Relation Between Brand-Name Linguistic Characteristics and Brand-Name Memory," *Journal of Advertising* (Fall 2003): 7–18; Eric Yorkston and Geeta Menon, "A Sound Idea: Phonetic Effects of Brand Names on Consumer Judgments," *Journal of Consumer Research* (June 2004): 43–52.
46. Sandra Blakeslee, "If Your Brain Has a 'Buy Button,' What Pushes It," nytimes.com, October 19, 2004.
47. Yuval Rottenstreich, Sanjay Sood, and Lyle Brenner, "Feeling and Thinking in Memory Versus Stimulus-Based Choices," *Journal of Consumer Research*, Vol. 33 (March 2007): 461–469.
48. For example, Jan Meller Jensen and Torben Hansen, "An Empirical Examination of Brand Loyalty," *Journal of Product & Brand Management,* Vol. 15 (7) (2006): 442–449.
49. Ivonne M. Torres and Elten Briggs, "Identification Effects on Advertising Response," *Journal of Advertising,* Vol. 36 (3) (Fall 2007): 97–109.
50. Marjolein Moorman, Peter C. Neijens, and Edith G. Smit, "The Effects of Program Involvement on Commercial Exposure and Recall in a Naturalistic Setting," *Journal of Advertising,* Vol. 36 (1) (Spring 2007): 121–138.
51. Mira Lee and Ronald J. Faber, "Effects of Product Placement in On-Line Games on Brand Memory," *Journal of Advertising,* Vol. 36 (4) (Winter 2007): 75–91.
52. Martin Holzwarth, Chris Janiszewski, and Marcus M. Neumann, "The Influence of Avatars on Online Consumer Shopping Behavior," *Journal of Marketing,* Vol. 70 (October 2006): 19–36.
53. Janet Rae-Dupree, "Let Computers Compute. It's the Age of the Right Brain," nytimes.com, April 6, 2008.
54. Herbert E. Krugman, "The Impact of Television Advertising: Learning Without Involvement," *Public Opinion Quarterly,* Vol. 29 (Fall 1965): 349–356; "Brain Wave Measures of Media Involvement," *Journal of Advertising Research,* Vol. 11 (February 1971): 3–10; "Memory Without Recall, Exposure Without Perception," *Journal of Advertising Research,* Vol. 1 (September 1982): 80–85.
55. George R. Franke, Bruce A. Huhmann, and David L. Mothersbaugh, "Information Content and Consumer Readership of Print Ads: A Comparison of Search and Experience Products," *Academy of Marketing Science Journal* (Winter 2004): 20+.
56. Spiros Gounaris and Vlasis Stathakopoulos, "Antecedents and Consequences of Brand Loyalty: An Empirical Study," *Journal of Brand Management,* (April 2004): 283–307.
57. 2013 Harris Poll EquiTrend® Rankings harrisinteractive.com/insights/equitrendrankings.aspx#Sports (accessed April 13, 2013).

Chapter 6

1. Felix Gillette, Diane Brady, and Caroline Winter," The Rise and Fall of Blackberry an Oral History", *The Economic Times*, Dec 7, 2013
2. Frank R Kardes, Thomas W Cline, and Maria L Cronley, "Consumer Behavior Science and Practice", Censage Learning, 2011.
3. Felix Gillette, Diane Brady, and Caroline Winter," The Rise and Fall of Blackberry an Oral History", *The Economic Times*, Dec 7, 2013.
4. Frank R Kardes,Thomas W Cline, and Maria L Cronley, "Consumer Behavior Science and Practice", Censage Learning, 2011.
5. Market study conducted by S. Ramesh Kumar and Nitya Gruvayurappan for a case study associated with a popular brand of toothpaste.
6. Ibid
7. Sanjay Vijayakumar and Sangeetha Kandavel, "Male celebrities Shine in Gold Endorsements as Cos change Tack" *The Economic Times*, Oct 18, 2012.
8. Preethi Chamikutty,"Can't be the Real thing", *The Economic Times*, Oct 17, 2012.
9. "Brand Boss", *The Economic Times*, February 29, 2012.
10. Mike McNamara (Q&A)," Tech too important to outsource: Tesco CIO" *The Economic Times*, Oct 25, 2013
11. Devendra Chawla,"Challenge is to engage consumers" *The Economic Times*, July 6, 2010
12. http://www.youtube.com/watch?v=u64lJ5EwdUE (accessed on January 15, 2014).
13. Geoffrey L. Cohen, Joshua Aronson, and Claude M. Steele, "When Beliefs Yield to Evidence: Reducing Biased Evaluation by Affirming the Self," *Personality & Social Psychology Bulletin*, 26 (9) (September 2000): 1151–1164.
14. Stuart Elliott, "As Technology Evolves, AT&T Adjusts a Theme," nytimes.com, April 8, 2012.
15. Rajiv Banerjee, "Rural Receipes" *The Economic Times*, July 20, 2011
16. Ibid
17. Martin Fishbein, "An Investigation of the Relationships Between Beliefs about an Object and the Attitude Toward the Object," *Human Relations*, 16 (1963): 233–240; Martin Fishbein, "A Behavioral Theory Approach to the Relations Between Beliefs about an Object and the Attitude Toward the Object," in *Readings in Attitude Theory and Measurement,*

ed. Martin Fishbein, pp. 389–400 (New York: John Wiley & Sons, 1967).

18. Shwu-Ing Wu, "The Relationship Between Consumer Characteristics and Attitude Toward Online Shopping," *Marketing Intelligence & Planning*, 21 (1) (2003): 37–44.
19. Terence A. Shimp and Alican Kavas, "The Theory of Reasoned Action Applied to Coupon Usage," *Journal of Consumer Research*, 11 (December 1984): 795–809; Blair H. Sheppard, Jon Hartwick, and Paul R. Warshaw, "The Theory of Reasoned Action: A Meta-Analysis of Past Research with Recommendations for Modifications and Future Research," *Journal of Consumer Research*, 15 (September 1986): 325–343; Sharon E. Beatly and Lynn R. Kahle, "Alternative Hierarchies of the Attitude-Behavior Relationship: The Impact of Brand Commitment and Habit," *Journal of the Academy of Marketing Science*, 16 (Summer 1988): 1–10; Richard P. Bagozzi, Hans Baumgartner, and Youjae Yi, "Coupon Usage and the Theory of Reasoned Action," in *Advances in Consumer Research*, 18, eds. Rebecca H. Holman and Michael R. Solomon, pp. 24–27 (Provo, UT: Association for Consumer Research, 1991); Hee Sun Park, "Relationships Among Attitudes and Subjective Norms: Testing the Theory of Reasoned Action Across Cultures," *Communication Studies*, 51 (2) (Summer 2000): 162–175; Hung-Pin Shih, "An Empirical Study on Predicting User Acceptance of e-Shopping on the Web," *Information & Management* (Amsterdam), 41 (January 2004): 351.
20. Richard P. Bagozzi and Paul R. Warshaw, "Trying to Consume," *Journal of Consumer Research*, 17 (September 1990): 127–140; Richard P. Bagozzi, Fred D. Davis, and Paul R. Warshaw, "Development and Test of a Theory of Technological Learning and Usage," *Human Relations*, 45 (7) (July 1992): 659–686; Anil Mathur, "From Intentions to Behavior: The Role of Trying and Control," in *1995 AMA Educators' Proceedings*, eds. Barbara B. Stern and George M. Zinkan, pp. 374–375 (Chicago: American Marketing Association, 1995).
21. Stephen J. Gould, Franklin S. Houston, and Jonel Mundt, "Failing to Try to Consume: A Reversal of the Usual Consumer Research Perspective," in *Advances in Consumer Research*, eds. Merrie Brucks and Deborah J. MacInnis, pp. 211–216 (Provo, UT: Association for Consumer Research, 1997).
22. Durriya Z. Khairullah and Zahid Y. Khairullah, "Relationships Between Acculturation, Attitude Toward the Advertisement, and Purchase Intention of Asian-Indian Immigrants," *International Journal of Commerce & Management*, 9 (3/4) (1999): 46–65.
23. Dan Petrovici and Marin Marinov, "Determinants and Antecedents of General Attitudes Towards Advertising: A Study of Two EU Accession Countries," *European Journal of Marketing*, 3 (4) (2007): 307–326.
24. "Discount does the magic, Honda Sells 850 Jazz in 3 Days"
25. Hoyar and McInnis," *Consumer Behavior*", Houghton Miffins, 118,126.
26. "Read Between the lines," *Wellness, The New Sunday Express*, April 1, 2012.
27. Ibid
28. Stuart Elliott, "Time to Eat Tuna? 'Wonder' No More," nytimes.com, March 7, 2011.
29. Daniel Katz, "The Functional Approach to the Study of Attitudes," *Public Opinion Quarterly*, 24 (Summer 1960): 163–191; Sharon Shavitt, "Products, Personality and Situations in Attitude Functions: Implications for Consumer Behavior," in *Advances in Consumer Research*, 16, ed. Thomas K. Srull, pp. 300–305 (Provo, UT: Association for Consumer Research, 1989); Richard Ennis and Mark P. Zanna, "Attitudes, Advertising, and Automobiles: A Functional Approach," in *Advances in Consumer Research*, 20, eds. Leigh McAlister and Michael L. Rothschild, pp. 662–666 (Provo, UT: Association for Consumer Research, 1992).
30. Barbara A. Lafferty and Ronald E. Goldsmith, "Cause-Brand Alliances: Does the Cause Help the Brand or Does the Brand Help the Cause?" *Journal of Business Research*, 58 (April 2005): 423–429.
31. Nora J. Rifon, Sejung Marina Choi, Carrie S. Tripble, and Hairong Li, "Congruence Effects in Sponsorship," *Journal of Advertising*, 33 (Spring 2004): 29–42.
32. Chan-Wook Park and Byeong-Joon Moon, "The Relationship Between Product Involvement and Product Knowledge: Moderating Roles of Product Type and Product Knowledge Type," *Psychology & Marketing* (November 2003): 977.
33. Richard E. Petty et al., "Theories of Attitude Change," in *Handbook of Consumer Theory and Research*, eds. Harold Kassarjian and Thomas Robertson (Upper Saddle River, NJ: Prentice Hall, 1991); Richard E. Petty, John T. Cacioppo, and David Schumann, "Central and Peripheral Routes to Advertising Effectiveness: The Moderating Role of Involvement," *Journal of Consumer Research*, 10 (September 1983): 135–146. Also see Curtis P. Haugtvedt and Alan J. Strathman, "Situational Product Relevance and Attitude Persistence," in *Advances in Consumer Research*, 17, eds. Marvin E. Goldberg, Gerald Gorn, and Richard W. Pollay, pp. 766–769 (Provo, UT: Association for Consumer Research, 1990); Scott B. Mackenzie and Richard A. Spreng, "How Does Motivation Moderate the Impact of Central and Peripheral Processing on Brand Attitudes

and Intentions?" *Journal of Consumer Research*, 18 (March 1992): 519–529.

34. Jon D. Morris, ChongMoo Woo, and A. J. Singh, "Elaboration Likelihood Model: A Missing Intrinsic Emotional Implication," *Journal of Targeting, Measurement & Analysis for Marketing*, 14 (1) (December 2005): 79–98.
35. Shin-Chieh Chuang and Chia-Ching Tsai, "The Impact of Consumer Product Knowledge on the Effect of Terminology in Advertising," *Journal of the American Academy of Business*, 6 (March 2005): 154–158; Jaideep Sgupta, Ronald C. Goldstein, and David S. Boninger, "All Cues Are Not Created Equal: Obtaining Attitude Persistence under Low-Involvement Conditions," *Journal of Consumer Research*, 23 (March 1997): 351–361.
36. James F. Engel, Roger D. Blackwell, and Paul W. Miniard, *Consumer Behavior*, 8th ed.(New York: The Dryden Press, 1995), 373–378.
37. Shin-Chieh Chuang and Chia-Ching Tsai, "The Impact of Consumer Product Knowledge on the Effect of Terminology in Advertising," *Journal of the American Academy of Business*, 6 (March 2005): 154–158, and Jaideep Sgupta, Ronald C. Goldstein, and David S. Boninger, "All Cues Are Not Created Equal: Obtaining Attitude Persistence Under Low-Involvement Conditions," *Journal of Consumer Research*, 23 (March 1997): 351–361.
38. Keith S. Coulter and Girish N. Punj, "The Effects of Cognitive Resource Requirements, Availability, and Argument Quality on Brand Attitudes," *Journal of Advertising*, 33 (Winter 2004): 53–64; and Keith S. Coulter, "An Examination of Qualitative vs. Quantitative Elaboration Likelihood Effects," *Psychology & Marketing*, 22, no. 1 (January 2005): 31–49.
39. Lefa Teng, Michel Laroche, and Huihuang Zhu, "The Effects of Multiple-Ads and Multiple-Brands on Consumer Attitude and Purchase Behavior," *Journal of Consumer Marketing*, 24, no. 1 (2007): 27–35.
40. Young "Sally" Kim, "Applications of the Cognitive Dissonance Theory to the Service Industry," *Services Marketing Quarterly*, 32 (2011): 96–112.
41. For example, David C. Matz and Wendy Wood, "Cognitive Dissonance in Groups," *Journal of Personality & Social Psychology*, 88 (January 2005): 22–37; Jillian C. Sweeney and Tanya Mukhopadhyay, "Cognitive Dissonance after Purchase: A Comparison of Bricks and Mortar and Online Retail Purchase Situations," *American Marketing Association Conference Proceedings: 2004 AMA Winter Educators' Conference*, 15, pp. 190–191 (Chicago: American Marketing Association, 2004); Martin O'Neill and Adrian Palmer, "Cognitive Dissonance and the Stability of Service Quality Perceptions," *Journal of Services Marketing*, 18 (6/7) (2004): 433–449; Robert A Wicklund and Jack W. Brehm, "Internalization of Multiple Perspectives or Dissonance Reduction?" *Theory & Psychology* (London), 14 (June 2004): 355–371; Alex R. Zablah, Danny N. Bellenger, and Westley J. Johnson, "Customer Relationship Management Implementation Gaps," *Journal of Personal Selling & Sales Management*, 24 (Fall 2004): 279–295.
42. Geoffrey N. Soutar and Jillian C. Sweeney, "Are There Cognitive Dissonance Segments?" *Australian Journal of Management*, 28 (December 2003): 227–239.
43. Phil Lampert, "Cognitive Dissonance," *Progressive Grocer*, 83 (May 15, 2004): 16.
44. Mohammed M. Nadeem, "Post-Purchase Dissonance: The Wisdom of the 'Repeat' Purchases," *Journal of Global Business Issues*, 1 (2) (Summer 2007): 183–193.
45. Edward E. Jones et al., *Attribution: Perceiving the Causes of Behavior* (Morristown, NJ: General Learning Press, 1972); Bernard Weiner, "Attributional Thoughts about Consumer Behavior," *Journal of Consumer Research*, 27 (3) (December 2000): 382–387.
46. Rifon et al., "Congruence Effects in Sponsorship," 29; Andrea C. Morales, "Giving Firms an 'E' for Effort: Consumer Responses to High-Effort Firms," *Journal of Consumer Research*, 3 (March 2005): 806–812.
47. S. Christian Wheeler, Richard E. Petty, and George Y. Bizer, "Self-Schema Matching and Attitude Change: Situational and Dispositional Determinants of Message Elaboration," *Journal of Consumer Research*, 31 (March 2005): 787–797.
48. For example, Leslie Lazar Kanuk, *Mail Questionnaire Response Behavior as a Function of Motivational Treatment* (New York: CUNY, 1974).
49. Angelos Rodafinos, Arso Vucevic, and Georgios D. Sideridis, "The Effectiveness of Compliance Techniques: Foot in the Door Versus Door in the Face," *Journal of Social Psychology*, 145 (April 2005): 237–239.
50. Harold H. Kelley, "Attribution Theory in Social Psychology," in *Nebraska Symposium on Motivation*, 15, ed. David Levine, p. 197 (Lincoln: University of Nebraska Press, 1967). Based on Andrea M. Sjovall and Andrew C. Talk, "From Actions to Impressions: Cognitive Attribution Theory and the Formation of Corporate Reputation," *Corporate Reputation Review,* 7 (Fall 2004): 277–289.

Chapter 7

1. Louise Story, "It's an Ad, Ad, Ad, Ad World," nytimes.com, August 6, 2007.

2. Ji Hee Song and George M. Zinkhan, "Determinants of Perceived Web Site Interactivity," *Journal of Marketing,* Vol. 72 (March 2008): 99–113.
3. Laura M. Holson, "In CBS Test, Mobile Ads Find Users," nytimes.com, February 6, 2008.
4. Edward Wyatt, "Publisher Aims at Cellphones," nytimes.com, February 18, 2008.
5. Louise Story, "Madison Avenue Calling," nytimes. com, January 20, 2007.
6. Shira Ovide, "Twitter to Target Ads Based on Interests," online.wsj.com, August 30, 2012.
7. Louise Story, "A TV Show's Content Calls the Commercial Plays," nytimes.com, December 21, 206.
8. Tim Arango, "Cable Firms Join Forces to Attract Focused Ads," nytimes.com, Match 10, 2008; Stephanie Clifford, "Cable Companies Target Commercials to Audience," nytimes.com, March 4, 2009.
9. Sravanthi Challapalli, "A touch of magic realism," *The Hindu Business Line*, March 15, 2012.
10. Rik Pieters, Michel Wedel, and Rajeev Batra, "The Stopping Power of Advertising: Measures and Effects of Visual Complexity," *Journal of Marketing*, Vol. 74 (September 2010): 48–60.
11. Stuart Elliott, "Paring Down Marketing to a Few Simple Basics," nytimes.com, July 26, 2012.
12. Richard Buda and Bruce H. Chamov, "Message Processing in Realistic Recruitment Practices," *Journal of Managerial Issues* (Fall 2003): 302+.
13. Jennifer L. Aaker and Angela Y. Lee, "'I' Seek Pleasure and 'We' Avoid Pains: The Role of Self-Regulatory Goals in Information Processing and Persuasion," *Journal of Consumer Research* (June 2001): 33–49.
14. Dena Cox and Anthony D. Cox, "Communicating the Consequences of Early Detection: The Role of Evidence and Framing," *Journal of Marketing* (July 2001): 91–103.
15. Baba Shiv, Julie A. Edell Britton, and John W. Payne, "Does Elaboration Increase or Decrease the Effectiveness of Negatively Versus Positively Framed Messages?" *Journal of Consumer Research* (June 2004): 199–209.
16. William E. Baker, Heather Honea, and Cristel Antonia Russell, "Do Not Wait to Reveal the Brand Name: The Effect of Brand-Name Placement on Television Advertising Effectiveness," *Journal of Advertising* (Fall 2004): 77–86.
17. Nathalie Dens and Patrick De Pelsmacker, "Consumer Response to Different Advertising Appeals for New Products: The Moderating Influence of Branding Strategy and Product Category Involvement," *Journal of Brand Management,* Vol. 18 (1) (2010): 50–65.
18. Marc Reinhard and Matthias Messner, "The Effects of Likeability and Need for Cognition on Advertising Effectiveness Under Explicit Persuasion," *Journal of Consumer Behavior,* Vol. 8 (2009): 179–191.
19. Kenneth C. Manning, Paul W. Miniard, Michael J. Barone, and Randall L. Rose, "Understanding the Mental Representations Created by Comparative Advertising," *Journal of Advertising* (Summer 2001): 27–39.
20. Chingching Chang, The Relative Effectiveness of Comparative Advertising: Evidence for Gender Differences in Information-Processing Strategies," *Journal of Advertising,* Vol. 36 (1) (Spring 2007): 21–36.
21. Shailendra Pratap Jain, Charles Lindsey, Nidhi Agrawal, and Durairaj Maheswaran, "For Better or For Worse? Valenced Comparative Frames and Regulatory Focus," *Journal of Consumer Research,* Vol. 34 (June 2007): 57–65.
22. Stephanie Clifford, "Best Soup Ever? Suits Over Ads Demand Proof," nytimes.com, November 21, 2009.
23. Ron Lennon, Randall Rentfro and Bay O'Leary, "Social Marketing and Distracted Driving Behaviors Among Young Adults: The Effectiveness of Fear Appeals," *Academy of Marketing Studies Journal*, Vol. 14 (2), (2010): 95–113.
24. Patrick De Pelsmacker, Verolien Cauberghe, and Nathalie Dens, "Fear Appeal Effectiveness for Familiar and Unfamiliar Issues," *Journal of Social Marketing*, Vol. 1 (3) (2011): 171–191.
25. Karen H. Smith and Mary Ann Stutts, "Effects of Short-Term Cosmetic Versus Long-Term Health Fear Appeals in Anti-Smoking Advertisements on the Smoking Behavior of Adolescents," *Journal of Consumer Behavior* (December 2003): 157+.
26. Andrea Morales, Eugenia Wu and Gavan Fitzsimons, "How Disgust Enhances the Effectiveness of Fear Appeals," *Journal of Consumer Research*, Vol. XLIX (June 2012): 383–393.
27. Martin Eisend, "How Humor in Advertising Works: A Meta-Analytic Test of Alternative Models," *Springer Science [plus] Business Media* (May 2010): 115–132.
28. Graeme Galloway, "Humor and Ad Liking: Evidence That Sensation Seeking Moderates the Effects of Incongruity-Resolution Humor," *Psychology and Marketing*, Vol. 26 (9) (September 2009): 779–792.
29. Thomas W. Cline, Moses B. Altsech, and James J. Kellaris, "When Does Humor Enhance or Inhibit Ad Responses? The Moderating Role of the Need for Humor," *Journal of Advertising* (Fall 2003): 31–46.
30. James J. Kellaris and Thomas W. Cline, "Humor and Ad Memorability: On the Contributions of Humor Expectancy, Relevancy, and Need for Humor," *Psychology and Marketing,* Vol. 24 (6) (June 2007): 497–509.

31. Thomas W. Cline and James J. Kellaris, "The Influence of Humor Strength and Humor-Message Relatedness on Ad Memorability: A Dual Process Model," *Journal of Advertising,* Vol. 36 (1) (Spring 2007): 55–68.
32. ChangHyun Jin and Jorge Villegas, "The Effect of the Placement of the Product in Film: Consumers' Emotional Responses to Humorous Stimuli and Prior Brand Evaluation," *Journal of Targeting, Measurement and Analysis for Marketing,* Vol. 15 (4) (2007): 244–255.
33. Elizabeth Olson, "Not Every Bad Day Needs to End With Ice Cream," nytimes.com, August 14, 2012.
34. Stuart Elliott, "The 'Moore' the Merrier, Paint Marketer Proclaims," nytimes.com, April 26, 2010.
35. Edward F. McQuarrie and David Glen Mick, "Visual and Verbal Rhetorical Figures Under Directed Processing Versus Incidental Exposure to Advertising," *Journal of Consumer Research* (March 2003): 579–588.
36. Stuart Elliott, "Is This a New 'Era' for Detergent Advertising?" nytimes.com, June 13, 2011.
37. Andrew Newman, "Small Carrier Gets Big Tailwind From Social Media," nytimes.com, April 6, 2011; Tanzina Vega, "From Zappos, an Unadorned Approach," nytimes.com, July 10, 2011.
38. Tom Reichert, Michael LaTour, and John Ford, "The Naked Truth: Revealing the Affinity for Graphic Sexual Appeals in Advertising," *Journal of Advertising Research* (June 2011): 436–448.
39. Iain Black, George Organ, and Peta Morton, "The Effect of Personality on Response to Sexual Appeals", *European Journal of Marketing*, Vol. 44 (9/10) (2010): 1453–1477.
40. Stuart Elliott, "Striving for Balance Between Losses and Laughs," nytimes.com, October 15, 2008.
41. Stephanie Clifford and Stuart Elliott, "Goodbye Seduction, Hello Coupons," nytimes.com, November 10, 2008.
42. Stuart Elliott, "Business District Tries Soft Selling for Holidays," nytimes.com, December 8, 2008.
43. Stuart Elliott, "Capitalizing on Consumer Anxiety, One Halloween Deal at a Time," nytimes.com, October 14, 2008.
44. Stuart Elliott, "Ads That Soothe When Banks Are Failing," nytimes.com, October 7, 2008; Stuart Elliott, "Down Economic Times Elicit Upbeat Consumers," nytimes.com, March 10, 2009; Vivian Toy, "Goodbye, Glitzy Condo Pitches," nytimes.com, August 20, 2010; Patricia Cohen, "Marketing Broadway: Selling Hope for a Song," nytimes.com, December 10, 2008; Andrew Newman, "Using Appeals to Emotions to Sell Paint," nytimes.com, June 7, 2010; Stuart Elliott, "In New Ads, Stirring Memories of Commercials Past," nytimes.com, January 12, 2012.
45. Delshad Irani, "An Affair To Remember," *The Economic Times*, August 31, 2011.
46. Ibid
47. Alexander Chernav, Ryan Hamilton, and David Gal (2011), "Competing for Consumer's Identity: Limits to Self Expression and Perils of Lifestyle Branding," *Journal of Marketing*, Vol.75 (3) (May 2011).
48. Susan Fournier, Felicia Miller, and Chris Allen, "Exploring Relationship Analogues in the Brand Space," In *Consumer-Brand Relationships: Theory and Practice*, edited by Susan Fournier, Michael Breazeale, and Marc Fetscherin, 30–56 (Oxon: Routledge, 2012)

Chapter 8

1. "Companies That 'Like' Facebook Ads," online.wsj.com, November 2, 2011.
2. S. Ramachandran, "Dish's Ads to End All Ads," online.wsj.com, May 16, 2012.
3. J. Jurgensen, "Binge Viewing: TV's Lost Weekends," online.wsj.com, July 12, 2012.
4. Miguel Helft and Tanzina Vega, "Retargeting Ads Follow Surfers to Other Sites," nytimes.com, August 29, 2010.
5. A. Efrati, "Google to Require Retailers to Pay," online.wsj.com, June 1, 2012.
6. Wikipedia.
7. J. Dohnert, "Consumers Most Annoyed by Ads on Social Networking Sites," *Incisive Interactive Marketing*, December 13, 2012.
8. J. Angwin and J. Singer-Vine, "Selling You on Facebook," online.wsj.com, April 8, 2012.
9. Ibid.
10. G. Fowler, "Are You Talking to Me?" online.wsj.com, April 25, 2011.
11. "McDonald's Social Media Director Explains Twitter Fiasco," paidContent.org, January 23, 2012.
12. E. Holmes, "Twitting Without Fear," online.wsj.com, December 11, 2011.
13. S. Elliott, "Selling New Wine in Millennial Bottles," nytimes.com, October 25, 2010.
14. J. Levere, "Cosmo Campaign Puts Viewers in the Photo Shoot," nytimes.com, September 29, 2010.
15. S. Kolesnikov-Jessop, "Selling a Watch via Social Media," nytimes.com, November 22, 2012.
16. E. Rusli and S. Banjo, "Facebook's Wal-Mart Gambit," online.wsj.com, December 16, 2012.
17. A. A. Newman, "Brands Now Direct Their Followers to Social Media," nytimes.com, August 3, 2011.
18. J. L. Levere, "A Mexican Beer Rides a Social Media Wave," nytimes.com, August 13, 2012; G. Schimdt, "A Product with Devotees Tries to Widen Its Niche," nytimes.com, August 15, 2012.

19. S. Elliott, "Early Kickoff for Marketers at Super Bowl," nytimes.com, December 11, 2012.
20. R. Rivera, "Social Media Strategy Was Crucial as Transit Agencies Coped with Hurricanes," nytimes.com, December 14, 2012.
21. T. Wayne, "Age Gap Narrows on Social Networking," nytimes.com, December 26, 2010.
22. G. A. Fowler, "Are You Talking to Me?" online.wsj.com, April 25, 2011; J. L. Levere, "Choosing a Marketing Plan: Traditional or Social Media?," nytimes.com, February 25, 2010.
23. L. Kwoh and M. Korn, "140 Characters of Risk: Some CEOs Fear Twitter," online.wsj.com, September 25, 2012.
24. Interactive Advertising Bureau (IAB), "Social Media Buyer's Guide," February 2010.
25. Ibid.
26. Masoom Gupte, "Social media makes it easier for brands to be more likeable," *Business Standard*, March 25, 2013.
27. K. M. Heussner, "U.S. to Top the World in Mobile Ad Spending for the First Time," gigaom.com/2012/08/01/us-to-top-the-world-in-mobile-ad-spending-for-the-first-time, August 1, 2012.
28. E. Rusli and S. Banjo, "Facebook's Wal-Mart Gambit," online.wsj.com, December 16, 2012.
29. M. Pihlstrom and G. J. Brush, "Comparing the Perceived Value of Information and Entertainment Mobile Services," *Psychology & Marketing*, Vol. 25 (8) (August 2008): 732–755.
30. C. Taylor and D. H. Lee, "Introduction: New Media: Mobile Advertising and Marketing," *Psychology & Marketing*, Vol. 25 (8) (August 2008): 711–713.
31. J. Mantel and Y. Sekhavat, "The Impact of SMS Advertising on Members of a Virtual Community," *Journal of Advertising Research* (September 2008): 363–373.
32. S. Ovide and G. Bensinger, "Mobile Ads: Here's What Works and What Doesn't," online.wsj.com, September 27, 2012.
33. C. C. Miller and S. Sengupta, "In Mobile World, Tech Giants Scramble to Get Up to Speed," online.wsj.com, October 22, 2012.
34. R. Stross, "Smartphones Ads and Their Drawbacks," nytimes.com, September 15, 2012.
35. B. Stone, "Amazon.com Invades the Apple App Store," nytimes.com, December 3, 2008.
36. Tim Arango, "Digital Sales Surpass CDs at Atlantic," nytimes.com, November 26, 2008.
37. Michael Grynbaum, "Taxi TV Screens Gain Ad Business in New York," nytimes.com, December 10, 2010.
38. Louise Story, "Madison Avenue Calling," nytimes.com, January 20, 2007.
39. Emily Steel and Jessica Vascellaro, "A Rare Apple Compromise," online.wsj.com, December 13, 2011.
40. Elizabeth Olson, "Bar Codes Add Detail on Items in TV Ads," nytimes.com, September 26, 2010.
41. S. Clifford and C. Miller, "Retailers Retool Sites to Ease Mobile Shopping," nytimes.com, April 17, 2011.
42. T. Vega, "Google Search That Leads to Brand Marketing," nytimes.com, November 15, 2010.
43. D. Mattioli, "Grocers Are Testing Smartphones," nytimes.com, October 11, 2011.
44. K. Belson, "With This App, a Souvenir Without the Stand," nytimes.com, August 26, 2011.
45. S. Elliott, "If You Can't Stand the Web Camera, Get Out of the Kitchen," nytimes.com, December 7, 2009.
46. D. Armano, "Six Social-Digital Trends for 2013," *Harvard Business Review*, (December 12, 2012): 34–47.
47. Ibid.
48. Shayndi Raice, "Inside Facebook's Push to Woo Big Advertisers," online.wsj.com, August 14, 2012.
49. "Social Media Ad Metrics Definitions," Interactive Advertising Bureau (IAB), May 2009.
50. www.comscore.com/Products_Services/Web_Analytics/Audience_Demographics (accessed August 1, 2012).
51. Louise Story, "How Many Site Hits? Depends Who's Counting," nytimes.com, October 22, 2007.
52. William Launder and Suzanne Vranica, "Nielsen to Branch Out with Arbitron," online.wsj.com, December 18, 2012.
53. Stu Woo and Geoffrey Fowler, "Daily Deals Rescue Local-Ad Market," online.wsj.com, June 14, 2011.
54. Stu Woo and Geoffrey Fowler, "Banner Ads and Other 'Local' Flops," online.wsj.com, June 14, 2011.
55. Compiled from data listed in Stuart Elliott, "Magazine Ad Pages Fell 3.1% in 2011, with a Weak End to the Year," nytimes.com, January 10, 2012.
56. http://www.nytimes.com/interactive/2009/01/30/business/20090201_metrics.html (accessed January 14, 2013).
57. Keach Hagey, "Magazines Cross the Digital Divide," online.wsj.com, January 18, 2013.
58. http://articles.timesofindia.indiatimes.com/2001-09-25/edit-page/27238333_1_jeweller-product-placement-brand (accessed on January 27, 2014.)
59. http://ijmtpublication.com/files/AOMR_2_1_2012/AOMR_2_1_2012_3.pdf (accessed on January 27, 2014).
60. Shannon Terlep and Suzanne Vranica, "GM to Forgo Pricey Super Bowl Ads," online.wsj.com, May 18, 2012.

61. Sam Schechner, "TV Networks See Key Audience Erode," online.wsj.com, May 27, 2011.
62. Shalini Ramachadram, "Evidence Grows on TV Cord-Cutting," online.wsj.com, August 7, 2012.
63. Miriam Gottfried, "Online Streaming Gives Cable Networks a Sporting Chance," online.wsj.com, August 15, 2012.
64. www.ensequence.com
65. Stephen Richard Dix, Steven Bellman, Hanadi Haddad, and Duane Varan, "Using Interactive Program-Loyalty Banners to Reduce TV Ad Avoidance: Is It Possible to Give Viewers a Reason to Stay Tuned during Commercial Breaks?" *Journal of Advertising Research* (June 2010): 154–161.
66. Barbara Chai, "'Person of Interest' Takes to Streets to Give People a Taste of the Show," online.wsj.com, September 12, 2011.
67. Stuart Elliott, "Hot Food, and Air, at Bus Stops," nytimes.com, December 2, 2008.
68. pqmedia, *Global Digital Out-of-Home Media Forecast 2012–2016*, "Executive Summary" (2011).
69. Doreen Carvajal, "Placing the Product in the Dialogue, Too," nytimes.com, January 17, 2006; Louise Story, "So That's Why They Drink Coke on TV," nytimes.com, December 9, 2007; Stuart Elliott, "Up Next, a Show from Our Sponsor," nytimes.com, June 12, 2008; Stephanie Clifford, "A Product's Place Is on the Set," nytimes.com, July 22, 2008.
70. Verolien Cauberghe and Patrick de Pelsmacker, "Advergames: The Impact of Brand Prominence and Game Repetition on Brand Responses," *Journal of Advertising,* Vol. 39 (1) (Spring 2010): 5–18.
71. Bhanu Pande and Sarah Jacob, "Tweet and make up," *The Economic Times*, August 30, 2010.
72. http://www.huffingtonpost.com/2012/10/04/facebook-1-billion-users_n_1938675.html
73. Claire Cain Miller, "YouTube gets the word out on tackling bad breath," *The Hindu Business Line*, September 30, 2010.
74. Christoph Burmann, "User generated branding," *Journal of Brand Management*, Vol. 18 (2010): 1–4.
75. R.B. Zajonc," Attitudinal Effects of Mere Exposure," *Journal of Personality and Social Psychology*, Vol. 9 (2, Pt.2) (Jun 1968): 1-27
76. Amrita Nayar-Ghaswallah, "HUL's not so secret sauce," *The Hindu Business Line*, July 12, 2013.
77. Anshul Dhamija, "Bangalore gets Puma Social club," *The Times of India*, July 12, 2013.
78. Venkat Ramaswamy and Francis Gouilllart, *Power of Co-creation: Build it with them to Boost Growth, Productivity and Profits* (New York: Free Press, 2010).
79. Ibid
80. Glued to internet? Scientists warn of identity crisis," *The Times of India*, July 31, 2011.
81. "The Skin Advisor App Enhanced Consumer-Brand Interaction: Ganesh Bangalore", Interview by Abhilasha Ojha, *Business Standard*, January 27, 2014.
82. Ibid
83. http://wearesocial.sg (accessed on May 30,2014).
84. Ibid

Chapter 9

1. Philipp Schmitt, Bernd Skiera, and Christophe Van den Bulte, "Referral Programs and Customer Value," *Journal of Marketing*, Vol. 75(1) (January 2011) (as reported in "Pays to Talk Knowledge @Wharton – BE exclusive, *The Economic Times*, September 22, 2010.)
2. Marina Krakovsky, "Less Wash, More Dry," *Scientific American* (November 2008): 28–29.
3. Andrew Adam Newman, "A Lucky Few, This Band of Brothers, and the Less Blood Shed the Better," nytimes.com, November 17, 2010.
4. R. Srinivasan, "A twist to the marketing tale," *The Hindu Business Line*, January 31, 2013.
5. Molly Soat, "Share and Share Alike," *American Marketing Association*, August 2013.
6. Times News Network, "Face recognition: The next big tech leap," *The Times of India*, November 26, 2013.
7. Peeter W. J. Verleigh, Ad Th. H. Pruyn, and Kim A. Peters, "Turning Shoppers into Sellers: Two Experiments on Member-Get-Member Campaigns," *Advances in Consumer Research,* 30 (2003): 346.
8. Charles Passy, "Waiting in Line: Good for the Ego, Bad for the Wallet," online.wsj.com, October 9, 2012.
9. Gary Kritz, Héctor R. Lozada, and Mary M. Long, "When Can Online Group Behavior Be an Aid: Can the Foodies Help Marketers Learn about Consumption?" *Journal of Business & Behavioral Sciences*, Vol. 24 (1) (Spring 2012): 58–71.
10. Bhanu Pande, "When a Crowd is Company," *The Economic Times*, January 25, 2012.
11. Namrata Singh, "Shaktimaans To Power Rural Reach," *The Times of India*, August 16, 2010.
12. Amit Bapna, "Tailing Trends," *The Economic Times*, 26 October, 2011.
13. Feng Zhu & Xiaoquan (Michael) Zhang, "Impact of Online Consumer Reviews on Sales: The Moderating Role of Product and Consumer Characteristics," *Journal of Marketing,* Vol. 74 (March 2010): 133–148.
14. Robert Madrigal, "The Influence of Social Alliances with Sports Teams on Intentions to Purchase Corporate Sponsors' Products," *Journal of Advertising,* 29 (Winter 2000): 13–24.

15. Katherine Rosman, "Books Women Read When No One Can See the Cover," online.wsj.com, March 14, 2012.
16. Srijana Mitra Das, "Do Nothing, Accomplish More: Deepak Chopra," *The Times of India*, January 23, 2012.
17. Jennifer Edson Escalas and James R. Bettman, "Self-Construal, Reference Groups, and Brand Meaning," Journal of Consumer Research, Vol. 32(3) (December 2005): 378–379.
18. Ravi Balakrishnan,' Strip Tees' *The Economic Times*, January 25, 2012.
19. Jennifer Edison Escalas and James R Bettman,' Self-Construal, Reference Group, and Brand Meaning *Journal of Consumer Research*, Vol. 32, December 2005.
20. George D. Deitz, Susan W. Myers, and Marla R. Stafford, "Understanding Consumer Response to Sponsorship Information: A Resource-Matching Approach," *Psychology & Marketing*, Vol. 29 (4) (April 2012): 226–239.
21. Jennifer Lemanski and Lee Hyung-Seok, "Attitude Certainty and Resistance to Persuasion: Investigating the Impact of Source Trustworthiness in Advertising," *International Journal of Business & Social Sciences*, Vol. 3 (1) (January 2012): 6675.
22. Zafer Erdogan, Michael J. Baker, and Stephen Tagg, "Selecting Celebrity Endorsers: The Practitioner's Perspective," *Journal of Advertising Research* (May/June 2001): 39–48.
23. Roobina Ohanian, "The Impact of Celebrity Spokespersons: Perceived Image on Consumers' Intention to Purchase," *Journal of Advertising Research* (February–March 1991): 46–54.
24. Carolyn Tripp, Thomas D. Jensen, and Les Carlson, "The Effects of Multiple Product Endorsements by Celebrities on Consumers' Attitudes and Intentions," *Journal of Consumer Research,* Vol. 20 (March 1994): 535–547; David C. Bojanic, Patricia K. Voli, and James B. Hunt, "Can Consumers Match Celebrity Endorsers with Products?" in *Developments in Marketing Science,* ed. Robert L. King (Richmond, VA: Academy of Marketing Science, 1991): 303–307.
25. Alan J. Bush, Craig A. Martin, and Victoria D. Bush, "Sports Celebrity Influence on the Behavioral Intentions of Generation Y," *Journal of Advertising Research* (March 2004): 108–118.
26. Ben Sisario, "In Beyoncé Deal, Pepsi Focuses on Collaboration," nytimes.com, December 9, 2012.
27. Suzanne Vranica, "Bringing Sexy Back to Golf?" online.wsj.com, January 24, 2012.
28. Brian Stelter, "After Apology, National Advertisers Are Still Shunning Limbaugh," nytimes.com, March 13, 2012.
29. Stuart Elliott, "A Noisy Casting Call as Thousands Quack for Aflac," nytimes.com, April 5, 2011.
30. Associated Press, "Nike Makes No Plans for Pistorius in Future Ads," online.wsj.com, February 18, 2013.
31. Kenneth E. Clow, Karen E. James, Sarah E. Sisk, and Henry S. Cole, "Source Credibility, Visual Strategy and the Model in Print Advertisements," *Journal of Marketing Development & Competitiveness,* Vol. 5 (3) (2011): 24–31.
32. Andria Cheng, "Marketers Seek Out Geeks," online.wsj.com, October 15, 2012.
33. Mathew Ingram, "Should You Care How High Your Klout Score Is?" GIGAOM, October 27, 2011; Meredith Popolo, "How to Boost Your Klout Score," online.wsj.com, November 2, 2011.
34. Jo Brown, Amanda J. Broderick, and Nick Lee, "Word of Mouth Communication within Online Communities: Conceptualizing the Online Social Network," *Journal of Interactive Marketing,* Vol. 21 (3) (Summer 2007): 2–20.
35. Shahana Sen and Dawn Lerman, "Why Are You Telling Me This? An Examination into Negative Consumer Reviews on the Web," *Journal of Interactive Marketing,* Vol. 21 (4) (Autumn 2007): 76–94.
36. Wu Paul and Wang Yun Chen, "The Influence of Electronic Word-of-Mouth Message Appeal and Message Source Credibility on Brand Attitude," *Asia Pacific Journal of Marketing & Logistics*, Vol. 23 (4) (2011): 448–472.
37. Ted Smith, James R. Coyle, Elizabeth Lightfoot, and Amy Scott, "Reconsidering Models of Influence: The Relationship Between Consumer Social Networks and Word-of-Mouth Effectiveness," *Journal of Advertising Research*, Vol. 47 (4) (December 2007): 387–397.
38. David Kirkpatrick and Daniel Roth, "Why There's No Escaping the BLOG," *Fortune,* January 10, 2005, 44–50.
39. John Jannarone, "When Twitter Fans Steer TV," online.wsj.com, September 16, 2012.
40. Stephanie Clifford, "Spreading the Word (and the Lotion) in Small-Town Alaska," nytimes.com, October 9, 2008.
41. Robert V. Kozinets, Kristine de Valck, Andrea C. Wojnicki, and Sarah J. S. Wilner, "Networked Narratives: Understanding Word-of-Mouth Marketing in Online Communities," *Journal of Marketing*, Vol. 74 (March 2010): 71–89.
42. Stuart Elliott, "Laugh at the Web Clips, Then Buy the Gel," nytimes.com, December 19, 2007.
43. Louise Story, "Facebook Is Marketing Your Brand Preferences (with Your Permission)," nytimes.com, November 7, 2007.

44. Keach Hagey, "The Advertorial's Best Friend," online.wsj.com, October 7, 2012.
45. Joseph E. Phelps, Regina Lewis, Lynne Mobilio, David Perry, and Niranjan Raman, "Viral Marketing or Electronic Word-of-Mouth Advertising: Examining Consumer Responses and Motivations to Pass Along Email," *Journal of Advertising Research* (December 2004): 333–348.
46. Kirthi Kalyanam, Shelby McIntyre, and Todd Masonis, "Adaptive Experimentation in Interactive Marketing: The Case of Viral Marketing at Plaxo," *Journal of Interactive Marketing,* Vol. 21 (3) (Summer 2007): 72–85.
47. Yang Hongwei, Liu Hui, and Zhou Liuning, "Predicting Young Chinese Consumers' Mobile Viral Attitudes, Intents and Behavior," *Asia Pacific Journal of Marketing & Logistics,* Vol. 24 (1) (2012): 59–77.
48. Rob Walker, "The Hidden (in Plain Sight) Persuaders," www.nytimes.com, December 5, 2004.
49. Katherine Rosman, "Big Marketers on Campus," nytimes.com, April 3, 2012.
50. Natasha Singer, "You've Won a Badge (and Now We Know All About You)," nytimes.com, February 4, 2012.
51. Eric Pfanner, "Taxi Drivers in London Take a Turn as Pitchmen," nytimes.com, January 21, 2008.
52. Thorsten Hennig-Thurau, Kevin P. Gwinner, Gianfranco Walsh, and Dwayne D. Gremler, "Electronic Word-of-Mouth Via Consumer-Opinion Platforms: What Motivates Consumers to Articulate Themselves on the Internet?" *Journal of Interactive Marketing* (Winter 2004): 38–52.
53. Eun-Ju Lee, Kyoung-Nan Kwon, and David W. Schumann, "Segmenting the Non-adopter Category in the Diffusion of Internet Banking," *International Journal of Bank Marketing,* Vol. 23 (5) (2005): 414–437.

Chapter 10

1. Pamela Kruger, "Why Johnny Can't Play," *Fast Company* (August 2000): 271–272. See also Daniel Thomas Cook, *The Commodification of Childhood: The Children's Clothing Industry and the Rise of the Child Consumer* (Durham, NC: Duke University Press, 2004).
2. Rafael Bravo, Elena Fraj, and Eva Martinez, "Intergenerational Influences on the Dimensions of Young Customer-Based Brand Equity," *Young Consumers,* Vol. 8 (1) (2007): 63.
3. Amy Rummel, John Howard, Jennifer M. Swinton, and D. Bradley Seymour, "You Can't Have That! A Study of Reactance Effects and Children's Consumer Behavior," *Journal of Marketing Theory & Practice* (Winter 2000): 38–45.
4. Jason E. Lueg and R. Zachary Finney, "Interpersonal Communication in the Consumer Socialization Process: Scale Development and Validation," *Journal of Marketing Theory & Practice,* Vol. 15 (Winter 2007): 25–39.
5. Based on Sabrina M. Neeley and Tim Coffey, "Understanding the 'Four-Eyed, Four-Legged' Consumer: A Segmentation Analysis of U.S. Moms," *Journal of Marketing Theory & Practice,* Vol. 15 (3) (Summer 2007): 251–261.
6. Lan Nguyen Chaplin and Deborah Roedder John, "Growing Up in a Material World: Age Differences in Materialism in Children and Adolescents," *Journal of Consumer Research,* Vol. 34 (December 2007): 480–493.
7. David B. Wooten, "From Labeling Possessions to Possessing Labels: Ridicule and Socialization among Adolescents," *Journal of Consumer Research,* Vol. 33 (September 2006): 188–198.
8. Marie J. Lachance and Frederic Legault, "College Students' Consumer Competence: Identifying the Socialization Sources," *Journal of Research for Consumers,* no. 13 (2007): 1–5.
9. Deborah Moscardelli and Catherine Liston-Heyes, "Consumer Socialization in a Wired World: The Effects of Internet Use and Parental Communication on the Development of Skepticism to Advertising," *Journal of Marketing,* Vol. 13 (3) (Summer 2005): 62–75; Maria Eugenia Perez, Dan Padgett, and Willem Burgers, "Intergenerational Influence on Brand Preferences," *Journal of Product & Brand Management,* Vol. 20 (1) (2011): 5–13.
10. John Fetto, "'Woof Woof' Means, 'I Love You,'" *American Demographics* (February 2002): 11; Sharon L. Peters, "Are American Crazy for Treating Our Pets Like Kids?" *USA Today*, December 18, 2011; available at http://yourlife.usatoday.com/parenting-family/pets/story/2011-12-18/Are Americans crazy...
11. See, for example, Carter A. Mandrik, Edward F. Fern, and Yeqing Bao, "Intergenerational Influence in Mothers and Young Adult Daughters," *Advances in Consumer Research,* Vol. 31 (2004): 697–699.
12. U.S. Census Bureau, "Average Annual Expenditures of All Consumer Units by Selected Major Types of Expenditures: 1990 to 2009," *Statistical Abstract of the United States: 2012,* Table 684. Available at http://www.census.gov/comendia/statab/2012/1250684.pdt.
13. Sheryll Alexander, "What Women Want... in a Car," CNN.com, March 14, 2008.
14. Ibid.
15. Sam Marsden, "Women Now in Charge of Major Financial Decisions," telegraph.co.uk, September 28, 2012.

16. John B. Ford, Michael S. LaTour, and Tony L. Henthorne, "Perception of Marital Roles in Purchase Decision Processes: A Cross-Cultural Study," *Journal of the Academy of Marketing Science,* Vol. 23 (2) (1995): 120–131; Tony L. Henthorne, Michael S. LaTour, and Robert Matthews, "Perception of Marital Roles in Purchase Decision Making: A Study of Japanese Couples," in *Proceedings of the AMA*, 321–322 (Chicago: American Marketing Association, 1995).
17. Yang Xia, Zafar U. Ahmed, Ng Kuan Hwa, Tan Wan Li, and Wendy Teo Chai Ying, "Spousal Influence in Singaporean Family Purchase Decision-Making Process: A Cross-Cultural Comparison," *Asia Pacific Journal of Marketing,* Vol. 18 (3) (2006): 201–222.
18. Michael J. Dotson and Eva M. Hyatt, "Major Influence Factors in Children's Consumer Socialization," *Journal of Consumer Marketing,* Vol. 22 (1) (2005): 35–42; Aviv Shoham, "He Said, She Said They Said: Parents' and Children's Assessment of Children's Influence on Family Consumption Decisions," *Journal of Consumer Marketing,* Vol. 22 (3) (2005): 152–160; L. A. Flurry and Alvin C. Burns, "Children's Influence in Purchase Decisions: A Social Power Theory Approach," *Journal of Business Research,* Vol. 58 (May 2005): 593–601.
19. Malene Gram, "Children as Co-decision Makers in the Family? The Case of Family Holidays," *Young Consumers,* Vol. 8 (1) (2007): 19–28.
20. Joyantha S. Wimalasiri, "A Cross-National Study on Children's Purchasing Behavior and Parental Response," *Journal of Consumer Marketing,* Vol. 21 (4) (2004): 274–284.
21. Michael A. Belch, Kathleen A. Krentler, and Laura A. Willis-Flurry, "Teen Internet Mavens: Influence in Family Decision Making," *Journal of Business Research,* Vol. 58 (May 2005): 569–575.
22. Stephanie Thompson, "Million-Dollar Baby," *Advertising Age,* May 30, 2005, 1, 50.
23. Bodil Stilling Blichfeldt, "A Nice Vacation: Variations in Experience Aspirations and Travel Careers," *Journal of Vacation Marketing,* Vol. 13 (2) (2007): 149–164.
24. U.S. Census Bureau, *Statistical Abstract of the United States, 2008*; available at http://www.census.gov/compendia/; U.S. Census Bureau, "American's Families and Living Arrangements, 2004, available at http://www.census.gov/prod/census2010/briefs/c2012br-14.
25. U.S. Census Bureau, "Households, Families, Subfamilies, and Married Couples: 1980 to 2006," and "Households by Age of Householder and Size of Household: 1990 to 2006," *Statistical Abstract of the United States: 2008,* Tables 58 and 61, accessed at www.census.gov/compendia/statab; U.S. Census Bureau, "Marital Status of People 15 Years and Over, by Age, Sex, Personal Earnings, Race, and Hispanic Origin, 2006," *Current Population Survey 2006, Annual Social and Economic Supplement*, March 27, 2007, Table A1.
26. Compiled from data at: U.S. Census Bureau, *Census 2010 Summary File 1 counts shown in American Fact Finder.* Available at http://www.comsus.gov/prod/cen2010/briefs/c2010br-14/.
27. Nabil Razzouk, Victoria Seitz, and Karen Prodigalidad Capo, "A Comparison of Consumer Decision-Making Behavior of Married and Cohabiting Couples," *Journal of Consumer Marketing,* Vol. 24 (5) (2007): 264–274.
28. Julie Tinson, Clive Nancarrow, and Ian Brace, "Purchase Decision Making and the Increasing Significance of Family Types," *Journal of Consumer Marketing,* Vol. 25 (1) (2008): 45–56.
29. Charles M. Schaninger and Sanjay Putrevu, "Dual Spousal Work Involvement: An Alternative Method to Classify Households/Families," *Academy of Marketing Science Review,* Vol. 10 (8) (2006): 1–21; Charles Schaninger and Sanjay Putrevu, "Dual Spousal Work Involvement," *European Advances in Consumer Research*, Vol. 8, ed. Stefania Borghinl, Mary Ann McGrath, and Cele Otnes (Duluth, MN: Association for Consumer Research, 2007): 80–86.
30. "Brand Stats: Market Focus—Instant Coffee," *Brand Strategy (London),* May 10, 2005, 50.
31. Takashina Shuji, "The New Inequality," *Japan Echo,* August 2000, 38–39.
32. *Source:* U.S. Census Bureau, *Statistical Abstract of the United States*, 2012, available at census.gov/prod/2011pubs/12statab/income.
33. Tamar Lewin, "A Marriage of Unequals," *New York Times,* May 19, 2005, A1, 14–15.
34. David Leonhardt, "The College Dropout Boom," *New York Times,* May 24, 2005, A1, 18–19.
35. Michael D. Yates, "A Statistical Portrait of the U.S. Working Class," *Monthly Review,* Vol. 56 (April 2005): 12–31.
36. *Source:* MRI Spring 2012, www.fwmedia.com, accessed July 16, 2012.
37. Robert B. Settle, Pamela L. Alreck, and Denny E. McCorkle, "Consumer Perceptions of Mail Phone Order Shopping Media," *Journal of Direct Marketing,* Vol. 8 (Summer 1994): 30–45.
38. W. Lloyd Warner, Marchia Meeker, and Kenneth Eells, *Social Class in America: Manual of Procedure for the Measurement of Social Status* (New York: Harper & Brothers, 1960).
39. *Methodology and Scores of Socioeconomic Status,* Working Paper No. 15 (Washington, DC: U.S. Bureau of the Census, 1963).

40. Janny Scott, "In America, Living Better and Living Longer Is a Major Factor in Health Care and the Gaps Are Widening," *International Herald Tribune,* May 17, 2005, 2.
41. Suniya S. Luthar and Shawn J. Latendresse, "Children of the Affluent; Challenges to Well-Being," *Current Directions in Psychological Science,* Vol. 14 (February 2005): 49.
42. Merrill Lynch and Capgemini, *World Wealth Report, 2008*, available at www.capgemini.com/resources/thought_leadership/world_wealth_report_2008; Merrill Lynch and Capgemini, *World Wealth Report, 2005*, available at www.capgemini.com/resources/thought_leadership/world_wealth_report_200.
43. James Davies, Susanna Sandstrom, Anthony Shorrocks, and Edward Wolff, "The World Distribution of Household Wealth," *World Institute for Development Economies Research of the United Nations University,* 2006, available at www.mindfully.org/WTO/2006/Household-Wealth-Gap5dec06.htm.
44. *The 2008 Mendelsohn Affluent Survey*, Ipsos Mendelsohn, 2008.
45. Ibid.
46. *The 2008 Mendelsohn Affluent Survey*, 2008.
47. *2011 Ipsos Mendelsohn Survey*.
48. Ibid.
49. *Statistical Abstract of the United States 2008,* Table 671.
50. www.factcheck.org/askfactcheck/is_there_a_standard_accepted_definition_of.html, accessed October 2008.
51. Gregory L. White and Shirley Leung, "Stepping Up," *Wall Street Journal*, March 29, 2002, A1.
52. Ellen Byron, "As Middle Class Shrinks, P&G Aims High and Low," online.wsj.com, September 12, 2011.
53. Gemma Charles, "The New Working-Class Brands: PizzaExpress, Tesco and BBC One," brandrepublic.com, July 7, 2011.
54. George Pitcher, "Being Super-Sized Boils Down to Personal Choice," *Marketing Week (London),* October 7, 2004, 33.
55. Owain Thomas, "Working Class Children Suffer Greater Risk of Obesity," covermagazine.co.uk, December 15, 2009.
56. Epictetus, "Discourses" (second century) in *The Enchiridion,* 2, trans. Thomas Higginson (Indianapolis: Bobbs-Merrill, 1955).
57. David Colman, "One Step Forward, Three Steps Back," nytimes.com, July 8, 2009.
58. Paul C. Henry, "Social Class, Market Situation, and Consumers' Metaphors of (Dis)Empowerment," *Journal of Consumersearch,* Vol. 31 (March 2005): 766–778.
59. Youn-Kyung Kim and Seunghae Han, "Perceived Images of Retail Stores and Brands: Comparison among Three Ethnic Consumer Groups," *Journal of Family & Consumer Sciences,* Vol. 92 (3) (2000): 58–61.
60. Randy Kennedy, "For Middle Class, New York Shrinks as Home Prices Soar," *New York Times,* April 1, 1998, A1, B6; "Two Tier Marketing," *Business Week,* March 17, 1997, 82–90; Keith Bradsher, "America's Opportunity Gap," *New York Times,* June 4, 1995, 4.
61. Jared Bernstein, "Income Picture: Median Income Rose as Did Poverty in 2007," *Economic Policy Institute* (August 26, 2008), available at www.epi.org/content.cfm/webfeatures_economindictors_income_20080826
62. Ibid.

Chapter 11

1. Elena Karahanna, J. Roberto Evaristo, and Mark Strite, "Levels of Culture and Individual Behavior: An Integrative Perspective," *Journal of Global Information Management,* Vol. 13 (April–June 2005): 1–20.
2. Tim Stock and Marie Lena Tupot, "Common Denominators: What Unites Global Youth?" *Young Consumers* (Quarter 1) (2006): 36–43.
3. Jeff Strieter and Jerald Weaver, "A Longitudinal Study of the Depiction of Women in a United States Business Publication," *Journal of the American Academy of Business,* Vol. 7 (September 2005): 229–235.
4. Asia Today," *BBC News*, October 18, 2010.
5. Hira Sheth, "The evolving face," *Business India*, October 18–November 2, 2010.
6. Preeti Khicha, "Tetra Pak: Packing a Punch," *Business Standard*, January 17, 2011.
7. Rajiv Banerjee, "Then and Now," *The Economic Times*, March 2, 2011.
8. Ibid
9. Ibid
10. Preeti Khicha, "Operation Dessert Storm," *Business Standard*, April 1, 2011.
11. Ibid
12. Virginia Richards, "Perpetuating Core Consumer Sciences," *Journal of Family & Consumer Sciences,* Vol. 97 (3) (September 2005): 8–10.
13. Kritsadarat Wattanasuwan, "Balancing the Hybrid Self in the Competing Landscapes of Consumption," *Journal of the American Academy of Business, Cambridge,* Vol. 11 (1) (March 2007): 9–17.
14. For a discussion of socialization, see Jason E. Lueg and R. Zachary Finney, "Interpersonal

Communication in the Consumer Socialization Process: Scale Development and Validation," *Journal of Marketing Theory & Practice,* Vol. 15 (1) (Winter 2007): 25–39.

15. Elizabeth C. Hirschman, "Men, Dogs, Guns, and Cars: The Semiotics of Rugged Individualism," *Journal of Advertising,* Vol. 32 (Spring 2003): 9–22.
16. Edward T. Hall, *Beyond Culture*, (New Jersey: Doubleday, 1976).
17. Dennis W. Rook, "The Ritual Dimension of Consumer Behavior," *Journal of Consumer Research,* Vol. 12 (December 1985): 251–264.
18. Sayantani Kar, "Garnering Volumes," *Business Standard*, October 18, 2010.
19. Dennis W. Rook, "The Ritual Dimension of Consumer Behavior," *Journal of Consumer Research,* Vol. 12 (December 1985): 251–264.
20. Bernard Berelson, *Content Analysis in Communication Research* (New York: Free Press, 1952).
21. Michael L. Maynard and Charles R. Taylor, "Girlish Images across Cultures: Analyzing Japanese versus U.S. *Seventeen* Magazine Ads," *Journal of Advertising,* Vol. 28 (1) (Spring 1999): 39–45.
22. Mindy F. Ji and James U. McNeal, "How Chinese Children's Commercials Differ from Those of the United States: A Content Analysis," *Journal of Advertising,* Vol. 30 (3) (Fall 2001): 79–92.
23. Lawrence Osborne, "Consuming Rituals of the Suburban Tribe," *New York Times Magazine*, January 13, 2002, 28–31; Margaret Littman, "Science Shopping," *Crain's Chicago Business,* January 11, 1999, 3; Marvin Matises, "Top of Mind: Send Ethnographers into New-SKU Jungle," *Brandweek*, September 25, 2000, 32–33.
24. Maria Kniazeva and Alladi Venkatesh, "Food for Thought: A Study of Food Consumption in Postmodern US Culture," *Journal of Consumer Behavior,* Vol. 6 (November–December 2007): 419–435.
25. Leonard V. Gordon, *Survey of Personal and Interpersonal Values* (Science Research Associates, 1976).
26. S. Ramesh Kumar, Nitya Guruvayurappan, and Madhurjya Banerjee, "Cultural Values and Branding in an Emerging Market—The Indian Context," *The Marketing Review*, 7 (Autumn 2007), 247–272.
27. As cited in Marieke de Mooij, *Global Marketing and Advertising: Understanding Cultural Paradoxes* (Thousand Oaks, CA and London: Sage Publications, 2007), 42–46.
28. As cited in Vijay Mahajan and Kamini Banga, *The 86% Solution: How to Succeed in the Biggest Market Opportunity of the Next Fifty Years* (Delhi: Pearson Power, 2006).
29. Data on Indian households and villages from The Marketing *Whitebook*, 2007–2008, *Businessworld*, 28–37.
30. Dennis W. Rook, "The Ritual Dimension of Consumer Behavior," *The Journal of Consumer Research*, 12, no. 3, 1985, 251–264.

Chapter 12

1. Carolyn A. Lin, "Cultural Values Reflected in Chinese and American Television Advertising," *Journal of Advertising*, Vol. 30 (3) (Winter 2001). Used with permission of M.E. Sharpe, Inc. All Rights Reserved. Not for reproduction.
2. Michel Laroche, Maria Kalamas, and Mark Cleveland, " 'I' Versus 'We': How Individualists and Collectivists Use Information Sources to Formulate Their Service Expectations," *International Marketing Review,* Vol. 22 (3) (2005): 279–308.
3. Kritika Kongsompong, "Cultural Diversities Between Singapore and Australia: An Analysis of Consumption Behavior," *Journal of the American Academy of Business,* Vol. 9 (2) (September 2006): 87–92.
4. Ultrich R. Orth, Harold F. Koenig, and Zuzana Firbasova, "Cross-National Differences in Consumer Response to the Framing of Advertising Messages," *European Journal of Marketing,* Vol. 41 (3/4) (2007): 327–348.
5. Julien Cayla and Giana M. Eckhardt, "Asian Brands and the Shaping of a Transnational Imagined Community," *Journal of Consumer Research,* Vol. 35 (August 2008): 216–230.
6. John A. McCarty, Martin I. Horn, Mary Kate Szenasy, and Jocelyn Feintuch, "An Exploratory Study of Consumer Style: Country Differences and International Segments," *Journal of Consumer Behaviour* (January–February 2007): 53–63.
7. *Source:* John A. McCarty, Martin I. Horn, Mary Kate Szenasy, and Jocelyn Feintuch, "An Exploratory Study of Consumer Style: Country Differences and International Segments," *Journal of Consumer Behaviour* (January–February 2007): 53–54. Copyright © 2007 John Wiley & Sons, Ltd.
8. Alexander Josiassen, "Consumer Disidentification and Its Effects on Domestic Product Purchases: An Empirical Investigation in the Netherlands," *Journal of Marketing,* Vol. 75 (March 2011): 124–140.
9. Jan-Benedict E. M. Steenkamp and Martijn G. de Jong, "A Global Investigation into the Constellation of Consumer Attitudes Toward Global and Local Products," *Journal of Marketing*, Vol. 74 (November 2010): 18–40.
10. Drew Martin and Paul Herbig, "Marketing Implications of Japan's Social-Cultural Underpinnings," *Journal of Brand Management,* Vol. 9 (3) (January 2002): 171–179.

11. Marion Issard, "To Tailor Burgers for France, McDonald's Enlists Baguette," online.wsj.com, February 24, 2012.
12. Annie Gasparro, "Domino's Sticks to Its Ways Abroad," online.wsj.com, April 17, 2012.
13. Liz Alderman, "In Europe, Starbucks Adjusts to a Café Culture," nytimes.com, March 30, 2012.
14. Christina Passariello, "Fitting Shades for Chinese," online.wsj.com, April 21, 2011.
15. Laurie Burkitt and Bob Davis, "Chasing China's Shoppers," online.wsj.com, June 14, 2012.
16. Jeff Bennett, "Chevrolet Ads to Take 'New Road,'" online.wsj.com, January 8, 2013.
17. Michael Wines, "Picking Brand Names in China Is a Business Itself," nytimes.com, November 11, 2011.
18. Suzanne Vranica, "PepsiCo Adds Fizz to Its Cola," online.wsj.com, March 29, 2012.
19. Leonidas Hatzithomas, Yorgos Zotos, and Christina Boutsouki, "Humor and Cultural Values in Print Advertising: A Cross-Cultural Study," *International Marketing Review,* Vol. 28 (1) (2011): 57–80.
20. Sukanlaya Sawang, "Sex Appeal in Advertising: What Consumers Think," *Journal of Promotion Management,* Vol. 16 (2010): 167–187.
21. Fang Liu, Hong Cheng, and Jianyao Li, "Consumer Responses to Sex Appeal Advertising: A Cross-Cultural Study," *International Marketing Review,* Vol. 26 (4/5) (2009): 501–520.
22. Jing Zhang, "The Persuasiveness of Individualistic and Collectivistic Advertising Appeals among Chinese Generation-X Consumers," *Journal of Advertising,* Vol. 39 (3) (Fall 2010): 69–80.
23. Simon Somogyi, Elton Li, Trent Johnson, Johan Bruwer, and Susan Bastian, "The Underlying Motivations of Chinese Wine Consumer Behavior," *Asia Pacific Journal of Marketing & Logistics,* Vol. 23 (4) (2011): 473–485.
24. Kawpong Polyorat and Dana L Alden, "Self-Construal and Need-for-Cognition Effects on Brand Attitudes and Purchase Intentions in Response to Comparative Advertising in Thailand and the United States," *Journal of Advertising* (Spring 2005): 37–49.
25. Yung Kyun Choi and Gordon E. Miracle, "The Effectiveness of Comparative Advertising in Korea and the United States," *Journal of Advertising* (Winter 2004): 75–88.
26. Rebecca Thurlow, "Australia Cigarette-Packaging Curbs Prompt Suit," online.wsj.com, November 21, 2011.
27. Chun Han Wong, "Singapore Tightens Rules on Casino Advertising," online.wsj.com, November 25, 2011.
28. Lilly Vitorovich, "Groupon Ads Draw U.K. Scrutiny," online.wsj.com, December 2, 2011.
29. Laurie Burkitt, "China Bans Ads in TV Dramas," online.wsj.com, November 29, 2011.
30. Laurie Burkitt, "In China, Air Cheow-DAN Cries Foul," online.wsj.com, February 24, 2012.
31. Chingching Chang, "The Effectiveness of Using a Global Look in an Asian Market," *Journal of Advertising Research* (June 2008): 199–214.
32. Natasha Singer, "At Estée Lauder, a Brand Is Developed Just for China," nytimes.com, September 24, 2012.
33. Douglas B. Holt, John A. Quelch, and Earl L. Taylor, "How Global Brands Compete," *Harvard Business Review* (September 2004): 68–75.
34. Ibid.
35. Carlos J. Torelli, Ay egül Özsomer, Sergio W. Carvalho, Hean Tat Keh, and Natalia Maehle, "Brand Concepts as Representations of Human Values: Do Cultural Congruity and Compatibility Between Values Matter?" *Journal of Marketing,* Vol. 76 (July 2012): 92–108.
36. Jessie H. Chen-Yu, Keum-Hee Hong, and Yoo-Kyoung Seock, "Adolescents' Clothing Motives and Store Selection Criteria: A Comparison between South Korea and the United States," *Journal of Fashion Marketing & Management,* Vol. 14 (1) (2010): 127–144.
37. Devon Maylie, "By Foot, by Bike, by Taxi, Nestlé Expands in Africa," online.wsj.com, December 1, 2011.
38. Both tables are based on: "Best Global Brands 2012," Interbrand Report, available at http://www.Interbrand.com/en/news-room/press-releases/2012-10-02-7543da7.aspx (accessed January 20, 2013).
39. Laurie Burkitt and Emily Glazer, "In China, Some Imports Get a Local Run for the Money," online.wsj.com, August 5, 2012.
40. Alokparna Basu Monga and Deborah Roedder John, "Consumer Response to Brand Extensions: Does Culture Matter?" *Advances in Consumer Research,* Vol. 31 (2004): 216–222.
41. Alokparna Basu Monga and Deborah Roedder John, "Cultural Differences in Brand Extension Evaluation: The Influence of Analytic versus Holistic Thinking," *Journal of Consumer Research,* Vol. 33 (March 2007): 529–536.
42. Shintaro Okazaki, "Searching the Web for Global Brands: How American Brands Standardize Their Web Sites in Europe," *European Journal of Marketing,* Vol. 39 (1/2) (2005): 87–109.
43. Andrew Browne, James T. Areddy, and Merissa Marr, "Katzenberg Unveils a China Film Project," online.wsj.com, April 19, 2013.
44. Laurie Burkitt, "Bling Toned Down in Beijing," online.wsj.com, August 6, 2012.

45. Andrew Kramer, "Russia Becomes a Magnet for U.S. Fast-Food Chains," nytimes.com, August 3, 2011.
46. Stephanie Clifford and Liz Alderman, "A New American Invasion," nytimes.com, June 16, 2011.
47. Hiroko Tabuchi, "Japanese Consumers Reconsidering Rice Loyalty," nytimes.com, July 19, 2012.
48. David Kesmodel, "Feeling Stale, Molson Reinvents Itself in Canada," online.wsj.com, April 13, 2011.
49. Moises Naim, "Can the World Afford a Middle Class?" *Foreign Policy,* Vol. 165 (March–April 2008): 95–96.
50. Peter Marber, "Globalization and Its Contents," *World Policy Journal* (Winter 2004–2005): 29–37.
51. Ann Veeck and Alvin C. Burns, "Changing Tastes: The Adoption of New Food Choices in Post-Reform China," *Journal of Business Research,* Vol. 58 (2005): 644–652.
52. R. Stephen Parker, Charles M. Hermans, and Allen D. Schaefer, "Fashion Consciousness of Chinese, Japanese and American Teenagers," *Journal of Fashion Marketing & Management,* Vol. 8 (2) (2004): 176–186.
53. Ibid., 182.
54. Energy BBDO, "The GenWorld Teen Study," available at www.businessfordiplomaticaction.com/learn/articles/genworld_leave_behind.pdf (accessed November 2008).
55. Based on: Becky Ebenkamp, "Creative Consciousness," *Brandweek,* January 16, 2006, 14.

Chapter 13

1. David Court, Dave Elzinga, Susan Mulder, and Ole JørgenVetvik, "The consumer decision Journey," The McKinsey Quarterly Vo.l 3 and David C. Ederlman," Branding in the digital age: You're Spending Your Money in All the Wrong places" HBR, Dec 2010 (accessed at www.hbr.org on Dec 13, 2010).
2. Gordon C. Bruner, II, "The Effect of Problem-Recognition Style on Information Seeking," *Journal of the Academy of Marketing Science*, Vol. 15 (Winter 1987): 33–41.
3. Matthew Klein, "He Shops, She Shops," *American Demographics* (March 1998): 34–35.
4. Sharon E. Beatty and Scott M. Smith, "External Search Effort: An Investigation across Several Product Categories," *Journal of Consumer Research,* 14 (June 1987): 83–95.
5. Niranjan V. Raman, "A Qualitative Investigation of Web-Browsing Behavior," in *Advances in Consumer Research*, eds. J. Brucks and S. MacInnis (Provo, UT: Association for Consumer Research, 1997): 511–516.
6. "Just the Facts," *Journal of Business Strategy*, Vol. 22 (2) (March/April, 2001): 3–4; Kuan-Pin Chiang, Ruby Roy Dholakia, and Stu Westin, "Needle in the Cyberstack: Consumer Search for Information in the Web-Based Marketspace," *Advances in Consumer Research,* Vol. 31 (2004): 88–89.
7. Kristy E. Reynolds, Judith Anne Garretson Folse, and Michael A. Jones, "Search Regret: Antecedents and Consequences," *Journal of Retailing*, 82, no. 4 (2006): 339
8. Reynolds, Folse, and Jones, "Search Regret."
9. Lan Xia, "Consumer Choice Strategies and Choice Confidence in the Electronic Environment," in *1999 AMA Educators Proceedings,* Vol. 10, eds. Stephen P. Brown and D. Sudharshan (Chicago: American Marketing Association, 1999): 270–277.
10. Henry Assael, "Consumer Behaviour: A Strategic Approach", Biztantra (2005): 88–117.
11. Sherif, Sherif and Nebergall, *Attitude and Attitude change: The Social Judgment-involvement Approach* (Westport: Greenwood Publishing, 1965)
12. M. Sherif and C.E. Hovland, *Social Judgment* (New Haven: Yale University Press, 1961).
13. Herbert E. Krugman, "The Impact of Television Advertising: Learning without Involvement," *Public Opinion Quarterly*, Vol.29 (Fall 1965): 349–356.
14. Petty, Cacioppo, and Schumann, "Central and Peripheral routes to Advertising Effectiveness: The Moderating Role of Involvement," *Journal of Consumer Research*, Vol. 10 (September 1983): 135–146.
15. Yuping Liu-Thompkeins and Leona Tom, "Not All repeat customers are the same: Designing Effective Cross-Selling Promotion on the Basis of Attitudinal Loyalty and Habit," *Journal of Marketing*, Vol. 77 (September 2013): 21–36.
16. John W. Pracejus, G. Douglas Olsen, and Thomas C. O'Guinn, "Nothing Is Something: The Production and Reception of Advertising Meaning through the Use of White Space," *Advances in Consumer Research,* Vol. 30, eds. Punam Anand Keller and Dennis W. Rook (Valdosta, GA: Association for Consumer Research, 2003): 174; Pamela Henderson, Joan Giese, and Joseph A. Cote, "Typeface Design and Meaning: The Three Faces of Typefaces," *Advances in Consumer Research,* Vol. 30 (2003): 175.
17. Ashley Lye, Wei Shao, and Sharyn Rundle-Thiele, "Decision Waves: Consumer Decisions in Today's Complex World," *European Journal of Marketing,* Vol. 39 (1/2) (2005): 216–230; see also Lam-Ying Huang and Ying-Jiun Hsieh, "Consumer Electronics Based on Innovation Attributes and Switching Costs: The Case of e-Book Readers," *Electronic Commerce Research & Applications,* Vol. 11 (2012): 218–228.

18. Jeffrey F. Durgee, "Why Some Products 'Just Feel Right,' or, the Phenomenology of Product Rightness," in *Advances in Consumer Research,* Vol. 22, eds. Frank R. Kardes and Mita Sujan (Provo, UT: Association for Consumer Research, 1995): 650–652.
19. Tulin Erdem and Joffre Swait, "Brand Credibility, Brand Consideration, and Choice," *Journal of Consumer Research,* Vol. 31 (June 2004): 191–198.
20. Laurie Peterson, "The Strategic Shopper," *Adweek's Marketing Week,* March 30, 1992, 18–20.
21. Emily Booth, "Getting Inside a Shopper's Mind," *Marketing (U.K.),* June 3, 1999, 33.
22. Kare Sandvik, Kjell Gronhaug, and Frank Lindberg, "Routes to Customer Retention: The Importance of Customer Satisfaction, Performance Quality, Brand Reputation and Customer Knowledge," in *AMA Winter Conference,* eds. Debbie Thorne LeClair and Michael Hartline (Chicago: American Marketing Association, 1997): 211–217.
23. Mohammed M. Nadeem, "Post-Purchase Dissonance: The Wisdom of the 'Repeat' Purchases," *Journal of Global Business Issues,* Vol. 1 (2) (Summer 2007): 183–193.
24. Raquel Sanchez-Fernandez and M. Angeles Iniesta-Bonillo, "Consumer Perception of Value: Literature Review and a New Conceptual Framework," *Journal of Consumer Satisfaction, Dissatisfaction & Complaining Behavior,* Vol. 19 (2006): 40–58.
25. Deirdre Shaw, Terry Newholm, and Roger Dickinson, "Consumption as Voting: An Exploration of Consumer Empowerment," *European Journal of Marketing,* Vol. 40 (9/10) (2006): 1049–1067.
26. Russell W. Belk and Gregory S. Coon, "Gift Giving as Agapic Love: An Alternative to the Exchange Paradigm Based on Dating Experiences," *Journal of Consumer Research,* Vol. 20 (December 1993): 393–417.
27. Julie A. Ruth, Cele C. Otnes, and Frédéric F. Brunel, "Gift Receipt and the Reformulation of Interpersonal Relationships," *Journal of Consumer Research,* Vol. 25 (March 1999): 385–402.
28. Adapted from Deborah Y. Cohn and Leon G. Schiffman, "Gifting: A Taxonomy of Private Realm Giver and Recipient Relationships" (Working Paper), City University of New York, Baruch College, 1996.
29. Deborah Y. Cohn and Leon G. Schiffman, "A Taxonomy of Consumer Gifting Relationships," in *Navigating Crisis and Opportunities in Global Markets: Leadership, Strategy and Governance, International Conference of the Global Business and Technology Association,* eds. Nejdet Delener and Chiang-nan Chaoin (June 8–12, 2004): 164–171.
30. Stephen J. Gould and Claudia E. Weil, "Gift-Giving and Gender Self-Concepts," *Gender Role,* Vol. 24 (1991): 617–637.
31. Tilottama G. Chowdhury, S. Ratneshwar, and Kalpesh K. Desai, "Do Unto Others as You Would Do Unto Yourself: Variety-Seeking Motives in Gift Giving," *Advances in Consumer Research,* Vol. 31, eds. Barbara E. Kahn and Mary Frances Luce (Valdosta, GA: Association for Consumer Research, 2004): 22–23.
32. Annamma Joy, "Gift Giving in Hong Kong and the Continuum of Social Ties," *Journal of Consumer Research,* Vol. 28 (2) (September 2001): 239–256.
33. Suri Weisfield-Spolter and Maneesh Thakkar, "A Framework for Examining the Role of Culture in Individuals' Likelihood to Engage in Self-Gift Behavior," *Academy of Marketing Studies Journal,* Vol. 16 (1) (2012): 39–52.
34. Leon G. Schiffman and Deborah Y. Cohn, "Are They Playing by the Same Rules? A Consumer Gifting Classification of Marital Dyads," *Journal of Business Research,* (forthcoming): 1054–1062.
35. Banwari Mittal, Morris Holbrook, Sharon Beatty, Priya Raghubir, and Arch Woodside, *Consumer Behavior – How Humans Think, Feel and Act in the Marketplace* (New York: Open Mentis, 2008)
36. Srividya Iyer, "Tweeting a serious business; Tweeters can earn up to Rs 1 lakh a month working for microblogging, promoting brands",http://economictimes.indiatimes.com/tech/internet/tweeting-a-serious-business-tweeters-can-earn-up-to-rs-1-lakh-a-month-working-for-microblogging-promoting-brands/articleshow/10084519.cms,accessed on September 23, 2011.
37. ET Q&A (2012), "Social media has transformed online travel planning," *The Economic Times*, May 3, 2012.
38. Saumya Prakash, "Luxor Group: Cleaning the Nano way," *Business Standard*, June 12, 2012.
39. Sayantini Kar, "The Italian Job," *Business Standard*, September 27,2010.
40. Jaclyn Trop, "Crowdfund a car, Test Drive on Google Street View", *The Economic Times*, November 29, 2013.
41. Hsiang Chen and Kevin Crowston, "Comparative Diffusion of the Telephone and the World Wide Web: An Analysis of Rates of Adoption," in *Proceedings of WebNet '97—World Conference of the WWW, Internet and Intranet,* eds. Suave Lobodzinski and Ivan Tomek, (AACE: Toronto, Canada): 110–115; see also Edward D. Conrad, Michael D. Michalisin, and Steven J. Karu, "Measuring Pre-Adoptive Behavior Towards Individual Willingness to Use IT Innovations," *Journal of Strategic Innovation and Sustainability,* Vol. 8 (1) (2012): 81–93.
42. Tariq Bhatti, "Exploring Factors Influencing the Adoption of Mobile Commerce," *Journal of Internet Banking & Commerce,* Vol. 12 (3) (2007): 1–13.

43. Susan H. Higgins and William L. Shanklin, "Seeding Mass Market Acceptance for High Technology Consumer Products," *Journal of Consumer Marketing*, Vol. 9 (Winter 1992): 5–14.

Chapter 14

1. Amanda Zimmerman and John Dahlberg, "The Sexual Objectification of Women in Advertising: A Contemporary Cultural Perspective," *Journal of Advertising Research*, Vol. 48 (1) (March 2008): 21–38.
2. Mike Esterl and Paul Ziobro, "Coke to Curb Ads to Kids, Push Diet Drinks," online.wsj.com, May 8, 2013.
3. Bill Tomson, "Caffeinated Snacks Draw FDA Scrutiny," online.wsj.com, April 30, 2013.
4. Ashok Prasad," Good Cause Hunting," *The Economic Times*, February 12, 2014.
5. Ibid
6. Deborah Roedder John, "Consumer Socialization of Children: A Retrospective Look at Twenty-Five Years of Research," *Journal of Consumer Research*, Vol. 26 (2) (1999): 183–213.
7. D. Borzekowski and T. Robinson, "The 30-Second Effect: An Experiment Revealing the Impact of Television Commercials on Food Preferences of Preschoolers," *Journal of American Dietetic Association*, Vol. 10 (1) (2001): 42–46.
8. K. Corfman and B. Harlam, "Relative Influence of Parent and Child in the Purchase of Products for Children," *Journal of Marketing Theory & Practice*, Vol. 12 (2) (2001): 132–146.
9. K. Palan and R. Wilkes, "Adolescent-Parent Interaction in Family Decision Making," *Journal of Consumer Research*, Vol. 24 (2) (1997): 159–169.
10. D. Marshall, S. O'Donohoe, and S. Kline, "Families, Food, and Pester Power: Beyond the Blame Game?" *Journal of Consumer Behaviour*, Vol. 6 (1) (2007): 164–181.
11. Kaiser Family Foundation, "Daily Media Use among Children and Teens up Dramatically from Five Years Ago" (January 20, 2010). News Release: http://www.kff.org/entmedia/entmedia012010nr.cfm (accessed August 11, 2012).
12. Institute of Medicine of the National Academies, *Food Marketing to Children and Youth* (Washington, DC: National Academies Press, 2005).
13. Center for Science in the Public Interest, "Pestering Parents: How Food Companies Market Obesity to Children" (November 2003).
14. www.caru.com (accessed August 11, 2012).
15. CARU New Releases: "Roseart Supports CARU and Children's Safety...," (January 5, 2005); "Nabisco Puts Safety First in TV Ads," (October 4, 2000); "Procter and Gamble Works with CARU on Pringles Commercial," (April 15, 2004). All available at www.caru.org/news/index.asp (accessed August 11, 2012).
16. Stuart Elliott, "McDonald's Ending Promotion on Jackets of Children's Report Cards," nytimes.com, January 18, 2008.
17. E. J. Schultz, "Advertisers Rebuke Obama Administration's Proposed Rules on Marketing Food to Kids," *Ad Age* online, April 28, 2011.
18. Mike Esterl, "Soda Makers to Post Calories on Vending Machines," online.wsj.com, October 8, 2012.
19. Brooks Barnes, "Promoting Nutrition, Disney to Restrict Junk-Food Ads," nytimes.com, June 5, 2012; Stephanie Storm, "McDonald's Menu to Post Calorie Data," nytimes.com, September 12, 2012.
20. Julie Jargon, "Success Is Only So Sweet in Remaking Cereals," online.wsj.com, October 11, 2011.
21. Jess Bravin, "California Can't Curb Children's Access to Videogames," online.wsj.com, June 28, 2011.
22. Melanie Warner, "The Food Industry Empire Strikes Back," nytimes.com, July 5, 2005.
23. Elizabeth S. Moore and Victoria J. Rideout, "The Online Marketing of Food to Children: Is It Just Fun and Games?" *Journal of Public Policy & Marketing*, Vol. 26 (2) (Fall 2007): 202–220; Kathleen Seiders and Ross D. Petty, "Taming the Obesity Beast: Children, Marketing, and Public Policy Considerations," *Journal of Public Policy & Marketing*, Vol. 26 (2) (Fall 2007): 236–242.
24. Jeremy Singer-Vine and Anton Troianovski, "How Kids Apps Are Data Magnets," online.wsj.com, June 27, 2013.
25. Stephanie Clifford, "Online Merchants Home In on Imbibing Consumer," nytimes.com, December 27, 2011.
26. Michael Moss, "The Extraordinary Science of Addictive Junk Food," nytimes.com, February 20, 2013.
27. Reuters, "Fat and Getting Fatter: U.S. Obesity Rates to Soar by 2030," September 19, 2012.
28. Rajagopal Raghunathan, Rebecca Walker Naylor, and Wayne D. Hoyer, "The Unhealthy = Tasty Intuition and Its Effects on Taste Inferences, Enjoyment, and Choice of Food Products," *Journal of Marketing*, Vol. 70 (October 2006): 170–184.
29. Brian Wansink and Koert van Ittersum, "Bottoms Up! The Influence of Elongation on Pouring and Consumption Value," *Journal of Consumer Research* (December 2003): 455–463; Brian Wansink, "Environmental Factors That Increase the Food Intake and Consumption Volume of Unknowing Consumers," *Annual Reviews* 24 (Nutrition, 2004): 455–479; Barbara E. Kahn and Brian Wansink, "The Influence of Assortment Structure on Perceived Variety and Consumption Quantities," *Journal of Consumer*

Research (March 2004): 519–534; Jennifer J. Argo and Katherine White, "When Do Consumers Eat More? The Role of Appearance Self-Esteem and Food Packaging Cues," *Journal of Marketing*, Vol. 76 (March 2012): 67–80.

30. "Credit Scores Plummet as Student Debt Rises," *Business Wire*, New York, April 8, 2005.
31. So-Hyun Joo, John E. Grable, and Dorothy C. Bagwell, "Credit Card Attitudes and Behaviors of College Students," *College Student Journal* (September 2003): 405–416.
32. "New York Law Targets Credit Card Ads at Universities," *Bank Marketing International* (December 2004): 1; Jonathan D. Glater, "Marketing Code for Student Lenders," nytimes.com, September 10, 2008.
33. Stephen F. Pirog III and James A. Roberts, "Personality and Credit Card Misuse among College Students: The Mediating Role of Impulsiveness," *Journal of Marketing Theory & Practice*, Vol. 15 (1) (Winter 2007): 65–77.
34. James A. Roberts and Stephen F. Pirog III, "A Preliminary Investigation of Materialism and Impulsiveness as Predictors of Technological Addictions among Young Adults," *Journal of Behavioral Addictions*, Vol. 2 (1) (March 2013): 56–62.
35. Anahad O'Connor, "The Problem with Serving Sizes," nytimes.com, August 2, 2011.
36. Gina S. Mohr, Donald R. Lichtenstein, & Chris Janiszewski, "The Effect of Marketer-Suggested Serving Size on Consumer Responses: The Unintended Consequences of Consumer Attention to Calorie Information," *Journal of Marketing*, Vol. 76 (January 2012): 59–75.
37. O'Connor, "The Problem with Serving Sizes."
38. Tara Parker-Pope, "Designing a Better Food Label," nytimes.com, July 28, 2011.
39. Stephanie Storm, "Lawsuit Forces General Mills to Defend the Accuracy of Its 'Natural' Labeling," nytimes.com, July 26, 2012.
40. Stephanie Storm, "Uneasy Allies in the Grocery Aisle," nytimes.com, September 13, 2012.
41. R. Stephen Parker and Charles E. Pettijohn, "Ethical Considerations in the Use of Direct-to-Consumer Advertising and Pharmaceutical Promotions: The Impact on Pharmaceutical Sales and Physicians," *Journal of Business Ethics* (December 2003): 279–287; Nat Ives, "Consumers Are Looking Past Commercials to Study Prescription Drugs," nytimes.com, March 25, 2005.
42. Stephanie Saul, "A Self-Imposed Ban on Drug Ads," nytimes.com, June 15, 2005.
43. Stephanie Clifford, "FDA Rules on Drug Ads Sow Confusion as Applied to Web," nytimes.com, April 16, 2009.
44. Duff Wilson, "As Generics Near, Makers Tweak Erectile Drugs," nytimes.com, April 13, 2011.
45. Thomas F. Stafford, "Alert or Oblivious? Factors Underlying Consumer Responses to Marketing Stimuli," *Psychology & Marketing* (September 2000): 745–760.
46. Serena Ng, "Toilet-Tissue 'Desheeting' Shrinks Rolls," online.wsj.com, July 24, 20–13.
47. Ibid.Plumps Margins,"
48. Kelly D. Martin and Craig Smith, "Commercializing Social Interaction: The Ethics of Stealth Marketing," *Journal of Public Policy & Marketing,* Vol. 27 (1) (Spring 2008): 45–56.
49. Michael A. Wiles & Anna Danielova, "The Worth of Product Placement in Successful Films: An Event Study Analysis," *Journal of Marketing*, Vol. 73 (July 2009): 44–63.
50. Ignacio Redondo, "The Behavioral Effects of Negative Product Placements in Movies," *Psychology & Marketing,* Vol. 29 (8) (August 2012): 622–635.
51. Haseeb Shabbir and Des Thwaites, "The Use of Humor to Mask Deceptive Advertising: It's No Laughing Matter," *Journal of Advertising,* Vol. 36 (2) (Summer 2007): 75–86.
52. Federal Trade Commission
53. Peter R. Darke, Laurence Ashworth, and Robin J. B. Ritchie, "Damage from Corrective Advertising: Causes and Cures," *Journal of Marketing,* Vol. 72 (November 2008): 81–97.
54. Nat Ives, "Advertisers Have a Deep Concern for the Truth, Especially When It Comes to a Rival's Claim," *New York Times,* September 21, 2004, C4.
55. Ibid.
56. Amy Schatz and Ilan Brat, "Dannon Settles Complaints over Yogurt Ads," online.wsj.com, December 16, 2010; Edward Eyatt, "Regulators Call Health Claims in Pom Juice Ads Deceptive," nytimes.com, September 27, 2010; Associated Press, "FDA Warns P&G for Adding Vitamin C to Nyquil," nytimes.com, October 14, 2009; Brent Kendall, "Skechers Settles with FTC over Deceptive Advertising of Toning Shoes," online.wsj.com, May 16, 2012; Anemona Hartocollis, "Dispute over City's Ads against Sodas," nytimes.com, October 28, 2010; Brent Kendall, "FTC Targets 'Ab Circle Pro' Ads," online.wsj.com, August 23, 2012; Jennifer Corbett Dooren and Emily Glazer, "FDA Rebukes Lancôme on Marketing," online.wsj.com, September 11, 2012; Danny Yadron and Shira Ovide, "FTC Says Tweet Ads Need Some Fine Print," online.wsj.com, March 12, 2013.
57. Martha Myslinski Tipton, Sundar Bharadwaj, and Diana Robertson, "Regulatory Exposure of Deceptive Marketing and Its Impact on Claimed Value," *Journal of Marketing* (November 2009): 230–243.

58. Ann Zimmerman, "Judge to Consider Zale's Brightest Diamond Claim," online.wsj.com, December 16, 2012.
59. Anemona Hartocollis, "E-Mails Reveal Dispute over City's Ad against Sodas," nytimes.com, October 28, 2010.
60. Dana Mattioli and Ryan Dezember, "Would-Be Buyers of Organix Naturally Hesitant on Name," online.wsj.com, April 30, 2013.
61. Suzanne Vranica, "Advertisers Practice for Super Bowl," online.wsj.com, February 3, 2012.
62. Jill K. Maher, Kenneth C. Herbst, Nancy M. Childs, and Seth Finn, "Racial Stereotypes in Children's Television Commercials," *Journal of Advertising,* Vol. 37 (1) (March 2008): 80–93.
63. Fred K. Beard, "How Product and Advertising Offend Consumers," *Journal of Advertising,* Vol. 37 (1) (March 2008): 13–21.
64. WSJ Staff, "Oh, Benetton. You and Your Controversial Ad Campaigns," online.wsj.com, November 16, 2011; Jonathan Hutchinson, "The Price of a Jersey Sets Rugby Fans against Adidas," nytimes.com, August 24, 2011; Andrew Newman, "A Line of Brews Draws a Star Endorser," nytimes.com, April 17, 2011; Abby Goodnough, "Caffeine and Alcohol Drink Is Potent Mix for Young," nytimes.com, October 26, 2010; Sarah Nir, "Nivea Pulls Ads after Online Outcry," nytimes.com, August 12, 2011.
65. Stuart Elliott, "Emphasizing Taste, and Not Just in Beer, at Super Bowl," *New York Times,* January 26, 2005, C1; Stuart Elliott, "Ad Reaction Claims Super Bowl Casualty," nytimes.com, February 3, 2005; Stuart Elliott, "Super Bowl Spot Provokes after Only One Broadcast," nytimes.com, February 8, 2005.
66. Richar Thaler, "Show Us the Data. (It's Ours, After All.)," nytimes.com, April 23, 2011.
67. Stephanie Clifford and Quentin Hardy, "Attention, Shoppers: Store Is Tracking Your Cell," nytimes.com, July 14, 2013.
68. Natasha Singer, "Secret E-Scores Chart Consumers' Buying Power," nytimes.com, August 18, 2012.
69. Edward Wyatt and Tanzina Vega, "F.T.C. Backs Plan to Honor Privacy of Online Users," nytimes.com, December 1, 2010; Edward Wyatt and Tanzina Vega, "U.S. Agency Seeks Tougher Consumer Privacy Rules," nytimes.com, March 26, 2012.
70. Tanzina Vega, "For Online Privacy, Click Here," nytimes.com, January 19, 2012.
71. Louise Story and Brad Stone, "Facebook Retreats on Online Tracking," nytimes.com, November 30, 2007.
72. Miguel Helft and Jenna Wortham, "Facebook Bows to Pressure over Privacy," nytimes.com, May 26, 2010.
73. Nathasha Singer, "When the Privacy Button Is Already Pressed," nytimes.com, September 15, 2012.
74. Noam Cohen, "An Ad Blocker Opens the Gate, Ever So Slightly," nytimes.com, January 1, 2012.
75. Somini Sengupta, "Study Finds Broad Wariness over Online Tracking," online.wsj.com, October 8, 2012.
76. Natasha Singer, "Do Not Track? Advertisers Say 'Don't Tread on Us,'" nytimes.com, October 13, 2012.
77. Tanzina Vega, "A New Tool in Protecting Online Privacy," nytimes.com, February 12, 2012.
78. Ian Sherr and Anton Troianovski, "Tracking-Software Maker Stirs Phone-Privacy Fears," online.wsj.com, December 2, 2011.
79. Stephanie Clifford, "Web Coupons Know Lots about You, and They Tell," nytimes.com, April 16, 2010.
80. Héctor R. Lozada, Gary H. Kritz, and Alma Mintu-Wimsatt, "The Challenge of Online Privacy to Global Marketers," *Journal of Marketing Development & Competitiveness* (2013; forthcoming).
81. Brooks Barnes, "Bowing to Pressure, Disney Bans Smoking in Its Branded Movies," nytimes.com, July 26, 2007.
82. Apisit Chattananon, Meredith Lawley, Jirasek Trimetsoontorn, Numachi Supparekchaisakul, and Lackana Leelayouthayothin, "Building Corporate Image through Societal Marketing Programs," *Society & Business Review,* Vol. 2 (3) (2007): 230–253.
83. Stefanie Rosen Robinson, Caglar Irmak, and Satish Jayachandran, "Choice of Cause in Cause-Related Marketing," *Journal of Marketing*, Vol. 76 (July 2012): 125–139.
84. Stuart Elliott, "A Push to Curb Casual Use of Ugly Phrases," nytimes.com, October 8, 2008.
85. Stephanie Clifford, "Teaching Teenagers about Harassment," nytimes.com, January 27, 2009.
86. Stuart Elliott, "Standing Up for Those Who Cannot," nytimes.com, September 29, 2008.
87. Stuart Elliott, "A New York Job Behind Every Light and Camera," nytimes.com, December 22, 2008.
88. Matt Richtel, "A Short-Circuit to Distracted Driving," nytimes.com, January 20, 2011.
89. Carolyn J. Simmons and Karen L. Becker-Olsen, "Achieving Marketing Objectives through Social Sponsorships," *Journal of Marketing,* Vol. 70 (October 2006): 154–169.
90. Xiaoli Nan and Kwangjun Heo, "Consumer Responses to Corporate Social Responsibility (CSR) Initiatives: Examining the Role of Brand-Cause Fit in Cause-Related Marketing," *Journal of Advertising,* Vol. 36 (2) (Summer 2007): 63–75.
91. Stacy Landreth Grau and Judith Anne Garreston Folse, "The Influence of Donation Proximity and Message-Framing Cues on the Less-Involved Consumer," *Journal of Advertising,* Vol. 36 (4) (Winter 2007): 19–34.

92. http://business.rediff.com/slide-show/2009/oct/29/slide-show-1-corporate-social-responsibility-india-ranks-4th.htm, accessed on May 10, 2010.
93. http://www.aashirvaad.com/about_ashirvaad/csr_movement.asp, accessed on May 10, 2010.
94. Carolyn J. Simmons and Karen L. Becker-Olsen, "Achieving Marketing Objectives Through Social Sponsorships," *Journal of Marketing*, 70 (October 2006): 154–169.
95. Xiaoli Nan and Kwangjun Heo, "Consumer Responses to Corporate Social Responsibility (CSR) Initiatives: Examining the Role of Brand-Cause Fit in Cause-Related Marketing," *Journal of Advertising*, 36, no. 2 (Summer 2007): 63–75.
96. Stacy Landreth Grau and Judith Anne Garreston Folse, "The Infl uence of Donation Proximity and Message-Framing Cues on the Less-Involved Consumer," *Journal of Advertising*, 36, no. 4 (Winter 2007): 19–34.
97. Oliver M. Freestone and Peter J. McGoldrick, "Motivations of the Ethical Consumer," *Journal of Business Ethics,* Vol. 79 (2008): 445–467.
98. Rajiv K. Sinha and Naomi Mandel, "Preventing Digital Music Piracy: The Carrot or the Stick?" *Journal of Marketing,* Vol. 72 (January 2008): 1–15.
99. David Segal, "Appalling Behavior, This Time by Customers," nytimes.com, July 10, 2010; Janet Morrissey, "Avoiding Luggage Fees," nytimes.com, February 6, 2012.
100. Times Network, "Look Before You Lick: Pickles, Biscuits Hide Health Hazards," *The Times of India*, February 9, 2014.
101. Shubham Batra, "Celebrity ads now get Govt's Goat," *The Economic Times*, February 11, 2014.

Chapter 15

1. Katherine Rosman, "Test-Marketing a Modern Princess," online.wsj.com, April 9, 2013.
2. Jon Gertner, "Our Rating, Ourselves," www.nytimes.com, April 10, 2005.
3. Ernest Dichter, "Whose Lifestyle Is It Anyway?" *Psychology & Marketing* (1986): 3; Ernest Dichter, *Handbook of Consumer Motivation* (New York: McGraw-Hill, 1964); Emanuel H. Demby, "A Remembrance of Ernest Dichter," *Marketing News,* Vol. 6 (January 6, 1992): 21. Also see Michelle R. Nelson, "The Hidden Persuaders: Then and Now," *Journal of Advertising*, Vol. 37 (Spring 2008): 113–126.
4. Stan Maklan, Simon Knox, and Lynette Ryals, "New Trends in Innovation and Customer Relationship Management: A Challenge for Market Researchers," *International Journal of Market Research*, Vol. 50 (2008): 221–238.
5. Nick Lee and Amanda J. Broderick, "The Past, Present and Future of Observational Research in Marketing," *Qualitative Market Research: An International Journal,* Vol. 10 (2007): 121–129.
6. Leslie Kaufman, "Enough Talk," *Newsweek*, August 19, 1997, 48–49.
7. Emily Nelson, "P&G Checks Out Real Life," *Wall Street Journal* (Eastern Edition), May 17, 2001, B1.
8. Ian Mount, "The Mystery of Duane Reade," *New York Magazine*, June 6, 2005, 28–31.
9. Kim S. Nash, "Casinos Hit Jackpot with Customer Data," *Computer World*, July 2, 2001, 16–17; *Modern Marvels: Casino Technology* [VHS videotape], 1999, A&E Television Networks.
10. Alex Salkever, "The Technology of Personalized Pitches," *Business Week Online*, June 22, 2004.
11. Constance L. Hays, "What Wal-Mart Knows about Customers' Habits," www.nytimes.com, November 14, 2004.
12. Melanie Wells, "In Search of the Buy Button," *Forbes*, September 1, 2003, 62.
13. Brian D. Till and Michael Busler, "The Match-Up Hypothesis: Physical Attractiveness, Expertise, and the Role of Fit on Brand Attitude, Purchase Intent and Brand Beliefs," *Journal of Advertising* (Fall 2000): 1–13.
14. Yoram Wind, "Marketing by Experiment," *Marketing Research* (Spring 2007): 10–16.
15. See the following for additional viewpoints: Jenny Clark, Clive Nancarrow, and Lee Higgins, "Using Consumer Panel Participants to Generate Creative New Product Ideas," *Journal of American Academy of Business,* Vol. 12 (September 2007): 139–144.
16. Nina Michaelidou and Sally Dibb, "Using Email Questionnaires for Research: Good Practice in Tackling Non-Response," *Journal of Targeting, Measurement & Analysis for Marketing*, Vol. 14 (July 2006): 289–296.
17. Thomas O. Jones and W. Earl Sasser, Jr., "Why Satisfied Customers Defect," *Harvard Business Review* (November–December 1995): 88–99.
18. A. Parasuraman, Valarie A. Zeithaml, and Leonard L. Berry, *Moving Forward in Service Quality Research: Measuring Different Customer-Expectation Levels, Comparing Alternative Scales, and Examining the Performance-Behavioral Intentions Link* (Report No. 94–114) (Cambridge, MA: Marketing Science Institute, 1994).
19. Michael M. Pearson and Guy H. Gessner, "Transactional Segmentation to Slow Customer Defections," *Marketing Management* (Summer 1999): 16–23.
20. Stuart Elliott, "Nielsen Presents a Research Plan to Quell Concerns about Accuracy," www.nytimes.com,

February 22, 2005; Stuart Elliott, "Nielsen Will Address Potential Undercounting of Minority TV Viewers," www.nytimes.com, March 24, 2005.

21. Solomon R.Michael, Consumer Behavior: Buying, Having and Being, Prentice Hall of India, New Delhi, 2002, p. 461.
22. W.D. Hoyer and D.J. MacInnis, Consumer Behavior, Houghton Mifflin, 1999, p. 409.
23. Consumer Behaviour, p. 461.
24. S. Ramesh Kumar, N. Guruvayurappan, and M. Banerjee, "Cultural Values and Branding in an Emerging Market," *The Marketing Review*, 7.3, 2007, pp. 243—272.
25. "Census of India," February 13, 2011, http://philatelynews.com/2011/india/census-of-india/, (accessed August 20, 2011).
26. T.J. Reynolds and D.B. Whitlark," Applying Laddering Data to Communications and Strategy and Advertising Practice," The Journal of Advertising Research, July/August 1995, pp. 9—17, http://belkfaculty.uncc.edu/jhanse15/Teaching/MeansEndTheory.pdf, accessed August 20, 2011.
27. Ramesh Kumar, et al., "Cultural Values and Branding in an Emerging Market."
28. "About Clean & Clear," www.cleanandclear.in/about-us, accessed August 20, 2011; "Clean & Clear: Foaming Face Wash," www.cleanandclear.in/product/foaming-face-wash/cleansers, accessed August 20, 2011.
29. "Clean & Clear Deep Action Cleanser Ad," www.youtube.com/watch?v=1xIucrG4lu8, accessed August 20, 2011.
30. "Clean & Clear's Foaming Face Wash Ad," www.youtube.com/watch?v=GZ4YWDg7Qxo&feature=related, accessed August 20, 2011.
31. "Clean & Clear Deep Action Cleanser Ad," www.youtube.com/watch?v=1xIucrG4lu8, accessed August 20, 2011.
32. "EverYuth's Light and Clear Face Wash Ad," www.youtube.com/watch?v=s0acI4xAWg8, accessed August 20, 2011.
33. "EverYuth Face Washes: Feel Fresh!" www.everyuth.com/face-wash.html, accessed August 20, 2011.
34. "EverYuth's Light and Clear Face Wash Ad," www.youtube.com/watch?v=s0acI4xAWg8, accessed August 28, 2011.
35. "EverYuth's Fruit Face Wash Ad," www.youtube.com/watch?v=_Qjk4TWEkIk&feature=related, accessed August 28, 2011.
36. "Himalaya Herbal Healthcare: Hydrating Face Wash Cream," www.himalayahealthcare.com/products/hydrating_facewash_cream.htm, accessed August 28, 2011.
37. "Himalaya Herbal Healthcare's Oil Balancing Face Wash Gel Ad," www.youtube.com/watch?v=EAiDlu8exC8&feature=related, accessed August 28, 2011.
38. "Himalaya Herbal Healthcare's Neem Face Wash Ad," www.youtube.com/watch?v=vdnzfpq1mu0&feature=related, accessed August 28, 2011.

Glossary

Absolute Threshold. The lowest level at which an individual experiences a sensation. The point at which a person can detect a difference between "something" and "nothing." *See Differential Threshold.*

Acculturation. Learning a new culture. *See Enculturation.*

Achievement Need. Regarding personal accomplishment as an end by itself, being self-confident, and enjoying taking calculated risks.

Actual Self-Image. The way individuals perceive themselves. *See Social Self-Image and Ideal Self-Image.*

Addressable Advertising. Customized messages that are sent to individual consumers and are based on the messages' receivers' prior shopping and surfing online, which marketers have tracked.

Adopter Categories. A classification showing where consumers stand in relation to other consumers in terms of the first time they had purchased an innovation (e.g., a new product or model). *See the five adopters' categories: Innovators, Early Adopters, Early Majority, Late Majority, and Laggards.*

Adoption. The final stage of Innovation Adoption, which is a term designating the process leading to a person's decision of whether or not to adopt an innovation. After becoming aware of and interested in the innovation, and evaluating and trying it, the person adopts (purchases) the innovation. If satisfied, he (or she) would buy the innovative product again. If not, there will be no repeat purchase. *See Innovation Adoption.*

Advergames. Brands embedded in video games played at homes, arcades, or online.

Advertising Wear-Out. Overexposure to repetitive advertising that causes individuals to become satiated, pay less attention to advertising, and remember fewer ads.

Advertorials. Printed ads that closely resemble content and editorial material.

Affect Referral Decision Rule. A decision rule by which consumers make product choices based on the products' overall ratings rather than considering specific product attributes. *See Noncompensatory Decision Rules.*

Affective Component. The second component of the Tri-Component Model of attitudes. It represents the person's *emotions* and *feelings* regarding the attitude object, which are considered *evaluations* because they capture the person's overall assessment of the attitude object (i.e., the extent to which the individual rates the attitude object as "favorable" or "unfavorable," "good" or "bad"). *See Likert Scale, Sematic Differential Scale, and Tri-Component Model.*

Affiliation Need. A psychological need that is similar to social need and reflects one's desire for friendship, acceptance, and belonging.

Affluent Market. Upscale market segment that consists of households with incomes that are, according to most definitions, over $ 100,000. However, what is considered "affluent" varies among geographic locations. *See Social Class.*

Aggresion. Responding aggresively when encountering frustration. *See Defense Mechanisms.*

Aggressive Individuals. One of three groups identified by Karen Horney (a neo-Freudian researcher), it designates persons who move against others, excel, and desire to be admired. *See Compliant Individuals and Detached Individuals.*

AIDA. An acronym of a cognitive learning model favored by advertisers, which states that product-related learning occurs in four stages: awareness, interest, desire, and action. *See Cognitive Learning.*

Aided Recall. A recognition test, that measures the effectiveness of learning and communications, where consumers are shown ads and asked whether or not they remember seeing them and can recall any of their salient points. *See Unaided Recall.*

Ambient Advertising (Experiential Marketing). *See Experiential Marketing.*

Ambush Marketing. Placing ads in places where consumers do not expect to see them and cannot avoid them readily.

American Core Values. Priorities and codes of conduct that both affect and reflect the character of American society. These values are: pervasive (i.e., a significant portion of the American people have accepted them); enduring (i.e., unlike fads, they have influenced Americans' actions over an extended period); and related to consumption behavior (i.e., in the context of this textbook). *See Culture.*

Anthropology. The comparative study of human societies' cultures and developments. *See Content Analysis, Culture, and Field Observation.*

Anthropomorphism. Assigning human characteristics to an object. *See Brand Personification.*

Approach Objects. Positive outcomes that people seek. *See Avoidance Objects.*

Apps (Applications). Chunks of software—installed on one's computer, tablet, or smartphone—that are gateways to games, online resources, and social networking.

Attitude. A learned predisposition to behave in a consistently favorable or unfavorable way toward a given object. *See Attitude Measures.*

Attitude-Toward-Behavior Model. A model stating that a consumer's attitude toward a specific behavior is a function of how strongly he or she believes that the action will lead to a specific outcome (either favorable or unfavorable).

Attitude-Toward-Object Model. A model stating that a consumer's attitude toward a product or brand is a function of the presence of certain attributes and the consumer's evaluation of those attributes.

Attitude-Toward-the-Ad Model. A model maintaining that a consumer form various feelings (affects) and judgments (cognitions) as the result of exposure to an advertisement, which, in turn, affects the consumer's attitude toward the ad and beliefs and attitudes toward the brand advertised.

Attribution Theory. A theory focused on how people assign causality to events and form or alter their attitudes after assessing their own or other people's behavior.

Authoritarian Parents. Parents who are very restrictive and not nurturing during their children's consumer socialization. *See Authoritative Parents, Indulgent Parents, and Neglecting Parents.*

Authoritative Parents. Parents who are very nurturing but also very restrictive during their children's consumer socialization. *See Authoritarian Parents, Indulgent Parents, and Neglecting Parents.*

Autonomic Decisions. Purchase decisions where either the husband or wife is the primary or only decision maker. *See Husband-Dominated Decisions, Joint Decisions, and Wife-Dominated Decisions.*

Avoidance Objects. Negative outcomes that people want to prevent. *See Approach Objects.*

Awareness. The first stage of Innovation Adoption, which is a term designating the process leading to a person's decision of whether or not to adopt an innovation. In this stage, the person becomes aware that the innovation is available. *See Innovation Adoption.*

Baby Boomers. The age cohort representing people born between 1946 and 1964. *See Subculture.*

Bachelorhood. In the context of the Family Life Cycle, individuals who are not married and have no children. *See Family Life Cycle.*

Behavior Intention Scale. An instrument that measures the likelihood that consumers will act a certain way in the future, such as if they will buy a product again or recommend it to friends. *See Quantitative Research.*

Behavioral Data. Behavioral segmentation data assembled through direct questioning (or observation) of consumers, and categorized using objective and measurable criteria, such as demographics. This information includes: (a) consumer-intrinsic dimensions (e.g., a person's age, gender, marital status, income, and education); (b) consumption-based behaviors (e.g., quantity of product purchased, frequency of leisure activities or the frequency of buying a given product). *See Cognitive Factors.*

Behavioral Learning (Stimulus-Response Learning). The premise that observable responses to specific external stimuli signal that learning has taken place. *See Classical Conditioning.*

Behavioral Targeting. Sending consumers personalized offers and promotional messages designed to reach specific persons and deliver to them highly relevant messages at the right time and more accurately than when using conventional segmentation techniques.

Benefit Segmentation. A segmentation approach based on the benefits that consumers seek from products and services.

Blog (Weblog). A discussion or informational site published on the Internet and consisting of discrete entries ("posts").

Brand Community. An online community formed by consumers who share an attachment to a brand.

Brand Equity. The intrinsic value of a brand name, which stems from consumers' perception of the brand's superiority, the social esteem that using it provides, and the customers' trust and identification with the brand.

Brand Loyalty. A measure of how often consumers buy a given brand, whether or not they switch brands and, if they do, how often, and the extent of their commitment to buying the brand regularly. *See Covetous Brand Loyalty, Inertia Brand Loyalty, and Premium Brand Loyalty.*

Brand Personification. Communicating human features of a brand in advertising. *See Anthropomorphism.*

Branded Entertainment. Featuring products within entertainment content or building entertainment content around promoted brands. *See Product Placement.*

Broad Categorizers. Low-risk perceivers who prefer to choose from a wide range of alternatives because they would rather face the consequences of a wrong decision than limit the number of alternatives from which they choose. *See Narrow Categorizers, Perceived Risk, and Risk Aversion.*

Buzz Agent. A consumer, employed by a marketer who promotes products clandestinely in exchange for (mostly) free product samples. *See Word-of-Mouth.*

Captive Advertising Screens. Promotional messages placed in locations where consumers spend time (and generally do not expect to see advertisements), such as elevators, cinemas, retail stores, restaurants, bars, fitness clubs, college campuses, and transit. *See Ambush Marketing.*

Cause-Related Marketing. Process in which a firm contributes a portion of its revenues from selling certain products to supporting needy groups, such as helping people with incurable diseases or hurt by inclement weather.

Celebrity Actor. A celebrity who plays a part in a commercial for a product.

Celebrity Endorsement. An ad where a celebrity appears of behalf of a product, with which he may or may not have direct experience or familiarity.

Celebrity Spokesperson. A celebrity who endorses a brand, social cause, or company over an extended period.

Celebrity Testimonial. A promotional message where a celebrity attests to the product's quality based on his or her usage of the product.

Central Route to Persuasion. A promotional approach maintaining that that highly involved consumers are best reached and persuaded through ads focused on the product's attributes. *See Elaboration Likelihood Model and Peripheral Route to Persuasion.*

Chunking. The process during which consumers recode what they have already encoded, which often results in recalling additional relevant information. "Chunks" are groupings of information.

Classical Conditioning. A form of behavioral learning stating that animal and human alike, can be taught behaviors and associations among stimuli through repetition. Some describe it as a "knee jerk" (or automatic) response to a drive that builds up through repeated exposure to a stimulus. *See Behavioral Learning, Conditioned Stimulus, and Conditioned Response.*

Closure. The instinct to organize pieces of sensory input into a complete image or feeling. Individuals need closure, which means that if they perceive that a stimulus is incomplete, they are compelled to figure out its complete meaning.

Cluster (Area) Sample. A probability sample where the population is divided into mutually exclusive groups (such as blocks), and the researcher draws a sample of the groups to study. *See Probability Sample.*

Cognitive Age. An individual's perceived, not chronological, age.

Cognitive Associative Learning. A learning theory that views classical conditioning as learning of associations among events that enable consumers to expect and anticipate and events, rather than being a reflexive action.

Cognitive Component. The first component of the Tri-Component Model of attitudes. It represents the person's *knowledge* and *perceptions* of the features of the attitude object, which, collectively, are the *beliefs* that the object possesses or does not possess specific attributes. *See Likert Scale, Semantic Differential Scale, and Tri-Component Model.*

Cognitive Dissonance. The mental discomfort that people experience when facing conflicting information about an attitude object. *See Post-Purchase Dissonance.*

Cognitive Factors. Segmentation data assembled through measures of psychological factors. This data includes: (a) consumer-intrinsic dimensions, such as personality traits, cultural values, and attitudes towards consumption and social issues; and (b) consumption-specific attitudes, behaviors and preferences, the benefits sought in products, and attitudes regarding many aspects of consumption. *See Behavioral Data.*

Cognitive Learning. The premise that learning occurs in the form of sequential, mental processing of information when people face problems that they wish to resolve. *See Innovation Adoption and Tri-Component Model.*

Communication. The process of imparting or exchanging information. In the context of consumer behavior, it is the transmission of messages from senders (the sources) to receivers (the consumers) via media (the channels of transmission). *See Formal Source, Impersonal Communications, Informal Source, and Interpersonal Communications.*

Communication Feedback. The responses of the receivers to communication messages that indicate to the senders as to whether their intended messages were received. *See Recall Test and Recognition Test.*

Comparative Advertising. An advertising appeal where marketers proclaim that their products are better than competing brands named in the ads. *See Two-Sided Message.*

Comparative Influence. A process that takes place when people compare themselves to others, whom they respect and admire, and then adopt their values or imitate their behaviors. *See Normative Influence and Reference Groups.*

Compatibility. One of the five characteristics identified as a determinant of consumer acceptance of a new product representing the degree to which potential customers perceive a new product as consistent with their present needs, values, and practices. *See the other four characteristics: Complexity, Observability, Relative Advantage, and Trial-ability.*

Compensatory Decision Rules. A group of decisions rules in which a consumer evaluates each brand in terms of each relevant attribute, weighted by the importance of that attribute, and then selects the brand with the highest weighted score. *See Noncompensatory Decision Rules.*

Complaint Analysis. Gathering complaints from unsatisfied customers and analyzing them in order to identify defects and improve the delivery of the product or service.

Complexity. One of the five characteristics identified as a determinant of consumer acceptance of a new product representing the degree to which a new product is difficult to understand or use. *See the other four characteristics: Compatibility, Observability, Relative Advantage, and Trial-ability.*

Compliant Individuals. One of three groups identified by Karen Horney (a neo- Freudian researcher), it designates persons who move toward others and desire to be loved, wanted, and appreciated. *See Aggressive Individuals and Detached Individuals.*

Compulsive Consumption. Addictive and out of control buying, that often has damaging consequences to the compulsive shoppers and those around them.

Conative Component. The third component of the Tri-Component Model of attitudes. It represents he *likelihood* that an individual will *behave in a particular way* with regard to the attitude object. In consumer behavior, the conative component is treated as an expression of the consumer's *intention to buy. See Behavior Intention Scale and Tri-Component Model.*

Conditioned Response. A response to conditioned stimulus. *See Conditioned Stimulus.*

Conditioned Stimulus. A stimulus that became associated with a particular event or feeling as a result of repetition. *See Classical Conditioning, Conditioned Respone, and Unconditioned Stimulus.*

Conjunctive Decision Rule. A noncompensatory decision rule in which consumers establish a minimally acceptable cutoff point for each product attribute evaluated. Brands that fall below the cutoff point on any attribute are not considered further. *See Noncompensatory Decision Rules.*

Consumer Behavior. The study of consumers' actions during searching for, purchasing, using, evaluating, and disposing of products and services that they expect will satisfy their needs.

Consumer Imagery. A term referring to consumers' perceptions of all the components of products, services, and brands, and to how consumers evaluate the quality of marketers' offerings. *See Perception.*

Consumer Involvement. The degree of personal relevance that the product or purchase holds for the consumer. *See High-Involvement Purchases and Low-Involvement Purchases.*

Consumer Learning. The process through which consumers acquire knowledge from experiences with products and observations of others' consumption, and use that knowledge in subsequent buying. *See Learning.*

Consumer Panels. A research method where a group of people are paid to record their purchases and/or media viewing habits in diaries, which are then compiled and analyzed to determine trends. *See Consumer Research and Primary Research.*

Consumer Research. The process and tools used to study consumer behavior. *See Qualitative Research and Quantitative Research.*

Consumer Socialization. The process by which children acquire the skills, knowledge, attitudes, and experiences necessary to function as consumers. *See Socialization and Socialization Agent.*

Content Analysis. Analyzing the content of verbal and/or pictorial communications of a given society in order to uncover its members' values, this method is often used in anthropological and sociological studies. *See Anthropology, Sociology, and Culture.*

Contextual Advertising. Targeted ads that originate in the web page a consumer is viewing or a search query the consumer has made.

Continuous Innovation. A new product that is an improved or modified version of an existing product rather than a totally new product, which therefore has very little disruptive influence on established consumption patterns. *See Discontinuous Innovation and Dynamically Continuous Innovation.*

Continuous Reinforcement. A method used in instrumental conditioning where a desired behavior is reinforced after every time it occurs. *See Instrumental Conditioning and Reinforcement.*

Controlled Experiment. An experimental design aimed at ensuring that any differences in the outcome (e.g., sales, a dependent variable) are due to different treatments of the variable under study (e.g., price, an independent variable) and not to extraneous factors (e.g., respondents' incomes). *See Experiments.*

Convenience Sample. A nonprobability sample where the researcher selects the most accessible people as the study's sample (e.g., students in a classroom). *See Nonprobability Sample.*

Corrective Advertising. A retraction or clarification a company must issue after it has made a false or misleading advertising claim because it was mandated to do so by the federal or local government.

Covert Marketing (Masked or Stealth Marketing). Marketing messages and promotional materials that appear to come from independent parties although, in fact, they come from marketers. *See Ambush Marketing.*

Covetous Brand Loyalty. Purchase behavior where consumers do not purchase the same brand consistently, but still have strong attachment and favorable predisposition toward the brand. *See Brand Loyalty.*

Cross-Cultural Analysis. A research method that compares the consumption patterns of members of different societies.

Cross-Screen Marketing. A promotional strategy that consists of tracking and targeting users across their computers, mobile phones, and tablets, and sending them personalized ads based on their interests, as observed by marketers.

Cues. Stimuli that direct motivated behavior. *See Learning.*

Culture. The collective values, customs, norms, arts, social institutions, and intellectual achievements of a particular society which express its principles, standards, and priorities. *See American Core Values, Content Analysis, and Field Observation.*

Customer Lifetime Value Profile. A forecasted estimate of how much a customer will spend on a particular product or service over the customer's entire "stay" with the offering's seller.

Customer Retention. Turning individual consumer transactions into long-term customer relationships.

Customer Satisfaction. Customers' perceptions of the performance of the product or service in relation to their expectations.

Customer Satisfaction Measurement. Quantitative and qualitative measures that gauge the level of customer satisfaction and its determinants.

Customer Satisfaction Survey. *See Customer Satisfaction Measurement.*

Customer Value. The ratio between customers' perceived benefits (i.e., economic, functional, and psychological) and the resources they have used to obtain those benefits (i.e., monetary, time, effort, psychological).

Data Aggregators. Data aggregation is an "information mining" process where data is searched, gathered and sold to marketers who use it to target customers. Data aggregators are organizations that compile information about consumers from many databases (including cookies that track online surfing) and use very sophisticated analysis to construct profiles of individual consumers or households.

Day-After Recall Test. A measure of ads' attention-getting and persuasive power where viewers of TV shows or listeners to radio broadcasts are interviewed a day after watching or listening to a given program, and asked to describe the commercials they recall. *See Unaided Recall.*

Daydreaming. Responding to frustration by fantasizing and imaginary gratification of unfilled needs. *See Defense Mechanisms.*

Deceptive Advertising. Marketing advertising claims that mislead consumers.

Defense Mechanisms. Cognitive and behavioral ways of handling frustration in order to protect one's self esteem. *See Aggression, Daydreaming, Identification, Projection, Rationalization, Regression, Repression, and Withdrawal.*

Defensive Attribution. Behavior or thoughts that occur when people accept (or take) credit for success (internal attribution), but assign failure to others or outside events (external attribution). *See Self-Perception Attribution.*

Demographic Segmentation. Dividing consumers according to age, gender, ethnicity, income and wealth, occupation, marital status, household type and size, and geographical location. These variables are objective, empirical, and can easily be determined through questioning or observation.

Depth Interview. A lengthy and unstructured interview designed to uncover a consumer's underlying attitudes and/or motivations. *See Discussion Guide and Qualitative Research.*

Detached Individuals. One of three groups identified by Karen Horney (a neo-Freudian researcher), it designates persons who move toward others and desire to be loved, wanted, and appreciated. *See Aggressive Individuals and Compliant Individuals.*

Differential Decay. A cognitive phenomenon where the memory of a low-credibility source decays faster than the contents of the message received from the source. *See Sleeper Effect.*

Differential Threshold (Just Noticeable Difference or JND). The minimal difference that can be detected between two similar stimuli. *See Absolute Threshold and Weber's Law.*

Diffusion of Innovations. The framework for exploring the evolution of consumers' acceptance of new products throughout the social system. *See Adopter Categories, Diffusion Process, Innovation, and Innovation Adoption.*

Discontinuous Innovation. A dramatically new product entry that greatly disrupts existing consumption behavior and requires the establishment of new practices. *See Continuous Innovation and Dynamically Continuous Innovation.*

Discussion Guide. A step-by-step outline that sets out the line of questioning the researcher needs to cover with the respondent in a depth interview, or a group of respondents in a focus group session. *See Depth Interview and Focus Group.*

Dissolution. The last stage of the Family Life Cycle where only one spouse survives. *See Family Life Cycle.*

Distributed Learning. Learning designed to take place over a period of time. *See Massed Learning.*

Dogmatism. A personality trait representing one's degree of cognitive rigidity—the opposite of being open-minded—towards information and opinions contradictory to one's own.

Door-in-the-Face Technique. A strategy aimed at changing attitudes where a large and costly first request—that is likely refused to be refused—is followed by a second, more realistic, and less costly request. *See Foot-in-the-Door Technique.*

Downward Mobility. Represented by people who have a lower social class level than their parents in terms of the jobs they hold, their residences, level of disposable income, and savings. *See Social Class and Upward Mobility.*

Dynamically Continuous Innovation. A new product entry that is sufficiently innovative to have some disruptive effects on established practices. *See Continuous Innovation and Discontinuous Innovation.*

E-Score. A digital calculation of people's buying power.

E-WOM. Word-of-mouth taking place online and occurring in social networks, brand communities, blogs, chat rooms, and twits.

Early Adopters. An adopter category designating consumers who buy new products within relatively short periods following the products' introductions, but not as early as the innovators. *See Adopter Categories, Innovators, Early Majority, Late Majority, and Laggards.*

Early Majority. An adopter category designating consumers who buy innovations after the early adopters had done so. *See Adopter Categories, Innovators, Early Adopters, Late Majority, and Laggards.*

Earned Social Media. Independent online media channels that are neither owned nor controlled by marketers.

Ego-Defensive Function. A functional approach to understanding attitudes where researchers believe that people replace doubt with feelings of security and confidence. *See Functional Approach.*

Ego. A Freudian term referring to the individual's conscious control in the form of an internal monitor that balances the impulsive demands of the id and the sociocultural constraints of the superego. *See Freudian Theory, Id, and Superego.*

Egoistic Needs. Psychological needs manifested in self-acceptance, self-esteem, success, independence, prestige, status, and recognition from others.

Elaboration Likelihood Model (ELM). The proposition that attitudes can be changed by either one of two different routes to persuasion—a central route or a peripheral route—and that the cognitive elaboration related to the processing of information received via each route is different. *See Central Route to Persuasion and Peripheral Route to Persuasion.*

Email Survey. Consumer research surveys conducted via email.

Emotional Bonds. Customers' high levels of personal commitment and attachment to a company and its products that extend beyond individual transactions. *See Transactional Bonds.*

Encoding. Assigning a word or visual image in order to represent an object during communications.

Enculturation. Learning one's own culture. *See Acculturation.*

Ethnocentrism. A personality traits representing one's tendency towards buying or not buying foreign-made products.

Evaluation. The third stage of Innovation Adoption, which is a term designating the process leading to a person's decision of whether or not to adopt an innovation. In this stage, the person evaluates the innovation and decides whether he (or she) wants to try using it. *See Innovation Adoption.*

Evoked Set. The specific brands (or models) a consumer considers during deciding which item to purchase within a particular product category. *See Inept Set and Inert Set.*

Experiential Marketing. Advertising designed to simulate consumers' sensory experiences with products by enabling them to physically interact with the products or providing sensory input (e.g., smell) that is part of the product.

Experiments. A consumer research approach designed to identify cause-and-effect relationships among purchase-related factors. *See Controlled Experiments, Quantitative Research, and Test Marketing.*

Exploratory Study. Research conducted before undertaking a full-scale market study.

Extended Family. A nuclear family with at least one grandparent or other relation living within the same household. *See Nuclear Family.*

Extensive Problem Solving. Purchase situations that occur infrequently and where the consumer does not have prior criteria to evaluate the product considered. *See Limited Problem Solving and Routinized Response Behavior.*

Extinction. A phenomenon that occurs when a learned response is no longer reinforced and the link between the stimulus and the expected reward is eliminated. *See Forgetting.*

Extrinsic Cues. Characteristics that are not physically inherent in the product, such as packaging, price and promotions. *See Intrinsic Cues.*

Family. Two or more persons related by blood, marriage, or adoption residing together. *See Nuclear Family, and Extended Family.*

Family Branding. Marketing a whole line of products under the same brand name, which is a marketing application of stimulus generalization. *See Stimulus Generalization.*

Family Life Cycle. A composite variable that includes marital status, size of family, age of family members (focusing on the age of the oldest or youngest child), and employment status of the head of household classifies the family into a "typical" stage. *See Bachelorhood, Honeymooners, Parenthood, Post-Parenthood, and Dissolution.*

Field Observation. A research method, used in anthropological and sociocultural studies, that consists of observing the daily behavior of selected members of a society in order to learn about its beliefs, values, and customs. *See Anthropology, Culture, Participant-Observers, and Sociology.*

Figure and Ground. An element of perception that describes the interrelationship between the stimulus itself (i.e., figure) and the environment or context within which is appears (i.e., ground).

Fixated Consumption. A personality trait referring to one's tendency to persistently buy items that are related to his or her collection or hobby and proudly display them for friends and other collectors.

Fixed Ratio Reinforcement. A method used in instrumental conditioning consisting of reinforcing a desired behavior every *n*th time (e.g., after every third time the behavior occurs). *See Instrumental Conditioning and Reinforcement.*

Focus Group. A method of qualitative research consisting of eight to ten participants who meet with a moderator-researcher-analyst and "focus on" or "explore" a particular product or product category (or any other topic or subject of research interest). *See Discussion Guide and Qualitative Research.*

Foot-in-the-Door Technique. A strategy aimed at changing attitudes consisting of getting people to agree to a large request after convincing them to agree to a small and modest request first. *See Door-in-the-Face Technique.*

Forgetting. A point at which the link between the stimulus and the expected reward seizes to exist because of lack of engagement in the applicable purchase situation for a lengthy period. *See Extinction.*

Formal Learning. Learning that occurs when parents, older siblings and other family members teach younger members "how to behave." *See Informal Learning and Technical Learning.*

Formal Source. A communication source that speaks on behalf of a company, such as an endorser, salesperson, or advertiser. *See Communication, Informal Source, and Source Credibility.*

Freudian Theory. A theory maintaining that unconscious needs or drives, especially biological and sexual ones, are at the heart of human motivation and personality. *See Ego, Id, and Superego.*

Frustration. The feeling that results from failure to achieve a goal. *See Defense Mechanisms.*

Functional Approach. An approach to changing attitudes by appealing to the reasons (or motivations) behind people's attitudes. These reasons are called "functions." *See Ego-Defensive Function, Knowledge Function, Utlitarian Function, and Value-Expressive Function.*

Generation X (Xers). The age cohort representing people born between 1965 and 1979.

Generation Y (Echo Boomers, Millennials). The age cohort representing people born between 1980 and 1996. Some definitions also include people born in the late 1970s and 1990s in this cohort.

Generation Z (Homeland Generation, Digital Natives). The age cohort representing people born from 1997 till the present.

Generic Goals. Outcomes that consumers seek in order to satisfy physiological and psychological needs. *See Product-Specific Goals.*

Geo-Demographic Segments. Segments identified through geodemographics.

Geodemographics. A hybrid segmentation scheme based on the premise that people who live close to one another are likely to have similar financial means, tastes, preferences, lifestyles, and consumption habits (as an old adage states, "Birds of a feather flock together").

Geofencing. Promotional alerts sent to the smartphones of customers, who opted into this service, when the customers near or enter the store.

Gestalt Psychology. The principles underlying perceptual organization. "Gestalt" means "pattern" or "configuration" in German. *See Perception.*

Gifting Behavior. Consumer behavior involving giving gifts.

Global Marketing Strategy. Selling the same product using the same positioning and communication approach globally. *See Hybrid Marketing Strategy and Local Marketing Strategy.*

Goals. Sought after outcomes of motivated behavior. *See Motivation.*

Google Analytics. A service offered by Google that enables advertisers to evaluate the effectiveness of their websites and profiles their users.

Gordon Survey of Personal and Interpersonal Values. A research instrument measuring the values that represent how people cope with their daily lives. *See Interpersonal Values and Personal Values.*

Grouping. People's instinctive tendency to group stimuli together and unite them into one entity. *See Perception.*

Halo Effect. An evaluation of an object based on only one (or several) positive dimension. Linguistically, the definition of "halo" signifies light, honor, and glory. Thus, in marketing, the term refers to a prestigious image of a product "rubbing on" other products marketed under the same brand name.

Hemispheric Lateralization (Split-Brain Theory). A theory whose premise is that the human brain is divided into two distinct cerebral hemispheres that operate together, but "specialize" in the processing different types of cognitions. The left hemisphere is the center of human language; it is the linear side of the brain and primarily responsible for reading, speaking, and reasoning. The right hemisphere of the brain is the home of spatial perception and nonverbal concepts; it is nonlinear and the source of imagination and pleasure. *See Passive Learning.*

High-Involvement Purchases. Purchases that are very important to the consumer and provoke a lot of perceived risk, and extensive problem solving and information processing. *See Consumer Involvement, Extensive Problem Solving, Low-Involvement Purchases, and Perceived Risk.*

Honeymooners. In the context of the Family Life Cycle, young and newly married couples. *See Family Life Cycle.*

Husband-Dominated Decisions. Purchase decisions where the husband's influence is greater than the wife's. *See Autonomic Decisions, Joint Decisions, and Wife-Dominated Decisions.*

Hybrid Marketing Strategy. While selling overseas, standardizing either the product or advertising message and customizing the other one. *See Global Marketing Strategy and Local Marketing Strategy.*

Id. A Freudian term referring to the "warehouse" of primitive and impulsive drives—basic physiological needs such as thirst, hunger, and sex—for which the individual seeks immediate satisfaction without concern for the specific means of satisfaction. *See Ego, Freudian Theory, and Superego.*

Ideal Self-Image. The way people like to see themselves.

Ideal Social Self-Image. The way people like others to see them.

Identification. Resolving frustration identifying with other persons who have experienced the same or similar frustrating situation. *See Defense Mechanisms.*

Impersonal Communications. Messages that companies (formal sources) develop and transmit through their marketing departments, advertising or public relations agencies, and spokespersons. *See Communication, Formal Source, and Interpersonal Communications.*

Impression-Based Targeting. A technique where advertisers specify the criteria of the persons they wish to reach online and then bid in real time for the opportunities to reach such people. A person reached is termed an "eyeball" or "impression." Impression-based ads often "follow" consumers online and thus keep reminding them about the products they were interested in. *See Real Time Bidding and Segment-Based Targeting.*

Index of Status Characteristics (Warner's ISC). A measure of social class in the form of a weighted index of occupation, source (not amount) of income, house type, and the quality of the dwelling area. *See Multivariable Index.*

Indulgent Parents. Parents who are very nurturing and highly permissive during their children's consumer socialization. *See Authoritarion Parents, Authoritative Parents, and Neglecting Parents.*

Inept Set. Brands (or models) that the consumer excludes from purchase consideration because they are unacceptable and often considered inferior. *See Evoked Set and Inert Set.*

Inert Set. Brands (or models) the consumer is indifferent toward because they are perceived as not having any particular advantages. *See Evoked Set and Inept Set.*

Inertia Brand Loyalty. Purchasing the same brand consistently because of habit and convenience, but without any emotional attachment to it. *See Brand Loyalty.*

Infomercials. Long commercials that appear to be documentaries rather than advertisements.

Informal Learning. Learning that occurs when children imitate the behaviors of selected others, such as family members, friends, or TV and movie heroes or characters. *See Formal Learning and Technical Learning.*

Informal Source. A person whom the message receiver knows personally, such as a parent or friend, or an individual met online, who provides the receiver with product information and advice. *See Communication, Formal Source, and Source Credibility.*

Information Overload. A situation that occurs when consumers receive too much information and find it difficult to encode and store it.

Inner-Directed. Consumers who rely on their own inner values and standards in evaluating new products, and are also likely to be consumer innovators. *See Other-Directed.*

Innovation. *See Continuous Innovation, Diffusion of Innovation, Discontinuous Innovation, and Dynamically Continuous Innovation.*

Innovation Adoption. A form of cognitive learning, developed by researchers of Diffusion of Innovations, this term designates the process leading to a person's decision of whether or not to adopt an innovation. This process consists of five stages. *See Awareness, Interest, Evaluation, Trial, and Adoption.*

Innovation Adoption Process. *See Innovation Adoption.*

Innovation Decision-Making. A form of cognitive learning, developed by researchers of Diffusion of Innovations, stating that learning about new products and deciding whether or not to adopt them occurs in the following manner: knowledge, persuasion, decision, and confirmation. This process is very similar to Innovation Adoption.

Innovativeness. The degree of a consumer's willingness to adopt new products and services shortly after they are they have been introduced. *See Innovators.*

Innovators. Consumers who are open to new ideas and are among the first to try new products, services, or practices. *See Innovativeness, Adopter Categories, Early Adopters, Early Majority, Late Majority, and Laggards.*

Institutional Advertising. Advertising that promotes a company's overall image without referring to specific products.

Instrumental Conditioning (Operant Conditioning). A form of behavioral learning based on the notion that learning occurs through a trial-and-error process, with habits formed as a result of rewards received for certain responses or behaviors. *See Behavioral Learning and Reinforcement.*

Instrumental Values. Within the Rokeach Value Survey, values that are defined as the "means" to achieve end goals. *See Rokeach Value Survey and Terminal Values.*

Interactive TV (iTV). A medium that combines TV broadcasts and the interactivity of the Internet. iTV and can be delivered to one's TV, computer, or mobile device in the form of a two-way communication between subscribers and providers of cable or satellite TV.

Interest. The second stage of Innovation Adoption, which is a term designating the process leading to a person's decision of whether or not to adopt an innovation. In this stage, the person begins to be interested in the innovation. *See Innovation Adoption.*

Internal Marketing. Marketing the organization to its personnel and treating them like "internal customers" in order to get them to "go the extra mile" in handling and retaining "real" customers.

Internet Survey. A research study conducted online.

Interpersonal Communications. Messages sent by either formal sources (e.g., a salesperson in a physical or virtual retail location) or informal sources (e.g., peers with whom the consumer communicates face to face or via electronic means). *See Communication, Formal Source, Impersonal Communications, and Informal Source.*

Interpersonal Values. Within Gordon's Survey of Personal and Interpersonal Values, measures of one's achievement need, goal orientation, and seeking new experiences. *See Gordon's Survey and Personal Values.*

Intrinsic Cues. Physical characteristics of the product itself, such as size, color, flavor, or aroma. *See Extrinsic Cues.*

JND (Just Noticeable Difference). *See Differential Threshold.*

Joint Decisions. Purchase decisions where the husband and wife's influence are equal. *See Autonomic Decisions, Husband-Dominated Decisions, and Wife-Dominated Decisions.*

Judgment Sample. A nonprobability sample where researchers use their own judgments to select the respondents. *See Nonprobability Sample.*

Key Informant Method. A technique of measuring opinion leadership that consists of gathering information from a person who is keenly knowledgeable about the nature of social communications among members of a specific group. *See Opinion Leadership.*

Klout Score. A numerical value that measures persons' influence online based on their ability to generate engagement with and feedback to their online postings.

Knowledge Function. A functional approach to studying attitudes where researchers maintain that people form attitudes because they have a strong need to understand the characters of the people, events, and objects they encounter. *See Functional Approach.*

Laggards. The very last consumers to adopt innovations. *See Adopter Categories, Innovators, Early Adopters, Early Majority, and Late Majority.*

Late Majority. People who buy innovations only after most other consumers have adopted them. *See Adopter Categories, Innovators, Early Adopters, Early Majority, and Laggards.*

Learning. Applying one's past knowledge and experience to present circumstances and behavior. *See Motivation, Cues, Response, and Reinforcement.*

Lexicographic Decision Rule. A noncopensatory decision rule where the consumer first ranks the attributes in terms of perceived relevance or importance. The consumer then compares the various alternatives in terms of the single attribute that is considered most important. *See Noncompensatory Decision Rules.*

Licensing. An application of stimulus generalization that contractually allows affixing a brand name to the products of another manufacturer. *See Stimulus Generalization.*

Likert Scale. The most popular form of attitude scale, where consumers are asked to check numbers corresponding to their level of "agreement" or "disagreement" with a series of statements about the studied object. The scale consists of an equal number of agreement/disagreement choices on either side of a neutral choice. *See Quantitative Research.*

Limited Problem Solving. Purchase decisions where consumers buy updated versions of products they have bought before and have set criteria to evaluate these items. *See Extensive Problem Solving and Routinized Response Behavior.*

Local Marketing Strategy. Customizing both the product and communication approach for overseas market. *See Global Marketing Strategy and Hybried Marketing Strategy.*

Long-Term Store. A location in the brain where information is retained for extended periods of time. *See Sensation, Sensory Store, and Short-Term Store.*

Low-Involvement Purchases. Purchases are not very important to the consumer, hold little relevance, have little perceived risk, and, thus, provoke very limited information processing. *See Consumer Involvement, High-Involvement Purchases, Perceived Risk, and Routinized Response Behavior.*

Magazine Readership Survey. A form of consumer survey. *See Starch Readership Ad Study.*

Mail Survey. A research study consisting of sending questionnaire by mail.

Market Research. A process that links the consumer, customer, and public to the marketer through information in order to identify marketing opportunities and problems, evaluate marketing actions, and judge the performance of marketing strategies.

Market Segmentation. The process of dividing a market into subsets of consumers with common needs or characteristics. Each subset represemts a consumer group with shared needs that are different from those shared by other groups.

Marketing. The activity, set of institutions, and processes for creating, communicating, delivering, and exchanging offerings that have value for customers, clients, partners, and society.

Marketing Concept. The premise that marketing consists of satisfying consumers' needs, creating value, and retaining customers, and that companies must produce only those goods that they have already determined that consumers would buy.

Marketing Ethics. Moral principles designed to guide marketers' behavior.

Marketing Mix (Four Ps). A business plan that includes four elements: the product (or service), price, place (or distribution), and promotion.

Marketing Myopia. A focus on the product rather than on the needs it presumes to satisfy.

Maslow's Hierarchy of Needs. A theoretical framework consisting of five levels of human needs, which rank in order of importance from lower-level (biogenic) needs to higher-level (psychogenic) needs. The theory states that individuals seek to satisfy lower-level needs before higher-level needs.

Massed Learning. Bunched up learning designed to teach people all at once. *See Distributed Learning.*

Materialism. A personality traits that gauges the extent to which an individual is preoccupied with the purchase and display of non-essential and often conspicuous luxury goods.

Media. The channels for transmitting communications. *See Communication.*

Media Exposure Effects. A measure of how many consumers were exposed to the message and their characteristics.

Membership Group. A group to which a person either belongs or can join and whose values he or she adopt. *See Reference Groups and Symbolic Group.*

Message. A thought, idea, attitude, image, or other information that the sender wishes to convey to the intended audience, and it can be verbal (spoken or written), nonverbal (a photograph, an illustration, or a symbol), or a combination of the two.

Microblog. A site that has less content than the traditional blog and allow users to exchange small elements of content, such as short sentences, individual images, and video links, mostly via Twitter. *See Blog.*

Mobile Ads. *See Mobile Advertising.*

Mobile Advertising. Sending promotional messages to consumers' cell phones, iPads, electronic readers, and other devices that people carry while on the go.

Motivation. The driving force within individuals that impels them to act.

Motivational Research. A "term of art" that refers to qualitative studies conducted by Dr. Ernest Dichter in the 1950s and 1960, which were designed to uncover consumers' subconscious or hidden motivations in the context of buying and consumption. *See Projective Techniques and Qualitative Research.*

Multi-Attribute Attitude Models. Models that portray consumers' attitudes as functions of their assessments of the objects' prominent attributes.

Multivariable Index. A measure of social class that combines several demographics to determine social class standing. *See Index of Status Characteristics and Socioeconomic Status Score.*

Mystery Shoppers. Professional observers who pose as customers and interact with and provide unbiased evaluations of the company's service personnel in order to identify opportunities for improving productivity and efficiency. *See Consumer Research.*

Narrow Categorizers. High-risk perceivers who prefer to limit their choices to a few safe alternatives rather than face the consequences of a wrong decision. *See Broad Categorizers, Perceived Risk, and Risk Aversion.*

Narrowcasting. Communication channels that enable marketers to send addressable, customized, interactive, and more response-measurable messages, to narrowly defined market segments.

National Brand. A brand that is available in all fifty states.

Need for Cognition (NFC). A personality traits that reflects a person's craving for or enjoyment of thinking.

Need for Humor. A person's tendency to enjoy, engage in, or seek out amusement.

Need for Self-Actualization (or Self-Fulfillment). An individual's desire to fulfill his or her potential—to becoming everything he or she is capable of becoming. *See Maslow's Hierarchy of Needs.*

Need for Uniqueness. Individuals' attempts to differentiate themselves through the acquisition of consumer goods that enhance their personal and social identities.

Need Recognition. The first step in the consumer decision-making process occurring when the consumer identifies and faces a "problem" that can be solved by buying a product or service.

Needs. Circumstances or things that that are wanted or required, and therefore direct the motivational forces. *See Motivation.*

Negative Disconfirmation of Expectations. A situation that occurs when a product's performance is below expectations and the consumer is dissatisfied. *See Positive Disconfirmation of Expectations.*

Negative Message Framing. A promotional message that stresses the benefits to be lost by not using the product. *See Positive Message Framing.*

Negative Reinforcement. Removing an unpleasant stimulus. *See Positive Reinforcement.*

Neglecting Parents. Parents who are very permissive, but provide their children with little or no nurturing during their children's consumer socialization. *See Authoritarian Parents, Authoritative Parents, and Indulgent Parents.*

Neo-Freudian Personality Theory. A theory based on the premise that social relationships play a crucial role in the development of personality, in addition to the aspects outlined by Freud.

Neuromarketing. The study of advertising's effects on brain activity. *See Physiological Measures.*

New Media. Online channels, social networks, and mobile electronic devices. Unlike traditional media, these channels allow marketers to send personalized messages to individual consumers who can respond to the messages immediately.

Non-Family Households. Living situations that are not legally defined as families. *See Family.*

Noncompensatory Decision Rules. A group of decision rules that do not allow consumers to balance positive evaluations of a brand on one attribute against negative evaluations on other attributes. *See Compensatory Decision Rules.*

Nonprobability Sample. Selecting study respondents in a nonrandom fashion based on researchers' judgments. *See Cluster Sample, Convenience Sample, Judgment Sample, and Quota Sample.*

Nontraditional Families. Families that do not readily fit into the Family Life Cycle. *See Family Life Cycle.*

Normative Influence. Learning and adopting a group's norms, values, and behaviors. *See Comparative Influence and Reference Groups.*

Nuclear Family. A married couple with one or more children. *See Extended Family.*

Objective Measures. Measures of social class that include one or more of the following variables: occupation, amount of income and education, and other related factors (e.g., source of income). *See Multivariable Index and Subjective Measures.*

Observability (Communicability). One of the five characteristics identified as a determinant of consumer acceptance of a new product representing the ease with which a product's benefits or attributes can be observed, imagined, or described to potential consumers. *See the other four characteristics: Compatibility, Complexity, Relative Advantage, and Trial-ability.*

Observational Learning (Modeling). Learning that occurs when people observe and later imitate observed behaviors.

Observational Research. A research tool where marketers because marketers gain an in-depth understanding of the relationship between people and products is by watching them in the process of buying and/or using the products. *See Quantitative Research.*

Occupational Prestige Ranking. Rankings that represent society's collective beliefs regarding the occupation's social worth and desirability, as stemming from the knowledge required to attain it (i.e., educational level) and the material rewards that occupants receive (i.e., income). *See Social Class and Social Status.*

One-Sided Message. A message that ignores competitors' products.

Online Display Ads. Fixed banners posted on websites.

Opinion Leadership. The process by which one person (the opinion leader) informally influences others, who might be either opinion seekers or recipients. This influence occurs between two or more people neither of whom represents a commercial seller nor would gain directly from providing advice or information. *See Buzz Agent and Word-of-Mouth.*

Optimum Stimulation Level (OSL). A personality traits that reflects the degree to which a person likes novel, complex and unusual experiences (i.e., high OSL), or prefers simple, uncluttered, and calm existence (i.e., low OSL).

Other-Directed. Consumers who look up to others for guidance as to what is appropriate or inappropriate and are unlikely to be consumer innovators. *See Inner-Directed.*

Out-of-Home Media. Communications vehicles that target consumers in captive and less cluttered environments outside of their homes.

Owned Social Media. Online communication channels that marketers control. *See Paid Social Media.*

Paid Social Media. Online communication channels that marketers pay for using. *See Owned Social Media.*

Parenthood. In the context of the Family Life Cycle, married couples with at least one child living at home. *See Family Life Cycle.*

Participant-Observers. Researchers who become active members of the society whose customs and values they are observing and studying. *See Field Observation.*

Passive Learning. *See Hemispheric Lateralization.*

Perceived Price. The customer's view of the value that he or she he receives from the purchase. *See Perception.*

Perceived Risk. The uncertainty that consumers face when they cannot foresee the consequences of their purchase decisions. The types of perceived risk include functional, physical, financial, psychological and time risks. *See Perception.*

Perception. The process by which individuals select, organize, and interpret stimuli into a meaningful and coherent picture of the world. It can be described as "how we see the world around us."

Perceptual Defense. A cognitive activity occurring when consumers subconsciously screen out stimuli that they find psychologically threatening, even though exposure has already taken place. *See Perception, Selective Attention, Selective Exposure, and Subliminal Perception.*

Perceptual Mapping. Constructing a maplike diagram representing consumers' perceptions of competing brands along relevant product attributes. Perceptual maps show marketers: (1) how consumers perceive their brand in relation to competition; (2) determine the direction for altering undesirable consumers' perception of their brands; and (3) find gaps, in the form of "un-owned" perceptual positions, that represent opportunities for developing new brands or products. *See Perception.*

Peripheral Route to Persuasion. A promotional approach maintaining that uninvolved consumers can be best persuaded by the ad's visual aspects rather than its informative copy (i.e., the product's attributes). *See Central Route to Persuasion and Elaboration Likelihood Model.*

Personal Interview Survey. A study where researchers interview respondents in person.

Personal Values. Within Gordon's Survey of Personal and Interpersonal Values, measures of one's leadership, desire to be recognized, and conformity. *See Gordon's Survey and Interpersonal Values.*

Personality. The inner psychological characteristics that both determine and reflect how we think and act.

Persuasion Effects. Measures that indicate whether the message was received, understood, and interpreted correctly.

Physiological Measures. Electronic instruments that track bodily responses to stimuli. *See Neuromarketing.*

Physiological Needs. Innate (biogenic, primary) motivational forces that sustains biological existence. They include the need for food, water, air, protecting the body from the outside environment (i.e., clothing and shelter), and sex. *See Psychological Needs.*

Physiological Observation. *See Physiological Measures.*

Portable People Meters (PPMs). Small devices, equipped with GPS, that consumers clip into their belts and wear all day (in exchange for monetary incentives). The devices monitor codes embedded in into the audio streams of media that consumers receive and can also capture visual images of the screens and written materials that consumers are exposed to.

Positioning. The process by which a company creates a distinct image and identity for its products, services and brands in consumers' minds. The image differentiates the company's offering from competition by communicating to the target audience that the product, service or brand fulfills the target consumers' needs better than alternatives. *See Repositioning.*

Positive Disconfirmation of Expectations. A situation that occurs when the product's performance exceeds expectations and the consumer is satisfied. *See Negative Disconfirmation of Expectations.*

Positive Message Framing. A promotional message that stresses the benefits to be gained by using a specific product. *See Negative Message Framing.*

Positive Reinforcement. Rewarding a particular behavior and strengthening the likelihood of a specific response during the same or similar situation in the future. *See Negative Reinforcement.*

Post-Parenthood. In the context of the Family Life Cycle, older couples with no children living at home. *See Family Life Cycle.*

Post-Purchase Dissonance. Cognitive dissonance that occurs after a purchase. *See Cognitive Dissonance.*

Power Need. A psychological force that is closely related to the egoistic need and reflects the individual's desire to control his or her environment, including controlling other persons and objects.

Pre-Purchase Search. A stage in the consumer decision-making process where the consumer tries to identify a product that will satisfy a recognized need better than other alternatives.

Predictive Analytics. Measures designed to predict consumers' future purchases on the bases of past buying information and other data, and also evaluate the impact of personalized promotions stemming from these predictions.

Premium Brand Loyalty. Solid attachment to the brand represented by continuous repeated purchases. *See Brand Loyalty.*

Price/Quality Relationship. A situation occurring when consumers rely on prices as indicators of product quality and view more expensive products as having higher quality and value. *See Perception.*

Primacy Effect. An indication that material presented first during communications is more noticeable and persuasive than subsequent materials. *See Recency Effect.*

Primary Research. New research especially designed and collected for purposes of a current research problem. *See Qualitative Research and Quantitative Research.*

PRIZM. A framework designed by Nielsen that is widely used in geodemographic segmentation. It consists of sixty-six segments classified according to ZIP codes and enables marketers to locate specific consumer groups readily.

Probability Sample. A method when studies' respondents are selected in such a way that every member of the population studied has a known, nonzero chance of being selected. *See Simple Random Sample, Stratified Random Sample, and Systematic Random Sample.*

Product Awareness Status. The degree of a consumer's awareness of the product and its features, and whether or not he or she intends to buy it reasonably soon.

Product Concept. A premise that consumers buy the product that offers them the highest quality, the best performance, and the most features.

Product Form Extensions. Offering the same product in a different form but under the same brand, which is a marketing application of stimulus generalization. *See Stimulus Generalization.*

Product Line Extensions. Additions of related items to an established brand because they are likely to be adopted, since they come under a known and trusted brand name, which is a marketing application of stimulus generalization. *See Stimulus Generalization.*

Product Placement. A form of promotion where marketers "disguise" promotional cues by integrating products (i.e., "figures") into TV shows, films or other entertainment content (i.e., "grounds"), or building entertainment content around products. *See Branded Entertainment and Figure and Ground.*

Product-Specific Goals. Sought outcomes to be achieved by using a given product or service. *See Generic Goals.*

Production Concept. A premise that consumers are mostly interested in product availability at low prices; its implicit marketing objectives are cheap, efficient production and intensive distribution of products.

Projection. Responding to frustration by projecting blame for failures and inabilities on other objects or persons. *See Defense Mechanisms.*

Projective Techniques. A research tool requiring respondents to interpret stimuli that do not have clear meanings, with the assumption that the subjects will "reveal" or "project" their subconscious, hidden motives into (or onto) the ambiguous stimuli. *See Qualitative Research.*

Psychographics (AIOs). Segmenting consumers according to their lifestyles, which consist of consumers' activities, interests, and opinions (i.e., AIOS).

Psychological Needs. Motivational forces that are learned from our parents, social environment, and interactions with others. *See Physiological Needs.*

Psychological Noise. Competing advertising messages or distracting thoughts that impact the reception of promotional messages.

Psychology. The study of the human mind and the mental factors that affect behavior (i.e., needs, personality traits, perception, learned experiences, and attitudes).

Qualitative Research. Studies that attempt to delve into the consumer's unconscious or hidden motivations. This research utilizes focus groups, depth interviews, motivational research, and projective techniques. *See Depth Interview, Focus Group, Motivational Research, and Projective Techniques.*

Quantitative Research. Gathering and analyzing statistical data, utilizing observational research, experimentation, and survey research. *See Behavior Intention Scale, Email Survey, Experiments, Internet Survey, Likert Scale, Mail Survey, Observational Research, Personal Interview Survey, Semantic Differential Scale, Rank Order Scale, and Telephone Interview Survey.*

Quota Sample. A nonprobability sample where the researcher interviews a prescribed number of people in each of several categories (e.g., 50 men and 50 women). *See Nonprobability Sample.*

Rank-Order Scale. A research instrument requiring participants in a study to rank items (e.g., products) in order of preference in terms of some criterion, such as overall quality or value for the money. *See Quantitative Research.*

Rationalization. Resolving frustration by inventing plausible reasons for being unable to attain goals or deciding that the goal is not really worth pursuing. *See Defense Mechanisms.*

Real Time Bidding. A technique that allows advertisers to reach the right user, in the right place, at the right time, and also sets the price that advertisers pay for each "eyeball" or "impression" (i.e., for each person reached). *See Impression-Based Targeting.*

Recall Test. *See Unaided Recall.*

Recency Effect. An indication that the material presented last during communications is more noticeable and persuasive than preceding materials. *See Primacy Effect.*

Recognition Test. *See Aided Recall.*

Reference Groups. Groups that serve as sources of comparison, influence, and norms for people's opinions, values, and behaviors. *See Comparative Influence, Membership Group, Normative Influence, and Symbolic Group.*

Regression. Reacting to a frustrating situation with childish or immature behavior. *See Defense Mechanisms.*

Rehearsal. The process that information in the short-term store undergoes, in the form of silent, mental repetition of information, after which the information is transferred to the long-term store.

Reinforcement. In learning, particularly in instrumental conditioning, it is a reward, in the form of pleasure, enjoyment, and other benefits, for a desired behavior. In consumer behavior, it is the benefits, enjoyment, and utilities that consumers receive from products purchased. *See Continuous Reinforcement, Fixed Ratio Reinforcement, Negative Reinforcement, Positive Reinforcement, and Variable Reinforcement.*

Relative Advantage. One of the five characteristics identified as a determinant of consumer acceptance of a new product representing the degree to which potential customers perceive a new product as superior to existing substitutes. *See the other four characteristics: Compatibility, Complexity, Observability, and Trial-ability.*

Reliability. A measure has reliability if the same questions, asked of a similar sample, produce the same findings. *See Validity.*

Repetition. In the context of consumer learning, the mechanism used continuously to establish and maintain associations between brands and unfulfilled needs. *See Classical Conditioning and Instrumental Conditioning.*

Repositioning. The process by which a company strategically changes the distinct image and identity of that its products, services, and brands. *See Positioning.*

Repression. Responding to frustration by "forcing" the failure to achieve a goal out of conscious awareness. *See Defense Mechanisms.*

Response. Reaction to a drive or cue. *See Learning.*

Retargeting. Ads for specific products that consumers have looked at online that "follow" these consumers repeatedly and show up whenever the consumers go online using the same computers.

Retrieval. The process by which people recover information from the long-term store, that is frequently triggered by external cues.

Risk Aversion. The reluctance to take risks and low tolerance of ambiguous situations.

Ritual. A symbolic activity consisting of a fixed sequence of steps that is repeated periodically.

Ritualistic Behavior. An action that has become a ritual.

Rokeach Value Survey. A self-administered, two-part values inventory. *See Instrumental Values and Terminal Values.*

Routinized Response Behavior. Purchase decisions that are "automatic" and made without much thought because the products involved are inexpensive and purchased frequently. *See Extensive Problem Solving and Limited Problem Solving.*

Safety and Security Needs. Psychological forces that are concerned not only with physical safety but also include order, stability, routine, familiarity, and control over one's life. *See Maslow's Hierarchy of Needs.*

Sales Effects. Measures that indicate whether the messages of a given campaign have generated the sales level defined in the campaign's objectives.

Sample. A presumably representative subset of the population under study that is used to estimate the entire population's characteristics. *See Nonprobability Sample and Probability Sample.*

Screener Questionnaire. A questionnaire designed to ensure that only individuals who fulfill a preset criteria are used as respondents in a research study. *See Consumer Research.*

Search Advertising. Placing online advertisements on Web pages that show results from search engine queries.

Secondary Data. Information that was gathered previously and not in the course of the study presently undertaken. *See Primary Research.*

Segment-Based Targeting. A atrategic method where advertisers pre-negotiate prices for advertising space in media (e.g., magazines or TV shows), whose audiences, presumably, largely (but never completely) match the profiles of the consumers the advertisers target. *See Impression-Based Targeting.*

Selective Attention. Consumers' heightened awareness of stimuli that meet their needs and interests and minimal awareness of stimuli irrelevant to their needs. *See Perception, Perceptual Defense, and Selective Exposure.*

Selective Exposure. Consumers seeking out sympathetic, pleasant messages and deliberately avoiding messages that they find painful or threatening. See *Perception, Perceptual Defense, and Selective Attention.*

Self-Construal. A trait that refers to how individuals perceive, comprehend, and interpret the world around them, particularly the behavior or action of others towards themselves.

Self-Designating Method. A technique of measuring opinion leadership that employs a self-administered questionnaire where respondents are asked to evaluate the extent to which they have provided others with information about a product or brand, or have otherwise influenced the purchase decisions of others. *See Opinion Leadership.*

Self-Image. *See Actual Self-Image.*

Self-Perception Attribution. A mental interpretation that reflects the way people see themselves when they form causalities about prior events, which consists of internal and external attributions. *See Defensive Attribution.*

Self-Reported Measures of Motives. Measures that consist of written statements, and where respondents are asked to indicate how relevant each statement is to them.

Selling Concept. A premise that marketers' primary focus should be selling the products that they have decided to produce through the "hard sell" approach.

Semantic Differential Scale. A measure consisting of a series of bipolar adjectives (such as "good/bad," "hot/cold," "like/dislike," or "expensive/inexpensive") anchored at the ends of an odd-numbered (e.g., five- or seven-point) continuum. *See Quantitative Research.*

Sensation. The immediate and direct response of the sensory organs to stimuli. *See Perception, Sensory Receptors, and Stimulus.*

Sensation Seeking. A personality traits that is closely related to OSL and reflects one's need for varied, novel, and complex sensations and experiences, and the willingness to take risks for the sake of such experiences.

Sensory Adaptation. Getting used to high levels of sensory input and therefore less able to notice a particular stimulus.

Sensory Receptors. The human organs (the eyes, ears, nose, mouth, and skin) that receive sensory inputs. Their sensory functions are to see, hear, smell, taste, and touch. *See Sensation and Stimulus.*

Sensory Store. A location in the brain where the sensory input lasts for just a second or two. If it is not processed immediately, it is lost. *See Long-Term Store and Short-Term Store.*

SERVQUAL Scale. Perceptual measure of the gap between customers' expectations of services and their perceptions of the actual service delivered, based on five dimensions: reliability, responsiveness, assurance, empathy, and tangibility. These dimensions are divided into two groups: the "outcome dimension," which focuses on the reliable delivery of the core service, and the "process dimension," which focuses on how the core service is delivered (i.e., the employees' responsiveness, assurance, and empathy in handling customers) and the service's tangible aspects.

Shaping. Reinforcement before the desired consumer behavior actually takes place, which increases the probability that the desired behavior will occur.

Short-Term Store (Working Memory). A location in brain where information is retained for a very short period. *See Long-Term Store, Sensation, and Sensory Store.*

Showrooming. Consumers using smartphones to scan the bar codes of products displayed in physical stores and then checking the items' prices online in order to purchase them at the lowest prices.

Simple Random Sample. A probability sample where every member of the population has a known and equal chance of being selected. *See Probability Sample.*

Sleeper Effect. A person's disassociation of the message from its source over time, which results in remembering only the message's content, but not its source. *See Differential Decay.*

Social Class. The division of members of a society into a hierarchy of distinct status classes, so that members of each class have relatively the same status and members of all other classes have either higher or lower status. *See Occupational Prestige Rankings, Social Class Consciousness, and Social Status.*

Social Media. Means of interactions among people in which they create, share, and exchange information and ideas in virtual communities and networks. Social media depend on mobile and Web-based technologies to create highly interactive platforms through which individuals and communities share, co-create, discuss, and modify user-generated content.

Social Needs. The psychogenic needs for love, affection, belonging, and acceptance. *See Maslow's Hierarchy of Needs.*

Social Network. Virtual community where people share information about themselves with others, generally with similar interests, with whom they had established relationships that, for the most part, exist only in cyberspace.

Social Self-Image. The image that reflects about how people believe others see them. *See Actual Self-Image.*

Social Status. The degree of prestige the members of one social class have in comparison with members of other social classes. Status is composed of several factors, including wealth (amount of economic assets), power (the degree of influence over others), and the amount of esteem one receives from others. *See Occupational Prestige Rankings and Social Class.*

Social-Class Consciousness. A person's level of identification with a given social class. *See Objective Measures.*

Socialization. The process by which people learn how to behave in ways that are acceptable to other members of their society. *See Socialization Agent.*

Socialization Agent. The person or organization involved in the socialization process because of frequency of contact with the individual being socialized and control over the rewards and punishments given to him or her. *See Consumer Socialization.*

Societal Marketing Concept. A premise that requires marketers to fulfill the needs of the target audience in ways that improve, preserve, and enhance society's well-being, while also meeting their business objectives.

Socioeconomic Status Score (SES). A measure of social class, developed by the U.S. Census Bureau, that combines occupation, family income, and educational attainment to determine social standing. *See Multivariable Index.*

Sociology. The study of the development, structure, functioning, and problems of human society. *See Content Analysis, Culture, and Field Observation.*

Sociometric Method. A technique of measuring opinion leadership that records person-to-person communications about a product or brand among members of a community where most people know each other by name. *See Opinion Leadership.*

Source Credibility. A source's persuasive impact, stemming from its perceived expertise, trustworthiness, and believability.

Starch Readership Ad Study. A research method that evaluates the effectiveness of magazine advertisements along three criteria: "Noticing" the ad, "associating" the ad with the brand advertised, and "involvement" with the ad (defined as having read most of the ad's text). *See Learning.*

Stereotypes. Biased notions that people carry in their minds about the meanings of various stimuli. When presented with these stimuli, people "add" these biases to what they see or hear and form mostly distorted impressions. *See Perception.*

Stimulus. Any input to any of the senses. *See Sensation and Sensory Receptors.*

Stimulus Discrimination. The strategy that is the opposite of stimulus generalization aimed at getting consumers to select a specific stimulus from among similar stimuli, whose objective is to position products and services in such a way that differentiates them effectively from competitive offerings. *See Positioning, Stimulus, and Stimulus Generalization.*

Stimulus Generalization. Responding the same way to slightly different stimuli. *See Stimulus and Stimulus Discrimination.*

Stratified Random Sample. A probability sample where the population is divided into mutually exclusive groups (such as age groups), and random samples are drawn from each group. *See Probability Sample.*

Subculture. A group that shares certain beliefs, values, and customes, stemming from ethnicity, religion, geographic location, age, or gender, while also being a part of a larger society.

Subjective Measures. Asking people to evaluate their own social class. *See Objective Measures and Social Class Consciousness.*

Subliminal Perception. A situation that occurs when the sensory receptors receive stimuli that are beneath the person's conscious awareness (i.e., the absolute threshold). *See Absolute Threshold, Perception, and Sensory Receptors.*

Superego. A Freudian term referring to the individual's internal expression of society's moral and ethical codes of "proper" or "correct" conduct. The superego's role is to see that individuals satisfy their needs in a socially acceptable fashion. Thus, the superego is a "brake" that restrains or inhibits the impulsive forces of the Id. *See Ego, Freudian Theory, and Id.*

Symbol. A verbal or non-verbal thing that represents or stands for something else.

Symbolic Group. A group to which an individual is unlikely to belong, but whose values and behaviors he or she adopts nevertheless. *See Membership Group and Reference Groups.*

Systematic Random Sample. A probability sample where members of the population are selected at random and then every nth person is selected. *See Probability Sample.*

Targeting. Selecting the segments that the company views as prospective customers and pursuing them.

Technical Learning. Learning that occurs when teachers instruct children about how to behave and "do things" in social and personal settings. *See Formal Learning and Informal Learning.*

Teens. The age cohort representing youngsters who are between 13 and 17 years old.

Telephone Interview Survey. A study conducted via the phone.

Terminal Values. Within the Rokeach Value Survey, values that reflect goals and desired states of existence (i.e., "ends). *See Instrumental Values and Rokeach Value Survey.*

Test Marketing. Selecting a geographic market, that it presumably representative of other markets, and then introducing a product (i.e., all the elements of the Marketing Mix) in order to examine consumers' responses to the offering under actual marketing conditions. *See Experiments.*

Thematic Apperception Test. Showing pictures to respondents and asking them to tell a story about each picture. *See Projective Techniques and Qualitative Research.*

Theory of Reasoned Action. An approach to studying attitudes that measures the "subjective norms" that influence a person's intention to act, which include his (or her) beliefs as to what relevant others (e.g., family, friends, roommates, co-workers) might think of the person's contemplated action.

Theory of Trying-to-Consume. An approach to studying attitudes referring to cases where positive attitudes lead to actions, although the personal and environmental impediments that the person faces may (or are even likely) to prevent the desired outcome.

Three-Hit Theory. A marketing assumption that just three exposures to an advertisement are needed in order for learning to take place: one to make consumers aware of the product, a second to show consumers the relevance of the product, and a third to remind them of its benefits.

Time Shifting. Electronic devices that enable consumers to skip commercials by pausing and resuming play during live broadcasts, or recording programs and viewing them later on.

Traditional Media. Impersonal, communication channels that are generally classified into print (newspapers, magazines, billboards) and broadcast (radio, television) media, where the communications' receivers get the same (one-way) message and cannot interact with the senders.

Trait Theory. A personality research approach focused on empirical measures of specific psychological characteristics (called traits) that distinguish people from one another.

Transactional Bonds. Convenience and transaction-related relationships between customers and companies. *See Emotional Bonds.*

Tri-Component Model. A model describing the structure of attitudes, it maintains that an attitude consists of three components. *See Affective Component, Cognitive Component, and Conative Component.*

Trial. The fourth stage of Innovation Adoption, which is a term designating the process leading to a person's decision of whether or not to adopt an innovation. After becoming aware and interested in the innovation, and undertaking a "mental trial" (or evaluation), the consumer tries the innovative product, either by buying it (while being able to return it) or receiving a free sample. *See Innovation Adoption.*

Trial ability. One of the five characteristics identified as a determinant of consumer acceptance of a new product representing the degree to which a new product can be tried on a limited basis. *See the other four characteristics: Compatibility, Complexity, Relative Advantage, and Observability.*

Trickle-Down Effect. Originally applied to fashion, the concept states that members of lower classes adopt the fashions of the upper class and maintain them even after the upper class has abandoned these fashions, presumably because they no longer reflect the exclusivity of the upper class. To "restore" their exclusivity, members of the upper class adopt new fashions, which are subsequently copied by the lower classes, and the cycle is repeated.

Truth-in-Advertising Laws. Laws designed to protect consumers against false advertising.

Tweens. The age cohort representing youngsters who are between 8 and 12 years old.

Twitter. An online social networking service and micro-blogging service that enables its users to send and read text-based messages of up to 140 characters, known as "tweets."

Two-Sided Message. A message that acknowledges competing products. *See Comparative Advertising and One-Sided Message.*

Umbrella Positioning. A statement or slogan that describes the universal benefit of a company's offerings. *See Positioning.*

Unaided Recall. A recall test, that measures the effectiveness of learning and communications, where consumers are asked whether or not they have read a particular magazine or have watched a particular TV show. Afterwards, they are asked whether they can recall any of the ads featured in these media and their salient points. *See Aided Recall.*

Unconditioned Stimulus. A stimulus that occurs naturally in response to given circumstances. *See Conditioned Stimulus.*

Upward Mobility. The opportunity to move from a lower social class to a higher one because of the availability of educational resources and free enterprise. *See Downward Mobility and Social Class.*

Usage Occasion Segmentation. A segmentation strategy based on the fact that many products are purchased and used in the context of specific occasions.

Usage Rate Segmentation. A segmentation strategy based on the differences among heavy, medium, and light users of a given product.

Utilitarian Function. A functional approach to understanding attitudes where researchers believe that that consumers' attitudes reflect the utilities that brands provide. *See Functional Approach.*

Validity. A measure has validity if it does, in fact, collects appropriate data needed to answer the questions or objectives stated in the first (objectives) stage of the research process. *See Reliability.*

VALS ™. An acronym for "values and lifestyles" representing a widely used segmentation method that classifies America's adult population into eight distinctive subgroups: innovators, thinkers, achievers, experiencers, believers, strivers, makers, and survivors.

Value-Expressive Function. A functional approach to studying attitudes where researchers believe that attitudes reflect people's values and beliefs. *See Functional Approach.*

Variable Ratio Reinforcement. A method used in instrumental conditioning consisting of reinforcing a desired behavior randomly. *See Instrumental Conditioning and Reinforcement.*

Variety and Novelty Seeking. Exploratory purchase behavior (e.g., switching brands to experience new, different, and possibly better alternatives), vicarious exploration (e.g., securing information about a new or different alternative and then contemplating buying it), and "use innovativeness" (using an already adopted product in a new or novel way).

Verbalizers. People who respond favorably to verbal messages and pay less attention to visual and pictorial messages. *See Visualizers.*

Viral Marketingv (Viral Advertising). A marketing techniques that uses social networks to increases brand awareness by encouraging individuals to pass along online email messages or other contents.

Visualizers. People who respond favorably to visual and pictorial messages and pay less attention to verbal messages. *See Verbalizers.*

Web-Search Ads. Ads generated by consumers' online searches.

Weber's Law. A principal stating that the stronger the initial stimulus, the greater the additional intensity needed for the second stimulus to be perceived as different. *See Differential Threshold and JND.*

Webisodes. Short videos featuring entertainment content centered around brands.

Wife-Dominated Decisions. Purchase decisions where the wife's influence is greater than the husband's. *See Autonomic Decisions, Husband-Dominated Decisions, and Joint Decisions.*

Withdrawal. Resolving frustration by withdrawing from the situation. *See Defense Mechanisms.*

Word Association Method. A projective research technique that consists of presenting respondents with words, one at a time, and asking them to say the first word that comes to mind. *See Projective Techniques and Qualitative Research.*

Word-of-Mouth. An oral or written communication in which satisfied customers tell others how much they like a business, product, service, or event. *See Buzz Agent and Opinion Leadership.*

World Brand. A brand that is sold and widely recognized globally.

Index

A

B